INDIANA
LAND ENTRIES

Volume 1
Cincinnati District
1801–1840

Margaret R. Waters

Southern Historical Press, Inc.
Greenville, South Carolina

Please direct all correspondence and book orders to:
SOUTHERN HISTORICAL PRESS, Inc.
PO Box 1267
Greenville, SC   29602-1267

Originally printed: Indianapolis, IN. 1948
ISBN #978-1-63914-122-7
Printed in the United States of America

CONTENTS

* See top of page iv

MAP ILLUSTRATING
THE PIONEER PERIODS IN INDIANA

S
DATE OF FIRST WHITE SETTLERS

O
DATE OF ORGANIZATION AS A COUNTY

C
DATE WHEN FIRST COURT CONVENED

L
DATE OF FIRST LAND ENTRY

+
EARLIER THAN

HEAVY BLACK LINES INDICATE BOUNDARIES OF THREE PIONEER PERIODS — THE HEAVY FIGURES — 1, 2, 3 INDICATE THE PIONEER PERIOD IN THE COUNTIES GROUPED WITHIN THE BOUNDARIES

COMPILED BY CHARLES NEBEKER THOMPSON FOR THE 1932 YEAR BOOK OF THE SOCIETY OF INDIANA PIONEERS

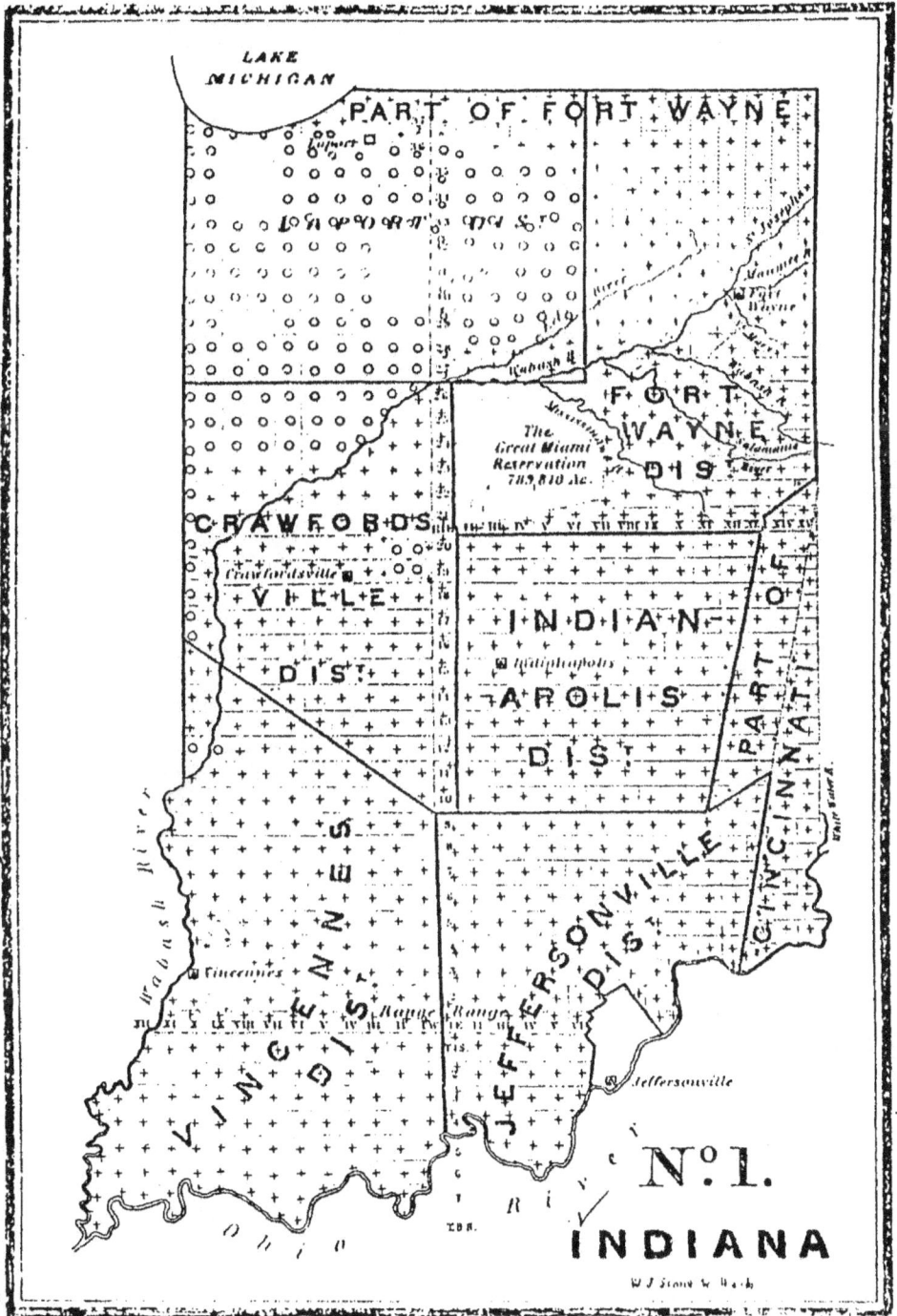

No. 1.

INDIANA

FOREWORD

Sharp, spirited, and steadfast, all deserving traits of a good genealogist, also highlight a description of Margaret R. Waters.

Miss Waters has been tracing family trees for over 40 years. A retired English teacher, she first became interested in genealogy when she had to write an autobiography for her high school English class. After the completion of her formal education by receiving degrees from Butler and Northwestern Universities, Miss Waters began her genealogical investigations with her own Waters family. Becoming one of the first professional genealogists in the country, she has since helped many other persons with their family history search.

Miss Waters has compiled several outstanding genealogical resource aids including *Revolutionary Soldiers Buried in Indiana*, Supplement.

This lovely lady who has given so much to the field of genealogy is not only an ardent supporter of the Indiana State Library but also a personal friend.

Carolyne L. Miller

Head Librarian, Genealogy Division

TO THE SEARCHER

A recent article in the Indiana History Bulletin for December 1947, published by the Indiana Historical Bureau, Indianapolis, and quoted by permission, gives an excellent account of the status of the public domain in Indiana Territory, created May 7, 1800.

- - - - -

"Prior to 1800 the only land owned by individuals in Indiana was either in and around Vincennes, where titles went back to French and Indian grants, or in Clark's Grant opposite the present Louisville, which had been allotted to the men who had served with George Rogers Clark in his Revolutionary War campaign against the British.

"Indian title to all the lands in Indiana was recognized at least nominally by the Federal government; and before any particular area was opened for sale, negotiations were opened with the chiefs of the tribes that claimed the land. Treaties were made whereby the Indians gave up their claims and accepted goods and money in exchange. The negotiations might be prolonged, but in the end the government always won out.

"The first such treaty affecting Indiana land was held in 1795, when the Indians ceded lands east of a line drawn from Fort Recovery in Ohio to a point on the Ohio River opposite the mouth of the Kentucky River. A triangular strip in what is now southeastern Indiana was thus opened for settlement; but it was not until six years later after the land had been surveyed and a land office was opened at Cincinnati, that it could be purchased. In the meantime, many settlers moved in and 'squatted' on the land, hoping to purchase their preferred site when the area was opened for sale.

"During the first two decades of government land sales in Indiana, purchasers had to buy at least 320 acres and pay a minimum of $2.00 per acre. Four years were allowed in which to complete payments. Land auctions were held when new areas were opened, and the land was sold to the highest bidder. Any tracts not sold at auction could be purchased at the land office for the minimum price. Many purchasers were forced to forfeit their lands when hard times came and payments could not be made. In 1820 a new land law was passed which placed the minimum price at $1.25 an acre and allowed purchasers to buy as little as 80 acres. The credit system was abolished in favor of cash payments. At the auction sales, choice land often sold for three and four times the minimum price. In the 1830's and 1840's, pre-emption acts were passed by Congress to give the 'squatter' who had settled and improved a piece of land the opportunity to purchase it at the minimum price before the public sale.

"The rectangular system of land surveys was used for the first time in what is now Ohio in the 1790's. The system was conceived by Thomas Hutchins in 1764 while on an expedition against the Indians."

- - - - -

The tract books for the several land offices in Indiana are deposited in the office of the Auditor of State, Indianapolis, and are in the care of the State Land Clerk. Eventually, it is my plan to copy all of these records through 1851 according to the chronological opening of the various land offices. The date 1851 was chosen to supplement information in the 1850 Census.

This first book contains the records of the Cincinnati District. The area covered is mainly a district known as the "wedge" or "gore", located in the southeastern part of the state and bounded roughly by the Ohio-Indiana State Line, the Ohio River, and the Greenville Treaty Line. The territory comprises all of the present counties of Ohio, Dearborn, Union, and Wayne; most of Switzerland, Fayette, Franklin, and Randolph; and a tiny section of Jay. Some entries in the region are given in the Indianapolis District, to be copied later. See map on page 1.

There are in Indiana two Principal Meridians---the first at the Ohio-Indiana State Line at approximately 84 degrees and 49 minutes longitude, the second about two-thirds of the way across the state to the west at approximately 86 degrees and 28 minutes longitude. Most descriptions of land are given as ranges east or west of the 2nd P.M. The Base Line is located in the southern part of the state at approximately 38 degrees and 28 minutes latitude. Townships are north or south of the Base Line.

These records have been copied solely for genealogical purposes to enable a searcher to learn if an ancestor did locate in Indiana; if so, where and when. Consequently, to save time and space, I have omitted giving the acreage and the final certificate numbers. Reference to my page 1 will, except in the case of fractional sections, give the acreage; and if anyone particularly cares for the final certificate number, he would probably want a signed letter from the Bureau of Land Management in Washington, D.C.

The land records for Indiana have never been published, copied, nor indexed by names. Therefore, they have been completely useless to searchers unless they knew the exact, or at least a close approximate, location of the land on which they suspected ancestors might have settled.

Since the 1820 Census is the first for Indiana, these records will, in a way, serve as a substitute for earlier censuses. The fact that a person entered land, however, does not necessarily mean that he ever actually lived on it. Also, some "squatter" residents may never have bought their land before they migrated to other places.

In copying the records, I have done so exactly as they appear in the originals---by location. By this, searchers may be able to identify other members of the family from nearby entries made by people of the same surname; also there is the possibility of a clue to neighboring families into which daughters might have married.

The searcher is warned against assuming, without other proof, that Sr. and Jr. necessarily mean father and son. In the early days, this often literally meant the "elder" and the "younger"---sometimes a man and his nephew, occasionally two unrelated men of the same name, coincidentally. A given name or middle name resembling a surname does not always positively indicate a relationship to that family. Children were often given the name of a neighbor. Of course, such names as George Washington Brown and Lorenzo Dow Green are self-explanatory!

The records of the Cincinnati District are contained in two books which I have called Volume I and Volume II. The earliest entries are on April 9, 1801, and the latest on August 1, 1840.

Volume I, the older, is unbound and is in very bad condition. The pages are brittle, and the ink is faded---in some places illegible. The handwriting is excellent, in the main. When a man relinquished his entry (did not complete his payments), a red R was placed beside his name; and the name of the later purchaser is also sometimes given. For example: "Powell Scott, NE¼-S6-T14N-R14E of 2nd P.M.; 4-2-1817. Rel.W½. To Jacob Deboy, 9-20-1827." Interpreted, this means that on April 2, 1817, Scott entered (started paying on) the NE¼, etc.; that he later relinquished his entry (stopped paying); and that on September 20, 1827, the W½-NE¼ was resold to Jacob Deboy. The R (for relinquished) does not always indicate whether the man gave up all of his land or only part; reference must be made to the same site in Volume II to see if anyone else bought the unmentioned part---in the above case, the E½-NE¼. Sometimes, a man later bought back all or part of what he had previously relinquished.

Volume II is largely a repetition of Volume I. In order to avoid copying the same names twice, I had to correlate the two volumes and copy them simultaneously. Volume II differs from Volume I in that: (a) it does not give the names of men who relinquished land, and these therefore are found only in Volume I; (b) it gives later entries; and (c) it gives the final certificate numbers.

Many discrepancies will be noted, particularly in names but sometimes in the descriptions. I have called attention to these but would not attempt to explain them except that in certain cases, I think that the Register copied part of a name from the line above or the line below. These discrepancies could probably be ironed out by writing the Bureau of Land Management.

The whimsical spelling of the two Registers has been given exactly as it appears. In the text itself, I have included all middle names and initials. However, in the index, to save space, I have used only the first name with the assumption that most men were called by it. If the searcher suspects that his ancestor might have used his middle name (and this is especially true of Germans), it would be wise to look up all given names listed under a surname.

In the index, I have occasionally made an attempt to standardize the spelling to make the names more easily found. I have also combined similar-sounding names such as Meyer-Meier-Myers. However, my interpretation of the handwriting, particularly in Volume II, may be faulty; so the searcher is advised to "look around" the alphabet. Names beginning with L-S-T, for instance, look much alike in some script. Also, remember that German names were often spelled interchangeably: B-P, C-G, C-K, D-T, F-P, F-V, K-N, S-Z.

ADDITIONAL NOTES

Some years ago, an abstractor who was working in the records labeled the county names on the original pages. I have copied these in my text, but I do not guarantee their accuracy. He did not label Ohio County, which was cut from the lower part of Dearborn County. The sections in Ohio County are very fractional because of the two rivers; but from an atlas, I have determined as best I can that Ohio County contains the following:

T 3 N, R 1 W   Sec. 1-10, 16-22 small fr. of 15 & 22
T 4 N, R 1 W   Sec. 7-10, 14-23, 25-36

T 3 N, R 2 W   Sec. 1-24
T 4 N, R 2 W   Sec. 21-29; 31-36 fr. 13 & fr. 30

T 3 N, R 3 W   Sec. 1-5 fr.; 8-17; fr. 18; 19-24

Page numbers in the text refer to page numbers in the two original volumes. Page numbers in the index refer to my page numbers.

ABBREVIATIONS

T township   P.M. Principal Meridian
R range   Rel. relinquished
S section, south   Fr. fractional
N north   pt. part
E east   cor. corner
W west

CORRECTIONS OF LAND ENTRIES

Lemuel Butler, Jessamine Co., Ky. SE-NE-Sfr-S28; 8-14-32.
  (Source said Jessamine Co., Ind., but no such Co. in Ind.)
Lemuel Butler, Jessamine Co., Ky. SE-NE-Sfr-S28; 8-14-32.
  (Source said Jessamine Co., Ind., but no such Co. in Ind.)
Lemuel Butler, Jessamine Co., Ky. SE-NE-Sfr-S28; 8-14-32.
  (Source said Jessamine Co., Ind., but no such Co. in Ind.)

ERRATA

Errata. After page 55, I numbered the next stencil page 57. I did not discover this error until page 82. To correct this, I numbered the next page 82a, thus making page 83 and the following pages in their correct sequence. Names are indexed accordingly.

December 21, 1946   Margaret R. Waters
        to
February 29, 1948

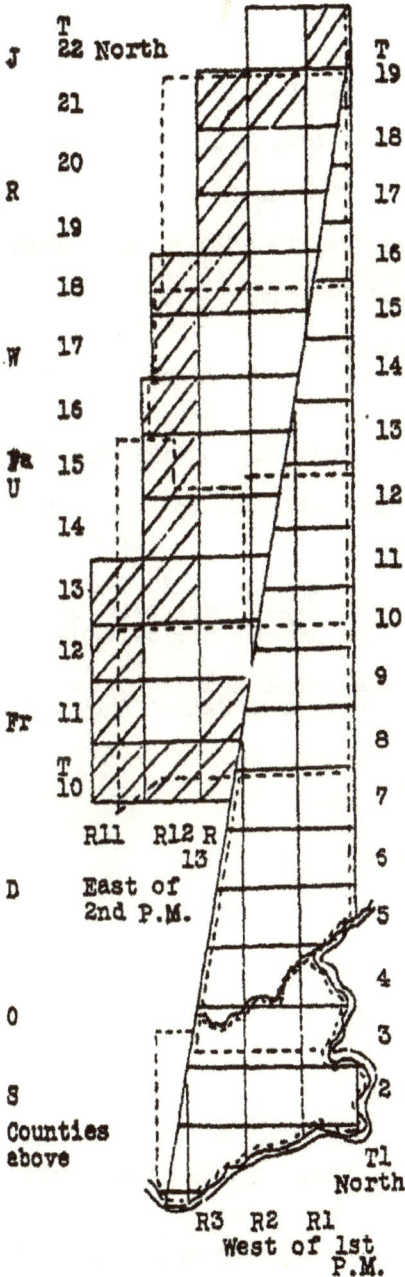

Arrangement of sections in a
"perfect" township, 36 sq. mi.

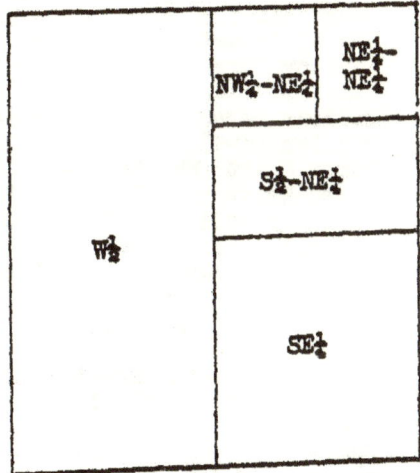

Dotted lines--counties.
Shaded sections--some entries
are in Indianapolis District.

Typical acreage divisions of a
"perfect" section:
    1 Section-640 ac., 1 sq. mi.
    W½ - 320 ac.
    SE¼ - 160 ac.
    S½-NE¼ - 80 ac.
    NE¼-NE¼ - 40 ac.
Acreage of fractional parts given
in tract book or plat book only.

Page 1.   T 1 N, R 1 E of 1st P.M.   **SWITZERLAND CO.**

John Andrews Pt. S5, 412.61 ac.; NE¼-S6; NW¼-S6; SE¼-S6; SW¼-S6;
Pt. S7, 428.73 ac.; Pt. S8, 30.90 ac.; Pt. S18, 3.60 ac.;
7-19-1809

Page 1.   T 2 N, R 1 E of 1st P.M.

Patrick Donahoe Pt. S29-30-32; S21; tot. 1411.90 ac.; 4-26-1804

Page 2.   T 1 N, R 1 W of 1st P.M.

John Buckhannon & William Philips Pt. S5-6 197.82 ac.; 9-18-1804

Page 2.   T 2 N, R 1 W of 1st P.M.

Thomas Stewart, Jr. NE¼-S1; 2-24-1816
James Quigley NW¼-S1; 3-24-1817. Rel.W½ to Jackson G. Douglass,
12-8-1829
John Quigley SE¼-S1; 2-27-1816
Ethan A. Brown SW¼-S1; 4-4-1818. Rel. E½ to William Williams,
Jr., 5-1-1832
Robert Hamilton NE¼-S2; 6-17-1818. Rel. E½ to Ralph Turner,
7-11-1827
Seth Sampson E½-NW¼-S2; 1-8-1818
William Campbell & William Ridgeley W½-NW¼-S2; 10-8-1817
Edward Hepburn & Henry Diffenderffer E½-SE¼-S2; 5-14-1818. Rel.
Edward Hepburn & Henry Diffenderffer W½-SE¼-S2; 5-14-1818. Rel.
John Vandorin SW¼-S2; 4-7-1817
Samuel Trousdel & Christopher Jones NE¼-S3; 1-21-1815
Pinkney James NW¼-S3; 8-7-1816. Rel.E½ to Samuel Jack,8-1-1831.
James Truesdell SE¼-S3; 7-2-1814
William Larew SW¼-S3; 9-16-1816
William Powell NE¼-S4; 6-21-1817
Henry Weist NW¼-S4; 6-19-1816
Henry Weist SE¼-S4; 6-19-1816
David Penwell SW¼-S4; 9-25-1816
Francis Hees NE¼-S5; 3-15-1816
John Bayne NW¼-S5; 4-4-1817
John D. Cook SE¼-S5; 4-12-1817
Aaron Tapley SW¼-S5; 5-19-1817. Rel.
Caleb Mounts NE¼-S6; 8-19-1812
Alexander Scott SE¼-S6; 10-23-1816
Robert Harris SW¼-S6; 11-10-1817
Thomas Dugan NE¼-S7; 12-2-1815
James Hamilton NW¼-S7; 11-17-1814
Jacob R. Harris E½-SE¼-S7; 4-20-1825
John Green W½-SE¼-S7; 6-9-1824
Cyrus N. Smith SW¼-S7; 5-27-1817. Rel. E½ to James Scott,
4-18-1832
Eli Penwell NE¼-S8; 10-9-1816
John Cunningham NW¼-S8; 3-25-1817. Rel. W½ to Supply Walker,
7-5-1831
John Cunningham SE¼-S8; 3-25-1817
Noah Smith SW¼-S8; 9-2-1815
Roderick Moore & Erastus Moore NE¼-S9; 3-24-1817

John McDowell NW¼-S9; 1-20-1817
John Cunningham SE¼-S9; 4-24-1817
Henry Munroe SW¼-S9; 3-25-1817
Samuel Jack NE¼-S10; 3-21-1816
Charles Wright NW¼-S10; 12-9-1816
Collen McNutt SE¼-S10; 3-3-1817
William McNutt SW¼-S10; 4-7-1817
James Moredock NE¼-S11; 2-21-1815
Samuel Jack NW¼-S11; 3-21-1816
Samuel West SE¼-S11; 5-9-1818. Rel. W½ to Cautious J. Choate,
    12-8-1829
Lemuel Searcy SW¼-S11; 9-8-1813
John Quigley NE¼-S12; 12-13-1813
Jacob Sherk NW¼-S12; 7-7-1817
Joshua Petty SE¼-S12; 11-10-1832
Robert Gaston SW¼-S12; 1-5-1816
Elisha Wade Pt. S13, 516.74 ac.; 2-25-1813
James Moore NE¼-S14; 7-7-1817
James Moredock NW¼-S14; 8-21-1815
James McIntire SE¼-S14; 4-17-1816. Rel. W½ to William B.
    Chamberlin, 8-21-1827
William Wade SW¼-S14; 6-26-1816
Austin Ames NE¼-S15; 11-9-1818. Rel   W½ to Arthur Humphrey,
    4-6-1830
John Patton NW¼-S15; 7-7-1817
Joel Bradford SE¼-S15; 8-13-1818
John Patton SW¼-S15; 4-7-1817. Vol. II, p. 3, says only the
    W½-SW¼
Auson A. Brown (illegible)-S15; 10-8-1824. Vol. II, p. 3, says
    the E½-SW¼
Ebenezer Humphrey (illegible)-S17; 5-8-1817. Vol. II, p. 3,
    says NE¼-S17

            Page 3. Bottom torn. Following supplied from
            Vol. II, page 3.

Zeally Moss NW¼-S17; 2-12-1816
Lewis Jones SE¼-S17; 8-3-1814
Zeally Moss SW¼-S17; 2-12-1816

            Page 3. T 2 N, R 1 W of 1st P.M.

Zeally Moss NE¼-S18; 1-7-1817. Rel. W½
Caleb White & David Cummins NW¼-S18; 6-22-1818. Rel. E½ to
    Jacob Rude Harris, 4-25-1832
Isaac Cook SE¼-S18; 8-13-1817. Vol. II, p. 4, says Jacob Cook.
Joseph Grose & Amariah Eveleth SW¼-S18; 7-28-1817. Rel. W½ to
    Adam Limeback, Nov. (illegible). Vol. II, p. 4, says 12-13-1831
Thomas Burk NE¼-S19; 5-19-1817
Caleb White & David Cummins NW¼-S19; 6-22-1818. Rel.
William McGinnis SE¼-S19; 1-3-1815
Thomas Burke SW¼-S19; 12-28-1816
William Campbell NW¼-S20; 5-19-1817
Amos Brown E½-SE¼-S20; 8-22-1814

Amos Brown W½-SE¼-S20; 8-22-1814
William Carver SW¼-S20; 7-28-1815
Peter Smith E½-NE¼-S21; 7-22-1829
William R. Wiley W½-NE¼-S21; 10-15-1824
John Patton E½-NW¼-S21; 4-7-1817
Amos A. Brown W½-NW¼-S21; 10-8-1824
Peter Smith SE¼-S21; 5-21-1818
Abraham Bledsoe SW¼-S21; 7-29-1815
Ethel B. Lyon NE¼-S22; 11-10-1818
Henry Weist NW¼-S22; 1-8-1818. Rel. Note adds to Henry Weist, 8-21-1827
William Sherman Buck SE¼-S22; 9-14-1818. Rel. E½ to William B Chamberlin, no date. (Vol. II, p.4, says 8-21-1827.) W½ to George Teague, 8-21-1827
George Tague SW¼-S22; 8-27-1817. Note adds to George Teague, 8-21-1827
Jacob Sherk E½-NE¼-S23; 4-3-1818
Peter Boas W½-NE¼-S23; 4-9-1818
Acklin D. Hart NW¼-S23; 1-24-1818
Levi James SE¼-S23; 8-7-1817
Samuel C. Vance E½-SW¼-S23; 4-11-1818. Rel. To Seth Storer Choat, 3-28-1832
Levi Hamblin W½-SW¼-S23; 2-2-1818
William Logg Pt. S24, 444.66 ac.; 10-24-1814. Vol. II, p.4, says Legg
James Taylor W½-S25; 6-9-1814
Patrick Donahoe S26; Pt. S35; tot. 1,127.32 ac.; 9-1-1804
Lewis Jones NE¼-S27; 7-15-1805
Amos Brown NW¼-S27; 2-18-1814
William Parson SE¼-S27; 5-9-1814. Rel. E½ to Arthur Humphrey, 12-8-1829. Vol. II, p.5, says Pierson
William Johnston SW¼-S27; 2-8-1812
Zealley Moss NE¼-S28; 10-31-1814
Christian Carver NW¼-S28; 6-11-1813
Martin Holden SE¼-S28; 6-22-1813. Vol. II, p.5, says Holder
Nicholas Keith SW¼-S28; 7-26-1813
George Teague NE¼-S29; 12-12-1814
Robert Willson NW¼-S29; 12-13-1814
Caleb Harris SE¼-S29; 2-25-1815
Eli Penwell SW¼-S29; 1-25-1816
Christian Cooper NE¼-S30; 12-31-1814
William McCreary NW¼-S30; 11-30-1816. Rel. W½ to Richardson Wiles, 3-30-1830
John Gilliland E½-SE¼-S30; 6-1-1818. Rel.
William Campbell W½-SE¼-S30; 9-6-1817
Jesse Kirk SW¼-S30; 5-8-1816
Levi James NE¼-S31; 7-28-1817
Albert Cosairt NW¼-S31; 12-11-1816. Rel. E½ to Richard Tilton Goddard, 11-13-1831
John B. Lindsay SE¼-S31; 9-9-1815
Benjamin Drake & Joseph Nelson SW¼-S31; 7-16-1814
William Campbell Pt. S32, 540 ac., 5-31-1814
Martin Baum Pt. S34, 370.95 ac.; 9-18-1804
Thomas Hopkins Pt. S36; Pt. S31; tot. 859.60 ac.; 7-2-1801

CINCINNATI DISTRICT --- VOL. I

Insert Page A. T 2 N, R 1 W of 1st P.M. (between pages 2 and 3)

SWITZERLAND

Robert Craig NE¼-NW¼-S6; 10-1-1832
Austin Seymour SE¼-S2; 1-3-1833
Delavzun DeForest W½-SW¼-S1; 1-3-1833
Robert Lyons NW¼-SW¼-S5; 1-9-1833
William Kelly SE¼-NW¼-S6; 5-15-1834
William R. Wiley SE¼-NW¼-S19; 6-12-1832. Vol. II, p. 4, gives middle name Royston
Elijah Rayl SE¼-SE¼-S30; 6-18-1832
Samuel Howard NE¼-SE¼-S30; 11-27-1834
Adam Limeback NW¼-NW¼-S19; 11-28-1834
Alexander Sebastian NE¼-NW¼-S19; 12-5-1834
Alexander Sebastian NE¼-SW¼-S18; 12-8-1834
Thomas Lonney SW¼-NE¼-S18; 12-8-1834
Jefferson Hiser SW¼-SW¼-S5; 6-30-1835
Martin Ruter Green NW¼-SW¼-S7; 8-4-1835
Polly Kelly NW¼-NW¼-S6; 8-10-1835
James V. Watson W½-NW¼-S18; 9-2-1835. Vol. II, p. 2, gives middle name Vaughn
James V. Watson NW¼-NE¼-S18; 9-2-1835
James V. Watson SW¼-SW¼-S7; 9-2-1835

Page 4. T 3 N, R 1 W of 1st P.M.

OHIO CO,

Davis & Chambers Pt. S1-2-3; 1010 ac.; 4-9-1801. Vol. II, p. 5, says Lewis Davis & Benjamin Chambers
David B. Close N½-S4; 2-11-1812
John James SE¼-S4; 8-18-1814
David Close SW¼-S4; 9-5-1814
John Payn NE¼-S5; 8-24-1814
Martin Stewart NW¼-S5; 7-4-1814
William Howlett SE¼-S5; 3-16-1813
John Dixon SW¼-S5; 6-28-1815
Peter White NE¼-S6; 6-9-1815
Hugh Beaty NW¼-S6; 5-17-1815
John Mounts SE¼-S6; 10-3-1815
John Barricklow & Robert Espy SW¼-S6; 10-3-1815
John Barricklow NE¼-S7; 9-25-1815
Hugh Espey NW¼-S7; 10-25-1815
Hugh Espey SE¼-S7; 9-23-1815
Hugh Espey SW¼-S7; 10-14-1814
John Dewit NE¼-S8; 7-4-1814
Robert Drake NW¼-S8; 6-18-1814
Hugh Moore SE¼-S8; 8-5-1817
Hugh Espey SW¼-S8; 7-29-1816
Peyton S. Symmes Pt. S15; 27.50 ac.; 10-1-1814. Vol. II, p. 6, says assigned to John James
Robert Rickets NE¼-S17; 11-28-1804
Stephen Stewart NW¼-S17; 7-5-1814
Robert Rickets SE¼-S17; 11-22-1813
Hugh Espey, Sr. SW¼-S17; 11-22-1814
Samuel S. Scott & Rufus Gordon NE¼-S18; 3-6-1816

John Dixon NW¼-S18; 12-4-1815
William Ross SE¼-S18; 8-31-1816
Dillard Drake SW¼-S18; 8-31-1816
Nathan Rickets NE¼-S19; 11-18-1814
Richard J. Hall NW¼-S19; 5-3-1815
Willis Bates SE¼-S19; 5-16-1816
Jacob Goodner SW¼-S19; 3-13-1815
Silas How NE¼-S20; 4-16-1816
William Ross NW¼-S20; 8-31-1816
Silas How SE¼-S20; 5-20-1817. Rel. E½ to Calvin Marble,
    8-21-1827
David Remer SW¼-S20; 3-7-1815
Lot North Pt. S21-22; 615.52 ac.; 12-7-1815
William Campbell Pt. S25; 449.50 ac.; 6-7-1814 SWITZERLAND CO.
William English Pt. S26; 454.78 ac.; 8-9-1814
Thomas North Pt. S27; 570.72 ac.; 5-31-1814
Thomas Mounts NE¼-S28; 8-17-1812
James Curry NW¼-S28; 1-23-1812
Levi James SE¼-S28; 9-11-1819. Rel. E½ to Arthur Humphrey,
    5-22-1828; W½ to Daniel Spore, 1-5-1829
Levi James SW¼-S28; 7-12-1817. Vol. II, p. 7, says to
    Thomas Mounts, 8-6-1814
Peter Lostutter NE¼-S29; 2-16-1815
Peter Lostutter NW¼-S29; 2-12-1816
Henry Wallick SE¼-S29; 8-1-1816. Vol. II, p. 7, says Walbeck
Edward Tidings SW¼-S29; 9-1-1815
William Kelly, Sr. NE¼-S30; 3-22-1817
Robert Hewitt NW¼-S30; 7-10-1817
Conrad Buck SE¼-S30; 2-24-1815
John Gibbins SW¼-S30; 10-16-1817
Martin Baum & James Findlay NE¼-S31; 8-9-1815. Rel. W½ to Henry
    Kelly, 8-9-1831; E½ to Peter Lostutter, 1-24-1832
Conrad Buck NW¼-S31; 8-16-1815
Daniel Hiser SE¼-S31; 8-25-1813
David Wilson SW¼-S31; 4-3-1818. Vol. II,.p. 7, says only W½-SW¼

Page 5. T 3 N, R 1 W of 1st P.M.   SWITZERLAND CO.

William Stewart NE¼-S32; 3-7-1815
James Hamilton NW¼-S32; 12-10-1814. Rel. Vol. II, p. 7, says
    redeemed 6-23-1831
Cornelius S. Harris SE¼-S32; 4-17-1817
Cyrus N. Smith SW¼-S32; 5-27-1817. Rel. To William Campbell,
    Aug. 1831. Vol. II, p. 7, says 8-9-1831
Cornelius McPhial NE¼-S33; 6-7-1817. Rel. W½
Thomas Stewart NW¼-S33; 8-3-1816. Vol. II, p. 7, says Jr.
Jacob Powell SE¼-S33; 6-21-1817. Rel. W½
William Vanhese SW¼-S33; 6-21-1817. Rel. E½ to John Stayback,
    5-26-1831
Ralph Turner E½-NE¼-S34; 7-14-1827
Ralph Turner W½-NE¼-S34; 7-14-1827
Lewis Hammond NW¼-S34; 9-7-1815
James Davis SE¼-S34; 1-3-1817
David Close SW¼-S34; 5-11-1819. Rel. To Reuben Stephens,
    12-4-1827

SWITZERLAND CO.

Archibald Meritt NE¼-S35; 7-19-1816. Rel. E½ to Archibald
   Meritt, 8-21-1827
Ralph Turner E½-NW¼-S35; 7-14-1827
Ralph Turner W½-NW¼-S35; 7-14-1827
Ralph Turner E½-SE¼-S35; 7-14-1827
Ralph Turner W½-SE¼-S35; 7-14-1827
James Butler SW¼-S35; 11-9-1815
John Hamilton,Jr. NE¼ & SW¼-S36; 1-17-1818. Rel. To Ralph
Turner, 7-14-1827. Vol. II, p. 8, adds SW¼ to Ralph Turner, too.
William Campbell NW¼-S36; 5-19-1817. Rel. W½ to Ralph Turner,
   7-14-1827
Peter Sheets SE¼-S36; 8-21-1817

Insert Page A. T 3 N, R 1 W of 1st P.M.
(between pages 2-3)

John P. Lillard W½-SE¼-S33; 12-1-1832. Vol. II, p. 7, says
   middle name Pullom
Henry Vandusen NE¼-SW¼-S31; 7-23-1833
Polly Kelly SE¼-SW¼-S31; 8-15-1835

Page 6. T 4 N, R 1 W of 1st P. M.   **DEARBORN CO.**

George P. Torrence Pt. S4; 254.36 ac.; 12-12-1810. See Vol. II,
   p. 8, Daniel Connor
Jesse L. Holeman NE¼-S5; 8-16-1810
James (?) W. Winkley NW¼-S5; 7-21-1813
John Walsh SE¼-S5; 4-27-1815
George Shinkle SW¼-S5; 5-20-1814
Isaac Conner NE¼-S6; 2-7-1815
Richard Norris NW¼-S6; 11-20-1813
Valentine Barton SE¼-S6; 5-3-1813
James Rambley SW¼-S6; 8-25-1812. Vol. II, p. 8, says Rumbley
Eli Greene NE¼-S7; 12-18-1812
Squire Paleet NW¼-S7; 6-14-1813. Vol. II, p. 8, says Poteet
Henry Grove SE¼-S7; 6-27-1812 [Part in Ohio Co.]
George Grove SW¼-S7; 6-5-1813. Vol. II, p. 8, says Groves
Oliver Ormsby S8 & Pt. S9; S10; 1,447.80 ac.; 12-3-1806.. See
   Vol. II, p. 8, Daniel Conner [Part in Ohio Co.]
Jesse Hunt Pt. S14-15-16; 1,247.89 ac.; 12-3-1806. See Vol. II,
   p. 8, Joseph Wilkinson   **OHIO CO.,**
Henry Miller NE¼-S17; 6-4-1814 [Part in Dearborn Co.]
Benjamin Miles NW¼-S17; 4-14-1813 [Part in Dearborn Co.]
Robert Taylor & Thomas Burns SE¼-S17; 1-24-1818
Benjamin Miles SW¼-S17; 7-2-1814
Michael Flake & William Flake NE¼-S18; 5-18-1813
Squire Poleet NW¼-S18; 11-18-1813 [Part in Dearborn Co.]
Jacob Smith & John Conner SE¼-S18; 8-10-1815
Richard Bailey SW¼-S18; 8-15-1814
John Hunt NE¼-S19; 2-8-1816
Farrington Barricklow NW¼-S19; 7-15-1816
James Burke SE¼-S19; 11-4-1813
John Barricklow & Farrington Barricklow SW¼-S19; 11-12-1813
James Warnock NE¼-S20; 10-9-1816

Joseph Warnock NW¼-S20; 10-1-1816
Thomas Stewart SE¼-S20; 9-5-1814
Abijah Goodrich SW¼-S20; 4-18-1816. Rel. E½ to William Higby, 7-5-1831
Hugh Moore NE¼-S21; 6-26-1816
John Barricklow NW¼-S21; 9-25-1815
William L. Cornelius & Joseph D. Miller S½-S21; 9-23-1814
Peyton Short S22 & Pt. S23; 1,052.53 ac.; 4-7-1807
Israel Loring Pt. S25; S26; 719.80 ac.; 5-27-1801
Jonathan Parks NE¼-S27; 5-18-1816
Alexander Abercrombie NW¼-S27; 5-13-1816
William Bills SE¼-S27; 7-1-1816
Abraham Dubois & Robert Dace SW¼-S27; 7-8-1816. Vol. II, p. 9, looks like Dare.
Robert Espey NE¼-S28; 9-18-1815
John McCollough NW¼-S28; 2-5-1814
James Stewart SE¼-S28; 10-23-1815
Charles English SW¼-S28; 9-19-1815
Ephraim Gard NE¼-S29; 6-1-1816
Samuel Steele NW¼-S29; 5-31-1816
James Hinds SE¼-S29; 5-28-1816. Rel. E½ to Isaac Dexter, 1-1-1830
Abraham Dubois SW¼-S29; 7-22-1817. Re. E½ to Henry Collins, 9-21-1831
John Barricklow & Farrington Barricklow NE¼-S30; 11-6-1813
John Barricklow & Farrington Barricklow NW¼-S30; 11-12-1813
Isaac Dexter SE¼-S30; 1-8-1814
Isaac Dexter SW¼-S30; 4-14-1815
Peter Lowsteller NE¼-S31; 1-27-1814
Peyton S. Symmes & Lewis Whiteman NW¼-S31; 10-2-1815
Asa Hamilton & James Buckhannon SE¼-S31; 8-18-1814
James Gibson SW¼-S31; 4-25-1814
Jonathan Huntington NE¼-S32; 12-30-1815
Noah Babbs & John Stewart SE¼-S32; 8-24-1814
Lot Abraham W½-S32; 4-15-1812. Rel.?
John English SW¼-S32; 9-19-1815
Benjamin Dubois NE¼-S33; 12-30-1816. Rel. To Samuel Montgomery Jelly, 8-9-1831
Robert Elliott NW¼-S33; 5-7-1817
Isaac Willcox SE¼-S33; 6-3-1815
Clabourn Allen SW¼-S33; 2-16-1813
David B. Close NE¼-S34; 3-27-1809
David Close NW¼-S34; 6-19-1815
Elnathan Keneper SE¼-S34; 9-24-1804. Vol.II, p.10, says Kemper
Samuel M. Jelly SW¼-S34; 5-20-1815
James Findley S35 & Pt. S36; 818.50 ac.; 4-27-1801

Insert Page A. T 4 N, R 1 W of 1st P.M.
(between pages 2-3)

Henry Collins SW¼-SE¼-S29; 1-28-1833
Elijah Lindsay NW¼-SE¼-S29; 3-2-1833

Page 7. T 5 N, R 1 W of 1st P.M.

Joseph Hays Pt. S1; 4-9-1801
G. Christ & H. Harding Pt. S2; 4-27-1801. Vol. II, p. 10, says
    George Christ & Hy. (Henry?) Harding
Barrent Eulick S3; 8-25-1802. Vol. II, p. 10, says Barnet
Timothy Davis NE¼-S4; 1-18-1815
John Howard NW¼-S4; 5-23-1812
William Caldwell SE¼-S4; 12-7-1812
John Ferris NE¼-S5; 12-24-1814
Thomas Townsen NW¼-S5; 12-24-1809. Vol.II, p.10, says Townsend
Samuel Bond SE¼-S5; 8-27-1808
Amos Way & Isaac Lemaster SW¼-S5; 11-7-1815
David Rees NE¼-S6; 9-13-1815
David Rees NW¼-S6; 9-13-1815
Jacob Brasher SE¼-S6; 3-16-1815
Leonard Chase SW¼-S6; 5-15-1815
Peyton S. Symmes & Lewis Whiteman NE¼-S7; 9-23-1815
Charles Dawson NW¼-S7; 2-9-1815
David Hogan SE¼-S7; 7-25-1814
Enoch James SW¼-S7; 7-4-1814
Caleb Pugh NE¼-S8; 12-19-1811
Enoch Pugh NW¼-S8; 11-22-1815
Jesse Laird SE¼-S8; 1-8-1817
David Rees SW¼-S8; 9-13-1815
Zebulon Pike NE¼-S9; 12-2-1816
Dele Elder NW¼-S9; 10-9-1811
Samuel Bond SE¼-S9; 8-27-1808
Samuel Bond SW¼-S9; 8-27-1808
John Brown S10 & Pt. S11-S12; 1,501.02 ac.; 12-3-1806. Vol. II,
    p. 11, says first to Zebulon Pike; then re-entered by Jesse
    Hunt, assignee of John Brown
Benjamin Chambers Pt. S13-S14; S15; 1,229.88 ac.; 12-3-1806.
    Vol. II, p. 11, says first to Samuel C. Vance, 7-23-1801
John Demos NE¼-S17; 7-15-1814
George Weaver NW¼-S17; 7-26-1814
David Dutton SE¼-S17; 12-15-1810
Adam Pate SW¼-S17; 10-16-1812
John Robinson NE¼-S18; 7-4-1814
Enoch James, Jr. NW¼-S18; 7-4-1814
Jahiel Buffington & Amer Bruce SE¼-S18; 6-28-1814
Enoch James SW¼-S18; 7-4-1814
David Rees NE¼-S19; 12-31-1806
Samuel Perry NW¼-S19; 6-28-1816
Francis Cheek SE¼-S19; 2-7-1812. Vol. II, p.11, says Cheek
Samuel Bond SW¼-S19; 8-17-1808
Page Cheek NE¼-S20; 4-9-1811. Vol. II, p. 11, says Cheek
Nathan C. Findlay SE¼-S20; 8-12-1806
David Rees W½-S20; 12-31-1806
David Rees S21; Pt. S22-23; 1,183.77 ac.; 12-3-1806. Vol. II,
    p. 11, says first to Charles Wilkins, 4-27-1801
Isaac Reynolds NE¼-S30; 8-29-1811
Eli Greene NW¼-S30; 12-11-1811
John Buffington SE¼-S30; 2-15-1811

Conrad Huffman SW¼-S30; 9-14-1809
Martin Cozine NE¼-S31; 12-12-1815
Abraham Carlough NW¼-S31; 1-31-1812
Richard Norris SE¼-S31; 10-27-1812
Richard Norris SW¼-S31; 3-19-1812
Charles Vattier Pt. S32-33; 551.44 ac.; 9-18-1804. Note says NE¼-S33 to Samuel Montgomery Jelly. Note struck off in red ink.

Page 8. T 6 N, R 1 W of 1st P.M.

Isaac Mills NE¼-S1; 8-4-1818. Rel. W½
Enoch Jackson NW¼-S1; 6-23-1817
John Garrison SE¼-S1; 12-11-1811
Michael Shanks SW¼-S1;,12-12-1809
John Harper NE¼-S2; 12-24-1814
Elijah Garrison NW¼-S2; 1-20-1814
Jacob R. Compton SE¼-S2; 3-8-1816
Joseph Harper SW¼-S2; 6-23-1815
George Farmer NE¼-S3; 6-2-1815
John Gibson NW¼-S3; 5-25-1816
James White SE¼-S3; 8-10-1814
Joseph Ramsburgh NE¼-S4; 9-2-1817
David Bowles NW¼-S4; 8-29-1817
Abner Graham SE¼-S4; 5-30-1818. Rel. W½ to Joseph White Allen, 8-20-1831
Thomas May SW¼-S4; 7-30-1818. Rel. E½ to William Vance,5-10-1832
Richard Weaver NE¼-S5; 4-8-1817
Richard Weaver SE¼-S5; 3-14-1817
William Barr W½-S5; 4-22-1818. Rel.
William Barr S6; 4-22-1818. Rel. NE¼, SE¼, NW¼. N½-SE¼ to Thomas Huddleston, no date
John Burke NE¼-S7; 1-16-1818
Robert Hunt NW¼-S7; 7-27-1815
Ebenezer Rogers SE¼-S7; 5-26-1815. Vol.II, p.12, says Rodgers
John Smith SW¼-S7; 10-3-1818
Ruliff Bogert NE¼-S8; 8-12-1817
Solomon Huchinson SE¼-S8; 1-6-1815. Vol.II, p.12, says Samuel Hutchinson
John Dawson SW¼-S8; 9-1-1813
Levi Bracken & Thomas Bracken NE¼-S9; 6-10-1816
William Green & Ruliff Bogert NW¼-S9; 1-6-1818. Rel. SE¼ to Caleb Osborn, 5-23-1832
Joseph White SE¼-S9; 6-4-1817
Reuben Sutton SW¼-S9; 1-6-1815
Jerry Murphey NE¼-S10; 10-3-1815
Aaron R. Bonham NW¼-S10; 7-5-1817
Joseph Strond SE¼-S10; 10-6-1815
Caleb White & David Cummins SW¼-S10; 7-10-1818. Rel. E½ to Daniel Wood, 10-5-1827
Isaac Henderson NE¼-S11; 12-11-1811
John White NW¼-S11; 12-13-1816
Noble Butler SE¼-S11; 10-22-1804
John Sheared SW¼-S11; 11-30-1812
Samuel McHenry NE¼-S12; 4-5-1817

Michael Shanks NW¼-S12; 12-12-1809
James Fuller SE¼-S12; 10-24-1815
John Barkaloo SW¼-S12; 8-26-1814
John Fuller & Sarah Fuller NE¼-S13; 4-1-1812
James White NW¼-S13; 7-1-1813
William Torrence & Thomas Fuller SE¼-S13; 2-13-1808
Thomas Miller SW¼-S13; 11-17-1804
Robert McConnel NE¼-S14; 10-2-1804
Jacob Parke NW¼-S14; 2-10-1817
Robert McConnel SE¼-S14; 10-31-1804
Robert McConnel SW¼-S14; 3-14-1815
Richard Dement NE¼-S15; 6-8-1818. Rel. W½ to Mathew Swan, 8-15-1831; E½ to James Smith, 9-19-1831
John A. Stephens NW¼-S15; 6-8-1818. Rel. E½ to Walter Hayes, 8-20-1829; W½ to Walter Hayes, 8-28-1829
Silas Garrison SE¼-S15; 6-29-1813
John A. Stephens SW¼-S15; 1-6-1818. Rel. E½ to John Goodwin, 10-23-1826; W½ to John Goodwin, 4-3-1830. John Goodwin looks more like Jehu Goodwin
Thomas Price NE¼-S17; 5-15-1817
John Ewbank NW¼-S17; 11-9-1811
John Ewbank SE¼-S17; 5-28-1817
John Ewbank SW¼-S17; 10-31-1811
John Ewbank NE¼-S18; 6-8-1817
Peter Higdon NW¼-S18; 1-27-1815
John Ewbank SE¼-S18; 11-7-1815
Robert Perret SW¼-S18; 7-3-1817

Page 9. T 6 N, R 1 W of 1st P.M.

Joseph Hall NW¼-S19; 9-18-1817
Micajah Dunn SE¼-S19; 2-18-1814
Samuel H. Dowden SW¼-S19; 2-19-1813
Nathaniel Tucker NE¼ & NW¼-S20; 6-17-1814. Vol.II, p.14, says NW¼ only, which seems likely; see following entry.
John Dawson & John Ewbank NE¼-S20; 5-28-1817
John Dawson SE¼-S20; 11-22-1814
John Davison SW¼-S20; 12-17-1816. Vol.II, p.14, says Dawson
Ezekiel Jackson W½-NE¼ & NW¼-S21; 1-21-1830. Rel. W½-NW¼ to Enoch Winchester Jackson, 9-1-1831; E½-NW¼ to Ezekiel Jackson, 9-1-1831
J. H. Piatt, John Armstrong, & Philip Granden SW¼-S21; 6-16-1818. Rel. E½ to John Leeper, 5-20-1826; W½ to Ezekiel Jackson, 9-5-1831
Joseph Parker E½-NE¼-S21; 2-22-1825. Vol.II, p.14, says Parke
Michael Shanks SE¼-S21; 11-25-1814
Abraham Garrison NE¼-S22; 9-28-1811
Ezekial Jackson NW¼-S22; 2-17-1815
Abijah Hays SE¼-S22; 3-23-1809
Ezekiel Jackson SW¼-S22; 2-17-1815
Joseph Hayes NE¼-S23; 8-13-1811
James Goodwin NW¼-S23; 7-4-1812
James Bennet SE¼-S23; 8-13-1811
Charles Dawson SW¼-S23; 9-18-1804

Thomas Hunt NE¼-S24; 10-5-1812
Levi Miller, asse. & David Gard NW¼-S24; 12-12-1811. Vol.II, p.14, omits David Gard
Micajah Park SE¼-S24; 9-11-1812
David Gard SW¼-S24; 2-29-1808. Vol.II, p.14, says Guard
Thomas Brannen N½-NE¼-S25 & Mary Muir S½-NE¼-S25; 6-22-1831
John Davis NW¼-S25; 6-22-1831
Daniel Perine SE¼-S25; 5-25-1815
Thomas Brannen W½-SW¼-S25 & Mary Muir E½-SW¼-S25; 6-22-1831
Charles Dawson S26; 8-22-1804
Thadeus Cooley NE¼-S27; 9-18-1804
Henry Coleman Smith NW¼-S27; 7-22-1806
Henry Coleman Smith SE¼-S27; 8-4-1806
John McCleave SW¼-S27; 1-30-1806
Jacob Blasdel & Archibald Stark S28; 8-6-1804
Jacob Blasdel NE¼-S29; 9-17-1804
Ephraim Kneeland NW¼-S29; 1-7-1818
John Dawson SE¼-S29; 11-22-1814
Demee Trustee SW¼-S29; 6-26-1815. Vol.II, p.15, looks like Demoe
Jacob Blasdel NE¼-S30; 1-16-1817
Thomas Darling NW¼-S30; 11-26-1816
William Barr & Edward Hepburn SE¼-S30; 4-22-1818. Rel. W½ to Samuel Elliott, 10-20-1831; E½ to Samuel Elliott, 4-30-1832
William P. Marshall SW¼-S30; 7-25-1815
Aaron Burrows NE¼-S31; 1-15-1817. Vol.II, p.15, says Burroughs
James Conner NW¼-S31; 9-16-1817
Charles Osgood SE¼-S31; 9-7-1816
Aaron Burrows SW¼-S31; 12-18-1816. Rel. W½ to Thomas Annis, 6-30-1831
John Frazer NE¼-S32; 11-29-1814. Vol.II, p.15, says Frisar
John Frazer NW¼-S32; 2-20-1816. Vol.II, p.15, says John Foster
James McClister SE¼-S32; 7-25-1814. Vol.II, p.15, says McClester
Joshua Stroud SW¼-S32; 9-19-1815
Stephen Ludlow NE¼-S33; 12-9-1814
Elijah Walder NW¼-S33; 8-7-1811. Vol.II, p.15, says Walden
Walter Armstrong SE¼-S33; 4-14-1814
Enoch Pugh SW¼-S33; 12-21-1811
Jacob Froman NE¼-S34; 12-6-1805
Stephen Ludlow NW¼-S34; 7-15-1814
Isaac Lee Masters SE¼-S34; 3-15-1806
Samuel Evans SW¼-S34; 8-19-1813
Robert Piatt NE¼-S35; 4-9-1811
James Hayse NW¼-S35; 6-13-1811
Thomas Miller SE¼-S35; 9-18-1804
Job Miller & Henry Hardin SW¼-S35; 12-11-1811
Joseph Hayse S36; 4-9-1801

Insert Page B. T 6 N, R 1 W of 1st P.M.
(between Pages 2-3)

John Jacobus W½-NE¼-S1; 1-7-1833. Vol.II, p.11, gives middle initial S
James Glasdon NE¼-SW¼-S5; 1-16-1833
William Liddle W½-NW¼-S9; 1-16-1833

William Smith SE¼-NW¼-S8; 3-2-1833
James Garrison NE¼-NW¼-S9; 1-23-1834
Isaac Fuller W½-SW¼-S10; 2-4-1834
Christopher Gibson NW¼-NW¼-S8; 11-1-1834
James A. Gootee E½-NW¼-S5; 1-5-1835. Vol.II, p.12, gives
   middle name Angevine
Levi B. Swan SW¼-NW¼-S5; 1-5-1835. Vol.II, p.12, gives Middle
   name Blakesley
James Garrison W½-SW¼-S4; 6-3-1835
Joseph Lynas S½-SW¼-S5; 7-27-1835
William Whitaker SW¼-NW¼-S8; 10-13-1835

Page 10. T 7 N, R 1 W of 1st P.M.

Stephen Falkington NE¼-S1; 11-30-1814
Samuel C. Vance NW¼-S1; 4-25-1818.Rel. W½ to John Garner, 2-14-
Hugh Moore SE¼-S1; 7-23-1816   1832
Obediah Ford SW¼-S1; 11-14-1811
James Remy NE¼-S2; 11-6-1812
George Larrison NW¼-S2; 9-23-1815. Rel. W½ to James McManaman,
   2-7-1832
James Backhouse SE¼-S2; 12-11-1811.Vol.II, p.16, says Blackhouse
Abraham Hyter E½-SW¼-S2; 2-6-1819. Rel. S½ to Nathan Canfield
   Wickham, 5-25-1832
Moses Wiley W½-SW¼-S2; 6-6-1818
James Kerby & Thomas R. Fosdick E½-NE¼-& W½-NW¼-S3; 10-1-1818.
   Rel. E½-NE¼ to Solomon Manwaring, 4-21-1829
Hugh Abbercrombie W½-NE¼ & E½-NW¼-S3; 6-9-1824. Rel.? Vol.II,
   p.16, shows final cert. issued
James Jones, Sr. SE¼-S3; 1-31-1816
James Jones, Sr. SW¼-S3; 10-26-1816
James Adair, Sr. E½-S4; 4-21-1803
James Jones NW¼-S4; 12-10-1810
Enoch Smith SW¼-S4; 12-12-1809
William Smith & Hugh Brison E½-S5; 12-12-1808
John Barber NW¼-S5; 8-1-1816
James Paris W½-SW¼-S5; 2-3-1818
John Clifton NE¼-S6; 7-21-1818. Rel. E½
John Clifton & Benjamin Clifton NW¼-S6; 3-11-1819. Vol.II, p.16,
   says Benjamin Cliffin
Cornelius Rinerson SE¼-S6; 4-16-1818
John Paterson E½-SW¼-S6; 7-1-1820. Vol.II, p.16, says John
   Peterson of N. Jersey
Jacob Coverdale NE¼-S7; 9-7-1818. Rel. E½ to Amos Sparks,
   1-6-1832; W½ to John Clifton, 10-19-1831; see Vol.II, p.16,
   Daniel Symmes Major
John Barkaloo SE¼-S7; 8-1-1818. Rel. E½ to Stephen Thorn, Jr.,
Robert Davidson W½-SW¼-S7; 1-4-1825   10-20-1831
John Barkaloo NE¼-S8; 7-9-1818
Phinehas Judd & Orrin Judd NW¼-S8; 8-12-1818
Samuel B. Looker & Carleton Clark SE¼-S8; 10-23-1815
William Smith & William S. White SW¼-S8; 2-20-1813
John Brown E½-S9; 8-13-1801
John Pursel NW¼-S9; 1-15-1812

John Hinkson SW¼-S9; 7-15-1814
Jacob Hackman E½-S10; 8-26-1803. Vol.II, p.17, says John
Richard Manwaring W½-S10; 7-14-1801
John Brown E½-S11; 8-29-1801
Lewis Deweese W½-S11; 8-13-1801
William Majors W½-S12; 6-5-1802
James Hartpence NE¼-S12; 11-1-1815
Alexander Dearmand SE¼-S12; 9-26-1804
Cave Johnson E½-S13; 8-22-1801
Bayless Ashby W½-S14; 9-16-1801
James McCoy NE¼-S14; 9-19-1804
James Cloud SE¼-S14; 11-25-1816. Rel. W½ to James Cloud, 6-6-1831
Thomas Skinner NE¼-S15; 1-2-1806
William Major NW¼-S15; 5-1-1813
Lewis Offield SE¼-S15; 11-9-1815. Rel. To Abram Briggs, 8-21-1827. Vol.II, p.17, says Abraham
William Major SW¼-S15; 5-14-1818
William Howell & Samuel Howell NE¼-S17; 3-19-1819. Rel. Vol.II, p.17, says Hallowell
William Horney SW¼-S17; 8-7-1818. Rel. E½
William Rowland NE¼-S18; 8-14-1818
John McMahon NW¼-S18; 12-8-1818
William Saighman SE¼-S18; 12-3-1816
Michael Moran SW¼-S18; 8-15-1818. Rel.

Page 11. T 7 N, R 1 W of 1st P.M.

John Lambdin NE¼-S19; 9-30-1814
Peyton S. Symmes & Hugh Moore SE¼-S19; 5-1-1816
William Cloud W½-S19; 5-21-1814
Michael Farran & Emery Hobbs NE¼-S20; 9-27-1816. Rel. E½ to Henry Murphey, 12-29-1829. Vol.II, p.18, says Henry Harpham
Emery Hobbs NW¼-S20; 4-4-1817. Rel. N½ to Abram Briggs, 12-8-1829. Vol.II, p.18, says Abraham
George P. Torrence SE¼-S20; 4-30-1814
James McClure SW¼-S20; 9-26-1814
Robert Bradshaw NW¼-S21; 6-28-1824
John Cassady E½-SE¼-S21; 2-15-1832
Anthony Broadrick W½-SE¼-S21; 9-1-1828
Dennis Clark SW¼-S21; 10-22-1814
Lewis Jolly E½-NE¼-S22; 2-4-1829
Elijah Lake W½-NE¼-S22; 2-15-1832
Jacob Shots & James Anderson E½-NW¼-S22; 3-3-1832
George Waldorf E½-SE¼-S22; 4-10-1832
Jacob Stoms W½-SE¼-S22; 3-24-1830
Anthony Harkness & Michael McDermot SW¼-S22; 8-21-1819. Rel. W½ to Anthony Harkness, 8-9-1831; E½ to Benjamin Morgan, Jr., 8-19-1831. Vol.II, p.18, omits Michael McDermot
William Purcil & Thomas Brackenridge E½-S23; 6-10-1818. Rel. E½-NE¼ to George Waldorf, 7-7-1828; W½-NE¼ to Benjamin Morgan, 11-26-1828. Rel. E½-SE¼
Alexander White NW¼-S23; 6-22-1818. Rel. E½ to Warren Tabb, 3-10-1830. (Tobb?)
Jacob Demaris SW¼-S23; 9-15-1818. Rel. W½

John Brown E½-S24; 4-9-1801
William Purcil NW¼-S24; 9-6-1811
Nathaniel Crookshanks SW¼-S24; 3-5-1818. Rel.
John Allen E½-NE¼ & W½-NE¼-S25; 8-5-1805
Ulick Burke & Elisha Burke NW¼-S25; 8-5-1818. Rel. S½ to Ulick
    Burke, 5-24-1832. See Vol.II, p.18, Ulick Burke
Jonas Crane SE¼-S25; 2-15-1815. Rel. E½ to David Holdron,
    7-11-1828. Vol.II, p.19, says Dennis Holdron
Daniel McKay SW¼-S25; 1-8-1819. Rel. W½ to William Smith
    Drewer, 4-5-1832
David Lathrop NE¼-S26; 7-20-1818. Rel. E½ to Ramey Scandler
    Cloud, 3-15-1832. Vol.II, p.19, says Scandlin
Enoch Morgan NW¼-S26; 7-2-1818
Henry Daggett SE¼-S26; 7-20-1818. Rel.
Absalom Cornelius SW¼-S26; 12-29-1817. Rel. E½
Willoughby Tibbs NE¼-S27; 6-1-1810
Joshua Pasuis NW¼-S27; 10-5-1814. Vol.II, p.19, says Paris
James Jones, Jr. SE¼-S27; 10-5-1814
James Cloud SW¼-S27; 10-6-1812
Baylis Cloud NE¼-S28; 11-29-1811
Matthew Lambdin & Samuel Lambdin NW¼-S28; 4-6-1814
Elijah Garrison SE¼-S28 2-22-1814
Joseph Wooley SW¼-S28; 8-30-1814
Joel Dicken NE¼-S29; 5-7-1814
John Gibson NW¼-S29; 5-25-1816
Robert Miers & Thomas Watts SE¼-S29; 1-1-1814. Vol.II, p.19,
    says Robert Myers & Thomas Walls
Nicholas Gro--ndyke SW¼-S29; 12-12-1818. Rel. W½ to John
    French, 7-5-1831; E½ to John French, 9-6-1831
Zedekiah Bonham & Jonathan Lewis NW¼-S30; 10-24-1815
Aquilla Cross SE¼-S30; 12-14-1815
Henry Miller E½-SW¼-S30; 12-10-1818
Israel W. Bonham W½-SW¼-S30; 3-5-1819
William Webb NE¼-S31; 10-26-1814
Aquilla Cross NW¼-S31; 1-22-1818. Rel. W½ to Isaac Taylor,
Stephen Wood SE¼-S31; 1-1-1818   3-29-1832
Ezekiel Jackson SW¼-S31; 7-10-1817
Casper Johnson NE¼-S32; 10-11-1817
Aquilla Cross SE¼-S32; 1-22-1818
George Tuttle E½-NW¼ & W½-NW¼-S32; 2-18-1832
William Stoms W½-SW¼-S32; 5-23-1832

Page 12. T 7 N, R 1 W of 1st P.M.

Aaron Bonham NE¼-S33; 10-5-1814. Vol.II, p.20, adds middle
James Cole NW¼-S33; 8-7-1815   initial R
John Ruffum & Henry Diffenderffer SE¼-S33; 7-21-1818
Sacker Nelson SW¼-S33; 12-22-1815
Benjamin Reily NE¼-S34; 9-10-1814
James Cloud NW¼-S34; 6-11-1817
Joseph Loyd SE¼-S34; 1-2-1815
Alexander White SW¼-S34; 2-2-1815
Gustavus A. Cone & Philip Barnet NW¼-S35; 7-29-1818. Rel. W½ to
    William McClure, 2-3-1832

Jacob Taylor SE¼-S35; 6-6-1818. Rel. (middle initial R.)
John Gibson SW¼-S35; 6-23-1817. Rel. E½ to Aaron Scoggin, 3-26-1832
Reuben Lewis NE¼-S36; 6-5-1816
Nicholas Longworth NW¼-S36; 9-30-1818 (all struck off). Rel. W½ to James Backhouse, 9-11-1828. E½, 3-7-1832 (struck off)
Benjamin Clark SE¼-S36; 6-26-1818. Rel. E½ to David Williams, 12-3-1831
James Backhouse W½-NW¼-S36; 9-11-1828
Stephen Burke & Elisha Burke E½-NW¼-S36; 3-7-1832

Page 12. T 8 N, R 1 W of 1st P.M. **FRANKLIN CO.**

John Wooley NE¼-S1; 6-10-1814
Benjamin Abraham NW¼-S1; 12-12-1811
John Caldwell SE¼-S1; 1-13-1808
John Allen SW¼-S1; 12-31-1811
Silas Wooley NE¼-S2; 6-10-1814
John Allen NW¼-S2; 12-31-1811
James Caldwell, Jr. & John Caldwell SE¼-S2; 12-10-1812. Vol.II, p.20, says James Caldwell & John Caldwell, Jr.
Abraham Bledsoe SW¼-S2; 8-1-1806
William Will NE¼-S3; 11-7-1814. Vol.II, p.20, says Well
William Wilson NW¼-S3; 4-7-1813
William Burke SE¼-S3; 5-19-1817
James Stewart SW¼-S3; 6-24-1815
Joseph Siers NE¼-S4; 5-2-1814
Matthew Sparks NW¼-S4; 10-27-1815
Nathaniel Milspaugh SE¼-S4; 6-9-1824. Rel.
William Lemmon SW¼-S4; 4-22-1818
Peter B. Milspaugh NE¼-S5; 4-9-1818
Jacob Fetter SE¼-S5; 3-26-1818. Vol.II, p.21, says Felter
Stephen Craig SW¼-S5; 4-21-1818. Rel.
Prince Jenkins NW¼-S5 & SE¼-S6; 12-9-1814
William McDonnel NE¼-S6; 12-11-1811
Thomas Milholland NW¼-S6; 4-2-1812
James Milholland SW¼-S6; 3-10-1813. Rel. NE¼ to Crocker Jenkins, 5-30-1832. Vol.II, p.21, shows final cert. 2131 to James Milholland for SW¼-S6
Timothy Parker & Housel Parker NW¼-S7; 2-7-1815. Rel. E½ to Britton Gant, 2-7-1828
John Taylor W½-SE¼-S7; 6-9-1824
John Welch SW¼-S7; 3-16-1814
Hugh Moore SE¼-S8; 9-11-1816
David Marshall SW¼-S8; 6-7-1819. Rel.
William Banes E½-SW¼-S8; 8-16-1831

Page 13. T 8 N, R 1 W of 1st P.M.

Joshua Guile NE¼-S9; 8-10-1815
Ebenezer Lewis NW¼-S9; 6-28-1815
Moses Wiley SE¼-S9; 1-18-1808
Joshua Guile SW¼-S9; 7-27-1815
Matthew Sparks NE¼-S10; 9-1-1814
William Buster NW¼-S10; 5-22-1813
Samuel Moore SE¼-S10; 8-5-1806

William Siers SW¼-S10; 3-16-1814
Joseph Siers NE¼-S11; 11-19-1805
William B. Allen & John S. Allen NW¼-S11; 3-2-1813
Allen Spencer & James Wiley SE¼-S11; 11-1-1811
William Romy SW¼-S11; 10-30-1811. Vol.II, p.22, says Remy
David Penwell & Eli Penwell NE¼-S12; 12-29-1812
Joseph Williams NW¼-S12; 8-13-1812
John Sater SE¼-S12; 10-12-1812
James Cloud SW¼-S12; 8-13-1811. Vol.II, p.22, says John
Philip Harwood NE¼-S13; 10-10-1811
Thomas McQueen NW¼-S13; 12-31-1811
John Wood SE¼-S13; 12-13-1814
Henry Ramey SW¼-S13; 7-9-1806
Thomas McQueen NE¼-S14; 11-21-1811
James A. Lowes & Josiah Lowes NW¼-S14; 12-2-1816
Peter Hann SE¼-S14; 4-8-1812
James Findlay SW¼-S14; 11-17-1814. Vol.II, p.22, says Finley
Isaac S. Swearingen E½-S15; 3-1-1815
William Lowes NW¼-S15; 6-9-1818
John Seely SW¼-S15; 6-24-1819
Philip Yost, Jr. NE¼-S17; 12-30-1818. Rel. E½ to William Starritt, 8-9-1831
Manuel Chambers NW¼-S17; 2-20-1816
David K. Este & Andrew Bailey SE¼-S17; 3-25-1815
George Rudisel SW¼-S17; 6-11-1813
Oliver Benton E½-NE¼-S18; 10-12-1816. Rel. E½. To William McClure & Joseph Bennet, 9-1-1831
Robert Taylor W½-NE¼-S18; 6-9-1824
John Sailor NW¼-S18; 1-10-1807
William Hudson SE¼-S18; 7-1-1815
Benjamin McCarty, James Price & Richard Conner SW¼-S18;3-21-1806
Jonathan Hunt NE¼-S19; 3-10-1813
Leonard Sayre & Elmore Williams NW¼-S19; 12-12-1809
Abijah Hays SW¼-S19; 8-1-1817. Rel. W½. To Moses Whitney, 12-28-1831
John McComb NE¼-S20; 7-12-1819. Rel.
Joseph Marmon NW¼-S20; 3-20-1817
Joseph Peters SE¼-S20; 1-13-1816. Rel. E½. To George Sutton, 2-28-1832
Thomas Clark SW¼-S20; 8-1-1816
Benjamin George NE¼-S21; 7-24-1817
Henry Teller NW¼-S21; 9-11-1812. Rel. E½. To Jacob Taylor, 11-5-1825
Michael Rudicil SE¼-S21; 2-3-1816
Sherman A. Buck E½-SW¼-S21; 8-7-1824
Elias Henderson W½-SW¼-S21; 1-21-1828
Isaac S. Swearingen NE¼-S22; 3-1-1815
David Mills NW¼-S22; 6-9-1824
Richard Hubble SE¼-S22; 5-8-1816
Richard Hubble, Jr. SW¼-S22; 6-5-1817
John Stansbury NE¼-S23; 9-10-1812
John Stansbury NW¼-S23; 6-1-1813
John Larison SE¼-S23; 11-8-1813
Israel Davis SW¼-S23; 9-9-1815
James Remey NE¼-S24; 5-23-1814
Henry Sater NW¼-S24; 9-10-1812
Joseph Summers SE¼-S24; 5-29-1813
William Ramey SW¼-S24; 1-28-1808
Morris Seeley NE¼-S25; 6-28-1814
James Remy NW¼-S25; 11-28-1812

Page 14. T 8 N, R 1 W of 1st P.M.

John Hays SE¼-S25; 5-27-1814
James Gold SW¼-S25; 5-2-1814
James Ramey NE¼-S26; 5-23-1814
Caleb Keeler NW¼-S26; 10-19-1814
Michael Rudicil SW¼-S26; 9-28-1807
Lemuel Snow NW¼-S27; 6-30-1814
Lemuel Snow SE¼-S27; 11-29-1814. Vol.II, p.24, adds Jr.
Lemuel Snow SW¼-S27; 6-30-1814
Samuel Webber NE¼-S28; 3-29-1813
John Vanblaricum NW¼-S28; 5-26-1814
Lemuel Snow SE¼-S28; 12-23-1814
George Larison SW¼-S28; 12-12-1814
John Vanblaricum NE¼-S29; 12-11-1811
John Allen NW¼-S29; 6-14-1806
Isaac Levi S½-S29; 9-19-1804
Robertson Jones & John Vanblaricum NE¼-S30; 3-5-1810
Robert McKoy & George M. Brown NW¼-S30; 8-4-1817. Rel. W½ to
     George Rudicel, 3-27-1832
James Jones, Sr. SE¼-S30; 2-17-1817
Robert McKoy & George M. Brown SW¼-S30; 8-4-1817. Rel.
John H. Rockafeller NE¼-S31; 3-20-1815
Thomas Manwaring SE¼-S31; 2-23-1816
James Jones, Jr. SW¼-S31; 6-3-1816. Rel. W½ to John Low Sparks,
     10-20-1832. Vol.II, p.24, says Joshua Low Sparks
Benjamin McCarty S32; 5-25-1803
Nathan Richardson NE¼-S33; 12-14-1814
Jonathan Watkins & William Watkins NW¼-S33; 5-6-1815
Alexander Abercrombie E½-SE¼-S33; 11-20-1817
Ralph Reiley W½-SE¼-S33; 9-14-1818. Rel.
Ralph Wildridge SW¼-S33; 1-6-1815. Rel. E½ to Ralph Wildridge,
Henry Garner NE¼-S34; 2-5-1814   10-18-1828
Benjamin Lewis NW¼-S34; 3-31-1818
James Gold W½-SE¼-S34; 1-21-1831
Abner Conner SW¼-S34; 12-14-1814
William Remy NE¼-S35; 8-10-1813
William Vanmeter NW¼-S35; 5-6-1805
Israel Davis SE¼-S35; 8-17-1813
Israel Davis & Frederick Shotts SW¼-S35; 4-5-1813
Robert M. Seely SE¼-S36; 11-3-1814
Jacob Hoops & Michael Flowers SW¼-S36; 1-2-1815. Rel. W½ to
     William Stone, 10-26-1827
Francis Charles Downing E½-SW¼-S36; 11-22-1831

Page 15. T 9 N, R 1 W of 1st P.M.

Samuel Bourn & Benjamin Crocker NE¼-S1; 8-24-1814
Ezra L. Bourne NW¼-S1; 11-18-1814
Matthew Smith, Jr. SE¼-S1; 9-15-1813
William Furguson SW¼-S1; 7-25-1814
Jeremiah Abbot NE¼-S2; 9-5-1814
Charles Burch NW¼-S2; 8-24-1812
Thomas Craven SE¼-S2; 11-3-1813

Alexander Tefor SW¼-S2; 8-7-1812. Vol.II, p.25, says Telford
Henry Burgett NE¼-S3; 8-25-1812
James Frel NW¼-S3; 8-22-1811. Vol.II, p.25, says Terrel
Stephen Gardner SE¼-S3; 7-20-1811
James McCan SW¼-S3; 6-29-1811
Lemuel Lemmon NE¼-S4; 2-11-1812
William P. Swett NW¼-S4; 5-3-1814
Gideon Wilkinson SE¼-S4; 7-22-1811. See Vol.II, p.25, Daniel Currie
Gideon Wilkinson SW¼-S4; 6-15-1811
John Smith NE¼-S5; 10-11-1815
William Nelson NW¼-S5; 4-12-1813
James Wood SE½-S5; 4-2-1813
Adam Reed SW¼-S5; 11-5-1810
Walter Tucker NE¼-S6; 9-7-1814
Daniel Reed SE¼-S6; 10-19-1810
John Wonderlick W½-S6; 12-20-1814
Daniel Reed NE¼-S7; 10-19-1810
Jacob Howel NW¼-S7; 11-1-1814. Rel. W½ tc James C. Tucker, 8-28-1826. Vol.II, p.26, says Joab Howell
William Hetdrick & Abraham Hetdrick SE¼-S7; 5-8-1812
William Hetdrick SW¼-S7; 6-6-1814
Jonathan Stout NE¼-S8; 9-30-1813
Adam Mow NW¼-S8; 8-7-1813
Enoch D. John SE¼-S8; 6-21-1814
Thomas Osborn SW¼-S8; 1-3-1812
Philip Jones, Jr. NE¼-S9; 7-20-1811
Gideon Wilkinson NW¼-S9; 6-15-1811
William Armstrong SE¼-S9; 8-7-1812
David Wason SW¼-S9; 4-15-1812. See Vol.II, p.26, Gideon Wilkinson
Cornelius Viley NE¼-S10; 8-27-1811
Richard Colliver NW¼-S10; 2-20-1812
Mitchel Fleming SE¼-S10; 9-9-1912. See Vol.II, p.26, Samuel McCray
John Milner SW¼-S10; 8-25-1812
Adam Carson NE¼-S11; 7-7-1812
Alexander Telfer NW¼-S11; 1-24-1815. Vol.II, p.26, says Tilford
Samuel C. Vance SE¼-S11; 5-1-1818. Rel. E½ to Abraham Lee, 7-5-1831. W½ to William Welch, 3-24-1832
Bryson Blackburn SW¼-S11; 11-2-1813
James Port NW¼-S12; 10-18-1817. Rel. W½ to Jacob Faussett, Jr., 12-15-1829
Thomas Bond SW¼-S12; 6-26-1815. Rel. W½ to James Kennedy, 5-22-1830; E½ to Judah Hinkley, 6-11-1830
Charles Cone E½-S12; 4-23-1813
Lewis Bond NE¼-S13; 5-26-1814
Mary Denny NW¼-S13; 6-6-1814
George Todd & James McNutt SE¼-S13; 2-28-1812
Andrew Shirk SW¼-S13; 1-3-1808
Moses Rarden NE¼-S14; 7-9-1812
Thomas Selfridge NW¼-S14; 8-7-1812
Moses Rarden SE¼-S14; 1-8-1810
William Ardery SW¼-S14; 11-2-1811
Elijah Atherton NE¼-S15; 9-21-1813
Enoch Buckingham NW¼-S15; 1-18-1815
Peter Updike & Elijah Updike E½-SE¼-S15; 8-6-1817

Samuel Shirk W½-SE¼-S15; 6-9-1824
Samuel F. Hunt & Jesse Hunt SW¼-S15; 9-10-1817
Robert John NE¼-S17; 6-21-1814. Rel. E½ to Elijah H. Tucker.
Andrew Shirk, Sr. NW¼-S17; 8-18-1812   10-20-1827
Lewis Bond SE¼-S17; 6-21-1814
Robert John SW¼-S17; 6-21-1814

Page 16. T 9 N, R 1 W of 1st. P.M.

Richard Kalb NE¼-S18; 7-10-1809. Vol.II, p.27, says Kobo
Abraham Timberman NW¼-S18; 12-15-1813
Walter Tucker SE¼-S18; 7-28-1812
John Stroube & Christopher Stroube SW¼-S18; 11-6-1813
James Goudie NE¼-S19; 8-9-1814
Peyton S. Symmes NW¼-S19; 9-1-1814
William Clark & Stephen Gregg SE¼-S19; 8-31-1813
William McDaniel SW¼-S19; 11-2-1811. Vol.II, p.27, says
Richard Cockey NE¼-S20; 8-8-1814   McDonald
John Carson NW¼-S20; 9-17-1814
Enoch D. John SE¼-S20; 6-21-1814
Thomas Gregg SW¼-S20; 5-6-1812
George Rab NE¼-S21; 6-21-1816
William Ruffin E½-NW¼-S21; 6-9-1824
Samuel Goudie W½-NW¼-S21; 6-9-1824
Enoch Buckingham SE¼-S21; 1-18-1815
Thomas Wainsley E½-SW¼-S21; 11-6-1828. Vol.II, p.27, says
John Misner W½-SW¼-S21; 12-17-1828   Wamsley
Andrew Shirk, Jr. NE¼-S22; 8-31-1813
Robert Luse NW¼-S22; 9-2-1814
Stephen Craig SE¼-S22; 11-29-1817
Cornelius Simons SW¼-S22; 11-29-1817. Rel. E½ to Minney W.
    Simonson & Charles H. Simonson, 12-8-1829. Vol.II, p.27, says
    Cornelius Simonson
James Rees NE¼-S23; 10-13-1813
William Ardery NW¼-S23; 11-21-1811
Edward White SE¼-S23; 3-2-1807
Joseph Cilley SW¼-S23; 4-17-1812
Josiah Beal NE¼-S24; 12-28-1811
Philip Wilkins NW¼-S24; 2-23-1809
Thomas Morgan SE¼-S24; 3-10-1807
Samuel Hamilton SW¼-S24; 5-31-1809
Isaac Wood NE¼-S25; 4-15-1812
John McGuire NW¼-S25; 7-30-1813
Benjamin Blue SE¼-S25; 2-19-1807
John Goldtrap SW¼-S25; 3-28-1814
Ithamer White NE¼-S26; 3-16-1813
Joseph Cilley NW¼-S26; 4-15-1812
Stanhope Royster SE¼-S26; 4-15-1812
Robert Gray SW¼-S26; 8-31-1813
Thomas Shaw NE¼-S27; 10-15-1813   * Samuel Stewart NE¼-S28;
Amos Atherton NW¼-S27; 8-25-1812   8-1-1816
Jacob Faussel SE¼-S27; 6-12-1813. Vol.II, p.28, says Fausset
John Ramsey & Robert Scantlin SW¼-S27; 10-13-1804. Vol.II, p.28,
    says Scantland
* (omission)

John Ramey SE¼-S28; 10-13-1804
James Heath SW¼-S28; 11-3-1806
Abner Leonard NE¼-S29; 11-19-1813
Dennis Dusky NW¼-S29; 6-20-1807
Stephen Davis SE¼-S29; 3-8-1815
Benjamin Hinds SW¼-S29; 7-27-1813
Richard Keene NE¼-S30; 9-3-1814
Joseph Carson NW¼-S30; 4-14-1813. Middle initial L
Archibald Talbott SE¼-S30; 6-22-1814
John Holliday SW¼-S30; 5-23-1814
William Seal NE¼-S31; 9-28-1813
George J.(I?) Wallace NW¼-S31; 4-19-1816
William Cloud SE¼-S31; 7-28-1806
James Seal SW¼-S31; 12-7-1813
Nixon Oliver NE¼-S32; 11-21-1815
John Crowel NW¼-S32; 7-23-1807
Henry R. Compton SE¼-S32; 11-18-1816
Benjamin Tucker SW¼-S32; 4-3-1817

Page 17. T 9 N, R 1 W of 1st P.M.

John Coulter & William Rayl E½-S33; 9-19-1806. Rel. E½-SW¼ to
    William H. Pawner, 12-11-1829. Vol.II, p.28, says Powner
John Clendening NW¼-S33; 7-23-1807
James P. Millspaugh W½-SW¼-S33; 3-8-1828. Vol.II, p.28, gives
    middle initial D
Robert Losset NE¼-S34; 10-29-1811. Vol.II, p.28, gives Fossett
John Rees NW¼-S34; 9-27-1813
David McGaughey SE¼-S34; 6-13-1814
Arthur Henry SW¼-S34; 1-2-1812
Chester Harrel NE¼-S35; 11-11-1811
Benjamin Wood NW¼-S35; 4-28-1813
Robert Blair SE¼-S35; 4-18-1814
James McCord SW¼-S35; 11-3-1813
Samuel Dugans NE¼-S36;; 1-7-1815
William Snodgrass NW¼-S36; 5-22-1813
Jacob Hiday SE¼-S36; 4-20-1813
Benjamin Abraham SW¼-S36; 12-15-1813

Page 17. T 10 N, R 1 W of 1st P.M.   UNION CO.

Joseph Harter NW¼-S1; 10-25-1815
John Miller SW¼-S1; 10-16-1810
Francis McClelland NE¼-S2; 11-29-1814
John Miller NW¼-S2; 12-4-1813
Jacob Darst SE¼-S2; 5-4-1807
Tobias Miller SW¼-S2; 1-15-1814
Matthew McCleerker NE¼-S3; 5-25-1809. Vol.II, p.29, looks
    like McClinkin
Thomas Sankey NW¼-S3; 11-18-1811
Thomas Harper, Sr. S½-S3; 3-9-1811
William Ogle NE¼-S4; 10-26-1813
William Miller SE¼-S4; 7-31-1813
William Ogle W½-S4; 9-23-1813

Joseph Hough NE¼-S5; 11-30-1814. Rel. W½ to James Macy 2-9-1828
William Miller, Jr. SE¼-S5; 7-12-1814
Robert Flack W½-S5; 7-26-1806
James Davis NE¼-S6; 9-8-1806
James Davis NW¼-S6; 12-11-1811
Samuel Shannon SE¼-S6; 4-14-1813
Samuel Shannon SW¼-S6; 7-26-1806
James Fordyce NE¼-S7; 2-28-1814
John Ray NW¼-S7; 8-26-1813
Peter Davis SE¼-S7; 7-19-1806
William Coe SW¼-S7; 1-13-1814
Morris Witham NE¼-S8; 3-23-1812
Joshua Williams NW¼-S8; 2-17-1812
Christopher Smith SE¼-S8; 1-7-1814
Peter Davis SW¼-S8; 7-19-1806
John Kell NE¼-S9; 1-25-1814
James Smiley & Thomas R. Smiley NW¼-S9; 4-1-1814
John McClucken SE¼-S9; 11-27-1811. Vol.II, p.30, says McClurken
William Deniston SW¼-S9; 12-31-1814
Cross Thompson NE¼-S10; 11-7-1814. Vol.II, p.30, says Closs
William Leper NW¼-S10; 3-17-1810
James Currie SE¼-S10; 8-16-1813
John Speer SW¼-S10; 11-18-1816
Thomas Harper, Sr. N½-S11; 3-9-1811
David Black S½-S11; 7-29-1814

Page 18. T 10 N, R 1 W of 1st P.M.

John Miller E½-S12; 2-26-1805
John Miller NW¼-S12; 10-16-1810
Abraham Durst SW¼-S12; 11-29-1805
John Denman NE¼-S13; 1-22-1808
William Crawford NW¼-S13; 10-28-1806
Abraham Hammon SE¼-S13; 6-14-1806
Jacob Bake SW¼-S13; 11-10-1806
John Miller NE¼-S14; 4-21-1810
William Stephens NW¼-S14; 9-22-1810
William Denniston SE¼-S14; 8-5-1809
Isaac Coon SW¼-S14; 9-22-1810
Boni Goble NE¼-S15; 1-26-1815. Vol.II, p.30, says Benone
Abner Goble SE¼-S15; 1-26-1815. Rel.E½ to John Orr, 8-7-1827
John Miller, Jr. E½-NW¼-S15; 2-10-1826
Andrew Himelick W½-NW¼-S15; 6-30-1829
David Orr W½-SW¼-S15; 8-28-1827
John W. Card NE¼-S17; 10-12-1814. May be McCord
James Stewart NW¼-S17; 6-22-1815
Jonathan W. Powers SE¼-S17; 4-20-1814
James Smith SW¼-S17; 2-26-1814
Samuel Howell NE¼-S18; 7-18-1806
Thomas Reeds NW¼-S18; 8-25-1806; Vol.II, p.30, says James
John Hetfield SE¼-S18; 8-17-1813
Joseph Nelson SW¼-S18; 8-25-1806

Page 18. T 10 N, R 1 W of 1st P.M.

John Flint & Nathan Garrett NE$\frac{1}{4}$-S19; 8-5-1811
Jonathan Copland & James Berry NW$\frac{1}{4}$-S19; 9-13-1806
Samuel Ayres SE$\frac{1}{4}$-S19; 9-3-1808
Moses Maxwell SW$\frac{1}{4}$-S19; 4-12-1810
James Dun, Jr. NE$\frac{1}{4}$-S20; 3-26-1816
John Flint NW$\frac{1}{4}$-S20; 7-10-1811
Thomas Reed SE$\frac{1}{4}$-S20; 3-13-1815
John Flint SW$\frac{1}{4}$-S20; 12-12-1811. Vol.II, p.31, adds Sr.
John Bake E$\frac{1}{2}$-NE$\frac{1}{4}$-S21; 6-9-1824
George Teagarden W$\frac{1}{2}$-NE$\frac{1}{4}$-S21; 6-9-1824
William Minear E$\frac{1}{2}$-NW$\frac{1}{4}$-S21; 8-4-1825
Robert Smith W$\frac{1}{2}$-NW$\frac{1}{4}$-S21; 10-24-1825
Thomas Capper E$\frac{1}{2}$-SE$\frac{1}{4}$-S21; 2-18-1825
Isaac A. Ogden W$\frac{1}{2}$-SE$\frac{1}{4}$-S21; 7-17-1827
Samuel Murphy E$\frac{1}{2}$-SW$\frac{1}{4}$-S21; 8-1-1826
John Flint W$\frac{1}{2}$-SW$\frac{1}{4}$-S21; 3-31-1826
Jacob Bell NE$\frac{1}{4}$-S22; 10-27-1813
Elijah H. Tucker E$\frac{1}{2}$-NW$\frac{1}{4}$-S22; 8-15-1826
William Bake W$\frac{1}{2}$-NW$\frac{1}{4}$-S22; 10-18-1827
Christopher Giston SE$\frac{1}{4}$-S22; 9-6-1814. Vol.II, p.31, says
Christian Girton
Andrew Himelick E$\frac{1}{2}$-SW$\frac{1}{4}$-S22; 6-9-1824
Andrew Himelick W$\frac{1}{2}$-SW$\frac{1}{4}$-S22; 1-23-1826
Joseph Lee NE$\frac{1}{4}$-S23; 10-9-1810
Christopher Smith NW$\frac{1}{4}$-S23; 1-20-1812
Jacob Ball SW$\frac{1}{4}$-S23; 1-22-1813. Vol.II, p.31, says Bell
James Crooks NE$\frac{1}{4}$-S24; 1-28-1806
Abraham Miller NW$\frac{1}{4}$-S24; 11-5-1805
Daniel Miller SE$\frac{1}{4}$-S24; 11-5-1805
David Hansel SW$\frac{1}{4}$-S24; 9-30-1805
Christopher Hansel NE$\frac{1}{4}$-S25; 11-16-1805
James Baxter NW$\frac{1}{4}$-S25; 2-1-1811
John Moss SE$\frac{1}{4}$-S25; 2-25-1811
Thomas Burke NE$\frac{1}{4}$-S26; 4-8-1806
Joseph Kingery NW$\frac{1}{4}$-S26: 11-23-1815
John Morris SW$\frac{1}{4}$-S26; 8-30-1816

Page 19. T 10 N, R 1 W of 1st P.M.

William Stephens NE$\frac{1}{4}$-S27; 9-22-1810
Christopher Hansel & George Hansel NW$\frac{1}{4}$-S27; 6-22-1813
William Forbes SE$\frac{1}{4}$-S27; 5-29-1815
Joshua Harris SW$\frac{1}{4}$-S27; 9-1-1814
John Ross NE$\frac{1}{4}$-S28; 5-4-1816
Andrew Orr & John Hatfield SE$\frac{1}{4}$-S28; 4-27-1816
Peter Sunderland W$\frac{1}{2}$-S28; 1-20-1817. Vol.II, p.32, says John
Robert Brisbin NE$\frac{1}{4}$-S29; 10-24-1814
John Chivington NW$\frac{1}{4}$-S29; 10-22-1814
John Flint, Sr. SE$\frac{1}{4}$-S29; 10-14-1813
Abiel Dare SW$\frac{1}{4}$-S29; 6-3-1812. Vol.II, p.32, says Abel
Chalfield Howell NE$\frac{1}{4}$-S30; 6-21-1806. Vol.II, p.32, says
Chatfield

Cormack Gellagan & Kepen Campeon NW¼-S30; 11-11-1806. Vol.II,
    p.32, says Charmick Gilligan & Hysen Campion
William Dubois SE¼-S30; 6-21-1806
Chelfield Howell SW¼-S30; 6-21-1806. Vol.II, p.32, says Chatfield
Adam Nelson NE¼-S31; 8-24-1813
Robert Pettycrew NW¼-S31; 9-21-1815
Benjamin Haregeder SE¼-S31; 8-16-1811. Vol.II, p.32, says
John Powers SW¼-S31; 4-26-1814   Hargerder
Samuel Kain NE¼-S32; 10-26-1813
John Howell & Chalfield Howell NW¼-S32; 10-24-1810. Vol.II, p.32,
Zachariah Davis SE¼-S32; 10-8-1814   says Chatfield
James Stephens NE¼-S33; 11-11-1815
Samuel Huston NW¼-S33; 8-14-1816. Rel. W½ to James Dailey,
    1-11-1828
John Carr SE¼-S33; 4-16-1813. See Vol.II, p.32, Samuel Huston
Lemuel Lemmon SW¼-S33; 10-28-1813
Robert Ross NE¼-S34; 5-4-1816
Samuel Huston NW¼-S34; 8-14-1816
Lemuel Lemmon SE¼-S34; 11-26-1812
William Goff SW¼-S34; 9-10-1813
William Ruffin NE¼-S35; 8-13-1816. Vol.II, p.32, says he
    assigned it to Jo. Pitman
Lemuel Lemmon NW¼-S35; 6-3-1815
Ephraim Tucker SE¼-S35; 1-4-1816
Alexander Furguson SW¼-S35; 7-25-1814
David Cray NE¼-S36; 7-11-1810
Christopher Hansel NW¼-S36; 9-10-1814
Abraham Lee SE¼-S36; 9-4-1807
Abraham Jones SW¼-S36; 6-13-1808

Page 20. T 11 N, R 1 W of 1st P.M.   UNION CO.

Anthony Williams NE¼-S1; 8-29-1806
John Penticost NW¼-S1; 1-13-1808
John Penticost, Jr. SE¼-S1; 2-8-1814
David Landis SW¼-S1; 9-8-1807
James Eggers NE¼-S2; 4-20-1813
Stephen Hayden & Benjamin Gard NW¼-S2; 4-13-1813
George Bridged SE¼-S2; 9-21-1813
Ephraim Brown SW¼-S2; 10-20-1813
William Eaton NE¼-S3; 1-13-1814
William Willis NW¼-S3; 4-14-1813
Thomas A. R. Eaton SE¼-S3; 1-25-1815
Matthew Tatem SW¼-S3; 9-15-1815
Richard Miner NE¼-S4; 12-2-1806
Isaac Swaford NW¼-S4; 1-20-1808
William Swaford SE¼-S4; 1-11-1808
Vincent Cromwell SW¼-S4; 1-11-1808
Jacob Skillman NE¼-S5; 2-2-1807
Samuel Lafuze & Joseph Vanvicter NW¼-S5; 9-28-1813. Vol.II,
    p.33, says Vanmeter
Thomas Miller SE¼-S5; 9-28-1813
Jonas Hunt & John Hunt SW¼-S5; 2-27-1815
Richard Arnold E½-S6; 2-12-1814

Aaron Staunton NW¼-S6; 9-1-1815
James Snodgrass SW¼-S6; 6-6-1815
George Dike NE¼-S7; 8-17-1811
George W. Crist NW¼-S7; 9-17-1814
David Hollingsworth SE¼-S7; 3-7-1808
George Williams SW¼-S7; 5-24-1814
Ruth Crane NE¼-S8; 4-7-1807
Samuel Tappen NW¼-S8; 4-7-1807
Zepheniah Burt SE¼-S8; 6-17-1814
Jonathan Crane SW¼-S8; 4-7-1807
John Wright NE¼-S9; 3-30-1814
Joab Brooks NW¼-S9; 11-17-1813
Henry Hollingsworth SE¼-S9; 3-30-1814
Uzal Ward SW¼-S9; 9-28-1813
William Cartwright NE¼-S10; 10-27-1815
Latham Stanton NW¼-S10; 10-21-1814
William Miller SE¼-S10; 12-20-1814
Isaac Gardner SW¼-S10; 4-28-1817
Asa Taler NE¼-S11; 9-12-1814
Jacob Maxwell NW¼-S11; 10-4-1814
Samuel McDill SE¼-S11; 9-28-1814
Thomas Miller SW¼-S11; 7-25-1814
Robert Elliott & Daniel Elliott NE¼-S12; 10-19-1814
John Miller NW¼-S12; 12-4-1813
John Wiley SE¼-S12; 12-26-1816
Samuel Rutter SW¼-S12; 3-2-1807. Vol.II, p.34, says Ratter
James McClurken NE¼-S13; 7-26-1813
Jacob Retter & John Retter NW¼-S13; 11-26-1811
Robert M. Miller SE¼-S13; 10-1-1818
Christopher Wetter SW¼-S13; 6-25-1806
Peter Lennen NE¼-S14; 4-17-1818. William Eaker crossed out and
    Peter Lennen written in
Asa Taler NW¼-S14; 9-12-1814
Joseph Kingery SE¼-S14; 12-7-1813
James Huston SW¼-S14; 12-7-1813
Benjamin Johnson E½-S15; 6-1-1818
William Macy W½-NW¼-S15; 5-16-1818
David Swain SW¼-S15; 11-8-1817
Joel Haworth E½-NW¼-S15; 12-14-1824
Ezekiel Hollingsworth NE¼-S17; 12-2-1817
Thomas Madden NW¼-S17; 9-2-1811
James Stanton SE¼-S17; 10-31-1811
Ebenezer How SW¼-S17; 11-22-1813

Page 21. T 11 N, R 1 W of 1st P.M.

John Macklin NE¼-S18; 8-27-1811
Henry Hunter NW¼-S18; 3-25-1814
Henry Hunter SE¼-S18; 4-14-1813
Daniel Parmer SW¼-S18; 1-13-1808. Vol.II, p.34, says Palmer
John Heavenridge NE¼-S19; 6-7-1811
Hugh Reid NW¼-S19; 7-23-1807
Reuben Scurlock SE¼-S19; 11-17-1813
James Greene & Thomas Brown SW¼-S19; 8-30-1817. Vol.II, p.34,
    says Grier

Elial Gardner NE¼-S20; 10-31-1811
James Hollingshead NW½-S20; 9-3-1813. Vol.II, p.34, says Hollingsworth
Aaron Stanton SE¼-S20; 12-24-1812
William Sparks SW¼-S20; 7-19-1809
Uriah Starbuck NE¼-S21; 7-2-1817
Rolland Coleman NW¼-S21; 4-24-1815
Isaac Gardner SE¼-S21; 8-2-1817
Isaac Gardner SW¼-S21; 10-24-1815
Joel Haworth NE¼-S22; 10-17-1816
Job Talbert NW¼-S22; 8-15-1817
William Riggsbee & William S. Clark E½-SE¼-S22; 6-9-1824
Moses Martindale W½-SE¼-S22; 9-2-1817
Silvanus Swain SW¼-S22; 8-9-1815
Joseph Kingery NE¼-S23; 9-24-1814
Christopher Wetter NW¼-S23; 11-22-1816. Vol.II, p.35, says Witter
Abraham Myers SE¼-S23; 5-26-1810
John Myers SW¼-S23; 5-9-1809
John Brown NE¼-S24; 10-4-1814
William Brown NW¼-S24; 12-18-1805
Samuel Bell SE¼-S24; 8-17-1814
John Wetter SW¼-S24; 7-2-1806
Samuel Kingery NW¼-S25; 12-28-1813
Christopher Wetter NE¼-S25; 6-25-1804. John Myers crossed off and Christopher Wetter written in
John Fisher SE¼-S25; 3-15-1805
John Fisher SW¼-S25; 8-2-1813
Joseph Kingery NE¼-S26; 3-16-1815
Martin Kingery NW¼-S26; 10-25-1809
Henry Brandenburg SE¼-S26; 9-28-1813
George Keffer SW¼-S26; 10-10-1806
Samuel Lennen & Peter Lennen NE¼-S27; 1-17-1815
Peter Lennen NW¼-S27; 10-11-1813
John Short SE¼-S27; 1-15-1808
David Pressley SW¼-S27; 8-2-1808. Vol.II, p.35, says Prestley
James Martin NE¼-S28; 2-4-1814
Jonathan Huddleston NW¼-S28; 8-8-1815
Jacob Giger SE¼-S28; 10-22-1814
William Beard SW¼-S28; 10-21-1815
Aaron Stanton NE¼-S29; 9-6-1813
John Furnes NW¼-S29; 4-12-1814
Hugh Maxwell SE¼-S29; 5-28-1813
Hugh Maxwell SW¼-S29; 5-28-1813
Abraham Hollingsworth NE¼-S30; 9-24-1808
Jesse Hunt NW¼-S30; 8-1-1816. See Vol.II, p.35, Thomas Brown
John Creek SE¼-S30; 12-12-1814
Solomon Beach SW¼-S30; 10-22-1816
John Creek NE¼-S31; 2-13-1808
John Creek NW¼-S31; 1-23-1814
John Creek SE¼-S31; 8-20-1810
Robert Gobel SW¼-S31; 7-12-1814
Thomas Wright NE¼-S32; 11-29-1814
John Creek NW¼-S32; 2-13-1808
Joseph Hough SE¼-S32; 11-30-1814
John Creek SW¼-S32; 8-20-1810
Samuel Bonner NE¼-S33; 8-18-1813
Samuel McDill NW¼-S33; 9-19-1914
David Bonner SE¼-S33; 12-7-1813
Andrew Nixon SW¼-S33; 6-3-1817

Page 22. T 11 N, R 1 W of 1st P.M.

Jacob Kingery NE¼-S34; 10-10-1806. Vol.II, p.36, adds Sr.
Matthew McClucken NW¼-S34; 11-27-1811. Vol.II, p.36, says
Adam Richey SE¼-S34; 10-21-1806   McClurken
William Ogle SW¼-S34; 10-4-1813
William Beard NE¼-S35; 8-2-1817
George Keffer NW¼-S35; 10-10-1806
Isaac Gardner & William Beard SE¼-S35; 8-4-1817
William Ramsey, Jr. SW¼-S35; 7-28-1808
John Myers NE¼-S36; 6-30-1806
John Allen NW¼-S36; 2-2-1815
Christley Kingery SE¼-S36; 11-2-1805
Joseph Rightnour SW¼-S36; 1-2-1815

Page 22. T 12 N, R 1 W of 1st P.M.   WAYNE CO.

John Thompson NE¼-S1; 11-26-1814
Bryan Leanly NW¼-S1; 6-11-1814. Vol.II, p.36, says Seaney
William S. Jones SE¼-S1; 4-18-1814
William H. McBoom SW¼-S1; 8-27-1817. Rel. E½ to Nicholas
   Drewley, 12-1-1825
John Lawman & Daniel Lawman NE¼-S2; 8-9-1817
Isaac Conley NW¼-S2; 10-9-1816
Thomas Wyatt SE¼-S2; 12-2-1811
Beni White SW¼-S2; 12-6-1813
David Fisher NE¼-S3; 7-27-1813
William Fouts NW¼-S3; 11-29-1806
Major Dodson SE¼-S3; 9-20-1813
Owen Sency SW¼-S3; 6-20-1808. Vol.II, p.37, says Seny
Peter Melender NE¼-S4; 4-14-1813
Isaac Esteb NW¼-S4; 8-12-1807
Abraham Lewis SE¼-S4; 10-30-1811
Samuel Job SW¼-S4; 4-14-1813
Edward Clanton NE¼-S5; 4-25-1812. Vol.II, p.37, says Clauson
Samuel Job NW¼-S5; 4-14-1813
Thomas Burke SE¼-S5; 7-23-1806
Jacob Little, Sr. SW¼-S5; 4-29-1807
Lewis Little NE¼-S6; 7-10-1807
Peter Smith NW¼-S6; 12-2-1805
Lewis Little SE¼-S6; 6-29-1807
John Hunt SW¼-S6; 4-14-1813

Page 22. T 12 N, R 1 W of 1st P.M.   UNION CO.

Thomas Burk NE¼-S7; 7-28-1806
John Smith NW¼-S7; 10-4-1806
William Holeman SE¼-S7; 7-24-1805
John Williams SW¼-S7; 9-18-1809
Joseph Powers NE¼-S8; 8-16-1808
Thomas Burk NW¼-S8; 7-23-1806
Walter S. Burgess SE¼-S8; 10-9-1811
Joseph Holeman SW¼-S8; 7-24-1806
Abraham Lewis NE¼-S9; 10-30-1811

Henry Hoover SE¼-S9; 2-17-1807
Abraham Lewis SW¼-S9; 7-3-1812
Isaac Eastop NE¼-S10; 1-23-1808
Major Dodson NW¼-S10; 11-28-1811
Isaac Medcalf, Richard Sedgwick & William Brown SE¼-S10; 1-13-1808
Zacheriah Stanley SW¼-S10; 11-28-1811

Page 23. T 12 N, R 1 W of 1st P.M.

Joel Moore NE¼-S11; 11-12-1810
Abraham Lewis NW¼-S11; 10-30-1811
Andrew Jones SE¼-S11; 9-8-1813
Isaac Medcalf, Richard Sedgwick & William Brown SW¼-S11; 1-13-1808
John Jordan NE¼-S12; 7-29-1812
Samuel Druley NW¼-S12; 11-14-1814
John Thompson SE¼-S12; 11-26-1814
David Brown SW¼-S12; 5-30-1817
Asa Elliott NE¼-S13; 4-8-1818. See Vol.II, p.38, Charles Gordon
Jacob House NW¼-S13; 10-5-1816
Henry Vanmiddlesworth S½-S13; 5-25-1818
William Wyatt NE¼-S14; 1-5-1814
David Wyatt NW¼-S14; 9-11-1813
John Stanley SE¼-S14; 6-1-1812
James Bedwell SW¼-S14; 6-6-1812
Nicholas Drewly NE¼-S15; 6-9-1824
Anthony Mabbett NW¼-S15; 8-17-1814
Martin Devenport E½-SE¼-S15; 10-7-1824
Andrew Jones W½-SE¼-S15; 3-1-1827
Joel Haworth SW¼-S15; 6-9-1824
Philip Woods NE¼-S17; 4-1-1812
William Hunt NW¼-S17; 2-8-1808
Samuel Job SW¼-S17; 6-29-1807
Andrew Fouts NE¼-S18; 8-29-1806
Bela Butler NW¼-S18; 7-23-1806. Vol.II, p.38, says Beale
John Beard SE¼-S18; 11-29-1806
Jesse Henly SW¼-S18; 8-29-1806
John Starr NE¼-S19; 6-27-1807
John Starr NW¼-S19; 9-11-1807
William Farlow SE¼-S19; 1-13-1808
John Farlow SW¼-S19; 4-14-1813
David T. Wyatt NE¼-S20; 12-9-1814. Vol.II, p.38, gives middle
     initial F
Robert Burnett NW¼-S20; 11-15-1814. Vol.II, p.38, says Bennett
John McEawan SE¼-S20; 9-16-1815
Robert Bennett SW¼-S20; 10-20-1808
Joel Haworth E½-SE¼-S21; 6-9-1824
Nicholas Drewly W½-SE¼-S21; 6-9-1824
Nicholas Drewly E½-SW¼-S21; 11-24-1825
Samuel McMahon W½-SW¼-S21; 10-27-1824
James Toney NE¼-S22; 7-6-1824
James McMahon E½-NW¼-S22; 12-23-1824
James McMahon W½-NW¼-S22; 10-27-1824
Jacob Strawn SE¼-S22; 2-16-1818
James Harvey E½-SW¼-S22; 12-16-1824

Joel Haworth W½-SW¼-S22; 6-9-1824
Joel House NE¼-S23; 12-3-1814. Vol.II, p.39, says Jacob
James Davis NW¼-S23; 11-28-1814
Lot Gard SE¼-S23; 6-12-1815
John McEawan SW¼-S23; 9-16-1815
Michael Snider NE¼-S24; 6-13-1808
William Moss NW¼-S24; 11-16-1814
William Moss SE¼-S24; 10-19-1808
Michael SW¼-S24; 1-13-1808   Surname Snider
Philip Lybrook E½-S25; 1-25-1808
Philip Lybrook NW¼-S25; 10-19-1808
Jacob Kingery SW¼-S25; 10-19-1808

Page 24. T 12 N, R 1 W of 1st P.M.

Jacob Kingery NE¼-S26; 11-16-1814
James Suler NW¼-S26; 9-7-1816. Vol.II, p.39, says Sulser
Henry Lybrook SE¼-S26; 10-31-1811
Jacob Roush SW¼-S26; 10-9-1816
Robert Harvey NE¼-S27; 9-16-1808
Francis Harvey NW¼-S27; 12-23-1813
John Kennady SE¼-S27; 11-26-1814
Aaron Gard SW¼-S27; 9-19-1814
William Fox NE¼-S28; 2-6-1808
David Drenan NW¼-S28; 1-24-1815. Rel. W½ to John Plummer, 9-1-
Joseph Nelson SE¼-S28; 11-6-1813   1827
John Plummer SW¼-S28; 1-13-1808
William Dunbar NE¼-S29; 2-15-1814
John Biggs SE¼-S29; 2-2-1814
Samuel Ritchet W½-S29; 9-5-1815. Vol.II, p.39, says Kitchel
Ebenezer Howe NE¼-S30; 7-19-1814
Daniel Miller NW¼-S30; 12-1-1808
Asa Elliott SE¼-S30; 2-25-1818
Henry Pearson NE¼-S31; 11-6-1816
John Reily NW¼-S31; 4-5-1815
Michael Culver SE¼-S31; 12-28-1813
David Dunham SW¼-S31; 11-29-1816
Robert Waddle NE¼-S52; 9-30-1813. Vol.II, p.40, says Waddell
Josiah Brodway NW¼-S32; 9-26-1814
Jacob Skillman S½-S32; 2-2-1807
Mary Miner NE¼-S33; 12-2-1806
Jacob Fouts NW¼-S33; 1-13-1808
Benjamin Nutter SE¼-S33; 12-2-1806
Antipas Thomas SW¼-S33; 12-9-1814
Nathan Ruder & Jeremiah Ruder NE¼-S34; 2-3-1814. Vol.II, p.40,
   says Reeder
Joseph Spencer NW¼-S34; 11-22-1811
David Gooding SE¼-S34; 2-2-1814. Vol.II, p.40, says Goodin
John Cartwright SW¼-S34; 12-2-1806
Benjamin Morris NE¼-S35; 12-7-1814   Josephus Gard S½-S36;
William Elder NW¼-S35; 11-28-1814   10-21-1806
Daniel Eggers, Jr. SE¼-S35; 12-11-1813
Enoch Boaling SW¼-S35; 11-28-1814. Vol.II, p.40, looks like
Philip Lybrook N½-S36; 10-15-1806   Booling

Page 25. T 13 N, R 1 W of 1st P.M. WAYNE CO.

Peter Fleming NE¼-S1; 9-23-1805
Robert Hill NW¼-S1; 12-12-1811
Matthew Flanegan SE¼-S1; 9-23-1805
Benjamin Small SW¼-S1; 12-4-1811
William Ellerman NE¼-S2; 6-7-1806
John Smith NW¼-S2; 8-18-1806
Thomas Hill SE¼-S2; 9-19-1806
John Smith SW¼-S2; 10-4-1806
Nathan Overman, Jr. NE¼-S3; 8-10-1813
Aaron Hill SE¼-S3; 9-18-1807
John Harvey W½-S3; 6-23-1807
James Johnston NE¼-S4; 4-14-1813. Vol.II, p.40, says Johnson
Thomas Roberts NW¼-S4; 8-11-1806
Ephraim Overman SE¼-S4; 4-14-1813
John Townsend SW¼-S4; 1-10-1807
John Smith NE¼-S5; 6-7-1806
Jeremiah Cox NW¼-S5; 6-25-1806
John Burgess S½-S5; 8-27-1806. Vol.II, p.41, says John Rogers
Jonas Randle NE¼-S6; 8-11-1806
Jeremiah Meek NW¼-S6; 7-30-1806
Samuel McKinley SE¼-S6; 7-30-1806
John Meek SW¼-S6; 7-30-1806
Joseph Woodcuck NE¼-S7; 7-30-1806
David Herman NW¼-S7; 7-12-1813. Vol.II, p.41, says Harman
Samuel McHenry SE¼-S7; 3-20-1817
David Gilbraith SW¼-S7; 12-11-1811.Vol.II, p.41, says Galbreath
John Davidson N½-S8; 2-9-1807
Daniel Trimble SE¼-S8; 8-18-1806
Jeremiah L. Meek SW¼-S8; 4-15-1812. Jacob Kesling crossed off and Jeremiah L. Meek written in
Samuel Walker NE¼-S9; 8-12-1806
John Meek, Jr. & Isaac Meek NW¼-S9; 9-3-1806. Vol.II, p.41, says Meeks
William Scearse SE¼-S9; 11-12-1806. Vol.II, p.41, says Scarce
Mary Everton SW¼-S9; 4-12-1805
Samuel Holmes NE¼-S10; 4-14-1813
John McClean, Sr. NW¼-S10; 1-9-1815
Nathaniel McClure SE¼-S10; 2-11-1808
Jasper Koons SW¼-S10; 11-19-1808
Nathan Small NE¼-S11; 10-4-1811. Vol.II, p.41, says Nathaniel
James Jacobs NW¼-S11; 12-13-1811
Jacob Fouts SE¼-S11; 1-24-1816
Jesse Devenport SW¼-S11; 3-7-1806
Samuel Walker NE¼-S12; 11-16-1808
Amos Higgins NW¼-S12; 10-23-1806
Jacob Fouts, Jr. SE¼-S12; 1-7-1806
Jacob Fouts SW¼-S12; 1-15-1807
William Fouts NE¼-S13; 3-7-1806
William Fouts NW¼-S13; 9-9-1807
Thomas C. Wade SE¼-S13; 2-1-1806
Thomas Bulla SW¼-S13; 3-7-1806
Thomas Bulla NE¼-S14; 11-5-1814
John Howard NW¼-S14; 9-3-1814

John Watts SE¼-S14; 8-1-1807
Nathan Pearson SW¼-S14; 12-15-1813
John Dugan NE¼-S15; 1-24-1816. Vol.II, p.41, says Dougan
William Edwards NW¼-S15; 6-9-1824
Nathaniel McClure, Jr. SE¼-S15; 7-25-1816
Henry Rue E½-SW¼-S15; 7-5-1824
John Davidson W½-SW¼-S15; 6-9-1824
George Holman NE¼-S17; 12-19-1804
John Turner NW¼-S17; 12-11-1811
Jeremiah Meek SE¼-S17; 4-12-1805
Richard Rice SW¼-S17; 12-19-1804. Vol.II, p.42, says Rue
Margaret McCoy E½-S18; 2-22-1805
David Harman & Andrew Harman NW¼-S18; 12-26-1814
Samuel Arnett SW¼-S18; 7-11-1805

Page 26. T 13 N, R 1 W of 1st P.M.

Thomas Consley NE¼-S19; 1-17-1807. Vol.II, p.42, says resold to
    Thomas Sloop, 4-15-1812
Samuel Henderson NW¼-S19; 12-16-1804
John Collins SE¼-S19; 1-13-1808
Peter Weaver SW¼-S19; 2-23-1807
Vincent Stephenson NE¼-S20; 4-15-1812
William Reynolds NW¼-S20; 10-1-1813
Henry Wingford SE¼-S20; 10-8-1806. Vol.II, p.42, says Wingfield
Joshua Meek SW¼-S20; 6-17-1813
William Williams NE¼-S21; 4-22-1814
Abraham Garr NW¼-S21; 11-15-1807
Samuel W. Stewart SE¼-S21; 6-9-1824
Wright Lancaster E½-SW¼-S21; 6-9-1824
David Bonine W½-SW¼-S21; 3-9-1825
Daniel Clark NE¼-S22; 1-30-1815
William Fouts NW¼-S22; 12-31-1808
Jeremiah Parker SE¼-S22; 8-22-1818
Thomas Bulla SW¼-S22; 6-21-1824
David Bailey NE¼-S23; 4-14-1813
John Watts NW¼-S23; 4-26-1813
James Hartup SE¼-S23; 12-15-1806
Catherine Price SW¼-S23; 11-3-1813
John Hardin NE¼-S24; 12-12-1805
Adam Zeek NW¼-S24; 6-8-1813
John Raper SE¼-S24; 10-30-1811
William Milner SW¼-S24; 6-11-1813
Thomas Hollett, Jr. NE¼-S25; 11-2-1813
Mark Hollett NW¼-S25; 11-18-1814
Thomas Taylor E½-SE¼-S25; 10-13-1825
Thomas Benton W½-SE¼-S25; 6-18-1829
George Hollett SW¼-S25; 1-22-1814
William Jones NE¼-S26; 11-10-1806.Vol.II, p.43, says N½-S26 only
Benjamin Hodges NW¼-S26; 10-20-1812. Vol.II, p.43, says N½-S26
    to William Jones, 11-10-1806; see it for Benjamin Hodges
Jacob Kesling SE¼-S26; 1-6-1809
George Jones SW¼-S26; 11-10-1806
Jacob Kesling NE¼-S27; 4-15-1812

George Jones SE$\frac{1}{4}$-S27; 11-10-1806
Jacob Kesling SW$\frac{1}{4}$-S27; 12-7-1808
David Heart NE$\frac{1}{4}$-S28; 1-13-1815. Vol.II, p.43, says Hart
William Grimes & James Grimes NW$\frac{1}{4}$-S28; 4-14-1813
Jacob Kesling SE$\frac{1}{4}$-S28; 12-7-1808
Elizabeth Miller SW$\frac{1}{4}$-S28; 3-30-1811
Hugh Cull NE$\frac{1}{4}$-S29; 10-9-1806
Bazil Meek NW$\frac{1}{4}$-S29; 1-8-1807
Washington Elliott SE$\frac{1}{4}$-S29; 9-22-1817
Isaac Beeson SW$\frac{1}{4}$-S29; 9-10-1806
Aaron Martin NE$\frac{1}{4}$-S30; 7-28-1806
Abraham Gaar NW$\frac{1}{4}$-S30; 1-13-1807. Vol.II, p.43, says Garr
Richard Rue SE$\frac{1}{4}$-S30; 7-5-1805
John Hunt SW$\frac{1}{4}$-S30; 9-27-1806
Jackson Rambo NE$\frac{1}{4}$-S31; 1-5-1809
Lazarus Whitehead NW$\frac{1}{4}$-S31; 8-8-1805
Daniel Osborn SE$\frac{1}{4}$-S31; 1-4-1814
John Whitehead SW$\frac{1}{4}$-S31; 12-11-1811
Benjamin Brown NE$\frac{1}{4}$-S32; 6-7-1813
John Whitehead NW$\frac{1}{4}$-S32; 1-11-1815
Abner Acree SE$\frac{1}{4}$-S32; 4-1-1815. Vol.II, p.43, says Acres
Washington Elliott SW$\frac{1}{4}$-S32; 12-6-1814
John Jordan NE$\frac{1}{4}$-S33; 11-25-1814
William Jones SE$\frac{1}{4}$-S33; 1-19-1808
John Townsend W$\frac{1}{2}$-S33; 10-23-1813

Page 27. T 13 N, R 1 W of 1st P.M.

George Holeman NE$\frac{1}{4}$-S34; 1-23-1807
Peter Demaree NW$\frac{1}{4}$-S34; 3-25-1807
William Holeman SE$\frac{1}{4}$-S34; 12-2-1806
Joseph Holderman SW$\frac{1}{4}$-S34; 12-2-1806
John Jordan E$\frac{1}{2}$-S35; 10-29-1814
George Holeman NW$\frac{1}{4}$-S35; 1-23-1807
Absalom Rambo SW$\frac{1}{4}$-S35; 11-11-1813
Wright Anderson E$\frac{1}{2}$-NE$\frac{1}{4}$-S36; 11-3-1825. Name Beck is added a short distance after Anderson; so Anderson may be middle name
Joshua Benton W$\frac{1}{2}$-NE$\frac{1}{4}$-S36; 9-25-1828
Felix Girton E$\frac{1}{2}$-NW$\frac{1}{4}$-S36; 10-18-1828
William Russey W$\frac{1}{2}$-NW$\frac{1}{4}$-S36; 12-10-1825
Nicholas Drewley E$\frac{1}{2}$-SW$\frac{1}{4}$ & W$\frac{1}{2}$-SW$\frac{1}{4}$-S36; 12-1-1825

Page 27. T 14 N, R 1 W of 1st P.M.

Samuel Henderson* E$\frac{1}{2}$-S1; 7-12-1808 * Jr.
Robert Morrison NW$\frac{1}{4}$-S1; 10-6-1810
Isaac Cummins SW$\frac{1}{4}$-S1; 8-10-1813. Vol.II, p.44, says Commons
Isaac Hiatt NE$\frac{1}{4}$-S2; 10-12-1816
John White NW$\frac{1}{4}$-S2; 10-18-1816
Jacob Boswell SE$\frac{1}{4}$-S2; 12-9-1814. Vol.II, p.44, says Isaac
Zacheriah Hiatt SW$\frac{1}{4}$-S2; 11-28-1814
Enos Grave NE$\frac{1}{4}$-S3; 7-18-1816
William Hiatt NW$\frac{1}{4}$-S3; 12-31-1816
John Thomas SE$\frac{1}{4}$-S3; 7-18-1816

William Hiatt SW¼-S3; 6-10-1813
Benjamin Harris NE¼-S4; 9-26-1807 Lawallen
Mashach Lawalling NW¼-S4; 4-14-1813. Vol.II, p.44, says Michael
William Strasback SE¼-S4; 1-11-1808. Vol.II, p.45, says Starback
John Addington SW¼-S4; 4-14-1813. Vol.II, p.44, says Joseph
James Morrison NE¼-S5; 4-14-1813
Tence Mossey NW¼-S5; 8-18-1817. Vol.II, p.44, says Massey
Benjamin Cox SE¼-S5; 6-23-1807
Jacob Hampton SW¼-S5; 11-28-1816
Andrew Hampton Fr. S6; 440.30 ac.; 7-3-1817
Jacob Hampton Fr. S7; 534.50 ac.; 11-28-1816
Thomas Addington NE¼-S8; 5-11-1807
Samuel Charles NW¼-S8; 1-3-1815
John Addington SE¼-S8; 12-3-1806
Isaac Barker SW¼-S8; 8-11-1808
Paul Starbuck NE¼-S9; 8-1-1816
Thomas Roberts NW¼-S9; 4-15-1812
Isaac Barker SE¼-S9; 1-25-1817
John Addington SW¼-S9; 5-11-1807
Lebini Hunt N½-S10; 1-15-1814. Vol.II, p.45, says Libni
James Wright SE¼-S10; 11-16-1814
Alexander Moore SW¼-S10; 12-5-1816
Henry Null NE¼-S11; 11-21-1806
Mariam Boswell NW¼-S11; 1-24-1818
Tabiatha White SE¼-S11; 10-14-1806
Tabiatha White SW¼-S11; 10-28-1806
Christian Pelafish NE¼-S12; 11-21-1806. Vol.II, p.45, says Petafish
Jeremiah Cox NW¼-S12; 4-7-1808
Conrad Roberts SE¼-S12; 6-21-1816
Bladen Ashby SW¼-S12; 4-15-1812

Page 28. T 14 N, R 1 W of 1st P.M.

William Alexander NE¼-S13; 12-23-1811
Joseph Pemberton NW¼-S13; 8-28-1816
Isaac Jessup SE¼-S13; 9-17-1814
Benjamin Smith SW¼-S13; 9-24-1813
John Morrow NE¼-S14; 10-19-1813
Mordecai Carter NW¼-S14; 8-2-1806
John Weeks SE¼-S14; 3-14-1814
Andrew Hoover SW¼-S14; 9-18-1807
William Bond NE¼-S15; 9-24-1816
William Williams NW¼-S15; 6-9-1824
Thomas Stafford SE¼-S15; 11-11-1813
Isaac Vore SW¼-S15; 11-26-1816
John Addington NE¼-S17; 11-3-1806
John Addington NW¼-S17; 5-13-1808
Susanna Butler SE¼-S17; 8-2-1806
William Meek SW¼-S17; 10-19-1815
Jacob Hampton NE¼-S18; 11-1-1817
Jacob Hampton NW¼-S18; 11-28-1816
Isaac Cook SE¼-S18; 12-13-1814
Isaac Martin SW¼-S18; 1-9-1815
Jonathan Mills NE¼-S19; 1-15-1814

Hardy Cain & Joseph Cain SE¼-S19; 9-22-1814
John Southerland, Jr. & William W. Pharis, Jr. W½-S19; 2-28-1816
Joshua Pigot NE¼-S20; 1-13-1808. Vol.II, p.45, says Piggot
Phineas Roberts NW¼-S20; 4-15-1812
Abijah Cain SE¼-S20; 4-14-1813
Benjamin Pearson SW¼-S20; 8-13-1811
Abner Clawson NE¼-S21; 9-17-1817
William Brown NW¼-S21; 8-23-1817
Josiah Clawson SE¼-S21; 10-9-1813
William Clawson SW¼-S21; 10-9-1815
Jesse Clark NE¼-S22; 1-14-1814
Alexander Moore NW¼-S22; 4-28-1817
Jesse Clark SE¼-S22; 12-28-1813
Jesse Clark SW¼-S22; 9-30-1813
John Wheeler NE¼-S23; 7-14-1814
Griffith Mendenhall NW¼-S23; 5-22-1815
Thomas Kindal SE¼-S23; 6-16-1817. Vol.II, p.47, says Kendal
William Thornbrough SW¼-S23; 10-16-1813
John Alexander NE¼-S24; 9-16-1807
Jonathan Wright & William Cook NW¼-S24; 10-6-1813
Archibald Wasson SE¼-S24; 9-6-1813
Isaac Jessop SW¼-S24; 11-29-1814
Andrew Bailey NE¼-S25; 9-15-1814
Conrad Roberts NW¼-S25; 2-5-1817
John Drake SE¼-S25; 8-27-1806
Joseph Wasson SW¼-S25; 3-21-1806
Benjamin Hill NE¼-S26; 11-5-1817
Jacob Jessop & Abraham Jessop NW¼-S26; 8-1-1817
Benjamin Hill SE¼-S26; 12-10-1806
John Wasson SW¼-S26; 1-2-1807
Ralph Wright NE¼-S27; 5-11-1807
Andrew Hoover NW¼-S27; 6-25-1806
Samuel Woods SE¼-S27; 6-9-1806
William Fouts SW¼-S27; 4-4-1806
Andrew Hoover NE¼-S28; 7-23-1806
Andrew Hoover W½ & SE¼-S28; 6-7-1806
John Small NE¼-S29; 7-4-1807
John Smith NW¼-S29; 6-25-1806
Andrew Hoover SE¼-S29; 6-7-1806
Moses Kelly SW¼-S29; 6-25-1806
Jonas Randle NE¼-S30; 6-27-1807
Thomas Lamb NW¼-S30; 4-14-1813
William Price SE¼-S30; 10-27-1814
Jonas Randle SW¼-S30; 8-11-1806

Page 29. T 14 N, R 1 W of 1st P.M.

Evins Shoemaker NE¼-S31; 10-7-1812
Mary Cook & Charity Cook NW¼-S31; 1-14-1807
Jonathan Roberts SE¼-S31; 8-11-1806
Jesse Bond SW¼-S31; 4-14-1813
John Smith NE¼-S32; 8-25-1807
John Smith NW¼-S32; 6-25-1806
John Meek SE¼-S32; 8-10-1805

John Smith SW¼-S32; 6-26-1807
John Hawkins NE¼-S33; 7-1-1807
Jeremiah Cox NW¼-S33; 1-10-1807
John Smith SE¼-S33; 1-27-1806
John Meek SW¼-S33; 8-10-1805
Amos Hawkins NE¼-S34; 8-3-1807
Hezekiah Viets NW¼-S34; 3-31-1817
Benjamin Morgan & Benjamin Maudlin SE¼-S34; 6-30-1807
John Harvey SW¼-S34; 6-23-1807
Robert Comer NE¼-S35; 7-1-1807
Benjamin Hill NW¼-S35; 3-25-1814
Robert Hill SE¼-S35; 8-5-1806
John Pool & Thomas Pool SW¼-S35; 6-30-1807
Richard Maxwell NE¼-S36; 9-23-1805
James Alexander NW¼-S36; 9-23-1805
Richard Maxwell SE¼-S36; 7-30-1806
John Ireland SW¼-S36; 9-23-1805

Page 30. T 15 N, R 1 W of 1st P.M.

Jacob Harlan E½-NE¼-S1; 3-21-1831
Silas Gist W½-NE¼-S1; 1-30-1832
William Vanhise E½-NW¼-S1; 1-16-1832
Samuel Watts W½-NW¼-S1; 5-26-1830
Nathan Harlan E½-SE¼-S1; 3-21-1831
Samuel M. Snodgrass W½-SE¼-S1; 11-27-1827
James Compton E½-SW¼-S1; 6-20-1817
John Withrow W½-SW¼-S1; 6-12-1824   7-5-1831
Isaac Huffman NE¼-S2; 8-25-1817. Rel. W½ to James Longfellow,
John Tharp E½-NW¼-S2; 1-13-1818. Vol.II, p.48, says Sharp
Benjamin Dobson W½-NW¼-S2; 4-19-1828
Gideon Harrison E½-SE¼-S2; 1-29-1828
James Winston W½-SE¼-S2; 3-5-1818. Rel. W½ to John Pool,
William Odell E½-SW¼-S2; 11-27-1817   10-27-1827
Amos Cadwalader W½-SW¼-S2; 3-21-1818. Rel. W½ to Michael Wolf,
William Arnold E½-NE¼-S3; 3-13-1832   11-9-1829
Cader Woodard W½-NE¼-S3; 4-12-1827
Joseph Draper E½-NW¼-S3; 9-24-1818. Rel. E½ to Jesse Overman,
Jesse Overman W½-NW¼-S3; 6-9-1824   8-9-1827
Levi Cassaday E½-SE¼-S3; 3-14-1828
James Holmes W½-SE¼-S3; 5-19-1831
John Pearson E½-SW¼ & W½-SW¼-S3; 12-16-1817
William Nixon NE¼-S4; 6-13-1817. Francis Thomas crossed off and
   William Nixon written in
William Nixon NW¼-S4; 12-13-1817
Samuel Nixon SE¼-S4; 10-6-1818
Hubbard Henderson E½-SW¼-S4; 12-5-1828
John Longfellow W½-SW¼-S4; 6-21-1828
John Longfellow Fr. S5; 251.52 ac.; 12-11-1813
John Hains & Malacha Moon Fr. S8; 409.16 ac.; 11-18-1811
Francis Thomas NE¼-S9; 6-13-1817
James Mendenhall NW¼-S9; 3-4-1817
Benjamin Morgan SE¼-S9; 8-15-1813
Benjamin Thomas SW¼-S9; 6-9-1815

James Homes NE$\frac{1}{4}$-S10; 5-28-1819. Rel. E$\frac{1}{4}$ to Isaac Mains, 7-5-1831
Archelaus Moorman NW$\frac{1}{2}$-S10; 1-3-1817
Thomas Wiley SE$\frac{1}{4}$-S10; 3-17-1818
Samuel Simons SW$\frac{1}{4}$-S10; 6-20-1817. Vol.II, p.48, says Symons
Charles Hardin NE$\frac{1}{4}$-S11; 10-31-1817. Rel. E$\frac{1}{2}$ to John Anderson,
   8-21-1827; W$\frac{1}{2}$ to John Anderson, 12-22-1827
Elizabeth Anderson NW$\frac{1}{4}$-S11; 3-7-1817. Rel. E$\frac{1}{2}$ to William
   Anderson, 8-21-1827; W$\frac{1}{2}$ to William Anderson, 7-5-1831
Samuel Thompson SE$\frac{1}{4}$-S11; 10-23-1816. Rel. W$\frac{1}{2}$ to Cornelius
David Anderson E$\frac{1}{2}$-SW$\frac{1}{4}$-S11; 8-17-1831   Vanhise, 12-11-1829
Silas Hubard W$\frac{1}{2}$-SW$\frac{1}{4}$-S11; 2-1-1828
Valentine Harlan NE$\frac{1}{4}$-S12; 9-30-1816
Elihu Harlan NW$\frac{1}{4}$-S12; 9-30-1816
Dennis Springer SE$\frac{1}{4}$-S12; 2-14-1817
Joshua Harlan SW$\frac{1}{4}$-S12; 9-30-1816. Rel. E$\frac{1}{4}$ to Isaac Compton,
Nathan Elliott NE$\frac{1}{4}$-S13; 4-6-1816   12-5-1827
Edward Strabuck NW$\frac{1}{2}$-S13; 5-29-1818. Vol.II, p.49, says Starbuck
James White SE$\frac{1}{4}$-S13; 10-14-1816
Tabitha White SW$\frac{1}{4}$-S13; 8-13-1817
John Withrow NE$\frac{1}{2}$-S14; 1-8-1824
Joseph Addleman E$\frac{1}{2}$-NW$\frac{1}{4}$ & W$\frac{1}{2}$-NW$\frac{1}{4}$-S14; 6-25-1827
Tabitha White SE$\frac{1}{4}$-S14; 8-13-1817
Edward Strabuck SW$\frac{1}{4}$-S14; 5-29-1818. Vol.II, p.49 says Starbuck
Joseph Addleman E$\frac{1}{2}$-NE$\frac{1}{4}$ & W$\frac{1}{2}$-NE$\frac{1}{4}$-S15; 6-25-1827
John M. Addleman E$\frac{1}{2}$-NW$\frac{1}{4}$-S15; 8-10-1827
John Thompson W$\frac{1}{2}$-NW$\frac{1}{4}$-S15; 10-5-1825
Benjamin Elliott E$\frac{1}{2}$-SE$\frac{1}{4}$ & W$\frac{1}{2}$-SE$\frac{1}{4}$-S15; 9-2-1825
Joseph Skinner E$\frac{1}{2}$-SW$\frac{1}{4}$-S15; 8-10-1827
Micajah Morgan W$\frac{1}{2}$-SW$\frac{1}{4}$-S15; 7-3-1827

Page 31. T 15 N, R 1 W of 1st P.M.

William Stafford NE$\frac{1}{4}$-S17; 10-26-1811
James Dwiggins SE$\frac{1}{4}$-S17; 10-20-1813
James Dwiggins W$\frac{1}{2}$-S17; 12-13-1810
Isaac Thomas NE$\frac{1}{4}$-S20; 10-20-1813
Solomon Thomas SE$\frac{1}{4}$-S20; 11-4-1814
Joseph Fulghum E$\frac{1}{2}$-NE$\frac{1}{4}$-S21; 10-22-1828
John Shugart W$\frac{1}{4}$-NE$\frac{1}{4}$-S21; 2-4-1831
Ebenezer Hiatt E$\frac{1}{2}$-NW$\frac{1}{4}$-S21; 10-30-1830. Vol.II, p.49, says
Daniel Puckett W$\frac{1}{2}$-NW$\frac{1}{4}$-S21; 2-1-1830   Eleazer
Solomon Meredith E$\frac{1}{2}$-SE$\frac{1}{4}$-S21; 12-7-1830
Paul Starbuck W$\frac{1}{2}$-SE$\frac{1}{4}$-S21; 1-21-1829
Josiah Unthank E$\frac{1}{2}$-SW$\frac{1}{4}$-S21; 10-30-1830
William Hough W$\frac{1}{2}$-SW$\frac{1}{4}$-S21; 2-1-1830
William Addleman NE$\frac{1}{4}$-S22; 12-30-1818
Abner Jones E$\frac{1}{2}$-NW$\frac{1}{4}$-S22; 1-25-1831
Joseph Fulghum W$\frac{1}{2}$-NW$\frac{1}{4}$-S22; 10-22-1828
Nathan Jones W$\frac{1}{2}$-SE$\frac{1}{4}$-S22; 10-15-1830
Edward Starbuck E$\frac{1}{2}$-SW$\frac{1}{4}$-S22; 5-12-1827
Edward Fisher W$\frac{1}{2}$-SW$\frac{1}{4}$-S22; 11-20-1828
Thomas Mason NE$\frac{1}{4}$-S23; 6-28-1817
Richard Williams NW$\frac{1}{4}$-S23; 8-20-1817
Samuel Williams SE$\frac{1}{2}$-S23; 4-10-1817

Henry Garrett SW¼-S23; 12-20-1817
John White NE¼-S24; 10-14-1816
Benjamin Parker & Joseph Skinner NW¼-S24; 4-30-1819
Richard Bunch SE¼-S24; 3-17-1817
Thomas Mason SW¼-S24; 5-5-1815
Henry Newton NE¼-S25; 10-21-1814
William Hunt NW¼-S25; 4-22-1816
James Newton SE¼-S25; 8-15-1816
Job Elliott SW¼-S25; 8-25-1814
Job Elliott NE¼-S26; 12-16-1817. Rel. W½ to Stephen Elliott,
Walter Roberds E½-NW¼-S26; 10-19-1831   9-24-1831
Gabriel Harrell SE¼-S26; 8-15-1816. Rel. W½ to John Bishop,
John Bishop E½-SW¼-S26; 10-19-1831   9-19-1831
Edward Starbuck W½-SW¼-S26; 2-12-1831
Jesse Stetler W½-NE¼-S27; 12-6-1827. Vol.II, p.50, looks like
Nathan Fisher NW¼-S27; 11-15-1817   Stetter
Edward Starbuck W½-SE¼-S27; 11-3-1830
Edward Starbuck SW¼-S27; 5-23-1817
Henry Duttarrow NE¼-S28; 9-24-1818
Samuel Pritchard E½-NW¼ & W½-NW¼-S28; 10-30-1830
William Hunt SE¼-S28; 10-20-1817
Peter Duttarrow SW¼-S28; 9-24-1818
Samuel Sanders NE¼-S29; 10-14-1818
Stephen Mendenhall SE¼-S29; 2-15-1817
Stephen Thomas, Sr. SW¼-S29; 11-9-1816
Charles Baldwin Fr. S30; 12-11-1813; 158.80 ac.
Elias Cabe Fr. S31; 300.80 ac.; 2-5-1822
Enos Grave NE¼-S32; 11-18-1816
Jonathan L. Grave NW¼-S32; 10-19-1816
John Turner SE¼-S32; 1-12-1808
John Turner SW¼-S32; 8-18-1817

Page 32. T 15 N, R 1 W of 1st P.M.

Thomas Fisher NE¼-S33; 6-16-1817
Hezekiah Jessop E½-NW¼-S33; 1-27-1820
Robert Macy W½-NW¼-S33; 5-10-1825
William Strasback SE¼-S33; 1-11-1808. Vol.II, p.51, says
James Johnston SW¼-S33; 4-4-1814   Starback
Phineas Robberds E½-NE¼-S34; 1-21-1829
Phillip Pedrick W½-NE¼-S34; 3-23-1827
Joseph Brown NW¼-S34; 1-16-1818
Joseph Addleman E½-SE¼-S34; 11-15-1827
Joseph Teas W½-SE¼-S34; 12-24-1825
John Venard SW¼-S34; 8-31-1816
James Wickersham NE¼-S35; 7-10-1817
Joseph Brown NW¼-S35; 1-16-1818
Zacheriah Hiatt SE¼-S35; 8-15-1816
John Nicholson SW¼-S35; 1-23-1818
John Zimmerman NE¼-S36; 9-13-1814
Elliott Pearson NW¼-S36; 8-25-1814
Samuel G. Mitchel SE¼-S36; 7-12-1808
Henry Paylen SW¼-S36; 8-16-1814. James Johnston crossed off
   and Henry Paylen written in

Page 32.   T 16 N, R 1 W of 1st P.M.   RANDOLPH CO.

Peter Crumrine NE¼-S1; 5-26-1819
Thornton Alexander E½-NW¼-S1; 8-23-1822
Ephraim Brown W½-NW¼-S2; 2-7-1818. Vol.II, p.51, says Bowen
Drewry Davis W½-SW¼-S2; 2-12-1818. Rel. To Stephen Davis,
    9-10-1831. Vol.II, p.52, says W½-SW¼ to Stephen Davis
Joshua Lazenby SE¼-S3; 2-11-1819
William Yates NE¼-S10; 1-19-1818
Obediah Small SE¼-S10; 9-17-1817. Rel. W½ to Clark Willcuts,
George F. Bowles W½-NE¼-S11; 5-6-1831   7-5-1831
Samuel H. Middleton W½-SE¼-S11; 4-10-1828

Page 33.   T 16 N, R 1 W of 1st P.M.

Henry Bailey W½-NW¼-S12; 11-4-1831
Staunton Bailey W½-NE¼-S14; 5-12-1823
Ephraim Overman NW¼-S14; 11-9-1816
John Ford W½-SE¼-S14; 9-22-1831
Cornelius Overman E½-SW¼-S14; 1-16-1832
Staunton Bailey W½-SW¼-S14; 10-21-1820
William McKim E½-NE¼ & W½-NE¼-S15; 11-4-1831
Benjamin Arnold E½-NW¼-S15; 11-16-1831
Henry Bailey E½-SE¼-S15; 11-10-1831
William McKim W½-SE¼-S15; 11-10-1831
Jesse Parker, Jr. E½-SW¼-S15; 11-14-1831
Daniel H. Miller W½-NE¼-S21; 3-22-1831
Peter Dervage E½-SE¼-S21, 4-8-1829
Allen Mann W½-SE¼-S21; 9-1-1831
Thomas Parker, Sr. E½-NE¼-S22; 10-26-1829
Ephraim Overman W½-NE¼-S22; 6-28-1827
Michael Fulghum E½-NW¼-S22; 2-20-1829
Malachi Nichols W½-NW¼-S22; 6-1-1829
William Wiggs E½-SE¼-S22; 4-15-1830
Elias Coleman W½-SE¼-S22; 10-22-1828
Robert Thompson E½-SW¼-S22; 11-14-1831
Jose Horn W½-SW¼-S22; 1-17-1827
Isaac Elliott W½-NE¼-S23; 10-17-1820
John Fellow E½-NW¼ & W½-NW¼-S23; 11-15-1831
Susannah Wiggs W½-SE¼-S23; 5-8-1830
Windsor Wiggs E½-SW¼-S23; 5-8-1830
John Schooley W½-SW¼-S23; 9-21-1821

Page 34.   T 16 N, R 1 W of 1st P.M.

Aaron Kelsey SE¼-S25; 7-6-1818. Rel. E½ to John Bates, 2-22-1832
William Arnold W½-NE¼-S26; 4-10-1830
Frederick Fulghum E½-NW¼-S26; 6-12-1823
Frederick Fulghum W½-NW¼-S26; 1-19-1831
Charles W. Swain W½-SE¼-S26; 4-12-1830
Jesse Parker E½-SW¼-S26; 4-10-1830
Joel Parker W½-SW¼-S26; 10-22-1828
Joshua Small NE¼-S27; 8-22-1818. Rel. W½ to Joshua Small,
    12-1-1828; E½ to Michael Fulghum, 10-15-1829

Ephraim Overman NW¼-S27; 8-23-1814
Absalom Thomas SE¼-S27; 1-31-1817
Nathan Overman SW¼-S27; 9-13-1815
Ephraim Brown NE¼-S28; 4-30-1814. Vol.II, p.55, says Bowen
Clark Wilcotts SE¼-S28; 1-19-1814
Samuel Mann W½-S28 & Fr.-S29; 349.28 ac., 6-28-1816
Thomas Parker Fr.-S32; 156.88 ac.; 8-16-1814
James Cammack NE¼ & SW¼-S33; 1-21-1814
John Thomas NW¼-S33; 7-28-1814
Eli Overman SE¼-S33; 12-13-1814
Ambrose Osborn E½-NE¼-S34; 5-11-1830
Harvey Harris W½-NE¼-S34; 3-30-1821
Levi Horner E½-NW¼-S34; 10-22-1827
Jason Overman W½-NW¼-S34; 2-15-1830
Jacob Horn E½-SE¼-S34; 11-5-1831
Jeremiah Arnold W½-SE¼-S34; 9-14-1831
Henry Bailey SW¼-S34; 8-14-1817
Samuel Jellison E½-NE¼-S35; 10-1-1831
Samuel Jellison W½-NE¼-S35; 6-25-1830
Ambrose Osborn W½-NW¼-S35; 11-21-1831
Elihu Harlan W½-SE¼-S35; 9-27-1831
George Thompson E½-SW¼-S35; 5-1-1832
Jacob Horn W½-SW¼-S35; 11-5-1831
William Odell E½-NE¼-S36; 8-2-1824
John Rogers W½-NE¼-S36; 2-15-1830   10-6-1831
Michael Arehart NW¼-S36; 6-26-1818. Rel. W½ to William Brown,
Gabriel Odell SE¼-S36; 11-26-1817.Rel. W½ to Hoel Ives, 1-5-1830
Andrew Arehart SW¼-S36; 6-26-1818.Rel. E½ to Hoel Ives, 1-5-1830

Page 35. T 17 N, R 1 W of 1st P.M.

William Kennon E½-NE¼-S11; 3-23-1831
David Wason E½-SW¼-S12; 1-3-1831

Page 36. T 17 N, R 1 W of 1st P.M.

William Chenowith SE¼-S24; 9-24-1817
William Chenowith S25; 9-24-1817. Rel. W½
Abraham Chenowith N½-S26; 9-24-1817
Abraham Chenowith SW¼-S26; 9-24-1817
James Lewis E½-NE¼ & W½-NE¼-S27; 10-15-1831
James Green N pt. & S pt.-NW¼-S27; 94.88 ac.; 9-20-1831
James Green N pt. & S pt.-SW¼-S27; 120.02 ac.; 9-10-1831
Ephraim L. Bowen E½-SE¼-S34; 12-28-1831
Samuel H. Middleton E½-SW¼-S34; 3-13-1832
William Jessop E½-NW¼-S35; 4-28-1831
John Addington W½-NW¼-S35; 1-5-1829
John Small SW¼-S35; 1-9-1818. Rel. E½
John Foster NE¼-S36; 12-1-1817
Robert Adams E½-SE¼-S36; 4-19-1832
Collier Simpson W½-SE¼-S36; 9-18-1830

Page 37. T 18 N, R 1 W of 1st P.M.   1831
Eli Noffsinger W½-SW¼-S13;9-21-1831.John Sheets W½-NW¼-S24;9-21-

Page 38.   T 1 N, R 2 W of 1st P.M.   SWITZERLAND CO.

Jared Mansfield Fr.-S1 & Fr.-S2; 795.50 ao.; 12-3-1806. See
 Vol.II, p.62, John J. Dufour
John Greiner Fr.-S4; 479.44 ao.; 3-31-1813
Dan Foot E½-NE¼-S5; 3-19-1818.Rel. E½ to Jacob Iler, 10-14-1829.
 Vol.II, p.62, says Jacob G. Iler
William Scott W½-NE¼-S5; 9-21-1824
John Blaney NW¼-S5; 7-20-1815
John Boisseau SE¼-S5; 5-27-1814
William Pickett SW¼-S5; 12-11-1824. Rel.   1828
Seth Stodder NE¼-S6; 11-6-1816. Rel. E½ to Thomas Smith, 10-25-
James Burke NW¼-S6; 7-14-1814. Rel. W½ to John B. Bosseau & Mary
 Peters, 2-26-1831
Jacob Misner SE¼-S6; 11-24-1813
Richard Folsom SW¼-S6; 1-6-1813
John J. Dufore Fr.-S7; Fr.-S18; 668.63 ao.; 9-14-1804. Vol.II,
 p.62, says Fr.-S2 & S18; gives middle name James; adds "and
 associates"
Charles Crutz, George Seanger & Peter Ming Fr.-S8; fr.-S9;
 315.98 ac.; 7-2-1812.Vol.II, p.62, looks like Krutz & Seariger

Page 38.   T 2 N, R 2 W of 1st P.M.

Jesse Embree & Edward Hepburn NE¼-S1; 6-2-1818. Rel.
Jesse Embree & Edward Hepburn NW¼-S1; 6-2-1818. Rel.
Seneca Lovelace & Allanson Rutter SE¼-S1; 10-22-1817
Robert Blacker SW¼-S1; 9-3-1817. Rel.
Jacob White NE¼-S2; 9-8-1817
John H. O'Neal NW¼-S2; 11-5-1816
Matthew Hueston E½-SE¼-S2; 7-2-1824
Matthew Hueston W½-SE¼-S2; 6-9-1824
David O'Neal SW¼-S2; 8-29-1816
Ebenezer Mixer NE¼-S3; 5-29-1815. Vol.II, p.63, says Mixter
George Barnard NW¼-S3; 8-15-1814. Vol.II, p.63, says Bernard
Ebenezer Mixer & Cornelius R. Sedam SE¼-S3; 1-13-1816. Rel. E½
 to John Dickeson, 12-11-1829. Vol.II, p.63, says Mixter
Benjamin M. Stephens SW¼-S3; 10-1-1814
Joseph Lassell E½-NE¼-S4; 4-20-1825
Pater Lock W½-NE¼-S4; 6-9-1825
William Smith NW¼-S4; 6-20-1814
Robert Drake SE¼-S4; 12-29-1813
John Dickason SW¼-S4; 2-8-1814. Vol.II, p.63, says Dickeson
Nathan Platt NE¼-S5; 6-20-1814
Cornelius R. Sedam NW¼-S5; 6-10-1815
Joseph Pugh & Cyrus Wood SE¼-S5; 9-5-1815. Vol.II, p.63, says
Samuel Buel NW¼-S6; 1-4-1817; also E½-S6   C. Moore
Nicholas Boyland SW¼-S6; 6-16-1818
Richard Baker NE¼-S7; 4-4-1825. Rel. But Vol.II, p.63, gives
 final certif. # 520
John Carter NW¼-S7; 10-16-1816
Marvin Bachus SE¼-S7; 10-1-1816
Marvin Bachus SW¼-S7; 10-1-1816
William Dickinson NE¼-S8; 7-1-1814. Vol.II, p.63, says Dickason

Thomas Cooper NW¼-S8; 1-12-1818
Aaron Chamberlain SE¼-S8; 1-27-1818
Thomas Cooper SW¼-S8; 1-12-1818
John Sherer NE¼-S9; 8-29-1816
Robert Bovard NW¼-S9; 9-29-1817
Richard Baker SE¼-S9; 4-4-1825
Daniel Dickerson NE¼-S10; 6-3-1817
George Wooley SW¼-S9; 9-27-1817
John Sherer NW¼-S10; 8-29-1816
John Dickerson SE¼-S10; 8-11-1817. Vol.II, p.63, says Dickson
Benjamin M. Stephens SW¼-S10; 12-9-1817. Rel. E½ to William
    Hedges, 12-8-1829
Jesse Hunt & Isaac Bates NE¼-S11; 10-20-1817
Lewis Bocock NW¼-S11; 7-8-1817
William Campbell SE¼-S11; 5-17-1817
Robert Kenady SW¼-S11; 8-16-1817. Rel.
Lewis Bocock E½-SW¼-S11; 2-14-1832

Page 39. T 2 N, R 2 W of 1st P.M.

Enos Ellis & Andrew Coffin NE¼-S12; 5-27-1817
William Means NW¼-S12; 5-27-1817
Edward Pocock SE¼-S12; 9-7-1816
Senaca Lovelace & Allanson Rutter SW¼-S12; 10-22-1817
James Pocock NE¼-S13; 8-26-1816
Robert Cunningham NW¼-S13; 3-26-1818. Rel.
William Scott SE¼-S13; 8-16-1815
Samuel Fenton SW¼-S13; 3-9-1818. Rel. W½
William Gard NE¼-S14; 10-23-1816
Levi James NW¼-S14; 7-11-1817
William McGarvey SE¼-S14; 2-1-1817
Jeremiah Reeder SW¼-S14; 4-16-1818. Rel.
Thomas Rayl, Jr. E½-SE¼-S15; 3-1-1832
William Brattle Chamberlin W½-SE¼-S15; 11-26-1831
Henry Scudder, Sr. SW¼-S15; 3-5-1819
William Barr NE¼-S17; 4-25-1818. Rel. W½ to Lemuel Montanye,
Jean Daniel Morerod NW¼-S17; 8-11-1814   5-14-1828
Zacheriah Montague SE¼-S17; 5-11-1818
Robert Bovard SW¼-S17; 12-2-1817
John F. Dufour NE¼-S18; 7-11-1814
Elijah Golay NW¼-S18; 7-11-1814. Vol.II, p.65, says Elisha
Robert Bovard SE¼-S18; 12-2-1817
Abraham Lindlay SW¼-S18; 6-24-1814
George Simonton NE¼-S19; 11-27-1817
Enos McIlroy NW¼-S19; 11-20-1817. Rel. W½ to Sayrs Gayley,
    2-13-1832; NE¼-NW¼ to Jeremiah Thomas, 5-30-1832
Theodore F. Talbot SE¼-S19; 7-27-1818. Rel.
Benjamin Warren SW¼-S19; 12-12-1817
Jonathan Shuff NE¼-S20; 5-25-1818. Rel. W½ to Jonathan Shuff,
William Campbell E½-SE¼-S20; 9-6-1817   9-3-1827
Noah Yates W½-SE¼-S20; 1-19-1818. Vol.II, p.65, says Gates
Samuel Lewis SW¼-S20; 4-13-1818. Rel.
John Johnson NE¼-S21; 9-22-1818. Rel. W½ to Elijah Lindsay Boyd,
    2-10-1832

James Boyd NW¼-S21; 1-14-1819. Rel. W½. Vol.II, p.65, shows
final certif. # 3655 to James Boyd for W½-NW¼
George Turner SE¼-S21; 3-11-1815
Riley Truitt SW¼-S21; 10-22-1817. Rel. W½ to Riley Truitt,
John Miller E½-NW¼-S22; 2-19-1831 1-19-1828
Andrew Dilman W½-NW¼-S22; 4-9-1828
Stephen Rhynebolt E½-SE¼-S22; 4-29-1825
Stephen Rhynebolt W½-SE¼-S22; 2-25-1825
George Midsker SW¼-S22; 11-30-1816. Vol.II, p.66, says Medsker
Abraham Burkdol NE¼-S23; 2-14-1816
Caleb Hays NW¼-S23; 9-3-1817. Rel.
Peter Vanblaricum SE¼-S23; 6-23-1817
Martin Crewell SW¼-S23; 1-14-1815. Vol.II, p.66, says Crowel
James Cunningham NE¼-S24; 3-26-1818. Rel. E½ to Simon Hageman,
William Campbell NW¼-S24; 5-19-1817 12-1-1829
Charles Phillips SE¼-S24; 10-15-1817
Nathan Nelson & Charles Nelson SW¼-S24; 3-21-1815
Charles Beatty NE¼-S25; 11-2-1816. Vol.II, p.66, says to
William Phillips, 1-31-1814
Samuel Fenton NW¼-S25; 7-22-1815
William White SE¼-S25; 12-25-1809
Luke Wiles SW¼-S25; 9-6-1816
Charles Phillips NE¼-S26; 8-17-1815
William Ryal NW¼-S26; 12-24-1814. Vol.II, p.66, says Rayl
Andrew Jelly SE¼-S26; 6-25-1816
David Fulton SW¼-S26; 6-20-1815

Page 40. T 2 N, R 2 W of 1st P.M.

James Mosley & Sally Hutchinson NE¼-S27; 6-20-1814. Vol.II, p.66,
William McCullough NW¼-S27; 8-8-1816 says Sarah
Abraham Scudder SE¼-S27; 10-27-1815. Vol.II, p.66, says Abner
Henry Loughman SW¼-S27; 12-17-1817
William Marsh NE¼-S28; 3-21-1815
John McCreary NW¼-S28; 1-19-1815
John Boisseau SE¼-S28; 6-6-1817
Samuel Hall NE¼-S29; 5-9-1817. Rel. NE¼-NE¼ to Newton H. Tapp,
5-24-1832. Vol.II, p.66, says Newton Harrison Tapp
Joseph Bentley NW¼-S29; 8-7-1818. Rel.
William Atkinson E½-SE¼-S29; 9-23-1824
Hugh Moore W½-SE¼-S29; 1-12-1818. Rel.
William McCullough SW¼-S29; 8-8-1816. Rel.
Robert McKim NE¼-S30; 7-2-1817. Rel.
John Boson, Sr. E½-NW¼-S30; 9-25-1818. Rel.
Isaac Levi W½-NW¼-S30; 9-8-1817
Joseph Croatt SE¼-S30; 6-4-1817. Vol.II, p.67, says Crawl
Joseph Bentley NE¼-S31; 7-20-1818 Rel. E½ to Isaac Matts, Jr.,
11-18-no year. Vol.II, p.67, says 1829
Paul Froman NW¼-S31; 2-18-1815
Hugh Moore SE¼-S31; 1-12-1818. Rel.
James Bates, Sr. SW¼-S31; 11-19-18
Newton H. Tapp NE¼-S32; 10-13-1815
Richard Weaver NW¼-S32; 12-16-1816 11-21-1831
James Pocock SW¼-S32; 8-26-1816. Rel. W½ to Walter Morris,

Solomon Nighswonger SE¼-S32; 7-20-1815. Rel. W½ to Isaac Matts, 8-20-1828; E½ to Isaac Matts, 9-10-1828
David McCormick E½-NE¼-S33; 8-24-1818
James Hadlock W½-NE¼-S33; 12-26-1817
Joshua Cook & Benjamin Beckett NW¼-S33; 12-1-1814. Vol.II, p.67, says Pickett
Benjamin Beckett NW¼-S33; 12-1-1814
David McCormick SE¼-S33; 7-1-1815
Barzilla Clark SW¼-S33; 10-23-1815. Vol.II, p.67, says Brazilla
Thomas Ramsey NW¼-S34; 10-3-1818. Rel.
James Taylor S½-S34; 7-21-1814
Lemon Dusky NW¼-S35; 9-13-1817
Daniel Crume SE¼-S35; 6-26-1812
John Gullion SW¼-S35; 3-16-1810
John Fenton NE¼-S36; 12-13-1809
John Bonta NW¼-S36; 12-11-1816
Joseph McFall SE¼-S36; 11-12-1812
John Miller SW¼-S36; 2-16-1813

Page 41. T 3 N, R 2 W of 1st P.M. Dearborn OHIO CO.

James A. Walton NE¼-S1; 7-4-1814
James A. Walton NW¼-S1; 7-4-1814
Robert Elliott SW¼-S1; 5-7-1817. Rel. W½ to Andrew Douglass, 8-27-1827
James Crane NW¼-S2; 7-18-1814
Luther Moad S½-S2; 7-4-1815. Vol.II, p.68, says Mead
Peyton S. Symmes ~~NE¼-S3; 8-20-1814~~
Joshua Scranton & Samuel Beckwith NW¼-S3; 1-30-1816
John Smith SE¼-S3; 10-26-1815
John Smith SW¼-S3; 10-26-1815
James Conley NE¼-S4; 6-19-1817
Joseph Richardson SE¼-S4; 6-20-1817
Joseph Barker SW¼-S4; 5-26-1818. Rel.
Jeremiah Mulford E½-NE¼-S5; 4-21-1818. Rel. E½ to Aquilla Carson, 3-27-1832
James Downey, Jr. W½-NE¼-S5; 4-21-1818
Amos Downey E½-NW¼-S5; 4-21-1818. Vol.II, p.68, says Donner
Daniel McLackey W½-NW¼-S5; 5-19-1818. Vol.II, p.68, says McLoskey
Henry Selwood E½-SE¼-S5; 3-9-1818. Rel. E½ to George Weaver, 4-2-1832
Samuel Records W½-SE¼-S5; 1-25-1818
Thomas Records E½-SW¼-S5; 1-26-1818
Hubbard Jones NE¼-S6; 7-29-1815
Robert Lyons NW¼-S6; 9-30-1816
Stephen Barrows SE¼-S6; 2-28-1818. Rel.
Stephen Barrows SW¼-S6; 2-28-1818. Rel.
Abraham Johnston NE¼-S7; 10-20-1817. Rel. W½. Vol.II, p.69, says Johnson
John Phelps E½-NW¼-S7; 5-9-1825
Nicholas Longworth & Moses Brooks W½-NW¼-S7; 7-12-1817. Rel.
John Downey NE¼-S8; 3-5-1818
Richard Downey NW¼-S8; 3-5-1818
Stephen Burrows W½-SE¼-S8, 2-28-1818. Rel. N½ to Richard Downey, 5-23-1832. See Vol.II, p.69, Richard Downey

David Cady SW¼-S8; 3-12-1818. Rel. E½ to Daniel Kittle,
    8-9-1831; NW¼-SW¼ to James Gibson Kittle, 5-28-1832
Jeremiah Mulford E½-SE¼-S8; 6-16-1824
John Hamilton NW¼-S9; 6-23-1818. Rel. Vol.II, p.69, shows
    final certif. # 73 for E½-NE¼ to John Hamelton
Andrew Tague W½-NE¼-S9; 7-21-1824   1831
John McKane S½-S9; 5-22-1816. Rel. W½-SE¼ to John McKane, 7-1-
Moses Daniel & Philip P. Taply N½-S10; 12-26-1815. Vol.II, p.70,
    gives middle initial Preston
Ezra Lambkin SE¼-S10; 11-14-1815
Elijah Thacher SW¼-S10; 1-24-1816
William Fisk NE¼-S11; 7-24-1817
Martin Scranton NW¼-S11; 6-25-1817
Ezra Webb SE¼-S11; 7-24-1817
Caleb A. Craft SW¼-S11; 3-10-1818. Rel. W½ to Judson Lambkin,
Hugh Bodle W½-NE¼-S12; 5-24-1830   3-10-1832
Jesse Embree & Edward Hepburn NW¼-S12; 6-2-1818
James Woods SE¼-S12; 10-28-1816
Jacob Wright, Jr. SW¼-S12; 8-7-1817. Rel. To James Boyle &
    Lydia Wright, 8-9-1831
George Newton NE¼-S13; 9-9-1814
Jesse Embree & Edward Hepburn NW¼-S13; 6-2-1818
Prince Athorn SE¼-S13; 12-27-1814. Vol.II, p.70, says Athearn
Benjamin Dubois SW¼-S13; 12-23-1816. Rel. W½
Felix Brandt NE¼-S14; 4-13-1818. Rel.
Julius James NW¼-S14; 2-18-1818. Rel.

Page 42. T 3 N, R 2 W of 1st P.M.

John Kemp SE¼-S14; 10-24-1817. Rel. E½ to John Goodner, 2-15-
Julius James SW¼-S14; 10-24-1817   1832
Lodowick Weller NE¼-S17; 2-27-1818
James M. Hill NW¼-S17; 2-23-1818
James S. Learned SE¼-S17; 7-1-1818. Rel.
Lodowick Weller SW¼-S17; 3-23-1818. Rel.
Caleb White NE¼-S18; 3-13-1818. Rel.
Ethan A. Brown NW¼-S18; 1-31-1818
Matthias Haynes & Joshua Haynes SE¼-S18; 3-16-1818. Rel.
Jacob Dennis N½-S19; 11-14-1817. Rel. E½-NE¼
Cornelius Culp SE¼-S19; 7-26-1817
John Gibbs SW¼-S19; 9-19-1817
Lodowick Weller E½-S20; 3-23-1818. Rel.
Catherine Hedger E½-NW¼-S20; 3-10-1818
Obadiah Walker & John Walker W½-NW¼-S20; 12-4-1817. Rel.
Nicholas Longworth & Moses Brooks E½-SW¼-S20; 1-19-1818
John Gibbs W½-SW¼-S20; 9-19-1817
William Brindle & James Murray NE¼-S21; 10-29-1817
William R. Goodwin NW¼-S21; 6-17-1819. Rel. E½ to Robert
    Gillespie, 8-21-1827; W½ to Robert Gillespie, 8-19-1829
Cyrus Cutter & Stephen Stewart SE¼-S21; 8-19-1817
Robert Gillespie SW¼-S21; 8-23-1819   5-16-1826
Joseph Ross NE¼-S22; 10-19-1818. Rel. E½ to William B. Phelps,
Joseph Hulick NW¼-S22; 4-23-1817. Vol.II, p.71, says Gulick
Robert Bovard SE¼-S22; 12-16-1817

Jacob Myers SW¼-S22; 3-1-1816
George Gale NE¼-S23; 6-21-1817. Rel. W½ to David Nickeson &
    Stewart Henry, 3-1-1832
John Thompson NW¼-S23; 8-28-1815
Garret Larew SE¼-S23; 8-5-1815
Benjamin Larew SW¼-S23; 8-5-1815
John Dewitt NE¼-S24; 2-18-1814
Jacob Light NW¼-S24; 1-17-1815
Robert Ricketts SE¼-S24; 11-26-1813. Vol.II, p.72,says Ricketty
Jacob Light SW¼-S24; 1-28-1814

Page 42. T 3 N, R 2 W of 1st P.M.   SWITZERLAND CO.

John Remer NE¼-S25; 4-15-1818. Rel. W½ to William Kelly,
    2-13-1830
Cyrus Cutte. NW¼-S25; 8-16-1817. Rel. E½ to Nathan Ricketts,
    9-22-1825; W½ to James M. Shepherd, 7-5-1831
Jacob Goodner SE¼-S25; 12-31-1817. Rel. W½ to Jacob Goodner,
John Rider SW¼-S25; 3-5-1818. Rel.   3-1-1832
John Hunter NE¼-S26; 8-28-1817
John Armstrong & William Kerr NW¼-S26; 11-15-1817
David Cummins SE¼-S26; 5-19-1818. Rel.
William Brindle SW¼-S26; 10-29-1817
Thomas Bishop NE¼-S27; 8-22-1816. Rel. W½ to William Brindle,
Abraham Parker NW¼-S27; 9-2-1815   7-5-1831
John Myers & Jonathan Myers SE¼-S27; 1-10-1818
Stephen Stewart & William Myers SW¼-S27; 10-1-1816. Rel. To
    William Brindle, 2-25-1830
Jonathan Myers NE¼-S28; 8-21-1815
Joseph Bell NW¼-S28; 7-2-1817
Amos Gilbert SE¼-S28; 5-24-1816
Jacob Suydam SW¼-S28; 7-15-1816
Nicholas Longworth & Moses Brooks NE¼-S29; 1-19-1818. Rel.
Isaac Jessup NW¼-S29; 1-22-1817
Simon Myers SE¼-S29; 10-1-1816
Charles McNutt SW¼-S29; 3-2-1816

Page 43. T 3 N, R 2 W of 1st P.M.

William Bell NE¼-S30; 2-3-1817. Rel. W½ to Joseph Culp, 7-11-
George Miller E½-NW¼-S30; 6-27-1818. Rel.   1831
Horace*Catlin W½-NW¼-S30; 4-8-1818. Rel. * middle initial R.
Justin Reynolds SE¼-S30; 4-1-1816. Vol.II, p.73, says Justice
Hiram Leek SW¼-S30; 1-23-1817. Vol.II, p.73, says Horman
Joseph Pugh NE¼-S31; 5-18-1815
Joel Clark NW¼-S31; 4-30-1817. Rel.NW¼-NW¼ to James Downey, Jr.,
Jesse Hunt SE¼-S31; 5-18-1815   5-28-1832
William T. Cullom SW¼-S31; 3-31-1817
John Sherer NE¼-S32; 8-29-1816
Jane Matherel NW¼-S32; 5-18-1815
Jesse Harrell SE¼-S32; 3-7-1815
Peter Demard SW¼-S32; 3-17-1815. Vol.II, p.73, says Demmaree
Peter Demard NE¼-S33; 1-29-1816. Vol.II, p.73, says Demaree
John Sherer NW¼-S33; 8-29-1816

SWITZERLAND CO.

Miner Roberts SE¼-S33; 7-31-1815
Caleb A. Craft NE¼-S34; 3-16-1818. Rel.
Benjamin Dubois NW¼-S34; 12-23-1816. Rel. To Thomas Cole, 8-9-1831
David Cummins SE¼-S34; 9-8-1817
Nicholas Longworth SW¼-S34; 9-30-1818
Edward White NE¼-S35; 8-22-1817. Rel.
Caleb A. Craft NW¼-S35; 3-16-1818. Rel.
Hardy Roper & David Cummins SE¼-S35; 9-8-1817. Rel.
Joseph McHendry SW¼-S35; 8-19-1817
Matthias Haynes & Joshua Haynes NE¼-S36; 3-16-1818. Rel. E½
John Lewis & John Courtney NW¼-S36; 5-11-1818
John Gest SE¼-S36; 3-31-1818. Rel.
Ralph Lotton, Sr. SW¼-S36; 6-5-1818

Page 43. T 4 N, R 2 W of 1st P.M. DEARBORN CO.

Daniel Huffman NW¼-S1; 3-3-1813
Joseph E. Milburn SE¼-S1; 11-2-1813
Jacob Moore SW¼-S1; 6-22-1813
James Lindsay NE¼-S2; 11-25-1812
Stephen Peters NW¼-S2; 3-4-1811
Samuel Walker SE¼-S2; 12-11-1811. Vol.II, p.74, says James
John Buffington SW¼-S2; 1-28-1811
Johiel Buffington NE¼-S3; 2-10-1815
George Moss Lindsay NW¼-S3; 11-6-1813. Vol.II, p.74, gives middle name Ross
Vincent Lindsay & Henry Peters SE¼-S3; 5-27-1813
John Wheeler SW¼-S3; 12-5-1817
Claborn Allen & Ira Allen NE¼-S4; 3-12-1817
Claborn Allen NW¼-S4; 7-7-1817
Jonathan Buffington SE¼-S4; 9-12-1814. Vol.II, p.74, says John
John Lewis SW¼-S4; 2-11-1815
Samuel Wheeler NE¼-S5; 8-19-1817. Rel. W½ to Elias Littell, 7-1-1831
Nathan Guilford & Samuel Todd NW¼-S5; 5-21-1819. Rel.
John Wheeler SE¼-S5; 5-30-1816
John Wheeler E½-SW¼-S5; 2-11-1818
Henry VanMiddlesworth N½-S6; 6-5-1820. Rel. E½-NE¼ to Michael Teney, 3-6-1832
William Ayer SW¼-S6; 5-15-1819. Rel.
John Davis & Dunham Davis NE¼-S7; 4-23-1818. Rel. W½
John Hubbart, Jr. NW¼-S7; 9-29-1818. Rel. W½ to Henry Teney, 1-11-1832
James B. Jones SE¼-S7; 10-3-1817
Samuel M. Ent SW¼-S7; 4-30-1818. Rel. W½

Page 44. T 4 N, R 2 W of 1st P.M.

David McKittrick NE¼-S8; 10-22-1813. Vol.II, p.75, says David M. Kettrick
James Hubbart NW¼-S8; 1-24-1818. Rel. W½
John Sutherland & James P. Ramsey W½-SE¼-S8; 9-23-1817. Rel. To William J. Fleming, 12-24-1827
Garret Swallow SW¼-S8; 9-22-1817
Christopher Briney E½-SE¼-S8; 5-4-1825. Rel.(?) Vol.II, p.75, shows final certif. #532 to him

Jahiel Buffington NE¼-S9; 4-6-1814
John Walker NW¼-S9; 12-29-1813
James Pritchard SE¼-S9; 9-1-1813
Caleb Mulford SW¼-S9; 4-24-1815. Rel. W½ to William Frazier, 8-21-1827
John Levingston NE¼-S10; 4-6-1806
John Walker NW¼-S10; 4-26-1815
Ralph Smith SW¼-S10; 6-29-1812
Henry Cloud E½-S11; 8-23-1803
Michael Horner NW¼-S11; 4-29-1805
Robert McKittrick, Jr. SW¼-S11; 10-22-1813
George Grave NE¼-S12; 4-29-1815. Vol.II, p.76, says Grove
Abraham Carbaugh NW¼-S12; 4-22-1813
Daniel Conway SE¼-S12; 4-9-1815. Vol.II, p.76, says Conaway.
Robert McKittrick SW¼-S12; 4-3-1815
John Brownson E½-S13; 1-24-1803 (Part in Ohio Co.)
Peter Allen NW¼-S13; 8-30-1814
Peter Allen SW¼-S13; 7-16-1811 (Part in Ohio Co.)
Daniel Conway NE¼-S14; 9-25-1812. Vol. II, p.76, says Conaway
George Nichols NW¼-S14; 7-4-1814
George Nichols SE¼-S14; 6-17-1812
George Nichols SW¼-S14; 1-25-1812
David Bowers NE¼-S15; 8-5-1815
Daniel Lynn SE¼-S15; 10-20-1813
Daniel Crume SW¼-S15; 5-12-1818. Rel. W½ to Benjamin Wilson, 8-22-1825
Garret Swallow NE¼-S17; 10-8-1817
Ezekiel Pritchard NW¼-S17; 1-24-1818. Rel. E½ to James Hainer, 8-21-1827
Alexander Fleming SE¼-S17; 6-11-1818. Rel. W½ to Robert Gullett, 8-29-1827; E½ to George Gordon, 9-3-1827
James Standiford SW¼-S17; 4-29-1818. Rel.
William Abbott NE¼-S18; 10-25-1817
Samuel Frazier NW¼-S18; 9-22-1817
Jesse Vandolak SE¼-S18; 8-24-1818
John Sutherland & James P. Ramsey SW¼-S18; 10-27-1817. Rel. W½ to Nehemiah Knap, 12-30-1829
Henry Britton NE¼-S19; 2-3-1818. Rel. W½ to Henry Brittain, 8-21-1827
Henry Britton NW¼-S19; 3-18-1818. Rel. W½ to William Smith, 8-21-1827
John Wilson Nixon SE¼-S19; 2-3-1818
Elijah Thatcher SW¼-S19; 1-24-1818
Daniel Crume NE¼-S20; 11-28-1817
Nathan Guilford & Samuel Todd NW¼-S20; 5-21-1819. Rel. W½
Matthias Whetstone W½-SW¼-S20; 1-22-1819. Rel. W½ to Samuel Harbert, 3-9-1832
Benjamin Willson NE¼-S21; 10-11-1811
Benjamin Willson NW¼-S21; 10-14-1812
Tetrich Fall SE¼-S21; 8-21-1812 (Part in Ohio Co.)
Daniel Crume SW¼-S21; 9-25-1810 (Part in Ohio Co.)
Henry Cloud NE¼-S22; 8-18-1812
William Spencer, Sr. NW¼-S22; 6-30-1812
William Blue SE¼-S22; 11-26-1811 (Part in Ohio Co.)
John James SW¼-S22; 11-5-1808 (Part in Ohio Co.)
John Brownson W½-S23; 1-24-1803
John Walker SE¼-S23; 5-7-1811
Benjamin Chambers NE¼-S23; 9-21-1802. See Vol.II, p.77, Benjamin Wilson

Page 45. T 4 N, R 2 W of 1st P.M.

Isaac Carlton NE¼-S24; 4-25-1814
John Walker & James Walker NW¼-S24; 11-6-1811 — (Part in Dearborn Co.)
James Allen SE¼-S24; 12-13-1816
Henry Anderson SW¼-S24; 4-20-1814
Joseph Oglevee NE¼-S25; 5-29-1815
John Walker NW¼-S25; 7-6-1815
John Davis SE¼-S25; 12-24-1813
John Walker SW¼-S25; 7-6-1815
William Cochran E½-NE¼ & W½-NE¼-S26; 10-?-1819. See Vol.II,
    p.77, John Walker
John Walker NW¼-S26; 7-6-1815
Thomas K. Coles SE¼-S26; 10-27-1817. Rel. E½ to Samuel Hannah,
John Walker & James Walker SW¼-S26; 8-4-1814   3-28-1832
William Blue NE¼-S27; 4-25-1815
David Blue NW¼-S27; 10-30-1812
John Walker SE¼-S27; 8-4-1814
David Blue SW¼-S27; 6-11-1817
John Walker NE¼-S28; 7-20-1815   2-28-1832
Joseph H. Coburn SE¼-S28; 1-21-1819. Rel. W½ to David Hufford,
John James W½-S28; 5-26-1808. Rel. W½-SE¼ (?) Vol.II, p.78,
    shows final certif. #6288 to him for full W½-S28 (Part in Dearborn Co.)
William Weathers NE¼-S29; 10-3-1812
Ebenezer Harbert NW¼-S29; 8-9-1815. Vol.II, p.78, says Herbert
  Tetrich Fall SE¼-S29; 6-1-1803. — See Vol.II, p.78, Daniel Crume
Robert Conway SW¼-S29; 1-21-1811 (Part in Dearborn Co.)   (Part in Dearborn Co.)
David Bevens E½-NE¼-S30; 4-10-1819. Rel.
Richard Smith W½-NE¼-S30; 5-22-1819
William S. Dart & George Dart E½-NW¼-S30; 6-10-1819. Rel.
Elijah Thatcher W½-NW¼-S30; 1-24-1818
James Hamilton & Michael Jones SE¼-S30; 7-10-1806 (Part in Dearborn Co.)
Nicholas Longworth SW¼-S30; 2-16-1819. Rel. SW¼-SW¼ to John
    Speer, 5-29-1832 (Part in Dearborn Co.)
Thomas Pursel NE¼-S31; 9-11-1806 (Part in Dearborn Co.)
Deckey Burkshire NW¼-S31; 11-15-1804. Vol.II, p.78, says Dickey
Simon Conway & Hubbard Jones SE¼-S31; 11-15-1817. Rel. E½ to
    Hubbard Jones, 3-16-1830
John Clements SW¼-S31; 8-13-1817
Robert Conway NE¼-S32; 11-4-1813
John Alexander NW¼-S32; 1-31-1818. Rel. E½ to John Weathers,
Jesse Weathers SE¼-S32; 4-4-1818. Rel.   2-23-1832
Joseph Frakes SW¼-S32; 8-28-1815
John Glass E½-NE¼-S33; 2-26-1818
James Conway NW¼-S33; 8-26-1816
William Babbs E½-SE¼-S33; 2-26-1818
James Boyle W½-SE¼-S33; 12-28-1818. Rel. To William Kittle,
William Gibson E½-SW¼-S33; 10-4-1818   8-21-1827
Otis Ellis W½-SW¼-S33; 3-14-1818. Rel.
Jacob Miller NE¼-S34; 3-15-1817
Joseph Woods NW¼-S34; 10-28-1816
James Gardner SE¼-S34; 7-11-1815
Ebenezer Harbert SW¼-S34; 2-28-1814
John Walker NE¼-S35; 3-19-1816

James Crane NW¼-S35; 7-4-1814 William Scranton NW¼-S36; 4-11-1814
John Espey SE¼-S35; 1-25-1814 John Barricklow SE¼-S36; 3-14-1814
Hugh Espey SW¼-S35; 8-1-1817
Benjamin Mills SW¼-S36; 2-28-1814. Vol.II, p.79, says Miles

Page 46. T 5 N, R 2 W of 1st P.M.   DEARBORN CO.

Ichabod Palmerton NE¼-S1; 12-3-1814
Elijah Piles NW¼-S1; 6-26-1812. Vol.II, p.79, says Pitts
Amer Bruce SE¼-S1; 12-21-1813
David Blue SW¼-S1; 3-22-1809. Vol.II, p.79, says Blane
James Vaughn NE¼-S2; 8-14-1813
James Vaughn NW¼-S2; 8-18-1817
John Ferris SE¼-S2; 12-24-1814
Robert McCracken E½-SW¼-S2; 2-17-1818
Ralph Hatch W½-SW¼-S2; 6-23-1818
John Stephenson NE¼-S3; 4-13-1816
Zebulon Dickinson NW¼-S3; 11-12-1817. Rel. W½
Benjamin Tibbets & John Tibbets SE¼-S3; 3-13-1817
Thomas C. Blake SW¼-S3; 4-19-1819. Rel. E½ to Elijah Thacher,
    5-13-1828; W½ to John C. Dickenson, 3-13-1832. Vol.II, p.79,
    says John Calvin (or Colvin) Dickinson
David Tibbets NE¼-S4; 9-1-1817
Moses Beckford NW¼-S4; 5-9-1818. Rel. W½
Samuel Roberts E½-SE¼-S4; 4-22-1818. Rel. E½ to Nathan Pettigrew,
Nathan Pettigrew W½-SE¼-S4; 7-30-1824   1-14-1832
Joel Bishop SW¼-S4; 6-3-1819. Rel.
John Tibbets E½-NE¼-S5; 12-4-1818. Rel. See Vol.II, p.80
John Odell E½-NW¼ & W½-NE¼-S5; 6-24-1818
Jeremiah Folsom E½-SE¼-S5; 12-31-1818. Rel.
Samuel Stage W½-SE¼-S5; 7-7-1819. Rel.
George Johnston W½-SW¼-S5; 12-17-1818. Rel.
Noyes Canfield W½-NE¼-S6; 11-26-1828
Lewis Whiteman NW¼-S6; 12-31-1817. Rel. W½ to Stephen Pain, 11-
    26-1827; E½ to Noyes Canfield, 11-26-1828. Vol.II, p.80, says
    Stephen J. Pain
James Mills, Jr. SE¼-S6; 11-10-1818
James Mills, Jr. E½-SW¼-S6; 5-24-1831
Alexander McKinstry & Hugh Alexander W½-SW¼-S6; 10-27-1831
Samuel Hamill E½-NE¼-S7; 1-26-1824
John Dashiell E½-NW¼ & W½-NW¼-S7; 9-6-1818. Rel.
John Dashiell SW¼-S7; 6-27-1818. Rel. E½ to Eli Musgrave,
Hugh McMullen NE¼-S8; 3-17-1818   1-25-1830
George Stephenson NW¼-S8; 6-12-1818
John Cotton Lewis SE¼-S8; 10-26-1818. Rel.
John R. Arnold SW¼-S8; 3-19-1818
John A. Stephens NE¼-S9; 8-24-1818. Rel.
Josiah Lewis NW¼-S9; 7-31-1819. Rel.
Robert Milburn SE¼-S9; 10-4-1815
Watkin Rumsey Watkins SW¼-S9; 8-19-1818
John Cundale E½-NE¼-S10; 6-9-1824   1826
Daniel Pate W½-NE¼-S10; 11-16-1816. Rel. To John Tibbets, 8-24-
David Johnson NW¼-S10; 1-16-1818. Rel. E½ to Townsend Dickinson,
    4-16-1832

Daniel Pate SE$\frac{1}{4}$-S10; 11-29-1816. Rel. W$\frac{1}{2}$ to Benniah B. Fifield & Evert Clindinin, March, no date. Vol.II, p.81, says 3-31-1829
John Johnson SW$\frac{1}{4}$-S10; 9-29-1814. Vol.II, p.81, says Johnston
Andrew Cook NE$\frac{1}{4}$-S11; 10-28-1815
Oliver Heustis NW$\frac{1}{4}$-S11; 8-6-1818
James Ince & George Mantle SE$\frac{1}{4}$-S11; 8-22-1818
Thomas Kyle SW$\frac{1}{4}$-S11; 5-14-1817
Henry Dils NE$\frac{1}{4}$-S12; 8-15-1817
James Leeson NW$\frac{1}{4}$-S12; 2-24-1818. Rel. W$\frac{1}{2}$ to James Leeson,
William Forbes SE$\frac{1}{4}$-S12; 2-3-1817 4-17-1832
David Hogan SW$\frac{1}{4}$-S12; 7-25-1818
Thomas Tanner NE$\frac{1}{4}$-S13; 9-16-1817
James Morgan NW$\frac{1}{4}$-S13; 11-13-1816
James Morgan SE$\frac{1}{4}$-S13; 10-28-1816
Michael Morgan E$\frac{1}{2}$-SW$\frac{1}{4}$ & W$\frac{1}{2}$-SW$\frac{1}{4}$-S13; 10-28-1816

Page 47. T 5 N, R 2 W of 1st P.M.

William Lewis NE$\frac{1}{4}$-S14; 8-22-1818
Joseph McKeney NW$\frac{1}{4}$-S14; 1-27-1815. Rel. E$\frac{1}{2}$. Vol.II, p.81, says McKinny
Lambkin McKenny SE$\frac{1}{4}$-S14; 6-1-1818. Vol.II, p.81, says Lumbkin
David G. Boardman SW$\frac{1}{4}$-S14; 8-24-1814 McKinney
William Shane E$\frac{1}{2}$-NE$\frac{1}{4}$-S15; 6-29-1824
George Clark W$\frac{1}{2}$-NE$\frac{1}{4}$-S15; 6-9-1824
Robert Milburn SE$\frac{1}{4}$-S15; 10-4-1815. Rel.(?) Vol.II, p.82, shows final certif. #11 for this
Bartholomew Caldwell E$\frac{1}{2}$-SW$\frac{1}{4}$-S15; 4-23-1832
John Caldwell & Bartholomew Caldwell W$\frac{1}{2}$-SW$\frac{1}{4}$-S15; 6-9-1824
William Arnold NE$\frac{1}{4}$-S17; 3-19-1818. Rel.
Nathan Todd W$\frac{1}{2}$-NW$\frac{1}{4}$-S17; 9-7-1830. Vol.II, p.82, says Nathaniel
David Osburn SE$\frac{1}{4}$-S17; 11-1-1816
Stephen Inman SW$\frac{1}{4}$-S17; 11-1-1817
Christian Harshey NE$\frac{1}{4}$-S18; 11-7-1816
John*Musgrave NW$\frac{1}{4}$-S18; 8-6-1817 * middle initial H
Jonathan Vail SE$\frac{1}{4}$-S18; 8-25-1817
Riley Truitt SW$\frac{1}{4}$-S18; 10-9-1817
Samuel B. Wood & Winslow J. Wood NE$\frac{1}{4}$-S19; 10-9-1817
David Kerr NW$\frac{1}{4}$-S19; 7-19-1817
Christian Harshey S$\frac{1}{2}$-S19; 11-7-1816
Thomas McIntire, Jr. NE$\frac{1}{4}$-S20; 11-18-1815
Moses Musgrave NW$\frac{1}{4}$-S20; 11-2-1816
Christian Harshey S$\frac{1}{2}$-S20; 11-6-1816
Peter Hennegin NW$\frac{1}{4}$-S21; 1-25-1819 1829
John McKinney SW$\frac{1}{4}$-S21; 10-22-1818. Rel. To Elias Conwell, 12-10-
Samuel Todd NE$\frac{1}{4}$-S22; 5-1-1819. Rel. W$\frac{1}{2}$
Henry Bruce E$\frac{1}{2}$-SE$\frac{1}{4}$-S22; 5-6-1829
Amer Bruce W$\frac{1}{2}$-SE$\frac{1}{4}$-S22; 8-21-1827. See Vol.II, p.83, John Bruce & Stephen Bruce
William Hendricks (assee. of ?) or (and ?) Elias Bedford Surplus in W$\frac{1}{2}$-S22; 11-8-1819. Rel.(?) No final certif. issued in Vol.II. See Vol.II, pp. 82-83, S22
Thomas Chancellor Porter NE$\frac{1}{4}$-S23; 10-12-1816
Benjamin Huffman NW$\frac{1}{4}$-S23; 6-29-1809

William Record SE¼-S23; 3-20-1812
James Bruce & Amar Bruce SW¼-S23; 6-7-1806
Priscilla Ruston NE¼-S24; 8-6-1816
Demas Moss NW¼-S24; 7-13-1816
James Bruce SE¼-S24; 12-12-1811
Benjamin Powell SW¼-S24; 1-11-1811
Jeremiah Hunt S26; 12-20-1803
Henry Bruce NE¼-S27; 1-14-1817
William Shane NW¼-S27; 8-10-1818
Daniel Odle SE¼-S27; 8-30-1814. Vol.II, p.83, says Odel
James Montgomery SW¼-S27; 4-18-1815

Page 48. T 5 N, R 2 W of 1st P.M.

John Montgomery NE¼-S28; 4-18-1815
James Reed NW¼-S28; 11-5-1817
Sylvester Richmond SE¼-S28; 10-25-1817
Martin Cozine W½-SW¼-S28; 6-3-1829
Edward O. Conner NE¼-S29; 4-7-1818. Rel.
Nathan Johnson & Nelson Burgess SE¼-S29; 12-22-1817. Rel.
John Knapp & Hiram Knapp W½-S29; 12-31-1817. Rel. SW¼ & E½-NW¼
Henry VanMiddlesworth NE¼-S30; 4-6-1819. Rel.
Jonathan Johnson & Nelson Burgess NW¼-S30; 7-12-1819. Rel.
Theodore Thompson SE¼-S30; 7-7-1819. Rel. E½ to Jonathan Parks,
Phineas L. King SW¼-S30; 7-7-1819   3-15-1830
Claiborne Allen NE¼-S31; 8-20-1819
William McClelland SE¼-S31; 9-23-1819. Rel.
William Olcott & Thomas Olcott W½-S31; 5-24-1819
James Lindsay NE¼-S32; 6-5-1819
James Lindsay NW¼-S32; 1-18-1819
John Jones SE¼-S32; 6-28-1819
Jesse Williams, Stephen Butler, & Elias P. Smith SW¼-S32; 12-18-
    1819. Rel. E½ to John Columbia, 9-22-1831
Isaac Allen NE¼-S33; 6-9-1818. Rel. W½
John Davis NW¼-S33; 7-31-1819.Rel. W½ to James Case, 6-30-1831
Isaac Allen SE¼-S33; 8-16-1809 Robert Milburn NE¼-S36; 11-2-1813
John Jones SW¼-S33; 8-26-1816
Jeremiah Hunt S34; 8-11-1813 John H. Piatt SE¼-S36; 8-13-1811
William Chamberlain NE¼-S35; 6-28-1814
William Strong & Phineas Hill NW¼-S35; 7-29-1813
Adam Flacke SE¼-S35; 6-21-1805   John Piatt SW¼-S36; 8-13-1811
Michael Flake & William Flake SW¼-S35; 1-19-1811
Michael Flake & William Flake NW¼-S36; 6-27-1812

Page 49. T 6 N, R 2 W of 1st P.M.

Paul Brown NE¼-S1; 11-19-1917
Caleb Williams NW¼-S1; 10-14-1816
Benjamin Southard SE¼-S1; 2-4-1817
James Angevine NW¼-S2; 7-31-1817
Conrad Row E½-SE¼-S2; 6-29-1818
David G. Layton W½-SE¼-S2; 8-4-1818. Rel.
John Davison W½ & E½-SW¼-S2; 7-31-1817
David Palmer NE¼-S3; 6-16-1817

Peter J. Bonta NW¼-S3; 1-5-1816. Vol.II, p.85, says Bonte
Ruliff Bogert SE¼-S3; 12-9-1815
Jane Bonta SW¼-S3; 12-21-1815. Vol.II, p.85, says Bonte
Edward Dwyger NE¼-S4; 10-10-1816. Vol.II, p.85, looks like
Patrick Diver NW¼-S4; 7-16-1818   Dwyzer
Aaron Port SE¼-S4; 8-8-1818. Rel. W½. Vol.II, p.85, says Post
Samuel McMath SW¼-S4; 11-26-1817
James Angevine S5; 7-25-1817
Samuel C. Vance NE¼-S6; 4-6-1818. Rel. E½
Samuel Y. Allaire NW¼-S6; 10-3-1817. Vol.II, p.85, gives middle
David Prudden SE¼-S6; 2-28-1818. Rel.   initial R
Thomas Smith SW¼-S6; 2-17-1818
Abraham Williams & Richard Mulford NE¼-S7; 5-7-1819. Rel.
Casper Michael NW¼-S7; 7-2-1818
Charles Dawson E½-SE¼-S7; 5-8-1817
Spencer Curtis (negro) W½-SE¼-S7; 6-9-1824   Shoemake
Blakeley Shoemaker SW¼-S7; 1-24-1818. Vol.II, p.85,says Blackly
Samuel Anderson NE¼-S8; 1-12-1818. Rel. W½ to Benjamin Morss,
Eli B. Mead W½-NW¼-S8; 6-19-1830   11-9-1831
John Bennett SE¼-S8; 8-17-1818
Philip Michael SW¼-S8; 10-21-1817. Rel. E½ to Philip Michael,
John H. Phillips NE¼-S9; 8-25-1818. Rel. W½   6-20-1831
Henry Likely NW¼-S9; 11-26-1817
John H. Phillips SE¼-S9; 9-10-1818
John H. Dixon SW¼-S9; 1-12-1818. Rel.
David Prince NE¼-S10; 12-9-1815. Vol.II, p.86, says Perine
James Colwell NW¼-S10; 5-6-1816
John Boice (?) SE¼-S10; 12-21-1815. Vol.II, p.86, looks like
John Malhollon SW¼-S10; 1-12-1818   Bovse
William Tharp NE¼-S11; 10-21-1816
Aaron Payne & Robert Jackson NW¼-S11; 7-21-1815
Cornelius Vanhorn SE¼-S11; 7-31-1817
Robert Rowe SW¼-S11; 8-16-1817
Robert Hunt NE¼-S12; 1-1-1817
Caleb White & David Cummins NW¼-S12; 7-13-1818. Rel.
William Green SE¼-S12; 8-15-1817. Rel. W½ to William Tucker,
     8-15-1831; E½ to William Tucker, 3-12-1832
Ruliff Bogert SW¼-S12; 8-12-1817   Jacob Norton SW¼-S14; 12-
Samuel C. Vance NE¼-S13; 8-27-1817   24-1818
William Bean NW¼-S13; 10-5-1818. Rel.
George Mantle & James Ince SE¼-S13; 8-10-1818. Rel. W½ to
     Thomas Hansell, 2-9-1827   William Shephard NE¼-S15;
William Harbert SW¼-S13; 8-8-1818. Rel. E½   12-23-1818
Thomas Hall NE¼-S14; 10-11-1817. Rel. E½   Benjamin Crouch E½ &
Jacob Norton NW¼-S14; 11-24-1818. Rel. E½ W½-SW¼-S15; 3-19-1832
William Barr SE¼-S14; 4-25-1818. Rel.
William Shephard & Robert Keightley SE¼-S15; 12-23-1818. Rel. W½

     Page 50. T 6 N, R 2 W of 1st P.M.

Israel Noyes NE¼-S17; 12-26-1817. Rel.
David Ketcham NW¼-S17; 10-22-1817
Israel Noyes SE¼-S17; 12-26-1817
David Ketcham & Gilbert Platt SW¼-S17; 10-22-1817

Samuel C. Vance NE¼-S18; 8-19-1817. Rel. E½ to John Bennett,
William Dawson NW¼-S18; 3-29-1817   4-22-1828
Gilbert Platt SE¼-S18; 10-22-1817
Jared Evans SW¼-S18; 10-30-1815
Daniel Miller NE¼-S19; 10-22-1817
Charles Dawson NW¼-S19; 4-11-1816
Pearse Shearer SE¼-S19; 10-9-1817.Vol.II, p.87, says Pars Sherer
Stephen Wood SW¼-S19; 12-30-1817
Israel Noyes NE¼-S20; 12-26-1817. Rel. W½ to George Clark,
   3-18-1830. Vol.II, p.87, shows final certif. #148 for whole
   NE¼ to Israel Noyes
Daniel Miller & James Miller, Jr. NW¼-S20; 10-22-1817
Anthony Brodrick SE¼-S20; 5-31-1816
John Kinsley SW¼-S20; 10-9-1817
Patrick Walsh & Ester Walsh NW¼-S21; 2-6-1819
John Darling E½-NE¼-S23; 5-25-1832. Rel. See Vol.II, p.88.
William Barr E½ & W½-NW¼-S23; 4-25-1818.Rel. W½ to Riley Elliott,
Niles Greenwood SE¼-S23; 8-16-1817. Rel.   3-9-1832
John Dawson SW¼-S23; 10-30-1817
Samuel Cunningham NE¼-S24; 7-13-1814
Caleb White & David Cummins NW¼-S24; 7-13-1818
John Hughes SE¼-S24; 3-26-1818
Seth Dunbar SW¼-S24; 2-18-1818. Rel. E½ to Thomas Hansell,
Jacob Darling NE¼-S25; 11-26-1817   1-22-1828
Abel True NW¼-S25; 6-9-1818. Rel. E½ to Reuben True, 12-3-1831
Ezekiel G. Harper SE¼-S25; 3-24-1814   11-26-1828
Stephen O. Brown SW¼-S25; 5-15-1817. Rel. W½ to Asa Jaquith,
William Shearer NE¼-S26; 3-15-1818. Vol.II, p.88, says Shearin
Abel True NW¼-S26; 6-9-1818   1831
James Cox SE¼-S26; 1-29-1818. Rel. W½ to Azariah Oldham, 8-23-
Joseph Hunter & Jonathan Bennet SW¼-S26; 5-28-1817
Nathan Pettigrew NE¼-S27; 5-9-1818. Rel. W½
David Woodward NW¼-S27; 1-26-1818
Thomas Littleton SE¼-S27; 2-16-1818. Rel. W½ to John Darling,
   3-5-1832; E½ to Joseph Roberts, 4-3-1832
Job Sylvester SW¼-S27; 1-15-1818
Stephen Wood E½-S28; 12-30-1817   1817
Matthew Millikan, Allen Millikan, & John Crocker NW¼-S28; 10-16-
John Crocker & William Tibbets SW¼-S28; 5-24-1817
Stephen Wood NE¼-S29; 12-30-1817
Minerva Swift NW¼-S29; 11-15-1817
Perin G. Northup SE¼-S29; 12-16-1815   1-19-1831
Roderick Moore SW¼-S29; 11-24-1815.Rel. W½ to Richard S. Freland,
John Cunningham NE¼-S30; 11-27-1815   John Feeland SE¼-S30;
Stephen Wood W½-S30; 10-25-1817   11-27-1815

                Page 51. T 6 N, R 2 W of 1st P.M.

William Barton NE¼-S31; 5-11-1818
David Roberts, Sr. NW¼-S31; 5-11-1818. Rel. W½
Noyes Canfield W½-SE¼-S31; 11-26-1828
Thomas Alloway SW¼-S31; 1-5-1818
Joseph Sylvester NE¼-S32; 2-28-1818
Elijah Rich NW¼-S32; 2-3-1818   9-2-1829
John Roll SW¼-S32; 6-20-1818. Rel. E½ to Samuel W. McMillen,
                          -53-

Caleb White & David Cummins SE¼-S32; 7-7-1818. Rel. SW¼-SE¼ to
*Hayes McMullen, 5-26-1832; NE¼-SE¼ to John Bliven Clark &
Sewell Plumer, 5-22-1832. * first name, William
Sarah Robert & Mack McCracken NE¼-S33; 7-28-1815. Vol.II, p.89,
says Mark McCormick
Job Sylvester NW¼-S33; 12-26-1817
Abner Tibbets SE¼-S33; 12-20-1814
Josiah Ferris SW¼-S33; 10-31-1815. Vol.II, p.89, says Isaiah
William B. Chamberlin NE¼-S34; 7-26-1817. Rel. W½ to Joseph
Roberts, 10-27-1829   2-22-1831
Joseph Plummer NW¼-S34; 10-22-1817. Rel. E½ to Oliver Heustis,
John Palmer SE¼-S34; 11-3-1815
Robert Hunt SW¼-S34; 7-27-1815
Laurence Lazieur N½-S35; 7-20-1815. Vol.II, p.89, says Lazieres
Gibens Bradbury SE¼-S35; 4-12-1814
James Vaughn SW¼-S35; 12-21-1813
Riley Elliott NE¼-S36; 11-6-1815
James Vaughan NW¼-S36; 3-16-1815
Jonathan Craw E½-SE¼-S36; 11-9-1824   1828
William Lewis W½-SE¼-S36; 1-29-1818. Rel. To Levi Hamblin, 2-21-
Samuel Wright SW¼-S36; 4-12-1816

Page 51. T 7 N, R 2 W of 1st P.M.

Hezekiah Coffin & Uzziah Kendall NE¼-S1; 10-18-1819. Rel. E½ to
William Hollowell, 9-17-1831
William Douglass NW¼-S1; 5-15-1818. Rel.
Daniel H. Lawrence W½-SE¼-S1; 5-11-1830
Valentine Lawrence SW¼-S1; 4-17-1818
Hallamus C. Vanhontin NE¼-S2; 5-6-1816. Rel. W½ to Obediah
Ellison, 11-13-1826; E½ to Abraham Funkhouser, 5-24-1832
Valentine Lawrence NW¼-S2; 8-29-1817   2-27-1832
Valentine Lawrence SE¼-S2; 4-17-1818. Rel. E½ to Jacob Mason,
Valentine Lawrence SW¼-S2; 1-10-1817
Daniel Taylor NW¼-S3; 3-1-1820. Rel. E½
Robert S. Hamilton SW¼-S3; 8-9-1819. Rel.
John Shivelay E½-SE¼-S4; 6-10-1818
Anthony McGinty W½-SE¼-S4; 6-16-1825
Thomas McClary SW¼-S4; 1-9-1821
Benjamin Brown E½-NE¼-S5; 10-13-1820
Thomas Coates W½-NE¼-S5; 10-13-1820
Seth Kelso SE¼-S5; 1-18-1819. Rel.

Page 52. T 7 N, R 2 W of 1st P.M.

James Lawrence W½-NE¼-S7; 2-28-1832
Isaac Lawrence E½-SE¼-S7; 4-29-1819
Isaac Lawrence W½-SE¼-S7; 6-16-1824
Daniel Lawrence SW¼-S7; 5-6-1818
Anthony McGinty NE¼-S8; 6-16-1825
Isaac Foster E½-NW¼-S8; 5-24-1832 Rel. N½
Isaac Lawrence SE¼-S8; 4-29-1819. Rel. E½ to Philip Lawrence,
8-1-1827; W½ to Joseph Yeager, 11-11-1831
Isaac Lawrence SW¼-S8; 9-19-1817

Thomas Bowman NE¼-S9; 8-23-1816   .1-3-1832
Frederick Hauptman NW¼-S9; 9-26-1818. Rel. To Joseph Yeager,
Philip Mason SE¼-S9; 4-17-1818   2-6-1830
James Foster SW¼-S9; 4-27-1818. Rel. E½ to Stephen Thom, Jr.,
George Lewis NE¼-S10; 2-26-1816. Rel. E½
William Lake NW¼-S10; 8-21-1816   * Omission:
Robert Davidson SE¼-S10; 5-22-1818   Edward Johnson &
Isaac Lawrence SW¼-S10; 9-19-1817   Basil Gaither
Durs Frey NE¼-S11; 11-3-1818. Rel. E½   NW¼-S11;
*Martin Benninger SE¼-S11; 11-3-1818   4-29-1816
Valentine Lawrence SW¼-S11; 1-10-1817
William Ashley NE¼-S12; 11-26-1819. Rel. E½
Daniel Lawrence NW¼-S12; 5-6-1818
Daniel Mason SE¼-S12; 5-7-1819
John Hall E½-SW¼-S12; 6-10-1824
John Hall W½-SW¼-S12; 11-26-1819
Thomas Hodge NE¼-S13; 10-27-1819. Rel. E½ to James Montgomery
    Martin, 12-30-1831; W½ to Joseph Butler, 3-16-1832
Peter McKeag NW¼-S13; 3-5-1819. Rel. E½
Samuel Caldwell E½-SE¼-S13; 8-16-1824
Samuel Pollock W½-SE¼-S13; 3-24-1817
Jeremiah Watkins SW¼-S13; 12-4-1815
Adam H. Lemon NE¼-S14; 10-26-1818·
Henry Beamer NW¼-S14; 5-1-1816
Joseph Adams SE¼-S14; 5-10-1816
Nathan Blodget SW¼-S14; 10-26-1818
Isaac Lawrence SE¼-S15; 6-16-1824·
George Mason SW¼-S15; 5-7-1819
Valentine Lawrence NE¼-S17; 4-17-1818
Isaac Lawrence NW¼-S17; 9-19-1817
Valentine Lawrence S½-S17; 8-29-1817
Isaac Lawrence NE¼-S18; 6-28-1819
John Sailer E½-NW¼-S18; 6-28-1822
Christopher Showalter W½-NW¼-S18; 6-13-1822
Simon Oler SE¼-S18; 10-28-1822. Vol.II, p.93, says Oeler
Isaac Lawrence SW¼-S18; 6-28-1819
John Leighty E½-NW¼-S19; 3-3-1823
Robert Terry SE¼-S19; 3-6-1818
Valentine Lawrence NE¼-S20; 8-29-1817
Joseph Gottstein E½-NW¼-S20; 6-15-1819
Joseph Gottstein W½-NW¼-S20; 2-8-1819   8-1-1831
William Leeper SE¼-S20; 4-19-1817. Rel. W½ to Sebastian Bohrer,

Page 53. T 7 N, R 2 W of 1st P.M.

George Mason W½-NE¼-S21; 7-24-1829
George Mason NW¼-S21; 12-6-1819
Johannes Lawrence W½-SE¼-S21; 4-9-1828
Ephraim Lewis E½-SW¼-S21; 5-26-1832. Rel. S½
George Lawrence, Sr. W½-SW¼-S21; 6-6-1828
Benjamin B. Bonham E½-NE¼-S22; 4-22-1825
Welcome Lewis & Richard Lewis W½-NE¼-S22; 6-10-1825
Martin Schnetz E½-NW¼-S22; 7-26-1824

Joseph Scharback W½-SE¼-S22; 7-2-1824
Jacob Burgett & Gregory Leithner E½-SW¼-S22; 10-20-1824
James Matthews & Michael O'Neil W½-SW¼-S22; 11-27-1830
James Colwell NE¼-S23; 5-10-1816
Jonathan Lewis NW¼-S23; 9-1-1817
James Colwell SE¼-S23; 8-6-1816
Jonathan Lewis SW¼-S23; 9-8-1817. Rel. E½ to Patrick McGuire & John Grogan, 7-6-1831
Thomas Danby NE¼-S24; 1-17-1815
Jacob Burnet SE¼-S24; 5-4-1815. See Vol.II, p.94, John Kelso
Joel Dickens W½-S24; 4-9-1816
William Cloud NE¼-S25; 3-6-1816
Henry McKenzie NW¼-S25; 5-3-1816
Peter I. Bonta SE¼-S25; 1-11-1819. Rel. E½ to Joseph Feger,
Joseph Adams SW¼-S25; 5-1-1816 3-1-1832
Caleb Johnston NE¼-S26; 5-3-1816
Jonathan Young NW¼-S26; 3-16-1818. Rel. E½
James Colwell SE¼-S26; 5-6-1816
Michael Sims, negro SW¼-S26; 2-4-1818. Rel.
Andrew B. Allaire NE¼-S27; 4-13-1818. Rel. E½
William Barr NW¼-S27; 4-25-1818. Rel.
Samuel C. Vance SW¼-S27; 8-27-1817. Rel.
Adam Miller NE¼- & W½-S28; 6-17-1817. Rel. E½-SW½ to Francis Anthony Walliser, 4-1-1828. Vol.II, p.94, says Walbiser
John McClure E½-SE¼-S28; 5-26-1817. Rel. To Gregory Stierlen,
Joseph Gottstein W½-SE¼-S28; 6-19-1824 4-1-1828
William McClure NE¼-S29; 4-19-1817
John Ulrick Geisser NW¼-S29; 12-2-1817
John McClure SE¼-S29; 4-19-1817
John Ulrick Engel SW¼-S29; 12-2-1817
Abraham Babinger NE¼-S30; 9-9-1817
Manning Hathaway NW¼-S30; 9-2-1817
Job A. Beach S½-S30; 9-2-1817
John Davison NE¼-S31; 7-31-1817
William Cairns SE¼-S31; 7-25-1817. Rel. W½ to John Wurts,
Samuel Y. Allaire W½-S31; 9-29-1817 8-16-1831
Adam Miller S32; 6-17-1817
Samuel C. Vance NE¼-S33; 8-27-1817. Rel. W½ to Robert Rowe, Jr., 1-19-1831. Vol. II, p. 95, omits Jr.
John McClure NW¼-S33; 4-19-1817
Robert Rowe SE¼-S33; 8-16-1817
Arthur Moore SW¼-S33; 12-6-1817. Rel. E½ to Robert Rowe, Jr.,
Abraham Tharp NE¼-S34; 1-12-1818 11-29-1825
William Green & Ruliff Bogert NW¼-S34; 1-6-1818
Peter J. (I.?) Bonta SE¼-S34; 12-6-1817. Rel.
Arthur Moore SW¼-S34; 6-24-1817
Hallamas C. Vanhouten NE¼ & W½-S35; 4-11-1816
Cyrus Cutter SE¼-S35; 12-12-1815
Edward Roberts NE¼-S36; 9-4-1818
Paul Brown NW¼-S36; 9-30-1815
Francis Dunlavy SE¼-S36; 11-22-1817. Rel. W½ to David Summers,
Paul Brown SW¼-S36; 4-6-1816 8-21-1827

There is no page 56 in this transcription.

Page 54.   T 8 N, R 2 W of 1st P.M.   Franklin Co.

Thomas Millholland E½-NE½-S1; 12-28-1814
Thomas Eldon W½-NE½-S1; 6-9-1824
William H. Eades NW½-S1; 1-23-1815
Briton Grant SE½-S1; 9-23-1811. Vol.II, p.96, says Gant
Giles Gant E½-SW½-S1; 4-7-1825
Henry Case NE½-S2; 7-17-1813
Seth Goodwine NW½-S2; 6-15-1805
John Quick SE½-S2; 12-22-1814
John Quick SW½-S2; 8-14-1810
James Adair NE½-S3; 3-22-1805
William Willson NW½-S3; 7-25-1805
John Milholland SE½-S3; 4-17-1805
Samuel Scott & Charles Scott SW½-S3; 9-3-1805
William Henderson NE½-S4; 9-22-1806
William Arnell NW½-S4; 12-27-1804. Vol.II, p.96, says Arnett
James McCoy SE½-S4; 10-22-1804
William Lynes SW½-S4; 2-13-1811
David Gayman NE½-S5; 1-11-1815
Thomas Henderson NW½-S5; 10-28-1816. Rel. E½
John Hall & Lewis Dewees SE½-S5; 12-31-1814. Rel. E½ to John
    Bradburn, 11-11-1827
Solomon Allen SW½-S5; 10-21-1816. Rel. W½
John Stafford NE½-S6; 7-31-1813. Rel. E½. Vol.II, p.96, says
Samuel C. Vance NW½-S6; 9-25-1817. Rel.   Hafford
Samuel C. Vance SE½-S6; 9-25-1817. Rel. E½
Elliot Herndon SW½-S6; 8-5-1813
Samuel C. Vance NE½-S7; 3-11-1818. Rel.
Stephen Butler & Elias P. Smith NW½-S7; 12-5-1817. Rel.
James Lyons, Abraham McCord, & Loring Morton SE½-S7; 6-4-1818
Nathaniel Herndon SW½-S7; 5-30-1814. Rel. E½
Solomon Shepard, Jr. NE½-S8; 4-26-1816
Daniel Hasbrook NW½-S8; 5-5-1816
Harvey Bates SE½-S8; 5-3-1816. Rel.
Thomas McColliscot SW½-S8; 5-3-1816. Rel.
Adam Nelson NW½-S9; 10-6-1817. Rel. E½
James Andrew & John Andrew SE½-S9; 6-10-1817
Ryleigh Woodworth SW½-S9; 2-18-1815. Rel. E½
Anthony Halberslude NE½-S10; 6-20-1806. Vol.II, p.97, says
Samuel Case NW½-S10; 6-6-1813   Halberstadt
John Leforge SE½-S10; 2-8-1812
William Eads NE½-S11; 4-23-1816. Rel. W½ to Thomas Shank & James
    Shank, 10-8-1828; E½ to John Quick, 10-27-1828
John Shank NW½-S11; 3-18-1812
John Fugit SE½-S11; 4-10-1816. Vol.II, p.97, says Fuget
John Conner SW½-S11; 8-14-1810
Timothy Parker & Housel Parker NE½-S12; 2-7-1815. Rel. E½. Vol.II
    p. 97, says Anselm Parker
William Jackman NW½-S12; 6-7-1814
Moses Congar SE½-S12; 2-22-1813
George Singhorse SW½-S12; 3-1-1813
William Helm NE½-S13; 1-14-1811
Thomas Clark SE½-S13; 12-11-1811
John Ward SW½-S13; 8-1-1816. Rel. W½ to Allen Backhouse, 1-12-1832

John Conner NE¼-S14; 8-14-1810
Stephen Gable NW¼-S14; 12-11-1811. Vol.II, p.98, says Goble
Allen Ramsey SE¼-S14; 2-20-1807
John Jasen SW¼-S14; 6-11-1816. Rel.
John Lefforge W½-NE¼-S15; 1-10-1829
John Lefforge E½-NW¼-S15; 1-10-1829
                Page 55. T 8 N, R 2 W of 1st P.M.
Joseph W. Morrison NE¼-S17; 10-28-1816. Rel.
Joseph K. Smith & Henry Rockey NW¼-S17; 7-6-1818. Rel.
David E. Wade SE¼-S17; 1-9-1817
John Stafford SW¼-S17; 5-22-1816. Rel. W½
Nathaniel Herndon NW¼-S18; 6-1-1814. Vol. II, p.98, says Nathan
Peter Prifagle SE¼-S18; 6-10-1816. Rel. E½
David James & James H. Speer SW¼-S18; 7-14-1818
George W. Matthews NE¼-S19; 9-24-1818. Rel. W½ to John Bradburn,
Jonathan Moore SE¼-S19; 2-5-1819. Rel.   11-12-1828
Nicholas Longworth S20; 1-3-1818. Rel. NW¼, SW¼, & E½-SE¼
James Howe E½-NW¼-S22; 5-28-1832
Robert Douglass SE¼-S22; 8-27-1818
Joseph Scoonover Whitney E½-SW¼-S22; 12-29-1831
John Hays NE¼-S23; 7-11-1817. Rel. E½
Jacob Hays SE¼-S23; 8-1-1817. Rel.
Lyons, McCord, & Nathaniel Finch W½-S23; 6-1-1818. Rel,
John B. Chapman & James Price NE¼-S24; 1-2-1817
John Ayres NW¼-S24; 7-21-1817
George Sutton E½-SE¼-S24; 5-16-1825
Abraham Hiler W½-SE¼-S24; 9-3-1831
John Page SW¼-S24; 7-26-1817. Rel. W½
Robertson Jones NE¼-S25; 5-8-1815
William Knowles NW¼-S25; 7-26-1817
Corbly Hudson SE¼-S25; 9-21-1816
Robertson Jones SW¼-S25; 11-13-1815
Levi Fortner NE¼-S26; 9-16-1817
Edward Carney NW¼-S26; 11-22-1814
William Ramsey SW¼-S26; 10-13-1814. Rel. Vol. II, p.100, says
   final certif. #1937 for it.
Eli Brooks NE¼-S27; 8-22-1816
William Cummings NW¼-S27; 10-26-1818. Rel.
John Mercer SE¼-S27; 10-13-1814
Samuel Price SW¼-S27; 7-19-1817
Uzziah Kendall NE¼-S28; 8-19-1818. Rel. W½
Thomas James NW¼-S28; 9-28-1818. Rel.
John Atkinson & William Walker SE¼-S28; 1-2-1815. Rel. E½ to
   Moses Dart & Amos Dart, 9-17-1831
Bradbury Catterell & James McCafferty SW¼-S28; 6-26-1818. Rel.
   E½ to Nancy Case, 1-2-1832
William Stephenson NE¼-S29; 8-19-1818
Phineas J. (I.?) Johnston NW¼-S29; 5-28-1818. Rel.
Job Harrison SE¼-S29; 8-5-1818
John Davis SW¼-S29; 8-19-1818
                Page 56. T 8 N, R 2 W of 1st P.M.
Charles Harrison W½-SE¼-S30, 10-28-1818. Rel.
Henry Dougherty E½-SW¼-S30; 10-28-1818. Rel.
George W. Shank NE¼-S31; 10-15-1818. Rel.

James Mason NW$\frac{1}{4}$-S31; 11-4-1818. Rel.
Edward Blackburn SE$\frac{1}{4}$-S31; 9-20-1819
Thomas Smith SW$\frac{1}{4}$-S31; 3-3-1820. Rel. 10-19-1831
Reuben Clearwater NE$\frac{1}{4}$-S32; 5-23-1817. Rel. W$\frac{1}{2}$ to Joseph Dart,
John Halberstadt NW$\frac{1}{4}$-S32; 9-12-1817. Rel. E$\frac{1}{2}$ to James McClary,
William Davis SW$\frac{1}{4}$-S32; 9-15-1819. Rel. W$\frac{1}{2}$ 9-22-1831
Nicholas Pumphery S33 & S34; 10-24-1814. Rel. E$\frac{1}{2}$-S33; SW$\frac{1}{4}$-S33; W$\frac{1}{2}$-S34; SE$\frac{1}{4}$-S34; SE$\frac{1}{4}$-S33 to James McClary, 1-18-1830; E$\frac{1}{2}$-NW$\frac{1}{4}$-S34 to John Peterson, 10-19-1831; E$\frac{1}{2}$-NE$\frac{1}{4}$-S33 to Philip Heck, 1-12-1832; W$\frac{1}{2}$-NE$\frac{1}{4}$-S33 to Richard Manwaring, 2-21-1832
Daniel Harty NE$\frac{1}{4}$-S35; 10-25-1814
Samuel Price & William Mints NW$\frac{1}{4}$-S35; 7-10-1817
William Mints SE$\frac{1}{4}$-S35; 8-4-1817
Corbly Hudson SW$\frac{1}{4}$-S35; 5-30-1818. Rel. E$\frac{1}{2}$ to William Spradling,
James Jones, Jr. NE$\frac{1}{4}$-S36; 5-13-1815 12-20-1827
Corbly Hudson NW$\frac{1}{4}$-S36; 5-30-1818 2-1-1832
Joseph L. Sparks SE$\frac{1}{4}$-S36; 3-10-1819. Rel. E$\frac{1}{2}$ to Joshua Low Sparks,
Ira Grover SW$\frac{1}{4}$-S36; 6-11-1819. Rel. W$\frac{1}{2}$ to Noah Swift, 10-19-1831

Page 56. T 9 N, R 2 W of 1st P.M.

John Wells NE$\frac{1}{4}$-S1; 10-21-1814
James Stevens NW$\frac{1}{4}$-S1; 1-12-1814
William Dubois SE$\frac{1}{4}$-S1; 10-13-1815
Ezekiel Powers & William Powers SW$\frac{1}{4}$-S1; 3-1-1814
Elias Baldwin NE$\frac{1}{4}$-S2; 12-12-1814
Jacob Stair NW$\frac{1}{4}$-S2; 11-8-1813
David Smith SE$\frac{1}{4}$-S2; 12-12-1814
Enoch Buckingham SW$\frac{1}{4}$-S2 & SE$\frac{1}{4}$-S3; 1-18-1815
Robert Glidwell NE$\frac{1}{4}$-S3; 6-7-1813
Agness Taylor NW$\frac{1}{4}$-S3; 10-23-1806
Lesmund Barye SW$\frac{1}{4}$-S3; 2-8-1812. Vol. II, p.103, says Lismund Easze
Robert Templeton E$\frac{1}{2}$-S4; 9-24-1804
Robert Templeton NW$\frac{1}{4}$-S4; 11-20-1804
Robert Templeton SW$\frac{1}{4}$-S4; 7-7-1812
Robert Templeton NE$\frac{1}{4}$-S5; 3-6-1816. Vol. II, p.103, adds Jr.
Peter Girard NW$\frac{1}{4}$-S5; 7-1-1816. Vol. II, p.103, says Gerard
John Tharp SE$\frac{1}{4}$-S5; 11-4-1814
William Eades SW$\frac{1}{4}$-S5; 12-10-1814. Vol. II, p.103, says Eads & adds middle initial H.
Robert Archibald Fr.S6; 9-10-1816. Rel. Fr. off S end; Lot 4-W$\frac{1}{2}$-SE$\frac{1}{4}$ to Miles G. Eggleston, 12-9-1829; Lot 5-SW cor.-Fr.S6 to Miles G. Eggleston, 12-9-1829
Thomas Skinner Fr.S7; 10-5-1810
John Tharp NE$\frac{1}{4}$-S8; 9-11-1811. Vol. II, p.103, says SE$\frac{1}{4}$ and reverses Lesmund Basye (2nd entry below)
Lesmund Basye SE$\frac{1}{4}$-S8; 8-20-1813. Vol. II, p.103, says NE$\frac{1}{4}$ and reverses John Tharp (2nd above)
David Bell NW$\frac{1}{4}$-S8; 11-22-1806. Vol. II, p.103, says SW$\frac{1}{4}$ and reverses with William Henderson (2nd below)
William Henderson SW$\frac{1}{4}$-S8; 10-22-1806. Vol. II, p.103, says NW$\frac{1}{4}$ and reverses with David Bell (2nd above)
John Logan NE$\frac{1}{4}$-S9; 10-9-1805
Blackslee Barnes NW$\frac{1}{4}$-S9; 11-29-1815
James Taylor S$\frac{1}{2}$-S9; 10-22-1804
William Morris & Stacy Fenton NE$\frac{1}{4}$-S10; 12-31-1814

James Logan NW¼-S10; 11-25-1813
Jacob Barckman SE¼-S10; 4-15-1811
Jacob Clearwater SW¼-S10; 10-19-1815. Rel. E½ to Elias Brook,
David Oliver NE¼-S11; 8-1-1817 12-17-1829
Jacob Craig NW¼-S11; 4-15-1811
Enoch Buckingham SE¼-S11; 1-2-1815
Richard Cockey SW¼-S11; 11-19-1814

Page 57. T 9 N, R 2 W of 1st P.M.

Peter Ambrose E½-S12; 9-30-1814
William Crooks NW¼-S12; 12-31-1814
David Haymond SW¼-S12; 6-26-1815. Rel. E½ to Samuel Goudie,
Job Stout NE¼-S13; 7-25-1814 1-29-1829
David Smith NW¼-S13; 12-31-1814
James Wallace SE¼-S13; 10-22-1814
Thomas Baldwin SW¼-S13; 1-2-1815
John Allen NE¼-S14; 12-17-1814
John Allen & Benjamin McCarty NW¼-S14; 12-5-1814
Alexander Cummings SW¼-S14; 4-20-1816
John Allen & Benjamin McCarty NE¼-S15; 12-17-1814
James McCalman NW¼-S15; 10-15-1816. Rel. E½ to James Gavin,
10-21-1826; W½ to Nicholas Weber, 3-21-1829
Jonathan McCarty E½-SE¼-S15; 12-8-1814
John R. Man W½-SE¼-S15; 8-28-1824
Lewis Bishop SW¼-S15; 5-8-1816
James Knight, Jr. NE¼-S17; 3-20-1811
James Knight NW¼-S17; 9-17-1808 says Ruffin
William Barr & William Buffin SE¼-S17; 4-12-1811. Vol. II, p.104,
James Knight & James McGinnis SW¼-S17; 8-1-1816. Rel.
Ferman Smith Fr.S18; 12-8-1814
John Norris NW¼-S19; 1-19-1808
Thomas Williams SE¼-S19; 11-17-1804
John Vincent SW¼-S19; 7-12-1806
Amos Butler NE¼-S20; 4-4-1806
Amos Butler NW¼-S20; 8-22-1808
Amos Butler SE¼-S20; 12-4-1804
Amos Butler SW¼-S20; 3-10-1806
William Butler NE¼-S21; 11-23-1814. Rel. W½ to Abner McCartney,
12-9-1829. Vol. II, p.104, says McCarty
Benjamin McCarty NW¼-S21; 11-5-1808
John Stockdale SE¼-S21; 12-14-1812
Amos Butler SW¼-S21; 12-4-1811
David E. Wade N½-S22; 6-12-1816
John Kelsey SE¼-S22; 12-17-1814
Anthony Halberstadt SW¼-S22; 12-4-1812 mid. init. G
Daniel Y. Templeton NE¼-S23; 10-2-1815. Vol. II, p.105, gives
David Graham NW¼-S23; 7-24-1815
David Black SE¼-S23; 7-30-1814
James Carson & Hanson Love SW¼-S23; 4-14-1813
David Hays NE¼-S24, 1-16-1815
Abel White NW¼-S24; 8-22-1815
Enoch Thompson SE¼-S24 8-6-1814
Enoch Buckingham SW¼-S24; 1-2-1815
Arthur Henry NE¼-S25; 10-9-1811. Vol. II, p.105, says Henroe
Andrew Reed NW¼-S25; 9-1-1813

James Gondier SE¼-S25; 10-13-1813. Vol. II, p.105, says Goudie
Amos Baldwin & Joseph Riche SW¼-S25; 8-18-1814
Archibald Talbott NE¼-S26; 6-22-1814
Peyton S. Symmes NW¼-S26; 7-27-1814
John Hedly S½-S26; 7-28-1814
Isaac Kimmey NE¼-S27; 7-25-1814
Solomon Tiner NW¼-S27; 1-8-1807
Isaac K. Finch SE¼-S27; 7-25-1814
David Penwell SW¼-S27; 1-19-1811
Micajah Park NE¼-S28; 1-5-1811
James McGinnis NW¼-S28; 5-20-1811. Vol. II, p.105, adds James Noble, assee. of James McGinnis
Ruggles Winchill SE¼-S28; 9-30-1811
John Kenedy SW¼-S28; 4-16-1811
John Allen NE¼-S29; 7-6-1805
Amos Butler & Jesse B. Thomas NW¼-S29; 7-11-1805
Amos Butler SE¼-S29; 3-18-1806
Amos Butler SW¼-S29; 10-1-1806

Page 58. T 9 N, R 2 W of 1st P.M.

James Moore NE¼-S30; 2-1-1808
Thomas Williams NW¼-S30; 1-19-1811
Jacob Hetdrick SE¼-S30; 6-13-1814
James Noble SW¼-S30; 12-2-1814
Eli Stringer NE¼-S31; 6-6-1814
Samuel F. Hunt & William C. Drew NW¼-S31; 9-19-1817. Rel.
Thomas Henderson SE¼-S31; 6-6-1814
Samuel F. Hunt & William C. Drew SW¼-S31; 9-19-1817
Samuel Arnett NE¼-S32; 7-24-1805
John Ramey SE¼-S32; 10-13-1804
Thomas Henderson W½-S32; 11-18-1805
John Richardson NE¼-S33; 1-11-1811
Solomon Tyner NW¼-S33; 11-30-1804
John Brown SE¼-S33; 7-22-1805
William Tyner SW¼-S33; 9-21-1804
David Clearwater NE¼-S34; 9-21-1814
John Penwell NW¼-S34; 1-13-1808
John Collins & William McCoy SE¼-S34; 11-28-1811
Abraham Hackleman SW¼-S34; 6-20-1806
David Bradford NW¼-S35; 6-15-1816
Charles Vancamp SE¼-S35; 8-18-1813. Rel. E½ to Jonathan Eads, 12-11-1829
John Collins SW¼-S35; 9-29-1814
Moses Pinch NW¼-S36; 8-24-1814. Vol. II, p.106, says Finch
Enoch McCarty SW¼-S36; 12-14-1814
Mary Milholland E½-S36; 11-8-1814

Page 58. T 10 N, R 2 W of 1st P.M. UNION CO.

Henry Shaffer NE¼-S1; 8-26-1813
Ebenezer Howard NW¼-S1; 8-16-1814
Abraham Rose SE¼-S1; 7-27-1814
James M. Gray & John G. Gray SW¼-S1; 6-25-1816
William Dunkin NE¼-S2; 1-6-1815
James Deakins NW¼-S2; 6-27-1814
Daniel Archer SE¼-S2; 5-24-1815. Vol. II, p.106, says David
Thomas Sackett SW¼-S2; 1-30-1815
Seth H. Bates NE¼-S3; 1-30-1815

Robert Hanna, Jr. NW¼-S3; 3-21-1818. Vol. II, p.106, shows final cert. #7419 to John Sample, 11-3-1813
John Bridges SE¼-S3; 1-22-1818
William Carter SW¼-S3; 5-9-1807
William Newcomb NE¼-S4; 5-24-1815. Vol. II, p.107, says Newnum
John Johnston SE¼-S4; 1-14-1814
John Templeton W½-S4; 9-24-1804
David Hueston Fr.S5; 1-14-1807
Thomas Thomas Fr.S8; 9-18-1816
Joseph Hanna N½-S9; 9-24-1804
George Hollingsworth SE¼-S9; 5-13-1806
James Taylor SW¼-S9; 10-23-1804
William Abernathy NE¼-S10; 2-17-1815
George Hollingsworth NW¼-S10; 9-12-1806
Hugh Moore SE¼-S10; 1-12-1818. Vol. II, p.107, shows final cert. #590 to Abraham Elwell, 10-6-1814
Reuben Scurlock SW¼-S10; 11-28-1814
William Dubois NE¼-S11; 6-21-1806
Jacob Dubois NW¼-S11; 12-11-1811
John Dickison SE¼-S11; 6-21-1806
Jacob Dubois SW¼-S11; 8-13-1811
Daniel Wilson NE¼-S12; 12-11-1811
Amasich Elwell NW¼-S12; 1-12-1808. Vol. II, p.107, says Ameriah
Alexander Dubois & Isaac Dubois SW¼-S12; 6-21-1806

Page 59. T 10 N, R 2 W of 1st P.M.

Clark Bates NE¼-S13; 1-11-1814
Clark Bates NW¼-S13; 12-11-1811
James Piper, Sr. & Joel Williams S½-S13; 8-11-1806
James Piper NE¼-S14; 12-4-1812
William Popenoe NW¼-S14; 12-30-1814
John Whitworth & John Reily SE¼-S14; 11-19-1814
Jacob Newkirk SW¼-S14; 4-28-1815
Ezekiel Rose NE¼-S15; 12-3-1818
Wilie Powell NW¼-S15; 2-28-1818
Charles Hall E½-SE¼-S15; 4-6-1825
James Osborn W½-SE¼-S15; 12-24-1818. Vol. II, p.107, says Osbon of W½
William H. Eads SW¼-S15; 1-7-1818
Jacob Bloyd NE¼-S17; 9-12-1806. Rel. N end/ to George Ferguson, 9-24-1828
Matthew Brown W½-Fr.S17; Fr.S18; 9-2-1816

* John Ewing SE¼-S17; 4-17-1805

Page 59. T 10 N, R 2 W of 1st P.M. FRANKLIN CO.

John Fisher Fr.S19; W½-S20; 3-2-1816
James Watters E½-S20; 2-21-1814
Thomas Osborne NE¼-S21; 11-5-1808
Isaac Willson & Benjamin Willson NW¼-S21; 2-2-1809
George Johnson SE¼-S21; 6-3-1812. Vol. II, p.108, says Johnston
Hugh Abernathy & William Rusing SW¼-S21; 4-19-1809
William Abernathy E½-NE¼-S22; 6-17-1825
William Hays W½-NE¼-S22; 5-24-1827
Thomas Osborn NW¼-S22; 8-25-1817
Charles Shriner E½-SE¼-S22; 12-6-1827
William Moore W½-SE¼-S22; 1-14-1828
Hezekiah Ogden & Matthew Hughes SW¼-S22; 2-21-1825
John Reily NE¼-S23; 5-31-1815
David Power NW¼-S23; 2-6-1815. Vol. II, p.108, says Powers

Robert Greene SE¼-S23; 1-15-1814
Vincent Davis SW¼-S23; 9-20-1814
Thomas J. Worman NE¼-S24; 3-1-1810
John Flint NW¼-S24; 10-18-1811. Vol. II, p.108, adds Sr.
Robert White S½-S24; 10-18-1811
John Smith NE¼-S25; 11-19-1812
Richard Freeman NW¼-S25; 2-2-1814
John Smith SE¼-S25; 11-19-1812
Daniel Osborn SW¼-S25; 3-11-1814
Isaac Sellars NE¼-S26; 10-7-1815
Joshua Butler NW¼-S26; 1-20-1814
Abraham Rose SE¼-S26; 7-27-1814
Elam Murray SW¼-S26; 3-16-1814
Daniel Powers NE¼-S27; 10-20-1814
Jonathan Bassett NW¼-S27; 4-16-1818
Archibald Morrow SE¼-S27; 10-9-1811
Henry Todd SW¼-S27; 3-4-1816
William Logan NE¼-S28; 12-4-1804
Robert Templeton NW¼-S28; 10-16-1804
Benjamin Nugent SW¼-S28; 10-30-1811
William Rusing NE¼-S29; 3-10-1814
Joel Belk NW¼-S29; 12-2-1814
Isaac Bulkley SE¼-S29; 9-4-1816. Vol. II, p.108, says Buckley
Thomas Harvey SW¼-S29; 12-6-1813
David Erb Fr.S30; 6-18-1816
James Gordon Fr.S31; 6-9-1817
Robert Hanna, Jr. & John Nugent NE¼-S32; 3-28-1814
Thomas Powers NW¼-S32; 6-23-1815
Ralph Williams SE¼-S32; 4-1-1811
Emery Hobbs SW¼-S32; 4-26-1814
Robert Hanna NE¼-S33; 9-24-1714
Robert Hanna NW¼-S33; 7-13-1811
John Huffman SE¼-S33; 1-3-1814
Obadiah Estes SW¼-S33; 8-1-1806
             Page 60. T 10 N, R 2 W of 1st P.M.
William Henry, Charlott Gibbs, & John Gibbs NE¼-S34; 6-11-1812
John Dickeson NW¼-S34; 11-25-1813
John Hornady SE¼-S34; 5-29-1811
Robert Gildewell SW¼-S34; 4-15-1806
William Sims NW¼-S35; 11-29-1813
Jacob Kiger & Christopher Kiger SE¼-S35; 10-23-1813
Aaron Frakes NW¼-S36; 10-13-1814
Stephen Gardner NE¼-S36; 3-8-1814
John Watts SE¼-S36; 12-31-1814
James Stephens & Joseph Stephens SW¼-S36; 3-2-1812
             Page 60. T 11 N, R 2 W of 1st P.M. Union   UNION CO.
Jacob Horner NE¼-S1; 12-30-1814
Jacob Horner NW¼-S1; 12-30-1814
Byrd Stiles SE¼-S1; 9-2-1813
William Cason SW¼-S1; 6-24-1814
Henry Peck NE¼-S2; 1-26-1814. Vol. II, p.109, says Beck
Thomas Cully NW¼-S2; 11-14-1814
William Cason SE¼-S2; 8-16-1814
James Tanner SW¼-S2; 2-1-1811

Thomas Cully NE¼-S3; 11-30-1814   1814.
John Andrews, Robert Burbridge, & Elijah Burbridge NW¼-S3; ~9-30~
Thomas Cully SE¼-S3; 11-30-1814
Elijah Carson SW¼-S3; 5-17-1816. Vol. II, p.109, says Cason
Zacheriah Furgerson Fr.S4; 3-13-1815
George Harlin Fr.S9; 1-23-1807
Robert Swann & James Nicholas NE¼-S10; 11-26-1814. Vol. II,
John Campbell NW¼-S10; 12-16-1816   p.110, says Nichols
Jacob Horner SE¼-S10; 12-30-1814
James Snowden SW¼-S10; 5-5-1815
Joshua Palmer NE¼-S11; 11-11-1814
Abraham Burkhalter NW¼-S11; 12-29-1810
Joshua Palmer SE¼-S11; 6-18-1807. Vol. II, p.110, adds Sr.
John Hollingsworth SW¼-S11; 9-1-1807. Vol. II, p.110, says
Wright Cook NE¼-S12; 12-18-1813   Jonathan
James Armstrong NW¼-S12; 11-15-1814
George W. Crist SE¼-S12; 9-19-1814
Jacob Horner SW¼-S12; 11-30-1814
Thomas Cook NE¼-S13; 12-12-1814
Isaac Cook NW¼-S13; 4-12-1814
Thomas Cook SE¼-S13; 4-14-1813
Jonathan Hollingsworth SW¼-S13; 9-17-1814
Joel Hollingsworth NE¼-S14; 9-14-1814
Joshua Harlin NW¼-S14; 1-23-1807
Isaac Hollingsworth SE¼-S14; 10-4-1813
Jonathan Hollingsworth SW¼-S14; 5-29-1807
William McMahan NE¼-S15; 9-12-1816
William King NW¼-S15; 9-30-1814. Vol. II, p.110, says Ring
William Greene SE¼-S15; 2-15-1814
John Campbell SW¼-S15; 6-28-1814
John Hanna & George Levingston Fr.S16; 10-16-1804
Thomas Nickels Fr.S20; 6-24-1815. Also W½-S21.
William Batkin & John McCutchin E½-S21; 12-18-1804. Vol. II,
William Logan NE¼-S22; 1-16-1807   p.110, says Botkin
William M. Greer NW¼-S22; 10-3-1814
Levi Hollingsworth SE¼-S22; 5-13-1806
Robert Swan SW¼-S22; 10-7-1805
          Page 61. T 11 N, R 2 W of 1st P.M.
Jacob Hollingsworth NE¼-S23; 9-22-1806
Richard Hollingsworth NW¼-S23; 10-5-1815
James Murdock SE¼-S23; 8-20-1814. Vol. II, p.110, says Mardock
Nathaniel Henderson SW¼-S23; 11-1-1814
Hugh Reid E½-S24; 7-23-1807. Vol. II, p.110, says Reed
James Hollingsworth E½-NW¼ & W½-NW¼-S24; 12-29-1813
Eli Henderson SW¼-S24; 7-1-1807
Eliab Gardner NE¼-S25; 11-2-1811
Eli Henderson NW¼-S25; 7-1-1807
John Creek SE¼-S25; 1-7-1815
John Brown, Jr. SW¼-S25; 4-14-1813
Willis Kelly NE¼-S26; 4-14-1813
William Norris NW¼-S26; 9-30-1814
Thomas Brown SE¼-S26; 11-14-1806
David Ewing SW¼-S26; 4-14-1813. Vol. II, p.111, says Daniel
David Hollingsworth NE¼-S27; 5-13-1806

John Hanna NW¼-S27; 10-16-1804
Joseph Hollingsworth SE¼-S27; 5-13-1806
John Hanna SW¼-S27; 1-4-1814
William Nichoals NE¼-S28; 5-13-1806. Vol. II, p.111, says
James Nichoals NW¼-S28; 6-25-1806 Nicholas
William Norris SE¼-S28; 4-8-1806
Mordecai McKinney SW¼-S28; 2-20-1807. Vol. II, p.111, says
William Ewing Fr.S29; 11-24-1806 McKinsey
Samuel Husten Fr.S32; 1-14-1807
George Morris NE¼-S33; 1-22-1814. Vol. II, p.111, says Norris
Martin Baum NW¼-S33; 10-19-1805
Robert A. Templeton SE¼-S33; 5-22-1813
William Cunningham SW¼-S33; 10-31-1804
Jacob Case NE¼-S34; 4-14-1813
Arthur Furgusson NW¼-S34; 10-14-1816
William Sparks SE¼-S34; 7-19-1809
Abraham Buckles SW¼-S34; 8-28-1815
Matthew Brown NW¼-S35; 8-26-1806
John Brown, Sr. NE¼-S35; 4-14-1813
John Burns SE¼-S35; 2-3-1815
Bennet Langston SW¼-S35; 9-4-1813
Solomon Beach NE¼-S36; 9-2-1814
Enos Bowlsley SE¼-S36; 8-15-1814. Vol. II, p.111, says Boulsby
James Snowden W½-S36; 12-30-1814

Page 62. T 12 N, R 2 W of 1st P.M. WAYNE CO.

Peter Smith NE¼-S1; 12-2-1805
George Hunt SE¼-S1; 3-25-1807
Charles Hunt W½-S1; 2-11-1807
David Railsback NE¼-S2; 3-13-1807
Timothy Hunt SE¼-S2; 10-6-1814
John Cox & Joseph Cox W½-S2 & Fr.S3; 12-11-1811

Page 62. T 12 N, R 2 W of 1st P.M. UNION CO.

Abraham Nave Fr.S10; 3-26-1806
Richard Denny NE¼-S11; 1-14-1811
Thomas Lewis NW¼-S11; 8-25-1806
Isaac Neley SE¼-S11; 1-2-1815. Vol. II, p.112, says Wiley
Thomas Lewis SW¼-S11; 8-25-1806
Smith Hunt NW¼-S12; 2-8-1808
Charles Hunt SE¼-S12; 2-11-1807
Henry Martin SW¼-S12; 1-7-1812
Charles Hunt NE¼-S13; 2-11-1807
Benjamin Boone NW¼-S13; 4-25-1808
Adam Ely SE¼-S13; 1-23-1807
Charles Gordon SW¼-S13; 10-29-1811
John Senoy NE¼-S14; 1-2-1815. Vol. II, p.112, looks like Siney
Abraham Nave NW¼-S14; 3-28-1806
Henry Martin SE¼-S14; 10-25-1814
William Marsh SW¼-S14; 6-6-1815
Joseph Cox & William Lewis Fr.S15; 8-25-1806
Thomas Hughes Fr.S22; 9-6-1809
Samuel Cunningham NE¼-S23; 2-24-1817
John Shelly NW¼-S23; 1-1-1814
Michael Snider SE¼-S23; 9-4-1813
John Emmitt SW¼-S23; 4-24-1816

Michael Snider SW¼ & NE¼-S24; 12-28-1812
John Myers NW¼-S24; 1-13-1808
Henry Miller SE¼-S24; 2-21-1807
Whiteley Wright NE¼-S25; 12-12-1814
William Fall NW¼-S25; 9-29-1807
Jacob Hoover SE¼-S25; 9-29-1807
William Kunt SW¼-S25; 9-16-1807. Vol. II, p.112, says Knitt
Francis Harvey NW¼-S26; 8-25-1815
David Canaday SE¼-S26; 12-15-1815
Henry Beck SW¼-S26; 12-2-1813
Thomas Martin E½-S27; 12-21-1816
Abner Chenarett W½-S27 & Fr.S28; 9-17-1813. Vol. II, p.113, says Chenault
James Oldham Fr.S33; 1-16-1815
William Riddle N½-S34; 3-13-1815
John D. Catterline SE¼-S34; 7-27-1815
Joel Kennady SW¼-S34; 3-13-1815
Edward J. Swanson & Michael Culver NE¼-S35; 12-28-1813
Whiteley Wright NW¼-S35; 12-12-1814
David Dunham SE¼-S35; 10-23-1816
Joseph Furguson SW¼-S35; 11-1-1814
Solomon Beck E½-S36; 12-2-1813
Richard Ring NW¼-S36; 12-2-1816
John Cromwell SW¼-S36; 12-1-1806

Page 63. T 13 N, R 2 W of 1st P.M. **WAYNE CO.**

John Townsend Fr.S1; 1-13-1808
Caleb Harvey Fr.S11 & W½-S12; 10-15-1808
Susanna Butler NE¼-S12; 8-2-1806
Israel Elliott SE¼-S12; 12-11-1811
Shadrick Henderson NE¼-S13; 12-5-1806
Hugh Endsley NW¼-S13; 1-11-1808
Shadrick Henderson S½-S13; 10-2-1806
Daniel Fisher Fr.S14; 5-12-1815. Vol. II, p.113, says David
Beale Butler Fr.S23; 7-29-1806
Jacob Lee NE¼-S24; 12-18-1804. Vol. II, p.113, says See
Alexander Miller NW¼-S24; 2-8-1812
Peter Fleming SE¼-S24; 12-18-1804
John Cox SW¼-S24; 7-30-1806
Joseph Wasson NE¼-S25; 12-18-1804
David Norton NW¼-S25; 9-2-1806
Andrew Endsley S½-S25; 6-3-1805
David Carson NE¼-S26; 5-28-1807
Abner Martin NW¼-S26; 4-23-1814
Lazarus Whitehead SE¼-S26; 5-6-1806
William Road SW¼-S26; 3-24-1812
John Ellis NW¼-S35; 11-9-1814
David Railsback SE¼-S35; 8-14-1811
David Railsback SW¼-S35; 12-27-1810
John Endsley NE¼-S36; 6-15-1805
James C. Morris SE¼-S36; 7-28-1806
Lazarus Whitehead SW¼-S36; 2-24-1806

Page 63. T 14 N, R 2 W of 1st P.M.

Isaac Julius & William Cox & B. Harvey Fr.S13 & Fr.S24; 11-7-1808
Nathan Morris Fr.S25; 10-6-1813
Thomas Neeley Fr.S36; 8-4-1814

Page 63. T 1 N, R 3 W of 1st P.M. **SWITZERLAND CO.**
William Stanley Fr.S5 & Fr.S6; 9-24-1804
Page 63. T 2 N, R 3 W of 1st P.M.
George Waltz NE¼-S1; 4-29-1814
Ralph Cotton, Jr. & Nathan Cotton NW¼-S1; 11-2-1812. Vol. II,
John Gilliland SE¼-S1; 11-17-1814. p.114, says Nathaniel
James Rickets, John McCrary, & William Keith SW¼-S1; 6-7-1813
Peter Lock NE¼-S2; 11-26-1811
Nathan Platt SE¼-S2; 7-30-1812
George Craig & Griffin Dickison W½-S2; 10-9-1804. Vol. II, p.114,
says to Stillwell Heady & Griffy Dickison
Peter Demaree & William Doston NE¼-S3; 5-29-1813. Vol. II, p.115,
Seth Stodder NW¼-S3; 11-6-1816 says Dotson
John Teague SE¼-S3; 10-27-1812
William Cotton & Jacob Burnett SW¼-S3; 11-1-1815
Marcus Bachus NE¼-S4; 8-28-1816. Vol. II, p.115, says Marvin
James Whitaker NW¼-S4; 2-1-1817
Seth Stodder SE¼-S4; 11-6-1816
Benjamin Headdy SW¼-S4; 5-9-1816. Rel. W½
James Baird W½-SW¼-S4; 9-6-1831
Page 64. T 2 N, R 3 W of 1st P.M.
Samuel Lamberson NE¼-S5; 7-23-1816
Joseph Orr NW¼-S5; 6-30-1817. Rel. W½
John Willis SE¼-S5; 6-16-1817. Rel. W½. W½ to John Willis,
Nicholas Davis SW¼-S5; 8-28-1815 4-7-1831
George Craig NE¼-S6; 12-9-1816
Samuel Heath NW¼-S6; 10-31-1814
Robert Rosebrough SE¼-S6; 8-28-1815. Rel. W½ to Simeon Conaway,
9-5-1828. Vol. II, p.115, says Simon
Benjamin D. Davis SW¼-S6; 12-4-1816. Rel. E½/ E½ to William
Nicholas Davis NE¼-S7; 11-8-1816 Lewis, 12-10-1828
William McKinstry NW¼-S7; 11-13-1816
Nicholas Longworth & David K. Este SE¼-S7; 12-18-1817
Hugh Moore SW¼-S7; 1-12-1818
John VanBriggle NE¼-S8; 10-2-1817 Rel. E½. To Samuel Leap.
Thomas Wright NW¼-S8; 12-9-1816 4-17-1832
John VanBriggle SE¼-S8; 10-4-1817
Robert Bakes SW¼-S8; 12-17-1817
Peter VanBriggle NE¼-S9; 6-9-1815
Joseph Orr NW¼-S9; 6-30-1817
George Craig SE¼-S9; 12-16-1815. Rel. E½ to Eli Ogle, 8-9-1831
Jacob Ramsiere SW¼-S9; 1-21-1817
Hiram Ogle NE¼-S10; 8-1-1817
Hugh Moore NW¼-S10; 6-26-1816
John Francis Dufour SE¼-S10; 12-1-1814
John Blaney SW¼-S10; 1-15-1814
Amos Gilbert NE¼-S11; 10-7-1812
Joseph Noble SE¼-S11; 10-25-1813
Philo Averill SW¼-S11; 11-19-1813
John J. Dufour & his associates Fr.S13; Fr.S23; S12; S14; 6-11-1802
John James Dufour Fr.S22; Fr.S27; S15; 12-1-1803
Robert Bakes NE¼-S17; 12-11-1816. Rel. W½
James Rous NW¼-S17; 4-29-1817
Robert Bakes SE¼-S17; 1-7-1814

Neil McCollum SW¼-S17; 1-28-1815
John Marling NE¼-S18; 6-21-1817
Philip Romeril NW¼-S18; 6-20-1817
Duncan McCallum SE¼-S18; 12-11-1816
Francis Louis Diserins SW¼-S18; 12-11-1816. Vol. II, p.116, looks
John Shaw NE¼-S19; 7-5-1817. Rel. E½ like Desereus
John Detraz NW¼-S19; 7-26-1817
Henry Peters SE¼-S19; 11-15-1816. Rel. E½
James Whitaker SW¼-S19; 12-17-1817. Rel. W½. To Michael Peters,
Felix Brandt NE¼-S20; 11-7-1817 9-5-1827
John L. Morcillon E½-NW¼-S20; 3-8-1819. Rel.
George Craig W½-NW¼-S20; 3-3-1818 4-18-1832
Gabriel Phillips SE¼-S20; 11-3-1817. Rel. E½. To Merritt Huser,
Cornelius Gonell E½-SW¼-S20; 3-21-1818. Vol. II, p.116, looks
Zachariah Cotton W½-SW¼-S20; 1-31-1818 like Youell
John P. Torrence & Lewis Whiteman NE¼-S21; 12-2-1814. Rel. E½ to
John James & Philip Schenck, 10-18-1831
Eugene Dutoit NW¼-S21; 11-6-1817. Vol. II, p.117, says Dutiel
John Mills SE¼-S21; 7-11-1814
David Latham SW¼-S21; 4-3-1818
Samuel Monnet Fr.S28; 4-8-1812. Vol. II, p.117, says Mennet
Frederick Louis Thiebaud NE¼-S29; 10-27-1817
Minor Roberts NW¼-S29; 9-7-1815
John James, Philip Schenck, & Daniel Buren SE¼-S29; 10-22-1817.
Vol. II, p.117, looks like Borem
George Craig SW¼-S29; 1-24-1817
Peter Peters NE¼-S30; 8-25-1812
Joseph Brown NW¼-S30; 4-30-1816
George Craig SE¼-S30; 11-29-1814
Thomas Davis SW¼-S30; 3-12-1814
Duncan McCullum NE¼-S31; 11-30-1819. Vol. II,p.117, says
McCallum. Rel. W½? See Vol. II, p.117, Moses Roberts
Aaron Culver NW¼-S31; 1-28-1818. Rel. E½. To George Hollcroft,
Abisha McCoy SE¼-S31; 3-8-1810 2-5-1828
Robert McCoy SW¼-S31; 9-18-1816. Rel. W½ to Mallory Lancaster,
3-2-1832; E½ to George Craig, 4-19-1832
George Craig Fr.S32; Fr.S33; 12-12-1809

Page 65. T 3 N, R 3 W of 1st P.M.

John Dickinson NE¼-S1; 2-26-1818. Rel. E½ to Horton Chamberlin,
8-9-1831; W½ to Horton Chamberlin, 8-9-1831
Thomas Smith NW¼-S1; 12-24-1817
Nicholas Longworth SE¼-S1; 7-10-1818. Rel. E½
Thomas Smith SW¼-S1; 12-24-1817
William Barr & Edward Hepburn NE¼-S2; 2-26-1818. Rel.
Presley Reno E½-NW¼-S2; 2-26-1818
John Rily W½-NW¼-S2; 2-27-1818
Robert Andrews E½-SE¼-S2; 9-8-1817 middle initial R.
Aaron Brown W½-SE¼-S2; 2-22-1822
William Cotton & Jacob Burnett E½-SW¼-S2; 3-18-1815. Rel.
Thomas Scott W½-SW¼-S2; 10-2-1824
Hugh Glenn & Edward Hepburn NE¼-S3; 3-5-1818. Rel.
John Dickinson NW¼-S3; 2-26-1818. Rel.? See Vol. II, p.118,
George Clark & 3 following
David Lee SE¼-S3; 2-23-1815

Stephen Peabody SW¼-S3; 8-22-1817
Arthur Andrews NE¼-S4; 9-17-1818
William Richards NW¼-S4; 5-24-1816
William Whitemore SE¼-S4; 11-16-1818
Ethan A. Brown SW¼-S4; 4-4-1818. Rel. E½
Abraham B. Dumont E½-NE¼-S5; 6-2-1818
Nicholas Lentz W½-NE¼-S5; 2-14-1818
Simeon Slawson E½-NW¼-S5; 8-11-1824
Robert Taylor W½-NW¼-S5; 2-14-1818. Rel.
Nicholas Lentz SE¼-S5; 6-8-1818. Rel. W½
William Mitchell SW¼-S5; 7-3-1818. Vol. II, p.118, adds middle initial C.
Gabriel Johnston Fr.S6; 3-14-1818
James McManaman Fr.S7; 8-28-1815
James Mapes NE¼-S8; 3-6-1818
Henry Burch NW¼-S8; 3-6-1818. Rel. W½
Charles Brewer SE¼-S8; 9-22-1815. Rel.
John Snook SW¼-S8; 9-23-1816
David Lester & Nicholas Lientz NE¼-S9; 10-1-1818. Rel. W½; Vol. II, p.119, says Leister
Isaac Bockus NW¼-S9; 5-6-1818. Rel.
Ralph Cotton SE¼-S9; 11-1-1815
Moses Brooks & James McGuire SW¼-S9; 12-28-1818. Rel.
William Lambdin & John B. Lindsey S10; 3-4-1815
Charles Leatherbury NE¼-S11; 9-4-1817
William Cotton & Jacob Burnett NW¼-S11; 3-18-1815
William Cotton & Jacob Burnett SE¼-S11; 3-18-1815
Allen Wiley SW¼-S10; 3-2-1815
James E. Brown NW¼-S12; 9-4-1817. Rel.
Peter Lock, Jr. NE¼-S12; 12-4-1815
Demas Moss SE¼-S12; 7-5-1816
John Teague SW¼-S12; 11-19-1817
Minor Chambers & John Pricket NE¼-S13; 7-5-1816. Rel. E½ to Lawrence Wilcell, 8-9-1831. Vol. II, p.119, says Wichell
John Coombs NW¼-S13; 6-2-1818. Rel. W½
John Teague SE¼-S13; 6-8-1814
Stephen Peabody SW¼-S13; 8-22-1817
George Arnold NE¼-S14; 9-5-1816. Rel. E½
William Cotton & Jacob Burnett NW¼-S14; 3-18-1815
Stephen Peabody SE¼-S14; 1-14-1818
Abraham B. Dumont SW¼-S14; 6-1-1818. Rel.
Hiram Ogle E½-SE¼-S15; 4-29-1816
Hiram Ogle W½-SE¼-S15; 5-16-1825
Ethan A. Brown NE¼-S17; 4-4-1818. Rel.
Hiram Ogle NW¼-S17; 4-11-1815. Rel. E½. To Daniel Blodget, 2-29-1832
Levi Orem SE¼-S17; 5-26-1817. Rel. E½
Michael Hildebrand SW¼-S17; 11-11-1816

Page 66. T 3 N, R 3 W of 1st P.M.

James Bowman NE¼-Fr.S18; 8-30-1824
David Imric NW pt.-S18; 9-9-1824
Joseph Bryant NE¼-S19; 3-26-1819. Rel. W½
Henry Rogers SE¼-S19; 8-10-1818
John Wright SW¼-S19; 12-26-1817
Michael Hildebrand NE¼-S20; 11-11-1816
George Butcher NW¼-S20; 12-9-1817

Robert Taylor. E½-SE¼-S20; 2-14-1818
Joseph Cole SE¼-S21; 6-24-1817
Martin Gillaspy NW¼-S22; 10-26-1818. Rel. W½
John Haynes NE¼-S23; 5-24-1817. Rel.
Caleb White & David Cummins NW¼-S23; 7-13-1818. Rel.
Nicholas Leintz SE¼-S23; 1-17-1815. Rel. W½/ Vol. II, p.121, shows final certif. #246 for all
James Dalmazzo SW¼-S23; 6-1-1816
Abraham Lindlay NE¼-S24; 6-24-1814
Lewis Michoud NW¼-S24; 7-19-1816
Joseph Noble SE¼-S24; 9-11-1815
John Nelson SW¼-S24; 3-23-1814
John Cochran NE¼-S25; 10-25-1816
Jonas Baldwin NW¼-S25; 9-11-1815
Seth Stodder SE¼-S25; 11-6-1816
Allen Burton SW¼-S25; 10-28-1815
William Huff NE¼-S26; 3-7-1815. Vol. II, p.121, adds middle initial T.
Jacob Hessler NW¼-S26; 8-1-1812
Daniel Pratt SE¼-S26; 9-17-1814
Andrew Stepleton SW¼-S26; 6-7-1813
Edward Coen NE¼-S27; 6-15-1814
Robert Rosebrough & Frederick Green NW¼-S27; 12-31-1817. Rel. E½ to George Emlen Pleasants, 7-25-1831
William Cotton SE¼-S27; 12-8-1814
Webster Marsh NE¼-S28; 9-17-1817
Silas Dascom NW¼-S28; 11-3-1817. Rel. E½
Adam Cole SE¼-S28; 6-10-1817
Thomas Davis SW¼-S28; 3-18-1818. Rel. E½ to Samuel Blodget, 7-9-1831
Daniel Burcham E½-NE¼-S29; 2-12-1824
Silas Smith W½-NE¼-S29; 11-27-1822
Silas Smith NW¼-S29; 9-25-1818
Stephen Rogers NE¼-S30; 5-14-1817. Vol. II, p.122, adds Sr.
Nicholas Longworth W½-NW¼-S30; 7-20-1818

Page 67. T 3 N, R 3 W of 1st P.M.

James Farrall SE¼-S30; 6-16-1817
Jackson Griffin SW¼-S30; 3-29-1817. Vol. II, p.122, says W. Jackson Griffith
Hugh Wilford NE¼-S31; 1-16-1816. Rel. W½. Vol. II, p.122, says Wilson & shows final certif. #8146 for all
John Gilliland NW¼-S31; 4-11-1815
Thomas Gilliland SW¼-S31; 5-23-1814
John Protsman SE¼-S31; SW¼-S32; 7-30-1814
Isaac Richards NE¼-S32; 5-1-1817. Rel. E½
Henry Hannas NW¼-S32; 4-8-1817
Isaac Richards SE¼-S32; 6-5-1817
Nicholas Davis NE¼-S33; 2-14-1817. Rel.
John Shaw NW¼-S33; 10-31-1817. Rel.
Nicholas Davis SE¼-S33; 1-29-1817. Rel. W½ to William Park, 8-10-1831
Joseph Dow E½-SW¼-S33; 1-13-1825
Nicholas Davis W½-SW¼-S33; 12-4-1816
Seth Stodder N½-S34; 11-11-1816
William Cotton SE¼-S34; 6-10-1805
Robert Cotton SW¼-S34; 10-7-1816
Jonathan Huntington NE¼-S35; 1-1-1814

SWITZERLAND CO.

Joseph Noble NW¼-S35; 11-13-1813
Paul Froman SE¼-S35; 12-15-1813
Henry Eaves SW¼-S35; 10-26-1813
Kimbrow Landers NE½-S36; 4-23-1814
Solomon Nighsworger NW¼-S36; 1-26-1814. Vol. II, p.123, says Mighswonger & adds Jr.
Andrew Baily SE¼-S36; 12-8-1814
Samuel McHenry SW¼-S36; 12-3-1814

Page 67. T 4 N, R 3 W of 1st P.M. **DEARBORN CO.**

Joseph Lyon NE¼-S1; 11-1-1814 (Part in Ohio Co.)
Felix Brandt SW¼-S1; 4-15-1818. Vol. II, p.123, says only W½-SW¼, (Part in Ohio Co.)
Samuel Purcell NE¼-S2; 3-31-1814 (Part in Ohio Co.)
Auston Hubbard NW¼-S2; 10-22-1814. Rel. W½ Part in Ohio Co.
Charles Brasher & Jacob Brasher SE¼-S2; 4-8-1812 (Part in Ohio Co.)
Peter Songer SW¼-S2; 3-20-1817
Griffin Tipsord SE¼-S3; 8-13-1811 (Part in Ohio Co.)
John Watts NW¼-S4; 4-2-1816
Nathan Flake SE¼-S4; 4-2-1816. Vol. II, p.124, says Frakes
John Watts SW¼-S4; 6-17-1815
Larkin Ryle Fr.S5; 9-4-1812. Vol. II, p.124, says Kyle
John Watts Fr.E½-S8; 4-3-1816 **DEARBORN CO.**
Thomas Rand E½-S9; 4-17-1811 (Part in Ohio Co.)
James Hamilton NW¼-S9; 8-13-1811 (Part in Dearborn Co.)
James McGuire SW¼-S9; 4-15-1815 (Part in Ohio Co.)
James McCarty NE¼-S10; 8-24-1812 (Part in Ohio Co.)
Jeremiah Pate NW¼-S10; 10-30-1815 (Part in Dearborn Co.)
Andrew Bailey SW¼-S10; 12-28-1814 **OHIO CO.**

Page 68. T 4 N, R 3 W of 1st P.M. **OHIO CO.**

Jesse Embree & Edward Hepburn NE¼-S11; 4-6-1818
William Woolery NW¼-S11; 6-1-1819. Vol. II, p.124, says Woolley
Jesse Embree & Edward Hepburn SE¼-S11; 4-7-1818
Jesse Embree & Edward Hepburn SW¼-S11; 4-7-1818
Henry L. Wilmer NE¼-S12; 7-16-1819
Jesse Embree & Edward Hepburn SE¼-S12; 6-2-1818
Edward Hepburn & Jesse Embree W½-S12; 4-7-1818
Hermon L. Margerum & Henry L. Wilmer NW¼-S13; 7-16-1819
Israel White SE¼-S13; 5-19-1818. Rel. * (William B. Phelps &
Richard Folsom SW¼-S13; 11-20-1818 (John Phelps SW¼-S24;
Eleazer Cole NE¼-S14; 11-8-1816. Rel. (10-5-1818.
William Barr & Edward Hepburn NW¼-S14; 2-26-1818 (Rel. W½
John Ernnout SE¼-S14; 9-21-1818. Rel.
John Aston SW¼-S14; 3-28-1818. Rel.
James McGuire E½-NE¼-S17; 12-7-1831
James McGuire W½-NE¼-S17; 4-9-1832
John Sherlock W pt. S17; Fr.S18; 4-1-1819. Rel. Vol. II, p.125, shows 180 ac. of Fr.S17 & Fr.S18 retained
Samuel Aston E½-S20; 3-28-1818. Rel. NE¼; E½-SE¼
James Reed SW¼-S20; 4-11-1818
Thomas Morgan & John Gifford NE¼-S23; 5-20-1817
Matthias Redding NW¼-S23; 1-29-1817
John Dickinson SE¼-S23; 2-26-1818. Rel.
Stephen Burrows SW¼-S23; 2-28-1818. Rel. E½ to John Clark, 8-21-1827
Peter Bear NE¼-S24; 7-7-1818
John Dickinson NW¼-S24; 2-26-1818 * see above

Page 69. T 4 N, R 3 W of 1st P.M. **SWITZERLAND CO.**

John McClutche NE¼-S25; 4-22-1818. Rel.
William Bell NW¼-S25; 3-18-1818. Rel. E½
James Stone SE¼-S25; 4-4-1818. Rel.
Samuel Stone SW¼-S25; 12-10-1817. Rel.
Nicholas Longworth & Moses Brooks N½-S26; SW¼-S26; 1-19-1818.Rel.
Nicholas Longworth & David K. Este SE¼-S26; 1-19-1818 NW¼
Nicholas Longworth & David K. Este NE¼-S27; 1-19-1818. Rel. W½
William Barr & Edward Hepburn NW¼-S27; 2-26-1818. Rel.
Stephen Burrows SE¼-S27; 2-28-1818. Rel.
John Dickinson SW¼-S27; 2-26-1818. Rel.
William Barr & Edward Hepburn NE¼-S28; 2-26-1818. Rel. E½
Stephen Burrows SE¼-S28; 3-11-1818. Rel.
James Stone SW¼-S28; 4-4-1818. Rel.
John Misner NE¼-S29; 6-1-1818. Rel.
Jesse Embree & Edward Hepburn NW¼-S29; 4-6-1818
William Barr SE¼-S29; 4-25-1818. Rel.
Jesse Embree & Edward Hepburn SW¼-S29; 4-6-1818. Rel.
William L. Callom Fr.S30; 5-2-1818. Rel. N½. Vol. II, p.128, says Cullom
Frederick Shaff Fr.S31; 4-9-1818. Vol. II, p.128, says Haff
John Gray NE¼-S32; 4-24-1818.Rel. W½. To Richard Lock, 6-28-1831
John F. Dufour & Robert Gullion NW¼-S32; 4-15-1815. Rel.
Peter Lock SE¼-S32; 5-4-1818.Rel. E½ to Benjamin Lock, 6-28-1831; W½ to Clark Jackewayse, 4-28-1829
Ethan A. Brown SW¼-S32; 4-4-1818. Rel. E½. To John Cole, Jr., 6-20-1831
Peter Lock NE¼-S33; 4-27-1818
James Stone NW¼-S33; 4-4-1818
William C. Mitchell SW¼-S33; 7-7-1818
Nicholas Longworth & Moses Brooks NE¼-S34; 11-23-1818
Jacob Froman & George Zinn SE¼-S34; 12-11-1816. No Rel., but see Vol. II, p. 129
Nicholas Longworth & Moses Brooks SW¼-S34; 2-15-1819
Joel Tousend E½-S35; 11-11-1817. Rel. NE¼
Samuel Stone W½-S35; 12-10-1817
Austin Clark NE¼-S36; 4-30-1817
Samuel Stone NW¼-S36; 12-10-1817. Rel. W½
Hugh Glenn & Edward Hepburn SE¼-S36; 3-5-1818. Rel.
John Dickinson SW¼-S36; 2-26-1818. Rel. E½

Page 70. T 5 N, R 3 W of 1st P.M. **DEARBORN CO.**

Samuel Bromlee NE¼-S1; 10-17-1815. Rel. E½ to William Noble & John Noble, 8-10-1831.
John Whitaker NW¼-S1; 5-20-1815
John Whitaker SE¼-S1; 1-31-1818. Rel.
Jesse Hunt, Samuel F. Hunt, & David Vanchoik SW¼-S1; 3-19-1819.Rel.
William Bennet NE¼-S2; 1-9-1818. Rel.
John C. Shuman E½-NW¼-S2; 9-4-1818
James McMakin W½-NW¼-S2; 1-22-1819. Rel.
Thomas Ansley E½-SE¼-S2; 2-18-1818. Rel.
Benjamin Biddel W½-SE¼-S2; 6-23-1818. Rel.
Henry Brocaw SW¼-S2; 12-9-1817
Samuel Flemings NE¼-S3; 10-27-1817. Vol. II, p.130, says Fleming
Samuel Flemings NW¼-S3; 11-5-1817. Rel. W½ to Robert Farran, 3-21-1827
Benjamin Parlee SE¼-S3; 10-21-1817

Philip Rowland SW$\frac{1}{4}$-S3; 10-21-1817
Samuel Flemings Fr.S4; Fr.S5; 10-18-1817
Jacob Baymiller & Thomas T. Benbridge Fr.S8; Fr.S9;8-17-1818 Rel. N end
Samuel Frazier NE$\frac{1}{4}$-S10; 6-3-1818
Archibald McCabe NW$\frac{1}{4}$-S10; 4-4-1818
James Loder & Azariah Jarman SE$\frac{1}{4}$-S10; 3-18-1818
Laban Bramble SW$\frac{1}{4}$-S10; 4-21-1818
George Abraham NE$\frac{1}{4}$-S11; 6-3-1818
James Burroughs Jones NW$\frac{1}{4}$-S11; 5-13-1818
Jesse Vandolah SE$\frac{1}{4}$-S11; 8-24-1818
Robert Smith SW$\frac{1}{4}$-S11; 3-30-1818
Ephraim Burroughs NE$\frac{1}{4}$-S12; 1-22-1819. Rel. W$\frac{1}{2}$
Daniel Wilson NW$\frac{1}{4}$-S12; 4-9-1818
William Randall SE$\frac{1}{4}$-S12; 2-27-1818
William Williamson SW$\frac{1}{4}$-S12; 3-20-1818
George Abrahams NE$\frac{1}{4}$-S13; 9-22-1817
Daniel Loder NW$\frac{1}{4}$-S13; 3-18-1818
John Sutherland & James P. Ramsey SE$\frac{1}{4}$-S13; 10-27-1817
William Frazier SW$\frac{1}{4}$-S13; 2-27-1818. Rel. E$\frac{1}{2}$. To James A. Loder, 8-21-1827
Daniel White NE$\frac{1}{4}$-S14; 1-31-1818
Nehemiah Knapp NW$\frac{1}{4}$-S14; 1-31-1818
Robert Smith SE$\frac{1}{4}$-S14; 3-30-1818
Peter Ramer SW$\frac{1}{4}$-S14; 3-20-1818
John Fleming Fr.S17; 5-1-1818
Felix Brandt Fr.S20; 4-13-1818
Theophilus Martin W$\frac{1}{2}$-SW$\frac{1}{4}$-S21; 3-25-1828
John Fleming E$\frac{1}{2}$-NE$\frac{1}{4}$-S23; 5-1-1818
John Fleming W$\frac{1}{2}$-NE$\frac{1}{4}$-S23; 8-22-1818

Page 71. T 5 N, R 3 W of 1st P.M.

Jacob Spangler E$\frac{1}{2}$-NW$\frac{1}{4}$-S23; 3-20-1818
Henry Parker W$\frac{1}{2}$-NW$\frac{1}{4}$-S23; 11-23-1818
David Williamson E$\frac{1}{2}$-SE$\frac{1}{4}$-S23; 5-7-1818
Robert Farran W$\frac{1}{2}$-SE$\frac{1}{4}$-S23; 10-26-1818. Rel.? See Vol. II, p.132, Herman Henry Nieman
Silas Shed SW$\frac{1}{4}$-S23; 8-7-1818. Rel.
Henry Smith NE$\frac{1}{4}$-S24; 12-3-1818. Rel. W$\frac{1}{2}$
Nehemiah Morehouse NW$\frac{1}{4}$-S24; 9-22-1818. Rel. E$\frac{1}{2}$
Elijah Thacher SE$\frac{1}{4}$-S24; 1-24-1818. Rel. W$\frac{1}{2}$
Robert Richards SW$\frac{1}{4}$-S24; 8-7-1818. Rel. W$\frac{1}{2}$ to Joseph Lenover, 8-10-1831
William S. Dart NE$\frac{1}{4}$-S25; 8-10-1818. Rel.
Benjamin Purcel SE$\frac{1}{4}$-S25; 3-3-1813
Tenent Huston & Robert Huston W$\frac{1}{2}$-S25; 8-7-1818
Jesse Embree & Edward Hepburn SE$\frac{1}{4}$-S26; 6-2-1818. Rel. W$\frac{1}{2}$
Nathaniel Wright NE$\frac{1}{4}$-S27; 6-16-1818. Rel. W$\frac{1}{2}$
Abel Johnson SW$\frac{1}{4}$-S27; 5-19-1818
John Watts NW$\frac{1}{4}$-S28; 3-31-1818. Rel. E$\frac{1}{2}$
George Pate & Daniel Kelsey SE$\frac{1}{4}$-S28; 12-17-1817
Martha Lemon SW$\frac{1}{4}$-S28; 4-17-1817
John Watts & Thomas Watts Fr.S29; 3-31-1818
Robert Ray Fr.S32; 4-3-1816
John Cole & Samuel Cole NE$\frac{1}{4}$-S33; 12-17-1817
Martha Lemon NW$\frac{1}{4}$-S33; 4-17-1817. Rel.
Felix Brandt S$\frac{1}{2}$-S33; 4-13-1818
Felix Brandt NE$\frac{1}{4}$-S34; 6-18-1818. Rel.

Ezra Slawson NW¼-S34; 2-11-1818
Lawrence Purcel SW¼-S34; 8-13-1817
Thomas Froman SW¼-S35; 5-24-1817. Rel.
Benjamin Purcel NE¼-S36; 6-29-1808 (Part in Ohio Co.
John Daugherty NW¼-S36; 6-17-1815
Solomon Stephens SE¼-S36; 11-18-1812 (Part in Ohio Co.)
James Burke SW¼-S36; 10-29-1816. Rel.

Page 72. T 6 N, R 3 W of 1st P.M.

Amer Bruce NE¼-S1; 11-22-1817
Stephen Wood NW¼-S1; 12-30-1817
Benjamin Johnson SW¼-S1; 7-26-1817. Rel. E½/To Stephen J. Pain.
Stephen Wood NE¼-S2; 12-30-1817 5-25-1829
Elisha Hancock NW¼-S2; 6-12-1818. Rel. W½
Benjamin Johnson SE¼-S2; 7-26-1817
Gilbert T. Givan E½-SW¼-S2; 6-12-1818
Nancy Davis W½-SW¼-S2; 6-12-1818
John Dashiell NE¼-S3; 6-12-1818
David Waddle E½-NW¼-S3; 12-27-1825
George Dean N end-Fr.S4; W½-NW¼-S3; 7-9-1824. Rel.
David Medsker SE¼-S3; 12-31-1811
Jesse B. Lord & Lemuel Moss S end-Fr.S4; SW¼-S3; 10-9-1817
Ebenezer Olmsted Fr.S9; 1-27-1818. Rel. S end. To John S. Olmsted,
Charles Dashiell NE¼-S10; 11-1-1817 12-9-1829
Samuel Knight & John Inman NW¼-S10; 10-27-1817
John Legget & Moses Musgrove SE¼-S10; 2-5-1818
James Anderson & Morton Justis SW¼-S10; 2-13-1818. Rel. E½. To Morton Justis, 8-21-1827
John Brumblay NE¼-S11; 11-17-1817
Riley Truitt NW¼-S11; SE¼-S11; 10-9-1817
Spencer Davis SW¼-S11; 2-3-1818
William Hancock NE¼-S12; 6-12-1818. Rel. E½
Amar Bruce NW¼-S12; 8-6-1817
Jonathan Vail SE¼-S12; 8-25-1817
Thomas Lambertson SW¼-S12; 9-20-1817
Jonathan Vail NE¼-S13; 8-25-1817. Rel. W½. To John Brewington,
Adam Flake NW¼-S13; 7-19-1817 11-12-1827
Jesse Williams, Stephen Butler, & Elias P. Smith SE¼-S13; 12-18-1817. Rel. E½ to Samuel Stage, 3-9-1832; W½ to James Dougherty & Charles Brewington, 9-3-1831
Joseph Churchill, Jr. SW¼-S13; 12-17-1817. Rel. E½. To Michael
David Osborn NE¼-S14; 11-13-1817 Flake, 5-30-1826
John Chance SE¼-S14; 3-7-1818. Rel. E½. To Thomas Baggs, 7-25-1825. Vol. II, p.135, says Boggs
Spencer Davis NW¼-S14; 11-17-1817
Benjamin Hinds SW¼-S14; 10-9-1824
Samuel B. Wood & Winslow J. Wood NE¼-S15; 10-9-1817
Ranna C. Stevens NW¼-S15; 5-25-1818. Rel. E½. To Willis Miller,
Robert Glass SE¼-S15; 3-7-1818. Rel. W½ 12-9-1829
John Lindsay SW¼-S15; 3-30-1818. Rel.
Samuel C. Vance Fr.S21; 7-17-1818. Rel. S end. Lot 2, S end-N½ to Samuel C. Vance, 7-1-1829. Lot 3, E pt.-S½ to Isaac Oathoudt, 7-5-1831
James S. Hogshire NE¼-S22; 7-2-1818. Rel. W½. Vol. II, p.136,
Thomas Lambertson NW¼-S22; 7-11-1818 says Hogsheare

Arnold Burch SE¼-S22; 7-13-1818
Sarah Daugherty E½-SW¼-S22; 8-4-1824. Vol. II, p.136, adds "late
Rufus Holcomb W½-SW¼-S22; 6-10-1824 Sarah Phillips"
Thomas Lambertson NE¼-S23; 6-29-1818
Josiah McKnight NW¼-S23; 6-29-1818
Asa Cloyd SE¼-S23; 6-4-1818
David Brown E½-SW¼-S23; 6-5-1818
Eliakim Jones W½-SW¼-S23; 7-2-1818
Samuel Snyder N½-S24; 6-23-1818. Rel. NE¼ & E½-NW¼. W½-NE¼ to Michael Flake, 5-30-1826; E½-NE¼ to Benjamin Brian, Jr., 7-17-1826; E½-NW¼ to Isaac McKnight, 9-4-1828. Vol. II, p.136, says
John Means SE¼-S24; 12-8-1817. Rel. Thomas McKnight
James S. Hogsheare SW¼-S24; 6-22-1818. Rel. E½
Lavinus King NE¼-S25; 10-11-1817
Stephan Burrows NW¼-S25; 12-1-1817
Theodorus Thompson SE¼-S25; 7-7-1817
George Hanes SW¼-S25; 11-28-1817
Peter Hancock NE¼-S26; 7-2-1818
Ebenezer H. Pierson NW¼-S26; 10-25-189. Rel. E½
Mary Faulkner E½-SE¼-S26; 7-10-1820
Robert Faulkner W½-SE¼-S26; 9-6-1822
Isaac T. Johnston SW¼-S26; 1-2-1819
Joseph Lee NE¼-S27; 9-9-1818
Peter Newcomer NW¼-S27; 9-12-1818

Page 73. T 6 N, R 3 W of 1st P.M.

John Snyder, Jr. SE¼-S27; 11-10-1818. Rel. W½
William Turner SW¼-S27; 1-25-1819
Jesse Hunt & Thomas Skillman Fr.S28; 12-30-1818
Mark Baker N½-Fr.S33; 11-16-1818. Rel. pt. of SE pt.
George Durham S½-SW¼-S33; 5-31-1832 1817 #
Jesse Williams, Stephen Butler, & Elias P. Smith NE¼-S34; 12-18-
William Lutchen NW¼-S34; 1-25-1819. Rel. To Henry Tency, 2-24-1832. Vol. II, p.137, says Teny
David Midsker SE¼-S34; 9-26-1817. *Vol. II, p.137, says Medsker
James Hayes SW¼-S34; 12-15-1817. Rel. W½. To James Hayes, 2-8-1832'
Sidney Robinson N½-S35; 11-13-1817
Adam D. Livingston S½-S35; 10-7-1817
Claiborne Allen NE¼-S36; 7-7-1817. Rel. W½. To William Tyler, 11-13-1817. Vol. II, p.137, says Tyier
Samuel Marshall NW¼-S36; 6-5-1820. Rel. W½
John Sutherland & James P. Ramsey SE¼-S36; 9-23-1817
Daniel Ansley SW¼-S36; 2-28-1818. Rel.

Page 73. T 7 N, R 3 W of 1st P.M.

Samuel C. Vance NE¼-S1; 3-11-1818. Rel. W½
Samuel C. Vance NW¼-S1; 10-26-1818. Rel.
Enoch Conger SE¼-S1; 9-14-1818. Rel. # Rel.
Michael Ehler SW¼-S1; 7-17-1818
Jacob Mendel NE¼-S2; 12-23-1816 * Rel. E½
Joseph Haines NW¼-S2; 12-23-1816
Mordecai Thurston E½-SE¼-S2; 7-11-1818. Rel.
Enoch Conger W½-SE¼-S2; 4-25-1818
Zachariah S. Conger SW¼-S2; 9-6-1816
Frederick Myers N½-Fr.S3; 6-4-1825
John Wilkinson S½-Fr.S3; 12-21-1816

William Hamilton Fr.S10; 12-1-1814
John P. Brown E½-NE¼-S11; 6-15-1825
Joseph Stateler W½-NE¼-S11; 1-27-1817
Thomas Hill NW¼-S11; 6-22-1816. Vol. II, p.138, says Phineas
James Babcock SE¼-S11; 3-18-1818
Cyrus Mills SW¼-S11; 9-6-1816
Jared Michael NE¼-S12; 8-21-1818. Rel. W½. To William Smith,
Ebenezer Westcott NW¼-S12; 8-27-1818   1-15-1828
Blakely Shoemaker SE¼-S12; 1-24-1818
Amos Morris, Jr. SW¼-S12; 7-3-1818. Rel. E½
Samuel C. Vance NE¼-S13; 10-10-1817.Rel. W½.ToBlakley Shoemaker,
    4-21-1828. Vol. II, p.138, says Blackley Shoemake, Jr.
Frederick Sand NW¼-S13; 7-30-1817. Rel. E½. To Jacob Michael,
    6-15-1827. Vol. II, p.138, says Frederick Swain
John Stephenson SE¼-S13; 11-4-1818
Jesse Stone SW¼-S13; 12-21-1818
David Conger NE¼-S14; 1-16-1818
Jacob Stetler NW¼-S14; 11-16-1816
Enoch Conger E½-SE¼-S14; 5-26-1827
Daniel Hathaway W½-SE¼-S14; 4-8-1825
Jesse Clements SW¼-S14; 2-13-1817. Rel. E½ to William Rood,2-6-
    1826; W½ to Enoch Conger, 1-27-1832. Vol. II, p.138, adds
    Enoch Congar of Dearborn Co.
William Hamilton Fr.S15; 12-1-1814
Joseph Ferris & John Freeland N½-Fr.S22; 1-28-1818
Jesse Embree & Edward Hepburn NE¼-S23; 4-6-1818. Rel.
Benjamin Beach, Sr. E½-NW¼-S23; 8-18-1819
John Doty W½-NW¼-S23; 8-10-1818
Joseph Andrew & Paul Huston SE¼-S23; 6-23-1818
Daniel Hathaway SW¼-S23; 3-12-1818
George Stephenson NE¼-S24; 11-4-1818.Rel.W½. To James Shoemaker,
Jesse Embree & Edward Hepburn NW¼-S24; 4-6-1818   4-16-1828
                Page 74. T 7 N, R 3 W of 1st P.M.
Jesse Embree & Edward Hepburn SW¼-S24; 4-6-1818
William Barr SE¼-S24; 4-25-1818. Rel.To Gersham Dunn,11-29-1831
Stephen Wood E½-S25; 10-25-1817
Sophia Fageley NW¼-S25; 3-6-1818
Godfrey Snow SW¼-S25; 12-1-1817
John George Howery & Michael Miller NE¼-S26; 3-6-1818. Rel. W½.
    To Edward Rownd, 5-19-1828
Benjamin Beach, Sr. E½-NW¼-S26; 1-23-1821
John Finch & Jonathan Finch SE¼-S26; 12-1-1817
George Givan SW¼-S26; 6-4-1825
Samuel Moss N pt.-Fr.S33-34; 1-3-1817.Vol.II, p.139, says Lemuel
Joshua Givan NE¼-S35; 6-4-1825
Blakely Shoemaker NW¼-S35; 1-24-1818. Rel.? See Vol. II, p.139,
    William Huls
David Roberts, Jr. SE¼-S35; 5-11-1818. Rel. E½ to Cyrus Cross,
    3-26-1828; W½ to Joseph P. King, 5-2-1828.Vol.II, p.139, says
John R. Rownd SW¼-S35; 6-15-1819. Rel. E½   John P. King
David G. Boardman N½-S36; 12-30-1817
Stephen Johnson Paine SE¼-S36; 11-24-1817
Robert McCrackin SW¼-S36; 1-21-1818

 DEARBORN CO.

Page 74. T 8 N, R 3 W of 1st P.M.
Joel Tucker E½-NW¼-S1; 11-24-1828
Lowry Foster W½-SE¼-S1; 9-20-1831
Christopher Showalter E½-SW¼-S1; 8-14-1823
Henry Kile, Jr. W½-NE¼-S12; 9-5-1831
Henry Kile E½-NW¼-S12; 7-31-1826
John K. Lawrence E½-NE¼-S13; 8-30-1830
Page 75. T 8 N, R 3 W of 1st P.M.
Jane Walker W pt.-S14; 12-10-1823
David Pettegrew Fr.S23; 6-4-1818. Rel. SE¼ & E½-NE¼. Lot 3-E½-SE fr. to Daniel Pettegrew, 2-20-1830
Daniel Pettegrew Lot 4-W½-SE¼-S23; 10-13-1831
Thomas Anderson S½-S24; 9-5-1817. Rel. W½-SW¼ to John Miller, 10-13-1831. Vol. II, p.141, shows final certif. #6350 for whole S½ to Thomas Anderson
Thomas Anderson S25; 9-5-1817
David Brown & George P. Torrence N end-Fr.S26-27; 8-19-1817.Rel.? Vol. II, p.141, shows final certif. #333 for Fr.S26-27
Isaac Alden E½-SE¼-S26; 10-13-1831
Samuel C. Vance Fr.S34; 8-19-1817. Rel. To John Boltz, 7-5-1831
Thomas Euart NE¼-S35; 4-2-1817. Rel.
Nathaniel Lambert NW¼-S35; 5-3-1817. Rel.? E½ to William Huls, 8-27-1827. Vol. II, p.142, says Nathan Lambert; shows final certif. #2779 to him for all
Eli Hill SE¼-S35; 3-10-1817
Ulysses Cooke SW¼-S35; 3-14-1817. Rel. W½ to John Ulrich Engle, 9-24-1831
Samuel Y. Allaire NE¼-S36; 10-3-1817
Samuel C. Vance SE¼-S36; 9-29-1817
Samuel Y. Allaire SW¼-S36; 10-3-1817

Page 75. T 9 N, R 3 W of 1st P.M. **FRANKLIN CO.**
William C. Drew & Isaiah Bisbee N pt.-NE¼-S1; 8-18-1817
Isaac Fuller Fr.S12; 9-6-1815
David Brown & Samuel C. Vance E½-Fr.S13; 9-10-1817.Rel.? Vol.II, p.142, shows final certif. #536 for it
Page 76. T 9 N, R 3 W of 1st P.M.
Benjamin Childres W½-NW¼-S36; 5-17-1825 Vol. II, p.143, says Childers
John Carson, Jr. E½-SW¼-S36; 12-19-1828
William Martin W½-SW¼-S36; 12-9-1826
Page 76. T 10 N, R 3 W of 1st P.M.
Benjamin McCarty Fr.S13-24; 7-22-1807
Patrick McCarty & Jonathan Gilmore Fr.S25; 3-7-1806. Vol. II, p.144, says Gilman
Samuel F. Hunt & William C. Drew S pt.-SE¼-S36; 9-8-1807

Page 76. T 1 N, R 4 W of 1st P.M. **SWITZERLAND CO.**
James McKay Fr.S1; 6-11-1810
Thomas Thompson Fr.S2; 9-25-1804
Page 76. T 2 N, R 4 W of 1st P.M.
Jacob Kann Fr.S1; 3-29-1815. Vol. II, p.144, says Kain
Philip Romeril Fr.S12; 12-10-1816
James Whitaker Fr.S13; 2-1-1817
Lewis F. Colay N pt.-S23 & NW¼-S24; 5-15-1817
William Piatt E½-S24; 11-18-1816. Rel. NE¼ & W½-SE¼. To Ezekial S. Haines, 4-20-1829
John Dunn E½-SW¼-S24; 11-25-1824

John Bray NE¼-S25; 3-5-1816
Elisha Burke & Edward Ray NW¼-S25; 10-18-1817
William J. Stewart SE¼-S25; 7-8-1816
George Gilmore SW¼-S25; 1-9-1817
Charles Johnston Fr.S26; 3-30-1816
Edward McIntire N pt.-Fr.S35; N pt. SE¼-S35; S pt.-SE¼-S35;7-26-
   1817. Rel. all. N½-Fr.S35 to Edward McIntire, 6-23-1829;
   S end-Fr.S35 to Joshua Cain, 9-7-1827; N pt.-SE¼-S35 to David
   Cain, 8-10-1831
Henry Lanham NE¼-S36; 1-29-1814
William Johnston NW¼-S36; 5-8-1816   1-27-1829
Charles Edward Romeril SE¼-S36; 6-27-1818. Rel. To James McKay,
Francis Louis Flotron SW¼-S36; 7-15-1818. Rel. E½ to James
   McKay, 3-21-1829
          Page 76. T 3 N, R 4 W of 1st P.M.
Robert Rutherford Fr.S24-25; 11-4-1816
Henry Hannas Fr.S36; 1-8-1814
          Page 77. T 10 N, R 11 E of 2nd P.M.   FRANKLIN CO.
Nicholas Longworth S pt.-Fr.S3; 8-10-1818
Nicholas Longworth & Moses Brooks N pt.-Fr.S10; 1-31-1818
Nicholas Longworth & Griffin Taylor NE¼-S11; 4-7-1818. Rel.
Nicholas Longworth & Griffin Taylor NW¼-S12; 4-7-1818. Rel.
Nicholas Longworth & Griffin Taylor SW¼-S12; 4-7-1818. Rel.
Nicholas Longworth & Griffin Taylor NW¼-S14; 4-7-1818. Rel.
          Page 78. T 10 N, R 11 E of 2nd P.M.
Nicholas Longworth & Moses Brooks SE¼-S27; 1-31-1818. Rel.
          Page 79. T 11 N, R 11 E of 2nd P.M.
Edmund Adams NW¼-S24; 9-8-1817. Rel. W½
Thomas Hendman SE¼-S25; 7-7-1817. Vol. II, p.150, says Hindman
Lyman B. House NE¼-S35; 7-11-1818. Rel.? See Vol. II, p.150
Joshua Riel NE¼-S36; 5-22-1815. Vol. II, p.151, says Rice
George W. Jones & George W. Himes NW¼-S36; 7-22-1818. Rel. W½ to
   Nathan Hawkins, 3-26-1832
          Page 80. T 12 N, R 11 E of 2nd P.M.
Timothy Allison N pt. & S pt.-NE¼-S1; 10-13-1829. Vol.II, p.151,
   says N½-S1
Robert Dickerson E pt.-S13; 5-31-1815. Rel. S end-E side.
   N½-SE pt. to William Egans, 2-21-1832. Vol. II, p.151, says
   Dickerson kept N½-NE pt.
Alexander Power NW pt.-S13; 3-8-1831
Henry Misner N pt.-SW¼-S13; 12-27-1828
Alexander Power S pt.-SW¼-S13; 3-8-1831
          Page 80. T 13 N, R 11 E of 2nd P.M.   FAYETTE CO.
Richard Stephen Fr.S25; 4-18-1832
          Page 81. T 10 N, R 12 E of 2nd P.M.   FRANKLIN CO.
James Hicks W½-SW¼-S2; 2-16-1829   3-3-1832
William Steele NW¼-S4; 6-24-1819. Rel. W½ to Andrew George,
William George SW¼-S4; 8-22-1817.Rel. W½ to William George,1-22-
Nicholas Longworth & Griffin Taylor SE¼-S8; 4-7-1818   1830
James Hicks W pt.-NE¼-Fr.S10; 2-16-1829
          Page 82. T 11 N, R 12 E of 2nd P.M.
Isaac Stip E½ & W½-NE¼-S4; 1-18-1814
John Hawkins SE¼-S4; 8-17-1815. Rel.
Alexander Speer SW¼-S4; 7-23-1811

Page 83. T 11 N, R 12 E of 2nd P.M.
Eli Allen NE¼-S8; 7-29-1815. Rel.
John Campbell SE¼-S8; 8-19-1814. Rel. W½
Eli Allen NW¼-S9; 12-16-1811
Andrew Speer SW¼-S9; 11-29-1811
Page 84. T 11 N, R 12 E of 2nd P.M.
Thomas Halston E½-SW¼-S15; 8-24-1824
David Lewis NE¼-S17; 1-21-1814
Henry Davies E½-NW¼-S17; 4-28-1828
Nathan Lewis SE¼-S17; 1-21-1814
John Miller SW¼-S17; 7-29-1815
William Martin NE¼-S20; 6-19-1815. Vol. II, p.159, says Marlin
Thomas Paine SE¼-S20; 4-19-1817. Rel. To Theodore Throckmorton,
    7-16-1828. Vol. II, p.159, says Joseph Throckmorton
James Fuller SW¼-S20; 8-6-1816. Rel. W½. Vol. II, p.159, shows
    final certif. #2333 to Jacob Burnet & A. Bailey for E½-SW¼;
David Nelson NE¼-S24; 11-28-1814   6-19-1815
John Alley NE¼-S25; 9-30-1817. Rel.
George Rasor E½-SW¼-S25; 1-27-1825
Page 85. T 11 N, R 12 E of 2nd P.M.
John Hawkins NW¼-S29; 12-17-1814. Rel. E½
John Miller SW¼-S29; 7-3-1816. Rel. E½
Joseph C. Reed W½-S30; 6-19-1815. Rel. SW¼ to Joseph Thompson,
Bartholomew Fitzpatrick SE¼-S30; 12-17-1814   8-25-1831
Jonathan Baker W½-NW¼-S33; 11-3-1817. Rel.
Page 86. T 11 N, R 12 E of 2nd P.M.
Jonathan Alley E½-SE¼-S35; 10-1-1831
Page 86. T 12 N, R 12 E of 2nd P.M.
Lewis S. Ray W½-NE¼-S1; 11-15-1828
Stephen Lee E½-NW¼-S1; 11-15-1828
Richard Dunkin NE¼-S2; 9-22-1815. Rel.? Vol. II, p.163, shows
    final certif. #4592 for it to Thomas Hedrick, 12-26-1834
Joseph Haffner E½-NW¼-S2; 10-12-1814. Rel.
Hugh Mead SW¼-S2; 2-12-1818. Rel. E½. To James Conwell, 12-22-
John Fouch W½-NW¼-S2; 9-9-1824   1831
Archibald Guthery NE¼-S3; 10-19-1811. Vol. II, p.165, says
Samuel Garrison NW¼-S3; 10-28-1811   Guthrew
William Smith SE¼-S3; 10-28-1811
Elijah Leympus SW¼-S3; 10-19-1811
Samuel Garrison NE¼-S4; 4-30-1817
James Conwell E½-NW¼-S4; 3-18-1829
Thomas Williams SE¼-S4; 10-4-1814
Zepaniah Stubbs E½-SW¼-S4; 1-17-1832
David N. Camp & Frederick Kellogg NW¼ & SE¼-S5; 8-5-1818. Rel. the
    NW¼. W½-NW¼ to Edward Toner, 1-?-1832; E½-NW¼ to Asberry
Thomas Williams W½-SW¼-S5; 8-18-1817   Allison, 1-?-1832
William Cox SW¼-S6; 9-13-1817
Page 87. T 12 N, R 12 E of 2nd P.M.
Benjamin Weston W½-NW¼-S8; 3-26-1832. Rel.? See Vol. II, p.164
William C. Drew & Isaiah Bisbee S½-S8; 8-27-1817. Rel. E½-SW¼
    to Benjamin Weston, 2-17-1832
William Maple NE¼-S9; 10-7-1814. Rel.? Vol. II, p.164, shows kept
Edward Tonee NW¼-S9; 10-20-1815. Rel.? Vol. II, p.164, shows
    final certif. #2724 for it to Edward Toner

James Agins SE¼-S9; 10-19-1811
Jesse Scott SW¼-S9; 10-28-1811. Vol. II. p.164. shows final cert. #2266 for it to Robert Russell, 10-28-1811
Horatio Mason NE¼-S10; 8-15-1817
John Arnold NW¼-S10; 12-2-1816
James Thomas SE¼-S10; 12-20-1813
Spencer Wiley & James Wiley SW¼-S10; 3-9-1814
James Conwell E½ & W½-NW¼-S11; 12-22-1831 8-10-1831
Harvy Lockwood SW¼-S11; 8-27-1815. Rel. W½ to William Potts,
David N. Camp & Frederick Kellogg SE¼-S11; NW¼-S12; 8-5-1818. Rel.? See Vol. II, p.165
Edward Brush NE¼-S14; 6-3-1815
Edward Brush NW¼-S14; 5-27-1815
William Rundle S½-S14; 12-11-1815. Rel. SW¼
James Chance W½-NE¼-S15; 1-26-1830
Edward Brush & Harvey Lockwood NW¼-S15; 3-22-1816
Jacob Burnett SE¼-S15; 10-28-1811. Rel.? Vol. II, p.165, shows final cert. #4518 to James Conwell, 10-31-1834
Otho Rench SW¼-S15; 11-14-1815. Rel.
Enoch Russel NE¼-S17; 12-14-1814
Joshua Rice SE¼-S17; 7-6-1815
Joshua Rice NE¼-S19; 7-6-1815
Joshua Rice NW¼-S19; 7-6-1815
Atwell Jackson SE¼-S19; 3-8-1815
John H. Faurct E½-SW¼-S19; 6-20-1831
Henry Teagarden NE¼-S20; 9-5-1812
James C. Smith NW¼-S20; 9-7-1813
Gideon Jinks E½-SE¼-S20; 3-15-1832
Jacob Faurot W½-SE¼-S20; 2-24-1832
Ephraim Young SW¼-S20; 5-20-1816

Page 88. T 12 N, R 12 E of 2nd P.M.

William Vanmeter NE¼-S21; 10-19-1811
James McCoy NW¼-S21; 10-19-1811
John Crist SE¼-S21; 2-29-1812
Hugh Brison SW¼-S21; 9-16-1816. Rel. W½/ To Gideon Jinks,
Allen Simpson NW¼-S22; 3-6-1818 3-15-1832
William Evans SE¼-S22; 6-13-1814
Hugh Brison SW¼-S22; 10-19-1811
Nehemiah Harp E½-SE¼-S23; 9-17-1817. Rel.
John Ferris SW¼-S23; 7-25-1814. Rel. Vol. II, p.167, shows W½-SW¼ to him, 11-28-1832
James Cole & Solomon Cole NE¼-S24; 9-3-1818. Rel. E½ to Ralph
James Russell SE¼-S24; 10-28-1811 Williams, 6-5-1828
John Curry SW¼-S24; 2-25-1817
William Gordon SE¼-S25; 1-19-1818
William Gordon SW¼-S25; 11-4-1811
Asahel Churchill NE¼-S26; 11-23-1811. See Vol. II, p.167
Artema D. Woodworth NW¼-S26; 4-2-1817 Rel. W½. To Arnold Murray, 9-27-1831
Artema D. Woodworth & Fielding Teter SE¼-S26; 12-17-1811. Vol. II, p.167, does not have Teter also
George Willson SW¼-S26; 10-28-1811
John Ferris NE¼-S27; 8-17-1813
John Conner NW¼-S27; 10-19-1811

James W. Bailey SE$\frac{1}{4}$-S27; 10-28-1811
George Crist SW$\frac{1}{4}$-S27; 10-19-1811
Michael Manan NE$\frac{1}{4}$-S28; 10-28-1811
John Brison SE$\frac{1}{4}$-S28; 3-13-1812
John Hiers W$\frac{1}{2}$-SW$\frac{1}{4}$-S28; 12-25-1825
William Maxwell W$\frac{1}{2}$-NW$\frac{1}{4}$-S29; 9-14-1821
Daniel Goodwin E$\frac{1}{2}$-SE$\frac{1}{4}$-S29; 10-5-1824
Stephen Bullock NE$\frac{1}{4}$-S30; 8-24-1814
Hugh Brison W$\frac{1}{2}$-NW$\frac{1}{4}$-S30; 9-11-1817

Page 89. T 12 N, R 12 E of 2nd P.M.

Jonathan Webb SE$\frac{1}{4}$-S32; 2-23-1814. Rel. E$\frac{1}{2}$
John Ferris NE$\frac{1}{4}$-S33; 9-2-1814. Rel. W$\frac{1}{2}$
Eli Stringer W$\frac{1}{2}$-SE$\frac{1}{4}$-S33; 10-19-1811. Vol. II, p.169, shows whole SE$\frac{1}{4}$, 10-21-1811
John C. Harley SW$\frac{1}{4}$-S33; 9-1-1813
David Mount NE$\frac{1}{4}$-S34; 10-7-1812
Jacob Manan NW$\frac{1}{4}$-S34; 11-30-1811
John Senour SE$\frac{1}{4}$-S34; 9-4-1813
Michael Manan SW$\frac{1}{4}$-S34; 6-30-1812
William Flood NE$\frac{1}{4}$-S35; 10-21-1811
George Adams NW$\frac{1}{4}$-S35; 10-19-1811
David Mounts SE$\frac{1}{4}$-S35; 7-6-1812
William Adams SW$\frac{1}{4}$-S35; 7-30-1814
George Guittner NE$\frac{1}{4}$-S36; 10-28-1811. Vol.II, p.169, says Guiltner
John Reed NW$\frac{1}{4}$-S36; 10-19-1811
Larkin Simes SE$\frac{1}{4}$-S36; 10-19-1811. Vol. II, p.169, says Sims
David Mounts SW$\frac{1}{4}$-S36; 10-21-1811

Page 89. T 13 N, R 12 E of 2nd P.M. **FAYETTE CO.**

Nathan Aldridge NE$\frac{1}{4}$-S1; 8-21-1813
Bazil Roberts NW$\frac{1}{4}$-S1; 6-27-1817
James Tweedy SE$\frac{1}{4}$-S1; 8-30-1813
Mathew Dixon NE$\frac{1}{4}$-S2; 10-21-1811. Vol. II, p.169, says Arthur Dixon
John Reed NW$\frac{1}{4}$-S2; 5-16-1812
Bazil Roberts & John Brison SE$\frac{1}{4}$-S2; 10-22-1811
William McCarty SW$\frac{1}{4}$-S2; 10-28-1811. Vol.II, p.169, says McCarley
Joshua Porter NE$\frac{1}{4}$-S3; 10-28-1811
Samuel Snodgrass NW$\frac{1}{4}$-S3; 9-8-1814
John Vance SE$\frac{1}{4}$-S3; 10-28-1811
James Kitchen SW$\frac{1}{4}$-S3; 1-17-1814
Thomas Cully NE$\frac{1}{4}$-S4; 10-21-1814
John Thomas NW$\frac{1}{4}$-S4; 9-3-1813
Joseph Vance SE$\frac{1}{4}$-S4; 3-19-1814
William Conner SW$\frac{1}{4}$-S4; 12-23-1813
William Murnan NE$\frac{1}{4}$-S5; 10-16-1813. Vol.II, p.170, says Marnan
James Heavren NW$\frac{1}{4}$-S5; 4-25-1814
John Thompson S$\frac{1}{2}$-S5; 9-10-1814
Benjamin Salor Fr.S6; S-10-1814
Samuel Todd & William C. Drew Fr.S7; 9-27-181
Benjamin McCarty NE$\frac{1}{4}$-S8; 8-2-1814
Samuel Logan NW$\frac{1}{4}$-S8; 6-10-1814
Samuel Newhouse SE$\frac{1}{4}$-S8; 8-16-1814
Caleb Smith SW$\frac{1}{4}$-S8; 7-29-1817
Benjamin McCarty NE$\frac{1}{4}$-S9; 2-3-1812
Robert Marshall NW$\frac{1}{4}$-S9; 4-9-1814

Benjamin McCarty SE¼-S9; 8-3-1814
Benjamin McCarty SW¼-S9; 8-9-1814
John Knox NE¼-S10; 6-22-1813
James Hamilton NW¼-S10; 11-29-1813
James Newhouse SE¼-S10; 10-4-1813
Christopher Ladd SW¼-S10; 12-23-1813
          Page 90. T 13 N, R 12 E of 2nd P.M.
William Willson NE¼-S11; 10-28-1811
William Harrel & Stephen Harrel NW¼-S11; 6-12-1813. Vol.II, p.170
    says William Stephen Harrel
John Vincent SE¼-S11; 12-16-1811
Benjamin Salor SW¼-S11; 8-30-1813
Samuel Fuller NE¼-S12; 1-8-1816
Moses Baker NW¼-S12; 10-22-1811
George Shaffer SE¼-S12; 1-28-1814
Samuel Fuller SW¼-S12; 10-22-1811
James Brownlee NE¼-S13; 8-5-1813
William Vardiman NW¼-S13; 3-21-1812
John Egar SE¼-S13; 12-10-1814. Vol.II, p.170, says Egan
John Julien SW¼-S13; 8-9-1814
Thomas Gillen NE¼-S14; 10-28-1811. Vol.II, p.170, says Gillam
Nicholas Regin NW¼-S14; 12-17-1811. Vol.II, p.170, says Reagan
John Agin SE¼-S14; 10-22-1811. Vol.II, p.170, says Eagin
William Agin SW¼-S14; 10-22-1811
Morgan Vardiman NE¼-S15; 3-21-1812
William Conner NW¼-S15; 6-17-1814
William Helm SE¼-S15; 8-2-1813
Benjamin Salor SW¼-S15; 9-28-1815. Rel. W½ to James Conwell,
    12-16-1831. Vol.II, p.170, shows whole SW¼ to Salor
James Buchanon NE¼-S17; 10-22-1814
Yale Hamilton NW¼-S17; 8-1-1817
Horatio Nelson Burguoyne E½-SE¼-S17; 2-1-1832
Robert Winchel SW¼-S17; 8-4-1814
Charles Hardy Fr.S18; 8-26-1814
John G. Gray, John Ronald, & John Coombs W½-NW¼-S19; 1-25-1822
Horatio Nelson Burguoyne E½ & W½-SE¼-S19; 2-21-1832
Wilson Wadams SW¼-S19; 9-2-1818. Rel. W½
Elijah Stevens NE¼-S20; 9-15-1814
Wilson Wadams NW¼-S20; 8-4-1814
John Bridges SE¼-S20; 12-21-1813
Elijah Stevens E½ & W½-SW¼-S20; 1-2-1832
Isaac Limpus W½-NW¼-S21; 2-4-1831
William Waddoms SE¼-S21; 7-5-1817. Rel. W½ to Willson Waddoms,
    3-30-1829; E½ to James Conwell, 12-16-1831
James Wiley SW¼-S21; 10-26-1815
Edward Webb NE¼-S22; 10-22-1811
John Conner NW¼-S22; 12-15-1814
William Gerrard SE¼-S22; 10-22-1811
Reuben Conner SW¼-S22; 11-17-1813
William Helm NE¼-S23; 1-13-1812
William Helm NW¼-S23; 10-22-1811
Daniel Greene SE¼-S23; 12-12-1811. Vol.II, p.171, says Greer
Gabriel Ginn SW¼-S23; 1-13-1812
Christopher Ladd NE¼-S24; 5-18-1816

Christopher Ladd NW¼-S24; 8-31-1816
John Baker SE¼-S24; 10-14-1813
Jacob Blacklidge SW¼-S24; 7-21-1814
Amos Askue NE¼-S25; 5-26-1815. Vol.II, p.171, says Askew
Morgan Vardeman NW¼-S25; 12-15-1814
John Lewis SE¼-S25; 12-4-1815
John McCabe W½-SW¼-S25; 11-1-1831
James Handley E½-NW¼-S26; 12-7-1831
Thomas Jefferson Crisler W½-NW¼-S26; 12-5-1831

Page 91. T 13 N, R 12 E of 2nd P.M.

Seth Dunbar SE¼-S26; 1-18-1816. Rel. E½ to John McCabe, 11-1-1831; W½ to William Wherrett, 12-12-1831
Edward Johnson SW¼-S26; 11-4-1816
John Crist NE¼-S27; 10-28-1811
William Conner NW¼-S27; 10-15-1814
Allen Crisler SE¼-S27; 11-17-1813
John Crisler SW¼-S27; 4-7-1818. Rel. E½. To William Wherrett, 1-27-1831. Vol.II, p.172, says Allen Crisler
Moses Martin NE¼-S28; 10-28-1811
Elijah Allen NW¼-S28; 9-28-1816
Enoch Limpus SE¼-S28; 9-7-1812
Charles Scott & Robert Russell SW¼-S28; 11-22-1811
Emery Hobbs NE¼-S29; 10-26-1816
Lewis Bishop NW¼-S29; 10-26-1816
Jonathan Gillman SE¼-S29; 10-2-1813. Vol.II, p.172, says Gillam
Cornelius Rinerson E½-SW¼-S29; 11-2-1831
Robert Glidewell, Jr. NE¼-S30; 10-20-1815. Vol.II, p.172, omits Jr.
Charles Stephens E½-NW¼-S30; 3-1-1832
Rinerd Rinerson E½-NE¼-S32; 7-5-1831
Moses Harrell W½-NE¼-S32; 1-26-1832
Moses Harrell E½-SE¼-S32; 1-3-1832
Moses Harrell W½-SE¼-S32; 3-17-1831
Edward Webb NE¼-S33; 11-4-1811
Horatio Mason E½-NW¼-S33; 4-28-1819
James Conwell W½-NW¼-S33; 12-16-1831
Enoch Limpus E½-SE¼-S33; 2-19-1818
Henry VanDalsam W½-SE¼-S33; 12-1-1831
Hugh Reed E½-SW¼-S33; 12-8-1831
Isaac Thomas W½-SW¼-S33; 12-22-1831
Elijah Limpus NE¼-S34; 11-2-1811
John Richardson NW¼-S34; 1-2-1812
Matthew Hueston & Henry Bryan SE¼-S34; 10-22-1811
Hugh Reed SW¼-S34; 10-22-1811
Benjamin Hoffner E½-NW¼-S35; 8-20-1814. See Vol.II, p.173
Orvill Gorden W½-NW¼-S35; 12-23-1824
James Conwell W½-SE¼-S35; 1-1-1831
Jacob Barnett SW¼-S35; 10-28-1811. Vol.II, p.173, says Burnett
Cyrus Haymond & Olive Clark NE¼-S36; 6-10-1817. Rel. E½ to Charles Melone, 1-19-1831; W½ to Charles Melone, 2-12-1828 3-23-1830
Sanford Keeler NW¼-S36; 6-14-1817. Rel. E½. To Charles Melone,

Page 92. T 14 N, R 12 E of 2nd P.M.

George Glaise N½-S1; 10-21-1811
Jacob Shidler SE¼-S1; 10-21-1811
Charles Royster SW¼-S1; 4-5-1813

Wear Cassady NE$\frac{1}{4}$-S2; 12-2-1816
James Dougherty NW$\frac{1}{4}$-S2; 10-21-1811
John White SE$\frac{1}{4}$-S2; 10-21-1811
John White SW$\frac{1}{4}$-S2; 10-21-1811
James Caldwell NE$\frac{1}{4}$-S3; 8-18-1814
James Caldwell NW$\frac{1}{4}$-S3; 10-21-1811
Isaac Hackleman SE$\frac{1}{4}$-S3; 6-30-1814
Jesse Webb SW$\frac{1}{4}$-S3; 8-31-1813
Alexander Dale NE$\frac{1}{4}$-S4; 10-28-1811
Joseph Caldwell NW$\frac{1}{4}$-S4; 12-11-1813
William Henderson SE$\frac{1}{4}$-S4; 9-17-1813
Joseph Dale SW$\frac{1}{4}$-S4; 3-9-1814
William McCarty & John McCarty Fr.S5; 12-9-1811
William Dickey Fr.S8; 10-22-1813
James Job NE$\frac{1}{4}$-S9; 2-22-1812
Alexander Dale NW$\frac{1}{4}$-S9; 9-9-1814
John Murphy E$\frac{1}{2}$ & W$\frac{1}{2}$-SE$\frac{1}{4}$-S9; 10-22-1814
John Lowder SW$\frac{1}{4}$-S9; 4-23-1814
Isaac Seward E$\frac{1}{2}$-NE$\frac{1}{4}$-S10; 10-13-1814
John Penwell W$\frac{1}{2}$-NE$\frac{1}{4}$-S10; 6-10-1824
William Cloud NW$\frac{1}{4}$-S10; 4-1-1814. See Vol.II, p.174
William Bell SE$\frac{1}{4}$-S10; 12-14-1814
Richard Tyner SW$\frac{1}{4}$-S10; 11-19-1814
Benjamin Salor NE$\frac{1}{4}$-S11; 8-30-1813
William Henderson SE$\frac{1}{4}$-S11; 9-17-1813
John Bradburn SW$\frac{1}{4}$-S11; 10-8-1812
George Hollingsworth NE$\frac{1}{4}$-S12; 7-29-1813
William Webb NW$\frac{1}{4}$-S12; 10-28-1811
Archibald Johnston SE$\frac{1}{4}$-S12; 8-30-1813
James Nichels, Sr. SW$\frac{1}{4}$-S12; 7-11-1812. Vol.II, p.174, omits Sr.
John McCormick NE$\frac{1}{4}$-S13; 10-22-1813
Samuel McCormick NW$\frac{1}{4}$-S13; 12-2-1816
Robert McCormick SE$\frac{1}{4}$-S13; 8-22-1812
John Perkins SW$\frac{1}{4}$-S13; 10-21-1811
Joel Dicker NE$\frac{1}{4}$-S14; 10-28-1811. Vol.II, p.175, says Dickens
Forrest Webb NW$\frac{1}{4}$-S14; 8-9-1814
Asa Stone SE$\frac{1}{4}$-S14; 8-22-1812
Lewis Johnson SW$\frac{1}{4}$-S14; 8-22-1811. Vol.II, p.175, says Johnston
Forrest Webb NE$\frac{1}{4}$-S15; 10-28-1811
Lewis Johnson SE$\frac{1}{4}$-S15; 10-22-1811
James Smith W$\frac{1}{2}$-S15; 9-2-1815
John Orr Fr.S17; 9-6-1813. Also Fr.S18
William Sparks Fr.S19; 3-7-1814. Also Fr.S30
Timothy Orr NE$\frac{1}{4}$-S20; 12-5-1811
Zacheriah Glover NW$\frac{1}{4}$-S20; 3-29-1813
John Henderson SE$\frac{1}{4}$-S20; 9-27-1813
William Denman SW$\frac{1}{4}$-S20; 10-9-1813
William Bennet NE$\frac{1}{4}$-S21; 8-5-1813
David Milton NW$\frac{1}{4}$-S21; 12-28-1811. Vol.II, p.175 says Melton
Paul Davis SE$\frac{1}{4}$-S21; 7-17-1813
Benjamin Booe SW$\frac{1}{4}$-S21; 5-4-1813
Richard Tyner NE$\frac{1}{4}$-S22; 10-21-1811
Plat B. Dickson NW$\frac{1}{4}$-S22; 2-15-1814
Adam Hamilton SE$\frac{1}{4}$-S22; 10-22-1814

James Denman SW¼-S22; 10-18-1813
John Conner NE¼-S23; 11-13-1812
Lewis Johnston NW¼-S23; 10-28-1811
Benjamin Taylor SE¼-S23; 8-7-1815. Vol.II, p.175 says Saylor
Larkin Simes & Andrew Bailey SW¼-S23; 9-25-1815
       Page 93. T 14 N, R 12 E of 2nd P.M.
Noah Beauchamp NE¼-S24; 12-14-1812
Jacob Hackleman NW¼-S24; 10-22-1811
Jacob Case SE¼-S24; 11-11-1811
Benjamin Taylor SW¼-S24; 10-22-1811. Vol.II, p.175 says Saylor
Andrew Tharp, assee., & Elihu Abbot NE¼-S25; 4-4-1812
John Conner NW¼-S25; 11-13-1812
Samuel Bealer SE¼-S25; 2-5-1814. See Vol.II, p.175
James Post NE¼-S26; 8-27-1814
John Perrin NW¼-S26; 5-9-1815
Jonas Williams SE¼-S26; 6-6-1815
Abiathar Hathaway SW¼-S26; 1-3-1814
Smith Lane NE¼-S27; 10-14-1814
John Henderson E½ & W½-NW¼-S27; 3-29-1813
William Hall SE¼-S27; 1-26-1815
Abner Ball SW¼-S27; 11-10-1813
John Fullin NE¼-S28; 11-8-1813. Vol.II, p.176 says Fallen
James Smith NW¼-S28; 4-10-1816
Thomas Smith SE¼-S28; 4-29-1815
James Alexander SW¼-S28; 5-3-1814
James Alexander NE¼-S29; 5-3-1814
Alexander Saxon NW¼-S29; 10-30-1813
James Smith SE¼-S29; 9-2-1815
James Williams SW¼-S29; 4-10-1816. Vol.II, p.176 says Jonas
                                              Williams, Sr.
Hezekiah Mounts Fr.S31; 2-3-1812
John Vance NE¼-S32; 12-25-1813
William Wier NW¼-S32; 10-11-1814
William Bridges SE¼-S32; 10-12-1816
James Greer SW¼-S32; 11-25-1813
Joseph Justice NE¼-S33; 10-22-1811
John Hughes NW¼-S33; 8-9-1814
Plat B. Dickson SE¼-S33; 6-27-1817
William Snodgrass SW¼-S33; 3-19-1814
Thomas Hinkson NE¼-S34; 5-3-1814
James Brownle NW¼-S34; 10-26-1813
Moses Lockhart SE¼-S34; 5-22-1813
Thomas Reed SW¼-S34; 10-26-1811
Elliott Herndon & Benjamin Salor NE¼-S35; 8-30-1813
John Perrin NW¼-S35; 1-3-1814
Joseph Miner SE¼-S35; 10-22-1811
John Russel SW¼-S35; 10-22-1811
William Denman NE¼-S36; 10-9-1813
Larkin Simes NW¼-S36; 10-22-1811
William Sparks SE¼-S36; 11-1-1811
Arthur Dixon SW¼-S36; 10-22-1811
       Page 94. T 15 N, R 12 E of 2nd P.M. Wayne Co.
James Rodgers NE¼-S1; 10-22-1811
Isaac Willets NW¼-S1; 10-22-1811
James Cawnover & John Cawnover SW¼-S1; 11-9-1811

Daniel Yount NE¼-S2; 10-22-1811
Benjamin McCarty NW¼-S2; 10-22-1811. See Vol.II, p.177
Debolt Hickle SE¼-S2; 10-22-1811
James Holdsclaw SW¼-S2; 10-28-1815
John Knips NE¼-S3; 11-2-1811
William Reynolds NW¼-S3; 7-10-1816
Moses Cooper, Sr. SE¼-S3; 5-8-1817
Peter Marts SW¼-S3; 12-9-1816

Page 94. T 15 N, R 12 E of 2nd P.M. FAYETTE CO.

Joab Reins Fr.S4; 2-25-1817
John Bell Fr.S9; 6-30-1817

Page 94. T 15 N, R 12 E of 2nd P.M. WAYNE CO.

James Cathcart NE¼-S10; 5-7-1817
John Bell NW¼-S10; 6-30-1817
Reuben Brownson SE¼-S10; 4-2-1814
David Shay SW¼-S10; 5-7-1817
Nimrod Furguson NE¼-S11; 10-22-1811
John Bell NW¼-S11; 6-3-1815
John Shaw SE¼-S11; 10-22-1811. Vol.II, p.177 says James
John Wallace SW¼-S11; 8-20-1813
John Knipe N½-S12; 10-22-1811
Thomas Beard SE¼-S12; 10-22-1811
James Shaw SW¼-S12; 10-22-1811
William Nelson NE¼-S13; 10-22-1811. Vol.II, p.177 says William Willson
Stephen Griffith NW¼-S13; 10-22-1811
Thomas Hardin SE¼-S13; 12-9-1811
Nimrod Furguson SW¼-S13; 10-22-1811
James Shaw NE¼-S14; 11-11-1811
John Wallace NW¼-S14; 3-11-1812
James Jackson SE¼-S14; 3-20-1817
John Wallace SW¼-S14; 8-20-1813
Richard Williams NE¼-S15; 2-20-1816
Jesse Munden NW¼-S15; 10-16-1816
Thomas Thomas SE¼-S15; 8-12-1813
Joseph Vanmeter SW¼-S15; 10-29-1811

Page 94. T 15 N, R 12 E of 2nd P.M. FAYETTE CO.

Amos Ascew & Samuel Heath Fr.S20 & W½-S21; 4-11-1814
Elisha Dennis NE¼-S21; 8-20-1812
William Lowry SE¼-S21; 8-9-1813

Page 94. T 15 N, R 12 E of 2nd P.M. WAYNE CO.

Jacob Bloyd NE¼-S22; 8-2-1814
Thomas Gillman NW¼-S22; 10-2-1813. Vol.II, p.178 says Gillam
Solomon Byrkit SE¼-S22; 11-11-1815. Vol.II, p.178 says Byrkill
Joseph Williams SW¼-S22; 10-9-1813
Samuel Easton NE¼-S23; 8-23-1814
William Holtzclaw NW¼-S23; 8-27-1814
Samuel M. George SE¼-S23; 8-14-1813.Vol.II, p.178 says McGeorge
Joseph Flint SW¼-S23; 9-10-1814
Joseph Spencer NE¼-S24; 10-22-1811
Benjamin Beeson NW¼-S24; 7-30-1812
Isaac Willson SE¼-S24; 10-22-1811
Joel Wright SW¼-S24; 8-13-1814
Nimrod Furguson N½-S25; 10-22-1811
Thomas Beard SE¼-S25; 10-22-1811

William Ross SW$\frac{1}{4}$-S25; 10-20-1814
John Baker NE$\frac{1}{4}$-S26; 9-10-1813
Isaac Willson NW$\frac{1}{4}$-S26; 9-2-1813
Thomas Neal SE$\frac{1}{4}$-S26; 12-20-1814
Abraham Vanmeter NE$\frac{1}{4}$-S27; 10-29-1811
Samuel Sanders NW$\frac{1}{4}$-S27; 7-16-1812
Adam Banks SE$\frac{1}{4}$-S27; 10-1-1813
Adam Jack SW$\frac{1}{4}$-S27; 1-24-1814

Page 95. T 15 N, R 12 E of 2nd P.M. **FAYETTE CO.**

George Manlove NE$\frac{1}{4}$-S28; 10-31-1811
Manlove Caldwell NW$\frac{1}{4}$-S28; 4-23-1814
John Caldwell SW$\frac{1}{4}$-S28; 3-4-1814
John Loder Fr.S29; 8-18-1814
William Baker Fr.S32; 2-15-1814
John Tyner NE$\frac{1}{4}$-S33; 10-28-1811
Richard Tyner NW$\frac{1}{4}$-S33; 10-28-1811
John Tyner SE$\frac{1}{4}$-S33; 10-22-1811
Joseph Caldwell SW$\frac{1}{4}$-S33; 10-22-1811
Isaac Willson NE$\frac{1}{4}$-S34; 10-2-1813
John Phillips NW$\frac{1}{4}$-S34; 10-22-1811
Solomon Horney SE$\frac{1}{4}$-S34; 7-16-1812
Thomas Caldwell SW$\frac{1}{4}$-S34; 10-22-1811
John Ward NE$\frac{1}{4}$-S35; 3-3-1814
William Willson NW$\frac{1}{4}$-S35; 12-7-1813
William Willson SE$\frac{1}{4}$-S35; 8-10-1814
Reason Davis & Charles Davis SW$\frac{1}{4}$-S35; 1-16-1812
Larkin Simes NE$\frac{1}{4}$-S36; 10-22-1811
Thomas Carter NW$\frac{1}{4}$-S36; 10-28-1811
Isaac Willson S$\frac{1}{2}$-S36; 10-22-1811

Page 95. T 16 N, R 12 E of 2nd P.M. **WAYNE CO.**

Ethan A. Brown NE$\frac{1}{2}$-S1; 5-2-1818. Rel. W$\frac{1}{2}$ to Andrew Jackson, 8-20-1828; E$\frac{1}{2}$ to Daniel Martin, 10-1-1828
Hannah Mater E$\frac{1}{2}$-NW$\frac{1}{4}$-S1; 11-1-1828
Abraham Cripe W$\frac{1}{2}$-NW$\frac{1}{4}$-S1; 3-19-1831
John Somers SE$\frac{1}{4}$-S1; 11-22-1811
Robert Badgley E$\frac{1}{2}$-SW$\frac{1}{4}$-S1; 12-18-1823
Abraham Cripe W$\frac{1}{2}$-SW$\frac{1}{4}$-S1; 3-19-1831
George Irwin Fr.S2-S3; 1-20-1815
Jesse Hill Fr.S10-S15; 2-4-1814
David Odum NE$\frac{1}{4}$-S11; 3-12-1814
Joseph Evans SE$\frac{1}{4}$-S11; 12-16-1811
John Pool SW$\frac{1}{4}$-S11; 1-3-1815
Thomas McCoy NE$\frac{1}{4}$-S12; 10-23-1811. Vol.II, p.179 says to Daniel Noland, assee. of McCoy
Elijah Spencer NW$\frac{1}{4}$-S12; 7-28-1814
Athwille Warrell SE$\frac{1}{4}$-S12; 10-23-1811. Vol.II, p.179 says Atterville
Sarah Symons & Lydia Symons SW$\frac{1}{4}$-S12; 10-19-1812
William Brown NE$\frac{1}{4}$-S13; 10-16-1812
Jehosaphat Morris NW$\frac{1}{4}$-S13; 10-28-1811
William Thorn SE$\frac{1}{4}$-S13; 11-9-1811
Barnett Starr SW$\frac{1}{4}$-S13; 10-23-1811
Robert Dickerson NE$\frac{1}{4}$-S14; 10-29-1811 Josiah
Abraham Small & Jonah Small NW$\frac{1}{4}$-S14; 8-16-1814. Vol.II, p.179 says
Daniel Noland SE$\frac{1}{4}$-S14; 10-28-1811

Abraham Crum SW¼-S14; 4-5-1815
Thomas Simons Fr.S22; 10-23-1811
John Nixon NE¼-S23; 11-8-1811
John Nixon NW¼-S23; 11-16-1811
George Vanbuskirk SW¼-S23; 4-18-1814
William Thorn NE¼-S24; 10-28-1811
Jesse Beard NW¼-S24; 10-23-1811
William Thorn SE¼-S24; 10-23-1811
Henry Brown SW¼-S24; 10-23-1811

Page 96. T 16 N, R 12 E of 2nd P.M.

John Shotridge S25; 10-23-1811
William Willetts NE¼-S26; 10-23-1811
Simon Powell NW¼-S26; 2-19-1814
Levi Willetts SE¼-S26; 10-23-1811
George Ash SW¼-S26; 5-11-1812. Vol.II, p.180 says Ish
John Hawkins, Sr. Fr.S27 & S28; 11-2-1811. Vol.II, p.180 omits Sr.
Joab Rains Fr.S33; 2-25-1817
Robert Taylor NE¼-S34; 10-23-1811. Vol.II, p.180 says to John
Thomas Stafford NW¼-S34; 10-23-1811 Bell. 10-24-1811
Boaze Tharp SE¼-S34; 10-23-1811
Samuel Drury SW¼-S34; 4-6-1814
George Glaize NE¼-S35; 10-23-1811
Thomas Simons NW¼-S35; 10-23-1811
Daniel Younts SE¼-S35; 10-23-1811
John Conner SW¼-S35; 10-23-1811
Samuel Beeler NW¼-S36; 10-23-1811
Nathan Richardson SE¼-S36; 10-23-1811
George Glaize SW¼-S36; 10-23-1811

Page 96. T 17 N, R 12 E of 2nd P.M.

John Haworth & Achillis Elmore Fr.S1; 8-23-1817. Vol.II, p.180
Jacob Virgil Fr.S12; 6-28-1815 says Archelaus
Joseph Hancock Fr.S13 & S14; 9-12-1815
Bartlett Woodward Fr.S23; 11-1-1813
James Reeder NE¼-S24; 2-15-1817
Samuel Hays NW¼-S24; 10-22-1817. Rel. E½
Howell Campbell SE¼-S24; 10-22-1817. Rel. W½
Philip Baltimore SW¼-S24; 10-31-1816
Enos Neal NE¼-S25; 1-11-1817
James Sturges SE¼-S25; 11-22-1817
Caleb Barrett SW¼-S25 & Fr.S26; 8-15-1816
John Clark Fr.S35; 5-21-1817
Elihu Harlan NE¼-S36; 2-26-1816
John W. Berry NW¼-S36; 9-2-1817
Peter Runyan SE¼-S36; 9-8-1817
John Miller W½-SW¼-S36; 11-14-1823

Page 96. T 18 N, R 12 E of 2nd P.M.

Leonard Stump Fr.S25 & S36; 10-23-1816

Page 97. T 11 N, R 13 E of 2nd P.M. FRANKLIN CO.

William Simes, Jr. Fr.S2; 10-23-1811. Vol.II, p.181 omits Jr.
John Bradley NE¼-S3; 10-23-1811. Vol.II, p.181 says William
John Neal NW¼-S3; 10-23-1811
John Brown SE¼-S3; 10-25-1811
William Wilson SW¼-S3; 10-23-1811
Harvey Brown NE¼-S4; 10-30-1811

William Amil NW¼-S4; 10-23-1811. Vol.II, p.181, says Arnett
Simpson Jones SE¼-S4; 10-23-1811
William Wilson SW¼-S4; 1-3-1815
Isaac Wilson NE¼-S5; 10-23-1811
William Arnold NW¼-S5; 10-23-1811
David Mounts SE¼-S5; 11-27-1812
Eli Stringer SW¼-S5; 9-22-1814
Alexander Miller NE¼-S6; 10-28-1811
William George NW¼-S6; 11-7-1812
Benjamin Taylor SE¼-S6; 10-5-1812. Vol.II, p.182, says Salor
Jonathan Orsborn NE¼-S7; 10-17-1812
Samuel Alley SE¼-S7; 10-5-1812
James Hobbs, Jr. SW¼-S7; 11-4-1817
William Wilson NE¼-S9; 1-3-1815
Joseph K. Smith NW¼-S9; 7-3-1818. Rel.
Caleb White SE¼-S9; 5-14-1818. Rel.
James Glenn SW¼-S9; 5-14-1818. Rel.
John Stafford NE¼-S10; 10-28-1811
Henry Calfer E½ & W½-NW¼-S10; 10-23-1811. Vol.II, p.182 says
John Wells SE¼-S10; 10-8-1814 Calfee
Benjamin Smith SW¼-S10; 7-23-1814
Samuel Brown & Stephen Martin Fr.S11; 10-23-1811
Amos Butler N end-Fr.S14; Fr.S23; 2-19-1817. Rel. Fr.S23 & S end-
Robert W. Halstead NE¼-S15; 4-10-1817 Fr.S14
Samuel C. Vance NW¼-S15; 10-3-1817. Rel.
Edmond Adams SE¼-S15; 7-12-1817. Rel.
Stephen Butler & Elias P. Smith SW¼-S15; 12-5-1817. Rel.
William B. Laughlin NE¼-S17; 11-18-1816
David Alley NE¼-S18; 9-25-1812
Cyrus Alley SE¼-S18; 10-12-1814
Jonathan Allen SW¼-S18; 1-28-1814. Rel. W½
James Alley NW¼-S19; 10-29-1812
Elisha Cragins SW¼-S19; 9-5-1814. Vol.II, p.183, says Cragun

Page 98. T 11 N, R 13 E of 2nd P.M.

William C. Drew & Samuel Todd NE¼ & E½-NW¼-S20; 4-22-1818. Rel.
Andrew Jackson SE¼-S20; 3-17-1817. Rel. E½
William C. Drew & Samuel Hunt SW¼-S20; 11-4-1817. Rel.
Daniel Gano & Aaron G. Gano NE¼-S21; 11-1-1817
William C. Drew & Samuel F. Hunt NW¼-S21; 11-4-1817. Rel.
Eli Stringer SE¼-S21; 8-14-1817
William C. Drew & Samuel Todd SW¼-S21; 9-27-1817
Jonathan Carlton & Daniel Brooks E pt.-Fr.S22; 3-21-1818
Samuel F. Hunt & William C. Drew Fr.S28; 12-11-1817. Rel. pt. off
Peter Alley NW¼-S30; 8-29-1814. Rel. E½ W side
William Conn SE¼-S30; 12-1-1815. Rel. E½
Caleb Cragun E½-SW¼-S30; 3-2-1819

Page 98. T 12 N, R 13 E of 2nd P.M.

John Brown Fr.S1; 10-17-1814
Joseph Glenn NW¼-S2; 12-2-1814
David Ewing SE¼-S2; 12-6-1813
Tyler McHorter SW¼-S2; 9-6-1814. Vol.II, p.185, says McWhartar
Samuel Steel NE¼-S3; 1-16-1815
Elizabeth Teagarden NW¼-S3; 6-12-1815
Martin Kingery SE¼-S3; 10-31-1814. Vol.II, p.185, says Michael

James Webb W½-SW¼-S3; 6-4-1831
Josiah Allen NE¼-S4; 8-26-1813
Solomon Shepperd NW¼-S4; 6-20-1814
John Allen, Jr. SE¼-S4; 8-26-1813
Ann Doughty SW¼-S4; 8-4-1814. Vol.II, p.185, says Dougherty
John R. Beaty NW¼-S5; 5-27-1814
Rhoda Crump SE¼-S5; 11-5-1814
William M. Worthington NE¼-S6; 3-24-1818. Rel. E½ to James Laird, 9-26-1831 (1837?)

Page 99. T 12 N, R 13 E of 2nd P.M.

Sarah Jones SE¼-S6; 12-11-1816. Rel. E½
Robert Cather, Sr. & Robert Cather, Jr. SW¼-S6; 3-24-1818. Rel. W½ to George Owen, 7-5-1831
Nathan Youngs NE¼-S7; 10-27-1818
Joseph Whitlock NW¼-S7; 1-9-1818
John Riggs NE¼-S8; 6-27-1815
William Richardson SE¼-S8; 4-6-1815
William Jones NE¼-S9; 7-7-1817. Rel. W½
John Riggs NW¼-S9; 6-27-1815
James Fordin SE¼-S9; 11-20-1815. Vol.II, p.186, says Fordice
James Winder SW¼-S9; 10-20-1815
James Webb NE¼-S10; 10-22-1814
Thomas Sherwood NW¼-S10; 9-2-1814
John Price SE¼-S10; 10-23-1813
James Sherwood SW¼-S10; 9-2-1814
William Harvey & James Harvey NE¼-S11; 10-10-1814
William Smith NW¼-S11; 9-3-1814
Charles Harvey SE¼-S11; 10-5-1815
William Skinner SW¼-S11; 10-22-1814
Benjamin Souder & Peter Dunkin Fr.S12; 1-6-1815. Vol.II, p.186, says P. Snowden instead of B. Souder
John Price, Jr. N pt.& S pt.-NW¼-S13; SW¼-S13; 3-12-1832
Simon Yanders NE¼-S14; 5-30-1818. Rel. W½. To John P. Williams
Malachi Swift NW¼-S14; 2-12-1817 3-15-1832
Emery Scotton SE¼-S14; 7-9-1816
John Delany SW¼-S14; 10-15-1814
George W. Miles & Matthew Farran NE¼-S15; 8-13-1814. Vol.II,
Alexander White NW¼-S15; 9-11-1813 p.187, says Millis
James Currie & Benjamin Norwell SE¼-S15; 9-14-1813
Christian Swift SW¼-S15; 8-23-1813. Vol.II, p.187, says
John Fisher NE¼-S17; 6-5-1819. Rel. W½ Christopher
Thomas Collier E½-NW¼-S17; 2-18-1830
Richard Clements SE¼-S17; 8-2-1814
Richard Williams SW¼-S17; 5-12-1814
Jacob Blacklidge NE¼-S19; 11-13-1811
Ralph Williams NW¼-S19; 10-23-1811
Calvin Kinsley NE¼-S20; 7-1-1817. Rel. W½
Warren Buck NW¼-S20; 7-11-1817. Rel. E½. Vol.II, p.188, says Burk
Michael Hinds SE¼-S20; 8-13-1817. Rel. W½ to Francis Holland,
Peter Hinds SW¼-S20; 8-13-1817. Rel. 9-28-1827
Henry Teagarden NE¼-S21; 10-4-1813
Calvin Kinsley NW¼-S21; 7-1-1817
Robert Morris W½-SE¼-S21; 10-1-1825

Page 100. T 12 N, R 13 E of 2nd P.M.

Nicholas Longworth & Moses Brooks SW¼-S21; 1-31-1818. Rel. E½ to Philip Jones, 5-23-1828
William Williams NE¼-S22; 2-24-1816
Thomas Slaughter SE¼-S22; 7-10-1817. Rel. W½
William Harper SW¼-S22; 4-4-1817
Henry Bruce NE¼-S23; 9-11-1815
Jacob Blacklidge NW¼-S23; 11-8-1813
Thomas Smith SE¼-S23; 9-22-1814
Thomas Slaughter SW¼-S23; 3-10-1815
Isaac Howard Fr.S24; 8-21-1816
Solomon Manwaring & Richard Manwaring Fr.S25; E½-S26; 11-24-1812
Henry M. Bonwill E½-NW¼-S26; 11-1-1825
James Blacklidge & Barnet McCombs W½-NW¼-S26; 3-10-1832
Thomas Heaton SW¼-S26; 6-14-1817. Rel. E½ to Samuel Goodwin, 11-1-1831
Garret Jones E½-NE¼-S27; 9-22-1820
Robert McKoy SW¼-S27; 10-2-1816. Vol.II, p.189, says McKay
Henry Hinds E½-S28; 7-11-1817. Rel. NE¼ & W½-SE¼. W½-SE¼ to William Chapman, 7-5-1831
John Melone NW¼-S28; 8-6-1817. Rel. W½ to Hiram Williams, 12-9-1831; E½ to James McWhorter, 11-9-1831
William Linn E½-NE¼-S29; 10-13-1831
Samuel Gustin NW¼-S29; 5-27-1817
Jonathan Chapman NE¼-S30; 7-14-1817. Rel. E½
Benajah Gustin NW¼-S30; 5-27-1817. Rel.
Hiram Pond W½-SE¼-S30; 7-10-1830
George Giltner & Asahel Giltner W½-SW¼-S30; 2-14-1832
John Kyger NE¼-S31; 12-14-1812
Philip Riche NW¼-S31; 7-23-1814
David Mounts SE¼-S31;10-23-1811
Richard Williams SW¼-S31; 10-28-1811
Hezekiah Mounts NW¼-S32; 11-22-1811
John McWhorter W½-SE¼-S32; 9-7-1831
Hezekiah Mounts SW¼-S32; 10-23-1811
Charles Collett NE¼-S33; 2-28-1817
Thomas Owsley NW¼-S33; 1-17-1814
William Wilson SE¼-S33; 10-23-1811
David Stoops SW¼-S33; 10-23-1811
Robert McKoy NE¼-S34; 10-2-1816
Henry Teagarden NW¼-S34; 9-4-1816
Thomas Owsley SE¼-S34; 8-25-1812
Charles Collett SW¼-S34; 6-10-1813
Corbly Hudson & Mary Hudson Fr.S35; 5-13-1815

Page 101. T 13 N, R 13 E of 2nd P.M. UNION CO.

Henry Nichols NE¼-S1; 10-11-1814
Jeremiah Woods NW¼-S1; 8-27-1814
John Fisher SE¼-S1; 7-11-1815
Martin Glidwell SW¼-S1; 5-20-1814

Page 101. T 13 N, R 13 E of 2nd P.M. FAYETTE CO.

Joseph Vanmeter NE¼-S2; 3-18-1814
Michael Brown SE¼-S2; 7-7-1814
Giles Mattix SW¼-S2; 11-8-1813
Joseph Vanmeter NW¼-S2; NE¼-S3; 8-30-1813
Jacob Tartar NW¼-S3; 4-9-1813

Samuel Fullen SE¼-S3; 10-28-1811
Andrew Barley SW¼-S3; 8-9-1814. Vol. II, p.190, says Bailey
Thomas Clark NE¼-S4; 8-4-1813
William Patton NW¼-S4; 11-22-1813
John Manley SE¼-S4; 6-18-1813
William Manley SW¼-S4; 3-10-1814
David Norris NE¼-S5; 3-28-1814
John Milner NW¼-S5; 10-3-1814
Cornelius Cummings SE¼-S5; 4-25-1815
John Milner SW¼-S5; 10-3-1814
Richard Thomas NE¼-S6; 9-15-1813
Samuel Harlin NW¼-S6; 10-23-1811
Thomas Bray SE¼-S6; 8-27-1814
Cornelius Williams SW¼-S6; 9-4-1813
Benjamin White NE¼-S7; 10-20-1815
John White NW¼-S7; 2-16-1816. Vol.II, p.191, says Benjamin
Samuel Harlin SE¼-S7; 11-2-1816
Nicholas Pumphrey SW¼-S7; 6-18-1816
David Farree NE¼-S8; 12-15-1815
Morgan Vandeman NW¼-S8; 4-2-1816. Vol.II, p.191, says Vardiman
James Newland SE¼-S8; 4-2-1814
Samuel Harlin SW¼-S8; 11-2-1816
Adam Pigman NE¼-S9; 1-13-1814
John Woods NW¼-S9; 8-28-1815
Jesse Pigman SE¼-S9; 1-13-1814
Harrod Newland SW¼-S9; 12-21-1814
John Bray NE¼-S10; 1-28-1814
Benjamin Elliott NW¼-S10; 1-4-1814
Ephraim Boreing SE¼-S10; 4-2-1814
John Huff SW¼-S10; 1-13-1814
Solomon Wise NE¼-S11; 4-14-1815
Henry Bray NW¼-S11; 2-7-1814
Jacob Mattix SE¼-S11; 3-23-1814
John Black SW¼-S11; 3-29-1814

Page 101. T 13 N, R 13 E of 2nd P.M. UNION CO.

Silas Anderson NE¼-S12; 7-22-1814
Nathan Crookshanks NW¼-S12; 10-28-1815. Vol.II, p.191, says Nathaniel
William Kirkpatrick SE¼-S12; 10-23-1811
John Norris SW¼-S12; 9-7-1814
David Noble, Sr. NE¼-S13; 12-2-1816
Harrod Newland NW¼-S13; 3-10-1814
Samuel Maize & David Maize SE¼-S13; 10-23-1811. Vol.II, p.191, says Maze
Alexander McCann SW¼-S13; 2-11-1814

Page 101. T 13 N, R 13 E of 2nd P.M. FAYETTE CO.

Harrod Newland NE¼-S14; 3-10-1814
Benjamin H. Hanson NW¼-S14; 9-10-1814
Elihu Crandel SE¼-S14; 1-19-1815. Vol.II, p.191, says Elisha
William Nugent & Robert Nugent SW¼-S14; 4-4-1816
Isaac Kelsey NE¼-S15; 4-15-1817. Rel. To William Price Bolton & James Alexander Bolton, 11-18-1831
John Huff NW¼-S15; 1-13-1814
Harrod Newland SE¼-S15; 12-21-1814
James Worster SW¼-S15; 9-10-1813
Levin Cambridge NE¼-S17; 6-25-1815

Zachariah Cooksey NW¼-S17; 8-21-1815
Levin Plummer SE¼-S17; 9-11-1816. Vol.II, p.191, says Levi
Levin Plummer SW¼-S17; 1-6-1817. Vol.II, p.191, says Levi
Samuel Harlan NE¼-S18; 12-10-1816
Moses Ladd NW¼-S18; 9-11-1816

Page 102. T 13 N, R 13 E of 2nd P.M.

Baruch Plummer & Noble Ladd SE¼-S18; 9-11-1816
John Plummer SW¼-S18; 10-23-1816
John Williams NE¼-S19; 12-27-1815
Elisha Stout & John Maple NW¼-S19; 8-22-1814
John Walker SE¼-S19; 11-11-1816. Vol.II, p.192, says Samuel
Thomas Farrer SW¼-S19; 8-28-1815.Vol.II,p.192,says Thomas Toner
Jacob Barckman NE¼-S20; 7-25-1814.Vol.II, p.192, says Barrackman
George Monroe NW¼-S20; 12-28-1812
John Richardson SE¼-S20; 11-4-1812
William Hopkins SW¼-S20; 10-27-1815
William Adams NW¼-S21; 8-24-1813
John Garvin NE¼-S21; 12-16-1814. Vol.II, p.192 says Thomas
John Morrow SE¼-S21; 3-27-1812
Eli Lee SW¼-S21; 1-31-1812
David Fallin NE¼-S22; 8-19-1814
Elijah Corbin NW¼-S22; 4-2-1814
James Morrow SE¼-S22; 11-13-1815
Thomas Stockdale SW¼-S22; 7-5-1814
William Beckett NE¼-S23; 12-10-1814
John Fisher NW¼-S23; 3-28-1817
John Fisher SE¼-S23; 6-6-1815
Isaac M. Johnston SW¼-S23; 10-24-1814.Vol.II,p.192 says Johnson.

Page 102. T 13 N, R 13 E of 2nd P.M. UNION CO.

John Mattocks NE¼-S24; 11-29-1813. Vol.II, p.192 says Matlock
John Huff NW¼-S24; 7-29-1814
William Clary SE¼-S24; 7-6-1814
John Harrel SW¼-S24; 1-22-1817
John Campbell Fr.S25; 10-27-1815

Page 102. T 13 N, R 13 E of 2nd P.M. FAYETTE CO.

Rowana Clark & Amaranda Clark NE¼-S36; 4-8-1817. Rel. E½. To Latham Stanton, 10-17-1827. Vol.II, p.192 says Amanda
Obediah Estes NW¼-S26; 7-16-1813
Simeon Grist SE¼-S26; 8-11-1815. Vol.II, p.192 says Simon
Robert T. Taylor SW¼-S26; 6-21-1814.Vol.II,p.192 says F.,not T.
David James & George Mattock NE¼-S27; 11-19-1811. Vol.II, p.192 seems to say David, George, & James Mallack
Thomas Stockdale NW¼-S27; 2-5-1814
Eli Stringer SE¼-S27; 10-23-1811
Thomas Henderson SW¼-S27; 10-23-1811
Hugh Moore NE¼-S28; 10-3-1816. Rel. W½ to John Starbuck, 9-16-1825; E½ to Charles Salyers & James Salyers, 2-4-1831
Sarah Lee NW¼-S28; 10-25-1814
Samuel Watters & Archibald Morrow SE¼-S28; 7-24-1813. Vol.II,
John Pollard SW¼-S28; 11-5-1813 p.193 says Wallers
Solomon Shepherd NE¼-S29; 7-18-1814
Edward McCew NW¼-S29; 10-6-1818. Rel. W½
Thomas Logan SE¼-S29; 1-13-1816
Daniel Logan SW¼-S29; 12-28-1815. Vol.II, p.193 says Samuel

Blackley Shoemaker W½-NE¼-S30; 1-15-1818. Vol.II, p.193 says Shoemake
Edward Simmons NW¼-S30; 11-22-1816. Rel. W½. To Elbert Walker, 1-19-1831
Joel Scott SE¼-S30; 10-17-1816
Calvin Kinsley SW¼-S30; 8-8-1817
Susannah Teagarden NE¼-S31; 11-11-1815
Stephen Lee E½-NW¼-S31; 11-15-1828
Joseph Whitelock E½-SE¼-S31; 6-27-1831
John Troth SW¼-S31; 9-15-1818
Hugh Abernath NE¼-S32; 6-21-1813. Vol.II, p.193 says Abernathy
John Norris NW¼-S32; 4-14-1815. Rel. To Joseph Whitelock, 8-10-1831
William Risk SE¼-S32; 10-10-1814
John Saylor NE¼-S33; 10-31-1811. Vol.II, p.193 says Tayler
Solomon Shepherd SE¼-S33; 6-20-1814
Thomas Risk SW¼-S33; 10-10-1814

Page 103. T 13 N, R 13 E of 2nd P.M.

Thomas Henderson NE¼-S34; 10-28-1811
Ebenezer Smith SE¼-S34; 12-4-1815
James Watters & John Watters SW¼-S34; 12-4-1812
Alexander Sims NE¼-S35; 5-4-1815
John McIlvain NW¼-S35; 3-19-1814
Edward Carney SE¼-S35; 12-5-1814
Ebenezer Smith SW¼-S35; 11-16-1813

Page 103. T 13 N, R 13 E of 2nd P.M. UNION CO.

Abraham Louderback Fr.S36; 9-11-1816

Page 103. T 14 N, R 13 E of 2nd P.M.

David Thomas NE¼-S1; 12-27-1816
Ephraim Thomas NW¼-S1; 4-3-1815
Thomas Osborn E½-SE¼-S1; 10-26-1821
James Baird, John Bond, & Edward B. Woodson W½-SE¼-S1; 3-26-1831
Thomas Osborn E½-SW¼-S1; 10-8-1822
Robert Holland W½-SW¼-S1; 2-24-1827

Page 103. T 14 N, R 13 E of 2nd P.M. FAYETTE CO.

Isaac Welliver NE¼-S2; 1-31-1825. Rel.
James Montgomery NW¼-S2; 10-23-1815
Robert Holland E½-SE¼-S2; 8-27-1819
Uriah Farlow W½-SE¼-S2; 3-21-1818
James N. Chambers SW¼-S2; 11-2-1815
Mordecai Morgan NE¼-S3; 6-14-1814
Anthony Wiley NW¼-S3; 6-14-1814
Josiah Lambert SE¼-S3; 3-19-1814
Abraham Vanmeter SW¼-S3; 6-14-1814
Abraham Vanmeter N½-S4; 6-14-1814
Matthias Dawson SE¼-S4; 6-23-1815
George P. Torrence & Lewis Whiteman SW¼-S4; 11-22-1815. Rel.
John McIntire NE¼-S5; 10-28-1811
John McIntire NW¼-S5; 10-28-1811
George Torrence SE¼-S5; 10-27-1815. Vol.II, p.194 says Middle initial P.
George P. Torrence & David Kilgore SW¼-S5; 10-28-1811. Vol.II, p.194 omits David Kilgore
John Grewell NE¼-S6; 10-23-1811
John Grewell NW¼-S6; 3-19-1812
Andrew Tharp SE¼-S6; 12-2-1816
Edward Webb SW¼-S6; 4-18-1817

Silas Gregg NE¼-S7; 10-24-1811
Edward Webb NW¼-S7; 10-23-1811
James Sutton, Jr. SE¼-S7; 6-28-1814
Zadock Smith SW¼-S7; 3-14-1812
Aaron Hougham NE¼-S8; 5-6-1815
Samuel Vance NW¼-S8; 6-22-1814
Aaron Hougham SE¼-S8; 5-6-1815
Ebenezer Heaton SW¼-S8; 3-11-1814
Daniel Heaton E½-S9; 1-7-1815
William Denniston & John Denniston NW¼-S9; 10-14-1817
Joseph White SW¼-S9; 8-8-1814
Jesse Dawson NE¼-S10; 8-29-1814
Benjamin Dungan NW¼-S10; 3-13-1815
Charles Collett SE¼-S10; 1-5-1814
Graves Hougham SW¼-S10; 7-28-1815. Vol.II, p.195 says Garvis
Christopher Wamsley NE¼-S11; 11-4-1817
Matthew Nicol NW¼-S11; 10-27-1815
John Ritter SE¼-S11; 12-18-1815
James Montgomery SW¼-S11; 9-29-1815
     Page 103. T 14 N, R 13 E of 2nd P.M.   **UNION CO.**
Daniel Trimbley NE¼-S12; 9-13-1822
James Dungan NW¼-S12; 9-9-1817
William Lewis SE¼-S12; 12-24-1813
Zadock Stephenson SW¼-S12; 2-13-1817
     Page 104. T 14 N, R 13 E of 2nd P.M.
Thomas Rambley NE¼-S13; 11-11-1815
John A. Ranck NW¼-S13; 6-7-1817
Thomas Madden SE¼-S13; 11-10-1814
William Hollingsworth SW¼-S13; 4-24-1815
     Page 104. T 14 N, R 13 E of 2nd P.M.   **FAYETTE CO.**
James Montgomery NE¼-S14; 8-4-1815
Thomas Cooper NW¼-S14; 5-31-1815
Joshua Simpson SE¼-S14; 12-16-1816
William Heirs SW¼-S14; 6-12-1815. Vol.II, p.195 says Hiers
Henry Holland NE¼-S15; 7-31-1813
James Rambley NW¼-S15; 8-22-1814. Vol.II, p.195 says Rumbley
Thomas Dawson SE¼-S15; 8-2-1813
Aaron DeLebar SW¼-S15; 4-29-1815
James Sutton NE¼-S17; 8-8-1814
Samuel Wilson NW¼-S17; 3-19-1812
Samuel Vance SE¼-S17; 6-24-1816
Archibald * SW¼-S17; 8-13-1814 *Reed
Zadock Smith NE¼-S18; 3-14-1812
Ebenezer * NW¼-S18; 10-30-1811 *Heaton
Archibald * SE¼-S18; 10-23-1811. Vol.II, p.195 adds SW¼. *Reed
Abraham Heaton NE¼-S19; 10-30-1811
Daniel Heaton NW¼-S19; 10-30-1811
Robert Brown SE¼-S19; 10-31-1811
Jacob Case SW¼-S19; 11-11-1811
George Death NE¼-S20; 9-29-1812
Ebenezer Howman NW¼-S20; 9-29-1812. Vol.II, p.196 says Homan
James Dearth SE¼-S20; 9-1-1812. Vol.II, p.196 adds Sr.
Robert Brown SW¼-S20; 10-25-1813.Vol.II,p.196 says Thomas Brown
John C. Death NW¼-S21; 9-29-1812

Crim Stoddard & Abel Robinson NE¼-S21; 2-14-1816. Vol.II, p.196
   says Orrin Stoddard
Jesse Fletcher SE¼-S21; 10-30-1813
Jonathan Hougham SW¼-S21; 8-24-1815
Abraham Vaneaton NE¼-S22; 8-5-1812
David Fletcher NW¼-S22; 10-27-1813
Samuel Hill & Stephen Oldham SE¼-S22; 10-22-1813
John Keeny SW¼-S22; 11-1-1811
Thomas Simpson NE¼-S23; 1-11-1814
Amos Sutton NW¼-S23; 8-23-1814
Valentine Harlan SE¼-S23; 3-4-1815
Valentine Harlan SW¼-S23; 12-10-1816

        Page 104. T 14 N, R 13 E of 2nd P.M.   **UNION CO.**
John Creek NE¼-S24; 12-12-1814
John Harlan NW¼-S24; 3-4-1815
Samuel Littret SE¼-S24; 8-10-1814
James Canaway SW¼-S24; 8-29-1815
William McMahan NE¼-S25; 9-12-1816. Rel. W½. To Benjamin Hillman,
James Canaway NW¼-S25; 8-29-1815   8-22-1827
Isaac Odell SE¼-S25; 1-13-1814
John Essley SW¼-S25; 1-9-1815

        Page 104. T 14 N, R 13 E of 2nd P.M.   **FAYETTE CO.**
Daniel Bayles, Jr. N½-S26; 9-2-1814
Lewis Noble SE¼-S26; 10-23-1811
William Knott SW¼-S26; 7-21-1813
Zachariah Davice NE¼-S27; 10-24-1816. Vol.II, p.196 says Davee
Samuel Riggs NW¼-S27; 10-30-1811
Michael Brown SE¼-S27; 6-7-1814
John Oldham SW¼-S27; 1-14-1815
James Smith & Daniel Conner NE¼-S28; 7-7-1813
James Ward NW¼-S28; 12-3-1814
John Keeney SE¼-S28; 3-8-1816
Robert Brown SW¼-S28; 11-30-1816
James Ward NE¼-S29; 12-3-1814
Isaac Martin NW¼-S29; 10-25-1813
Joel White SE¼-S29; 10-7-1813
Phineas McCray SW¼-S29; 1-18-1815

        Page 105. T 14 N, R 13 E of 2nd P.M.
Robert Brown NE¼-S30; 10-23-1811   Samuel Wilson NE¼-S35;
George Frazer NW¼-S30; 10-24-1811   2-9-1815
John Hughes SE¼-S30; 11-28-1811   Robert Abernathy NW¼-S35;
George Ross Adair SW¼-S30; 12-23-1811   3-10-1814
Samuel Harlin S31; 10-28-1811   Robert Abernathy SE¼-S35;
Robert Williams NW¼-S32; 11-15-1815   11-26-1814
David Conner SE¼-S32; 7-30-1814   Joseph Dungan SW¼-S35;
James Freal SW¼-S32; 1-7-1814   3-13-1815
Samuel Bell NE¼-S33; 10-12-1813
Samuel Bell, Sr. NW¼-S33; 1-6-1815
Samuel Bell SE¼-S33; 1-7-1814
Phineas McCray SW¼-S33; 2-2-1814
Thomas Patton NE¼-S34; 10-10-1814
Peggy Shields NW¼-S34; 11-6-1813
Richard Colliver SE¼-S34; 9-8-1814
Jacob Tartar SW¼-S34; 11-27-1813

Page 105.   T 14 N, R 13 E of 2nd P.M.   UNION CO.
John McMacken NE¼-S36; 2-7-1814
Samuel Wilson NW¼-S36; 1-6-1815. Vol.II,p.197 says William Wilson
William Nichols SE¼-S36; 10-11-1814
Hugh Bell SW¼-S36; 4-1-1814
Page 105.   T 15 N, R 13 E of 2nd P.M.   WAYNE CO.
Lewis Thomas NE¼-S1; 8-8-1816
Henry Bryan NW¼-S1; 10-24-1811
Job Huddleston SE¼-S1; 10-25-1816
Andrew Bailey & Thomas Danby SW¼-S1; 6-20-1814
Peter Bonta NW¼-S2; 12-2-1816
Elisha Dennis SE¼-S2; 8-22-1814
Thomas McCoy SW¼-S2; 10-28-1811
Joseph Gillispie & Samuel Beck NE¼-S3; 7-11-1817. Rel. W½. To
     Peter Miller, 7-5-1831   10-1829
Edward Thornton NW¼-S3; 6-7-1816.Rel. E½. To Henry Hartman, 12-
Joseph Waling SW¼-S3; 11-30-1814.Rel. To Abram G. Hannah. 12-10-
John McCarty NE¼-S4; 3-11-1816.Vol.II. p.198, says Job   1829
Jesse Willets NW¼-S4; 10-23-1816
Martin Fisher SE¼-S4; 2-7-1816
Jesse Willets & Elisha Willets SW¼-S4; 4-6-1814
Samuel Black N½-S5; 10-24-1811
Levi Willets SE¼-S5; 10-24-1811.Vol.II,p.198 says William Willets
Robinson McIntire SW¼-S5; 10-24-1811. Vol.II, p.198 says to
John Kilbourn NE¼-S6; 10-24-1811   Levi Willets
Levi Willets SE¼-S6; 10-24-1811
John Wallace SW¼-S6; 10-24-1811
Samuel C. Vance NE¼-S7; 1-11-1818
William H. Harrison NW¼-S7; 7-4-1814
Andrew Crouch SE¼-S7; 10-30-1811
John Andrews SW¼-S7; 7-30-1817
Isaac Waters & William Cummings NE¼-S8; 2-1-1814
Abraham Miller NW¼-S8; 10-24-1811
James N. Chambers SE¼-S8; 12-13-1811
Samuel Bealor SW¼-S8; 3-1-1814
Page 106.   T 15 N, R 13 E of 2nd P.M.
William McLucas NE¼-S9; 3-17-1813
James McGrew NW¼-S9; 12-2-1811
Peter Little SE¼-S9; 10-24-1811
Silas Dunn SW¼-S9; 12-20-1813
William Beeson NE¼-S10; 11-2-1811
Daniel Moland NW¼-S10; 11-20-1811
Wright Lancaster SE¼-S10; 10-24-1811
Jacob Little SW¼-S10; 10-24-1811   John Spahr
John Conely W½-S11; NE¼-S11; 4-2-1812. See Vol.II, p.198-199,
John Spake SE¼-S11; 11-27-1811. Vol.II, p.198-199, says Spahr &
     gives the rest of S11, 4-2-1812
John Jones NE¼-S12; 11-2-1816. Rel. E½ to Spencer Stephens,
William Black SE¼-S12; 2-2-1816   8-27-1827
John Doddridge W½-S12; 12-25-1813
Henry Hendrix NE¼-S13; 8-26-1815
David Day SE¼-S13; 8-26-1815
Phineas McCray W½-S13; 9-24-1813
John Henwood NE¼-S14; 12-24-1812

John Spake W½-S14; 11-27-1811. Vol.II, p.199, says Spahr
Wright Lancaster NE¼-S15; 10-24-1811
John Post E½ & W½-NW¼-S15; 10-24-1811
Philip Doddridge SE¼-S15; 4-20-1814
John Post SW¼-S15; 12-13-1811
David Stephenson NE¼-S17; 3-4-1814
George Farlow NW¼-S17; 2-1-1814
John Miller SE¼-S17; 4-14-1814
Stephen Griffith SW¼-S17; 12-2-1817
Richard Hendray NE¼-S18; 10-30-1811
John Fix NW¼-S18; 10-28-1811
Samuel Brown SE¼-S18; 9-13-1813
David Lamme SW¼-S18; 10-24-1811. Vol.II, p.199 says Lamb
George Miller NE¼-S19; 1-15-1814
Thomas Bond NW¼-S19; 10-24-1811. Vol.II, p.199 says Beard
Isaac Miller SE¼-S19; 1-15-1814
John Dodson SW¼-S19; 12-2-1816
John Simmons & George Farlow NE¼-S20; 12-23-1812
Thomas Beard NW¼-S20-12-12-1811
Joseph Flint SE¼-S20; 10-24-1811
William Montgomery SW¼-S20; 1-11-1814
Jonathan Gilbert NE¼-S21; 11-21-1811
Samuel Sterrett NW¼-S21; 10-24-1811
Thomas Beard & Jacob Weymire SE¼-S21; 3-5-1812
Philip Fox SW¼-S21; 10-24-1811
David Jenkins E½-S22; 4-2-1812
William Walter NW¼-S22; 4-20-1814
Thomas Endley & Edward Hunt SW¼-S22; 2-23-1814. Vol.II, p.200 says
John Shetterly & George Miser NE¼-S23; 1-3-1818 Endsley
John Spahr NW¼-S23; 12-13-1813
John Benefield SE¼-S23; 4-12-1814
William Jarrett NE¼-S24; 4-23-1817. Vol.II, p.200 says Garrett
John Doddridge NW¼-S24; 4-20-1814
James McClain SE¼-S24; 11-16-1816 1829
Smith Lane SW¼-S24; 1-7-1817. Rel. E½. To John Hunsicker.1-7-

Page 105. T 15 N, R 13 E of 2nd P.M. UNION CO.

Jonathan Hill NE¼-S25; 3-2-1814
Robert Benefield NW¼-S25; 4-15-1814
John Shelby SE¼-S25; 3-14-1814
Ephraim Brown SW¼-S25; 7-2-1814

Page 106. T 15 N, R 13 E of 2nd P.M. WAYNE CO.

Robert Benefield NE¼-S26; 4-12-1814
Simeon Summers NW¼-S26; 8-26-1815
Jonas Huffman SE¼-S26; 11-17-1814
John Summers SW¼-S26; 9-8-1815

Page 107. T 15 N, R 13 E of 2nd P.M.

Platt Montgomery NE¼-S27; 4-15-1814
Josias Lambert NW¼-S27; 1-3-1814
John Simmons SE¼-S27; 9-23-1814
William Dyer SW¼-S27; 12-28-[illegible]
Thomas Clark NE¼-S28; 8-12-1813
John Fox NW¼-S28; 10-24-1811
Joseph Hoult SE¼-S28; 7-8-1816
William Shaw SW¼-S28; 10-24-1811

Robert Montgomery NE¼-S29; 6-11-1812
Robert Montgomery NW¼-S29; 3-19-1814
Joseph Watts SE¼-S29; 10-24-1811
Matthias Parson SW¼-S29; 8-19-1812
Asa Gruwell NE¼-S30; 1-6-1814
Jonathan Higgins NW¼-S30; 12-28-1816. Rel. Vol.II, p.200 shows final certif. for it
Hugh Moore SE¼-S30; 3-20-1817
Ralph Wright SW¼-S30; 12-7-1811

Page 107. T 15 N, R 13 E of 2nd P.M. **FAYETTE CO.**

Samuel Grewell NE¼-S31; 11-11-1811
John Beard NW¼-S31; 10-24-1811
John Hardin SE¼-S31; 10-24-1811
Eliakim Harding SW¼-S31; 3-12-1812
John Sharp NE¼-S32; 10-24-1811. Vol.II, p.201 looks like Tharp
William P. Smith NW¼-S32; 2-7-1812
Matthias Dawson SE¼-S32; 10-24-1811
Thomas Sloo, Jr. SW¼-S32; 10-28-1811
Jonathan Higgins NE¼-S33; 9-6-1813
Jonathan Coleman NW¼-S33; 12-6-1813
James Parker SE¼-S33; 9-6-1813
Nathan Roysdam SW¼-S33; 12-21-1813. Vol.II, p.201 says Roysdon
John Steeth NE¼-S34; 10-8-1814. Vol.II, p.201 says Sleeth
Abraham Vanmeter NW¼-S34; 6-14-1814
Abraham Vanmeter SE¼-S34; 6-26-1816
Abraham Vanmater SW¼-S34; 6-14-1814
Robert Huffman NE¼-S35; 11-17-1814
Andrew Huffman NW¼-S35; 12-3-1814
Willis P. Miller SE¼-S35; 10-21-1815
John M. Laycon SW¼-S35; 10-30-1815. Vol.II, p.201 says Layson

Page 107. T 15 N, R 13 E of 2nd P.M. **UNION CO.**

John Doddridge NE¼-S36; 6-18-1814
Jacob Helmick SE¼-S36; 8-2-1818
John Doddridge W½-S36; 4-28-1814

Page 108. T 16 N, R 13 E of 2nd P.M. **WAYNE CO.**

Jonathan Cloud NE¼-S1; 9-3-1814
John Harvey, Sr. NW¼-S1; 10-4-1815
William Pike SE¼-S1; 8-19-1814
Eli Brown SW¼-S1; 5-16-1816
Absalom Williams NE¼-S2; 10-3-1814
Isaac Mendenhall NW¼-S2; 5-17-1814
William Frazier SE¼-S2; 12-16-1815
Nathan Hill SW¼-S2; 2-5-1818
Peter Hoover NE¼-S3; 10-24-1811. Vol.II, p.201 says Henry
John Fincher NW¼-S3; 10-24-1811
Peter Hoover SW¼-S3; 10-24-1811
John Fincher E½-NE¼-S4; 9-15-1817
Jane Fincher W½-NE¼-S4; 6-25-1824
Samuel Leonard NW¼-S4; 1-3-1816. Rel. E½. To James Ridge, 2-11-1831
William Fincher SE¼-S4; 10-24-1811
John Harvey, Jr. SW¼-S4; 10-4-1815
Samuel Leonard NE¼-S5; 12-2-1816
John Harvey NW¼-S5; 10-24-1811
Joseph Warrell SE¼-S5; 10-24-1811

Samuel Leonard NE¼-S6; 10-24-1811
Samuel Boyd NW¼-S6; 10-24-1811
Andrew Wood SE¼-S6; 10-24-1811
Walter Buel SW¼-S6; 10-24-1811
Samuel Woods NE¼-S7; 10-24-1811
Henry Brown NW¼-S7; 10-24-1811
Samuel Woods SE¼-S7; 11-23-1811
John Irwin SW¼-S7; 12-2-1816
William Smith NE¼-S8; 12-30-1811
James Brown NW¼-S8; 10-24-1811
Michael Swope SE¼-S8; 5-27-1816
Robert Lovell SW¼-S8; 10-24-1811
Elijah Fox NE¼-S9; 10-24-1811
William Hosier NW¼-S9; 9-27-1815
James Boyd SE¼-S9; 10-24-1811
James Boyd SW¼-S9; 8-18-1817. Rel. W½. Vol.II, p.202 shows he re-entered the W½, 6-21-1832
William Hozier NE¼-S10; 8-12-1814
James John Fox NW¼-S10; 10-24-1811. Vol.II, p.202 says John Joseph Fox
John Pegg SE¼-S10; 8-12-1814
Henry Hoover SW¼-S10; 11-8-1811
John Garrett NE¼-S11; 5-4-1815
Josiah Bundy NW¼-S11; 5-28-1815
John Harvey, Sr. SE¼-S11; 10-4-1815. Vol.II, p.202 omits Sr.
Robert Gilbraith SW¼-S11; 5-4-1815
John Garrett NE¼-S12; 5-4-1815
Nathan Garrett NW¼-S12; 5-26-1817
Joseph Cox SE¼-S12; 9-20-1814
William Hosier SW¼-S12; 1-22-1817
Jonathan Jessup NE¼-S13; 9-6-1814
Nathan Cook & Isaac Martin NW¼-S13; 7-18-1816
William Cummings SE¼-S13; 12-11-1811
William Hosier SW¼-S13; 9-12-1816
Nathan Hill NE¼-S14; 7-10-1816
Robert Hill NW¼-S14; 9-27-1815
Charles Cordon, Sr. SE¼-S14; 11-9-1816. Rel. W½.To Bazel Wingfield, 4-6-1827. Vol.II, p.203 omits Sr., and says Winfield
Susan Reed SW¼-S14; 7-17-1815
William Hosier NE¼-S15; 11-1-1814
Joseph Evans NW¼-S15; 12-16-1811
Jacob Reed SE¼-S15; 10-24-1814
John Harvey SW¼-S15; 4-12-1814

Page 109. T 16 N, R 13 E of 2nd P.M.

Richard Leason NE¼-S17; 3-7-1816. Middle initial L.
Thomas J. Worman NW¼-S17; 10-24-1811
Joseph Shank & William Larrue SE¼-S17; 5-27-1816
James Daugherty SW¼-S17; 5-27-1816
John McKee E½-S18; 10-24-1811
Asa Provo NW¼-S18; 1-24-1814
David Embree SW¼-S18; 10-28-1811. Vol.II, p.203 says Davis
William Thorn NE¼-S19; 10-28-1811
William Thorn NW¼-S19; 10-24-1811
James Parsonett & Jonathan S. Davis SE¼-S19; 4-11-1816
William Thorn SW¼-S19; 10-24-1811

Isaac Willets NE¼-S20; 4-10-1816
Isaac Morris NW¼-S20; 8-30-1815
Benjamin Morgan SE¼-S20; 9-27-1815
Josiah Bundy SW¼-S20; 10-28-1815
Lewis Hozier NE¼-S21; 10-24-1811
Isaac Willets NW¼-S21; 10-24-1811   Thorn, assee.
William Sanders SE¼-S21; 10-28-1811.Vol.II,p.203 says to William
William Rooker SW¼-S21; 10-28-1811.Vol.II,p.203 says to William
Ezekiel Commons NE¼-S22; 8-12-1814   Thorn, assee.
John Beck NW¼-S22; 10-24-1811
George Brown SE¼-S22; 8-25-1815
Samuel Boyd SW¼-S22; 10-24-1811
John Harvey, Jr. NE¼-S23; 8-31-1816. Vol.II, p.203 omits Jr.
Nathan Commons NW¼-S23; 12-11-1817. Rel. E½. To Isaac Martin,
Zachariah Hiatt SE¼-S23; 8-20-1816   11-3-1827
Ethan A. Brown SW¼-S23; 1-20-1818. Rel. To Richard C. Parker,
John Harvey NE¼-S24; 10-24-1811   12-15-1826
Nathan Hill NW¼-S24; 10-3-1814
William Harvey SE¼-S24; 10-24-1811
Greenbury Cornelius SW¼-S24; 12-11-1813
Robert Blair NE¼-S25; 7-1-1812
William Irwin NW¼-S25; 10-24-1811
Isaac Julian SE¼-S25; 10-24-1811
John McIntire SW¼-S25; 10-24-1811
Isaac Julian NE¼-S26; 7-8-1817
Henry Harvey NW¼-S26; 3-4-1817
John McIntire SE¼-S26; 12-7-1812
Achillis Morris SW¼-S26; 8-30-1817. Rel. W½ to Christian Ray,
     6-6-1827; E½ to Peter Deardorf, 6-16-1827
John Harvey E½-NE¼-S27; 6-12-1824
Daniel Stone W½-NE¼-S27; 12-10-1816
Reuben Waggoner NW¼-S27; 4-1-1814
Joel Reed SE¼-S27; 12-25-1816
Isaac Hicks SW¼-S27; 1-9-1815
Isaac Willets NE¼-S28; 11-4-1811
Isaac Willets NW¼-S28; 10-24-1811
John Woodward SE¼-S28; 8-16-1814
Edward Drury SW¼-S28; 10-24-1811
John Lacy NE¼-S29; 9-20-1814
Richard Wharton SW¼-S29; 8-15-1814
George Ish SE¼-S29; 1-28-1815
Aaron Manan NW¼-S29; 8-15-1814
Samuel C. Vance NE¼-S30, 4-11-1818. Rel. E½ to Thomas Brumfield,
     10-18-1827; W½ to John Lacy, 3-7-1828
Johosaphat Morris NW¼-S30; 10-28-1811. Vol.II, p.204 says to
William G. Reynolds SE¼-S30; 1-20-1816   William Thorn, assee.
Andrew Woods SW¼-S30; 10-24-1811
George Shotridge NE¼-S31; 4-20-1812
Samuel Beeler NW¼-S31; 10-24-1811
Joseph Hobson SE¼-S31; 6-22-1812
Samuel Beeler SW¼-S31; 10-24-1811
John Cawnover NE¼-S32; 1-28-1815
Jacob Oldakers NW¼-S32; 1-23-1815   George Ish SW¼-S32;
Edward Drury SE¼-S32; 10-28-1811   5-11-1812

Page 110. T 16 N, R 13 E of 2nd P.M.

Samuel Shortridge NE¼-S33; 12-10-1816
William Campbell NW¼-S33; 10-24-1811
Samuel Shortridge SE¼-S33; 9-9-1816
Henry Bryan SW¼-S33; 12-2-1816
James Tucker NE¼-S34; 11-7-1814
Samuel C. Vance NW¼-S34; 4-11-1818
Michael Hooke & George Miser SE¼-S34; 11-26-1817
Runnels Wright SW¼-S34; 1-14-1814
John Harvey NE¼-S35; 10-24-1811
Susannah Booker E½-NW¼-S35; 10-28-1824
Samuel Crawford W½-NW¼-S35; 11-29-1816.Rel. To Daniel Welshhous,
Thomas McCoy SE¼-S35; 10-24-1811   2-1-1828
Thomas McCoy SW¼-S35; 10-26-1816
Harman Waivam NE¼-S36; 1-31-1812. Vol.II, p.305 says Wairam
Henry Bryan NW¼-S36; 10-24-1811
Robert Black SE¼-S36; 12-10-1813
Henry Bryan SW¼-S36; 10-24-1811

Page 110. T 17 N, R 13 E of 2nd P.M.

Pleasant Winston NE¼-S1; 11-15-1817. Rel. E½ to William Fowler,
    9-14-1827; W½ to Joseph Boon, 8-29-1828
William Ballenger NW¼-S1; 10-24-1816
Seth Way SE¼-S1; 6-27-1817
Thomas Way E½-SW¼-S1; 11-5-1831
Thomas Lilly W½-SW¼-S1; 10-20-1820
Joshua Ballenger E½-S2; 11-7-1815
Benjamin Hutchens E½-NW¼-S2; 11-22-1830
Benjamin Hutchens W½-NW¼-S2; 10-25-1830
Luke Dillon SW¼-S2; 1-18-1815
Jesse Dillon NE¼-S3; 1-18-1815   7-25-1815
Joseph Lewis NW¼-S3; 1-8-1817.Vol.II, p.305 says to John Bailey,
Thomas Lamb SE¼-S3; 5-17-1814. Rel. E½. To John Bailey, 12-10-.
John Bailey SW¼-S3;9-1-1817. Rel.W½. To Thomas Lindsey,   1829
Charles Williams E½-NE¼-S4; 3-21-1831   11-24-1831
Jonathan Williams W½-NE¼-S4; 5-1-1829
Henry Steddam NW¼-S4; 3-26-1818
John W. Berry SW¼-S4; 9-2-1817
James Farrall NE¼-S5; 8-15-1816
Jacob French NW¼-S5; 8-12-1812
Hezekiah Manning SE¼-S5; 3-27-1816
John Mounts SW¼-S5; 8-22-1816
Solomon Hodgson NE¼-S6; 11-15-1816
William Williams NW¼-S6; 3-30-1816
Dilwin Bales SE¼-S6; 5-29-1816
Nathan Williams SW¼-S6; 8-30-1816. Rel. W½
Dilwin Bales NE¼-S7; 12-5-1815
James Moore SE¼-S7; 1-26-1816
William Murray NE¼-S8; 8-22-1816. Rel. E½. To Bordan Hanson,
John Williams E½-SE¼-S8; 6-10-1831   7-5-1831
Levi Cox W½-SE¼-S8; 6-10-1831
Henry Franch SW¼-S8; 11-25-1811
William P. Smith NW¼-S8; 12-24-1813
Daniel Bradberry E½-NE¼-S9; 12-31-1828   James Porter NW¼-S9;
Jonathan Macy W½-NE¼-S9; 8-26-1831   10-25-1814

Page 111. T 17 N, R 13 E of 2nd P.M.

Daniel Bradberry E½-SE¼-S9; 12-31-1828
William Elliott W½-SE¼-S9; 8-29-1831
Stephen Cox E½ & W½-SW¼-S9; 6-10-1831
William Elliott NE¼-S10; 2-12-1816
John Cain NW¼-S10; 8-2-1814
William Demitt SE¼-S10; 1-20-1815
Samuel Smith SW¼-S10; 12-8-1813. Rel. E½. To John Gardner, 1-14-
James Ballenger E½-NE¼-S11; 12-23-1826   1830
Henry Study W½-NE¼-S11; 11-25-1829
Henry Oler NW¼-S11; 8-5-1814
Benjamin Ballenger E½-SE¼-S11; 2-27-1826
James Harris W½-SE¼-S11; 10-25-1831
Joshua Albertson SW¼-S11; 1-7-1815
William Dimmitt NE¼-S12; 12-21-1814
Henry Study E½-NW¼-S12; 1-31-1821
Henry Study W½-NW¼-S12; 5-28-1823
Moses Martindale SW¼-S12; 9-15-1817
William Underhill NE¼-S13; 10-22-1814. Vol.II, p.207 gives NW¼
    instead; and gives NE¼ to Daniel Clark, 10-25-1811
Samuel Jones SE¼-S13; 12-2-1816
David Brown SW¼-S13; 3-20-1817
William Burroughs NE¼-S14; 8-6-1816.Rel. E½ to John Baldwin, Sr.,
    3-16-1826; W½ to Isaac Baldwin, 11-14-1827
George Renberger NW¼-S14; 10-21-1817
Thomas Nixon SE¼-S14; 4-25-1816
Henry Willitts E½ & W½-SW¼-S14; 6-7-1827
Thomas Dimmitt NE¼-S15; 12-27-1816
Archibald Beall NW¼-S15; 3-21-1814
Elias Bradfield E½-SE¼-S15; 12-15-1830
Samuel Walcup W½-SE¼-S15; 11-16-1830
Andrew Hoover SW¼-S15; 4-21-1815
Josias Lambert NE¼-S17; 9-22-1815
Michael Fouts NW¼-S17; 11-15-1811
Samuel McCollough SE¼-S17; 4-30-1816.Rel. E½. To John McCullough,
Isaac Harvey SW¼-S17; 11-2-1811   8-29-1831
Samuel McCollough NE¼-S18; 4-30-1816. Rel. W½. To Samuel 1832
Bonham Runyan SE¼-S18; 3-15-1816   McCullough, 1-23-
James Hill NE¼-S19; 5-29-1815
John Small S½-E½-NW¼-S19; 5-30-1832
John Mell W½-NW¼-S19; 10-6-1820
James Porter SE¼-S19; 11-8-1811
Matthias Pearson, Jr. SW¼-S19; 8-20-1816
John Moore NE¼-S20; 4-14-1815
Jacob Hughell SE¼-S20; 2-6-1812
Jacob Galycan W½-S20; 10-28-1811.Vol.II, p.208 says NW¼ to Jacob
    Galyean & SW¼ to Thomas Galyean
Josiah Bradbury NE¼-S21; 7-9-1814
Jonathan Shaw, Jr. NW¼-S21; 8-30-1815. Vol.II, p.208 says Sr.
William Young SE¼-S21; 7-6-1815
David Bradbury SW¼-S21; 3-23-1814
John Sutton NE¼-S22; 9-28-1818   1-26-1831
Aaron R. Sayres NW¼-S22; 2-3-1817. Rel. E½. To Michael Wolf,
Joshua Benny SE¼-S22; 2-1-1816. Vol.II, p.208 says Binney

Enos Neal SW¼-S22; 1-11-1817
Henry Garrett NE¼-S23; 12-2-1815
William Bulla NW¼-S23; 2-3-1815
William Fox SE¼-S23; 10-24-1811
James Spray SW¼-S23; 12-11-1815
          Page 112. T 17 N, R 13 E of 2nd P.M.
Jeremiah Elliott & Abraham Elliott NE¼-S24; 10-24-1811
Henry Garrett NW¼-S24; 10-24-1811
James O. Dill SE¼-S24; 11-9-1811. Vol.II, p.208 says Dell
James O. Dill SW¼-S24; 10-24-1811. Vol.II, p.208 says Dell
Stephen Gullefer NE¼-S25; 10-23-1812
Abraham Elliott NW¼-S25; 2-19-1812. Vol.II, p.208 adds Jr.
Nathan Hill SE¼-S25; 10-20-1814
Abel Jenny NE¼-S26; 10-24-1811
Thomas Hatfield NW¼-S26; 3-26-1812
James Martindale SE¼-S26; 10-24-1811
Jonas Hatfield SW¼-S26; 10-24-1811
Samuel Evans NE¼-S27; 9-6-1817
Enos Neal NW¼-S27; 1-11-1817. Vol.II, p.208 says Peal
Miles Dimmitt SE¼-S27; 12-27-1816
Mason Fithian SW¼-S27; 10-16-1817
William Bulla NE¼-S28; 2-3-1815. Rel. E½ to Jesse Martindale,
   11-26-1825; W½ to Ezekial Bradbury, 1-5-1828
Caleb Morris NW¼-S28; 5-18-1815
Mills Murphy SE¼-S28; 2-3-1815. Vol.II, p.209 says Miles
Nathan Morris SW¼-S28; 5-18-1815
James O. Dell NE¼-S29; 10-24-1811
John Martindale NW¼-S29; 10-24-1811
Jeremiah Cox SE¼-S29; 10-24-1811
John Harvey SW¼-S29; 10-24-1811
Robert Ewing NE¼-S30; 10-24-1811
William Martindale NW¼-S30; 7-10-1816
Samuel Baldridge SE¼-S30; 12-2-1816
Hugh Allen SW¼-S30; 6-5-1812   Eli Frazier SW¼-S36;
Ethan Stone NE¼-S31; 10-28-1811   10-10-1816
James Wilcox NW¼-S31; 10-27-1817
Peter Cossairt SE¼-S31; 2-6-1812
James Ralston SW¼-S31; 9-24-1817. Rel. W½. To Peter Runyan,
Nathaniel Leonard NW¼-S32; 4-6-1814   5-26-1829
John Scott SE¼-S32; 3-25-1812
Ephraim Clark SW¼-S32; 10-16-1812
Cornelius Rutliff NE¼-S33; 2-3-1815. Vol.II, p.209 says Ratliff
William Steel NW¼-S33; 4-8-1818
David Hoover, son of Jacob SE¼-S33; 10-26-1816
John Scott SW¼-S33; 10-9-1815
Thomas Kersey NE¼-S34; 12-12-1811
David Peacock NW¼-S34; 11-18-1817. Rel. W½. To David Peacock,
Eli Milliken SE¼-S34; .12-12-1811   12-10-1829
John Foland SW¼-S34; 7-6-1814   Cornelius Ratliff NW¼-S36;
James Martindale NE¼-S35; 10-24-1811   10-21-1814
Peter Quakenbush NW¼-S35; 10-24-1811 Eli Frazier SE¼-S36;9-20-
Jesse Bond SE¼-S35; 6-10-1814   1816. Rel.W½/ To Wil-
Jacob Julien SW¼-S35; 10-24-1811   liam M. Doughty,1-14-
Joseph Thornborough NE¼-S36; 7-31-1816   1830

Page 113. T 18 N, R 13 E of 2nd P.M.
Joseph Hollingsworth W½-NW½-S2; 10-10-1818
Jesse Cox SW½-S2; 10-16-1817
Hugh Botkin NE½-S3; 9-29-1817. Rel. E½. To Hugh Botkin, 7-4-1831
Stephen Brewer E½-NW½-S3; 1-17-1831
Joshua Wright & James Wright SE½-S3; 9-20-1817
Thomas Cox E½-SW½-S3; 2-2-1829
Benjamin Cox W½-SW½-S3; 2-2-1829
Achillis Morris NW½-S4; 8-30-1817. Rel.
Joseph Macy S½-SE½-S5; 3-28-1832
William Smith W pt.-S5; Fr.S6; 5-8-1817
Isaac Barnes Fr.S7; 7-6-1815
Cornelius Shane NE½-S8; 7-6-1815
John E. Hodge NW½-S8; 7-6-1815
Thomas Crawford SE½-S8; 9-30-1816
William Blount SW½-S8; 4-10-1815
John Cox NE½-S9; 9-14-1818
Charles McMannus NW½-S9; 12-3-1817. Rel.
William Smith SE½-S9; 4-7-1818. Rel. E½
Achillis Morris SW½-S9; 8-30-1817. Rel. E½
Ephraim D. Williams NE½-S10; 11-7-1817   Rel. E½
Joseph Thornburgh, Sr. & Morgan Thornburgh NW½-S10; 9-26-1817. /
Thomas Biggs SE½-S10; 11-20-1817. Rel. W½ to Joseph Hollings
Seth Rodibough SW½-S10; 2-23-1818   worth, 4-4-1831
Daniel Jones E½-S11; 6-4-1818
Joseph Hollingsworth NW½-S11; 6-3-1818
Moses Martindale SW½-S11; 9-15-1817. Rel. W½. To Christen Edman,
Thomas Phillips NE½-S12; 7-21-1819   7-1-1831
James Burns NW½-S12; 9-15-1817
Josiah Rogers SE½-S12; 6-20-1818. Vol.II, p.211 says Isaiah
Joseph Rogers, Jr. SW½-S12; 6-4-1818. Vol.II, p.211 omits Jr.
Martin Hardwick W½-NE½-S13; 1-10-1831
Reuben Norcross NW½-S13; 6-8-1818
Jeremiah Kirkling W½-SE½-S13; 1-2-1832
Moses Martindale SW½-S13; 9-15-1817
William Peacock NE½-S14; 12-22-1818
Samuel Rogers NW½-S14; 7-21-1819. Rel.
Moses Martindale SE½-S14; 9-2-1817. Rel. W½
Page 114. T 18 N, R 13 E of 2nd P.M.
Jonathan Cox NW½-S15; 10-16-1817
Jesse Cox SE½-S15; 10-16-1817. Rel. W½ to William Cox, 1-3-1832
Jonathan Cox SW½-S15; 11-5-1817
James Malcom NE½-S17; 10-12-1816
Job Huddeston NW½-S17; 5-3-1815
Amy Hall SE½-S17; 10-11-1815. Rel. E½. (?) W½ to Thomas Worth,
David Moore SW½-S17; 5-4-1816   9-26-1827
John Jones Fr.S18; 5-3-1815
Page 114. T 18 N, R 13 E of 2nd P.M.   **WAYNE CO.**
John Jordan Fr.S19; 4-21-1815
William Fife NE½-S20; 1-7-1817
Jonathan Thornburgh E½-NW½-S20; 1-19-1829
John Jordan W½-NW½-S20; 2-17-1818
William Barnes SE½-S20; 5-17-1814   3-31-1829
George Hobson SW½-S20; 1-31-1816. Rel. W½. To George Hobson,

Thomas Marshall NE¼-S21; 10-7-1815
Thomas Crawford NW¼-S21; 9-25-1815
Elihu Swain SE¼-S21; 9-25-1815
Samuel Baldridge SW¼-S21; 8-4-1814
Charles W. Starr W½-S22; 1-11-1819. Rel. W½-SW¼ to Isaiah Osburn,
    12-10-1827; E½-SW¼ to Elihu Swain, Jr., 1-22-1829; W½-NW¼ to
    Aaron Marshill, 1-29-1829; E½-NW¼ to William Cox, 11-5-1829
Joseph Jackson W½-NE¼-S22; 6-1-1831
Josiah Johnson W½-SE¼-S22; 5-1-1829
Isaac Mills NE¼-S23; 9-23-1816
Obed Ward E½-NW¼-S23; 5-21-1830
John Mills SE¼-S23; 9-4-1816
Landlott McJunkins E½-NE¼-S24; 10-14-1830
William Fowler W½-NE¼-S24; 1-10-1831
Obed Ward W½-NW¼-S24; 11-18-1830
Denson Hutchens E½-SE¼-S24; 2-7-1831
James Cook W½-SE¼-S24; 3-28-1828
William Taylor E½-SW¼-S24; 8-12-1830
Jonathan Hutchins W½-SW¼-S24; 11-30-1828
William Cook NE¼-S25; 8-11-1817. Rel. W½. To Cornelius Cook,
Cornelius Cook E½-NW¼-S25; 9-15-1831   5-20-1828
John Meek W½-NW¼-S25; 5-10-1830
William Ladd E½-SE¼-S25; 11-25-1829
William Ladd W½-SE¼-S25; 12-3-1830
Henry Hollingsworth E½ & W½-SW¼-S25; 9-28-1829
William Burroughs NE¼-S26; 8-6-1816
Jesse Baldwin SE¼-S26; 5-22-1819
Obed Ward E½-SW¼-S26; 5-19-1829
Thomas Ratcliff W½-SW¼-S26; 7-1-1831
Hervey Coffin E½-NE¼-S27; 11-19-1831
Zachariah Hodson W½-NE¼-S27; 6-12-1829
William Lock NW¼-S27; 12-3-1818
Zachariah Hodson W½-SE¼-S27; 6-12-1829
Charles W. Starr SW¼-S27; 1-7-1819. Rel. W½ to Joshua Johnson,
    3-29-1828; E½ to Samuel Moore, 2-1-1830. Vol.II, p.214 says
Isaac Mills NE¼-S28; 11-11-1814   Josiah Johnson
John Bailey NW¼-S28; 4-15-1814
Samuel Moore SE¼-S28; 1-13-1816
Henry Mills & Moses Mills SW¼-S28; 11-11-1814   12-19-1826
Robert Canaday NE¼-S29; 10-28-1815. Rel. W½. To Robert Canaday,
Nathan Stalker NW¼-S29; 8-30-1817. Rel. E½. To Miles Marshill,
    1-1-1829
              Page 115. T 18 N, R 13 E of 2nd P.M.
Richard Williams SE¼-S29; 8-12-1814
William Blunt SW¼-S29; 3-3-1814
Walter Thornburgh NE¼-S30; 12-10-1814
Richard Mills SE¼-S30; 9-7-1815
John Gwin & Seth Mills W½-S30; 11-23-1814
David Osborn NE¼-S31; 9-7-1815
Jesse Greenstreet NW¼-S31; 8-17-1815
Jesse Pugh SE¼-S31; 10-2-1815
Jason Howell SW¼-S31; 3-4-1817
Jesse Willis NE¼-S32; 9-20-1815. Rel. E½. To Jonathan Macy,
William Blunt NW¼-S32; 4-15-1814   8-22-1827

James Warren SE¼-S32; 9-7-1815
James Warren SW¼-S32; 11-8-1813
John Moffitt NE¼-S33; 6-23-1819.Rel. To Caleb Cowgill, 1-30-1832
John Canaday NW¼-S33; 11-15-1816
Daniel Jones E½-SE¼-S33; 2-15-1831
Azariah Williams W½-SE¼-S33; 5-20-1831
Hezekiah Williams SW¼-S33; 6-28-1814
John Haworth & Archelaus Elmore N½-S34; 8-23-1817
Samuel Jay SE¼-S34; 8-23-1817
John Davis SW¼-S34; 8-13-1817
Charles W. Starr NE¼-S35; 1-7-1819
Spencer Elliott E½-NW¼-S35; 5-30-1831
William Riley W½-NW¼-S35; 11-8-1831
Eli Gapen SE¼-S35; 12-1-1815
Benjamin Hutchins E½-SW¼-S35; 10-25-1830
George D. McPherson W½-SW¼-S35; 11-22-1830
James Hollingsworth E½-NE¼-S36; 11-28-1829
James Newton Ladd W½-NE¼-S36; 11-20-1828
Abraham Elliott NW¼-S36; 10-2-1816
Jacob Study SE¼-S36; 12-3-1818
Nathan Reily SW¼-S36; 10-24-1816

Page 115. T 19 N, R 13 E of 2nd P.M. **RANDOLPH CO.**

Jeremiah Rinard NE¼-S3; 3-24-1818
Zachariah Puckett NW¼-S3; 4-7-1819
Uriah Moorman E½-NE¼-S4; 5-2-1825
Isaac Moor W½-SE¼-S4; 4-12-1832

Page 116. T 19 N, R 13 E of 2nd P.M.

Joseph Hollingsworth Fr.S8; W½-Fr.S9; 10-13-1819
Thomas Gillum E½-S9; 4-29-1818
Andrew Lykins SE¼-S12; 12-6-1817
Andrew Lykins NE¼-S13; 12-6-1817
Thomas Johnston W½-NW¼-S13; 2-5-1830. Vol.II, p.216 says Johnson
John Adamson NW¼-S15; 12-9-1820 -S20
William Denton N pt.-SE¼ & S pt.-SE¼/(called S½ by the Register);
11-1-1828. Vol.II, p.217 says S½-Fr.S20
John Sumwalt E½ & W½-NW¼-S21; 4-14-1820.Rel. W½. To William Hunt,
Oliver Walker SE¼-S21; 5-5-1819. Rel. E½ 7-4-1831
Oliver Walker SW¼-S21; 3-27-1819
Oliver Walker SW¼-S22; 5-5-1819. Rel.

Page 117. T 19 N, R 13 E of 2nd P.M.

Oliver Walker N½-S28; 3-27-1819. Rel. W½-NW¼
Jonas Heaton SW¼-S28; 3-27-1819. Rel. E½. To Samuel Heaton, 5-3-
1831. Vol.II, p.218 says Jonah Heaton
Benjamin F. Powers & William C. Drew S end-S32; 9-29-1817
John Jackson W½-NE¼-S33; 6-17-1819
Bazil Hunt E½-NW¼-S33; 11-2-1829
John Jackson W½-NW¼-S33; 3-13-1819
John H. Denton W½-SE¼-S33; 10-13-1829

Page 118. T 19 N, R 13 E of 2nd P.M.

Peter Botkin W½-SE¼-S34; 12-1-1831

Page 119. T 20 N, R 13 E of 2nd P.M.

Joseph K. Smith NE¼-S13; 1-1-1819
John Clark SE¼-S13; 1-8-1816

Tarleton Moorman SW¼-S13; 10-19-1816
David Fairfield, Sr. & Robert Atkinson SE¼-S14; 1-12-1819
Robinson McIntire SW¼-S14; 1-21-1819. Rel. To Walter Ruble, 6-5-
Godfrey Sumwalt Fr.S28; Fr.S21; 9-6-1820   1831
William Way NE¼-S22; 6-5-1816
Henry Way NW¼-S22; 6-5-1816
William C. Way SE¼-S22; 8-12-1817. Rel. E½. To Moorman Way, 7-5-
   1831. Vol.II, p.221 says William Way, Sr.
Henry H. Way SW¼-S22; 8-12-1817.Vol.II, p.221 says middle initial
Albert Banta E½-NE¼-S23; 2-7-1818   K.
William Diggs W½-NE¼-S23; 4-15-1818
Robinson McIntire E½-NW¼-S23; 8-13-1819
William Way, Jr. W½-NW¼-S23; 2-7-1818
Isaac Barber SE¼-S23; 6-4-1817. Vol.II, p.221 says Barker
James Moorman SW¼-S23; 11-21-1817
William Diggs, Jr. NE¼-S24; 9-27-1816
John Wright NW¼-S24; 6-10-1817
James Wright SE¼-S24; 6-10-1817. Rel. E½. Vol.II, p.221 says
William Haworth SW¼-S24; 12-7-1816   Joseph
Daniel Puckett NW¼-S25; 10-26-1818
Tarleton Moorman SW¼-S25; 4-15-1819
Thomas Puckett NE¼-S26; 10-26-1818
Paul W. Way NW¼-S26; 8-7-1818. Rel. E½. To Paul W. Way, 7-5-1831
George Hayworth SE¼-S26; 9-10-1818
John Wright SW¼-S26; 12-7-1816
Henry H. Way NE¼-S27; 10-29-1816
Jesse Greene NW¼-S27; 12-5-1816
John Ballinger SE¼-S27; 12-5-1816
Thomas Gillam SW¼-S27; 12-5-1816
William Search & Phillip Search Fr.S33; 11-20-1820
Isom Puckett E½-NE¼-S34; 4-2-1832
Isom Puckett W½-NE¼-S34; 11-20-1820
James Spray, Jr. NW¼-S34; 10-4-1817
Jesse Ballinger SE¼-S34; 6-4-1817
John Puckett SW¼-S34; 1-18-1819. Vol.II, p.222 says Joseph
          Page 120. T 20 N, R 13 E of 2nd P.M.
Jesse Moorman NE¼-S35; 4-15-1819
Joseph Crew NW¼-S36; 4-15-1819
          Page 120. T 21 N, R 13 E of 2nd P.M.
Mashack Lawellen Fr.S1; Fr.S12; 7-19-1817.Rel. Fr.S1 & E side of
Solomon Horney NW¼-S13; 12-11-1817. Rel. W½   Fr.S12
Samuel Sanders SW¼-S13; 1-19-1818. Rel.
John Armstrong, Philip Grandin, Benjamin Piatt, & John H. Piatt
   Fr.S11; N end-S14; 6-29-1818
Jacob Sanders NE¼-S23; 12-11-1817. Rel. E½
William Sanders NW¼-S26; 5-29-1818. Rel.
          Page 121. T 13 N, R 14 E of 2nd P.M.   UNION CO.
John Ward Fr.S6; 8-5-1814
John Hanna, Sr. Fr.S7; 11-11-1811. Vol.II, p.225 omits Sr.
Adam Maze, Eli Maze, & Samuel Maze Fr.S18; Fr.S19; 7-2-1812
          Page 121. T 14 N, R 14 E of 2nd P.M.
Benjamin McCarty Fr.S4; Fr.S5; 4-7-1812
Powell Scott NE¼-S6; 4-2-1817.Rel. W½. To Jacob Deboy, 9-20-1827
John Kain E½-NW¼-S6; 3-19-1823

Jacob Deboy W½-NW¼-S6; 11-13-1828
John Starr SE¼-S6; 10-25-1811
Samuel Walker SW¼-S6; 9-8-1817
John Myers NE¼-S7; 10-25-1811
George Paris NW¼-S7; 9-8-1814
John Sumey SE½-S7; 10-25-1811
William Lewis SW¼-S7; 9-2-1813
James Batton Fr.S8; 10-20-1814. Vol.II, p.225 looks like Bolton
Zachariah Furguson Fr.S17; 2-16-1815
Aaron Ashbrook NE¼-S18; 12-13-1811
Charles McGlathlen SE¼-S18; 11-23-1811
David Hollingsworth SW¼-S18; 11-23-1811
James Leviston NE¼-S19; 10-28-1811
Joshua Harlin NW¼-S19; 10-25-1811
John Morris SE½-S19; 10-25-1811. Vol.II, p.225 says Norris
Samuel Littrell SW¼-S19; 10-25-1811
George Harlan Fr.S20; Fr.S29; 12-16-1811
Whitely Wright NE¼-S30; 3-1-1817
James McKinney NW¼-S30; 9-21-1815
Joseph Keeney SE¼-S30; 12-17-1814
John Esley E½-SW¼-S30; 10-24-1817
James Noble W½-SW¼-S30; 10-1-1817
Abijah Shields Fr.S31; Fr.S32; 9-28-1816.Rel. 220 ac. off S end.
   Lots 3 & 11, SW cor.-Fr.S31 to Robert Abernathy, 12-10-1829;
   Lot 2, SE pt.-Fr.S31 to Abel Abernathy, 12-14-1829
             Page 122. T 15 N, R 14 E of 2nd P.M. Wayne Co.
Hiram Butler & Beal Butler Fr.S3; 9-28-1816
William M. Worthington NE¼-S4; 3-24-1818. Rel. E½ to Zachariah
   Dicks, 11-7-1827; W½ to Zachariah Dicks, 1-28-1829
Henry Vanmiddlesworth NW¼-S4; 3-21-1818.Rel. E¼ to Henry Wiltse,
   9-27-1829; W½ to Philip Lykins, 4-2-1832
Zachariah Dicks SE¼-S4; 12-2-1816
Thomas Cornell SW¼-S4; 2-20-1816
Henry Vanmiddlesworth NE¼-S5; 3-21-1818. Rel. W½ to Jonathan
   Wilson, 7-5-1831
Benjamin Jones NW¼-S5; 1-17-1817. Rel. E½ to Bentley Jarrett,
   5-13-1829; W½ to Bentley Jarrett, 9-15-1829
Thomas Greenstreet & John Potter E½-SE¼-S5; 9-30-1817
William Butler W½-SE¼-S5; 9-1-1817
William Junkin SW¼-S5; 12-11-1817.Rel. W½. To Jeptha Meek, 12-10-
Alexander C. Black NE¼-S6; 1-20-1816   1829
Isaac Williams NW¼-S6; 10-3-1814
John Jones, Sr. S½-S6; 1-17-1817
William Jones N½-S7; SE¼-S7; 11-2-1816. Rel. E½-NE¼. To Caleb
Hillary Jones SW¼-S7; 11-2-1816   Lewis, 7-28-1828
George Jarrett NE¼-S8; 10-20-1817
Lawrence H. Brannon NW¼-S8; 3-21-1818
Levi Jarrett SE¼-S8; 10-20-1817
Joseph Prior & Allen Prior SW¼-S8; 12-26-1817
Moses Robbins Fr.S9; Fr.S10; 7-3-1817. Rel. W½-NW¼-Fr.S9. To
   Joseph Meek, 9-15-1827. Rel. E½-NW¼-Fr.S9.To Moses Robbins,Jr.
David Railsback NE¼-S17; 12-26-1815   12-12-1827
William Jarrett NW¼-S17; 1-17-1817
Gabriel Fender SE¼-S17; 3-13-1815

Henry Long SW¼-S17; 1-13-1817
Edward Jones NE¼-S18; 1-17-1817. Vol.II, p.227 says Edmund
John Ellis NW¼-S18; 4-22-1815
Spencer Stevens SE¼-S18; 12-26-1815
Samuel Shelton SW¼-S18; 1-17-1817. Rel. W½ to Eli Jarrett, 1-12-
     1826; E½ to Alexander C. Black, 1-12-1826. Vol.II, p.227 says
     Eli Garsett
William M. Worthington N½-S19; 3-24-1818. Rel. E½-NE¼ to Samuel
     McCullough, 4-1-1828; W½-NE¼ to Adam Smith, 3-19-1828
Daniel Clevenger SE¼-S19; 2-10-1816
Jeremiah Allen SW¼-S19; 11-19-1814
Henry Long NE¼-S20; 1-13-1817
Jeremiah Allen NW¼-S20; 10-15-1816. Rel. To John Wright, 1-22-
     1831. Vol.II, p.227 shows final certif. to Allen
Benson Minor SE¼-S20; 9-29-1815
Daniel Alexander SW¼-S20; 12-7-1815
Henry Fender Fr.S21; 10-6-1813
          Page 122. T 15 N, R 14 E of 2nd P.M. Union Co.
Thomas Moffitt Fr.S28; Fr.S33; 11-5-1811
Thomas R. Chunn NE¼-S29; 1-23-1817
Henry Whittenger NW¼-S29; 7-31-1815
John Whittenger SE¼-S29; 6-11-1814
Jacob Bowman E½-SW¼-S29; 8-31-1826
Isaac Rambo W½-SW¼-S29; 11-12-1825
William M. Worthington NE¼-S30; 3-24-1818. Rel. To Elijah Young,
Joseph Shelby NW¼-S30; 12-29-1813   9-1-1827
William M. Worthington SE¼-S30; 3-24-1818. Rel. W½ to William
     Dunkin, 10-26-1827; E½ to William Wood, 11-1-1827
Joel Hill SW¼-S30; 9-19-1817
Alexander Wood, Sr. NE¼-S31; 12-24-1818
Benjamin Clark E½-NW¼-S31; 8-5-1819. Rel. To William Wood, 11-1-
Josiah Welliver W½-NW¼-S31; 6-10-1825   1827
Benjamin McCarty SE¼-S31; 4-2-1816
Jeremiah Oliver E½-SW¼-S31; 5-5-1826
John Gilliland W½-SW¼-S31; 8-19-1822
John Myers NE¼-S32; 10-25-1811
William Walker NW¼-S32; 7-14-1817. Rel. W½. To William Walker,
Samuel Stover SE¼-S32; 12-18-1811   1-24-1826
John Miller SW¼-S32; 8-27-1814
          Page 123. T 16 N, R 14 E of 2nd P.M.   WAYNE CO.
Thomas Lamb Fr.S2; Fr.S11; 11-15-1815
Patrick Moore NE¼-S3; 9-9-1817
William Rider SE¼-S3; 8-30-1817. Rel. E½. To Joseph Brown, 9-24-
Joseph Hough & Samuel Milikin SW¼-S3; 1-20-1816   1827
Joseph Hough & Samuel Milikin E½-S4; 1-20-1816
John King SW¼-S4; 4-2-1817
John Bailey NE¼-S5; 10-25-1811. Vol.II, p.228 says Henry
Joseph Holman NW¼-S5; 9-13-1815
Joseph King SE¼-S5; 1-15-1816
John Coapland SW¼-S5; 6-28-1814
Robert Gilbraith NE¼-S6; 5-4-1815
Thomas Nixon NW¼-S6; 8-12-1814
Exum Elliott SE¼-S6; 11-6-1815
Henry Bailey SW¼-S6; 3-1-1814

Joseph Holeman & Eli Overman NE¼-S7; 3-19-1812
Benjamin Mudlin NW¼-S7; 11-11-1813
Matthew Hastings SE¼-S7; 11-23-1811. Vol.II, p.228 says William
Henry Bailey SW¼-S7; 5-9-1815
Archibald Beall NE¼-S8; 10-8-1816
Daniel King NW¼-S8; 2-9-1816
Francis Culbertson SE¼-S8; 3-21-1814
Jacob Griffin SW¼-S8; 1-19-1814. Vol.II, p.228 says Graffin
Alexander McAllister NE¼-S9; 11-27-1815
William Beall NW¼-S9; 11-23-1816
James Black SE¼-S9; 7-15-1815
Joshua Eliason SW¼-S9; 3-17-1814
David Davis NW¼-S10; 12-14-1815
William Davis SE½-S10; 7-8-1817. Rel. W½. To David Vinnedge, 2-10-1827
James Black SW¼-S10; 12-10-1813
John Sutherland, William Irwin, & Thomas Sloo Fr.S14; Fr.S15;
    5-5-1812. Vol.II, p.229 says F. Sloo, Jr.
John Maxwell NE¼-S17; 10-31-1811
Nathan Garrett NW¼-S17; 10-25-1811
John Bell SE½-S17; 8-21-1812
John Harvey SW¼-S17; 8-7-1812
William Peterson NE¼-S18; 10-25-1811.Vol.II, p.229 says Patterson
James Townsend NW¼-S18; 12-12-1811
John Garrett & Robert Gilbraith SE¼-S18; 10-25-1811
Robert Harvey SW¼-S18; 10-25-1811
Jacob Sinks NE¼-S19; 10-25-1811
William Haizier NW¼-S19; 10-25-1811. Vol.II, p.229 says Hosier
Ethan Stone SE¼-S19; 10-28-1811
Nathan Overman SW¼-S19; 12-16-1811
Jacob Burnett NE¼-S20; 10-28-1811
Jacob Burnett NW¼-S20; 10-28-1811
Evins Shoemaker SE¼-S20; 9-16-1813
Israel Elliott SW¼-S20; 9-27-1813
Ewell Kendell & John Turner NE¼-S21; 1-22-1812
Eli Butler NW¼-S21; 1-31-1814
James Thompson SE¼-S21; 4-20-1817
Joseph Kibby SW¼-S21; 2-1-1814
John Smith Fr.S22; 12-11-1811
Samuel Walker Fr.S27; 9-27-1813
John Sutherland E½-NE¼-S28; 8-13-1824
John Sutherland W½-NE¼-S28; 6-16-1824
Peyton S. Symmes NW¼-S28; 10-2-1815
Jesse Thomas SE¼-S28; 11-22-1817   1828
John Lough SW¼-S28; 10-25-1816. Rel. W½. To Henry Bryan, 10-13-
            Page 124. T 16 N, R 13 E of 2nd P.M.
Samuel King NE¼-S29; 1-17-1814
James Black, Jr. NW¼-S29; 3-8-1814. Vol.II, p.229 omits Jr.
Elisha King SE¼-S29; 2-19-1814
Spencer (a free man of color) SW¼-S29; 7-15-1813. Vol.II, p.229
    gives surname Free
Christopher Roddy NE¼-S30; 7-8-1814
Robert Culbertson NW¼-S30; 1-17-1814
David Gilbraith SE¼-S30; 7-1-1813
James Junker SW¼-S30; 12-10-1813. Vol.II, p.229 says Junkin

John Gilbraith NW¼-S31; 7-1-1813
Enos Butler SE¼-S31; 9-17-1816. (Query: Amos? M.R.W.)
Lewis Thomas SW¼-S31; 12-6-1815
Spencer (a free man of color) NE¼-S32; 10-19-1815. Vol.II, p.230
gives surname Free
Joseph Aikin NW¼-S32; 7-11-1814
Enos Butler SE¼-S32; 9-17-1816. (Query: Amos? M.R.W.)
Hiram Butler SW¼-S32; 9-28-1816 1831
William Barr NE¼-S33; 4-9-1818. Rel. W½ to William H. Bundy, 7-5-
William Barr E½-NW¼-S33; 4-9-1818. Rel. To James S. Crabb, 1-28-
Moses Martindale W½-NW¼-S33; 9-15-1817 1828
Solomon Madden SE¼-S33; 11-20-1817
Henry Vanmiddlesworth SW¼-S33; 5-1-1818. Rel.
Hiram Butler & Beal Butler Fr.S34; 9-28-1816

Page 124. T 17 N, R 14 E of 2nd P.M.

George Sugent & Jonathan Hough Fr.S1; 11-11-1811. Vol.II, p.230
Abraham Hampton NE¼-S2; 7-3-1817 says Shugart
Thomas Potter NW¼-S2; 4-18-1817
Joseph Wood & Ira Hunt SE¼-S2; 3-12-1817
Abijah Jones SW¼-S2; 3-21-1814
Hartshorn White NE¼-S3; 11-30-1819
Jesse Haisley E½-NW¼-S3; 11-1-1827
Jesse Haisley W½-NW¼-S3; 11-8-1822
Tristram Croggeshall SE¼-S3; 11-25-1815
David Bowles SW¼-S3; 8-29-1817
Micajah Weesner E½-NE¼-S4; 11-10-1827
Isaac Clements W½-NE¼-S4; 10-22-1827
Sarah Ferguson E½ & W½-NW¼-S4; 11-1-1826
Micajah Weesner E½-SE¼-S4; 11-1-1827
Joseph Haisley W½-SE¼-S4; 11-8-1822
Moses Hockett E½-SW¼-S4; 6-27-1827
Moses Hockett W½-SW¼-S4; 10-19-1827
Seth Way NE¼-S5; 10-25-1811
John Tawell NW¼-S5; 11-16-1811. Vol.II, p.230 says Towel
Stephen Johnson SE¼-S5; 5-25-1815
Peter Dumont SW¼-S5; 10-28-1811. Vol.II, p.230 says to James O.
Thomas Craner NE¼-S6; 9-13-1813 Dell, 10-28-1811
Henry Way NW¼-S6; 8-2-1815
Henry Way SE¼-S6; 10-25-1811
Seth Way SW¼-S6; 9-13-1815
James Lindlay NW¼-S7; 10-25-1811
Anthony Chamness SE¼-S7; 11-2-1811
John Lewis SW¼-S7; 10-25-1811. Vol.II, p.231 says Richard Lewis
Joshua Craner NE¼-S8; 5-25-1815
William P. Smith NW¼-S8; 12-24-1813. Vol.II, p.231 says to Jacob
James Harris SE¼-S8; 4-21-1818 French, 11-22-1811
John Lewis SW¼-S8; 4-7-1815
John Phillips E½-NE¼-S9; 10-24-1827
Hesekiah Pattison W½-NE¼-S9; 11-10-1827

Page 125. T 17 N, R 14 E of 2nd P.M.

Henry Catey NW¼-S9; 8-25-1821
Nathan Jessop SE¼-S9; 9-14-1816 1-1827
Willas Whitson SW¼-S9; 1-9-1818. Rel.W½. To Owen Williams, 11-
Tristram Croggeshall NE¼-S10; 11-25-1815

Zachariah Hiatt SE¼-S10; 7-10-1817
Jacob Jessop SW¼-S10; 9-8-1817
Thomas Tharp NE¼-S11; 12-4-1811
Josiah Lamb NW¼-S11; 6-19-1815
Obediah Harris SE¼-S11; 11-7-1811
Daniel Baldwin SW¼-S11; 9-22-1813
Francis Thomas Fr.S12; 10-28-1811
Jonathan Marine Fr.S13; 2-15-1817
Jonathan Marine NE¼-S14; 10-28-1811
Thomas Baldwin NW¼-S14; 11-11-1811
John Baldwin SE¼-S14; 6-10-1811
John Baldwin SW¼-S14; 11-18-1811
Ira Hough NE¼-S15; 11-28-1816
John Scott NW¼-S15; 12-7-1816
Joseph Hallen SE¼-S15; 11-9-1811. Vol.II, p.231 says Joseph Bond
Joseph Bond SW¼-S15; 10-30-1816
John Scroggy NE¼-S17; 11-5-1817
Joseph Lewis NW¼-S17; 4-7-1817. Rel. E½. To Benjamin Satter-
Edward Bond SE¼-S17; 11-15-1817   thwaite, 12-10-1829
John Beverlin SW¼-S17; 12-28-1815
Micajah Symons NE¼-S18; 11-11-1811
Richard Lewis NW¼-S18; 10-25-1811
Joseph Evans SE¼-S18; 12-16-1811
Jesse Johnston & Joshua Murphy SW¼-S18; 11-2-1811
Joseph Evans S19; S20; 12-16-1811
Joseph Teagle NE¼-S21; 2-22-1817
Thomas T. Teagle NW¼-S21; 2-22-1817
Drury Walls & Samuel Howard SE¼-S21; 11-6-1817
Henry Hawkins SW¼-S21; 1-22-1817
William Thorn NE¼-S22; 10-25-1811
Samuel Bond NW¼-S22; 5-21-1814
Edward Bond SE¼-S22; 11-9-1811
Benjamin Evans SW¼-S22; 11-18-1811
Isaac Jessop W½-S23; 10-16-1816
Jacob Hampton E½-S23; Fr.S24; 11-28-1816
John Stedman & John Jay Fr.S26; 11-1-1817
Stephen Comer NE¼-S27; 9-8-1813
Nathan Hawkins SE¼-S27; 11-29-1813
Willis Whitson W½-S27; 10-25-1811
Isaac Jessop, Jr. NE¼-S28; 10-19-1816
Thomas Carson, Jr. NW¼-S28; 3-14-1816
Henry Hawkins SE¼-S28; 11-17-1814
William Thornborough SW¼-S28; 9-9-1816
Joseph Evans NE¼-S29; 12-16-1811
Richard W. Cheeseman NW¼-S29; 12-16-1811
Marian Nixon SE¼-S29; 5-18-1815. Vol.II, p.232 says Miriam
William Commons SW¼-S29; 10-22-1814
John McLane, Jr. NE¼-S30; 8-15-1816
John Pearson NW¼-S30; 5-16-1815
Thomas Carson SE¼-S30; 2-29-1816. Vol.II, p.232 says Cason, Jr.
Martin Martindale SW¼-S30; 12-11-1815
Archibald Beall NE¼-S31; 1-13-1816
Archibald Beall NW¼-S31; 2-10-1814
Edward Burbon SE¼-S31; 7-20-1814. Vol.II, p.232 says Benbow

David Bailey & Thomas Nixon SW¼-S31; 12-21-1813
Timothy Jessup NW¼-S32; 1-3-1815
William McClain NE¼-S32; 3-4-1817
Robert Culbertson SE¼-S32; 3-21-1814
John McClain, Sr. SW¼-S32; 2-7-1817

Page 126. T 17 N, R 14 E of 2nd P.M.

Benjamin Evans NE¼-S33; 11-18-1811
John King NW¼-S33; 3-21-1814. Rel. E½. Vol.II, p.233 says kept whole NW¼
Benjamin Harvey SE¼-S33; 1-7-1814
William McClain SW¼-S33; 11-19-1811
Michael Harvey NE¼-S34; 8-23-1813
William Harvey NW¼-S34; 8-23-1813
Benjamin Harvey SE¼-S34; 11-9-1816
Eli Overman & Reuben Overman SW¼-S34; 8-23-1813
Joseph Canby Fr.S35; 5-20-1818

Page 126. T 18 N, R 14 E of 2nd P.M. RANDOLPH CO.

Enos Hodson E½-NW¼-S1; 3-1-1828
Thomas Clevenger W½-NW¼-S1; 11-25-1823
John Melton W½-SE¼-S1; 11-25-1823
Jesse Johnston SW¼-S1; 4-29-1818. Rel. E½. To Enoch Beard, 4-16-1832
James Frazer NE¼-S2; 11-13-1816
Paul Beard W½-NW¼-S2; 9-3-1830
David Kenworthy SE¼-S2; 11-2-1816
Jesse Johnston SW¼-S2; 11-28-1816
Thomas Pierson W½-NW¼-S3; 11-23-1830
William Smith E½-SE¼-S3; 4-25-1831
William Pierson NE¼-S4; 7-29-1818
Joseph Hocket NW¼-S4; 10-25-1816
David Hammer SE¼-S4; 7-22-1818
Isaac Hocket SW¼-S4; 2-8-1817
Edward Thornburgh NE¼-S5; 8-13-1819
John Fowler E½-NW¼-S5; 7-27-1818
Edward Thornburgh W½-NW¼-S5; 9-10-1818
Stephen Hocket SE¼-S5; 2-8-1817
William Hocket SW¼-S5; 9-12-1817
Edward Thornburgh NE¼-S6; 8-12-1819
Hur Hodgson SE¼-S6; 11-3-1817. Rel. W½
Isaac Beeson E½-SW¼-S6; 11-5-1821
Hezekiah Hocket E½-S7; 10-25-1816
Samuel Smith NW¼-S7; 2-10-1818
Nathaniel Case SW¼-S7; 1-6-1818
Stephen Hocket NE¼-S8; 2-8-1817
Thomas Hester NW¼-S8; 3-25-1818
John Osburn SE¼-S8; 6-1-1815
Daniel Osburn SW¼-S8; 1-12-1818. Rel. W½. To Daniel Osburn, 8-22-1827
Barnet Frost NE¼-S9; 12-21-1816
Gideon Frazier NW¼-S9; 10-17-1815. Vol.II, p.234 says George
Isaac Cook SE¼-S9; 10-8-1816
John Johnston SW¼-S9; 3-2-1816
Paul Beard NE¼-S10; 8-9-1815
Thomas Frazier NW¼-S10; 4-29-1818
Francis Adcock SE¼-S10; 10-19-1814
Obediah Harris, Jr. SW¼-S10; 5-8-1815. Vol.II, p.234 omits Jr.

Page 127. T 18 N, R 14 E of 2nd P.M.
Jesse Johnson NE¼-S11; 10-2-1817. Rel. E½. To Silas Johnson,
Paul Beard NW¼-S11; 8-9-1815   6-30-1831
Peter Mills SE¼-S11; 2-14-1818. Rel. E½. To Daniel Shoemaker,
   7-4-1826. Vol.II, p.235 says Peter Mills, assee. of D.Shoemaker
Curtis Glenny SW¼-S11; 1-7-1815. Vol.II, p.235 says Clenny
John Boon, Jr. W½-NW¼-S12; 4-10-1828
John Ham E½-SE¼-S12; 2-12-1831. Vol.II, p.235 looks like Hain
George Dyer W½-SE¼-S12; 3-5-1832
Willis C. Willmore E½-SW¼-S12; 7-25-1831
Hur Hodson W½-SW¼-S12; 6-12-1824
Abner Cadwallader E½-NE¼-S13; 1-20-1831
Willis C. Willmore W½-NE¼-S13; 7-25-1831
Pharaoh Clark E½-NW¼-S13; 1-19-1831
Miles Rhoads W½-NW¼-S13; 1-17-1829
Peter Pearson SE¼-S13; 12-16-1817
Aaron Mills E½-SW¼-S13; 11-22-1830
Sampson Shoemaker W½-SW¼-S13; 2-16-1830   1830
James Norton NE¼-S14; 5-22-1820. Rel. E½. To Elias Norton, 1-9-
Francis Adcock NW¼-S14; 5-14-1817. Vol.II, p.235 says Travis Ad-
Tibi Merine E½-SE¼-S14;11-21-1828.Vol.II,p.235 says Ziba . cock
David M. Harris W½-SE¼-S14; 11-13-1826
William Milner SW¼-S14; 5-8-1817
Obadiah Harris, son of Obadiah NE¼-S15; 10-4-1815
Seth Cook NW¼-S15; 10-8-1816
Isaac Hutchins SE¼-S15; 12-7-1816
Susanna Moorman SW¼-S15; 7-7-1817
Mordecai Mendenhall N½-S17; 8-11-1817
Enoch Nichols SE¼-S17; 12-27-1822
John Pigg SW¼-S17; 11-7-1816. Vol.II, p.235 says Pegg
Eleazer Smith NE¼-S18; 11-7-1816
Morgam McQueary NW¼-S18; 1-6-1818
Zimri Lewis SE¼-S18; 4-17-1818
William Lewis SW¼-S18; 4-17-1818

Page 127. T 18 N, R 14 E of 2nd P.M.   WAYNE CO.
Henry Steddam NE¼-S19; 12-19-1821
Henry Steddam NW¼-S19; SE¼-S19; 12-3-1821
Samuel Steddam W½ & E½-SW¼-S19; 8-21-1829
John Poole & Micajah Henley NE¼-S20; 11-2-1816
Elijah Brock E½-NW¼-S20; 4-29-1818
William Mills, Jr. W½-NW¼-S20; 10-23-1818
Eleazer Smith SE¼-S20; 11-7-1816
Eleazer Smith E½-SW¼-S20; 11-25-1829
Valentine Pegg W½-SW¼-S20; 9-25-1830. Vol.II, p.236 says Pigg
Thomas Moorman NE¼-S21; 7-28-1814
Isaac Gardner NW¼-S21; 10-22-1814
John Pegg SE¼-S21; 8-12-1814
Thomas Tharp SW¼-S21; 7-28-1814
Thomas Moorman NE¼-S22; 2-7-1818
Huldah Way NW¼-S22; 9-9-1815
Daniel Baldwin, Jr. SE¼-S22; 3-14-1818. Rel. W½. To William
Abraham Platt E½-SW¼-S22; 1-8-1825   Price, 9-20-1827
Clark Willents W½-SW¼-S22; 2-24-1818.Vol.II, p.236 says Willcutt
Moses Parker W½-NE¼-S23; 8-2-1819

John Jeffrey E½-NE¼-S23; 10-26-1829
Stephen Williams E½-NW¼-S23; 2-7-1818
Elias Norton W½-NW¼-S23; 3-4-1819
George Wilson SE¼-S23; 6-5-1819. Rel. E½. To James Moorman, 1-18-1828
John Moorman SW¼-S23; 12-20-1817
Esau Lamb E½-NE¼-S24; 7-14-1828
Nicholas Tucker W½-NE¼-S24; 6-3-1826
Hiram Bailey E½-NW¼-S24; 11-12-1829
John Barnes W½-NW¼-S24; 9-6-1820

Page 128. T 18 N, R 14 E of 2nd P.M.

Charles Marine SE¼-S24; 8-2-1819
James Moorman SW¼-S24; 4-15-1819
John James NE¼-S25; 2-7-1818
John Fisher NW¼-S25; 1-3-1817
Thomas Knight SE¼-S25; 10-17-1814
John Peal SW¼-S25; 9-25-1816
John Robertson NE¼-S26; 10-27-1817
Edward Price SE¼-S26; 10-27-1817
William Lacy W½-S26; 10-24-1817
William Massey E½-NE¼-S27; 1-15-1822
James Brittain W½-NE¼-S27; 4-29-1829
John Kenworthy NW¼-S27; 7-2-1818
John Lacy & Thomas Mills SE¼-S27; 3-16-1818
John Potter E½-SW¼-S27; 11-29-1822
John Kenworthy W½-SW¼-S27; 11-1-1822
John Frazer NE¼-S28; 9-20-1814
Isaac Hutchins NW¼-S28; 11-21-1811
Abraham Platt E½-SE¼-S28; 1-8-1825
James Jay W½-SE¼-S28; 12-28-1821
Samuel Charles SW¼-S28; 9-30-1813
Isaiah Case NE¼-S29; 3-13-1819
Paul Way NW¼-S29; 8-11-1817. Rel. E½. To Moses Davis, 6-27-1831
Isaiah Case SE¼-S29; 11-4-1811
Lewis Stegall E½-SW¼-S29; 1-18-1825
Benjamin Brittain W½-SW¼-S29; 8-16-1828
John Pierson E½-NE¼-S30; 11-27-1819
John Green W½-NE¼-S30; 11-25-1829
John R. Kirkling E½-NW¼-S30; 12-29-1821
Elijah Wright W½-NW¼-S30; 4-9-1818
Tristram Starbuck SE¼-S30; 11-15-1816
Jeremiah Stegall E½-SW¼-S30; 1-1-1819
John Barner W½-SW¼-S30; 2-8-1820
Joseph Ladd NE¼-S31; 5-3-1815
Jonathan Stegall E½-NW¼-S31; 9-6-1826
Thornton S. Freeman W½-NW¼-S31; 11-28-1829
Benjamin Hutchens SE¼-S31; 9-10-1814
Thomas Hutchens E½ & W½-SW¼-S31; 3-21-1826
Henry Way NE¼-S32; 10-25-1811
Abel Lamax NW¼-S32; 11-11-1815
Charles Moffett SE¼-S32; 11-16-1811
James Morrison SW¼-S32; 12-20-1811
James Brittain E½-NE¼-S33; 10-28-1826
John Baldwin W½-NE¼-S33; 12-20-1817
Henry Way NW¼-S33; 1-31-1814

James Brittain E½-SE½-S33; 10-28-1826
Levi Horner W½-SE½-S33; 9-18-1818
Isaac Gardner SW½-S33; 10-22-1814
Joel Jeffery NE½-S34; 8-12-1820
Jacob Cook NW½-S34; 11-21-1817
John Jeffery SE½-S34; 8-23-1820
John Potter SW½-S34; 11-29-1822
Thomas Price NE½-S35; 10-27-1817   12-10-1829
Samuel Horner NW½-S35; 3-9-1818. Rel. W½. To Samuel Horner, Jr.,
Job Horner SE½-S35; 4-18-1817. Rel. W½. To Caleb Cowgill, 9-18-
Job. S. Jeffery SW½-S35; 4-18-1817   1827
Stephen Thomas Fr.S36; 8-12-1814
   Page 129. T 19 N, R 14 E of 2nd P.M.
Nicholas Longworth W½-NE½-S2; 6-15-1818
Albert Banta E½-NW½-S2; 4-27-1818. Rel.
William Kennedy W½-NW½-S2; 2-6-1818
Nicholas Longworth SW½-S2; 8-5-1818. Rel.
Henry Monfort NE½-S3; 4-27-1818
Jesse Brewer SE½-S3; 3-23-1818. Rel. E½
Albert Banta SW½-S3; 4-21-1818. Rel. W½
Jeremiah Meek N½-S4; 6-30-1817. Rel. W½-NE½ to Eli Edwards,
 2-15-1831; NW½ to Jacob A. White, 7-4-1831
Nicholas Longworth SW½-S4; 8-5-1818. Rel.
George W. Himes NE½-S5; 7-15-1818
Moses Brooks & Nicholas Longworth E½-NW½-S5; 7-30-1818. Rel.
Moses Brooks & Nicholas Longworth E½-SE½-S5; 7-30-1818
John Eltzroth N½-S6; 7-2-1818
Thomas Garred SE½-S6; 12-4-1819
David Heaston E½-SW½-S6; 2-15-1831
Andrew Lykins S7; 12-6-1817
Nicholas Longworth NE½-S10; 8-5-1818. Rel.
Albert Banta NW½-S10; 3-20-1818. Rel. W½
Henry Wysong SE½-S10; 4-27-1818. Rel. E½
Moses Brooks SW½-S10; 7-15-1818
   Page 130. T 19 N, R 14 E of 2nd P.M.
Nicholas Longworth NW½-S14; 4-4-1818
Albert Banta NE½-S15; 3-20-1818. Rel. E½
James Clark SE½-S15; 6-30-1818. Rel. W½ to David Frazer, 9-27-
David Frazer E½-SW½-S15; 4-22-1831   1831
James Lykins NW½-S18; 7-9-1818
   Page 131. T 19 N, R 14 E of 2nd P.M.
David Frazer E½-SE½-S21; 4-22-1831
William Johnson E½-NE½-S22; 9-11-1821
Levi Stout E½-SW½-S22; 9-22-1831
Jacob Jessop, Jr. SW½-S24; 4-21-1820. Vol.II, p.242 shows it to
Stephen Melton SE½-S27; 4-2-1818 Joseph Derickson,2-1-1837
Enoch Pilsher SW½-S27; 1-9-1817
James Abshire W½-SW½-S28; 1-13-1827
Curtis Beals E½-NW½-S29; 12-22-1831
Joseph Grass SE½-S29; 8-11-1817. Rel. E½. To James Abshire,
 1-13-1827. Vol.II, p.243 says Gass
   Page 132. T 19 N, R 14 E of 2nd P.M.
William Reece NE½-S32; 11-5-1816   Hoskins
Jonathan Haskin NW½-S32; 4-26-1818. Rel. W½. Vol.II,p.244 says

Jonathan Willis SE¼-S32; 2-12-1819
Joseph Thornburgh SW¼-S32; 8-12-1819
William Connor NE¼-S33; 1-11-1817
John Harris E½-NW¼-S33; 9-3-1830
James Abshier E½-SE¼-S33; 6-30-1819
Isaac Pearson W½-SE¼-S33; 8-14-1818
Nathan Thornburg SW¼-S33; 10-25-1816
Caleb Reece W½-NW¼-S33; 2-14-1818
John Baxter NW¼-S34; 1-9-1817. Rel. E½. To John Baxter, 7-1-1831
Abraham Hunt & Edward Hunt SW¼-S34; 10-2-1817. Rel. E½
William Benson E½-SE¼-S35; 2-19-1830
Abraham Hunt E½-SW¼-S35; 4-16-1832. See Vol.II, p.245   1831
David Frazer SW¼-S36; 7-3-1819. Rel. W½. To Henry Benson, 6-30-
      Page 133. T 20 N, R 14 E of 2nd P.M.
Jeremiah Moffitt SE¼-S3; 9-3-1818. Rel.
Charles Conway W½-SW¼-S6; 2-6-1832

      Page 134. T 20 N, R 14 E of 2nd P.M.
Jesse Murdick E½-NE¼-S9; 8-22-1823. Middle initial H.
James Maguire SE¼-S9; 11-27-1818
Nicholas Longworth SW¼-S9; 11-22-1818. Rel.   10-28-1831
Jeremiah Moffitt NE¼-S10; 4-23-1818. Rel. W½ to Seth Moffitt,
Joseph Moffitt SE¼-S10; 4-23-1818. Rel. W½. Vol.II, p.247 shows
    all to him
John Eltzroth NE¼-S13; 7-29-1818. Rel. W½ to Joseph Hickman,
    9-2-1831; E½ to Isaac Collett, 9-13-1831
Richard Mendenhall NW¼-S13; 3-24-1818
Nicholas Longworth & Griffin Taylor SW¼-S13; 4-7-1818. Rel.
Daniel Hodgson NE¼-S14; 11-19-1817   Wright,11-15-1817
Benjamin Cox NW¼-S14; 11-19-1817. Vol.II, p.248 says to Isaac
John Cox & Absalom Gray SE¼-S14, 1-7-1820. Rel. E½ to Horace
    Rawson, 8-13-1828; W½ to Simon Cox, 4-8-1831
John C. Cox SW¼-S14; 9-11-1817. Vol.II, p.248 omits C.
Samuel Charles NW¼-S15; 4-15-1818
Benjamin Cox SE¼-S15; 9-11-1817
John Dodson SW¼-S15; 7-31-1817
James Wright NE¼-S17; 12-4-1816
Solomon Wright NW¼-S17; 12-4-1816
Antipas Thomas SE¼-S17; 12-4-1816
William Haworth SW¼-S17; 10-19-1816
Shubal Ellis NE¼-S18; 11-13-1816
John Way NW¼-S18; 3-21-1820. Rel. W½
John Moore SE¼-S18; 12-7-1816
Armsby Diggs SW¼-S18; 6-26-1817
Moses Brooks & Nicholas Longworth NE¼-S19; 7-30-1818
Jesse Moorman NW¼-S19; 11-21-1817
Christopher Hiatt SE¼-S19; 9-17-1817
Moses Brooks & Nicholas Longworth SW¼-S19; 7-30-1818
John Wright NE¼-S20; 11-4-1816
David Wright NW¼-S20; 11-4-1816
Charles Conway SE¼-S20; 7-1-1817
David Stout SW¼-S20; 9-15-1817
Jonathan Hiatt NE¼-S21; 9-17-1817
John Wright & Daniel Petty NW¼-S21; 5-8-1817

Christian Shell SE¼-S21; 1-19-1818
Isaac Everett SW¼-S21; 10-22-1817
Frederick Barnard NE¼-S22; 5-8-1817
Jeremiah Moffit NW¼-S22; 12-1-1817
Page 135. T 20 N, R 14 E of 2nd P.M. 1831
Jeremiah Meek SE¼-S22; 1-30-1817. Rel. W½. to Moses Hiatt, 7-20-
Zachariah Hiatt SW¼-S22; 1-8-1818. Rel. E½ to Moses Hiatt, 1-28-
Isaac Wright NE¼-S23;9-14-1818.Rel.W½ to John Coats,8-22-1827.1830
Nicholas Longworth & Moses Brooks NW¼-S23; 1-21-1818. Rel. E½ to
Enoch Davis, 11-7-1831
Nicholas Longworth SE¼-S23; 8-5-1818. Rel.
Isaac Julian SW¼-S23; 1-19-1818.Rel. W½ to Thomas*Coats,7-5-1831
Isaac Coats E½-NE¼-S24; 2-25-1832 *middle initial W.
Richard Mendenhall SE¼-S24; 3-24-1818
Jesse Brewer NE¼-S25; 3-23-1818
Nicholas Longworth NW¼-S25; 6-15-1818. Rel. E½ to Rebecca
John Piggott W½-SE¼-S25; 11-1-1831 Pickett, 7-5-1831
Benjamin Cox SW¼-S25; 2-6-1818
Albert Banta NE¼-S26; 2-6-1818. Rel.
Rene Julian NW¼-S26; 1-19-1818 1826
Albert Banta SE¼-S26; 2-7-1818. Rel. E½ to Absalom Grey, 6-13-
Nicholas Longworth & Moses Brooks SW¼-S26; 1-21-1818. Rel.
Zachariah Hiatt NE¼-S27; 1-8-1818. Rel. W½
John Smith NW¼-S27; 9-1-1817
Ethan A. Brown SE¼-S27; 1-20-1818. Rel. 7-5-1831
Ethan A. Brown SW¼-S27; 1-20-1818. Rel. E½ to George Knight,
Ethan A. Brown E½-S28; 1-20-1818. Rel. NE¼ & SE¼. E½-NE¼ to
Jehu Robinson, 1-27-1830
Jacob Miller NW¼-S28; 7-31-1817
Thomas Sinnard SW¼-S28; 3-6-1818.Vol.II, p.250 shows only W½-SW¼
Charles Conway NE¼-S29; 5-6-1817
Jonathan Edwards NW¼-S29; 9-29-1817
Caleb Wickersham SE¼-S29; 7-1-1817
Nicholas Longworth & Griffin Taylor SW¼-S29; 4-7-1818. Rel. E½.
Vol.II, p.250 shows whole SW¼ kept
Moses Brooks & Obediah Walker E½-NE¼-S30; 4-6-1818. Rel.
Moses Brooks W½-NE¼-S30; 6-8-1818. Rel.
Nicholas Longworth & Griffin Taylor NW¼-S30; 4-7-1818
Moses Brooks E½-SE¼-S30; 5-20-1818.
Moses Brooks W½-SE¼-S30; 6-8-1818.
Nicholas Longworth SW¼-S30; 8-5-1818. Rel.
Nicholas Longworth NE¼-S31; 8-5-1818
Thomas Garrard SE¼-S31; 12-6-1817
William Hockett NE¼-S32; 9-12-1817
Mashack Laweller NW¼-S32; 7-1-1817
Valentine Wysong SE¼-S32; 2-25-1818. Rel. W½
John Eltzroth SW¼-S32; 7-2-1818
Nicholas Longworth NE¼-S33; 4-20-1818
Nicholas Longworth* NW¼-S33; 1-21-1818. And Moses Brooks
John Eltzroth SE¼-S33; 7-15-1818
Amos Hodgson SW¼-S33; 11-3-1817 p.251
Nicholas Longworth & Moses Brooks N½-S34; 1-21-1818. See Vol.II,
Valentine Wysong SE¼-S34; 2-25-1818. Rel. W½ to Thomas Hinshaw,
Nicholas Longworth SW¼-S34; 8-5-1818. Rel. 4-12-1830

Jeremiah Cox NE$\frac{1}{4}$-S35; 2-6-1818
Nicholas Longworth & Moses Brooks NW$\frac{1}{4}$-S35; 1-21-1818. Rel.
Nicholas Longworth & Griffin Taylor SE$\frac{1}{4}$-S35; 4-7-1818
Valentine Wysong SW$\frac{1}{4}$-S35; 2-25-1818. Rel. W$\frac{1}{2}$
Nicholas Longworth NW$\frac{1}{4}$-S36; 8-5-1818.Rel. W$\frac{1}{2}$ to Rebecca Pickett,
John Hickman W$\frac{1}{2}$-SW$\frac{1}{4}$-S36; 7-5-1831   7-5-1831
         Page 136. T 21 N, R 14 E of 2nd P.M.
John Hall SW$\frac{1}{4}$-S4; 10-15-1818. Rel.
Henry Welch E$\frac{1}{2}$ & W$\frac{1}{2}$-SE$\frac{1}{4}$-S5; 2-23-1832
John Hall NE$\frac{1}{4}$-S7; 9-6-1819. Rel. E$\frac{1}{2}$ to Burket Pierce, 3-5-1832
Benjamin Lawellin SE$\frac{1}{4}$-S7; 6-10-1817
Jacob Grave SW$\frac{1}{4}$-S7; 6-19-1817. Vol.II, p.253 says Groves
Daniel Kite NE$\frac{1}{4}$-S8; 6-10-1817
Robert Taylor NW$\frac{1}{4}$-S8; 3-23-1818
Daniel Kite SE$\frac{1}{4}$-S8; 6-10-1817
James Jacobs & John Jacobs SW$\frac{1}{4}$-S8; 5-10-1817
Joel Canaday NE$\frac{1}{4}$-S9; 6-10-1817
James Reed NW$\frac{1}{4}$-S9; 6-10-1817
David Conner SE$\frac{1}{4}$-S9; 7-10-1817
James Reed SW$\frac{1}{2}$-S9; 6-10-1817
Tence Massey SE$\frac{1}{4}$-S10; 1-24-1818. Vol.II, p.253 says only E$\frac{1}{2}$-SE$\frac{1}{4}$
James Wilson W$\frac{1}{2}$-S10; 6-10-1817. Rel. E$\frac{1}{2}$-SW$\frac{1}{4}$
         Page 137. T 21 N, R 14 E of 2nd P.M.
William R. Goodwin & William Waters SE$\frac{1}{4}$-S11; 10-19-1819. Rel.
James Massey SW$\frac{1}{4}$-S11; 1-24-1818. Rel. E$\frac{1}{2}$. To Edward Thurber,
Eli Blount SE$\frac{1}{4}$-S12; 10-12-1819. Rel. E$\frac{1}{2}$ 8-26-1831
Daniel Richardson & Isaac Richardson SW$\frac{1}{4}$-S12; 5-21-1817. Vol.II,
    p.254 says only E$\frac{1}{2}$-SW$\frac{1}{4}$
James Strain S13; 10-16-1816
Joseph Cravens NE$\frac{1}{4}$-S14; 5-11-1819. Rel. W$\frac{1}{2}$
Willis Whitson NE$\frac{1}{4}$-S15; 6-5-1818. Rel.
Joseph Hinshaw NE$\frac{1}{4}$-S17; 6-23-1817. Vol.II, p.255 says Henshaw
John S. Reed NW$\frac{1}{4}$-S17; 8-28-1817. Rel. W$\frac{1}{2}$. To Thomas Pierce, 7-5-
James Jacobs NE$\frac{1}{4}$-S18; 7-18-1817   1831
Martin Boots E$\frac{1}{2}$-NE$\frac{1}{4}$-S20; 3-28-1820
John Hale E$\frac{1}{2}$-SE$\frac{1}{4}$-S20; 11-25-1819.Rel. To Martin Overly; 3-5-1832
Richard Beeson NE$\frac{1}{4}$-S21; 11-5-1818
William Jackson SE$\frac{1}{4}$-S21; 10-2-1819
Samuel Cain SW$\frac{1}{4}$-S21; 10-26-1818. Rel. W$\frac{1}{2}$
Robert Taylor NW$\frac{1}{4}$-S22; 3-23-1818. Rel.
         Page 137. T 21 N, R 14 E of 2nd P.M.
Ruley Marshall E$\frac{1}{2}$-NE$\frac{1}{4}$-S23; 11-10-1819. Rel. To Daniel B. Miller,
James Massey NW$\frac{1}{4}$-S24; 11-5-1818   7-5-1831
Samuel Helm · E$\frac{1}{2}$-SW$\frac{1}{4}$-S24; 4-29-1831
Jacob Weaver NE$\frac{1}{4}$-S28; 12-8-1819
John Hale NW$\frac{1}{4}$-S28; 11-18-1819. Rel. W$\frac{1}{2}$
John Weaver E$\frac{1}{2}$-SE$\frac{1}{4}$-S28; 4-23-1822
Jeremiah Lindsey SW$\frac{1}{4}$-S28; 11-26-1819. Rel. E$\frac{1}{2}$
henry Kizer NW$\frac{1}{4}$-S29; 10-21-1820
Benjamin Nordyke SW$\frac{1}{4}$-S29; 11-12-1818. Rel.
Henry Kizer E$\frac{1}{2}$-SE$\frac{1}{4}$-S30; 5-4-1822
Henry Kizer NE$\frac{1}{4}$-S31; 10-21-1820
         Page 139. No entries

Page 140. T 18 N, R 15 E of 2nd P.M.   Randolph Co.
Allen Man NE pt.-S7; 9-11-1830
James Clark E½-NW¼-S7; 9-8-1831
Clark Willcutts SE pt.-S7; 12-5-1828
William Hill W½-SW¼-S7; 4-8-1829
Rice Price Fr.S18; 11-14-1817
Page 140. T 18 N, R 15 E of 2nd P.M.   WAYNE CO.
Joseph Cox Fr.S19; 6-27-1816
Page 141. T 19 N, R 15 E of 2nd P.M.   RANDOLPH CO.
Joshua Buckingham E½-NE¼-S6; 8-11-1825
Joshua Buckingham W½-NE¼-S6; 6-4-1831
Nathan Freeman W½-SE¼-S6; 4-6-1832
Stanton Bailey Fr.S9;*10-4-1831. Also Fr.30 & Fr.31·
Page 142. No entries
Page 143. T 20 N, R 15 E of 2nd P.M.
Jeremiah Moffit NW¼-S18; 12-1-1817
Jeremiah Cox SE¼-S18; 5-29-1818
Jeremiah Cox S19; 2-6-1818
Christopher Baker SE¼-S20; 5-17-1819. Rel. E½
Solomon Cox E½-NE¼-S29; 5-16-1826
Amy Cox W½-NE¼-S29; 9-24-1824
Abraham Peacock NE¼-S30; 4-15-1818
Joshua Cox W½-NW¼-S30; 12-10-1822   to him, 8-24-1836
Henry Hill SE¼-S30; 4-15-1818. Rel. W½. Vol.II, p.265 shows W½
Page 144. T 20 N, R 15 E of 2nd P.M.
Amos Peacock NE¼-S31; 4-15-1818. Rel. W½ to Benoni Hill, 8-9-
   1831. Vol.II, p.265 shows W½ to James S. Armstrong, 5-21-1838
Benoni Hill SE¼-S31; 4-15-1818. Rel. W½. Vol.II, p.266, shows
   W½ to him, 8-9-1831
Page 144. T 21 N, R 15 E of 2nd P.M.
Micajah Weasner SW¼-S6; 12-17-1819. Rel.
Page 145. T 21 N, R 15 E of 2nd P.M.
Charles Dashiell SE¼-S7; 10-26-1816. Rel.
John Abercrombie SW¼-S7; 10-16-1816
John C. Dunham E½-S8; 8-18-1819   3-5-1832
James Williams NW¼-S10; 11-30-1819. Rel. W½ to Jasper Jacobs,
William Simmons W½-NE¼-S20; 6-5-1820. Rel. To James Simmons,
   5-10-1831
Page 146. T 21 N, R 15 E of 2nd P.M.
John Laverty SW¼-S20; 12-22-1816. Rel. E½
John Jones W½-NW¼-S21; 8-27-1830
Pages 147-148-149-150. No entries.

END OF CINCINNATI DISTRICT --- VOLUME I

Page 1. T 1 N, R 1 E of 1st P.M. Switzerland Co.
Oliver Ormsby Fr.S5; S6; Fr.S7; Fr.S8; 12-2-1806
Thomas Hopkins Fr.S31; 7-2-1801

Page 2. T 2 N, R 1 W of 1st P.M.
William Brattle Chamberlin E½-S5; 8-9-1831
Archibald D. Scott SW¼-NW¼-S6; 9-29-1837

Page 4. T 2 N, R 1 W of 1st P.M.
Thomas Lonney SW¼-NE¼-S18; 12-8-1834
James Vaughn Watson NW¼-NE¼-S18; 9-2-1835
James Vaughn Watson W½-NW¼-S18; 9-2-1835
Alexander Sebastian NE¼-SW¼-S18; 12-8-1834
Thomas Lonney SE¼-SW¼-S18; 5-11-1836
William Royston Wiley SE¼-NW¼-S19; 6-12-1832
Thomas Carter SW¼-NW¼-S19; 4-12-1836
Alexander Sebastian NE¼-NW¼-S19; 12-5-1834
Adam Limeback NW¼-NW¼-S19; 11-28-1834   4-19-1813
David McClure E½-S25; Fr.S30, T 1 R 1 (description not clear);

Page 5. T 2 N, R 1 W of 1st P.M.
Elijah Rayl SE¼-SE¼-S30; 6-18-1832
Samuel Howard NE¼-SE¼-S30; 11-27-1834
Joseph Nelson & John Nelson Fr.S33; 2-17-1814
Patrick Donahoe Fr.S35; 9-4-1804

Page 6. T 3 N, R 1 W of 1st P.M.
Henry Cadbury S9; Fr.S10; Fr.S11; 1-25-1802 -   **OHIO CO.**

Page 7. T 3 N, R 1 W of 1st P.M.
Thomas Mounts SW¼-S28; 8-6-1814. Final cert. #1118; however,
see Levi James, Vol.I, p.4 [Part in Switzerland Co.]
Providence Mounts W½-NE¼-S33; 1-18-1830

Page 8. T 4 N, R 1 W of 1st P.M.   **DEARBORN CO.**
Daniel Connor Fr.S4; 9-18-1804. Resold to G.P. Torrence, 12-12-1810
Daniel Conner S8; Fr.S9; 4-22-1801. Re-entered by O. Ormsby,
Dec. 1805   [Part in Ohio Co.]
Joseph Wilkinson Fr.S14; S15; S16; 7-20-1801. Re-entered by
Jesse Hunt, Dec. 1806   **OHIO CO**

Page 9. T 4 N, R 1 W of 1st P.M.
James Hinde W½-SW¼-S29; 5-28-1816   **OHIO CO.**
Frederick Waldo NW¼-S32; 8-18-1814

Page 10. T 5 N, R 1 W of 1st P.M.   **DEARBORN CO.**
Samuel Bond SW¼-S4; 11-13-1809

Page 11. T 5 N, R 1 W of 1st P.M.
James Conn Fr.S27; S28; S29; 12-19-1801

Page 11. T 6 N, R 1 W of 1st P.M.
John S. Jacobus W½-NE¼-S1; 1-7-1833

Page 12. T 6 N, R 1 W of 1st P.M.
John McConnel SW¼-S3; 7-30-1814
Levi Blakesley Swan NW¼-NW¼-S5; 1-22-1835
George Cook W½-SW¼-S5; 2-1-1836
Thomas Huddleston NE¼-S6; NW¼-S6; SE¼-S6; 10-20-1831
William Barr W½-SW¼ & E½-SW¼-S6; 4-22-1818
William Smith NE¼-NW¼-S8; 1-16-1836

Page 14. T 6 N, R 1 W of 1st P.M.
Nathaniel Tucker NE¼-S19; 6-17-1814

Page 15. T 7 N, R 1 W of 1st P.M.
Jesse Whipple NW¼-NW¼-S3; 8-29-1832

Reese Stroud SW¼-NW¼-S3; 11-4-1833
John Barber NE¼-SW¼-S5; 10-21-1834
William Chappelaw SE¼-SW¼-S5; 12-2-1835
John Clifton E½-NE¼-S6; 10-9-1831
John Henry Ohlman W½-SW¼-S6; 11-2-1835
Daniel Symmes Major W½-NE¼-S7; 1-27-1836
Frederick Henry Wohlking & Christopher Henry Medorn (sp?) NW¼-S7;
Isaac Barkhurst W½-SE¼-S7; 5-6-1835   5-24-1834
Herman Freak Spangenburg NE¼-SW¼-S7; 4-25-1836
Robert Davidson SE¼-SW¼-S7; 12-23-1834

          Page 17. T 7 N, R 1 W of 1st P.M.
William Hallowell & Samuel Hallowell NE¼-S17; 3-19-1819
James Harvey Bonham NE¼-NW¼-S17; 10-7-1835
James Harvey Bonham NW¼-NW¼-S17; 5-2-1836
Jesse Sparks SW¼-NW¼-S17; 11-5-1835
Daniel Symmes Major SE¼-NW¼-S17; 3-10-1836
Jonathan Hallowell E½-SE¼-S17; 1-18-1836
Jonathan Hallowell W½-SE¼-S17; 10-13-1835
Alfred Alonzo Stoms E½-SW¼-S17; 1-26-1836
William Dunn & William Burgoine E½-SW¼-S18; 8-6-1833
William Dunn & William Burgoine W½-SW¼-S18; 5-9-1834

          Page 18. T 7 N, R 1 W of 1st P.M.
Jacob Rudicel NW¼-NE¼-S21; 5-22-1834
Jacob Rudicel NE¼-NE¼-S21; 5-25-1836
William Cassaday SE¼-NE¼-S21; 9-29-1835
William Alwath Bodine SW¼-NE¼-S21; 9-29-1835
Francis J. Smith SW¼-NW¼-S22; 8-1-1832
James Markland NW¼-NW¼-S22; 4-17-1833
Thomas McElrath Brackenridge SE¼-SE¼-S23; 2-20-1833
Joseph Williamson Waldorf NE¼-SE¼-S23; 5-21-1835
George Waldorf W½-SW¼-S23; 1-24-1835
John Snyder E½-SW¼-S24; 2-7-1833
John Snyder W½-SW¼-S24; 2-13-1833
Ulick Burk SE¼-SW¼-NW¼-S25; 5-24-1832
William Waldorf N½-NW¼-S25; 8-27-1835

          Page 19. T 7 N, R 1 W of 1st P.M.
John Henderson, Jr. E½-SW¼-S25; 3-17-1834
John McCannon NE¼-SE¼-S26; 10-23-1832
John Henderson, Jr. SE¼-SE¼-S26; 3-17-1834
Robert Cassady W½-SE¼-S26; 10-22-1835
Enoch Morgan E½-SW¼-S26; 4-24-1833
John L. Watkins NE¼-S30; 10-7-1815
William Davis E½-SW¼-S32; 1-3-1835

          Page 20. T 7 N, R 1 W of 1st P.M.
Aaron Scogin E½-NW¼-S35; 5-30-1833
Eli Scogin SE¼-S35; 5-2-1833
Isaac Prudden E½-NE¼-S35; 8-13-1832
William Harper Lloyd SW¼-NE¼-S35; 9-1-1835
Benjamin Morgan, Jr. NW¼-NE¼-S35; 1-28-1836
David Williams NW¼-SE¼-S36; 1-22-1833
John Lewis Hull SW¼-SE¼-S36; 2-6-1834
Hiram Henderson & Silas Henderson E½-SW¼-S36; 7-17-1832
Aaron Scogin W½-SW¼-S36; 5-30-1833

Page 21. T 8 N, R 1 W of 1st P.M.
Crocker Jenkins NE1/4-SW1/4-S5; 5-30-1832
Oren Jenkins NW1/4-SW1/4-S5; 6-23-1832
William Ashton SE1/4-SW1/4-S5; 6-11-1834
William Kerr SW1/4-SW1/4-S5; 6-11-1834
John Linn, Jr. SW1/4-NW1/4-S7; 6-13-1832
George Gant NW1/4-NW1/4-S7; 2-25-1836
William Heap SE1/4-SE1/4-S7; 6-26-1832
John Beeslay NE1/4-SE1/4-S7; 2-15-1836
Isaac Beesley NE1/4-NE1/4-S8; 8-10-1832
John Mary Courcier NW1/4-NE1/4-S8; 5-10-1833. (Query: John and Mary?)
William Wright SE1/4-NE1/4-S8; 9-25-1833
William Hart SW1/4-NE1/4-S8; 1-21-1836
Isaac Soper NE1/4-NW1/4-S8; 10-10-1832
William Ashton NW1/4-NW1/4-S8; 7-21-1834
William Kerr SW1/4-NW1/4-S8; 11-19-1834
Alexander Boyd SE1/4-NW1/4-S8; 10-9-1835
William Heap SW1/4-SW1/4-S8; 6-26-1832
William Kerr NW1/4-SW1/4-S8; 1-22-1836

Page 22. T 8 N, R 1 W of 1st P.M.
Jacob Otto W1/2-NE1/4-S17; 11-12-1833
Nathan Porter SE1/4-S19; 3-22-1806

Page 23. T 8 N, R 1 W of 1st P.M.
Jacob Fausset & Samuel S. Fausset W1/2-SE1/4-S20; 7-15-1836
George Michael Rudicel NE1/4-NE1/4-S20; 2-27-1834
Philip Rudicel SE1/4-NE1/4-S20; 4-21-1835
George Terry NW1/4-NE1/4-S20; 2-9-1836
George Terry SW1/4-NE1/4-S20; 2-12-1836
Michael Rudicel NW1/4-NW1/4-S21; 2-22-1836
Samuel Evans SW1/4-NW1/4-S21; 7-26-1836
William Smith & Simon Gulleys SE1/4-S26; 10-26-1815
John Foutsch NE1/4-S27; 7-21-1813

Page 24. T 8 N, R 1 W of 1st P.M.
Joseph Bennett SE1/4-NW1/4-S30; 3-2-1833
George Rudicel NE1/4-NW1/4-S30; 8-2-1836
Charles Theodore Meyncke E1/2-SW1/4-S30; 1-21-1835
Charles Theodore Meyncke NW1/4-SW1/4-S30; 1-21-1835
Daniel Symmes Major SW1/4-SW1/4-S30; 2-6-1836
Samuel Boutcher NW1/4-SE1/4-S33; 8-22-1832
Thomas Bowman SW1/4-SE1/4-S33; 9-20-1833
William McManaman E1/2-SE1/4-S34; 12-14-1833

Page 25. T 8 N, R 1 W of 1st P.M.
Andrew Bailey NE1/4-S36; 11-1-1814
William Lewis NW1/4-S36; 4-24-1815

Page 25. T 9 N, R 1 W of 1st P.M.
Daniel Currie SE1/4-S4; 7-22-1811

Page 26. T 9 N, R 1 W of 1st P.M.
Gideon Wilkinson SW1/4-S9; 7-22-1811
Samuel McCray SE1/4-S10; 11-29-1811

Page 28. T 9 N, R 1 W of 1st P.M.
Isaac Wamsley NW1/4-S28; 8-6-1813

Page 29. T 10 N, R 1 W of 1st P.M. UNION CO.
Cornelius Wiley NE1/4-S1; SE1/4-S1; 12-8-1804

Page 31. T 10 N, R 1 W of 1st P.M.
James Baxter SE¼-S23; 11-18-1809
John Harper SW¼-S25; 11-18-1809
James Baxter SE¼-S26; 11-18-1809
Page 32. T 10 N, R 1 W of 1st P.M.
Andrew Cornelison SW¼-S32; 1-19-1810
David Jones E½-NW¼-S33; 1-11-1815
Samuel Huston SE¼-S33; 8-14-1816
Page 35. T 11 N, R 1 W of 1st P.M. **UNION CO.**
Thomas Brown NW¼-S30; 9-6-1810. Resale to Jesse Hunt, Aug. 1816
Page 37. T 12 N, R 1 W of 1st P.M.
John Star NW¼-S9; 9-16-1809
Page 38. T 12 N, R 1 W of 1st P.M.
Thomas Bradbury SE¼-S17; 5-17-1814
James Richardson NE¼-S21; NW¼-S21; 10-8-1817. Assee. of George Cort, assee. of Annanias E. Stafford, a Canadian volunteer located this under Act of 5th March 1816
Page 39. T 12 N, R 1 W of 1st P.M.
George Fall SW¼-S30; 8-1-1817
Page 43. T 13 N, R 1 W of 1st P.M. **WAYNE CO.**
Benjamin Hodges NW¼-S27; 10-20-1812. See Vol. I
Page 44. T 13 N, R 1 W of 1st P.M.
Aaron Harding SE¼-S36; 11-30-1814
Page 49. T 15 N, R 1 W of 1st P.M.
Benjamin Thomas W½-S19; Fr.S19; 6-10-1811
Abner Clawson E½-SE¼-S22; 2-7-1833
Page 50. T 15 N, R 1 W of 1st P.M.
Abner Clawson W½-NW¼-S26; 2-28-1833
David Meredith E½-NE¼-S27; 9-8-1831
Edward Starbuck E½-SE¼-S27; 9-8-1831
Matthew Aldman NW¼-S29; 1-31-1814
Page 51. T 16 N, R 1 W of 1st P.M. **RANDOLPH CO.**
Alfred Smith NW¼-NW¼-S1; 6-6-1833
John Alexander SW¼-NW¼-S1; 8-24-1836
Ezekiel Lewis NE¼-SE¼-S1; 12-5-1836
Benjamin Tann (negro) SE¼-SE¼-S1; 4-21-1837
Thornton Alexander W½-SE¼-S1; 3-11-1835
Thornton Alexander NE¼-SW¼-S1; 8-6-1832
Thornton Alexander SE¼-SW¼-S1; 9-25-1833
Gabriel Alexander & John Alexander W½-SW¼-S1; 8-6-1832
John Peele E½-NE¼-S2; 12-21-1836
William N. Jackson W½-NE¼-S2; 12-21-1836
James Jackson E½-NW¼-S2; 6-25-1834
Page 52. T 16 N, R 1 W of 1st P.M.
Allen Davis SW¼-SE¼-S2; 1-3-1835
James Moorman NW¼-SE¼-S2; 6-11-1836
James Moorman E½-SE¼-S2; 1-12-1835
Jacob Rogers E½-SW¼-S2; 11-29-1833
Joseph Jackson E½-NE¼-S3; 6-23-1834
Ahaz Cartwright W½-NE¼-S3; 8-9-1836
Humphrey Loyd NE¼-NW¼-S3; 9-12-1836
John Gross SE¼-NW¼-S3; 10-10-1836
William N. Jackson W½-NW¼-S3; 6-20-1836
Nathaniel Teagle Ford SE¼-SW¼-S3; 12-13-1834

John Gross NE$\frac{1}{4}$-SW$\frac{1}{4}$-S3; 10-10-1836
John Flater W$\frac{1}{2}$-SW$\frac{1}{4}$-S3; 10-8-1836
John Flater Fr.S4; 10-6-1836
David Bell S end -S$\frac{1}{2}$-Fr.S9; 11-7-1834
Josiah Bell N end-S$\frac{1}{2}$-Fr.S9; 11-7-1834
William Chenoweth N$\frac{1}{2}$-Fr.S9; 11-7-1834
Ahaz Cartwright E$\frac{1}{2}$-NW$\frac{1}{4}$-S10; 11-8-1833
William McKim W$\frac{1}{2}$-NW$\frac{1}{4}$-S10; 1-23-1835
Robert Love E$\frac{1}{2}$-SW$\frac{1}{4}$-S10; 1-24-1834
Jeremiah Plew W$\frac{1}{2}$-SW$\frac{1}{4}$-S10; 6-10-1834
John Randle SE$\frac{1}{4}$-NE$\frac{1}{4}$-S11; 11-16-1835
Jacob Rogers NE$\frac{1}{4}$-NE$\frac{1}{4}$-S11; 9-15-1834
Henry Davis E$\frac{1}{2}$-NW$\frac{1}{4}$-S11; 1-21-1834
Jacob Rogers NE$\frac{1}{4}$-NW$\frac{1}{4}$-S11; 5-27-1836
Jacob Rogers W$\frac{1}{2}$-NW$\frac{1}{4}$-S11; 11-29-1833
Samuel Harrison Middleton SE$\frac{1}{4}$-SE$\frac{1}{4}$-S11; 7-7-1834
Samuel Harrison Middleton NE$\frac{1}{4}$-SE$\frac{1}{4}$-S11; 1-12-1835
Pleasant Winston SW$\frac{1}{4}$-S11; 11-15-1817
Charles Mason, Jr. (negro) NE$\frac{1}{4}$-NE$\frac{1}{4}$-S12; 10-29-1835
Gabriel Alexander NW$\frac{1}{2}$-NE$\frac{1}{4}$-S12; 9-8-1836
William Atkins S$\frac{1}{2}$-NE$\frac{1}{4}$-S12; 12-26-1836
          Page 53. T 16 N, R 1 W of 1st P.M.
Thornton Alexander, Jr. NE$\frac{1}{4}$-NW$\frac{1}{4}$-S12; 5-27-1834
William Atkins SE$\frac{1}{4}$-NW$\frac{1}{4}$-S12; 12-26-1836
William Atkins E$\frac{1}{2}$-SE$\frac{1}{4}$-S12; 12-13-1836
John Randle W$\frac{1}{2}$-SE$\frac{1}{4}$; E$\frac{1}{2}$-SW$\frac{1}{4}$-S12; 2-16-1836
James Moorman W$\frac{1}{2}$-SW$\frac{1}{4}$-S12; 1-3-1835
William Atkins E$\frac{1}{2}$-NE$\frac{1}{4}$-S13; 12-13-1836
John Randle W$\frac{1}{2}$-NE$\frac{1}{4}$; E$\frac{1}{2}$-NW$\frac{1}{4}$-S13; 12-20-1834
James Toles NW$\frac{1}{4}$-NW$\frac{1}{4}$-S13; 11-27-1835
George Anderson SW$\frac{1}{4}$-NW$\frac{1}{4}$-S13; 9-15-1836
James Gray E$\frac{1}{2}$-SE$\frac{1}{4}$-S13; 2-22-1836
Asa Woodmansee W$\frac{1}{2}$-SE$\frac{1}{4}$-S13; 5-16-1836
Henry Derry Jellison SE$\frac{1}{4}$-SW$\frac{1}{4}$-S13; 6-16-1835
Henry Miley NE$\frac{1}{4}$-SW$\frac{1}{4}$-S13; 9-2-1835
William Susser W$\frac{1}{2}$-SW$\frac{1}{4}$-S13; 2-20-1836
James Toles NE$\frac{1}{4}$-NE$\frac{1}{4}$-S14; 11-27-1835
George Anderson SE$\frac{1}{4}$-NE$\frac{1}{4}$-S14; 9-15-1836
Samuel Buzzard E$\frac{1}{2}$-SE$\frac{1}{4}$-S14; 12-26-1835
William Blizzard Borders SW$\frac{1}{4}$-NW$\frac{1}{4}$-S15; 9-25-1834
Jabez Murray NW$\frac{1}{4}$-NW$\frac{1}{4}$-S15; 11-7-1834
Malachi Nichols SW$\frac{1}{4}$-SW$\frac{1}{4}$-S15; 12-21-1833
Malachi Nichols NW$\frac{1}{4}$-SW$\frac{1}{4}$-S15; 3-14-1834
Richard Corbitt NE$\frac{1}{4}$-NE$\frac{1}{4}$-S21; 2-20-1836
James Collier Bowen SE$\frac{1}{4}$-NE$\frac{1}{4}$-S21; 4-11-1833
          Page 54. T 16 N, R 1 W of 1st P.M.
John Mann Lot 2-S$\frac{1}{2}$-SW$\frac{1}{4}$-Pt.-SW$\frac{1}{4}$-S21; 11-8-1833
John Mann Lot 2-N$\frac{1}{2}$-SW$\frac{1}{4}$-Pt.-SW$\frac{1}{4}$-S21; 3-14-1834
Nathan Elliott E$\frac{1}{2}$-NE$\frac{1}{4}$-S23; 7-26-1836   Jabez Murray
Taylor Thorn SE$\frac{1}{4}$-SE$\frac{1}{4}$-S23; 2-13-1835   Pt.-NW$\frac{1}{4}$-S21;
John Moore NE$\frac{1}{4}$-SE$\frac{1}{4}$-S23; 4-13-1836   11-7-1834
Asa Woodmansee E$\frac{1}{2}$-NE$\frac{1}{4}$-S24; 2-22-1836
Nathan Elliott W$\frac{1}{2}$-NE$\frac{1}{4}$-S24; 5-23-1834
Adam Frase NE$\frac{1}{4}$-NW$\frac{1}{4}$-S24; 3-31-1835

John Carman SE¼-NW¼; W½-NW¼-S24; 8-22-1836
Benjamin Cardon Davis E½-SE¼-S24; 2-22-1836
Walter Roberds W½-SE¼-S24; 3-6-1834
John Moore NW¼-SW¼-S24; 4-13-1836
Andrew Walker E½ & SW¼-SW¼-S24; 7-19-1836
Hiram Odell NW¼-NE¼-S25; 2-12-1834
William Lanham Gott SE¼-NE¼-S25; 1-16-1835
Nero Bristow SW¼-NE¼-S25; 1-17-1835
William Atkins NE¼-NE¼-S25; 12-13-1836
Stephen Barnes SE¼-NW¼-S25; 10-22-1833
William Odell NE¼-NW¼-S25; 2-12-1834
Isaac Cooper SW¼-NW¼-S25; 12-15-1834
Joseph Gray NW¼-NW¼-S25; 2-19-1836
William Nettler W½-SE¼-S25; 4-26-1833
        Page 55. T 16 N, R 1 W of 1st P.M.
Jeremiah Corbet E½-SW¼-S25; 1-9-1833
Thomas Brown W½-SW¼-S25; 9-6-1833
Joseph Galloway SE¼-NE¼-S26; 2-11-1836
John Wade NE¼-NE¼-S26; 5-5-1836
Dorsey Ryan SE¼-SE¼-S26; 8-21-1833
Isaac Cooper NE¼-SE¼-S26; 12-15-1834
Josiah Bundy NE¼-NW¼-S35; 4-24-1833
Josiah Bundy SE¼-NW¼-S35; 9-30-1833
John Peden E½-SE¼-S35; 12-24-1832
        Page 56. T 16 N, R 1 W of 1st P.M.
Elijah Harris SE¼-NW¼-S36; 8-16-1832
Daniel Thomas NE¼-NW¼-S36; 7-6-1833
        Page 56. T 17 N, R 1 W of 1st P.M.
Jesse Williams & John Wayne Cooper NE¼-S1; 7-13-1836
John Tilman NW¼-S1; SE¼-S1; 1-13-1836
Thomas Bezley SE¼-SW¼-S1; 9-4-1835
Samuel Hettzel NE¼-SW¼-S1; 10-19-1837
Joseph Harkriader W½-SW¼-S1; 10-12-1835
David Robison E½ & NW¼-NW¼-S2; 10-18-1836
Francis A. Cunningham SW¼-NE¼-S2; 5-14-1838
Thomas Beesley SE¼-SE¼-S2; 9-4-1835
Silas Dixson SW¼-SE¼-S2; 10-12-1835
Joseph Harkriader NE¼-SE¼-S2; 1-26-1836
John Dixson NW¼-SE¼-S2; 12-14-1837
Philip Powell N½ & S½-Pt.S10; 11-30-1836
Samuel Downing N½-N½-Fr.S15; 12-30-1836
Harvey Harrison S½-N½-S15; 1-30-1837
Eleazer Williamson N end-S½-S15; 11-9-1837
        Page 57. T 17 N, R 1 W of 1st P.M.
Samuel Snodgrass S end-S½-Fr.S15; 1-20-1837. Middle initial M.
John Dixon W½-NE¼-S11; 2-2-1835
William Polly E½-NW¼-S11; 11-5-1836
William Anderson W½-NW¼-S11; 9-28-1838
Robert Perkins E½-SE¼-S11; 12-26-1833
Robert Perkins SW¼-SE¼-S11; 3-30-1835
Ezekiel Pritchett NW¼-SE¼-S11; 12-17-1836
Ezekiel Gullet SE¼-SW¼-S11; 1-19-1837
Isaac Gullet NE¼-SW¼-S11; 3-23-1837
David Polly W½-SW¼-S11; 3-23-1837

Samuel Hettzel NE¼-NE¼-S12; 1-26-1837
Christina Jane Flash SE¼-NE¼-S12; 8-16-1838
Peter Hoover, Jr. W½-NE¼-S12; 8-15-1835
Peter Hoover E½-NW¼-S12; 6-17-1834
George Gullett W½-NW¼-S12; 2-2-1835
David Wason NW¼-SE¼-S12; 6-7-1836
Christina Jane Flash NE¼-SE¼-S12; 8-16-1838
Benjamin Murphy S½-SE¼-S12; 2-13-1837
Isaac Gullett NW¼-SW¼-S12; 7-8-1836
John H. Martin SW¼-SW¼-S12; 8-5-1836
Samuel Morrison NE¼-S13; 7-21-1836
Robert Murphy NE¼-NW¼-S13; 1-30-1834
Martin Cox SE¼-NW¼-S13; 6-7-1836
Martin Cox SW¼-NW¼-S13; 9-19-1835
Robert Murphy NW¼-NW¼-S13; 6-7-1836
William M. Irvin SE¼-S13; 9-17-1836
John Lowder NW¼-SW¼-S13; 11-25-1835
Samuel Fosdick SW¼-SW¼; E½-SW¼-S13; 1-2-1836
George Brown NE¼-S14; 4-7-1836
Smith G. Masterson NE¼-NW¼-S14; 6-2-1836
Samuel Downing SE¼-NW¼; W½-NW¼-S14; 12-10-1836
Martin Cox E½-SE¼-S14; 9-19-1835
George Brown W½-SE¼-S14; 4-7-1836
James W. Masterson SW¼-SW¼-S14; 1-4-1837
Samuel Fosdick E½-SW¼; NW¼-SW¼-S14; 1-2-1837
Edmund P. Dailey NE¼-S22; 1-13-1836

Page 58. T 17 N, R 1 W of 1st P.M.

Edmund P. Dailey N½-SE¼-S22; 1-13-1836
Edmund P. Dailey S½-SE¼-S22; 9-21-1836
Samuel Snodgrass Fr.NW¼-S22; 1-20-1837. Middle initial M.
Samuel Snodgrass N½-Fr.SW¼-S22; 1-30-1837. Middle init. W. (prob. error for M.)
Richard C. Warrick S½-Fr.SW¼-S22; 7-24-1833
Jefferson L. Summers NW¼-NE¼-S23; 4-12-1836
Jefferson L. Summers SW¼-NE¼-S23; 2-24-1837
Martin Cox E½-NE¼-S23; 8-15-1836
Stephen M. Irvin W½ & NE¼-NW¼-S23; 9-17-1836
Branson Anderson SE¼-NW¼-S23; 12-21-1836
Jacob Chenoweth NE¼-SE¼-S23; 1-15-1834
Branson Anderson SE¼-SE¼-S23; 10-14-1835
Abraham Chenoweth W½-SE¼-S23; 4-14-1834
John B. Tullis SW¼-S23; 6-10-1836
Thomas Dunn NE¼-S24; 2-17-1837
Eleazer Williams NE¼-NE¼-S24; 9-28-1837
Robert Gibbs W½-NE¼-S24; 3-20-1837
William M. Irvin NW¼-S24; 9-17-1836
John L. (S.?) Dunn SE¼-SW¼-S24; 3-25-1835
John L. (S.?) Dunn NE¼-SW¼-S24; 6-7-1836
Jacob Chenoweth W½-SW¼-S24; 4-14-1834
Jacob Chenoweth NW¼-NW¼-S25; 1-29-1836
Hamilton White SW¼-NW¼; E½-NW¼-S25; 11-7-1836
Hamilton White E½-SW¼-S25; 11-7-1836
William N. Jackson SE¼-SW¼-S25; 8-23-1836
William N. Jackson W½-SW¼-S25; 3-12-1836

Moses Thompson SE¼-S27; 3-9-1835

Nathaniel Adams E½-SE¼-S26; 12-26-1835

Edwin Lee Poore W½-SE¼-S26; 12-28-1833

Page 59. T 17 N, R 1 W of 1st P.M.

Stephen W. Dukes   Fr.S33; 1-5-1837
Jason Boswell   NE¼-NE¼; NW¼-NE¼-S34; 6-20-1836
Samuel Farrens   SE¼-NE¼-S34; 4-5-1832; 10-4-1832, (2 dates)
Samuel Farrens   SW¼-NE¼-S34; 8-2-1835
John McKim   W½-SE¼-S34; 1-23-1835
John Loyd   W½-SW¼-S34; 6-10-1836
Mahlon Clawson   E½-NW¼-S34; 6-27-1833
Hezekiah Luck   SW¼-NW¼-S34; 5-21-1836
John Gross   NW¼-NW¼-S34; 2-22-1839
Thornton Alexander, Jr.   SW¼-NE¼-S35; 1-27-1834
Abraham Patterson   NW¼-NE¼-S35; 11-14-1836
Joseph McMaken   E½-NE¼-S35; 9-23-1836
James Holland   E½-SE¼-S35; 11-11-1836
Jesse Bright   W½-SE¼-S35; 6-20-1836
Jesse Bright   SE¼-SW¼-S35; 6-2-1834
Thomas Grandy   NE¼-SW¼-S35; 11-7-1834
Flemmin Tucker   SE¼-NW¼-S36; 11-3-1835
Abraham Patterson   NE¼-NW¼-S36; 2-19-1838
Joseph McMaken   W½-NW¼-S36; 9-23-1836
Collier Simpson   SE¼-SW¼-S36; 9-18-1832
Peter Holland   SW¼-SW¼-S36; 2-13-1837
Collier Simpson   NE¼-SW¼-S36; 9-7-1834
Fleming Tucker   NW¼-SW¼-S36; 11-3-1835

Page 59. T 18 N, R 1 W of 1st P.M.

Henry Smith   N½-NW¼; S½-NW¼-S1; 4-12-1837

Page 60. T 18 N, T 1 W of 1st P.M.

David A. Frankfather   N½ & S½-SW¼-S1; 4-12-1837
Joshua Harlan   E½-SE¼-S1; 1-26-1837
James Harlan   W½-SE¼-S1; 2-22-1837
Henry Smith   NE¼-S1; 4-12-1837
Thomas Wiley   Fr.S11; 9-9-1835
Abraham Smith   NE¼-S12; 4-12-1837
John Hoke   SE¼-S12; .10-7-1836
Abraham Smith   E½-NW¼-S12; 4-12-1837
Elihu Harlan   W½-NW¼-S12; 12-12-1836
Thomas Wiley   SE¼-SW¼-S12; 9-9-1835
David A. Frankfather   NE¼-SW¼-S12; 4-12-1837
Thomas Wiley, Jr.   W½-SW¼-S12; 3-15-1834
George Smith   E½-NE¼-S13; 6-8-1837
Valentine Harlan   W½-NE¼-S13; 12-12-1836
James Wickersham   SW¼-NW¼-S13; 7-29-1835
Thomas Loring   NW¼-NW¼; E½-NW¼-S13; 9-9-1835
Abraham Royer   E½-SE¼-S13; 1-30-1837
Abraham Royer   W½-SE¼-S13; 8-10-1836
Eli Noffsinger   E½-SW¼-S13; 6-24-1834
Peyton S. Symmes   N½-Fr.S14; 3-1-1837
Peyton S. Symmes   S½-Fr.S14; 3-1-1837
Peyton S. Symmes   N pt.-N½-S23; 3-1-1837
Francis Parrott & Thomas Parrott   S pt.-N½-S23; 9-19-1836
David Potter   N pt.-S½-S23; 8-15-1836
Jacob Emmick   SE¼-SE¼-S23; 1-15-1833
Thomas Henderson   SW¼-SW¼-S23; 8-1-1840
John Flory   NE¼-S24; 11-7-1836

John Sheets SE¼-NW¼-S24; 7-6-1833
Perry Sheets NE¼-NW¼-S24; 8-30-1836
John Hoke E½-SE¼-S24; 4-12-1837
Emanuel Flory, Sr. W½-SE¼-S24; 9-22-1836
John Sheets NW¼-SW¼-S24; 7-7-1835
John Finney SW¼-SW¼-S24; 9-14-1836
Emanuel Flory, Sr. E½-SW¼-S24; 9-22-1836

Page 61. T 18 N, R 1 W of 1st P.M.

John Crumrine NE¼-S25; 6-22-1836
Zachariah Overly NW¼-NW¼-S25; 8-11-1835
John Emrick SW¼-NW¼-S25; 8-11-1835
John Crumrine E½-NW¼-S25; 2-1-1836
John Crumrine SE¼-S25; 6-22-1836
John Crumrine E½-SW¼-S25; 2-1-1836
John Royer W½-SW¼-S25; 9-21-1825
John Emrick Lot 1-NE pt.-N½-Fr.S26; 1-15-1833
Robert Ewing Lot 2-NW pt.-N½-S26; Lot 3-SW pt.-N½-S26; 8-20-1836
John Emrick Lot 4-SE pt.-N½-S26; 3-22-1834
Thomas Peeden Lot 5-NE pt.-S½-S26; 10-2-1832
Robert Ewing Lot 6-NW pt.-S½-S26; 8-20-1836
John Kunkle Lot 7-SW pt.-S½-S26; 5-11-1836
Thomas Peeden Lot 8-SE pt.-S½-S26; 10-2-1832
John Kunkle Lot 1-N½-NW¼-Fr.S35; NW¼-NE¼-S35; 4-14-1836
Warren Butterfield SW¼-NE¼-S35; 2-4-1837. Middle initials W.F.
Elizabeth Robison E½-NE¼-S35; 2-4-1837
Christian Anngst Lot 2-S½-NW¼; Lot 3-N½-SW¼; Lot 4-S½-SW¼-S35; 5-24-1837
Alfred Ayers SE¼-S35; 1-27-1837
John Royer NW¼-NW¼-S35; 10-27-1836
John Root NE¼-NW¼-S35; 10-27-1836
Samuel Cole S½-NW¼-S35; 5-20-1837
John Tilman SW¼-S36; 1-13-1836
Abraham Root NE¼-S36; 8-29-1836
John A. Wiseman SE¼-S36; 7-1-1837

Page 61. T 19 N, R 1 W of 1st P.M. JAY CO.

Thomas Anderson Fr.S13; 8-1-1840

Page 61. T 19 N, R 1 W of 1st P.M. RANDOLPH CO

Benjamin Drake N½-Fr.S24; 11-4-1837
Demas Lindley Lots 3-4, S½-S24; 6-19-1837
Daniel Lindley S½-S25; 7-6-1837
John A. Wiseman N½-S25; 7-11-1837
John Stout E½-NE¼-S36; 6-22-1837
Isaiah P. Thomas Lots 1-2, W pt.-N½-Fr.S36; 8-21-1838
Nathan Harlan Lots 1-2, SW¼-Fr.S36; 10-5-1837
John Gittinger SE¼-S36; 6-6-1837

Page 62. T 1 N, R 2 W of 1st P.M. SWITZERLAND CO.

John J. Dufour Fr.S1; Fr.S2; 4-10-1801. Resold to Jared Mansfiel 12-3-1806, but given up again. Resale No. 4. (see Vol. I)
Thomas Hopkins Fr.S3; 7-14-1801
James Burke NW¼-S6; 7-24-1814

Page 62. T 2 N, R 2 W of 1st P.M.

Aaron F. Cochran N½-SW¼-S1; 6-15-1836
James Kelley NE¼-NE¼-S1; 4-30-1836
Samuel Hass SE¼-NE¼-S1; 8-17-1833
Nathan Ricketts NW¼-NE¼-S1; 8-22-1833
Elisha Lander Hess SW¼-NE¼-S1; 2-27-1833
Jesse Bradford S½-SW¼-S1; 10-16-1833

Page 63. T 2 N, R 2 W of 1st P.M.
Samuel Buel SW$\frac{1}{4}$-S5; 5-19-1817
Page 64. T 2 N, R 2 W of 1st P.M.
Lewis Bocock & Hezekiah Spoque(?) NW$\frac{1}{4}$-SW$\frac{1}{4}$-S11; 1-7-1833. Surname of Hezekiah is illegible
Josiah Woodruff SW$\frac{1}{4}$-SW$\frac{1}{4}$-S11; 3-13-1835
Benjamin Smith NE$\frac{1}{4}$-NW$\frac{1}{4}$-S13; 8-9-1832
Robert Chandler NW$\frac{1}{4}$-NW$\frac{1}{4}$-S13; 8-14-1832
Benjamin Smith SE$\frac{1}{4}$-NW$\frac{1}{4}$-S13; 9-20-1836
Robert Chandler SW$\frac{1}{4}$-NW$\frac{1}{4}$-S13; 12-13-1833
John Lampton SW$\frac{1}{4}$-SW$\frac{1}{4}$-S13; 9-20-1836
William Hastie NW$\frac{1}{4}$-SW$\frac{1}{4}$-S13; 10-29-1836
Thomas Champion NE$\frac{1}{4}$-SW$\frac{1}{4}$-S14; 12-25-1835
John H. Gilbert SE$\frac{1}{4}$-SW$\frac{1}{4}$-S14; 10-10-1836
William Reilly SW$\frac{1}{4}$-SW$\frac{1}{4}$-S14; 1-18-1836
Isaac Shuff NW$\frac{1}{4}$-SW$\frac{1}{4}$-S14; 8-18-1836
James Rayl NE$\frac{1}{4}$-NE$\frac{1}{4}$-S15; 11-7-1832
James Rayl SE$\frac{1}{4}$-NE$\frac{1}{4}$-S15; 1-26-1833
Nathaniel G. Hedges NW$\frac{1}{4}$-NE$\frac{1}{4}$-S15; 2-23-1836
Thomas Wright SW$\frac{1}{4}$-NE$\frac{1}{4}$-S15; 5-21-1836
Charles Emerson Hedges NE$\frac{1}{4}$-NW$\frac{1}{4}$-S15; 12-30-1835
Eli Murphy NW$\frac{1}{4}$-NW$\frac{1}{4}$-S15; 12-30-1835
Charles Emerson Hedges SE$\frac{1}{4}$-NW$\frac{1}{4}$-S15; 5-14-1836
Thomas Wright SW$\frac{1}{4}$-NW$\frac{1}{4}$-S15; 5-21-1836
Walter Armstrong SE$\frac{1}{4}$-NE$\frac{1}{4}$-S17; 10-26-1835
Lemuel Montanye NE$\frac{1}{4}$-NE$\frac{1}{4}$-S17; 7-16-1832
Page 65. T 2 N, R 2 W of 1st P.M.
William Lawrence SE$\frac{1}{4}$-NW$\frac{1}{4}$-S19; 8-10-1835
James Dunlap NE$\frac{1}{4}$-SE$\frac{1}{4}$-S19; 8-21-1835
Walter Armstrong SE$\frac{1}{4}$-SE$\frac{1}{4}$-S19; 10-26-1835
William Lawrence W$\frac{1}{2}$-SE$\frac{1}{4}$-S19; 12-29-1834
Jacob Shuff NE$\frac{1}{4}$-NW$\frac{1}{4}$-S20; 7-16-1832
Claude Pasquier NW$\frac{1}{4}$, SE$\frac{1}{4}$, & SW$\frac{1}{4}$-NW$\frac{1}{4}$-S20; 3-17-1834
Zachariah Montanye NE$\frac{1}{4}$-SW$\frac{1}{4}$-S20; 2-20-1833
Lemuel Montanye SE$\frac{1}{4}$-SW$\frac{1}{4}$-S20; 2-4-1835
Walter Armstrong W$\frac{1}{2}$-SW$\frac{1}{4}$-S20; 10-26-1835
Thomas Rayl, Jr. SW$\frac{1}{4}$-NE$\frac{1}{4}$-S22; 6-18-1832
William Linebak SE$\frac{1}{4}$-NE$\frac{1}{4}$-S22; 9-24-1832
John Miller N$\frac{1}{2}$-NE$\frac{1}{4}$-S22; 3-19-1836
Page 66. T 2 N, R 2 W of 1st P.M.
Abia Luckey S$\frac{1}{2}$-NW$\frac{1}{4}$-S23; 9-24-1832
William Moore NE$\frac{1}{4}$-NW$\frac{1}{4}$-S23; 6-10-1835
John Rayl NW$\frac{1}{4}$-NW$\frac{1}{4}$-S23; 2-24-1836
Jesse VanMeter Dailey E$\frac{1}{2}$-SE$\frac{1}{4}$-S23; 3-20-1835
William Phillips NE$\frac{1}{4}$-S25; 1-31-1814. Vol.I says to Charles Beatty, 11-2-1816
Mordecai Jackson SW$\frac{1}{4}$-S28; 5-20-1815
John Spears NW$\frac{1}{4}$-NE$\frac{1}{4}$-S29; 9-8-1833
Robert Hatton SE$\frac{1}{4}$-NE$\frac{1}{4}$-S29; 4-20-1835
John Campbell Brown SW$\frac{1}{4}$-NE$\frac{1}{4}$-S29; 3-3-1836
Henry Boyd SW$\frac{1}{4}$-NW$\frac{1}{4}$-S29; 3-2-1833
Walter Armstrong NW$\frac{1}{4}$-NW$\frac{1}{4}$-S29; 10-26-1835
Jacob Boisseau NE$\frac{1}{4}$-NW$\frac{1}{4}$-S29; 4-6-1833
John Boyd SE$\frac{1}{4}$-NW$\frac{1}{4}$-S29; 2-25-1836

Page 67. T 2 N, R 2 W of 1st P.M. **SWITZERLAND CO**

William Atkinson SW¼-SE¼-S29; 7-2-1832
William Atkinson NW¼-SE¼-S29; 2-25-1836
David McCormick E½-SW¼-S29; 4-14-1834
David McCormick W½-SW¼-S29; 2-25-1836
Solomon Stow NE¼-NE¼-S30; 2-4-1835
Walter Armstrong NW¼-NE¼-S30; 10-26-1835
Parker Tawitt(?) S½-NE¼-S30; 9-24-1832. Surname illegible
Joseph Walton E½-NW¼-S30; 6-21-1834
Duncan McCallum SW¼-S30; 6-28-1815
Thomas Jefferson Bays W½-NE¼-S31; 1-23-1833
David Allen SW¼-SE¼-S31; 11-8-1832
David Allen NW¼-SE¼-S31; 10-25-1833
Walter Armstrong NE¼-SE¼-S31; 10-26-1835
Levi Gibson SE¼-SE¼-S31; 8-12-1833
Robert Gullion & David Miller NE¼-S34; 9-6-1816
Charles Beaty NE¼-S35; 11-2-1816

Page 68. T 3 N, R 2 W of 1st P.M. **OHIO CO.**

Robert Elliott E½-SW¼-S1; 5-7-1817
David Herron NW¼-SE¼-S1; 9-23-1833
John Wesley Herron SW¼-SE¼-S1; 12-23-1834
David Herron NE¼-SW¼-S1; 9-23-1833
Andrew Douglass SE¼-SW¼-S1; 11-12-1834
James Curry & Jesse Drake NE¼-S2; 1-20-1810
Robert Conaway E½-NW¼-S4; 3-1-1836
Diodat Dart SW¼-NW¼-S4; 12-8-1837
William C. Kittle NW¼-NW¼-S4; 11-3-1838
Samuel Tinker NE¼-SW¼-S4; 4-23-1833
George Smith SE¼-SW¼-S4; NW¼-SW¼-S4; 1-13-1837
Hugh T. Collins SW¼-SW¼-S4; 4-13-1837

Page 69. T 3 N, R 2 W of 1st P.M.

Chester Thayer NW¼-SW¼-S5; 1-13-1837
Silvanus Stevenson SW¼-SW¼-S5; 1-15-1839
Simon Conaway SW¼-SE¼-S6; 5-29-1833
Daniel Conaway NW¼-SE¼-S6; 2-25-1836
Leonard Bailey NE¼-SE¼; SE¼-SE¼-S6; 9-30-1837
Simon Conaway SE¼-SW¼-S6; 5-29-1833
Hiram Barker NE¼-SW¼; NW¼-SW¼; SW¼-SW¼-S6; 2-22-1839
Moses Johnson NW¼-NE¼-S7; 3-7-1836
Moses Johnson SW¼-NE¼-S7; 5-7-1836
James Gibson Kittle NE¼-SE¼-S7; 3-2-1833
Richard Downey SE¼-SE¼-S7; 1-25-1838
John Gibbs W½-SE¼-S7; 7-16-1830
John Gibbs NE¼-SW¼-S7; 7-7-1832
John Dunn SE¼-SW¼-S7; 1-6-1838
Richard Downey NW¼-SE¼-S8; 5-23-1832
Alexander C. Downey SW¼-SE¼-S8; 8-18-1836
Richard Downey SW¼-SW¼-S8; 9-19-1836
David Marsh SE¼-NW¼-S9; 12-5-1835
Edward Doughty NE¼-NW¼-S9; 4-6-1837
William Gray W½-NW¼-S9; 4-30-1836

Page 70. T 3 N, R 2 W of 1st P.M.

Thomas Lotton E½-SW¼-S11; 8-27-1833
James Wishard NE¼-NE¼-S12; 3-18-1834

William Gray SE¼-NE¼-S12; 3-18-1834
James T. Pollock W½-SW¼-S13; 11-26-1832
Isaac Read NW¼-NE¼-S14; 1-15-1834
Samuel Turner SW¼-NE¼-S14; 8-24-1835
Samuel Harrison Mitchele SE¼-NE¼-S14; 1-18-1834
Isaac Reed NE¼-NE¼-S14; 1-11-1836
Charles Marsh NE¼-NW¼-S14; 8-20-1832
Ames Main York SE¼-NW¼-S14; 2-22-1834
John Kemp NW¼-NW¼-S14; 3-18-1834
John Johnson Hueston SW¼-NW¼-S14; 4-23-1834
James Gibson NE¼-SE¼-S17; 1-22-1833
Phineas Kittle SE¼-SE¼-S17; 5-21-1833
William Gibson W½-SE¼-S17; 8-8-1832

Page 71. T 3 N, R 2 W of 1st P.M.

John Vanosdol NE¼-SW¼-S17; 5-24-1833
Joseph Watson SE¼-SW¼-S17; 1-24-1837
Joseph Edwards W½-SW¼-S17; 9-19-1836
Vallorus Morse E½-NE¼-S18; 4-21-1836
John Gibbs NW¼-NE¼-S18; 4-25-1836
John Myers, Jr. SW¼-NE¼-S18; 5-21-1838
Enoch Cochran SW¼-SE¼-S18; 1-21-1836
John Myers NW¼-SE¼-S18; 9-3-1838
Benjamin Moulton SE¼-SE¼-S18; 9-10-1836
Benjamin Moulton NE¼-SE¼-S18; 6-11-1836
James Mulford Downey S½-SW¼-S18; 3-20-1834
Bethuel Riggs N½-SW¼-S18; 12-8-1836
Stephen Ranson Tinker SE¼-NE¼-S19; 4-19-1833
Richard Downey NE¼-NE¼-S19; 1-25-1838
Isaac McHenry NE¼-NE¼; NW¼-NE¼-S20; 4-20-1835
Norman Sloan SE¼-NE¼-S20; 10-9-1832
George Sloan SW¼-NE¼-S20; 10-6-1832
William Moulton NW¼-NW¼-S20; 5-27-1836
William Moulton SW¼-NW¼-S20; 9-10-1836
Edward Miller SE¼-SE¼-S20; 2-8-1834
Henry Brierton N½-SE¼-S20; 4-14-1836
Walter Jessup SW¼-SE¼-S20; 9-25-1834

Page 72. T 3 N, R 2 W of 1st P.M.

William Dorrel NE¼-NE¼-S23; 7-26-1833
Thomas Winn SE¼-NE¼-S23; 7-2-1832

Page 72. T 3 N, R 2 W of 1st P.M. SWITZERLAND CO.

James McHenry NW¼-SW¼-S25; 8-24-1835
James McHenry SW¼-SW¼-S25; 1-7-1833
Michael Smith NE¼-SW¼-S25; 9-18-1834
Michael Smith SE¼-SW¼-S25; 12-17-1835
James McHenry E½-SE¼-S26; 5-7-1833
Joseph McHenry SW¼-SE¼-S26; 6-22-1833
Joseph McHenry NW¼-SE¼-S26; 4-9-1835

Page 73. T 3 N, R 2 W of 1st P.M.

Isaac Jessup SW¼-NE¼-S29; 8-19-1833
Eli Jessup NW¼-NE¼-S29; 9-23-1833
David Jessup SE¼-NE¼; NE¼-NE¼-S29; 4-11-1834
James Downey, Jr. SE¼-NW¼-S30; 12-30-1833
Ezra Jessup SW¼-NW¼-S30; 8-14-1837
Erastus Sylvester Bascom N½-NW¼-S30; 7-8-1834

SWITZERLAND CO.

John Irby NE¼-NW¼-S31; 2-2-1837
William Morrow S½-NW¼-S31; 5-23-1836
Justice Carley SW¼-S33; 4-4-1816
Joel Myers NE¼-NE¼-S34; 12-11-1834
Hugh McHenry SE¼-NE¼-S34; 9-21-1835
Daniel Heath NW¼-NE¼-S34; 9-16-1833
Francis McBeth SW¼-NE¼-S34; 2-21-1833
Samuel Adkinson SW¼-NE¼-S35; 6-22-1833
Daniel Conner NW¼-NE¼-S35; 1-2-1835
Samuel Adkinson SE¼-NE¼-S35; 12-11-1833
Daniel Conner NE¼-NE¼-S35; 12-17-1833

Page 74. T 3 N, R 2 W of 1st P.M.

Abraham Adkinson SE¼-NW¼-S35; 8-26-1833
Henry Surber NE¼-NW¼-S35; 3-26-1836
Timothy Conner W½-NW¼-S35; 12-17-1833
Michael Dunning NE¼-SE¼-S35; 1-28-1834
Henry Surber NW¼-SE¼-S35; 11-9-1832
Enos Ellis SE¼-S35; SW¼-S35; 9-18-1832
Andrew Hodges SE¼-NE¼-S36; 7-29-1835
Andrew Hodges NE¼-NE¼-S36; 12-29-1835
Alfred Pugh NE¼-SE¼-S36; 12-14-1833
Michael Duning NW¼-SE¼-S36; 10-14-1832
Robert Nesbit SE¼-SE¼-S36; 6-8-1835
Michael Duning SW¼-SE¼-S36; 6-26-1836

Page 74. T 4 N, R 2 W of 1st P.M.

DEARBORN CO.

Iry (Ivy?) White NE¼-S1; 4-3-1812

Page 75. T 4 N, R 2 W of 1st P.M.

John Hubbart NW¼-NW¼-S5; 6-6-1836
Elias Littell E½-NW¼-S5; 6-6-1836
John Hubbart SW¼-NW¼-S5; 5-16-1837
James W. Whitaker SW¼-SW¼-S5; 6-6-1836
Lewis Nichols NW¼-SW¼-S5; 3-1-1837
Lewis B. Hunt W½-NE¼-S6; 11-3-1836
Henry VanMiddlesworth W½-NW¼-S6; 6-5-1820
John L. Bailey Lot 1-E½-NW¼-S6; 2-22-1837
Harrison Alfred SW¼-SE¼-S6; 10-16-1837
Ellis Kincaid NW¼-SE¼-S6; 3-28-1839
Arthur F. Roberts E½-SE¼-S6; 12-17-1838
Henry Leasure NW¼-SW¼-S6; 6-15-1836
William C. Birdzell SE¼-SW¼-S6; 9-16-1836
Henry Leasure SW¼-SW¼-S6; 11-12-1836
Ellis Kincaid NE¼-SW¼-S6; 3-28-1839
John Kerr SW¼-NE¼-S7; 1-31-1837
Harrison Alfred NW¼-NE¼-S7; 10-16-1837
William C. Birdzell NE¼-NW¼-S7; 9-16-1836
William B. Miller SE¼-NW¼-S7; 11-3-1836
William Abbot SW¼-SW¼-S7; 4-14-1835
James McClain NW¼-SW¼-S7; 1-18-1836
James Smith SW¼-NW¼-S8; 1-22-1834
James W. Whiteaker NW¼-NW¼-S8; 6-6-1836
Christopher Briney E½-SE¼-S8; 5-4-1825

Page 76. T 4 N, R 2 W of 1st P.M.

William Frazier W½-SW¼-S9; 8-21-1827
John Hubbart, Sr. SE¼-S10; 8-30-1811

Samuel C. Vance, assee. of Romulus Riggs, assee. of Moses Jewett, assee. of George Hiatt, a private in the Canadian volunteers, located NW¼-S15; 7-31-1819
David Abbott NE¼-SW¼-S17; 10-11-1832
Ezekiel Harper SE¼-SW¼-S17; 4-17-1839
John Kneeland W½-SW¼-S17; 3-1-1837
John Vandolak SE¼-SW¼-S18; 8-21-1833
David Kerr NE¼-SW¼-S18; 2-3-1836

Page 77. T 4 N, R 2 W of 1st P.M.

John Wilson Nixon SE¼-NE¼-S19; 2-26-1836
Henry Darby NE¼-NE¼-S19; 3-25-1837
George W. S. Mitchell NW¼-NW¼-S20; 3-25-1837
Henry Martin SW¼-NW¼-S20; 9-13-1837
James Wilson E½-SE¼-S20; 7-3-1832
Thomas Guion W½-SE¼-S20; 4-4-1833
John Hughes NE¼-SW¼-S20; 4-3-1833
Samuel Harbert SE¼-SW¼-S20; 10-22-1835
Benjamin Wilson NE¼-S23; 9-26-1804
John Walker NE¼-S26; 7-5-1814. Final cert. #1386. OHIO CO.
p.45, William Cochran

Page 78. T 4 N, R 2 W of 1st P.M.

Daniel Crume SE¼-S29; 12-12-1809. Final cert. #3346. See Vol.I, p.45, Tetrick Fall [Part in Dearborn Co.]
Thomas Guion SE¼-NE¼-S30; 5-13-1836 DEARBORN CO.
Jonathan Hill NE¼-NE¼-S30; 12-11-1837 DEARBORN CO.
Charles Linch Pate SE¼-NW¼-S30; 1-27-1834 DEARBORN CO.
Richard Smith NE¼-NW¼-S30; 2-25-1836 DEARBORN CO.
Charles Linch Pate N½-SW¼-S30; 12-30-1835 [Part in Ohio Co.]
Martha Speer SE¼-SW¼-S30; 6-6-1832 [Part in Ohio Co.]
Samuel Giffin SW¼-SE¼-S31; 5-21-1833 OHIO CO.
Samuel Giffin NW¼-SE¼-S31; 10-22-1833
John Watts Ray SW¼-NW¼-S32; 9-4-1835
Thomas Purcel, Jr. NW¼-NW¼-S32; 5-17-1836 [Part in Dearborn Co.]
John Conaway N½-SE¼-S32; 10-6-1832
Renselear Willey SE¼-SE¼; SW¼-SE¼-S32; 2-6-1836

Page 79. T 4 N, R 2 W of 1st P.M.

David Hufford W½-NE¼-S33; 5-2-1836
William Alexander NE¼-S36; 7-6-1814

Page 79. T 5 N, R 2 W of 1st P.M. DEARBORN CO.

Abner Tibbets, Jr. W½-NW¼-S3; 9-7-1831

Page 80. T 5 N, R 2 W of 1st P.M.

George W. Clark & Moses M. Roberts W½-NW¼-S4; 1-23-1836
Nathan Pettegrew NE¼-SW¼-S4; 1-16-1836
David Milburn SE¼-SW¼-S4; 1-16-1836
Richard Oliver NW¼-SW¼-S4; 1-28-1836
Wesley Caldwell SW¼-SW¼-S4; 1-29-1836
John Tibbetts E½-NE¼-S5; 12-4-1818. Final cert. #2768
Ira Tinker NW¼-NW¼-S5; 3-10-1836
Samuel Roberts SW¼-SW¼-S5; 6-30-1836
James Fox SE¼-SE¼-S5; 6-14-1832
George W. Clark NE¼-SE¼-S5; 2-17-1836
William Hewitt W½-SE¼-S5; 6-2-1836
Francis Vinson E½-SW¼-S5; 4-4-1836
John Vinson W½-SW¼-S5; 11-18-1831

John Ellis NE¼-NE¼-S6; 2-9-1836
William Hewitt SE¼-NE¼-S6; 6-2-1836
James Hodgson NW¼-NE¼-S7; 7-8-1833
James Byers SW¼-NE¼-S7; 6-24-1834
Alexander Low SW¼-NW¼-S7; 7-20-1833
Thomas McKinstrey NW¼-NW¼-S7; 11-14-1836
Aaron Valentine SE¼-NW¼-S7; 12-15-1836
Joseph E. Baker NE¼-NW¼-S7; 5-2-1836
John Dunkin Bowin SW¼-SE¼-S7; 10-14-1835
Henry Hancock NW¼-SE¼; SE¼-SE¼-S7; 3-9-1836
            Page 81. T 5 N, R 2 W of 1st P.M.
William Rumsey N½-SE¼-S8; 9-16-1835
William Hewitt SW¼-SE¼-S8; 10-24-1836
David Durham SE¼-SE¼-S8; 3-1-1837
William Gregory NE¼-NE¼-S9; 9-5-1835
Jedde Clark NW¼-NE¼-S9; 10-1-1832
George Johnston SE¼-NE¼-S9; 6-3-1834
Zebulon Harman Robarts SW¼-NE¼-S9; 3-2-1833
John Rumsey SW¼-NW¼-S9; 8-1-1832
Thomas Heckilburn NW¼-NW¼-S9; 1-27-1836
Isaac Tindal SE¼-NW¼-S9; 8-20-1834
Jedde Clark NE¼-NW¼-S9; 1-27-1836
Armour Stevenson E½-NW¼-S14; 6-19-1832
            Page 82. T 5 N, R 2 W of 1st P.M.
Samuel C. Vance, assee. of Romulus Riggs, assee. of Moses Jewett,
    assee. of Anthony Benoit, a private in the Canadian volunteers,
    located NW¼-S15; 7-31-1819
Gilbert T. Givan NE¼-S17; 3-9-1836
Thomas Bishop Cook SE¼-NW¼-S17; 8-3-1832
Thomas Bishop Cook NE¼-NW¼-S17; 5-26-1836
Samuel C. Vance, assee. of Romulus Riggs, assee. of Benjamin M.
    Hopkins, assee. of William Martin, Jr., a private in the
    Canadian volunteers, located NE¼-S21; 7-31-1819
Samuel C. Vance, assee. of Romulus Riggs, assee. of Moses Jewett,
    assee. of Samuel Austin, a private in the Canadian volunteers,
    located SE¼-S21; 7-21-1819
Amer Bruce W½-NE¼-S22; 8-21-1827
John Brice, Jr. NE¼-NW¼-S22; 4-17-1833
Andrew Stevenson NW¼-NW¼-S22; 3-26-1833
John Snider SW¼-NW¼-S22; 4-22-1833
Andrew Stevenson SE¼-NW¼-S22; 4-1-1833
Caleb Coledin NW¼-SW¼-S22; 9-5-1833
Caleb Coledin NE¼-SW¼-S22; 4-1-1834
            Page 83. T 5 N, R 2 W of 1st P.M.
Timothy Kimball S½-SW¼-S22; 2-12-1835
John Bruce NW¼-SE¼-S22; 5-31-1836. Final cert. #5592. See Vol.I,
    p.47, Amer Bruce
Stephen Bruce SW¼-SE¼-S22; 5-31-1836. Final cert. #5591. See
    Vol.I, p.47, Amer Bruce
Amos Boardman & D. G. Boardman S25; 11-25-1809
Asa Jackson E½-SW¼-S28; 1-24-1833
John Pritchard NW¼-NE¼-S29; 8-3-1832
John Pritchard SW¼-NE¼-S29; 8-13-1832
Nancy Higbee NE¼-NE¼; SE¼-NE¼-S29; 11-23-1832

Smith Thompson NE¼-NW¼-S29; 1-15-1833
Benjamin Brewington SE¼-NW¼-S29; 12-31-1835
Nancy Higbee SE¼-S29; 11-23-1832
Thomas Record SW¼-SW¼-S29; 6-20-1832
Armour Flake NE¼-SW¼-S29; 11-8-1832
Nancy Higbee SE¼-SW¼-S29; 8-10-1836
Thomas Record NW¼-SW¼-S29; 12-13-1836
Thompson Dean NE¼-NE¼-S30; 5-16-1836
Wilson L. Wheeler SW¼-NE¼-S30; 6-27-1836
Wilson L. Wheeler NW¼-NE¼-S30; 3-24-1837
John Christy SE¼-NE¼-S30; 11-6-1837

Page 84. T 5 N, R 2 W of 1st P.M.

Joseph Carpenter SW¼-NW¼-S30; 8-22-1832
Piercy Wheeler NW¼-NW¼-S30; 3-24-1836
George Cornelius NE¼-NW¼-S30; 3-1-1837
Aaron Foulk SE¼-NW¼-S30; 10-6-1832
Lorenzo Wright E½-SE¼-S31; 1-23-1833
Michael Flake W½-SE¼-S31; 9-13-1831
James Lindsey NW¼-SW¼-S32; 9-20-1832
Peter Rough SW¼-SW¼-S32; 10-16-1837
George Golding NW¼-NE¼-S33; 6-5-1832
Lewis Nichols SW¼-NE¼-S33; 4-12-1836
George Golding NE¼-NW¼-S33; 2-3-1834
James Case SE¼-NW¼-S33; 5-30-1831

Page 85. T 6 N, R 2 W of 1st P.M.

James Slaats, Jr. SW¼-S1; 8-7-1817
Hallamds(?) C. Vanhouton NE¼-S2; 5-6-1816
William Kleinmann
Israel Ketcham W½-SE¼-S4; 6-17-1833
John Wollising(?) NE¼-NE¼-S6; 9-12-1833
Christiana Wictor(?) SE¼-NE¼-S6; 5-15-1834
Isaac Freeman NW¼-SE¼-S6; 7-25-1832
Francis Wictor(?) SW¼-SE¼-S6; 5-5-1834
John Snell NE¼-SE¼; SE¼-SE¼-S6; 7-29-1833
John Roth E½-NE¼-S7; 7-2-1835
Peter J. Bonte W½-NE¼-S7; 6-16-1834
Joseph Ritter NE¼-NE¼-S8; 7-26-1833
David Buckel SE¼-NE¼-S8; 4-4-1834
John Adam Keyser E½-NW¼-S8; 1-20-1835

Page 86. T 6 N, R 2 W of 1st P.M.

John Henry Peter Shawger (sp.?) NW¼-NE¼-S9; 5-20-1834. May be John Henry & Peter
Daniel Michael SW¼-NE¼-S9; 7-8-1834
Magdalina Siefert NE¼-SW¼-S9; 6-6-1833
Jacob Wilhelm SE¼-SW¼-S9; 7-13-1835
Francis Korcher, Jr. NW¼-SW¼-S9; 9-6-1834
John N. Herman SW¼-SW¼-S9; 9-19-1835
John Smith, Jr. SE¼-NW¼-S12; 10-10-1832
Samuel Bolser NE¼-NW¼-S12; 6-13-1833
William Tucker W½-NW¼-S12; 10-4-1832
Daniel Landen Chidester N½-NW¼-S13; 10-1-1832
Riley Elliott SE¼-NW¼; SW¼-NW¼-S13; 3-13-1834
William Sawden, Jr. E½-SW¼-S13; 3-2-1833
John Lamb NE¼-NE¼-S14; 6-14-1834
John Feist SE¼-NE¼-S14; 6-14-1834

Page 87. T 6 N, R 2 W of 1st P.M.
Robert Carson E$\frac{1}{2}$-NW$\frac{1}{4}$-S14; 9-6-1833
Samuel Hanson Dowden N$\frac{1}{2}$-SE$\frac{1}{4}$-S14; 3-2-1833
William Davies SE$\frac{1}{4}$-SE$\frac{1}{4}$-S14; 1-11-1836
William Davies SW$\frac{1}{4}$-SE$\frac{1}{4}$-S14; 12-16-1833
Matthias Buckel NW$\frac{1}{4}$-S15; 4-4-1834
Thomas Jefferson Darling W$\frac{1}{2}$-SE$\frac{1}{4}$-S15; 3-7-1834
Silas Landers NW$\frac{1}{4}$-NE$\frac{1}{4}$-S17; 9-13-1832
David Hall SW$\frac{1}{4}$-NE$\frac{1}{4}$-S17; 4-15-1836
Samuel Shoemake NE$\frac{1}{4}$-NE$\frac{1}{4}$-S17; 1-26-1836
Blackley Shoemake SE$\frac{1}{4}$-NE$\frac{1}{4}$-S17; 2-19-1836
Isaac Ferris, assee. of a Canadian volunteer NE$\frac{1}{4}$-S21; 6-29-1819
Isaac Ferris, assee. of a Canadian volunteer SE$\frac{1}{4}$-S21; 6-29-1819
Samuel C. Vance, assee. of Canadian volunteer SW$\frac{1}{4}$-S21; 7-31-1819
Isaac Ferris (assee. of ?), a Canadian volunteer NE$\frac{1}{4}$-S22;6-29-1819
Isaac Ferris (assee. of?), a Canadian volunteer NE$\frac{1}{4}$-S22;6-29-1819
Isaac Ferris, assee. of Canadian volunteer NW$\frac{1}{4}$-S22; 6-29-1819
Isaac Ferris (assee. of?), Canadian volunteer SE$\frac{1}{4}$-S22; 6-29-1819
Isaac Ferris, assee. of Canadian volunteer SW$\frac{1}{4}$-S22; 6-29-1819

Page 88. T 6 N, R 2 W of 1st P.M.
John Darling SE$\frac{1}{4}$-NE$\frac{1}{4}$-S23; 5-25-1832
George Thompson NE$\frac{1}{4}$-NE$\frac{1}{4}$-S23; 11-12-1834
Isaac Ferris (assee. of?), Canadian volunteer W$\frac{1}{2}$-NE$\frac{1}{4}$-S23;6-29-1819
Tobias Mann E$\frac{1}{2}$-NW$\frac{1}{4}$-S23; 3-25-1836
George Snell NW$\frac{1}{4}$-SE$\frac{1}{4}$-S23; 2-27-1834
John Taylor SW$\frac{1}{4}$-SE$\frac{1}{4}$-S23; 4-5-1834
Hiram Fairbanks SE$\frac{1}{4}$-SE$\frac{1}{4}$-S23; 4-1-1834
James Murray NE$\frac{1}{4}$-SE$\frac{1}{4}$-S23; 1-19-1836
George Clark W$\frac{1}{2}$-NE$\frac{1}{4}$-S27; 3-18-1830
Stephen Wood SE$\frac{1}{4}$-S28; 12-30-1817

Page 89. T 6 N, R 2 W of 1st P.M.
Asahel Tynel (sp.?) SW$\frac{1}{4}$-NW$\frac{1}{4}$-S31; 3-2-1833
Walter Pardun NW$\frac{1}{4}$-NW$\frac{1}{4}$-S31; 3-9-1836
William Barton, Jr. NE$\frac{1}{4}$-SE$\frac{1}{4}$-S31; 3-19-1836
Edwin Canfield SE$\frac{1}{4}$-SE$\frac{1}{4}$-S31; 4-4-1836
David McCoy NW$\frac{1}{4}$-SE$\frac{1}{4}$; SW$\frac{1}{4}$-SE$\frac{1}{4}$-S32; 5-26-1832
John Roll SW$\frac{1}{4}$-S32; 6-20-1818. Rel. E$\frac{1}{2}$ to Samuel W. McMillen, 9-2-1829. Vol.II, p.89 says McMullen. (This entry was in Vol.I)
Daniel Hays McMullen NW$\frac{1}{4}$-SW$\frac{1}{4}$-S32; 11-28-1832
Luther Plumer SW$\frac{1}{4}$-SW$\frac{1}{4}$-S32; 10-14-1835

Page 90. T 7 N, R 2 W of 1st P.M.
Maria Rapp W$\frac{1}{2}$-NE$\frac{1}{4}$-S1; 10-2-1835
Michael Shranck E$\frac{1}{2}$-NW$\frac{1}{4}$-S1; 5-25-1835
Samuel Cook W$\frac{1}{2}$-NW$\frac{1}{4}$-S1; 5-22-1834
Conrad Frech SE$\frac{1}{4}$-SE$\frac{1}{4}$-S1; 10-12-1835
John Henry Ohlman NE$\frac{1}{4}$-SE$\frac{1}{4}$-S1; 11-2-1835
Adam Bohl & Philip Jacob Kuhn NE$\frac{1}{4}$-S3; 3-15-1833
Joseph Hahn SE$\frac{1}{4}$-NW$\frac{1}{4}$-S3; 5-30-1834
James Spradling NE$\frac{1}{4}$-NW$\frac{1}{4}$-S3; 3-18-1836
Joseph Hahn E$\frac{1}{2}$-SE$\frac{1}{4}$-S3; 6-24-1833
Frederick Hoffer W$\frac{1}{2}$-SE$\frac{1}{4}$-S3; 1-22-1834
Peter Stone NW$\frac{1}{4}$-SW$\frac{1}{4}$-S3; 1-30-1833
Henry Scott SW$\frac{1}{4}$-SW$\frac{1}{4}$-S3; 3-8-1834
Peter Renner NE$\frac{1}{4}$-SW$\frac{1}{4}$-S3; 2-6-1834

Henry Scott SE¼-SW¼-S3; 3-8-1834
Sebastian Messersmith E½-NE¼-S4; 4-4-1835
Christian Conrad W½-NE¼-S4; 9-14-1835
Tousaint Poirot NW¼-S4; 8-7-1834

Page 91. T 7 N, R 2 W of 1st P.M.

Andrew Bohle NW¼-NW¼-S5; 1-16-1835
George P. Buell SW¼-NW¼-S5; 2-1-1836
George Pearson Buell E½-NW¼-S5; 11-7-1835
Isaac Hazen SW¼-SE¼-S5; 5-15-1834
Perry Coverdale NE¼-SE¼-S5; 10-29-1834
Archibald Stewart SE¼-SE¼-S5; 11-20-1834
Isaac Hazen NW¼-SE¼-S5; 11-20-1834
John Hazen E½-SW¼-S5; 11-20-1834
George Pearson Buell W½-SW¼-S5; 2-1-1836
Abraham Lawrence NE¼-NE¼-S6; 7-2-1834
Jacob Clemens SE¼-NE¼-S6; 7-17-1835
Jacob Clemens W½-NE¼-S6; 1-3-1835
Joseph Yeager NW¼-S6; 1-1-1835
John Whitehead SW¼-SE¼-S6; 1-16-1834
Michael Whitehead SE¼-SE¼-S6; 1-28-1835
Jesse Whitehead N½-SE¼-S6; 6-5-1835
Adam Clemens SE¼-SW¼-S6; 12-6-1833
Jacob Clemens NE¼-SW¼-S6; 9-2-1834
Jacob Clemens NW¼-SW¼-S6; 7-17-1835
Jacob Clemens SW¼-SW¼-S6; 3-8-1834
Daniel Lawrence E½-NE¼-S7; 5-31-1833
Michael Whitehead NE¼-NE¼-S7; 1-28-1835
Joseph Issenman E½-NW¼-S7; 6-4-1833
David Bolay W½-NW¼-S7; 1-23-1834
Daniel Lawrence SW¼-NW¼-S8; 5-31-1833
Joseph Carnon(?) NE¼-NW¼-S8; 1-5-1835
Nicholas Yeager NW¼-NW¼-S8; 11-5-1834 (1835?)

Page 92. T 7 N, R 2 W of 1st P.M.

George Hodge, for himself & the other heirs of Thomas Hodge, deceased E½-NE¼-S10; 1-14-1831
Joseph Mason NE¼-NE¼-S11; 1-28-1833
Thomas Foster SE¼-NE¼-S11; 10-17-1833
Edward Johnson & Basil Gaither NW¼-S11; 4-29-1816. (This entry was in Vol.I.) Vol.II, p.92, says Johnston
Daniel Mason SE¼-NE¼-S12; 3-22-1833
Henry Sheland NE¼-NE¼-S12; 11-2-1835
Joseph Shough, Jr. NE¼-NW¼-S13; 3-26-1833
John Pocqueneur SE¼-NW¼-S13; 3-28-1834
Samuel C. Vance, assee. of a Canadian volunteer NE¼-S15;7-31-1819
Samuel C. Vance, assee. of Romulus Riggs, assee. of Moses Jewett, assee. of Wells Hiatt, a musician in the Canadian volunteers NW¼-S15; 7-31-1819

Page 93. T 7 N, R 2 W of 1st P.M.

Anthony Smith NE¼-NE¼-S19; 2-8-1833
Abraham Showalter SE¼-NE¼-S19; 9-19-1834
Jacob Leighty W½-NE¼-S19; 8-17-1838
John Leighty W½-NW¼-S19; 8-30-1831
Frederick Meister SE¼-SW¼-S19; 8-8-1832
Arbagoost Froliger & John Brunner NE¼-SW¼-S19; 12-28-1832

Christopher Welsh NW¼-SW¼ & SW¼-SW¼-S19; 10-19-1832
Daniel Symmes Major W½-NW¼-S20; 3-10-1836
John Greener SW¼-S20; 2-27-1818
Daniel Clenoy & John Mahony E½-NE¼-S21; 7-3-1833
Gregori Stierlen E½-SE¼-S21; 2-1-1833
Gregori Stierlen SE¼-SW¼-S21; 2-1-1833

Page 94. T 7 N, R 2 W of 1st P.M.

Laurence McGuire E½-SE¼-S22; 8-24-1832
John Kelso SE¼-S24; 6-15-1814
John Felix SW¼-SE¼-S25; 8-20-1832
George Lewis NW¼-SE¼-S25; 9-22-1832
William Davis SE¼-NW¼-S26; 2-6-1833
Edward Rigney NE¼-NW¼-S26; 6-27-1833
Richard Hyland SW¼-S26; 8-24-1832
Daniel McKay NE¼-NE¼-S27; 7-27-1832
Edward Rigney SE¼-NE¼-S27; 6-27-1833
Henry Houschantt & Jacob Cook NW¼-S27; 7-5-1833
Hallamus C. Vanhouten E½-SE¼-S27; 5-6-1816
Martin Hofard SW¼-SE¼-S27; 9-13-1832
William Ashford NW¼-SE¼-S27; 10-20-1832
John Hall SE¼-SW¼-S27; 7-28-1832
Balthasar Hammerle NE¼-SW¼-S27; 1-9-1833
John Blattner W½-SW¼-S27; 8-29-1831

Page 95. T 7 N, R 2 W of 1st P.M.

Barbara Eckendorff Shaffer W½-SW¼-S33; 8-28-1832
William Tucker SE¼-SE¼-S34; 10-29-1832
Philip Michael NE¼-SE¼-S34; 7-24-1834
John Henry Bush W½-SE¼-S34; 8-14-1832
Armstead Blevins Reed NE¼-SE¼-S36; 10-8-1832
David D. Davis SE¼-SE¼-S36; 6-21-1838

Page 96. T 8 N, R 2 W of 1st P.M. **FRANKLIN CO.**

Cyrus Quick W½-SW¼-S1; 2-10-1836
Spencer Wiley SE¼-NW¼-S5; 3-2-1835
Jacob Lefforge NE¼-NW¼-S5; 5-29-1835
Spencer Wiley NW¼-SW¼-S5; 3-2-1835
John Robeson & Gideon Herndon SW¼-SW¼-S5; 8-29-1836
Jacob Lefforge SE¼-NE¼-S6; 11-18-1835
Thomas Herndon NE¼-NE¼-S6; 1-22-1836
James Mewhinney NE¼-NW¼-S6; 9-21-1836
Gideon Herndon NW¼-NW¼-S6; 8-29-1836
Thomas Herndon SE¼-NW¼-S6; 10-6-1832
Jacob Remlinger SW¼-NW¼-S6; 11-24-1836
Gideon Herndon SE¼-SE¼-S6; 8-21-1836
Peter Riedlinger NE¼-SE¼-S6; 11-23-1836. May be Remlinger; see 2nd entry above

Page 97. T 8 N, R 2 W of 1st P.M.

Samuel Mewhinney SE¼-NE¼-S7; 11-12-1835
John Robeson & Gideon Herndon NE¼-NE¼-S7; 8-29-1836
Samuel Mewhinney W½-NE¼-S7; 12-14-1835
James Mewhinney & William M. McCarty E½-NW¼-S7; 2-9-1836
James Mewhinney SW¼-NW¼-S7; 2-9-1836
Lewis Shockey NW¼-NW¼-S7; 8-25-1836
Thomas Herndon SE¼-SW¼-S7; 10-4-1832
Gideon Herndon NE¼-SW¼-S7; 8-29-1836

Lorenzo Dow Morgan E½-SE¼-S8; 9-16-1833
John T. McKinney W½-SE¼-S8; 1-29-1836
Jonathan Shaw N½-SW¼-S8; 1-28-1836
John T. McKinney SE¼-SW¼ & SW¼-SW¼-S8; 1-29-1836
John Hackleman & Jacob Hackleman NE¼-S9; 9-17-1816
Hiram Fay SE¼-NW¼-S9; 10-15-1832
William Lyons, Jr. NE¼-NW¼-S9; 10-17-1835
Samuel Shirk NE¼-SW¼-S9; 9-25-1832
Samuel Shirk SE¼-SW¼-S9; 6-14-1833
Zachariah Cooksey SW¼-S10; 3-18-1817
Britton Gant NE¼-NE¼-S12; 6-13-1832
Giles Gant SE¼-NE¼-S12; 2-3-1837

Page 98. T 8 N, R 2 W of 1st P.M.

John Conner NW¼-S13; 8-14-1810
John Harden NE¼-SW¼-S14; 3-25-1833
James Forester SE¼-SW¼-S14; 4-1-1834
James Forester NW¼-SW¼-S14; 8-17-1835
James Forester SW¼-SW¼-S14; 1-18-1834
Alexander Crawford NE¼-NE¼-S15; 3-31-1834
Timothy Gennings SE¼-NE¼-S15; 8-13-1835
Milton Dearmond W½-NW¼-S15; 8-28-1832
Ward Davis SW¼-SE¼-S15; 11-13-1834
Highland Jacobs NW¼-SE¼-S15; 3-6-1835
David Usher SE¼-SE¼-S15; 3-6-1835
Timothy Jennings NE¼-SE¼-S15; 8-13-1835
Milton Dearmond NW¼-SW¼-S15; 2-18-1833
Joseph Richards SW¼-SW¼-S15; 4-22-1834
Highland Jacobs NE¼-SW¼-S15; 12-30-1834
Ward Davis SE¼-SW¼-S15; 5-12-1835
Enoch McCarty N½-NE¼-S17; 3-11-1835
William M. McCarty S½-NE¼-S17; 1-28-1836
Lewis Shockey S½-NW¼-S17; 2-1-1836 Sterrett
William Stervolt N½-NW¼-S17; 7-5-1836. Might be Sterrolt or
Conrad Schamber SW¼-SW¼-S17; 9-29-1834
Christian Floor NW¼-SW¼-S17; 3-29-1836
John Robeson, Jr. NW¼-NE¼-S18; 1-22-1836
Henry Maseger SW¼-NE¼-S18; 3-29-1836. Might be Mareger
Jacob Rosenbaum SE¼-NE¼-S18; 7-7-1836
George Holcher NE¼-NE¼-S18; 7-7-1836

Page 99. T 8 N, R 2 W of 1st P.M.

Peter Prefogle NE¼-SE¼-S18; 8-31-1834
Henry Masemaor & Frederick Klanke SE¼-SE¼-S18; 4-18-1836
Henry Maschger & Frederick Maschger S½-SW¼-S18; 2-8-1836
James Robeson NE¼-SW¼-S18; 2-4-1836
Abraham Robeson NW¼-NW¼-S19; 2-4-1836
Joel Keeler SE¼-NW¼-S19; 2-4-1836
Joshua Lyons SW¼-NW¼-S19; 2-22-1836
Joel Keeler NE¼-NW¼-S19; 2-22-1835
William McAnally NW¼-SE¼-S19; 12-6-1834
William McAnally NE¼-SE¼-S19; 2-13-1836
John Stockinger S½-SE¼-S19; 10-13-1835
Catharine Ripp E½-SW¼-S19; 2-20-1836
John Rudolph Dearkhusing W½-SW¼-S19; 9-11-1835
William Robeson SE¼-NW¼-S20; 12-13-1832

Henry Wolber NE$\frac{1}{4}$-NW$\frac{1}{4}$-S20; NW$\frac{1}{4}$-NW$\frac{1}{4}$-S20; 10-29-1834
Frederick Wolber SW$\frac{1}{4}$-NW$\frac{1}{4}$-S20; 10-29-1834
Herman Frederick Dobbeling E$\frac{1}{2}$-SE$\frac{1}{4}$-S20; 10-23-1834
William Robeson NE$\frac{1}{4}$-SW$\frac{1}{4}$-S20; 12-13-1832
Adam Foosner SE$\frac{1}{4}$-SW$\frac{1}{4}$-S20; 1-2-1837
Joshua Baker SW$\frac{1}{4}$-SW$\frac{1}{4}$-S20; 1-15-1834
Frederick Wolber NW$\frac{1}{4}$-SW$\frac{1}{4}$-S20; 10-29-1834
Michael Klein NW$\frac{1}{4}$-NE$\frac{1}{4}$-S21; 8-9-1834
Christian Pinger SW$\frac{1}{4}$-NE$\frac{1}{4}$ & E$\frac{1}{2}$-NE$\frac{1}{4}$-S21; 4-29-1835
John Stockinger E$\frac{1}{2}$-NW$\frac{1}{4}$-S21; 7-30-1834
Philip Waldorf W$\frac{1}{2}$-NW$\frac{1}{4}$-S21; 9-5-1834
Daniel Symmes Major E$\frac{1}{2}$-SE$\frac{1}{4}$-S21; 3-10-1836
John Henry Ellerman W$\frac{1}{2}$-SE$\frac{1}{4}$-S21; 2-1-1836
Parker Wise SW$\frac{1}{4}$-SW$\frac{1}{4}$-S21; 10-4-1834
Joshua Parvis NW$\frac{1}{4}$-SW$\frac{1}{4}$-S21; 10-6-1834
Henry Beckman E$\frac{1}{2}$-SW$\frac{1}{4}$-S21; 10-23-1834

Page 100. T 8 N, R 2 W of 1st P.M.

Peter Hiler S$\frac{1}{2}$-NE$\frac{1}{4}$-S22; 3-1-1833
Henry Scott NE$\frac{1}{4}$-NE$\frac{1}{4}$-S22; 2-18-1836
John Scott NW$\frac{1}{4}$-NE$\frac{1}{4}$-S22; 2-18-1836
Thomas Howe SW$\frac{1}{4}$-NW$\frac{1}{4}$-S22; 4-9-1833
Thomas Howe NW$\frac{1}{4}$-NW$\frac{1}{4}$-S22; 12-5-1835
Joseph Schoonover Whitney NW$\frac{1}{4}$-SW$\frac{1}{4}$-S22; 6-13-1832
Samuel Ward SW$\frac{1}{4}$-SW$\frac{1}{4}$-S22; 1-9-1834
John Harden NE$\frac{1}{4}$-NE$\frac{1}{4}$-S23; 1-26-1836
Daniel Symmes Major SE$\frac{1}{4}$-NE$\frac{1}{4}$-S23; 2-6-1836
David Usher E$\frac{1}{2}$-NW$\frac{1}{4}$-S23; 12-13-1833
John Johnson W$\frac{1}{2}$-NW$\frac{1}{4}$-S23; 1-5-1833
William Spradling SW$\frac{1}{4}$-SE$\frac{1}{4}$-S23; 6-14-1833
Hamilton Shaw NW$\frac{1}{4}$-SE$\frac{1}{4}$; NE$\frac{1}{4}$-SE$\frac{1}{4}$; SE$\frac{1}{4}$-SE$\frac{1}{4}$-S23; 3-26-1836
Calvin Owen SE$\frac{1}{4}$-SW$\frac{1}{4}$-S23; 1-5-1833
Calvin Owen NE$\frac{1}{4}$-SW$\frac{1}{4}$-S23; 2-6-1836
Thomas Bennet SW$\frac{1}{4}$-SW$\frac{1}{4}$-S23; 12-15-1834
John Scott NW$\frac{1}{4}$-SW$\frac{1}{4}$-S23; 1-27-1836
Allen Backhouse W$\frac{1}{2}$-SW$\frac{1}{4}$-S24; 1-23-1836
William Fread SE$\frac{1}{4}$-S26; 5-15-1815

Page 101. T 8 N, R 2 W of 1st P.M.

Isaac Hart SW$\frac{1}{4}$-NW$\frac{1}{4}$-S27; 8-11-1832
Philip Heck NW$\frac{1}{4}$-NW$\frac{1}{4}$-S27; 2-27-1836
Henry Speckman E$\frac{1}{2}$-NW$\frac{1}{4}$-S27; 10-3-1835
Henry Wilmers SW$\frac{1}{4}$-NE$\frac{1}{4}$-S28; 10-23-1834
Henry Miller NW$\frac{1}{4}$-NE$\frac{1}{4}$-S28; 10-10-1835
Henry Meier E$\frac{1}{2}$-NW$\frac{1}{4}$-S28; 10-23-1834
Samuel Wise W$\frac{1}{2}$-NW$\frac{1}{4}$-S28; 10-4-1834
Wilhelm Fischer SW$\frac{1}{4}$-SE$\frac{1}{4}$-S28; 11-13-1833
Henry Poppe NW$\frac{1}{4}$-SE$\frac{1}{4}$-S28; 10-23-1834
Perry Coverdale SW$\frac{1}{4}$-NW$\frac{1}{4}$-S29; 12-9-1835
Henry Speckman E$\frac{1}{2}$-NW$\frac{1}{4}$-S29; 2-1-1836
Martin Baker NW$\frac{1}{4}$-NW$\frac{1}{4}$-S29; 3-22-1836
Valentine Dill SE$\frac{1}{4}$-NE$\frac{1}{4}$-S30; 2-15-1836
Catherine Ripp NE$\frac{1}{4}$-NE$\frac{1}{4}$-S30; 2-20-1836
Valentine Fuller W$\frac{1}{2}$-NE$\frac{1}{4}$-S30; 2-7-1835
Sarah Keeler NW$\frac{1}{4}$-NW$\frac{1}{4}$-S30; 2-17-1836
Catherine Ripp SW$\frac{1}{4}$-NW$\frac{1}{4}$-S30; 2-20-1836

Catherine Ripp E½-NW¼-S30; 2-20-1836
Henry William Kise E½-SE¼-S30; 9-30-1833
Nicholas Siefert W½-SE¼-S30; 9-30-1833
Ignatz Ripperger E½-SW¼-S30; 9-30-1833
Alvis Bauer W½-SW¼-S30; 10-28-1833
Michael Ripperger NE¼-S31; 9-30-1833
Ignatz Ripperger E½-NW¼-S31; 9-30-1833
John Anthony Fusner W½-NW¼-S31; 9-30-1833
Ignatz Ripperger E½-SW¼-S31; 9-30-1833
John Anthony Fusner W½-SW¼-S31; 9-30-1833
     Page 102. T 8 N, R 2 W of 1st P.M.
Henry William Kise W½-NW¼-S32; 9-30-1833
William Henry Harrison Halberstadt NW¼-SE¼-S32; 10-30-1834
George Pearson Buell SW¼-SE¼-S32; 2-1-1836
Arnold, Henry, Julius, & Charles Weigler E½-S32; 7-13-1835
Henry William Kise W½-SW¼-S32; 9-30-1833
John Wolf NE¼-SW¼-S33; 4-11-1835
Michael Hammann SE¼-SW¼-S33; 10-5-1835
Arnold, Henry, Julius, & Charles Weigler W½-SW¼-S33; 7-13-1835
John Peterson NW¼-NW¼-S34; 5-24-1832
Joseph Price SW¼-NW¼-S34; 10-30-1834
William Jackman SE¼-S34; 2-20-1834
James Hamilton NW¼-SW¼-S34; 9-5-1832
Daniel Taylor SW¼-SW¼-S34; 1-30-1833
Frederick Watts Ice NE¼-SW¼-S34; 4-15-1834
Daniel Taylor SE¼-SW¼-S34; 10-4-1832
John Spradling SW¼-SW¼-S35; 3-2-1833
Solomon Allen NW¼-SW¼-S35; 3-8-1834
John Little NE¼-SW¼-S36; 1-26-1835
Valentine Walter SE¼-SW¼-S36; 10-5-1835
     Page 103. T 9 N, R 2 W of 1st P.M.
Enoch Buckingham SE¼-S3; 1-18-1815
James S. Powers Lot 6-SE pt.-N½-Fr.S6; 6-17-1836. * Omission:
William McCleery Lot 3-E½-SE¼-S6; 1-20-1836   James S. Powers
     Page 104. T 9 N, R 2 W of 1st P.M.   Lot 2-SW pt.-
Andrew Bailey SE¼-S14; 12-31-1814   N½-Fr.S6;
John T. McKinney SW¼-S17; 10-26-1833   7-25-1835
John Kenneday NE¼-S19; 9-13-1808
     Page 105. T 9 N, R 2 W of 1st P.M.
Jeremiah Woods N½-NW¼-S31; 12-25-1835
John Iff & John Simon S½-NW¼-S31; 7-25-1836
     Page 106. T 9 N, R 2 W of 1st P.M.
George Anthony NE¼-S35; 9-27-1811
     Page 107. T 10 N, R 2 W of 1st P.M.   UNION CO.
William Coomes SE¼-S12; 7-27-1814
     Page 108. T 10 N, R 2 W of 1st P.M.   FRANKLIN CO.
Robert Hanna SE¼-S28; 9-24-1804
     Page 109. T 10 N, R 2 W of 1st P.M.
Daniel Powers NE¼-S35; 10-20-1814
William Harvey SW¼-S35; 5-1-1815
     Page 113. T 12 N, R 2 W of 1st P.M.   UNION CO.
Peter Emmard NE¼-S26; 1-11-1809
     Page 114. T 13 N, R 2 W of 1st P.M.   WAYNE CO.
John Read, assee. of Thomas Lewis NE¼-S35; 8-25-1806
John Lee NW¼-S36; 2-24-1806

Page 115. T 2 N, R 3 W of 1st P.M. **SWITZERLAND CO.**

John Orr W½-NW¼-S5; 5-10-1832
John Kunkle E½-SE¼-S6; 10-20-1832
George Washington Heady NW¼-SE¼-S9; 6-3-1833
George Washington Heady SW¼-SE¼-S9; 3-2-1833

Page 116. T 2 N, R 3 W of 1st P.M.

William Dickeson & John Dickeson NW¼-S11; 11-25-1811
James Malco_____ NW¼-NE¼-S17; 1-18-1833. Might be McCallum; see following entries
Gabriel Hall SW¼-NE¼-S17; 6-21-1836
George Hollcroft SE¼-NE¼-S19; 9-26-1832
Moses B. Pearson NE¼-NE¼-S19; 8-26-1836
Andrew Roberts SE¼-SE¼-S19; 9-3 -1832
Moses B. Pearson NE¼-SE¼-S19; 8-24-1836
William Means NE¼-NW¼-S20; 7-1-1836
James Dalmazzo SE¼-NW¼-S20; 8-13-1836
John William Wright W½-NE¼-S21; 7-7-1832

Page 117. T 2 N, R 3 W of 1st P.M.

Moses Roberts W½-NE¼-S31; 4-2-1836
Winthrop Robinson E½-SE¼-S1; 12-10-1833
John Cunningham NE¼-NE¼-S2; 1-30-1833
Moses Porter SE¼-NE¼-S2; 9-15-1834
Isaac Fredenburgh, Jr. W½-NE¼-S2; 6-26-1832

Page 118. T 3 N, R 3 W of 1st P.M.

James Porter NE¼-SW¼-S2; 11-30-1832
James Porter SE¼-SW¼-S2; 6-3-1833
Lemuel Wiley NE¼-NE¼-S3; 11-23-1833
James Hallinan NW¼-NE¼-S3; 7-21-1834
David Lee SE¼-NE¼-S3; 2-26-1833
Minor Chambers SW¼-NE¼-S3; 9-25-1832
George Clark SE¼-NW¼-S3; 9-25-1832
James Hallinan NE¼-NW¼-S3; 7-21-1834
Harvey Pease NW¼-NW¼-S3; 1-11-1834
Harvey Pease SW¼-NW¼-S3; 11-16-1833
Isaac Richards, Jr. NE¼-SW¼-S4; 5-3-1834
Martin Potter SE¼-SW¼-S4; 4-11-1836
Henry Mitchell NW¼-NW¼-S5; 2-12-1834
William Clark Mitchell SW¼-NW¼-S5; 6-24-1834
Martin Reese NW¼-SE¼-S5; 12-7-1832
William C. Mitchell SW¼-SE¼-S5; 8-19-1836
Emsley Shadday SW¼-NW¼-S8; 10-22-1832
John Gardner NW¼-NW¼-S8; 6-26-1834
James Riley, Jr. NE¼-SE¼-S8; 9-19-1835
Daniel Loudon NW¼-SE¼-S8; 5-16-1836. Might be London
John Protsman SE¼-SE¼-S8; 6-13-1836
James Riley, Jr. SW¼-SE¼-S8; 7-18-1836

Page 119. T 3 N, R 3 W of 1st P.M.

William Lee NW¼-NE¼-S9; 3-16-1835
John F. Cotton SW¼-NE¼-S9; 9-14-1836
Joseph Allen Cole NW¼-NW¼-S9; 6-8-1832
Joseph Kincaid E½-NW¼; SW¼-NW¼-S9; 5-18-1836
David Cain N½-SW¼-S9; 9-10-1836
John F. Cotton SE¼-SW¼-S9; 9-14-1836
Thomas Hamel SW¼-SW¼-S9; 10-8-1836

SWITZERLAND CO.

Thomas Walter Imel NE¼-NW¼-S12; 11-30-1832
Samuel Forwood NW¼-NW¼-S12; 9-29-1832
Charles Leatherbury SE¼-NW¼-S12; 3-23-1836
Robert Imel SW¼-SW¼-S12; 8-10-1835
Lawrence Nichell W½-NE¼-S13; 2-3-1836
Michael Lawrence W½-NW¼-S13; 6-29-1836
William Brown E½-NE¼-S14; 6-11-1832
Henry Mitchell NE¼-SW¼-S14; 9-29-1832
Melville Wiley NW¼-SW¼-S14; 11-15-1833
Hiram Peabody SE¼-SW¼-S14; 2-12-1834
Joel Wilson SW¼-SW¼-S14; 4-14-1834
James Richardson, assee. of Jonathan Baird, a Canadian volunteer,
    located per Act of 15 March 1814 NE¼-S15; 10-8-1817
        Page 120. T 3 N, R 3 W of 1st P.M.
Solomon Freeman NE¼-NW¼-S15; 12-23-183__ (looks like 1836)
Henry Scudder SE¼-NW¼-S15; 9-10-1836
Frederick Green W½-NW¼-S15; 6-11-1836
Solomon Freeman NE¼-SW¼-S15; 3-14-1836
Henry Scudder NW¼-SW¼-S15; 9-10-1836
Thomas Hamel S½-SW¼-S15; 9-24-1836
Daniel Blodget NW¼-NE¼-S17; SE¼-NE¼-S17; 7-20-1833
Nicholas Lientz NE¼-NE¼-S17; 3-15-1836
Ora Blodget SW¼-NE¼-S17; 10-18-1836
Zenas Sisson E½-SE¼-S17; 7-9-1836
James Bowman NE¼-S18; 8-30-1824
George W. Heady SE¼-S18; 1-26-1837
William Prewitt N½-SW fr.-S18; 10-11-1834
William Graham S½-SW fr.-S18; 8-22-1836
Joseph Bryant SW¼-NE¼-S19; 12-28-1833
Thomas C. Bryant NW¼-NE¼-S19; 8-25-1837
Joseph Bryant NW¼-S19; 2-26-1836
Joseph Blodget NW¼-SE¼-S20; 1-31-1833
Isaac Gray SW¼-SE¼-S20; 5-30-1836
James Graham SW¼-SW¼-S20; 8-20-1832
John Graham, Sr. NW¼-SW¼-S20; 5-19-1836
Daniel Loudon SE¼-SW¼-S20; 4-4-1836. May be London
Stillwell Graham NE¼-SW¼-S20; 5-19-1836
        Page 121. T 3 N, R 3 W of 1st P.M.
John Spears NW¼-NE¼-S21; 3-19-1836
John Spears NE¼-NE¼-S21; 3-15-1836
Silas S. Cole SE¼-NE¼-S21; 3-15-1836
John Lewis SW¼-NE¼-S21; 3-15-1836
Martin R. Cole S½-NW¼-S21; 3-21-1836
William Whitmore NE¼-NW¼-S21; 8-16-1836
Thomas Hamel NW¼-NW¼-S21; 9-24-1836
Mary Frazer, widow of Samuel Frazer, a private in the Canadian
    volunteers SW¼-S21; 6-14-1821
James Richardson, assee. of a Canadian volunteer NE¼-S22; 10-8-1817
Joseph Cole, Jr. SW¼-NW¼-S22; 12-30-1835
Thomas Hamel NW¼-NW¼-S22; 9-24-1836
James Richardson, assee. of a Canadian volunteer SE¼-S22; 10-8-1817
James Richardson, assee. of a Canadian volunteer SW¼-S22; 10-8-1817
Edwin Story NE¼-S23; 5-5-1832
Walter Armstrong NE¼-NW¼; NW¼-NW¼-S23; 10-26-1835

Joel Wilson SE¼-NW¼-S23; 9-29-1832 **SWITZERLAND CO.**
Walter Armstrong SW¼-NW¼-S23; 10-26-1835
Daniel Wilcox, Jr. W½-NW¼-S27; 6-3-1834
Friend Thrall E½-SW¼-S27; 12-13-1816
Francis Silvers W½-SW¼-S27; 9-1-1832

Page 122. T 3 N, R 3 W of 1st P.M.

David Shull E½-NW¼-S28; 3-2-1833
Daniel Burcham NW¼-SW¼-S28; 4-19-1834
Solomon Losey SW¼-SW¼-S28; 7-18-1836
William Bright NE¼-SE¼-S29; 6-13-1832
John Lock NW¼-SE¼-S29; 6-13-1832
Stephen R. Garrard SE¼-SE¼-S29; 2-18-1837
Moses R. Brandon SW¼-SE¼-S29; 5-30-1836
Samuel Husk Pavy NE¼-SW¼-S29; 12-2-1835
George E. Pleasants NW¼-SW¼-S29; 4-20-1837
Joseph Malin S½-SW¼-S29; 10-15-1833
John Sigmon E½-NE¼-S32; 7-2-1835
Rosanna Richards E½-NE¼-S33; 9-3-1833
Mary Griffith W½-NE¼-S33; 9-3-1833
John Brandon SE¼-NW¼-S33; 12-15-1832
James Gray NE¼-NW¼-S33; 3-4-1835
John Sigmon W½-NW¼-S33; 10-8-1832
Arad Silvers NE¼-SE¼-S33; 9-1-1832
William Park SE¼-SE¼-S33; 12-10-1833

Page 123. T 4 N, R 3 W of 1st P.M. **DEARBORN CO.**

Joseph Lyons NW¼-S1; 11-27-1811 (Part in Ohio Co.)
Samuel Graham NW¼-SE¼-S1; 6-3-1836 **OHIO CO.**
James Lyons NE¼-SE¼-S1; 9-12-1836
Samuel Graham SW¼-SE¼; SE¼-SE¼-S1; 12-26-1837
Samuel Graham E½-SW¼-S1; 6-3-1836
Charles B. Pate SW¼-NW¼-S2; 2-22-1836 (Part in Dearborn Co.)
Lewis Pate NW¼-NW¼-S2; 1-18-1837 (Part in Dearborn Co.
Charles B. Pate NE¼-NE¼-S3; 2-22-1836 **DEARBORN CO.**
George Pate, Jr. NW¼-NE¼-S3; 9-21-1836
Randol R. Pate SW¼-NE¼; SE¼-NE¼-S3; 9-21-1836
Herod H. Y. Ellerman NW¼-NW¼-S3; 12-26-1838
Henry Probst E½-NW¼-S3; 6-17-1839
Frederick Wolber SW¼-NW¼-S3; 6-17-1839

Page 124. T 4 N, R 3 W of 1st P.M.

Abraham Bills E½-SW¼-S3; 6-24-1814
Frederick Wolber NW¼-SW¼; SW¼-SW¼-S3; 6-17-1839
Frederick Probst E½-NE¼; NW¼-NE¼-S4; 12-26-1838
Frederick Probst SW¼-NE¼-S4; 6-17-1839
David Pate N½-NW¼-S8; 8-15-1836 **OHIO CO.**
John Henry Libbert S½-NW¼-S8; 12-31-1839 Part in Dearborn Co.)
George Pate NE¼-SE¼-S10; 5-22-1836 **OHIO CO.**
Henry S. Pate NW¼-SE¼-S10; 5-28-1836
William Patmore E½-SW¼-S11; 7-22-1833
George Pate SW¼-SW¼-S11; 5-23-1836
Cornelius S. Terwilliger NW¼-SW¼-S11; 2-28-1839
John J. Feely N½-NE¼-S13; 2-12-1839

Page 125. T 4 N, R 3 W of 1st P.M.

James F. Johnson SE¼-SE¼-S13; 4-15-1834
Timothy Ward Graham N½-NE¼-S14; 10-6-1832

George Carpenter SE¼-NE¼-S14; 5-29-1837
John Elder SW¼-NE¼-S14; 1-28-1836
Norman Sloan NE¼-SE¼-S14; 3-1-1837
Azor N. Sloan SE¼-SE¼-S14; 4-21-1837
Daniel Woolcott W½-SE¼-S14; 9-20-1836
James Wymond SW¼-S14; 3-7-1834
Ezra G. Bear SE¼-NE¼-S15; 9-5-1836
Thomas Jones NE¼-NE¼-S15; 7-3-1837
Ezra Mulford W½-NE¼-S15; 4-2-1838
Hiram Barker NW¼-S15; 2-22-1839
Timothy Ward SE¼-SE¼-S15; 9-29-1836
Timothy Ward NE¼-SE¼-S15; 5-13-1834
Timothy Ward W½-SE¼-S15; 10-2-1833
Hugh Cole S½-SW¼-S15; 10-27-1836
William Winscott NW¼-SW¼-S15; 10-27-1836
Joseph Q. Frazee NE¼-SW¼-S15; 12-18-1837
Benjamin Dolph NE¼-SE¼-S17; 10-7-1833
Albert Voris S½-SE¼-S17; 6-20-1836
John McGuire Lot 1-NE pt.-NW¼-Fr.S17; 12-26-1837
John McGuire Lot 2-SE pt.-NE¼-S17; 5-5-1838
Benjamin S. Hildebrand Lot 3-NE pt.-SW¼-S17; 3-9-1839
William M. Gardner Lot 4-SE pt.-SW¼-S17; 1-27-1838
George Fallis SE¼-NE¼-S20; 3-14-1836
Luther Hotchkiss NE¼-NE¼-S20; 7-5-1836
Luther Hotchkiss W½-NE¼-S20; 6-15-1836
Martin David Fallis SE¼-SE¼-S20; 3-14-1836
Madison Vanosdol NE¼-SE¼-S20; 6-20-1836

Page 126. T 4 N, R 3 W of 1st P.M.

Henry Demaree SE¼-NW¼-S20; 6-30-1836
William Brown SW¼-NW¼-S20; 12-7-1838
Jacob Boyd N½-Fr.S19; 12-7-1838
John Campbell Marfort S½-Fr.S19; 6-13-1833
James Wilson E½-NE¼-S21; 11-7-1834
John Fallis NW¼-NE¼-S21; 4-24-1839
William Murphey SE¼-NW¼-S21; 8-17-1835
George Fallis SW¼-NW¼-S21; 3-1-1837
Samuel Fallis NE¼-NW¼-S21; 3-1-1837
Edward Roberts NW¼-NW¼-S21; 2-2-1838
William Armstrong SW¼-SE¼-S21; 12-15-1837
Marshall Elliott NW¼-SE¼-S21; 5-21-1830
Joseph B. Glenn E½-SE¼-S21; 2-23-1839
Martin David Fallis SW¼-SW¼-S21; 2-24-1837
Richard Fallis NW¼-SW¼-S21; 10-6-1838
John Gross E½-SW¼-S21; 8-28-1839
Peter Gordon Daubenheyer NE¼-NE¼-S22; 1-20-1836
Peter Gordon Daubenheyer SE¼-NE¼-S22; 5-13-1834
Orlando Walker W½-NE¼-S22; 8-6-1833
Benaiah Harmon Walker E½-NW¼-S22; 8-6-1833
Christian Cooper W½-NW¼-S22; 8-11-1832
Peter Jordan Daubenheyer NE¼-SE¼-S22; 5-13-1834
Joseph Culp SE¼-SE¼-S22; 6-11-1834
Isaac Gilson Bascum W½-SE¼-S22; 9-2-1833
Christian Cooper N½-SW¼-S22; 10-13-1832
Joshua Sutton SE¼-SW¼-S22; 8-20-1834

Eli Cooper SW¼-SW¼-S22; 9-5-1836
Harvey Thatcher NW¼-SE¼-S23; 1-12-1836
Harvey Thatcher NE¼-SE¼-S23; 12-8-1836
David Brown SW¼-SE¼-S23; 2-28-1837
Eleazer Smith SE¼-SE¼-S23; 3-27-1837

Page 127. T 4 N, R 3 W of 1st P.M.

John Gibbs E½-SE¼-S24; 10-23-1837
James Fox W½-SE¼-S24; 3-21-1837
Jacob Harris SW¼-SW¼-S24; 9-27-1836
John Clark NW¼-SW¼-S24; 12-22-1838

Page 127. T 4 N, R 3 W of 1st P.M. SWITZERLAND CO.

Asa Jessup SE¼-NE¼-S25; 5-24-1833
William B. Hey NE¼-NE¼-S25; 6-12-1839
Jacob R. Harris NW¼-NE¼-S25; 9-27-1836
Joseph Emanuel SW¼-NE¼-S25; 4-30-1840
Jacob R. Harris E½-NW¼-S25; 9-27-1836
Walter Jessup NE¼-SE¼-S25; 7-8-1836
Hugh B. Darney(?(SE¼-SE¼-S25; 9-3-1836
William Lesure SW¼-SE¼-S25; 10-26-1836
Walter Jessup NW¼-SE¼-S25; 12-27-1837
Thomas Warenski & Peter Roscheshoski NE¼-SW¼-S25; 11-15-1837
Albert Cusmiercik SE¼-SW¼-S25; 4-30-1838
James Huntei W½-SW¼-S25; 12-20-1834
Valloms Morse NW¼-NW¼-S26; 6-26-1832
Thomas Davis SW¼-NW¼-S26; 4-2-1834
Michael Dunning NE¼-NW¼; SE¼-NW¼-S26; 12-13-1836
David Brown NW¼-NE¼-S27; 8-20-1834
Levi Traver SW¼-NE¼-S27; 12-24-1834
John Sutton NE¼-NW¼-S27; 2-19-1834
William Andrews SE¼-NW¼-S27; 6-13-1836
William Armstrong W½-NW¼-S27; 6-29-1836
William Peck NE¼-SE¼-S27; 2-23-1833
Samuel F. Ford SE¼-SE¼-S27; 8-30-1836
Peter Pelsor W½-SE¼; E½-SW¼-S27; 5-25-1833

Page 128. T 4 N, R 3 W of 1st P.M.

James Burroughs SW¼-SW¼-S27; 9-27-1836
James L. Burroughs NW¼-SW¼-S27; 1-28-1837
Amos D. Hammond NE¼-NE¼-S28; 11-27-1837
Peter Sherman SE¼-NE¼-S28; 9-3-1839
Joseph Lassell NW¼-S28; 11-19-1836
John H. Chittenden SW¼-SE¼-S28; 10-19-1836
James Lewis NW¼-SE¼-S28; 10-19-1836
William Lassell & John T. Swift E½-SE¼-S28; 12-13-1836
Jeremiah Richards SE¼-SW¼-S28; 4-25-1834
James Lewis NE¼-SW¼-S28; 11-9-1836
Presley Q. Reno NW¼-SW¼-S28; 2-10-1837
Lewis A. Clarke SW¼-SW¼-S28; 10-13-1836
Daniel Voris W½-NE¼-S29; 2-2-1836
Daniel Voris SE¼-NE¼-S29; 7-5-1836
Daniel Goodner E½-SE¼-S29; 6-23-1834
Daniel Goodner W½-SE¼-S29; 4-25-1836
William Austin SW¼-SW¼-S29; 1-20-1835
John Kephart NW¼-SW¼-S29; 4-12-1833
Jacob Goodner SE¼-SW¼; NE¼-SW¼-S29; 6-23-1834

SWITZERLAND CO.

Henry Demaree Lot 3-N end-Fr.N½-Fr.S30; 5-30-1833
Henry Voris Lot 2-S pt.-N end-Fr.N½-Fr.S30; 6-13-1833
Thomas Jones Davis E½-NW¼-S32; 12-5-1832
William Austin W½-NW¼-S32; 1-20-1835
Isaac Richards SE¼-S33; 6-14-1817

Page 129. T 4 N, R 3 W of 1st P.M.

James Hallinan NW¼-S34; 7-21-1834
Allen Wiley SE¼-SE¼-S34; 6-1-1835
Delaney Wiley NE¼-SE¼-S34; 6-3-1836
Francis S. Lindley W½-SE¼-S34; 3-28-1836
Abraham Higbie SW¼-NE¼-S35; 10-10-1833
James Hunter NW¼-NE¼-S35; 1-6-1835
John Cunningham NE¼-NE¼-S35; SE¼-NE¼-S35; 2-22-1834
Patrick Kelly W½-NW¼-S36; 7-12-1834
Martin Potter SE¼-S36; 4-15-1833
Peter Althiser SE¼-SW¼-S36; 4-22-1833
Patrick Kelly NE¼-SW¼-S36; 7-12-1834

Page 129. T 5 N, R 3 W of 1st P.M. DEARBORN CO.

James Noble SW¼-NE¼-S1; 6-26-1834
Jacob E. Johnson NW¼-NE¼-S1; 2-6-1837
Elijah Miller NW¼-SE¼-S1; 6-20-1836
Elijah Miller NE¼-SE¼-S1; 10-24-1836
Jeduthan Hart S½-SE¼-S1; 3-1-1837
Harrison Alfred NW¼-SW¼-S1; 9-1-1836
Christian Weist SW¼-SW¼-S1; 9-1-1836
William L. Thornton NE¼-SW¼-S1; 3-15-1839
George W. Thornton NW¼-NE¼-S2; 2-3-1836
Jacob Wakeman SW¼-NE¼-S2; 2-1-1837
Edward Eugene Ravers(?) E½-NE¼-S2; 9-29-1836

Page 130. T 5 N, R 3 W of 1st P.M.

John Carpenter Shuman SW¼-NW¼-S2; 5-23-1832
Humphrey Cain NW¼-NW¼-S2; 4-5-1837
George H. Shuman NE¼-SE¼-S2; 6-28-1836
Jacob E. Johnson SE¼-SE¼-S2; 9-2-1836
Jacob Wakeman NW¼-SE¼-S2; 2-1-1837
John Winsor SW¼-SE¼-S2; 1-4-1833
James Oliver Smith SE¼-NW¼-S3; 5-25-1832
John J. Akin NE¼-NW¼-S3; 8-21-1837
Oliver Lee Lyon N end-Fr.S8; 9-5-1836
Philip Rowland NE¼-NE¼-S9; 1-9-1833
John McCabe SE¼-NE¼-S9; 5-27-1834
Philip Rowland W½-NE¼-S9; 3-24-1836
Joachim Williamson N½-NW¼-S9; 3-9-1836
Ayers L. Bramble SE¼-NW¼; SW¼-NW¼-S9; 4-2-1836
Laban Bramble Lot 2-N end-SE¼-S9; 5-1-1834
John Owings Lot 3-N end-SW¼-S9; 8-17-1836
Ephraim Burroughs SW¼-NE¼-S12; 5-9-1835
Jeduthan Hart NW¼-NE¼-S12; 5-21-1838

Page 131. T 5 N, R 3 W of 1st P.M.

William Headley NE¼-S21; 2-26-1836
Joseph Cossins NW¼-NW¼-S21; 2-26-1836
John Headley NE¼-NW¼-S21; 2-4-1837
Enoch Bostick S½-NW¼-S21; 3-27-1837
William Headley SW¼-SE¼-S21; 1-16-1837

Henry Petersohen E½-SE¼-S21; 5-3-1838
Young Johnson SE¼-SW½-S21; 1-19-1836
Theophilus Martin NE¼-SW½-S21; 1-25-1837
George Grove, Jr. NE¼-NE¼-S22; 8-6-1836
Henry Parker NW½-NE¼-S22; 12-9-1836
Rice Cowles S½-NE¼-S22; 1-12-1838
Isaac Jones NW¼-NW½-S22; 3-23-1836
George Grove, Jr. SW½-NW½-S22; 1-12-1837
George Grove, Jr. SE¼-NW½-S22; 1-27-1837
John Miller NE¼-NW¼-S22; 2-3-1837
Benjamin Fowler NW¼-SE¼-S22; 4-16-1838
John Ruthop SW¼-SE¼-S22; 5-3-1838
George Grove, Jr. E½-SE¼-S22; 8-1-1836
Benjamin Fowler NE¼-SW¼-S22; 4-16-1838
John Ruthop SE¼-SW½-S22; 5-3-1838
Henry Petersohen W½-SW¼-S22; 5-3-1838

Page 132.   T 5 N, R 3 W of 1st P.M.

Herman Henry Nieman W½-SE¼-S23; 4-23-1838
John Brinkman NW¼-SW½-S23; 12-20-1838
James Grove SW½-SW½-S23; 3-21-1838
Peter Tasset E½-SW¼-S23; 4-25-1833
John Henry Vosten(?) W½-NE½-S24; 4-25-1838
John E. Goodert SE¼-NW¼-S24; 10-13-1837
Henry Probst NE¼-NW¼-S24; 12-25-1838
John Henry Barket W¼-SE½-S24; 4-25-1838
John E. Goodert NE¼-SW¼-S24; 10-13-1837
John Henry Barket SE¼-SW¼-S24; 4-25-1838
James Abdon E½-NE½-S25; 6-23-1837
Herman Shafer W½-NE¼-S25; 4-25-1838
John Williamson NE¼-NE¼-S26; 2-26-1834
Henry Probst W½-NE¼; SE¼-NE¼-S26; 4-23-1838
Young Johnson SW¼-NW¼-S26; 7-29-1836
Henry Probst SE¼-NW¼-S26; 4-23-1838
Charles Droge N½-NW¼-S26; 4-23-1838
William Turner SW¼-SE¼-S26; 1-6-1838
Henry Probst NW¼-SE¼-S26; 4-26-1838
Peter Spangler NE¼-SW¼-S26; 8-11-1836
Peter Spangler NW¼-SW¼-S26; 8-18-1836
Frederick Wolber S½-SW¼-S26; 4-23-1838
Charles Droge W½-NE¼-S27; 4-23-1838
Daniel Kelsey SW½-NW½-S27; 7-5-1836
Charles Droge E½-NW¼; NW¼-NW¼-S27; 4-23-1838

Page 133.   T 5 N, R 3 W of 1st P.M.

James Lenover SE¼-SE¼-S27; 2-10-1837
James P. Johnson NW¼-SE¼-S27; 2-27-1837
Abel Johnson SW¼-SE¼-S27; 6-17-1839
William Johnson SE½-NE¼-S28; 12-18-1832
Charles Droge NE¼-NE¼; W½-NE¼-S28; 4-23-1838
William Patterson E½-NW¼-S28; 2-25-1837
Daniel Kelsey E½-NW¼-S33; 4-19-1833
Daniel Kelsey NW½-NW¼-S33; 7-5-1836
Harvey Cole SW½-NW¼-S33; 9-4-1838
Abraham C. Hart SE¼-NE¼-S34; 2-23-1838
Henry Wolber NE¼-NE¼-S34; 4-24-1838

William S. Pate W$\frac{1}{2}$-NE$\frac{1}{4}$-S34; 1-18-1837
Jacob Froman & George Zinn SE$\frac{1}{4}$-S34; 12-14-1816
Turpin K. Bradley SE$\frac{1}{4}$-NE$\frac{1}{4}$-S35; 4-8-1837
Herod Henry Ellerman NE$\frac{1}{4}$-NE$\frac{1}{4}$-S35; NW$\frac{1}{4}$-NE$\frac{1}{4}$-S35; 4-23-1838
William Patterson SW$\frac{1}{4}$-NE$\frac{1}{4}$-S35; 10-9-1837
Abraham C. Hart SW$\frac{1}{4}$-NW$\frac{1}{4}$-S35; 11-7-1837
Henry Wolber NW$\frac{1}{4}$-N $\frac{1}{4}$-S35; 4-24-1838
John Frederick Bartel E$\frac{1}{2}$-NW$\frac{1}{4}$-S35; 5-14-1838
William Patterson NW$\frac{1}{4}$-SE$\frac{1}{4}$-S35; 10-9-1837
William L. Pate NE$\frac{1}{4}$-SE$\frac{1}{4}$-S35; 1-9-1838
John Liggett S$\frac{1}{2}$-SE$\frac{1}{4}$-S35; 5-21-1838
Robert Turner SW$\frac{1}{4}$-SW$\frac{1}{4}$-S35; 4-17-1835
William Turner NW$\frac{1}{4}$-SW$\frac{1}{4}$-S35; 1-11-1837
Jared Brush E$\frac{1}{2}$-SW$\frac{1}{4}$-S35; 6-7-1837

Page 134. T 5 N, R 3 W of 1st P.M.

James Lyons NE$\frac{1}{4}$-SW$\frac{1}{4}$-S36; 9-12-1836
James Lyons NW$\frac{1}{4}$-SW$\frac{1}{4}$-S36; 1-2-1837
Charles Thomas Adney SE$\frac{1}{4}$-SW$\frac{1}{4}$; SW$\frac{1}{4}$-SW$\frac{1}{4}$-S36; 10-3-1832

Page 134. T 6 N, R 3 W of 1st P.M.

Samuel McKinstry NE$\frac{1}{4}$-SE$\frac{1}{4}$-S1; 8-12-1833
Samuel McKinstry SE$\frac{1}{4}$-SE$\frac{1}{4}$-S1; 2-29-1836
Thomas Lamberson SW$\frac{1}{4}$-SE$\frac{1}{4}$-S1; 6-20-1836
George H. Johnson NW$\frac{1}{4}$-SE$\frac{1}{4}$-S1; 5-16-1837
Henry Johnson W$\frac{1}{2}$-NW$\frac{1}{4}$-S2; 4-2-1836

Page 135. T 6 N, R 3 W of 1st P.M.

John McKinstry NE$\frac{1}{4}$-NE$\frac{1}{4}$-S12; 7-2-1834
John Alexander SE$\frac{1}{4}$-NE$\frac{1}{4}$-S12; 7-7-1836
Caleb Green Ward SW$\frac{1}{4}$-SE$\frac{1}{4}$-S15; 1-4-1836
Robert Glass NW$\frac{1}{4}$-SE$\frac{1}{4}$-S15; 1-16-1836
Reizen Hinds NW$\frac{1}{4}$-SW$\frac{1}{4}$-S15; 1-11-1836
Levi Boyd SE$\frac{1}{4}$-SW$\frac{1}{4}$-S15; 1-1-1836
Alexander Walker SW$\frac{1}{4}$-SW$\frac{1}{4}$-S15; 5-28-1832
James Lamberton NE$\frac{1}{4}$-SW$\frac{1}{4}$-S15; 3-17-1836
Seth Heaton Lot 4-W pt.-S$\frac{1}{2}$-SW$\frac{1}{4}$-S21; 12-15-1832
John J. Livingston Lot 4-W pt.-N$\frac{1}{2}$-SW$\frac{1}{4}$-S21; 6-13-1836

Page 136. T 6 N, R 3 W of 1st P.M.

Elhanan Burroughs Lot 4-N$\frac{1}{2}$-SW pt.-S33; 5-12-1833
James Dolson SW$\frac{1}{4}$-NE$\frac{1}{4}$-S22; 7-20-1832
Caleb Green Ward NW$\frac{1}{4}$-NE$\frac{1}{4}$-S22; 1-4-1836
Samuel Ewan NE$\frac{1}{4}$-SE$\frac{1}{4}$-S24; NW$\frac{1}{4}$-SE$\frac{1}{4}$-S24; 7-1-1836
Piercy Wheeler SE$\frac{1}{4}$-SE$\frac{1}{4}$-S24; 6-18-1836
William Wheeler SW$\frac{1}{4}$-SE$\frac{1}{4}$-S24; 10-13-1832
Levin Warren Riggin E$\frac{1}{2}$-SW$\frac{1}{4}$-S24; 9-13-1832
John Jacob Goyer(?) NE$\frac{1}{4}$-NW$\frac{1}{4}$-S26; 12-15-1832
Jacob Faulkner SE$\frac{1}{4}$-NW$\frac{1}{4}$-S26; 2-1-1836

Page 137. T 6 N, R 3 W of 1st P.M.

John Montgomery Patrick W$\frac{1}{2}$-SE$\frac{1}{4}$-S27; 1-21-1836
John Montgomery Patrick NE$\frac{1}{4}$-NE$\frac{1}{4}$-S34; 5-25-1832
Alexander Walker NW$\frac{1}{4}$-NE$\frac{1}{4}$-S34; 2-6-1836
James Hays S$\frac{1}{2}$-NE$\frac{1}{4}$-S34; 3-22-1837
Armstead Abbitt NE$\frac{1}{4}$-SE$\frac{1}{4}$-S34; 11-7-1836
Philip Rowland SE$\frac{1}{4}$-SE$\frac{1}{4}$-S34; 1-26-1837
Thomas G. Benson NW$\frac{1}{4}$-NW$\frac{1}{4}$-S36; 8-30-1836
Allen Perry SW$\frac{1}{4}$-NW$\frac{1}{4}$-S36; 12-30-1837

Perry Bixby SW¼-SW¼-S36; 1-10-1837
Perry Bixby NW¼-SW¼-S36; 1-18-1837
Thomas Nelson NE¼-SW¼-S36; 10-14-1837
Harrison Alfred SE¼-SW¼-S36; 10-20-1837

Page 138. T 7 N, R 3 W of 1st P.M.
Enoch Conger E½-SE¼-S2; 9-22-1832
Amos Morris, Jr. E½-SW¼-S12; 3-2-1833

Page 139. T 7 N, R 3 W of 1st P.M.
Jonah Lewis W½-NW¼-S26; 4-6-1835
Ira Wilson N½-NW¼-Fr.S27; 2-22-1836
Ira Wilson S½-NW¼-Fr.S27; 5-9-1833
Ammi Willson NE¼-NE¼-Fr.S27; 12-22-1834
Joseph French, Jr. NW¼-NE¼-Fr.S27; 12-25-1834
Jonah Lewis SE¼-NE¼-Fr.S27; 4-6-1835
Ira Wilson SW¼-NE¼-Fr.S27; 2-22-1836
Stephen Muson(?) Day NE¼-SE¼-Fr.S27; 2-5-1836
Daniel Hall SE¼-SE¼; SW¼-SE¼-Fr.S27; 5-10-1836
Stephen Munson Day NW¼-SE¼-Fr.S27; 5-6-1836
Harvey Moss S end-Fr.S33; W½ off S end-Fr.S34; 11-27-1833
Adam Moore E½-S end-Fr.S34; 9-9-1835
William Huls E½-NW¼-S35; 8-27-1827
William Huls W½-NW¼-S35; 5-26-1836
John R. Round E½-SW¼-S35; 4-4-1836

Page 140. T 7 N, R 3 W of 1st P.M.
John Jackson & Stephen Munson Day SE¼-SE¼; NE¼-SE¼-Fr.S22; 5-20-1837
Luther Cleveland NW¼-SE¼-Fr.S22; 3-10-1836
Luther Cleveland SW¼-SE¼-Fr.S22; 3-10-1836
Winslow Y. Wood N½-SW pt.-Fr.S22; 4-20-1836
Luther Cleveland S½-SW pt.-Fr.S22; 4-6-1836

Page 140. T 8 N, R 3 W of 1st P.M.
Isaac Lawrence SW¼-NE¼-S1; 8-17-1832
Isaac Lawrence NW¼-NE¼-S1; 4-10-1833
John Hool NE¼-NE¼; SE¼-NE¼-S1; 7-9-1836
Conrad Weiler W½-NW¼-S1; 7-29-1833
John Hool E½-SE¼-S1; 7-9-1836
John Showalter NW¼-SW¼-S1; 6-26-1833
John Showalter SW¼-SW¼-S1; 10-7-1835
Joseph Goll N pt.-N½-Fr.S2; 7-20-1833
Adam Schlicht S pt.-N½-Fr.S2; 6-26-1833
George Nicholas Hornberger N & S pt.-S½-Fr.S2; 6-22-1833
George Nicolas Hornberger N pt.-N½ & S pt.-N½-Fr.S11; 11-25-1833
George Nicolas Hornberger N pt.-S½ & S pt.-S½-Fr.S11; 6-3-1833
Augustin Philips E½-NE¼-S12; 1-23-1834
John Kile W½-NW¼-S12; 6-22-1833
John Kenk(?) Lawrence SE¼-SE¼-S12; 8-17-1832
Nathaniel Hazen NE¼-SE¼-S12;. 5-22-1833
Philip Jacob Kuhn W½-SE¼-S12; 4-29-1833
Jacob Showalter E½-SW¼-S12; 9-7-1831
George Nicolas Hornberger W½-SW¼-S12; 6-22-1833

Page 141. T 8 N, R 3 W of 1st P.M.
Nathaniel Hazen NW¼-NE¼-S13; 1-27-1834
Archibald Stewart SW¼-NE¼-S13; 12-4-1835
Jacob Mailine NE¼-NW¼-S13; 7-20-1833
Amos Jones SE¼-NW¼-S13; 7-1-1834

Amos Jones NW¼-NW¼; SW¼-NW¼-S13; 7-1-1834
George Adam Faber SE¼-SE¼-S13; 6-3-1833
George Adam Faber NE¼-SE¼-S13; 6-15-1833
John Suesey NW¼-SE¼-S13; 6-22-1833
Adam Denies SW¼-SE¼-S13; 1-23-1834
John Swesey NE¼-SW¼-S13; 6-22-1833
Adam Denies SE¼-SW¼-S13; 1-23-1834
George Knorr NW¼-SW¼-S13; 10-28-1835
Andreas Logee E½-NE¼-S14; 12-24-1835
Peter Kline W½-NE¼-S14; 4-24-1835
William Griswold SE¼-SE¼-S14; 9-13-1833
Isaac Alden NE¼-SE¼-S14; 4-1-1835
Frederick Nagel W½-SE¼-S14; 6-26-1833
Lemuel Connelly SE¼-NE¼-S23; 10-3-1832
Ezekiel Pettegrew & Ephraim Lollar NE¼-NE¼-S23; 10-11-1833
Joseph Meister SW¼-NW¼-S24; 12-20-1834
Daniel Symmes Major E½-NW¼; NW¼-NW¼-S24; 3-10-1836
             Page 142. T 8 N, R 3 W of 1st P.M.
Frederick Bealer E½-SW¼-S26; 7-18-1833
John Millar W½-SW¼-S26; 10-13-1831
Ahrend Henry Poppe S end-Fr.S27; 10-1-1833
Thomas Ewart Wood SW¼-NE¼-S35; 3-17-1834
Salman P. Chase NW¼-NE¼-S35; 2-29-1836
Thomas Morgan NW¼-S36; 5-27-1817
             Page 142. T 9 N, R 3 W of 1st P.M.   FRANKLIN CO.
John Iff Lot 1-SE pt.-N½-Fr.S1; 3-25-1837
Frederick Minneman & Marie Meirs Lot 2-SW pt.-N½ & Lot 3-NW pt.-
             S½ & Lot 4-NE pt.-S½-S1; 8-25-1836
John Frederick Ahlers Lot 5-SE¼-SE¼ & Lot 6-SW¼-SE¼-S1; 8-25-1836
Gerhard Hy. Allerman & John Hy. Factor Lot 7-SW cor.-S½-S1; 9-8-
Henry Robeson Lot 1-NE¼-SW¼-Fr.S13; 1-13-1834   1836
John Pyle Lot 2-NW¼-SW¼-S13; 2-17-1836
James Robeson Lot 5-SE¼-SW¼-S13; 2-4-1836
William Baker Lot 6-SW¼-SW¼-S13; 10-7-1836
George Adam Eppig N½-NW¼-S13; 11-26-1836
Adam Sam Lot 3-SE¼-NW¼ & Lot 4-SW¼-NW¼-S13; 11-26-1836
             Page 143. T 9 N, R 3 W of 1st P.M.
Willson Poe NW¼-NE¼-S24; 2-17-1836
Nicholas Seifert SW¼-NE¼-S24; 11-28-1836
John Bauer E½-NE¼-S24; 2-22-1836
Henry Stallman NE¼-SE¼-S24; 2-8-1836
Henry Rottinghaus W½-SE¼-S24; 2-8-1836
John Rudolph Dearkhumig(?) SE¼-SE¼-S24; 9-11-1835
James Golding NE¼-NW¼-S24; 11-9-1833
Shelby Baker SW¼-NW¼-S24; 11-25-1833
John Knecht Lot 1-NW¼-NW¼-S24; 2-1-1837
Shelby Baker SE¼-NW¼-S24; 2-27-1836
George Bohrer E½-SW¼; NW¼-SW¼-S24; 11-23-1835
George Siebendollar SW¼-SW¼-S24; 12-5-1833
Michael Ripperger Fr.S23; 2-1-1837
George Adam Ripp NE¼-S25; 4-3-1835
George Siebendollar NW¼-NW¼-S25; 10-24-1833
John Nerrick SW¼-NW¼-S25; 7-21-1835
Christian Bohrer E½-NW¼-S25; 11-23-1835

Ignatz Ripperger NE¼-SE¼-S25; 11-11-1833
Michael Ripperger SE¼-SE¼-S25; 9-10-1836
John Sheet W½-SE¼-S25; 7-2-1834
Philip Siebendollar SW¼-SW¼-S25; 8-19-1833
Philip Siebendollar NW¼-SW¼-S25; 12-26-1833
John Hoffmann NE¼-SW¼-S25; 11-23-1835
John Hoffmann SE¼-SW¼-S25; 5-16-1834
Henry Huber Fr.S26; 8-7-1833
George Henry Fettig N pt.-N½ & S pt.-N½ & N pt.-S½-Fr.S35; 3-1-1834
Aloisius Kegler S pt.-S½-Fr.S35; 11-9-1833
Sebastian Miller SW¼-NE¼-S36; 11-27-1833
Michael Hummel NW¼-NE¼-S36; 7-2-1834
William Bals E½-NE¼-S36; 9-26-1836
James Gary, Jr. SE¼-NW¼-S36; 8-3-1832
Jacob Klein NE¼-NW¼-S36; 11-4-1833
William Bals E½-SE¼-S36; 9-26-1836
Sebastian Miller W½-SE¼-S36; 11-27-1833

Page 144. T 10 N, R 3 W of 1st P.M.

Lemuel Zeter Lots 1-2--N end-Fr.S36; no date

Page 144. T 2 N, R 4 W of 1st P.M. SWITZERLAND CO.

William Shaw S pt.-Fr.S23; W½-SW¼-S24; 7-14-1835

Page 145. T 2 N, R 4 W of 1st P.M.

Edward Combs NW¼-SW¼-S36; 9-4-1836
Moses McKay SW¼-SW¼-S36; 6-15-1835

Page 146. T 10 N, R 11 E of 2nd P.M FRANKLIN CO.

Charles Throckmorton E½-NE¼-S1; 2-5-1836
Joseph Throckmotron W½-NE¼-S1; 2-5-1836
John Henry Plaspohl(?) E½-NW¼-S1; 2-6-1837
Benjamin Drake W½-NW¼-S1; 2-1-1837
Aaron Case E½-SE¼-S1; 2-1-1836
Elisha Davis W½-SE¼-S1; 2-1-1836
Elisha Davis E½-SW¼-S1; 3-28-1836
Benjamin Drake W½-SW¼-S1; 2-1-1837
Benjamin Boyer NE¼-NW¼-S2; 4-11-1834
James Love NW¼-NW¼-S2; 6-6-1837
Isrel Love SE¼-NW¼-S2; 6-23-1837
Cenzens(?) Shrimp(?) SW¼-NW¼-S2; 10-12-1837
Benjamin Higdon SW¼-SW¼-S2; 8-26-1836
John J. Lightner NW¼-SW¼-S2; 10-2-1837
Herman Henry Dukme (Dukine?) E½-SW¼-S2; 4-8-1837
Horace Pease Lot 1-N end-Fr.S3; 6-20-1836
Lorenzo Dow Garrison Lot 2-S pt.-N½-S3; 6-21-1836
Herman Henry Rieckelman Lot 1-NE pt.-S end-S10; 4-7-1837
Enoch Abraham Lot 2-NW pt.-S end-S10; 8-4-1836
John Herman Torline Lot 3-SW pt.-S end-S10; 4-7-1837
Herman Henry Rieckelman Lot 4-SE pt.-S end-S10; 4-7-1837
Benjamin Drake E½-NE¼-S11; 2-1-1837
Armistead Kerrick W½-NE¼-S11; 3-1-1837
Bernard Henry Stehr E½-NW¼-S11; 4-5-1837
John Herman Goos W½-NW¼-S11; 4-5-1837
John Butt E½-SE¼-S11; 5-23-1836
John Henry Plaspohl W½-SE¼-S11; 1-26-1837
John Henry Plaspohl E½-SW¼-S11; 1-13-1837
John Frederick Bartel W½-SW¼-S11; 3-1-1837
Aaron Case E½-NE¼-S12; 2-1-1836

Page 147. T 10 N, R 11 E of 2nd P.M.
Aaron Case NW¼-NE¼-S12; 2-10-1836
Peter Case SW¼-NE¼-S12; 3-30-1836
Peter Case E½-NW¼-S12; 3-30-1836
Benjamin Drake W½-NW¼-S12; 2-1-1837
Henry Brewater E½-SE¼-S12; 10-21-1836
Christopher Albers W½-SE¼-S12; 10-21-1836
John Butt SW¼-S12; 5-23-1836
Christopher Albers NE¼-S13; 10-21-1836
James K. Davis NW¼-S13; 3-30-1836
John Alvah Church NE¼-SE¼-S13; 6-17-1836
Herman Dickman SE¼-SE¼-S13; 10-27-1836
Christopher Albers W½-SE¼-S13; 11-21-1836
John H. W. Borchelt SW¼-SW¼-S13; 10-17-1836
John F. Wisman SE¼-SW¼-S13; 10-21-1836
John F. Busch NW¼-SW¼-S13; 10-17-1836
John F. Busch NE¼-SW¼-S13; 10-18-1836
Henry Butt, Jr. NE¼-S14; 5-23-1836
John Henry Plaspohl E½-NW¼-S14; 1-12-1837
Auson Balkley W½-NW¼-S14; 11-26-1836
Henry Otta E½-SE¼-S14; 10-17-1836
John Henry Schutta W½-SE¼-S14; 10-15-1836
Giles Davis E½-SW¼-S14; 7-28-1836
Henry Butt, Jr. W½-SW¼-S14; 7-28-1836
John Hy. Buckman & John Hy. Brewater E½-NE¼-Fr.S15; 1-12-1837
Bernard Hesse NW¼-NE¼-S15; 1-12-1837
Thomas Wilson NW¼-SE¼-S15; 2-8-1836
William Habadank SW¼-SE¼-S15; 11-15-1836
John Frederick Nienaber NE¼-SE¼; SE¼-SE¼-S15; 11-15-1836
Bernard Hesse NW¼-S15; 1-12-1837
Thomas Wilson Lots 1-2--SW¼-S15; 1-11-1836
Enoch Lashire Goodwin N½-NW¼-S22; 12-29-1835
Samuel Fosdick S½-NW¼-S22; 1-2-1837
Joseph Worman Lots 1-2--S½-SW¼-S22; 10-28-1836
James Wilson NE¼-S22; 10-17-1836
Joseph Powers E½-SE¼-S22; 9-9-1836
Joseph Worman W½-SE¼-S22; 10-28-1836

Page 148. T 10 N, R 11 E of 2nd P.M.
John Frederick Uhlhom NE¼-S23; 10-14-1836
Henry Butt, Sr. NW¼-S23; 7-28-1836
Henry William Goldmeier E½-SE¼-S23; 10-14-1836
Christian Henry Meyers W½-SE¼-S23; 10-15-1836
Thomas Cooksey NE¼-SW¼-S23; 9-7-1836
Oner R. Powell SE¼-SW¼-S23; 10-14-1836
Oner R. Powell W½-SW¼-S23; 10-14-1836
Eli Martin NW¼-SE¼; S½-SE¼; E½-SW¼-S24; 4-24-1835
Thomas Hamson W½-SW¼; SW¼-NW¼-S24; 9-22-1836
John Koch E½-NE¼-S24; 10-27-1836
Herman Dickman W½-NE¼; E½-NW¼; NW¼-NW¼-S24; 10-27-1836
James Ripley NE¼-SE¼-S24; 10-29-1836
Henry Christian Dickman Lots 7-8--Fr.S25; 10-19-1836
Thomas H. Brookbank Lots 11-12--W½-SW¼-S26; 10-11-1836
Frederick Lilie Lot 10-E½-SW¼-S26; 10-22-1836
Frederick Lilie Lot 9-W pt.-SE¼-S26; 10-29-1836

John Henry Ohlman Lots 5-6-7-8--NE pt.-Fr.S26; 10-14-1836
Oner R. Powell NW¼-S26; 10-14-1836
Isabella Matthews NE¼-S27; 8-26-1836
John Boyle NW¼-S27; 10-14-1836
Isaac N. Powell S½-S27; 10-13-1836
Isaac N. Powell Fr.S28; 10-15-1836. Decatur penciled in.
William Scoles N½-Fr.S33; 10-15-1836. Decatur penciled in.
Elisha Dwelle S½-Fr.S33; 8-29-1836. Decatur penciled in.
Samuel Heath Lot 6-E pt.-E½-Fr.S34; 9-20-1836
William Scoles Lots 7-8-9-10-11--W½-S34; W pt.-E½-S34; 10-13-1836
Thomas H. Brookbank Fr.S35; 10-11-1836

Page 149. T 11 N, R 11 E of 2nd P.M.

John Simonson, of Preble Co. (Ohio, obviously. MRW) NE¼-S1;
Alexander Davison NW¼-NW¼-S1; 1-7-1833 2-15-1836
Aaron Ailes SW¼-NW¼-S1; 2-12-1836
John Milton Allen SE¼-NW¼-S1; 2-13-1836
William Simonson NE¼-NW¼-S1; 2-15-1833
Henry George SE¼-S1; 5-12-1836
Alexander Dinkins NW¼-SW¼-S1; 2-12-1836
Robert Pugh E½-SW¼-S1; 2-12-1836
William Scudder SW¼-SW¼-S1; 9-13-1836
Daniel Gard Lots 1-2--E pt.-N½-Fr.S2; 2-12-1836
Henderson S. Brown E½-S end-Fr.S2; 2-20-1836
Philip Cupp Lots 3-4--W½-S end-Fr.S2; 8-20-1836
William Scudder W pt.-N½-Fr.S2; 9-13-1836
William Scudder NE¼-Fr.S11; 10-24-1836
William Angur(?) SE¼-Fr.S11; 12-19-1836
William Scudder W½-Fr.S11; 12-19-1836
Stephen Schooley NE¼-S12; 9-13-1836
William Scudder NW¼-S12; 9-13-1836
John Bernet Neman N½-SE¼-S13; 11-20-1837
Joseph H. York SE¼-SE¼-S13; 7-12-1836
Joseph York SW¼-SE¼-S13; 3-27-1834
Joseph York SE¼-SW¼-S13; 3-2-1833
Joseph H. York NE¼-SW¼-S13; 3-1-1837
Joab Sentenay W½-SW¼-S13; 9-10-1836
Charles Marlin NE¼-SE¼-S14; 6-22-1832
Benjamin Smathers SE¼-SE¼-S14; 2-19-1836
Benjamin Smathers NW¼-SE¼-S14; 1-15-1836
John Quin SW¼-SE¼-S14; 12-27-1836
Mathias Davis N½-SW¼-S14; 9-16-1833
P. S. Symmes N½-S14; 8-1-1840

Page 150. T 11 N, R 11 E of 2nd P.M.

William Marlin W½-SE¼; E½-SW¼-S23; 10-28-1836
Joseph Roberts & John Roberts N½-SW¼; W½-SW¼-Fr.S22; E½-SE¼-S23;
John Ricketts N½-NE¼-S24; 4-6-1837 12-24-1836
John Hy. Nobbe SE¼-NE¼-S24; 10-7-1837
John Henry Gramann SW¼-NE¼-S24; 5-7-1838
William Jones NW¼-NW¼-S24; 6-20-1836
Jacob Bren SW¼-NW¼-S24; 11-20-1837
John Diedrig Klostarman E½-SE¼-S24; 5-2-1837
John Henry Klostarman W½-SE¼-S24; 5-2-1837
Wesley Marlin SE¼-SW¼-S24; 10-28-1836
John Willen NE¼-SW¼-S24; 10-28-1837

John B. Hy. Timmerman W½-SW¼-S24; 5-1-1837
John Diederick Lesche E½-NE¼-S25; 5-1-1837
Bernard Henry Lesche W½-NE¼-S25; 5-1-1837
Wesley Marlin NE¼-NW¼-S25; 10-28-1836
Barnet Hy. Mucherlierd SE¼-NW¼-S25; 4-28-1837
Barnet Hy. Devinger(?) W½-NW¼-S25; 4-28-1837
Henry Joseph Bardleman SW¼-S25; 4-28-1837. See 11th entry below
Joseph Roberts & John Roberts NE¼-NW¼-S26; 12-24-1836
John Roberts, Sr. SE¼-S26; SW¼-S26; 12-27-1836
Joseph Roberts & John Roberts Fr.S27; 12-24-1836
Horace Pease Lot 4-S end-Fr.S34; 1-29-1836
Horace Pease Lot 3-N½-S½-Fr.S34; 1-9-1837
Francis Hy. Grava(?) N½-Fr.S34; 5-17-1837
Nathan Hawkins SE¼-NE¼-S35; 8-31-1836
Nathan Hawkins NE¼-NE¼-S35; 2-14-1837
John Roberts, Sr. W½-NE¼-S35; 12-27-1836
John Hawkins SW¼-NW¼-S35; 2-22-1836
John Hy. Bardleman & Joseph Bardleman NW¼-NW¼-S35; 5-7-1836. Given names may be listed wrong; see entry above
Joshua Jones NE¼-NW¼-S35; 9-6-1836
John D. Mute SE¼-NW¼-S35; 11-9-1836
John Albert Nienaber SE¼-S35; 5-1-1837

Page 151. T 11 N, R 11 E of 2nd P.M.

Thomas White SW¼-SW¼-S35; 1-12-1836
Thomas White NW¼-SW¼-S35; 6-6-1836
John Raver E½-SW¼-S35; 5-1-1837
Samuel Wilson SE¼-NW¼-S36; 3-1-1837
Giehard Hy. Nienaber NE¼-NW¼-S36; 8-28-1837
Charles Throckmorton, Jr. SE¼-SE¼-S36; 9-16-1836
John Henry Plaspohl NE¼-SE¼; W½-SE¼-S36; 1-10-1837
John Henry Plaspohl E½-SW¼-S36; 2-6-1837
John Henry Duhme W½-SW¼-S36; 4-8-1837

Page 151. T 12 N, R 11 E of 2nd P.M.

Job Scott Lot 4-SE cor.-Fr.S1; 2-11-1836
Charles Milone Lot 1-NE pt.-S½; Lot 3-SW pt.-S½-S1; 10-12-1836
Charles Milone Lot 2-NW pt.-S½-S1; 12-13-1836
Edward Scott NE¼-NE¼-Fr.S12; 7-10-1832
John Linville SE¼-NE¼-S12; 1-20-1836
James Wallace W½-NE¼-S12; 7-25-1832
Elisha Ellison Fr.NW¼-S12; 10-22-1834
Elisha Ellison Lot 1-N½-SW¼-S12; 1-6-1835
John Houston Scott Lot 3-S½-SW¼-S12; 1-25-1836
David Ballenger NW¼-SE¼-S12; 3-18-1835
Orange Hide Neff NE¼-SE¼-S12; 1-25-1836
John Walker S½-SE¼-S12; 1-25-1836
Alexander Power NW pt.-Fr.S13; 3-8-1831
William Egans S½-NE pt.-S13; 6-8-1832
Christopher Misner S½-SE pt.-S13; 10-11-1832
Elisha Misner E½-NE¼-S24; 10-11-1832
John Bishop W½-NE¼-S24; 3-17-1834
William Faurot(?) SW¼-SE¼-S24; 11-19-1836
William Neff NW¼-SE¼; E½-SE¼-S24; 12-15-1836

Page 152. T 12 N, R 11 E of 2nd P.M.

William Nichols E½-NW¼-S24; 1-8-1836

William Morris Powers NW¼-NW¼-S24; 1-7-1836
Hardin Burk SW¼-NW¼-S24; 10-1-1833
James Simpson Gwinnup SE¼-SW¼-S24; 10-3-1833
William Neff NE¼-SW¼-S24; 12-15-1836
Hausberry Burk NW¼-SW¼-S24; 10-1-1833
James Simpson Gwinnup SW¼-SW¼-S24; 10-3-1833
William Neff Fr.S23; 12-15-1836
John H. Faurot E½-NE¼-S25; 11-5-1836
William Neff NW¼-NE¼-S25; 12-15-1836
Samuel Miers SW¼-NE¼-S25; 11-2-1835
John Thomas NW¼-NW¼-S25; 9-29-1835
John Holliday Faurot NE¼-NW¼-S25; 10-12-1835
Samuel Miers SE¼-NW¼-S25; 11-2-1835
John Thomas SW¼-NW¼-S25; 1-8-1836
William Neff SE¼-S25; SW¼-S25; 12-15-1836
James Hildreth Lot 1-N pt.-Fr.S26; 10-31-1836
William Neff Lot 2-N½-S pt.; Lot 3-S½-S pt.-S26; 12-15-1836
William Neff Lot 1-N½-N end-Fr.S35; 12-15-1836
Edward Yates Lot 2-S½-N end-Fr.S35; 1-8-1836
William Neff Lot 3-N½-S end-Fr.S35; 12-15-1836
William Pruet Lot 4-S½-S end-Fr.S35; 2-20-1836
Simon Brown NW¼-S36; 5-9-1836
William Neff NE¼-NW¼; W½-NW¼-S36; 12-15-1836
James Simpson Gwinnup E½-SE¼-S36; 2-15-1836
William Neff NW¼-SE¼-S36; 12-15-1836
William Simonson SW¼-SE¼-S36; 2-15-1836
William Neff NE¼-S36; 12-15-1836
Mason Palmer SW¼-SW¼-S36; 9-19-1833
Samuel Stubbs N½-SW¼-S36; 5-9-1836
William Simonson SE¼-SW¼-S36; 2-15-1836

Page 153. T 13 N, R 11 E of 2nd P.M.

John Klum Fr.S24; 6-14-1832
Richard Stephen Fr.S25; 4-18-1832
James Conwell Lot 1-N end-N½; Lot 2-S end-N½-Fr.S36; 9-19-1834
James Conwell Lot 3-N end-S½-Fr.S36; 9-19-1834
John Linville Lot 4-S end-S½-Fr.S36; 6-19-1834

Page 153. T 10 N, R 12 E of 2nd P.M.

Joseph Roberts & John Roberts E pt. & E side-W½; W side-W½-Fr.S1; 11-3-1836
Jesse Petty N½-NE pt.-S2; 11-16-1836
Andrew Alley SW¼-NE¼-S2; 9-7-1836
Joseph Roberts & John Roberts SE¼-NE¼-S2; 11-17-1836
Jane Rader NW¼ or cor. of NW¼-S2; 10-3-1832
Joseph Roberts & John Roberts NE¼ or cor. of NW¼-S2; 11-17-1836
James Hicks SW¼-NW¼-Fr.S2; 3-25-1836
Joseph Roberts & John Roberts SE¼-NW¼-Fr.S2; 11-17-1836
Henry Brees NW¼-SE¼-Fr.S2; 7-14-1835
Joseph Roberts & John Roberts SW¼-SE¼; Lot 1-E pt.-SE¼-Fr.S2; 11-17-1836
Henry Brees NE¼-SW¼-S2; 7-14-1835
Joseph Roberts & John Roberts SE¼-SW¼-S2; 11-17-1836
Richard Pippen Fr.S11; 2-23-1833
James Hicks S side-E½-Fr.S10; 3-25-1836
Herman Henry Asmann NW¼-S10; 11-11-1836
Bernard Hinnenkamp Fr.S15; SW¼-S10; 11-11-1836
Joseph Schreiber NE¼-S3; 9-15-1836

Anthony Schreiber NW¼-S3; 9-15-1836
Elizabeth Jane Hobbs E½-SE¼-S3; 11-2-1835
John Henry Steinemann W½-SE¼-S3; 11-15-1836
Henry Schreiber E½-SW¼-S3; 9-15-1836
Jacob Hirt W½-SW¼-S3; 9-15-1836
John Albert Tholking E½-NE¼-S4; 11-11-1836
John Henry Ronnebaum W½-NE¼-S4; 11-11-1836

Page 154. T 10 N, R 12 E of 2nd P.M.

John Stottle E½-NW¼-S4; 10-28-1836
Gallus Schock SE¼-SE¼-S4; 11-4-1836.
John Henry Ronnebaum NE¼-SE¼-S4; 11-11-1836
Anthony Stottle W½-SE¼-S4; 10-28-1836
William George E½-SW¼-S4; 8-22-1817
Herman Henry Booing(?) E½-NE¼-S5; 11-11-1836
John Herman Ronnebaum W½-NE¼-S5; 11-11-1836
Henry Brockamp E½-NW¼-S5; 11-11-1836
John Henry Nurre W½-NW¼-S5; 11-11-1836
John Henry Ronnebaum SE¼-S5; 11-11-1836
Joseph Schuegman · SW¼-S5; 11-11-1836
John Herman Bodeker E½-NE¼-S6; 11-11-1836
Joseph Throckmorton W½-NE¼-S6; 9-16-1836
Charles Throckmorton NW¼-S6; 2-22-1836
John Herman Bodaker E½-SE¼-S6; 11-11-1836
Bernard Fehrmann W½-SE¼-S6; 11-11-1836
Elisha Davis SW¼-S6; 3-28-1836
Henry Kalmeyer NE¼-S7; 10-21-1836
Aaron Case NW¼-S7; 2-1-1836
William Miller E½-SE¼-S7; 10-21-1836
Frederick Colthoff W½-SE¼-S7; 10-21-1836
Henry Havekotte SW¼-S7; 10-21-1836
Hannibal Sutton SE¼-NE¼-S8; 3-21-1836
Christopher Decker NE¼-NE¼; W½-NE¼-S8; 11-12-1836
James P. Wilson E½-NW¼-S8; 9-30-1836
John Henry Buckman W½-NW¼-S8; 10-21-1836
William Nenthorp(?) E½-SW¼-S8; 10-21-1836
John Henry Vosbrynck W½-SW¼-S8; 10-21-1836
John Henry Berte NE¼-NE¼-S9; 11-11-1836
Gabriel Ferry SE¼-NE¼-S9; 10-10-1836
Elisha Misner W½-NE¼-S9; 9-9-1836
Anthony Babst E½-NW¼-S9; 10-3-1836
Atolf Greanwalt W½-NW¼-S9; 10-3-1836
Siegfried Keller E½-SE¼-S9; 1-11-1836
Michael Schloser W½-SE¼-S9; 10-3-1836

Page 155. T 10 N, R 12 E of 2nd P.M.

John Bachus E½-SW¼-S9; 10-3-1836
Ludan Wagner W½-SW¼-S9; 10-3-1836
John Frederick Prus E½-NW¼-Fr.S17; 10-21-1836
John Albert Plumer W½-NW¼-Fr.S17; 10-21-1836
John Frederick Prus W½-NE¼-Fr.S17; 10-21-1836
John Herman Schwegman E½-NE¼-Fr.S17; 10-29-1836
John Herman Kessens E½-SW¼-Fr.S17; 10-29-1836
Henry Kramer W½-SW¼-Fr.S17; 10-29-1836
John Albert Plumer Lot 1-E pt.-SE¼; Lot 2-W pt.-SE¼-Fr.S17; 11-15-1836
John Albert Plumer E½-NE¼-S18; 10-21-1836

Christopher Albers W½-NE¼-S18; 10-21-1836
Henry Havekotte NW¼-S18; 10-21-1836
Henry Meirose SE¼-S18; 10-21-1836
John Alvah Church SW¼-S18; 6-17-1836
Martin Stehlin Lot 1-NE¼-NE¼; Lot 2-NW¼-NE¼-Fr.S19; 11-14-1836 36
George Henry WiemanLot 3-N end; Lot 4-S end-W pt -Fr.S19;10-27-18
John Henry Ohlman, Henry Havekotte, & John Koch Lot 5-SE pt.-
     Fr.S19; 11-15-1836
John Roberts Fr.S20; 11-5-1836
          Page 155.   T 11 N, R 12 E of 2nd P.M.
Henry Pond NE¼-NE¼-S1; 5-23-1832
Thomas Wilson Smith NW¼-NE¼-S1; 10-1-1832
Hiram Pond SE¼-NE¼-S1; 2-9-1836
William Holland SW¼-NE¼-S1; 10-15-1836
Timothy Brown NE¼-NW¼-S1; 12-30-1835
Joseph Roberts & John Roberts SE¼-NW¼; W½-NW¼-S1; 12-2-1836
William Holland E½-SE¼-S1; 7-14-1836
Samuel Clark SW¼-SE¼-S1; 9-2-1836
Joseph Roberts & John Roberts NW¼-SE¼-S1; 12-2-1836
David Mount SW¼-SW¼-S1; 1-18-1836
William Pelson NW¼-SW¼-S1; 9-19-1836
Joseph Roberts & John Roberts E½-SW¼-S1; 12-2-1836
Peter Mount SE¼-NE¼-S2; 9-8-1836
Joseph Roberts & John Roberts NE¼-NE¼; W½-NE¼-S2; 12-2-1836
          Page 156.   T 11 N, R 12 E of 2nd P.M.
John Reed SW¼-NW¼-S2; 4-9-1835
Joseph Roberts & John Roberts NW¼-NW¼-S2; 12-2-1836
David Mount NE¼-NW¼-S2; 5-18-1836
Joseph Roberts & John Roberts SE¼-NW¼-S2; 12-2-1836
David Mount E½-SE¼-S2; 1-18-1836
Joseph Roberts & John Roberts W½-SE¼-S2; 12-2-1836
John Reed NW¼-SW¼-S2; 4-9-1835
Elias Brock SW¼-SW¼-S2; 10-12-1836
Joseph Roberts & John Roberts E½-SW¼-S2; 12-2-1836
Elias Brock SE¼-NE¼-S3; 10-12-1836
John Senour NE¼-NE¼-S3; 10-31-1836
George G. Shoup W½-NE¼-S3; 12-15-1836
Rachael A. Knight E½-NW¼-S3; 4-21-1836
Isaac Goble SW¼-NW¼-S3; 5-27-1836
George G. Shoup NW¼-NW¼-S3; 12-15-1836
James McCash SW¼-S3; 11-21-1836
Spencer Coffey E½-SE¼-S3; 9-7-1836
Adamston Pruet W½-SE¼-S3; 10-26-1836
William Henderson NW¼-S4; 10-21-1811
Samuel Davidson NE¼-SE¼-S4; 9-12-1836
Alexander Davidson NW¼-SE¼-S4; 10-1-1832
Edward Dodson SE¼-SE¼; SW¼-SE¼-S4; 12-16-1836
James Halsey N½-NE¼-S5; 4-24-1833
William Scudder SE¼-NE¼; SW¼-NE¼-S5; 10-11-1836
Stephen Shepherd NW¼-S5; 8-18-1836
James Halsey E½-SE¼-S5; 3-12-1836
Stephen Schooley W½-SE¼; SW¼-S5; 9-13-1836
Daniel Hoffman NE¼-S6; 5-12-1836
William Dola & Fletcher Ailes NW¼-S6; 2-22-1836

William Shepherd SW¼-SE¼-S6; 8-23-1836
Henry L. Reeder NW¼-SE¼; E½-SE¼-S6; 9-13-1836
Daniel Hoffman SW¼-S6; 5-12-1836
Henry L. Reeder NE¼-S7; 9-18-1836
Page 157. T 11 N, R 12 E of 2nd P.M.
Stephen Schooley NW¼-S7; 9-13-1836
Henry L. Reeder SE¼-S7; 12-24-1836
John Quin SW¼-S7; 12-22-1836
Daniel Dotson SW¼-NE¼-S8; 2-12-1836
Jesse York SE¼-NE¼-S8; 3-26-1836
Stephen Schooley N½-NE¼-S8; 9-13-1836
Stephen Schooley NW¼-S8; 9-13-1836
Morgan Lewis W½-SE¼-S8; 3-1-1836
John Quin SW¼-S8; 12-22-1836
William McCash NE¼-S9; 11-21-1836
James McCash E½-SE¼-S9; 11-21-1836
John Quin W½-SE¼-S9; 12-22-1836
John Lipscomb E½-NE¼; NW¼-NE¼-S10; 10-31-1836
John Ferris SW¼-NE¼-S10; 11-21-1836
Reuben Hawkins NE¼-NW¼-S10; 9-12-1836
John Ferris SE¼-NW¼-S10; 11-21-1836
Archibald Woodruff, Jr. W½-NW¼-S10; 11-21-1836
John Ferris SE¼-S10; SW¼-S10; 11-21-1836
David Mount NE¼-S11; 1-18-1836
William Pilson E½-NW¼-S11; 10-31-1836
Thomas J. Wade W½-NW¼-S11; .11-15-1836
Blair N. Pumphrey NE¼-SE¼-S11; 10-21-1836
Matthew Lewis NW¼-SE¼-S11; 10-10-1832
Thomas Wilson SE¼-SE¼-S11; 10-24-1836
John S. Biggs SW¼-SE¼-S11; 10-26-1836
John S. Biggs SW¼-S11; 10-25-1836
Thomas Clark NE¼-NE¼-S12; 2-12-1836
Matthew Hawkins Pruit SE¼-NE¼-S12; 5-3-1836
James Rembert NW¼-NE¼-S12; 10-19-1836
John S. Biggs SW¼-NE¼-S12; 11-17-1836
David Mount W½-NW¼-S12; 1-18-1836
Joseph Roberts & John Roberts E½-NW¼-S12; 12-19-1836
Page 158. T 11 N, R 12 E of 2nd P.M.
Thomas Wilson NE¼-SE¼-S12; 10-9-1832
Bazel Wilson NW¼-SE¼-S12; 8-19-1836
John S. Biggs SE¼-SE¼-S12; 10-26-1836
John Griffin SW¼-SE¼-S12; 11-17-1836
Joseph Roberts & John Roberts SW¼-S12; 12-19-1836
John S. Biggs NE¼-S13; 11-18-1836
Thomas Biggs NW¼-S13; 11-17-1836
John S. Biggs SW¼-NW¼-S13; 12-6-1836
John Herman Bodeker E½-NW¼-S13; 7-6-1837
Thomas W. Alley SE¼-SE¼-S13; 12-1-1836
David Abley, Jr. NE¼-SE¼-S13; 12-7-1836
Daniel Lawrence NW¼-SE¼-S13; 9-19-1837
Philip Lawrence SW¼-SE¼-S13; 9-19-1837
Frederick Gisser E½-SW¼-S13; 8-2-1837
Gerhard Hinkin W½-SW¼-S13; 7-12-1857
Ithamer Hickman E½-NE¼; SW¼-NE¼-S14; 12-5-1836

Joseph Roberts & John Roberts NW$\frac{1}{2}$-NE$\frac{1}{4}$-S14; 12-22-1836
Joseph Roberts & John Roberts NW$\frac{1}{4}$-S14; 12-19-1836
John Henry Enderreadon E$\frac{1}{2}$-SE$\frac{1}{4}$-S14; 9-15-1837
Joseph Roberts & John Roberts W$\frac{1}{2}$-SE$\frac{1}{4}$; E$\frac{1}{2}$-SW$\frac{1}{4}$-S14; 12-22-1836
Stephen Gant W$\frac{1}{2}$-SW$\frac{1}{4}$-S14; 2-4-1836
John Morford E$\frac{1}{2}$-NE$\frac{1}{4}$-S15; 6-5-1834
George Milholland W$\frac{1}{2}$-NE$\frac{1}{2}$-S15; 1-22-183f
Thomas Matston SE$\frac{1}{4}$-NW$\frac{1}{4}$-S15; 2-3-1836
Aaron Malson SW$\frac{1}{4}$-NW$\frac{1}{4}$-S15; 11-3-1836
John Ferris N$\frac{1}{2}$-NW$\frac{1}{4}$-S15; 11-21-1936
Stephen Gant SE$\frac{1}{4}$-S15; 1-22-1836
Thomas Matston NW$\frac{1}{2}$-SW$\frac{1}{4}$-S15; 2-3-1836
John Bernard & Henry Asmann SW$\frac{1}{4}$-SW$\frac{1}{4}$-S15; 5-15-1837
Joshua York, Jr. SW$\frac{1}{2}$-NW$\frac{1}{2}$-S17; 11-17-1836
John Quin NW$\frac{1}{4}$-NW$\frac{1}{2}$-S17; 12-22-1836
    Page 159. T 11 N, R 12 E of 2nd P.M.
John Quin NE$\frac{1}{4}$-S18; NW$\frac{1}{2}$-S18; 12-22-1836
James Curby E$\frac{1}{2}$-SE$\frac{1}{4}$-S18; 8-12-1836
James Curby SW$\frac{1}{2}$-SE$\frac{1}{4}$-S18; 10-28-1836
John Quin NW$\frac{1}{4}$-SE$\frac{1}{4}$-S18; 12-22-1836
William Pain SE$\frac{1}{2}$-SW$\frac{1}{4}$-SW$\frac{1}{4}$-S18; 7-10-1832
John Ricketts NE$\frac{1}{4}$-NW$\frac{1}{4}$-SW$\frac{1}{4}$-S18; 7-29-1836
John Henry Kordenbrock E$\frac{1}{2}$-NE$\frac{1}{4}$-S19; 7-25-1837
John William Heheman W$\frac{1}{2}$-NE$\frac{1}{4}$-S19; 8-12-1837
William Baty N$\frac{1}{2}$-NW$\frac{1}{4}$-S19; 11-8-1836
Herman Henry Pillenessel S$\frac{1}{2}$-NW$\frac{1}{4}$-S19; 9-14-1837
Benjamin Abraham E$\frac{1}{2}$-SE$\frac{1}{4}$-S19; 1-5-1837
John Henry Pount W$\frac{1}{2}$-SE$\frac{1}{4}$-S19; 7-18-1837
Herman Henry Pillenessel N$\frac{1}{2}$-SW$\frac{1}{4}$-S19; 9-4-1837
Bartholomew Fitchpatrick S$\frac{1}{2}$-SW$\frac{1}{4}$-S19; 3-24-1837
William Amack, Jr. E$\frac{1}{2}$-NW$\frac{1}{4}$-S20; 1-7-1837
John Anthony Brinkman W$\frac{1}{2}$-NW$\frac{1}{4}$-S20; 7-11-1837
Jacob Burnet & A. Bailey E$\frac{1}{2}$-SW$\frac{1}{4}$-S20; 6-19-1815
Thomas Cooksey SW$\frac{1}{4}$-SW$\frac{1}{2}$-S20; 11-25-1833
Jonathan G. Cooksey NW$\frac{1}{2}$-SW$\frac{1}{4}$-S20; 3-1-1837
John Bernard & Henry Asmann E$\frac{1}{2}$-NE$\frac{1}{2}$-S21; 5-15-1837
Anthony Daus W$\frac{1}{2}$-NE$\frac{1}{4}$-S21; 3-27-1837
Joseph Throckmorton SW$\frac{1}{2}$-NW$\frac{1}{2}$-S21; 2-22-1837
Samuel G. Marlin NW$\frac{1}{2}$-NW$\frac{1}{2}$-S21; 7-22-1837
Charles Marlin E$\frac{1}{2}$-NW$\frac{1}{2}$-S21; 3-24-1837
William Marlin E$\frac{1}{2}$-SE$\frac{1}{4}$-S21; 10-28-1836
William Marlin W$\frac{1}{2}$-SE$\frac{1}{4}$-S21; 3-24-1837
Henry Will E$\frac{1}{2}$-SW$\frac{1}{4}$-S21; 3-27-1837
Joseph Throckmorton N$\frac{1}{2}$-SW$\frac{1}{4}$-S21; 2-22-1837
Thomas Milholland NE$\frac{1}{4}$-S22; 2-4-1836
Wesley Reynolds SE$\frac{1}{4}$-NW$\frac{1}{4}$-S22; 10-22-1836
P. S. Symms W$\frac{1}{2}$-NE$\frac{1}{2}$-S22; 8-1-1840
Henry Amthauser E$\frac{1}{2}$-SE$\frac{1}{2}$-S22; 9-19-1836
George Milholland W$\frac{1}{2}$-SE$\frac{1}{4}$-S22; 3-26-1836
William Marlin SW$\frac{1}{4}$-SW$\frac{1}{4}$-S22; 5-28-1833
Henry Kienker NW$\frac{1}{4}$-SW$\frac{1}{2}$-S22; 2-20-1837
William Marlin E$\frac{1}{2}$-SW$\frac{1}{4}$-S22; 2-5-1836
    Page 160. T 11 N, R 12 E of 2nd P.M.
Thomas Upjohn NE$\frac{1}{4}$-S23; 4-6-1837

Hartshorn Cole SW¼-SE¼-S23; 2-1-1836
Thomas Upjohn NW¼-SE¼-S23; 4-6-1837
John Norton NE¼-SE¼-S23; 3-29-1837
Charlotte Upjohn SE¼-SE¼-S23; 4-6-1837
Nicholas Gloshon SE¼-SW¼-S23; 3-28-1837
Thomas Upjohn NE¼-SW¼-S23; 4-6-1837
Peter Bohl W½-SW¼-S23; 9-19-1836
Thomas Upjohn NW¼-S24; 4-6-1837
David Allen SE¼-SE¼-S24; 3-2-1833
Joseph Roberts & John Roberts NE¼-SE¼-S24; 11-17-1836
Joseph Roberts & John Roberts SW¼-SE¼-S24; 12-2-1836
John Allen, Sr. NW¼-SE¼; NE¼-SW¼-S24; 9-7-1836
Joseph Roberts & John Roberts SE¼-SW¼-S24; 12-2-1836
John Norton W½-SW¼-S24; 3-29-1837
William Alley NE¼-NE¼-S25; 6-6-1832
William Alley SE¼-NE¼-S25; 2-16-1836
Nicholas Quals NW¼-NE¼-S25; 3-5-1836
Nicholas Quals SW¼-NE¼-S25; 9-15-1832
Joseph Roberts & John Roberts E½-NW¼-S25; 11-17-1836
Joseph Roberts & John Roberts W½-NW¼-S25; 2-1-1837
John M. Quals NW¼-SE¼-S25; 6-30-1836
George Rasor SW¼-SE¼-S25; 9-5-1836
Joseph Roberts & John Roberts E½-SE¼-S25; 11-17-1836
George Rasor SW¼-SW¼-S25; 2-22-1836
Joseph Roberts & John Roberts NW¼-SW¼-S25; 11-17-1836
Joseph Roberts & John Roberts NE¼-S26; NW¼-S26; 11-18-1836
Joseph Roberts & John Roberts SE¼-S26; SW¼-S26; 11-3-1836
John Turner NW¼-NE¼-S27; 6-4-1832
William Pilson SW¼-NE¼-S27; 9-19-1836
John Hirt E½-NE¼-S27; 9-14-1836
Sebastian Bechel E½-NW¼-S27; 10-3-1836
Wesley Reynolds W½-NW¼-S27; 7-22-1835

Page 161. T 11 N, R 12 E of 2nd P.M.

Joseph Hirt E½-SE¼-S27; 9-14-1836
Joseph Huegel W½-SE¼-S27; 9-10-1836
Charles Marlin SW¼-S27; 5-28-1833
Sebastian Bechel E½-SW¼-NE¼-S28; 10-3-1836
Stephen Bolinger NW¼-NE¼-S28; 4-13-1837
Henry Sack E½-NW¼-S28; 2-22-1837
John Henry Kleinmann W½-NW¼-S28; 2-22-1837
Charles Marlin NE¼-SE¼-S28; 2-5-1836
Cicero Marlin SE¼-SE¼-S28; 10-28-1836
Samuel Fosdick W½-SE¼-S28; 1-2-1837
Samuel Fosdick E½-SW¼-S28; 1-2-1837
John Gross W½-SW¼-S28;.10-27-1836
James Abraham SW¼-NE¼-S29; 1-5-1837
Joseph Throckmorton NW¼-NE¼-S29; 10-6-1832
George Cary (negro) SE¼-NE¼; NE¼-NE¼-S29; 10-12-1836
Benjamin Abraham NE¼-NW¼-S29; 2-22-1836
James Abraham SE¼-NW¼-S29; 3-24-1836
James Abraham NW¼-SE¼-S29; 9-6-1836
Francis Stines SW¼-SE¼-S29; 1-9-1837
John Gross E½-SE¼-S29; 10-27-1836
Hiram George NE¼-SW¼-S29; 2-24-1834

Francis Stiens SE¼-SW¼-S29; 1-9-1837
James Abraham E½-NE¼-S30; 3-24-1836
Robert Wilson W½-NE¼-S30; 6-18-1836
Theodore Sprengelmeier N½-NW¼-S30; 5-15-1837
Samuel Wilson S½-NW¼-S30; 3-1-1837
Bartholomew Fitchpatrick NW¼-NE¼-S31; 5-24-1836
Gerhard Kramer & Henry Stalman SW¼-NE¼; E½-NE¼-S31; 1-9-1837
Joseph Thompson N½-NW¼-Fr.NE¼-S31; 3-1-1837
Henry Curry E½-SE¼-S31; 1-7-1837
Bernard Meyer W½-SE¼-S31; 1-7-1837

Page 162. T 11 N, R 12 E of 2nd P.M.

William Marlin E½-NE¼-S32; 8-9-1836
James Henry Plaspohl W½-NE¼-S32; 1-2-1837
John Frilling E½-NW¼-S32; 1-13-1837
Hiram George W½-NW¼-S32; 8-19-1836
Bernard Rolfes NE¼-SE¼-S32; 11-12-1836
John Henry Recke SE¼-SE¼-S32; 11-15-1836
Joseph Heneke W½-SE¼-S32; 11-11-1836
Herman Henry Ortman E½-SW¼-S32; 11-11-1836
Bernard VanHandorf W½-SW¼-S32; 1-7-1837
Lewis Huigel E½-NE¼-S33; 8-12-1836. (May be Hingel)
William Miller W½-NE¼-S33; 10-28-1836
William Marlin SW¼-NW¼-S33; 7-2-1836
Joseph Henry NW¼-NW¼-S33; 1-31-1837
Henry Huntmann E½-NW¼-S33; 11-25-1836
Bernard Berns E½-SE¼-S33; 11-12-1836
Joseph Berns W½-SE¼-S33; 11-12-1836
John Henry Plaspohl SW¼-S33; 12-8-1836
Michael Huber NE¼-S34; NW¼-S34; 8-12-1836
Michael Huber, Sr. SE¼-S34; 11-9-1836
Michael Huber SW¼-S34; 8-12-1836
Robert Hobbs SE¼-NE¼-S35; 10-29-1835
Elisha Hobbs NE¼-NE¼-S35; 4-5-1836
John Gloshon NW¼-NE¼-S35; 9-6-1836
William Neff SW¼-NE¼-S35; 8-1-1840
John Gloshon NE¼-NW¼-S35; 2-13-1836
Stephen Hunnemann SE¼-NW¼; W½-NW¼-S35; 2-7-1837
Caleb Cragun NW¼-SE¼-S35; 2-20-1836
David Alley SW¼-SE¼-S35; 10-10-1836
John Rader SW¼-SW¼-S35; 2-11-1833
Henry Thoble NW¼-SW¼-S35; 2-1-1837
John Rader SE¼-SW¼-S35; 2-17-1836
John Henry Plaspohl NE¼-SW¼-S35; 2-9-1837
Henry Schwigmann W½-NE¼; SE¼-NE¼-S36; 4-19-1837
Henry Schwigmann NE¼-NE¼-S36; 7-3-1837
Joseph Roberts & John Roberts E½-NW¼-S36; 11-17-1836
Elisha Hobbs W½-NW¼-S36; 4-5-1836
John Roberts, Sr. SE¼-S36; 12-27-1836
Joseph Roberts & John Roberts SW¼-S36; 11-17-1836

Page 163. T 12 N, R 12 E of 2nd P.M.

Thomas Hedrick E½-NE¼-S1; 12-26-1834
Edward Johnson W½-NW¼-S1; 12-26-1834
Thomas Hedrick SE¼-S1; 12-26-1834
Milton Ladd Crawley NW¼-SW¼-S1; 8-28-1834

Milton Ladd Crawley SW$\frac{1}{4}$-SW$\frac{1}{4}$-S1; 11-13-1835
Thomas Hedrick E$\frac{1}{2}$-SW$\frac{1}{4}$-S1; 12-26-1834
James Conwell E$\frac{1}{2}$-NW$\frac{1}{4}$-S2; 11-28-1832
Edward Johnson SE$\frac{1}{4}$-S2; 12-26-1834
Hugh Mead W$\frac{1}{2}$-SW$\frac{1}{4}$-S2; 2-12-1818
James Conwell W$\frac{1}{2}$-NW$\frac{1}{4}$-S4; 10-31-1834
John W. McReynolds W$\frac{1}{2}$-SW$\frac{1}{4}$-S4; 10-31-1834
James Conwell E$\frac{1}{2}$-NE$\frac{1}{4}$-S5; 10-31-1834
James Conwell W$\frac{1}{2}$-NE$\frac{1}{4}$-S5; 1-3-1833
James Conwell E$\frac{1}{2}$-SW$\frac{1}{4}$-S5; 5-23-1832
Buckley C. Harris E$\frac{1}{2}$-NW$\frac{1}{4}$-NE$\frac{1}{4}$-S6; 8-19-1836
Francis A. Conwell SW$\frac{1}{4}$-NE$\frac{1}{4}$-S6; 12-10-1836

Page 164. T 12 N, R 12 E of 2nd P.M.

Thomas Cox SE$\frac{1}{4}$-NW$\frac{1}{4}$-S6; 2-20-1836
David Stilwell SW$\frac{1}{4}$-NW$\frac{1}{4}$-S6; 9-2-1836
William Neff N$\frac{1}{2}$-NW$\frac{1}{4}$-S6; 12-10-1836
John Sterling Russell SE$\frac{1}{4}$-SE$\frac{1}{4}$-S6; 2-11-1836
James Allison NE$\frac{1}{4}$-SE$\frac{1}{4}$-S6; 11-17-1836
Francis A. Conwell W$\frac{1}{2}$-SE$\frac{1}{4}$-S6; 12-10-1836
Francis A. Conwell NE$\frac{1}{4}$-S7; 6-16-1836
William Neff NE$\frac{1}{4}$-NW$\frac{1}{4}$-S7; 12-10-1836
Charles Smith SE$\frac{1}{4}$-NW$\frac{1}{4}$-S7; 10-8-1836
Nathan Springer W$\frac{1}{2}$-NW$\frac{1}{4}$-S7; 1-25-1836
William Alfred Anderson NE$\frac{1}{4}$-SE$\frac{1}{4}$-S7; 1-26-1836
Thomas Cox SW$\frac{1}{4}$-SW$\frac{1}{4}$-S7; 12-7-1836
William Neff SE$\frac{1}{4}$-NW$\frac{1}{4}$-SE$\frac{1}{4}$-S7; 12-10-1836
Weden Williams NW$\frac{1}{4}$-SW$\frac{1}{4}$-S7; 1-25-1836
Jonathan Russell SW$\frac{1}{4}$-SW$\frac{1}{4}$-S7; 1-25-1836
Charles Smith NE$\frac{1}{4}$-SW$\frac{1}{4}$-S7; 10-8-1836
Thomas Cox SE$\frac{1}{4}$-SW$\frac{1}{4}$-S7; 12-7-1836
James Conwell E$\frac{1}{2}$-NE$\frac{1}{4}$-S8; 10-11-1834
James Conwell W$\frac{1}{2}$-NE$\frac{1}{4}$-S8; 10-31-1834
William Creekmore N$\frac{1}{2}$-NW$\frac{1}{4}$-S8; 10-4-1834
James Conwell SE$\frac{1}{4}$-NW$\frac{1}{4}$; SW$\frac{1}{4}$-NW$\frac{1}{4}$-S8; 10-31-1834
Robert Russell NE$\frac{1}{4}$-SE$\frac{1}{4}$-S8; 10-9-1834
Stephen Maple SE$\frac{1}{4}$-SE$\frac{1}{4}$-S8; 10-25-1832
Levi Wood SW$\frac{1}{4}$-SE$\frac{1}{4}$-S8; 2-4-1834
James Conwell NW$\frac{1}{4}$-SE$\frac{1}{4}$-S8; 10-31-1834
Benjamin Weston W$\frac{1}{2}$-SW$\frac{1}{4}$-S8; 3-26-1832
Edward Johnson S$\frac{1}{2}$-NE$\frac{1}{4}$-S11; 1-30-1836
William Neff N$\frac{1}{2}$-NE$\frac{1}{4}$-S11; 12-10-1836

Page 165. T 12 N, R 12 E of 2nd P.M.

John Debaun SE$\frac{1}{4}$-SE$\frac{1}{4}$-S11; 10-12-1835
Matthew Smith NE$\frac{1}{4}$-SE$\frac{1}{4}$-S11; 10-22-1835
James Potts SW$\frac{1}{4}$-SE$\frac{1}{4}$-S11; 9-29-1836
William Neff NW$\frac{1}{4}$-SE$\frac{1}{4}$-S11; 12-10-1836
Otho Selby E$\frac{1}{2}$-SW$\frac{1}{4}$-S11; 8-18-1832
Henry Harpham NE$\frac{1}{4}$-S12; 4-2-1836
Henry D. Smith E$\frac{1}{2}$-NW$\frac{1}{4}$-S12; 10-8-1836
James Crawley NW$\frac{1}{4}$-NW$\frac{1}{4}$-S12; 9-12-1832
James Crawley SW$\frac{1}{4}$-NW$\frac{1}{4}$-S12; 5-28-1833
Anderson Warner E$\frac{1}{2}$-SE$\frac{1}{4}$-S12; 1-18-1836
Francis A. Conwell W$\frac{1}{2}$-SE$\frac{1}{4}$; E$\frac{1}{2}$-SW$\frac{1}{4}$-S12; 12-10-1836
James Potts W$\frac{1}{2}$-SW$\frac{1}{4}$-S12; 1-15-1836

David Blazer E½-NE¼; NW¼-NE¼-S13; 1-28-1836
William Neff SW¼-NE¼-S13; 12-10-1836
William Neff E½-NW¼-S13; 12-10-1836
Martin Warner W½-NW¼-S13; 11-9-1836
William Neff SE¼-S13; 12-10-1836
John Currey E½-SW¼-S13; 1-22-1836
Ralph Williams W½-SW¼-S13; 5-10-1834
Edwin Burr. Babbitt NE¼-SW¼-S14; 6-19-1832
James Conwell SE¼-SW¼-S14; 10-31-1834
James Conwell NW¼-SW¼; SW¼-SW¼-S14; 10-31-1834
James Conwell E½-NE¼-S15; 11-28-1832
Edward Brush & H. Lockwood NW¼-S15; 3-22-1816
James Conwell E½-SW¼-S15; 11-28-1832
James Conwell W½-SW¼-S15; 12-16-1831
James Conwell E½-NW¼-S17; 10-31-1834

Page 166. T 12 N, R 12 E of 2nd P.M.

Jacob Smith NW¼-NW¼-S17; 2-2-1835
Henry D. Smith SW¼-NW¼-S17; 6-16-1836
George Grove Shoup SW¼-S17; 12-19-1835
Thomas Cooper NE¼-S18; 12-10-1835
John Small Springer E½-NW¼-S18; 1-25-1836
Atwell Jackman W½-NW¼-S18; 1-25-1836
William Cahill SE¼-SE¼-S18; 7-21-1835
William Cahill NE¼-SE¼-S18; 1-25-1836
John Cones W½-SE¼-S18; 8-23-1836
Gideon Jinks E½-SW¼-S18; 2-6-1836
Aaron Matthews (negro) W½-SW¼-S18; 10-29-1835
John B. Lockwood NW¼-SW¼-S19; 6-27-1836
Summers Q. Smith SW¼-SW¼-S19; 9-30-1836
James Conwell NE¼-S22; 3-21-1836
John Chance NE¼-NE¼-S23; 2-4-1836
John Chance SE¼-NE¼-S23; 1-1-1835
John Chance W½-NE¼-S23; 3-2-1833
James Conwell NW¼-S23; 10-31-1834
Andrew Murray E½-SE¼-S23; 2-6-1836
Jacob Miller NW¼-SE¼-S23; 12-3-1833
Jacob Miller SW¼-SE¼-S23; 3-4-1834

Page 167. T 12 N, R 12 E of 2nd P.M.

James Eads McClure NE¼-SW¼-S23; 2-3-1834
Arnold Murray SE¼-SW¼-S23; 1-22-1836
Hiram Bennett Langston W½-NE¼-S24; 1-22-1836
Alexander Simpson SW¼-NW¼-S24; 1-1-1835
James Chance NW¼-NW¼-S24; 10-26-1835
Arnold Murray NE¼-NW¼-S24; 1-22-1836
John Walls Garrison SE¼-NW¼-S24; 1-15-1835
John Currey NW¼-NE¼-S25; 6-7-1833
William Gordon SW¼-NE¼-S25; 10-15-1836
William Neff NE¼-NE¼; SE¼-NE¼-S25; 12-15-1836
William Gordon, assee. of Thomas Curry NW¼-S25; 11-4-1811
Artema D. Woodworth, assee. of Charls (sp.?) NE¼-S26; 11-23-1811. See Vol. I, Aschel Churchill
Thomas Deford SW¼-NW¼-S28; 2-8-1836
Jared Lockwood E½-NW¼-S28; 4-22-1836
James Wiley E½-SW¼-S28; 10-21-1835

John Crist NE¼-NE¼-S29; 6-12-1834
Randall Pitt & Chandler Barwick (possibly just one name) SE¼-NE¼-S29; 5-19-1836
Coburn Murray W½-NE¼-S29; 10-20-1835
Stephen Hart NE¼-NW¼-S29; 11-19-1833
Thomas Maxwell, Jr. SE¼-NW¼-S29; 9-2-1836

Page 168. T 12 N, R 12 E of 2nd P.M.

James Catlin NW¼-SE¼-S29; 7-30-1836
John Cox SW¼-SE¼-S29; 12-5-1836
Nicholas Anselm Stroube NE¼-SW¼-S29; 6-22-1835
Jeffrey Hildrith NW¼-SW¼-S29; 8-23-1836
John Moniker S½-SW¼-S29; 11-21-1836
Charles W. Ryckman SE¼-NW¼-S30; 2-2-1836
Jesse Williams NE¼-NW¼-S30; 10-28-1836
David Wilson SE¼-S30; 11-7-1836
Uriah Lefter E½-SW¼-S30; 6-7-1836
William Neff W½-SW¼-S30; 12-15-1836
John Simpson SW¼-NE¼-S31; 6-26-1834
George Q. Shoup NW¼-NE¼-S31; 12-15-1836
Benjamin G. Goodwin E½-NE¼-S31; 9-12-1836
John Simpson SE¼-NW¼-S31; 6-20-1836
George Q. Shoup NE¼-NW¼-S31; 12-15-1836
William Neff W½-NW¼-S31; 12-15-1836
Robert McNutt N½-SE¼-S31; 8-5-1836
Thomas S. Bank S½-SE¼-S31; 11-28-1836
Elliott Mefford SW¼-SW¼-S31; 1-24-1834
Robert McNutt NW¼-SW¼; E½-SW¼-S31; 7-28-1836
Joel J. Buckler SW¼-NE¼-S32; 2-4-1836
George Q. Shoup NW¼-NE¼-S32; 12-15-1836
John Hiers NE¼-NE¼-S32; 3-4-1836
Benjamin G. Goodwin SE¼-NE¼-S32; 9-12-1836
James Beel NE¼-NW¼-S32; 9-12-1836
George Q. Shoup SE¼-NW¼-S32; 12-15-1836
Curtis Condon NW¼-NW¼-S32; 10-5-1836
George Q. Shoup SW¼-NW¼-S32; 12-15-1836
Thomas Clark SE¼-SE¼-S32; 10-2-1832
George Q. Shoup NE¼-SE¼-S32; 12-15-1836
David Weston SE¼-SW¼-S32; 2-7-1834
David Weston NE¼-SW¼-S32; 4-20-1835
John George SW¼-SW¼-S32; 3-4-1836
John Cook NW¼-SW¼-S32; 9-1-1836

Page 169. T 12 N, R 12 E of 2nd P.M.

James Wiley W½-NE¼-S33; 10-21-1835
John Hiers NW¼-NW¼-S33; 8-3-1832
Patrick Adams SW¼-NW¼-S33; 10-24-1835
Benjamin Deford Goodwin SE¼-NW¼-S33; 3-17-1834
James Wiley NE¼-NW¼-S33; 10-21-1835

Page 169. T 13 N, R 12 E of 2nd P.M. FAYETTE CO.

Jeremiah Warham SW¼-S1; 12-19-1811

Page 171. T 13 N, R 12 E of 2nd P.M.

William Chiles Plummer NW¼-SE¼-S17; 6-12-1832
James Conwell SW¼-SE¼-S17; 3-2-1835
Benjamin Franklin Utter E½-NE¼-S19; 7-10-1834
James Conwell W½-NE¼-S19; 3-2-18[illegible]
George Klum SE¼-NW¼-S19; 6-14-1832

James Conwell NE¼-NW¼-S19; 3-2-1835
William Jacobs W½-SW¼-S19; 5-3-1832
James Conwell NE¼-S21; 11-24-1834
James Conwell E½-NW¼-S21; 11-24-1834

Page 172. T 13 N, R 12 E of 2nd P.M.

John McCabe NE¼-SW¼-S25; 5-30-1832
Greenberry Steele SE¼-SW¼-S25; 1-3-1837
Daniel Green NE¼-S26; 12-16-1814
Cornelius Rinerson NW¼-SW¼-S29; 7-19-1833
Rinerd Rinerson SW¼-SW¼-S29; 2-7-1834
Booz Tharp SW¼-NW¼-S30; 9-28-1835
Job Waltz NW¼-NW¼-S30; 1-25-1836
James Conwell E½-SE¼-S30; 11-27-1834
James Conwell W½-SE¼-S30; SW¼-S30; 12-10-1835
James Moore NW¼-NE¼-S31; 1-25-1836
Charles Melone SW¼-NE¼-S31; 12-13-1836
James Linville E½-NE¼-S31; 12-7-1836
Charles Morrow E½-NW¼-S31; 12-7-1836
Charles Melone W½-NW¼-S31; 12-13-1836
Charles Melone SE¼-S31; 10-12-1836

Page 173. T 13 N, R 12 E of 2nd P.M.

Rinerd Rinerson NE¼-NW¼-S32; 2-7-1834
Moses Harrell SE¼-NW¼-S32; 1-3-1835
John J. Shaver NW¼-NW¼-S32; 5-17-1834
Francis A. Conwell SW¼-NW¼-S32; 11-17-1836
Francis A. Conwell SE¼-SW¼-S32; 11-17-1836
James Webb, Jr. NE¼-SW¼-S32; 12-25-1834
Francis A. Conwell W½-SW¼-S32; 11-17-1836
James Conwell E½-NE¼-S35; 10-31-1834
Jeremiah Conwell W½-NE¼-S35; 3-15-1833
Elbert Walker E½-NW¼-S35; 10-3-1834
Joseph Crawley NE¼-SE¼-S36; 5-28-1832
Michael Null SE¼-NE¼-S36; 7-28-1836
James Conwell W½-SE¼-S36; 11-27-1834
James Conwell SW¼-S36; 11-27-1834

Page 174. T 14 N, R 12 E of 2nd P.M.

Eli Scotten NW¼-S10; 3-26-1814
Samuel Dehavan NW¼-S11; 10-7-1812

Page 175. T 14 N, R 12 E of 2nd P.M.

Alexander Saxon SE¼-S25; 12-8-1811
James Adair, Jr. SW¼-S25; 10-23-1811

Page 177. T 15 N, R 12 E of 2nd P.M. WAYNE CO.

Jacob Burnett SE¼-S1; 10-28-1811
Richard Williams NW¼-S2; 10-22-1811

Page 178. T 15 N, R 12 E of 2nd P.M.

E. Brown SW¼-S26; 11-5-1814

Page 178. T 15 N, R 12 E of 2nd P.M. FAYETTE CO.

Richard Kobb SE¼-S28; 11-21-1812

Page 179. T 16 N, R 12 E of 2nd P.M. WAYNE CO.

Benjamin Roberts NW¼-S11; 6-2-1815

Page 180. T 16 N, R 12 E of 2nd P.M.

John Hoover SE¼-S23; 11-26-1811
Isaac Willson NE¼-S36; 10-23-1811

Page 181. T 17 N, R 12 E of 2nd P.M.
James Swift NE¼-NW¼-S24; 6-17-1833
James Powell SE¼-NW¼-S24; 1-24-1835
Joseph Bowen SW¼-SE¼-S24; 3-1-1834
William Murray NW¼-SE¼-S24; 3-10-1835
William Codington NW¼-S25; 8-15-1817
John Clemans E½-SW¼-S36; 5-28-1832

Page 182. T 11 N, R 13 E of 2nd P.M.   FRANKLIN CO.
William Morford SE¼-SW¼-S6; 12-1-1832
James Renhart SW¼-SW¼-S6; 12-1-1832
Henry Pond NE¼-SW¼-S6; 7-4-1836
Warren S. Pond NW¼-SW¼-S6; 6-25-1836
Thomas Clark NW¼-S7; 2-6-1836
Louis Morgan Clark E½-NE¼-S8; 1-11-1836
Louis Morgan Clark W½-NE¼-S8; 11-14-1836
William Stringer NW¼-NW¼-S8; 5-13-1833
John S. Biggs SW¼-NW¼-S8; 12-20-1836
Charles Wilson SE¼-NW¼-S8; 3-3-1836
John S. Biggs NE¼-NW¼-S8; 12-20-1836
Samuel Sering SE¼-S8; 1-2-1836
Jonathan Alley SW¼-SW¼-S8; 2-10-1836
Charles Wilson NE¼-SW¼-S8; 3-3-1836
Jonathan Alley NW¼-SW¼-S8; 10-7-1836
Calvin A. Gant SE¼-SW¼-S8; 10-12-1836
James Calfee E½-NW¼-S9; 8-8-1835
Louis Morgan Clark W½-NW¼-S9; 1-11-1836
Robert Wade Halsted SE¼-S9; 1-27-1836
Robert Wade Halsted E½-SW¼; SW¼-SW¼-S9; 12-8-1834
Louis Morgan Clark NW¼-SW¼-S9; 1-11-1836
Fielding Jeter Lot 1-NE cor.-S pt.-Fr.S14; Lot 2-NW cor.-S pt.-
   Fr.S14; Lot 3-SW cor.-Fr.S14; 1-29-1836
Fielding Jeter Lot 4-SE cor.-Fr.S14; 1-9-1834
David Virtue E½-NW¼-S15; 3-3-1836

Page 183. T 11 N, R 13 E of 2nd P.M.
Fielding Jeter W½-NW¼-S15; 1-25-1836
Fielding Jeter W½-SE¼-S15; 1-9-1834
Nathan D. Gallion & William T. Beeks E½-SE¼-S15; 1-26-1836
David Virtue E½-SW¼-S15; 3-3-1836
Fielding Jeter W½-SW¼-S15; 1-25-1836
Calvin A. Gant N½-NW¼-S17; 7-7-1836
Joseph Roberts & John Roberts S½-NW¼-S17; 12-22-1836
Ansel Terry E½-SE¼-S17; 12-5-1836
Joseph Roberts & John Roberts W½-SE¼-S17; 12-22-1836
Isaac Cooley NW¼-SW¼-S17; 10-19-1836
Thomas Halsted NE¼-SW¼-S17; 11-24-1836
Elizabeth Jones SW¼-SW¼-S17; 12-1-1836
Joseph Roberts & John Roberts SE¼-SW¼-S17; 12-2-1836
James Mitchell Alley E½-NW¼-S18; 1-11-1836
John S. Biggs W½-NW¼-S18; 11-18-1836
Elisha Hobbs SW¼-SW¼-S18; 3-5-1836
John S. Biggs NW¼-SW¼-S18; 11-18-1836
David Alley NW¼-NE¼-S19; 2-20-1856
Joseph Roberts & John Roberts SW¼-NE¼; E½-NE¼-S19; 11-17-1836
Philip Laurence E½-SE¼-S19; 6-5-1835

Joseph Roberts & John Roberts W$\frac{1}{2}$-SE$\frac{1}{4}$-S19; 11-17-1836
Joseph Roberts & John Roberts E$\frac{1}{2}$-NW$\frac{1}{4}$-S20; 12-2-1836
Joseph Roberts & John Roberts W$\frac{1}{2}$-NW$\frac{1}{4}$-S20; 11-17-1836
Thomas Coen SE$\frac{1}{4}$-SE$\frac{1}{4}$-S20; 5-29-1832
Josiah Coen NE$\frac{1}{4}$-SE$\frac{1}{4}$-S20; 9-17-1835
Josiah Coen SE$\frac{1}{4}$-SW$\frac{1}{4}$-S20; 9-14-1836
Joseph Roberts & John Roberts NE$\frac{1}{4}$-SW$\frac{1}{4}$-S20; 12-2-1836
Philip Laurence W$\frac{1}{2}$-SW$\frac{1}{4}$-S20; 12-19-1834
George Laurence E$\frac{1}{2}$-NW$\frac{1}{4}$-S21; 3-26-1834

Page 184. T 11 N, R 13 E of 2nd P.M.

Ansel Terry SW$\frac{1}{4}$-NW$\frac{1}{4}$-S21; 9-25-1835
John Knecht NW$\frac{1}{4}$-NW$\frac{1}{4}$-S21; 2-1-1837
Fielding Jeter Lots 6-7--W$\frac{1}{2}$-NW$\frac{1}{4}$-Fr.S22; 1-29-1836
Henry Treitline Lot 5-NE pt.-W side-S22; 5-20-1837
Valentine Weis Lot 8-SE pt.-NW$\frac{1}{4}$-S22; SW cor.-NE$\frac{1}{4}$-S22; 5-24-1837
Nicholas Diel Lot 9-W pt.-SE$\frac{1}{4}$-S22; 5-25-1837
Valentine Dill Lot 10-E$\frac{1}{2}$-SW$\frac{1}{4}$-S22; 5-23-1837
Valentine Fuller Lot 11-NW$\frac{1}{4}$-SW$\frac{1}{4}$-S22; 5-22-1837
Nicholas Seibert Lot 12-SW$\frac{1}{4}$-SW$\frac{1}{4}$-S22; 5-24-1837
Hadley D. Johnson Fr.S23; 5-4-1837
Nicholas Seibert Fr.S27; 5-24-1837
Aaron Robeson Lyons Lot 2-NE$\frac{1}{4}$-NW$\frac{1}{4}$-Fr.S28; 11-11-1835
Aaron R. Lyons Lot 3-NW$\frac{1}{4}$-NW$\frac{1}{4}$-S28; 1-28-1834
Jonathan Smith Lot 4-SW$\frac{1}{4}$-NW$\frac{1}{4}$-S28; 9-25-1833
Samuel Bennet Lot 5-SE pt.-W$\frac{1}{2}$-S28; 2-9-1836
Jonathan Smith Lot 6-SW cor.-Fr.S28; 1-28-1834
Philip Laurence E$\frac{1}{2}$-NE$\frac{1}{4}$-S29; 1-28-1834
Philip Laurence W$\frac{1}{2}$-NE$\frac{1}{4}$-S29; 3-18-1834
Philip Laurence E$\frac{1}{2}$-NW$\frac{1}{4}$-S29; 6-6-1834
Philip Laurence W$\frac{1}{2}$-NW$\frac{1}{4}$-S29; 12-19-1834
Daniel Morgan Fleming E$\frac{1}{2}$-SW$\frac{1}{4}$-S29; 5-26-1837
William Egbert W$\frac{1}{2}$-SW$\frac{1}{4}$-S29; 2-9-1838
Tyra Stafford Lot 1-E$\frac{1}{2}$-SE$\frac{1}{4}$-Fr.S29; 1-28-1834
Philip Laurence Lot 2-NW$\frac{1}{4}$-SE$\frac{1}{4}$; Lot 3-SW$\frac{1}{4}$-SE$\frac{1}{4}$-S29; 6-5-1835
James Alley SE$\frac{1}{4}$-NE$\frac{1}{4}$-S30; 10-10-1836
Joseph Roberts & John Roberts NE$\frac{1}{4}$-NE$\frac{1}{4}$-S30; 12-2-1836
Joseph Roberts & John Roberts W$\frac{1}{2}$-NE$\frac{1}{4}$-S30; 11-3-1836
Susanna Rhea SE$\frac{1}{4}$-NW$\frac{1}{4}$-S30; 3-20-1834
Joseph Roberts & John Roberts NE$\frac{1}{4}$-NW$\frac{1}{4}$-S30; 12-2-1836
Stephen Henry Wellmann E$\frac{1}{2}$-SE$\frac{1}{4}$-S30; 8-1-1837

Page 185. T 11 N, R 13 E of 2nd P.M.

Joseph Roberts & John Roberts W$\frac{1}{2}$-SW$\frac{1}{4}$-S30; 11-3-1836
James Hornback SE$\frac{1}{4}$-NE$\frac{1}{4}$-S31; 10-1-1832
William Pilson NE$\frac{1}{4}$-NE$\frac{1}{4}$-S31; 9-19-1836
Milton Hutchinson SW$\frac{1}{4}$-NE$\frac{1}{4}$-S31; 1-18-1833
Elisha Balwin Jones NW$\frac{1}{4}$-NE$\frac{1}{4}$-S31; 11-5-1835
Milton Hutchinson SE$\frac{1}{4}$-NW$\frac{1}{4}$-S31; 1-28-1833
James Alley NE$\frac{1}{4}$-NW$\frac{1}{4}$-S31; 3-25-1833
John S. Riggs Fr.S6: Lots 10-11-12--SW$\frac{1}{4}$-W$\frac{1}{2}$-SE$\frac{1}{4}$-Fr.S31; 10-10-1836
Joseph Roberts & John Roberts W$\frac{1}{2}$-NW$\frac{1}{4}$-S31; 11-3-1836
Daniel M. Fleming Lot 5-E pt.; Lot 6-W pt.-Fr.S32; 6-21-1836

Page 185. T 12 N, R 13 E of 2nd P.M.

Richard Dunkin NE$\frac{1}{4}$-S2; 9-22-1815
Samuel McHenry E$\frac{1}{2}$-SW$\frac{1}{4}$-S3; 8-1-1816

Daniel Teagarden NE$\frac{1}{4}$-S5; 4-20-1814
John R. Beaty SW$\frac{1}{4}$-S5; 5-27-1814
James Laride E$\frac{1}{2}$-NE$\frac{1}{4}$-S5; 9-26-1831
Ezekiel Nichols Serrin W$\frac{1}{2}$-NE$\frac{1}{4}$-S5; 11-14-1832

Page 186. T 12 N, R 13 E of 2nd P.M.

Thomas Campbell Whitelock SE$\frac{1}{4}$-NW$\frac{1}{4}$-S6; 11-23-1832
Stephen Schooley NE$\frac{1}{4}$-NW$\frac{1}{4}$; NW$\frac{1}{4}$-NW$\frac{1}{4}$-S6; 9-13-1836
Samuel Dudley Owen SW$\frac{1}{4}$-NW$\frac{1}{4}$-S6; 11-3-1834
Abraham Whitelock SE$\frac{1}{4}$-SE$\frac{1}{4}$-S6; 11-23-1832
William W. Whitelock NE$\frac{1}{4}$-SE$\frac{1}{4}$-S6; 12-24-1832
John Crouel SE$\frac{1}{4}$-SE$\frac{1}{4}$-S7; 11-25-1836
William Neff NE$\frac{1}{4}$-SE$\frac{1}{4}$-S7; 12-15-1836
Thomas Smith Webb W$\frac{1}{2}$-SE$\frac{1}{4}$-S7; 2-4-1836
Isaiah Clemmons Tuttle NE$\frac{1}{2}$-SW$\frac{1}{4}$-S7; 9-26-1833
Darlin Tuttle S$\frac{1}{2}$-SW$\frac{1}{4}$-S7; 1-23-1836
Charles Whitelock NW$\frac{1}{4}$-SW$\frac{1}{4}$-S7; 2-13-1836
Caleb B. Clements NW$\frac{1}{4}$-S8; 6-23-1814
Ralph Williams NE$\frac{1}{4}$-NW$\frac{1}{4}$-S8; 5-26-1832
Lazarus Dannell(?) Rasnick SE$\frac{1}{4}$-SW$\frac{1}{4}$-S8; 1-21-1836
George W. C. Miller SW$\frac{1}{4}$-SW$\frac{1}{4}$-S8; 2-4-1836
Henry Harpham W$\frac{1}{2}$-NE$\frac{1}{4}$-S9; 3-2-1833

Page 187. T 12 N, R 13 E of 2nd P.M.

James Swift SW$\frac{1}{4}$-NE$\frac{1}{4}$-S17; 10-11-1833
William Jefferson Townson NW$\frac{1}{2}$-NE$\frac{1}{4}$-S17; 3-17-1835
William Neff W$\frac{1}{2}$-NW$\frac{1}{4}$-S17; 12-15-1836
Samuel V. Hubartt NE$\frac{1}{4}$-NE$\frac{1}{4}$-S18; 1-14-1836
John Hubartt SW$\frac{1}{4}$-NE$\frac{1}{4}$-S18; 1-14-1836
William Neff NW$\frac{1}{4}$-SE$\frac{1}{4}$-S18; 12-15-1836
Anderson Warner NW$\frac{1}{4}$-NW$\frac{1}{4}$-S18; 1-18-1836
Simeon Broadbury E$\frac{1}{2}$-NW$\frac{1}{4}$; SW$\frac{1}{4}$-NW$\frac{1}{4}$-S18; 10-7-1836
Jacob Blacklidge SE$\frac{1}{4}$-SE$\frac{1}{4}$-S18; 5-25-1833
William Neff NE$\frac{1}{4}$-SE$\frac{1}{4}$-S18; 12-15-1836
Orvill Gorden W$\frac{1}{2}$-SE$\frac{1}{4}$-S18; 1-13-1836
William Neff NE$\frac{1}{4}$-SW$\frac{1}{4}$; NW$\frac{1}{4}$-SW$\frac{1}{4}$; SE$\frac{1}{4}$-SW$\frac{1}{4}$-S18; 12-15-1836
James Patterson SW$\frac{1}{4}$-SW$\frac{1}{4}$-S18; 10-1-1832
Orville Gorden SW$\frac{1}{4}$-SE$\frac{1}{4}$-S19; 5-14-1835
Orville Gorden NW$\frac{1}{4}$-SE$\frac{1}{4}$-S19; 12-24-1835
Orville Gorden E$\frac{1}{2}$-SE$\frac{1}{4}$-S19; 1-13-1836
Jacob Blacklidge NW$\frac{1}{2}$-SW$\frac{1}{4}$-S19; 5-25-1833
William Neff SW$\frac{1}{4}$-SW$\frac{1}{4}$-S19; 12-15-1836
Ralph Williams E$\frac{1}{2}$-SW$\frac{1}{4}$-S19; 6-7-1833
William Wiggans, Jr. SW$\frac{1}{4}$-NE$\frac{1}{4}$-S20; 10-23-1833
Thomas Hughell NW$\frac{1}{4}$-NE$\frac{1}{4}$-S20; 4-11-1834

Page 188. T 12 N, R 13 E of 2nd P.M.

William Fleweling NE$\frac{1}{4}$-NW$\frac{1}{4}$-S20; 5-23-1835
William Wright SE$\frac{1}{4}$-NW$\frac{1}{4}$-S20; 10-29-1835
Richard Thomas SE$\frac{1}{4}$-SE$\frac{1}{4}$-S20; 10-6-1835
Daniel Lounsbury NE$\frac{1}{4}$-SE$\frac{1}{4}$-S20; 12-11-1835
Richard Thomas NE$\frac{1}{4}$-SW$\frac{1}{4}$-S20; 12-18-1832
Daniel Lounsbury NW$\frac{1}{4}$-SW$\frac{1}{4}$-S20; 12-11-1835
John Williams SE$\frac{1}{4}$-SW$\frac{1}{4}$-S20; 10-6-1832
Joshua Sylvester Kiorn(?) SW$\frac{1}{4}$-SW$\frac{1}{4}$-S20; 10-29-1835
John Newman NE$\frac{1}{4}$-SE$\frac{1}{4}$-S21; 12-6-1833
Martin Williams SE$\frac{1}{4}$-SE$\frac{1}{4}$-S21; 1-26-1836

Hiram Williams SW¼-SW¼-S21; 4-4-1834
Philip Jones NW¼-SW¼-S21; 10-1-1834
Joseph Hughell, Jr. NW¼-S22; 9-28-1814
Stanford Jones SW¼-SE¼-S22; 1-6-1834
John Newman NW¼-SE¼-S22; 11-9-1835
James Blacklidge W½-SW¼-S26; 12-19-1835
Jeremiah Schoonover SW¼-NE¼-S27; 8-7-1835
William Pilson NW¼-NE¼-S27; 9-9-1836
Henry Cater & Gerhard Hollrah E½-NW¼-S27; 7-5-1836
Asa Schoonover W½-NW¼-S27; 8-7-1835

Page 189. T 12 N, R 13 E of 2nd P.M.
James Blacklidge S½-SE¼-S27; 7-2-1836
William Pilson N½-SE¼-S27; 9-9-1836
Thomas Jefferson Norvill SE¼-NE¼-S28; 6-1-1832
Adam Williams NE¼-NE¼-S28; 8-26-1834
Samuel Lewis W½-NE¼-S28; 4-4-1834
William Chapman E½-SW¼-S28; 5-29-1832
John Gross W½-SW¼-S28; 10-12-1836
Alexander W. Barnes W½-NE¼-S29; 10-25-1836
William Lynn SE¼-SE¼-S29; 3-8-1836
William Gorden NE¼-SE¼-S29; 3-13-1835
William Gorden W½-SE¼-S29; 3-13-1835
Henry Armstrong SW¼-S29; 1-27-1836
Thomas Swiggett NE¼-NE¼-S30; 6-15-1832
Richard Swift SE¼-NE¼-S30; 11-9-1835
George Giltner & Asahel Giltner E½-NW¼-S30; 10-6-1832
Harvey Blacklidge NW¼-NW¼-S30; 7-20-1835
Solomon Pierce SW¼-NW¼-S30; 12-16-1835
William Gorden E½-SE¼-S30; 1-13-1836
Harvey Blacklidge E½-SW¼-S30; 11-2-1835
Joseph Schoonover NE¼-S32; 7-30-1835
Joseph Schoonover SE¼-NE¼-S32; 2-4-1836
William Gorden W½-NE¼-S32; 1-13-1836
Isaac Wilson SE¼-SE¼-S32; 6-2-1832
James Linn NE¼-SE¼-S32; 2-2-1836

Page 193. T 13 N, R 13 E of 2nd P.M.   FAYETTE CO
Jesse Ward SW¼-NW¼-S29; 5-24-1832
Jesse Ward NW¼-NW¼-S29; 11-26-1832
Isaac Tuttle Riggs E½-NE¼-S30; 11-14-1834
John Hanley Carmichael SW¼-NW¼-S31; 1-19-1835
Enoch Youngs NW¼-NW¼-S31; 1-7-1837
Michael Null W½-SE¼-S31; 7-28-1836
Peter Jackson Massey NW¼-SW¼-S32; 3-2-1838
William Risk S½-SW¼-S32; 12-10-1836
John Spenser NE¼-SW¼-S32; 11-16-1836
James Craig NW¼-S33; 3-10-1813
Thomas Henderson NW¼-S34; 10-28-1811

Page 197. T 14 N, R 13 E of 2nd P.M.
John Wilson NE¼-S32; 2-24-1815

Page 198. T 15 N, R 13 E of 2nd P.M.   WAYNE CO.
John Knipe NE¼-S2; 10-24-1811
John Patterson SE¼-S3; 10-24-1811
Alexander Gray NW¼-S6; 10-24-1811

Page 199. T 15 N, R 13 E of 2nd P.M.
John Conely SE¼-S14; 4-2-1812
Page 200. T 15 N, R 13 E of 2nd P.M.
David Jenkins SW¼-S23; 12-25-1813
Page 201. T 16 N, R 13 E of 2nd P.M.
Henry Hoover SE¼-S3; 11-8-1811
Page 202. T 16 N, R 13 E of 2nd P.M.
Robenson McIntire SW¼-S5; 10-24-1811
Page 206. T 17 N, R 13 E of 2nd P.M.
Perry Hurst E½-SE¼-S4; 10-12-1833
Job Ratcliff W½-SE¼-S4; 6-28-1832
James A. Dawson W½-SW¼-S6; 2-5-1833
Jeremiah Bowen E½-NW¼-S7; 3-25-1834
Philander Fowler W½-NW¼-S7; 6-13-1833
Page 207. T 17 N, R 13 E of 2nd P.M.
William Clawson SE¼-S12; 10-24-1811
Isaac Peirce E½-NW¼-S18; 2-1-1836
William Brown W½-NW¼-S18; 2-8-1836
William Brown SW¼-S18; 2-8-1836
Page 208. T 17 N, R 13 E of 2nd P.M.
Samuel Bundy NE¼-NW¼-S19; 10-9-1834
Jesse Albertson SW¼-S25; 10-21-1814
Page 209. T 17 N, R 13 E of 2nd P.M.
James Holliday NE¼-S32; 2-7-1812
Page 210. T 18 N, R 13 E of 2nd P.M.   **RANDOLPH CO.**
William Doherty SW¼-NE¼-S1; 2-1-1836
Joseph Mills E½-NE¼; NW¼-NE¼-S1; 9-17-1836
Henry Mills NW¼-S1; 6-8-1836
Temple Smith SE¼-SE¼-S1; 3-26-1835
James Taylor Nicholson NE¼-SE¼-S1; 3-1-1837
Henry Mills W½-SE¼-S1; 6-8-1836
James Ballinger SW¼-SW¼-S1; 5-27-1835
Miles Hunt NW¼-SW¼-S1; 2-18-1837
Henry Mills E½-SW¼-S1; 6-8-1836
Stanley Frazer NE¼-NE¼-S2; 5-1-1835
Robert Willis NW¼-NE¼-S2; 9-15-1835
Peter Swerer(?) SW¼-NE¼-S2; 2-7-1837
Peter Swerer(?) SE¼-NE¼-S2; 2-15-1837
Thomas Craner(?) E½-NW¼-S2; 8-27-1833
Miles Hunt NE¼-SE¼-S2; 2-18-1837
James Ballinger SE¼-SE¼-S2; 4-21-1836
Stephen Brewer W½-SE¼-S2; 2-26-1834
Samuel W. Fenimore W½-NW¼-S3; 4-20-1836
Benjamin Cox SE¼-NE¼-S4; 2-17-1835
John Harvey W½-NE¼; NE¼-NE¼-S4; 11-19-1835
Elijah Arnold NW¼-NW¼-S4; 6-4-1833
Charles Gallaher SW¼-NW¼-S4; 9-8-1835
John Beck NE¼-NW¼-S4; 7-1-1835
John Harvey SE¼-NW¼-S4; 11-19-1835
Washington Craner SE¼-SE¼-S4; 12-1-1835
Thomas Washington Craner NE¼-SE¼-S4: 2-6-1836
Abraham Adamson W½-SE¼-S4; 3-1-1837
Elijah Mendenhall E½-SW¼-S4; 3-1-1837
Joseph Macy W½-SW¼-S4; 2-11-1836

Page 211. T 18 N, R 13 E of 2nd P.M.
William Locke N½-NE¼-S5; 2-1-1836
Ira Swain Lot 4-SE¼-NE¼-Fr.S5; 1-23-1836
Jeramiah Smith Lot 3-SW¼-NE¼-Fr.S5; 4-11-1838
Elijah Arnold NE¼-SE¼-S5; 6-4-1833
Joseph Macy NW¼-SE¼-S5; 6-3-1835
David Hutchins NW¼-NW¼-S9; 1-23-1836
Miles Hunt & George Bailey SW¼-NW¼; E½-NW¼-S9; 2-18-1837
James Stanley, Jr. E½-SE¼-S9; 7-20-1832
Barnabas Lamb E½-SW¼-S9; 4-15-1837
Albert Macy SE¼-NW¼-S10; 6-24-1833
Albert Macy NE¼-NW¼-S10; 1-24-1835
William Catey E½-SE¼-S10; 12-13-1833
Daniel Jones SE¼-S11; 6-4-1818
Robert H. Millman SE¼-NE¼-S13; 3-27-1837
Evan Jay NE¼-NE¼-S13; 10-10-1836
          Page 212. T 18 N, R 13 E of 2nd P.M.
George Brittain E½-SE¼-S13; 2-24-1835
Elias Davison SE¼-NW¼-S14; 10-8-1835
Silvanus Davison SW¼-NW¼-S14; 12-3-1836
Christian Edmond NE¼-NW¼-S14; 3-27-1837
Silvanus Davison NW¼-NW¼-S14; 10-26-1838
Moses Davison W½-SE¼-S14; 12-12-1836
William Price E½-SW¼-S14; 3-9-1835
William Davidson W½-SW¼-S14; 7-13-1830
Archelaus Stanley SW¼-NE¼-S15; 1-23-1836
James Weeks NW¼-NE¼-S15; 1-12-1837
Jonathan Hutchens E½-NE¼-S15; 3-27-1837
William Cox E½-SE¼-S15; 6-6-1833
Amos Elliston NE¼-SW¼-S17; 7-9-1833
David Moore SE¼-SW¼-S17; 12-22-1835
          Page 213. T 18 N, R 13 E of 2nd P.M.   **WAYNE CO.**
Robert Burns E½-NE¼-S22; 1-23-1835
Henry Mullonick E½-SE¼-S22; 1-23-1835
Samuel W. Fenimore W½-NW¼-S23; 4-20-1836
David Maulsby SW¼-S23; 3-12-1836
Thomas Douglass Neal SE¼-NW¼-S24; 9-10-1833
John Hardwick NE¼-NW¼-S24; 10-8-1835
Asbury Arnett E½-NW¼-S26; 9-14-1835
Joseph Lomax W½-NW¼-S26; 6-18-1832
          Page 214. T 18 N, R 13 E of 2nd P.M.
Joseph Lomax E½-SE¼-S27; 6-18-1832
          Page 215. T 19 N, R 13 E of 2nd P.M.   **RANDOLPH CO.**
Amos A. Hulett W½-NE¼-S1; 12-28-1836
Charles Smith E½-NE¼-S1; 2-27-1837
Nathan Cook NW¼-S1; 4-6-1836
Jemima Kelly E½-SE¼-S1; 2-6-1837
Samuel Lasley W½-SE¼-S1; 12-28-1836
Moses Lasley NE¼-SW¼-S1; 4-6-1833
Moses Lasley NW¼-SW¼-S1; 6-17-1836
Eli Lasley S½-SW¼-S1; 6-17-1836
Nathan Cook E½-NE¼-S2; 4-6-1836
Samuel Fosdick W½-NE¼-S2; 1-2-1837
Solomon Knight NW¼-S2; 6-8-1833

Jemima Kelly SW¼-SE¼-S2; 3-2-1835
Joseph Rainier NW¼-SE¼-S2; 2-27-1837
Walter Starbuck E½-SE¼-S2; 1-11-1837
Solomon Knight E½-SW¼-S2; 6-3-1835
Owen Bevan W½-SW¼-S2; 11-16-1836
Solomon Rinard W½-SE¼-S3; 6-13-1836
Solomon Rinard NE¼-SE¼-S3; 7-11-1836
Thomas Gilliam NW¼-SW¼-S3; 9-20-1833
Hiram Mendenhall SW¼-SW¼-S3; 1-7-1835
Hiram Mendenhall E½-SW¼-S3; 1-7-1835
John Dolby SW¼-NE¼-S4; 9-12-1833
Nelson Smith Bale NW¼-NE¼-S4; 3-30-1835
Thomas Gillum E½-SE¼-S4; 3-1-1833
          Page 216. T 19 N, R 13 E of 2nd P.M.
Thomas Gillum NW¼-Fr.S4; 9-20-1833
Thomas Gillum SW¼-S4; 4-21-1836
Elwell Black NE¼-NE¼-S10; 1-18-1837
John Starbuck NW¼-NE¼-S10; 12-15-1836
Nathan Mendenhall, Jr. S½-NE¼-S10; 6-6-1835
John Starbuck SE¼-NW¼-S10; 6-22-1833
Hiram Mendenhall NE¼-NW¼-S10; 1-7-1835
Hiram Mendenhall W½-NW¼-S10; 1-7-1835
Hiram Mendenhall SE¼-S10; 6-18-1836
Elwell Black SW¼-S10; 8-13-1833
Henry Johnson E½-NE¼-S11; 5-28-1832
Enoch Light NW¼-NE¼-S11; 3-2-1833
Enoch Light SW¼-NE¼-S11; 3-24-1834
Carter Kersey NW¼-S11; 1-24-1835
George Washington Vanderburgh E½-SE¼-S11; 1-28-1835
George Washington Vanderburgh W½-SE¼-S11; 1-25-1836
David Hoilman E½-SW¼; NW¼-SW¼-S11; 1-8-1835
Augustis Hopkins SW¼-SW¼-S11; 7-2-1836
John Lykins NE¼-S12; 4-21-1836
Elwell Black NW¼-S12; 1-18-1837
Elwell Black E½-SW¼-S12; 1-18-1837
George Washington Vanderburgh W½-SW¼-S12; 1-28-1835
David B. Lamb E½-NW¼-S13; 1-9-1837
James Butler E½-SE¼-S13; 1-9-1837. Might be Butter
Benjamin Harris W½-SE¼-S13; 12-5-1836
Benjamin Harris SW¼-S13; 2-8-1836
Silas A. Crapper N½-NE¼-S14; 1-9-1837
Wright Haynes S½-NE¼-S14; 1-20-1835
Timothy Clark Beach S½-NW¼-S14; 1-3-1835
Allison Pollard N½-NW¼-S14; 1-8-1835
Wright Hayhes SE¼-S14; 1-20-1835
Timothy Clark Beach SW¼-S14; 10-14-1834
          Page 217. T 19 N, R 13 E of 2nd P.M.
John Shearer NE¼-NE¼-S15; 2-3-1834
William Smith SE¼-NE¼-S15; 2-11-1835
John Shearer W½-NE¼-S15; 2-3-1834
Jonas Lykins SE¼-S15; 6-8-1833
Thomas Gillum SE¼-SW¼-S15; 9-20-1833
Hiram Mendenhall NE¼-SW¼-S15; 12-30-1835
James McNutt W½-SW¼-S15; 8-16-1833

James Denton Hunt N½-Fr.S17; 1-8-1833
William Hunt S½-Fr.S17; 1-14-1833
William Hunt S pt.-N½-Fr.S20; 1-14-1833
Clark Nickerson N pt.-N½-Fr.S20; 8-27-1834
Allison Pollard E½-NE¼-S21; 9-11-1833
Bela Walker Crapper W½-NE¼; E½-NW¼-S21; 5-17-1833
Joseph Yates Crapper SE¼-SE¼-S21; 9-11-1833
Benjamin Edwards NE¼-SE¼-S21; 1-13-1834
Stephen Haynes E½-NE¼-S22; 1-19-1835
Hiram Whetsel W½-NE¼-S22; 11-11-1834
Isaac Locke NW¼-NW¼-S22; 12-26-1833
Allison Pollard SW¼-NW¼-S22; 1-8-1835
Hiram Whetsel E½-NW¼-S22; 11-11-1834
Wright Haynes SE¼-S22; 1-20-1835
David Ashly SW¼-S22; 10-13-1834
John Harris E½-NE¼-S23; 2-8-1836
Stephen Haynes W½-NE¼; NW¼-S23; 1-19-1835
George Bailey NW¼-SE¼-S23; 9-24-1836
Bazel Hunt SW¼-SE¼-S23; E½-SE¼-S23; 11-29-1836
John Harris SW¼-S23; 2-8-1836
Joseph Goodwin E½-NE¼-S24; 2-1-1837
David B. Lamb W½-NE¼-S24; 1-9-1837
John Harris NW¼-S24; 2-8-1836
David B. Lamb E½-SE¼-S24; 1-9-1837
William H. Cummins W½-SE¼-S24; 1-9-1837
      Page 218.   T 19 N, R 13 E of 2nd P.M.
William H. Cummins E½-SW¼-S24; 9-20-1836
Absalom H. Orin W½-SW¼-S24; 8-22-1836. May be Horin
William Acrell(?) Lamb NE¼-S25; NW¼-S25; 2-8-1836
Nathan Garrett Lamb SE¼-S25; 2-8-1836. May be Ganett
Ephraim Oren SW¼-S25; 1-30-1836
Philip Campbell NE¼-S26; 9-14-1836
John Hill NW¼-S26; 11-10-1836
Henry Gilpin SE¼-S26; 1-30-1836
Bazel Hunt E½-SW¼-S26; 11-8-1836
Andrew Farquhar W½-SW¼-S26; 1-6-1836
Asa Haynes NE¼-S27; 1-19-1835
Miles Hunt SW¼-NW¼-S27; 11-5-1833
Nathaniel Gray NW¼-NW¼-S27; 6-20-1834
Miles Hunt E½-NW¼-S27; 7-1-1834
Parker Jewett SE¼-S27; 6-15-1835
Nathaniel Gray NW¼-SW¼-S27; 6-20-1834
Jane Mumbower SW¼-SW¼-S27; 2-16-1835
Parker Jewett E½-SW¼-S27; 6-15-1835
James Botkin SW¼-NW¼-S28; 10-19-1833
Benjamin Edwards NW¼-NW¼-S28; 1-4-1834
Miles Hunt & Basel Hunt E½-SE¼-S28; 12-2-1833
Bazaleel Hunt W½-SE¼-S28; 12-23-1833
James Pugh SE¼-NE¼-S29; 1-11-1834
James Pugh NE¼-NE¼-S29; 1-26-1835
Lewis Wilson Denton NW¼-NE¼-S29; 1-19-1835
James Pugh SW¼-NE¼-S29; 10-31-1836
William Hunt SE¼-S29; 2-1-1836
Bazel Hunt NW¼-S29; 9-9-1834

Eli Wood SW-S29; 1-20-1934
James Kirk N end-SE¼-S32; 12-29-1838
Barton Andrews Lot 2-N pt.-SW¼; S pt.-NW¼-S32; 11-18-1833

Page 219. T 19 N, R 13 E of 2nd P.M.

Abel Briggs E½-SE¼-S33; 1-8-1835
John Pingry E½-SW¼-S33; 10-27-1832
Bazel Hunt W½-SW¼-S33; 11-2-1832
Dwight Beach E½-NE¼-S34; 1-24-1835
Miles Hunt W½-NE¼-S34; 7-21-1836
Miles Hunt E½-NW¼-S34; 7-12-1836
Jane Mumbower W½-NW¼-S34; 12-5-1834
Peter Botkin SE¼-SE¼; NE¼-SE¼-S34; 7-12-1836
John Mills E½-SW¼-S34; 12-5-1834
Abel Briggs W½-SW¼-S34; 1-8-1835
David Stalker NE¼-S35; 1-30-1836
Bazel Hunt E½-NW¼-S35; 11-29-1836
Dwight Beach W½-NW¼-S35; 1-24-1835
Stanley Frazer SE¼-SE¼-S35; 3-26-1835
Joseph Gilpin N½-SE¼-S35; 2-18-1836
Robert Willis SW¼-SE¼-S35; 9-15-1835
Pryor Harvey E½-SW¼-S35; 9-15-1835
Thomas Gilpin SW¼-SW¼-S35; 10-18-1836
Bazel Hunt NW¼-SW¼-S35; 11-29-1836
Jacob Ladd Oren NE¼-S36; 2-17-1836
Jacob Ladd Oren NE¼-NW¼-S36; 2-17-1836
Joseph Mills SE¼-NW¼; W½-NW¼-S36; 9-17-1836
Joseph Mills SE¼-S36; 9-17-1836
Mahlon Farquhar SW¼-S36; 8-12-1836

Page 220. T 20 N, R 13 E of 2nd P.M.

Jonah F. Randolph SW¼-S1; 10-7-1836
Joseph Floyd SE¼-NE¼-S2; 9-16-1836
Jesse Huffman NW¼-NE¼-S2; 10-10-1836
James Helms NE¼-NE¼; SW¼-NE¼-S2; 8-11-1837
William R. Wright NW¼-NW¼-S2; 11-27-1835
Rees Wright SW¼-NW¼-S2; 9-3-1836
Nelson Clark E½-NW¼-S2; 12-14-1836
Jonah F. Randolph SE¼-S2; 10-7-1836
Nelson Clark E½-SW¼-S2; 12-14-1836
Henry Duggins W½-SW¼-S2; 10-10-1836
Moses Markley Lots 1 & 4-E½-NE¼-Fr.S3; Lots 2-3--NW¼ pt.-Fr.S3; 11-5-1836
Henry D. Huffman E½-SE¼-S3; 10-20-1836
Moses Markley Lots 5-6--SW¼ pt.-Fr.S3; 11-5-1836
John Markley NE¼-Fr.S10; 11-5-1836
Jonathan Robberds NW¼-Fr.S10; 11-24-1836
Joseph Kerns SE¼-Fr.S10; 11-5-1836
Amos Whitson SW¼-Fr.S10; 11-24-1836
Jacob Huffman NE¼-S11; 1-17-1837
Harnit E. Yager NW¼-S11; 2-10-1837
Jacob Huffman SE¼-S11; 1-17-1837
George Ruble SE¼-SW¼-S11; 2-14-1837
Benjamin Drake W½-SW¼-S11; 4-10-1837
Benjamin Drake NE¼-SW¼-S11; 4-10-1837
Nelson Clark NE¼-S12; 12-14-1836
Jonah F. Randolph NW¼-S12; 10-7-1836
Augustus Hopkins E½-SE¼-S12; 11-14-1836
Nelson Clark W½-SE¼-S12; 12-14-1836
Henry Diggs SE¼-SW¼-S12; 3-28-1836

Robert Edwards
NE¼-SW¼-S12;
3-28-1836
Asel Driggs
SW¼-SW¼-S12; 2-6-1837
Michael Aker
NW¼-SW¼-S12
2-6-1838

Page 221. T 20 N, R 13 E of 2nd P.M.
Augustus Hopkins NW¼-S13; 9-5-1836
David K. Este NE¼-S14; 1-18-1837
David K. Este E½-NW¼-S14; 1-18-1837
Chester Lee W½-NW¼-S14; 12-20-1836
Israel Wright SW¼-SW¼-S14; 4-6-1835
Israel Wright NW¼-SW¼-S14; 10-5-1836
James Pursley SW¼-NE¼-S15; 11-2-1836
John Gross NW¼-NE¼-S15; 4-17-1839
Chester Lee E½-NE¼-S15; 12-20-1836
Jacob Fisher SE¼-SE¼-S15; 7-1-1834
Jacob Fisher NE¼-SE¼-S15; 10-17-1836
Samuel D. Woodworth W½-SE¼-S15; 9-29-1836
Hudson Pursley E½-NW¼-S15; 11-2-1836
John Sample W½-NW¼-S15; 4-6-1835
Simon Leighdy SE¼-SW¼-S15; 11-9-1832
John Sample NE¼-SW¼-S15; 10-17-1836
John Sample NW¼-SW¼-S15; 4-6-1835
James Pursley SW¼-SW¼-S15; 10-25-1832
George Michael Rytz (Retz?) E½-SE¼-S24; 10-31-1833

Page 222. T 20 N, R 13 E of 2nd P.M.
John Retz NW¼-NE¼-S25; 5-27-1836
William Retz SW¼-NE¼-S25; 10-3-1836
Benjamin D. Diggs E½-NE¼-S25; 10-5-1836
Perry Williams E½-SE¼-S25; 10-8-1836
Samuel Fosdick W½-SE¼-S25; 1-18-1837
Jesse Moorman E½-NW¼-S35; 10-19-1836
Isom Puckett W½-NW¼-S35; 3-17-1836
Isaac Wright NE¼-SE¼-S35; 11-7-1836
Lewis Wooton SW¼-SE¼-S35; 11-7-1836
Enos Pray NW¼-SE¼-S35; 12-30-1836
John Gross SE¼-SE¼-S35; 4-24-1839
Benjamin Puckett NE¼-SW¼-S35; 6-28-1834
Lewis Wooton SE¼-SW¼-S35; 11-7-1836
John Harbuck W½-SW¼-S35; 8-18-1834
Jonathan Johnson SW¼-NE¼-S36; 3-28-1836
Michael Aker NW¼-NE¼-S36; 2-8-1837
John S. Cloud E½-NE¼-S36; 10-17-1836

Page 223. T 20 N, R 13 E of 2nd P.M.
Jonathan Johnson NW¼-SE¼-S36; 3-28-1836
James Kelly SW¼-SE¼-S36; 10-29-1839
Enoch Light E½-SE¼-S36; 9-24-1836
William Wickersham E½-SW¼-S36; 3-3-1836
James Wright W½-SW¼-S36; 2-24-1836

Page 223. T 21 N, R 13 E of 2nd P.M.
Edward McCue S½-Lot 3-SE cor.-Fr.S12; 3-22-1833
Sebastian Bruengart S½-Lot 2 & N½-Lot 3-E pt.-Fr.S12; 5-13-1833
Thomas James Phillips N½-Lot 2-E pt. & Fr. Lot 1-Fr.S12; 9-16-1834
William Hollowell S pt.-N½-S14; 9-6-1838
Robert McCracken SE¼-S14; 6-1-1837
Luke Hollowell SW¼-S14; 8-30-1838
Moses Gard E½-NE¼-S13; 3-24-1837
Joab Ward W½-NE¼-S13; 11-4-1836
Joab Ward W½-NW¼-S13; 7-17-1837

James S. Armstrong SE¼-S13; 5-21-1838
James Hickman NE¼-SW¼-S13; 4-15-1836
James Hickman NW¼-SW¼-S13; 10-3-1836
James S. Armstrong S½-SW¼-S13; 5-21-1838
Uriah Woolman E½-NE¼-S23; 10-16-1837
William Huntington E½-SE¼-S23; 10-30-1838
Thomas Addington W½-SE¼-S23; 11-24-1836
Jesse Addington SW¼-S23; Fr.S22; 6-25-1834
Elijah Harris E½-NW¼-Fr.S23; 3-28-1837
John Gross W½-NW¼-S23; 4-24-1839
John Culp SE¼-NE¼-S24; 10-5-1835
Daniel Gard NE¼-NE¼-S24; 3-1-1837
George Vance SE¼-SE¼-S24; 8-23-1836
Henderson S. Brown NE¼-SE¼-S24; 3-27-1837
Henderson S. Brown W½-SE¼-S24; 3-1-1837

Page 224. T 21 N, R 13 E of 2nd P.M.

Uriah Woolman SW¼-S24; 3-1-1837
Clayton Brown E½-NE¼-S25; 3-24-1837
Joseph Campbell W½-NE¼-S25; 10-30-1838
David Crawford SW¼-NW¼-S25; 5-21-1838
Jehu Hiatt NW¼-NW¼-S25; 10-24-1838. Might be John
Joseph Campbell E½-NW¼-S25; 10-30-1838
James S. Armstrong E½-SE¼-S25; 5-21-1838
Mark Peele W½-SE¼; E½-SW¼-S25; 2-2-1837
Mary Whitson W½-SW¼-S25; 2-2-1837
Jehu Hiatt NE¼-NE¼-S26; 10-24-1838
David Crawford SE¼-NE¼-S26; 5-21-1838
Thomas Addington W½-NE¼-S26; 3-25-1837
Thomas Addington NW¼-S26; 5-27-1834
Willis Arnett N½-SE¼-S26; 3-22-1837
Nathan Wooters S½-SE¼-S26; 6-13-1836
Mark Peele E½-SW¼-S26; 4-22-1836
Thomas Green W½-SW¼-S26; 4-7-1834
Thomas Green S½-Fr.S27; 6-12-1834
Seth Elliott N½-Fr.S27; 1-24-1835
James Addington Lots 1-2--N½-Fr.S34; 4-25-1835
Joseph Addington Lots 3-4-5--S½-Fr.S34; 8-19-1835
John McNees NW¼-NW¼-S35; 4-7-1834
Jesse Moorman SW¼-NW¼-S35; 11-4-1836
Thomas Addington E½-NW¼-S35; 8-19-1835
Pardon Shearman SW¼-SE¼-S35; 6-13-1836
William Huffman NW¼-SE¼-S35; 10-10-1836
Peter Myers E½-SE¼-S35; 2-4-1837
William Huffman SE¼-SW¼-S35; 10-10-1836
Pardon Shearman NE¼-SW¼-S35; 6-13-1836
Simon Leighdy W½-SW¼-S35; 3-11-1836
George Huffman NW¼-NE¼-S35; 5-13-1836
George Huffman NE¼-NE¼-S35; 10-3-1836
Curtis W. Keener(?) S½-NE¼-S35; 2-16-1837
Jesse Arnett E½-NE¼-S36; 2-2-1837
Willis Arnett W½-NE¼-S36; 2-2-1837
John Huffman NW¼-NW¼-S36; 10-3-1836
Benjamin Drake SW¼-NW¼-S36; 10-2-1837
Benjamin Drake E½-NW¼-S36; 2-1-1837

Page 225. T 14 N, R 14 E of 2nd P.M. UNION CO.
Richard Brock NW¼-S18; 11-5-1814
Page 226. T 15 N, R 14 E of 2nd P.M. WAYNE CO.
William Shotridge E½-NE¼-S5; 5-10-1834
Page 227. T 15 N, R 14 E of 2nd P.M.
John Wright NW¼-S19; 1-22-1831
Page 228. T 16 N, R 14 E of 2nd P.M.
William Davis NW¼-S3; 7-8-1817. Shows no final certif. issued
Asa Prevo NW¼-S4; 2-20-1815
Patrick Moore NE¼-S10; 9-9-1817
Page 230. T 16 N, R 14 E of 2nd P.M.
Archibald Beall NE¼-S31; 2-10-1814
Lot Bloomfield E½-NE¼-S33; 5-14-1832
Page 231. T 17 N, R 14 E of 2nd P.M.
John Lewis NE¼-S7; 10-25-1811
John Studdom NW¼-S10; 8-12-1817
Page 233. T 18 N, R 14 E of 2nd P.M. RANDOLPH CO.
John Jeffrey Reynolds E½-NE¼-S1; 6-3-1835
Annual Hodson SW¼-NE¼-S1; 9-9-1835
Demsey Linton NW¼-NE¼-S1; 10-2-1835
Benjamin Thomas E½-SE¼-S1; 1-10-1834
Robert Hodson SE¼-NW¼-S2; 7-3-1834
William B. Miller NE¼-NW¼-S2; 7-7-1836
Phebe Hinshaw SE¼-NE¼-S3; 9-20-1832
Phebe Hinshaw NE¼-NE¼-S3; 1-28-1836
Elijah H. Platt NW¼-NE¼-S3; 6-30-1836
Paul Beard SW¼-NE¼-S3; 7-7-1836
Jacob Shoemaker E½-NW¼-S3; 10-1-1836
Jesse Johnson W½-SE¼-S3; 2-19-1835
Page 234. T 18 N, R 14 E of 2nd P.M.
William Reece NW¼-SW¼-S3; 2-3-1834
Henry Way SW¼-SW¼-S3; 1-15-1836
William Beard SE¼-SW¼-S3; 1-17-1835
William Beard NE¼-SW¼-S3; 12-21-1836
Thomas Kersey NW¼-S6; 12-5-1836
Isaac Hodgson W½-SE¼-S6; 3-26-1835
Isaac Hockett W½-SW¼-S6; 3-2-1833
Page 235. T 18 N, R 14 E of 2nd P.M.
William Thomas, Jr. SE¼-NE¼-S12; 6-11-1834
James Odell SW¼-NE¼-S12; 8-13-1835
John Thomas N½-NE¼-S12; 4-8-1835
Pierce Hollingsworth E½-NW¼-S12; 1-9-1834
Page 238. T 19 N, R 14 E of 2nd P.M. WAYNE CO.
Benjamin Drake E½-NE¼-S1; 2-6-1838
Charles W. Antrim W½-NE¼-S1; 1-21-1837
Joseph Hickman NW¼-NW¼-S1; 12-15-1836
David North SW¼-NW¼-S1; 3-1-1837
Charles W. Antrim E½-NW¼-S1; 1-21-1837
Joshua Robinson SE¼-SE¼-S1; 6-13-1836
John Robinson NE¼-SE¼-S1; 1-10-1837
David North W½-SE¼-S1; 3-1-1837
Benjamin Drake E½-SW¼-S1; 3-1-1837
Benjamin Drake W½-SW¼-S1; 3-1-1837
Joseph Keys NE¼-NE¼-S2; 3-17-1836

Robert A. Tindel SE¼-NE¼-S2; 1-23-1837
Joseph Keys SE¼-NW¼-S2; 12-5-1832
Charles Wesley Wheeler NE¼-NW¼-S2; 5-29-1834
Robert A. Tindel NW¼-SE¼-S2; 2-16-1837
Thomas North SW¼-SE¼; E½-SE¼-S2; 3-1-1837
Sylvester Pruden W½-SW¼; NE¼-SW¼-S2; 9-24-1835
Ann Maria Williams SE¼-SW¼-S2; 9-24-1835
Pierce Hollingsworth NW¼-S3; 11-22-1836
          Page 239. T 19 N, R 14 E of 2nd P.M.
Alfred Benge NE¼-SE¼-S3; 9-26-1833
Thomas Carter SE¼-SE¼-S3; 2-13-1836
Robert Irvin SW¼-SW¼-S3; 5-1-1835
Robert Irvin NW¼-SW¼-S3; 4-21-1836
Jonathan Harlan E½-NE¼-S4; 5-25-1835
Joseph Lewis NE¼-SE¼-S4; 6-24-1835
John Irvin, Jr. SE¼-SE¼-S4; 3-28-1836
James S. Armstrong W½-SE¼-S4; 5-21-1838
Richard Bittle E½-SW¼-S4; 6-8-1836
Thomas Miller W½-SW¼-S4; 12-7-1836
John Irvin NE¼-NW¼; W½-NW¼-S5; 1-28-1836
Elisha Jarrell, Jr. SE¼-NW¼-S5; 11-14-1836. Jarrett?
David Wysong W½-SE¼-S5; 1-30-1836
David E. Heston NW¼-SW¼-S5; 3-28-1836
Michael Jones SW¼-SW¼-S5; 3-28-1836
Elisha Jarrell, Jr. E½-SW¼-S5; 11-14-1836
Benjamin Hill NW¼-SW¼-S6; 6-22-1835
Benjamin Hill SW¼-SW¼-S6; 3-28-1836
Nelson Johnson NE¼-NE¼-S8; 9-18-1834
David M. Pruden SE¼-NE¼-S8; 9-26-1836
David Lasley W½-NE¼-S8; 6-17-1836
Michael Jones NW¼-NW¼-S8; 10-29-1836
Jacob B. Miles E½-NW¼; SW¼-NW¼-S8; 1-7-1837
David M. Pruden NE¼-SE¼-S8; 9-26-1836
John S. Biggs SE¼-SE¼-S8; 10-25-1836
Jacob B. Mills W½-SE¼-S8; 10-26-1836
David Lasley E½-SW¼-S8; 3-28-1836
Jacob B. Mills W½-SW¼-S8; 10-26-1836
          Page 240. T 19 N, R 14 E of 2nd P.M.
John Irvin, Jr. NE¼-NE¼-S9; 3-28-1836
Jacob B. Mills SE¼-NE¼-S9; 1-7-1837
Benjamin Hollingsworth W½-NE¼-S9; 10-26-1836
Robert Decan(?) NW¼-S9; 10-26-1836
John S. Biggs SE¼-S9; SW¼-S9; 10-11-1836
John S. Biggs SE½-NE¼-S10; 10-25-1836
Philip Bendel NE¼-NE¼-S10; 10-17-1835
Philip Bendel W½-NE¼-S10; 3-7-1835
Joel Rute SW¼-NW¼-S10; 9-3-1836
George Irvin NW¼-NW¼-S10; 9-3-1836
William Henderson Freeman SE¼-SE¼-S10; 10-12-1835
William Bittle NE¼-SE¼-S10; 6-8-1836
John Thompson NE¼-S11; 2-15-1836
Richard Bittle NW¼-S11; 5-23-1836
Lannen Mullin E½-SE¼-S11; 8-29-1836
John Thompson W½-SE¼-S11; 2-15-1835

Alexander Helton SW¼-SW¼-S11; 10-12-1835
Richard Bittle NW¼-SW¼-S11; 5-23-1836
John Thompson E½-SW¼-S11; 2-15-1836
Jesse Johnson E½-NE¼-S12; 4-4-1836
William Evans W½-NE¼-S12; 1-30-1837
Amos Manning NW¼-S12; 12-5-1836
Hyronimous Dyke NE¼-SE¼-S12; 1-19-1837
Alexander Oursler SE¼-SE¼-S12; 1-30-1837
Rachel Shockney NW¼-SE¼-S12; 12-30-1837
Alexander Oursler SW¼-SE¼-S12; 12-30-1837
Ann Manning SW¼-S12; 12-5-1836
William Schieds NE¼-S13; 2-27-1837
Alexander Dubois E½-NW¼-S13; 8-29-1836
Isaac Dubois, Jr. W½-NW¼-S13; 8-29-1836
Eli Hollingsworth E½-SE¼-S13; 10-4-1836
John B. Chenoweth W½-SE¼-S13; 10-14-1837
William Frost Young SW¼-SW¼-S13; 5-5-1835
Philip Brown NW¼-SW¼-S13; 6-27-1836
John B. Chenoweth E½-SW¼-S13; 10-14-1837
            Page 241. T 19 N, R 14 E of 2nd P.M.
Horace Wells NE¼-S14; 10-5-1835
David Karnes SE¼-S14; 6-8-1836
Alfred Berge E½-SW¼-S14; 2-15-1836
Leroy Davis W½-SW¼-S14; 11-11-1834
William Henderson Freeman NE¼-NE¼-S15; 12-9-1834
Joseph Teas SE¼-NE¼-S15; 4-29-1835
James Abshire SE¼-NW¼-S15; 1-28-1835
James Abshire NE¼-NW¼-S15; 3-17-1836
John Gross W½-NW¼-S15; 10-12-1836
Joseph Teas E½-SE¼-S15; 3-22-1834
John Gross W½-SW¼-S15; 10-12-1836
John Gross NE¼-S15; 10-11-1836
Benjamin Hornbaker NW¼-S17; 12-17-1835
John Gross SE¼-S17; 10-11-1836
William Rockhill SW¼-S17; 6-6-1836
Josiah Conger NE¼-S18; 12-17-1835
William Rockhill SE¼-S18; 6-11-1836
Joseph Goodwin E½-SW¼-S18; 1-18-1837
Job Smith W½-SW¼-S18; 1-18-1837
Thomas Gordon E½-NE¼; NW¼-NE¼-S19; 9-6-1836
Daniel Puckett SW¼-NE¼-S19; 12-30-1836
Badger Longfellow NW¼-S19; 10-6-1836
Stacy Rainier E½-SE¼; SW¼-SE¼-S19; 9-10-1836
Daniel Puckett NW¼-SE¼-S19; 12-30-1836
Benjamin Hill SW¼-S19; 11-10-1836
Benjamin Miller SE¼-NE¼-S20; 4-2-1834
Thomas Miller NE¼-NE¼-S20; 6-17-1836
Thomas Smith, Jr. W½-NE¼-S20; 8-12-1836
John N. Smith NW¼-S20; 8-12-1836
Pleasant Beals SE¼-SE¼-S20; 1-28-1836
John Beals NE¼-SE¼-S20; 6-11-1836
Pleasant Beals SW¼-SE¼-S20; 8-22-1836
Daniel Puckett NW¼-SE¼-S20; 12-30-1836

Page 242. T 19 N, R 14 E of 2nd P.M.

Francis A. Wilkins SW¼-SW¼-S20; 10-17-1835
Obadiah Harris NW¼-SW¼-S20; 8-15-1836
Cary(?) Bradfield E½-SW¼-S20; 10-18-1836
John S. Biggs E½-NE¼-S21; 10-11-1836
James Pike W½-NE¼-S21; 10-11-1836
Jonathan Johnson E½-NW¼-S21; 10-11-1836
Benjamin Miller W½-NW¼-S21; 8-18-1832
Nathan Butler W½-SE¼-S21; 10-5-1836
Nathan Butler SE¼-SW¼-S21; 10-11-1836
George Washington Daly NE¼-SW¼-S21; 9-17-1836
George Washington Daly W½-SW¼-S21; 1-26-1836
Abel Hinshaw SW¼-NE¼-S22; 11-13-1834
Abel Hinshaw NW¼-NE¼-S22; 1-1-1836
David Frazer NE¼-NW¼-S22; 11-13-1834
Joseph Frazer SE¼-NW¼-S22; 7-11-1836
Jesse Kenworthy W½-NW¼-S22; 2-22-1834
Absalom Hinshaw SE¼-SE¼-S22; 1-26-1836
Philip Brown NE¼-SE¼-S22; 7-9-1836
Abel Hinshaw W½-SE¼-S22; 11-13-1834
Gibson Teas W½-SW¼-S22; 3-3-1834
Philip Brown E½-NE¼-S23; 5-26-1836
Chester Ball W½-NE¼; E½-NW¼-S23; 8-18-1836
Richard Bittle W½-NW¼-S23; 6-8-1836
Norton D. Hartley E½-SE¼-S23; 12-30-1836
Thomas Titus W½-SE¼-S23; 10-3-1836
Milass Hogston SE¼-SW¼-S23; 10-24-1836
William Barnes NE¼-SW¼-S23; 10-11-1836
Wittoes(?) Odell W½-SW¼-S23; 6-8-1836
Enos Thomas E½-NE¼-S24; 2-1-1837
Joseph Derickson W½-NE¼-S24; 2-1-1837
David Fudge E½-NW¼-S24; 6-1-1836
David Hudlow W½-NW¼-S24; 3-2-1833
Joseph Derickson SE¼-S24; 2-1-1837
Lewis Ellis E½-NE¼-S25; 11-29-1836
Isaiah Ellis W½-NE¼-S25; 11-29-1836

Page 243. T 19 N, R 14 E of 2nd P.M.

John Frazer NW¼-S25; 11-24-1836
Lewis Ellis E½-SE¼-S25; 11-29-1836
Philip Hill W½-SE¼-S25; 1-23-1837
Bevan Ellis SE¼-SW¼-S25; 10-4-1836
John Frazer NE¼-SW¼-S25; 4-6-1837
James Longfellow W½-SW¼-S25; 10-18-1836
John Erwin NE¼-S26; NW¼-S26; 5-26-1836
Abraham Platt SE¼-SE¼-S26; 2-19-1836
John Erwin NE¼-SE¼; W½-SE¼-S26; 5-26-1836
John Erwin SW¼-S25; 5-26-1836
Manliff Jarrell NE¼-S27; 4-8-1835
Nathan Thornberry E½-NW¼-S27; 1-23-1835
Thomas Frazer, Jr. W½-NW¼-S27; 4-25-1835
Thomas Frazer NW¼-NW¼-S27; 7-2-1835
Joseph Teas E½-NE¼-S28; 3-22-163±
Nathan Thornberry SW¼-NE¼-S28; .-29-1836
William Benson & Michael Benson NW¼-NE¼-S28; 9-19-1836

Levi Stout SW$\frac{1}{4}$-NW$\frac{1}{4}$-S28; 5-13-1836
Thomas Mills NW$\frac{1}{4}$-NW$\frac{1}{4}$-S28; 11-1-1836
William Benson & Michael Benson E$\frac{1}{2}$-NW$\frac{1}{4}$-S28; 9-19-1836
Jonathan Willis E$\frac{1}{2}$-SE$\frac{1}{4}$-S28; 1-23-1835
Benjamin Bond W$\frac{1}{2}$-SE$\frac{1}{4}$; E$\frac{1}{2}$-SW$\frac{1}{4}$-S28; 11-29-1836
Thomas Miller NE$\frac{1}{4}$-NE$\frac{1}{4}$-S29; 12-11-1832. Note name below
Thomas Mills SE$\frac{1}{4}$-NE$\frac{1}{4}$-S29; 6-7-1833. May be same man as above
Jacob B. Mills NW$\frac{1}{4}$-NE$\frac{1}{4}$-S29; 8-15-1836
Joseph Wilkins SW$\frac{1}{4}$-NE$\frac{1}{4}$-S29; 10-17-1833
Richard Conarroe(?) W$\frac{1}{2}$-NW$\frac{1}{4}$-S29; 10-15-1836
Samuel Richards Chadwick E$\frac{1}{2}$-SW$\frac{1}{4}$-S29; 3-10-1835
Henry Green W$\frac{1}{2}$-SW$\frac{1}{4}$-S29; 10-3-1836

Page 244. T 19 N, R 14 E of 2nd P.M.

Henry Green NE$\frac{1}{4}$-S30; 10-3-1836
John Longgrear E$\frac{1}{2}$-NW$\frac{1}{4}$-S30; 8-24-1836
Andrew Hill W$\frac{1}{2}$-NW$\frac{1}{4}$-S30; 11-10-1836
Jesse Brumfield SE$\frac{1}{4}$-S30; SW$\frac{1}{4}$-S30; 8-24-1836
Jonathan Willis SE$\frac{1}{4}$-NE$\frac{1}{4}$-S31; 1-28-1836
Daniel Puckett NE$\frac{1}{4}$-NE$\frac{1}{4}$-S31; 12-30-1836
Henry Green W$\frac{1}{2}$-NE$\frac{1}{4}$-S31; 10-3-1836
Henry Green NW$\frac{1}{4}$-S31; 10-3-1836
Levi Coffin SE$\frac{1}{4}$-S31; 11-28-1836
Thomas Kersey SW$\frac{1}{4}$-S31; 12-5-1836
William Hammar SW$\frac{1}{4}$-NW$\frac{1}{4}$-S32; 1-28-1836
Daniel Puckett NW$\frac{1}{4}$-NW$\frac{1}{4}$-S32; 12-30-1836
Ezekiel Robins E$\frac{1}{2}$-NE$\frac{1}{4}$-S34; 10-28-1836
Samuel Nixon NW$\frac{1}{4}$-NE$\frac{1}{4}$-S34; 12-30-1836
Ezekiel Robins SW$\frac{1}{4}$-NE$\frac{1}{4}$-S34; 1-2-1831
Solomon Hinshaw SE$\frac{1}{4}$-SE$\frac{1}{4}$-S34; 6-28-1836
John Randle NE$\frac{1}{4}$-SE$\frac{1}{4}$-S34; 7-7-1836
Samuel Platt W$\frac{1}{2}$-SE$\frac{1}{4}$-S34; 10-28-1836
Abraham Hunt E$\frac{1}{2}$-SW$\frac{1}{4}$-S34; 4-16-1832
James Frazer SE$\frac{1}{4}$-NE$\frac{1}{4}$-S35; 1-23-1835
James Frazer NE$\frac{1}{4}$-NE$\frac{1}{4}$-S35; 7-14-1836
Samuel Robins W$\frac{1}{2}$-NE$\frac{1}{4}$-S35; 1-2-1837
John Boon SW$\frac{1}{4}$-NW$\frac{1}{4}$-S35; 1-28-1836
John Erwin NW$\frac{1}{4}$-NW$\frac{1}{4}$; E$\frac{1}{2}$-NW$\frac{1}{4}$-S34; 5-26-1836

Page 245. T 19 N, R 14 E of 2nd P.M.

John Johnson W$\frac{1}{2}$-SE$\frac{1}{4}$-S35; 7-7-1836
Joseph Frazer NW$\frac{1}{4}$-SW$\frac{1}{4}$-S35; 9-24-1834
Philip Brown SW$\frac{1}{4}$-SW$\frac{1}{4}$-S35; 7-9-1836
Francis Frazer SE$\frac{1}{4}$-SW$\frac{1}{4}$-S35; 7-14-1836
Ezekiel Robins NE$\frac{1}{4}$-SW$\frac{1}{4}$-S35; 1-9-1837
Jacob W. Pearce NE$\frac{1}{4}$-NE$\frac{1}{4}$-S36; 6-29-1836
John Williams SW$\frac{1}{4}$-NE$\frac{1}{4}$-S36; 11-26-1836
Merely Pearce SE$\frac{1}{4}$-NE$\frac{1}{4}$-S36; 1-9-1837
Thomas Cadwallader, Jr. NW$\frac{1}{4}$-NE$\frac{1}{4}$-S36; 4-15-1837
Josiah Crew S$\frac{1}{2}$-NW$\frac{1}{4}$-S36; 6-25-1835
George Fox Bowls NW$\frac{1}{4}$-NW$\frac{1}{4}$-S36; 10-3-1836
Levi Kenworthy NE$\frac{1}{4}$-NW$\frac{1}{4}$-S36; 9-25-1838
Thomas Jeffrey SE$\frac{1}{4}$-SE$\frac{1}{4}$-S36; 4-8-1835
John Williams N$\frac{1}{2}$-SE$\frac{1}{4}$-S36; 8-22-1836
Thomas Clevenger SW$\frac{1}{4}$-SE$\frac{1}{4}$-S36; 5-13-1836

Page 245. T 20 N, R 14 E of 2nd P.M.
John McDonald E½-NE¼-S1; 9-21-1837
Adam Bousman W½-NE¼-S1; 5-21-1838
Margaret Almourod(?) E½-NW¼-S1; 5-13-1837
David Almourod(?) W½-NW¼-S1; 5-13-1837
Henry Whitesel E½-SE¼-S1; 11-15-1838
Nathan P. Woodberry W½-SE¼-S1; 4-19-1838
William L. Campbell NE¼-SW¼-S1; 9-21-1837
James Coats SE¼-SW¼-S1; 6-30-1837
Washington Bousman W½-SW¼-S1; 5-13-1837
Andrew Fottrell NE¼-S2; 4-3-1837
Andrew Fottrell E½-NW¼-S2; 5-30-1837
Jesse Tomlinson W½-NW¼-S2; 10-17-1836
Benjamin Drake SE¼-S2; 6-10-1837
Margaret Smith E½-SW¼-S2; 7-7-1837
John Nicoll W½-SW¼-S2; 7-7-1837
Jesse Tomlinson E½-NE¼-S3; 10-17-1836
William Coats W½-NE¼-S3; 3-1-1837
David Allen NW¼-S3; 5-31-1837

Page 246. T 20 N, R 14 E of 2nd P.M.
John Kerschner E½-SE¼-S3; 2-24-1837
Seth Moffitt W½-SE¼-S3; 12-5-1832
Zimri Moffitt E½-SW¼-S3; 6-22-1833
Daniel Charles W½-SW¼-S3; 3-1-1837
James Ramsey E½-NE¼-S4; 12-15-1836
David Ramsey NW¼-NE¼-S4; 5-29-1837
George Allen SW¼-NE¼-S4; E½-NW¼-S4; 5-31-1837
James G. Birney W½-NW¼-S4; 11-26-1836
James Ramsey E½-SE¼-S4; 12-15-1836
Nathan P. Woodberry W½-SE¼; E½-SW¼-S4; 5-31-1837
James G. Birney W½-SW¼-S4; 11-26-1836
James G. Birney E½-NE¼-S5; 11-26-1836
William Stratton NW¼-NE¼-S5; 10-9-1838
Andrew Smith SW¼-NE¼-S5; 8-31-1837
George W. Kennady NW¼-S5; 4-29-1837
John Flavel Wright SE¼-S5; 7-28-1836
Samuel Williams SW¼-S5; 7-27-1836
Amos Murphy E½-NE¼-S6; 2-21-1837
John Huffman W½-NE¼; E½-NW¼-S6; 11-28-1836
Enoch Baker W½-NW¼-S6; 5-16-1837
Amos Hiatt SW¼-SE¼-S6; 3-28-1836
Amos Hiatt NW¼-SE¼-S6; 11-4-1836
Cyrenius Wysong SE¼-SE¼-S6; 2-14-1837
Cyrenius Wysong NE¼-SE¼-S6; 3-28-1837
James R. Lewis W½-SW¼-S6; 5-16-1837
Jacob Riley E½-SW¼-S6; 11-28-1836
Samuel Ward Sutton SW¼-NE¼-S7; 1-5-1835
John D. Stewart NW¼-NE¼-S7; 9-2-1836
William Brown E½-NE¼-S7; 6-4-1836   James G. Birney
John D. Stewart NW¼-S7; 9-2-1836   E½-NW¼-S8;
Francis Wright SE¼-S7; 12-17-1835   8-15-1836
James G. Birney E½-SW¼-S7; 8-30-1835   James G. Birney
Stephen Allbaugh W½-SW¼-S7; 5-30-1836   W½-NW¼-S8;
James G. Birney NE¼-S8; 7-29-1836   7-29-1836

Page 247. T 20 N, R 14 E of 2nd P.M.
William Holderman SE¼-SE¼-S8; 5-1-1835
James G. Birney NE¼-SE¼-S8; W½-SE¼-S8; 8-30-1836
James G. Birney E½-SW¼-S8; 8-30-1836
Michael Harmond W½-NE¼-S9; 9-23-1836
Joshua Cox S½-NW¼-S9; 11-4-1836
James G. Birney NW¼-NW¼-S9; 11-26-1836
Matthias Honour NE¼-NW¼-S9; 6-29-1837
Elias Kizer NE¼-SW¼-S9; 9-24-1836
Francis Hickman NW¼-SW¼-S9; 1-30-1836
Jesse Tomlinson S½-SW¼-S9; 1-10-1834
Benjamin Drake E½-NE¼-S10; 6-10-1837
Seth Moffitt E½-NW¼-S10; 3-1-1837
Seth Moffitt W½-NW¼-S10; 10-17-1836
Joseph Moffitt NE¼-SW¼-S10; 11-4-1836
Josephus Harris SW¼-SW¼-S10; 12-15-1836
Thomas M. Davis SE¼-SW¼-S10; 1-21-1837
Thomas H. Johnson NW¼-SW¼-S10; 10-1-1838
David Allen NW¼-NE¼-S11; 5-31-1837
Andrew Smith NE¼-NE¼-S11; 7-7-1837
Enoch Davis S½-NE¼-S11; 3-1-1837
Samuel Kellum E½-NW¼-S11; 1-23-1837
Benjamin Smith W½-NW¼-S11; 6-23-1837
Alexander Johnson, Sr. E½-SE¼-S11; 2-24-1837
Nathan P. Woodberry W½-SE¼-S11; 4-19-1838
Thomas Pierce SW¼-SW¼-S11; 1-14-1837
Benjamin Drake NW¼-SW¼-S11; 4-2-1838
Thomas Pierce E½-SW¼-S11; 4-1-1837
William Hickman SW¼-NE¼-S12; 11-4-1837
William Huntington E½-NE¼-S12; 10-30-1838
Stephen Allbaugh NW¼-NE¼-S12; 11-16-1838
Francis Hickman E½-NW¼-S12; 3-1-1837
Jacob Bolinger W½-NW¼-S12; 7-13-1837
Samuel Kellum S½-SE¼-S12; 1-23-1837

Page 248. T 20 N, R 14 E of 2nd P.M.
Levi Coffin NE¼-SE¼-S12; 1-30-1838
Philip Nester NW¼-SE¼-S12; 9-9-1837
Joseph Hickman E½-SW¼-S12; 4-1-1837
John Shank W½-SW¼-S12; 2-24-1837
Jacob Hickman NW¼-SE¼-S13; 12-15-1836
Joshua Cox SW¼-SE¼-S13; 11-16-1838
Michael Matthews E½-SE¼-S13; 2-15-1837
Durant Smith N½-SW¼-S13; 2-12-1836
John Coats SE¼-SW¼-S13; 3-1-1837
Elisha Martin SW¼-SW¼-S13; 4-10-1837
Joshua Cox NE¼-S15; 11-19-1817
Rebecca Goodrich SW¼-NW¼-S18; 12-5-1832
Stephen Allbaugh NW¼-NW¼-S18; 5-30-1836

Page 249. T 20 N, R 14 E of 2nd P.M.
Joseph Hubbard NE¼-NE¼-S23; 2-10-1837
Thomas W. Coats SE¼-NE¼-S23; 11-2-1838
Benjamin Cox, Sr. NW¼-NW¼-S23; 12-6-1836
Willis L. Harris SW¼-NW¼-S23; 1-23-1837
Absalom Gray SW¼-SE¼-S23; 1-30-1836

William Coats SE$\frac{1}{4}$-SE$\frac{1}{4}$-S23; 12-15-1836
Stephen Coffin NW$\frac{1}{4}$-SE$\frac{1}{4}$-S23; 1-30-1837
Thomas W. Coats NE$\frac{1}{4}$-SE$\frac{1}{4}$-S23; 6-30-1837
Simeon Harris SE$\frac{1}{4}$-SW$\frac{1}{4}$-S23; 8-11-1832
Simeon Harris NE$\frac{1}{4}$-SW$\frac{1}{4}$-S23; 12-21-1836
Levi B. Rawson SW$\frac{1}{4}$-NE$\frac{1}{4}$-S24; 3-1-1837
Seth Moffit NW$\frac{1}{4}$-NE$\frac{1}{4}$-S24; 11-2-1838
Andrew Nesbitt N$\frac{1}{2}$-NW$\frac{1}{4}$-S24; 11-4-1836
Coonrod G. Harns S$\frac{1}{2}$-NW$\frac{1}{4}$-S24; 1-25-1838
John Cox SW$\frac{1}{2}$-SW$\frac{1}{4}$-S24; 12-15-1836
Stephen Moffitt SE$\frac{1}{4}$-SW$\frac{1}{4}$-S24; 11-2-1838
Coonrod G. Harns N$\frac{1}{2}$-SW$\frac{1}{4}$-S24; 1-25-1838
Benjamin Cox NW$\frac{1}{4}$-NW$\frac{1}{4}$-S25; 10-7-1835
Benjamin P. Keys SW$\frac{1}{4}$-NW$\frac{1}{4}$-S25; 3-17-1836
Amos J. Bishop E$\frac{1}{2}$-SE$\frac{1}{4}$-S25; 2-21-1837
          Page 250. T 20 N, R 14 E of 2nd P.M.
Cader Woodard W$\frac{1}{2}$-NE$\frac{1}{4}$; SE$\frac{1}{4}$-NE$\frac{1}{4}$-S26; 2-2-1837
Benjamin Cox, Sr. NE$\frac{1}{4}$-NE$\frac{1}{4}$-S26; 3-1-1837
Joseph W. Davis W$\frac{1}{2}$-SE$\frac{1}{4}$-S26; 8-29-1836
John Cooper SW$\frac{1}{4}$-SW$\frac{1}{4}$-S26; 7-2-1836
Samuel Williams NW$\frac{1}{4}$-SW$\frac{1}{4}$-S26; 7-28-1836
Samuel Morrison E$\frac{1}{2}$-SW$\frac{1}{4}$-S26; 7-28-1836
Samuel Copeland SW$\frac{1}{4}$-NE$\frac{1}{4}$-S27; 1-1-1835
Zimri Moffitt NW$\frac{1}{4}$-NE$\frac{1}{4}$-S27; 1-30-1836
Nicholas Dull NE$\frac{1}{4}$-SE$\frac{1}{4}$-S27; 5-27-1836
John Cooper SE$\frac{1}{4}$-SE$\frac{1}{4}$-S27; 7-2-1836
John Dull W$\frac{1}{2}$-SE$\frac{1}{4}$-S27; 11-9-1835
Thomas Aker W$\frac{1}{2}$-SW$\frac{1}{4}$-S27; 5-20-1833
Isaac Roll W$\frac{1}{2}$-NE$\frac{1}{4}$-S28; 10-8-1834
Joseph Abbot Badgley SE$\frac{1}{4}$-S28; 1-4-1833
Jehiel Hull E$\frac{1}{2}$-SW$\frac{1}{4}$-S28; 1-4-1833
Jonathan C. Hiatt NE$\frac{1}{4}$-NE$\frac{1}{4}$-S30; 12-5-1832
William Edwards SE$\frac{1}{4}$-NE$\frac{1}{4}$-S30; 2-23-1833
David Heaston NW$\frac{1}{4}$-NE$\frac{1}{4}$-S30; 8-20-1835
Jonathan Edwards SW$\frac{1}{4}$-NE$\frac{1}{4}$-S30; 10-5-1835
John Monks SE$\frac{1}{4}$-SW$\frac{1}{4}$-S30; 5-1-1835
William Woolf SW$\frac{1}{4}$-SW$\frac{1}{4}$-S30; 10-17-1836
Nathan R. Edwards N$\frac{1}{2}$-SW$\frac{1}{4}$-S30; 5-27-1836
          Page 251. T 20 N, R 14 E of 2nd P.M.
William Woolf N$\frac{1}{2}$-NW$\frac{1}{4}$-S31; 10-5-1836
John Bolender SW$\frac{1}{4}$-NW$\frac{1}{4}$-S31; 11-1-1836
George Nostodt SW$\frac{1}{4}$-NW$\frac{1}{4}$-S31; 11-1-1836
Thomas Garrard E$\frac{1}{2}$-SW$\frac{1}{4}$-S31; 2-24-1834
Madison Wheeler W$\frac{1}{2}$-SW$\frac{1}{4}$-S31; 3-21-1836
David Wysong W$\frac{1}{2}$-SE$\frac{1}{4}$-S32; 1-18-1833
Stephen Allbaugh E$\frac{1}{2}$-NE$\frac{1}{4}$-S34; 5-30-1835
Madison Harbour SE$\frac{1}{4}$-SE$\frac{1}{4}$-S34; 1-25-1837
Thomas Hinshaw NE$\frac{1}{4}$-SE$\frac{1}{4}$-S34; 3-1-1837
Benjamin Drake E$\frac{1}{2}$-SW$\frac{1}{4}$-S34; 2-1-1837
John Neff W$\frac{1}{2}$-SW$\frac{1}{4}$-S34; 12-20-1834
Jehu Robinson NE$\frac{1}{4}$-NW$\frac{1}{4}$-S35; 6-12-1834
William Robinson SE$\frac{1}{4}$-NW$\frac{1}{4}$-S35; 9-24-1836
Joseph W. Davis W$\frac{1}{2}$-NW$\frac{1}{4}$-S35; 8-29-1836
Charles Wesley Wheeler SW$\frac{1}{4}$-SW$\frac{1}{4}$-S35; 5-29-1834

Thomas Hinshaw NW¼-SW¼-S35; 3-1-1837
John Pickett SW¼-NE¼-S36; 12-15-1836
Peter Forris NW¼-NE¼-S36; 2-13-1838
David Summers E½-NE¼-S36; 12-16-1837
William McKim E½-NW¼-S36; 1-5-1837
                Page 252. T 20 N, R 14 E of 2nd P.M.
Jacob Fleming NW¼-SE¼-S36; 12-15-1836
William McKim SW¼-SE¼-S36; 1-5-1837
John Hickman E½-SE¼-S36; 2-16-1837
William McKim E½-SW¼-S36; 1-5-1837
                Page 252. T 21 N, R 14 E of 2nd P.M.
Hiram Daines SE¼-NE¼-S1; 5-27-1836
John Alexander NE¼-NE¼-S1; 6-18-1836
John Alexander W½-NE¼-S1; 10-18-1836
Jesse Oyster NW¼-S1; 5-24-1837
James Porter SE¼-SE¼-S1; 10-6-1836
James Porter NE¼-SE¼-S1; 1-28-1837
Mary Constable W½-SE¼-S1; 1-23-1837
Mary Constable E½-SW¼-S1; 1-23-1837
Thomas J. Constable W½-SW¼-S1; 4-12-1837
George Shinfilt E½-NE¼-S2; 4-14-1837
Zedekiah Ross W½-NE¼-S2; 5-11-1837
John Brennaman E½-NW¼-S2; 4-25-1837
David Stansbaugh W½-NW¼-S2; 4-5-1837
Benjamin Drake E½-SE¼-S2; 4-10-1837
Benjamin Drake W½-SE¼-S2; 4-10-1837
John Stansbaugh SW¼-S2; 4-5-1837
Nancy Denmoyer NE¼-S3; 3-1-1837
John Watson NW¼-NW¼-S3; 5-5-1836
Peter D. Green SW¼-NW¼-S3; 3-1-1837
Peter D. Green E½-NW¼-S3; 1-30-1837
Samuel Hick E½-SE¼-S3; 4-5-1837
David K. Este W½-SE¼-S3; 1-18-1837
Peter D. Green E½-SW¼-S3; 1-30-1837
Peter D. Green W½-SW¼-S3; 11-23-1836
Isom Boswell NE¼-NE¼-S4; 4-21-1836
Peter D. Green SE¼-NE¼; W½-NE¼-S4; 7-22-1836
Platt Voris SW¼-NW¼-S4; 5-23-1836
Peter D. Green NW¼-NW¼-S4; 7-22-1836
Platt Voris E½-NW¼-S4; 7-6-1836
                Page 253. T 21 N, R 14 E of 2nd P.M.
Peter D. Green SE¼-S4; 11-23-1836
Platt Voris NW¼-SW¼-S4; 5-23-1836
Isaac Cherry NE¼-SW¼-S4; 10-8-1836
James F. Bryson S½-SW¼-S4; 7-21-1836
Peter D. Green NE¼-Fr.S5; 7-22-1836
Joseph C. Orcutt E½-NW¼-S5; 1-4-1837
Samuel Fosdick W½-NW¼-S5; 1-2-1837
Samuel Hodges SE¼-SW¼-Fr.S5; 10-17-1836
Samuel Fosdick NE¼-SW¼; W½-SW¼-S5; 1-2-1837
David K. Este NE¼-Fr.S6; SE¼-Fr.S6; 1-18-1837
Philip Lennard Lot 9-E pt. & Lot 10-W pt.-W½-S6; 8-13-1837
Jeremiah Lindsey Mock SW¼-NE¼-S7; 4-28-1834
Burkett Peirce NW¼-NE¼-S7; 10-17-1836

Burkett Peirce E½-NW¼-S7; 11-27-1833
Burkett Peirce SW¼-NW¼-S7; 9-20-1834
Burkett Peirce NW¼-NW¼-S7; 6-17-1836
Allen Wall SE¼-NE¼-S10; 12-5-1832
Samuel Stick NE¼-NE¼-S10; 4-5-1837
James W. Bowers W½-NE¼-S10; 7-23-1836
Peter D. Green W½-SE¼-S10; 6-15-1836
Peter D. Green E½-SW¼-S10; 6-15-1836

Page 254. T 21 N, R 14 E of 2nd P.M.

John Alexander N½-NE¼-S11; 8-28-1832
Hiram Daines S½-NE¼-S11; 8-28-1832
Edward Thurber SW¼-NW¼-S11; 10-12-1833
Solomón Wall NW¼-NW¼-S11; 11-1-1836
Edward Thurber SE¼-NW¼-S11; 2-6-1837
Sarah Wall NE¼-NW¼-S11; 5-27-1837
Augustus Hopkins SE¼-S11; 7-21-1836
Lansford Fields NW¼-NE¼-S12; 6-14-1834
Elias Kizer SW¼-NE¼-S12; 10-7-1836
William Simmons E½-NE¼-S12; 1-28-1837
Benjamin Pursail NE¼-NW¼-S12; 6-18-1836
John Pursail SE¼-NW¼-S12; 1-20-1837
Benjamin Pursail W½-NW¼-S12; 2-27-1836
William Simmons NE¼-SE¼-S12; 6-18-1836
John Baugh SE¼-SE¼-S12; 12-15-1836
Benjamin Pursail NW¼-SW¼-S12; 2-27-1836
Ernestus Putman SW¼-SW¼-S12; 12-18-1838
Ephraim Bragg SW¼-NE¼-S14; 1-20-1837
Israel Taylor NW¼-NE¼-S14; 5-21-1838
Wiley Lauson NW¼-NW¼-S14; 3-11-1836
William Fields, Jr. SE¼-NW¼-S14; 8-23-1836
Charles Wellner SW¼-NW¼-S14; 11-23-1837
Israel Taylor NE¼-NW¼-S14; 5-21-1838
William Fields NW¼-SE¼-S14; 6-14-1834
Andrew Key NE¼-SE¼-S14; 1-30-1836
Andrew Key SE¼-SE¼-S14; 1-4-1837
Robert Poage SW¼-SE¼-S14; 8-6-1838
John B. Warren SW¼-S14; 7-21-1836
Duncan Cameron Coffin NW¼-NE¼-S15; 5-6-1833
Peter D. Green S½-NE¼-S15; 7-22-1836
Wiley Lawson NE¼-NE¼-S15; 3-11-1836
Peter D. Green E½-NW¼-S15; 7-13-1836
Augustus Hopkins W½-NW¼-S15; 7-21-1836

Page 255. T 21 N, R 14 E of 2nd P.M.

Samuel Morrison SE¼-S15; 7-21-1836
Charles Wellner E½-SW¼; W½-SW¼-S15; 7-21-1836
Sylvester Miller SE¼-SE¼-S17; 2-27-1836
John B. Clapp NE¼-SE¼-S17; 8-23-1836
Peter D. Green W½-SE¼-S17; 8-23-1836
Jemah (Jonah?) Tomlinson SW¼-S17; 8-22-1836
David Riddlesbarger NE¼-NW¼-S18; 3-28-1836
Samuel Fosdick SE¼-NW¼-S18; 1-18-1837
Ernestus Putnam W½-NW¼-S18; 1-20-1837
James G. Roberts E½-SE¼-S18; 10-1-1836
William Odle W½-SE¼-S18; 8-23-1836

Robert L. Jack SW¼-S18; 5-16-1837
William Odle E½-NE¼-S19; 10-1-1836
Benjamin Drake W½-NE¼-S19; 12-1-1837
John Sumption S½-NW¼-S19; 12-15-1836
Daniel Gard N½-NW¼-S19; 3-1-1837
John Baker E½-SE¼-S19; 9-3-1836
Rufus Gilpatrick W½-SE¼-S19; 5-18-1837
Enoch Baker & James R. Lewis E½-SW¼-S19; 5-16-1837
Robert L. Jack W½-SW¼-S19; 5-16-1837
Anthony Reitenour NW¼-NE¼-S20; 1-7-1837
Benjamin Drake SW¼-NE¼-S20; 3-1-1837
Matthew Makin NW¼-S20; 11-1-1836
Samuel Evans W½-SE¼-S20; 10-17-1836
Theodore Fry E½-SW¼-S20; 3-1-1837
Thompson Fry W½-SW¼-S20; 3-1-1837
Peter D. Green E½-NW¼-S21; 11-23-1836
John Jewell W½-NW¼-S21; 8-23-1836

Page 256. T 21 N, R 14 E of 2nd P.M.

Sylvester Miller NW¼-SW¼-S21; 11-9-1833
Adjet McGuire SW¼-SW¼-S21; 6-17-1836
John A. Wiseman NE¼-S22; 2-21-1837
Jackson Fields NW¼-NW¼-S22; 1-4-1837
John Gross SW¼-NW¼-S22; 4-24-1837
David Puderbaugh E½-NW¼-S22; 5-18-1837
John Michael SW¼-S22; 5-29-1837
Robert Poage W½-NE¼-S23; 11-19-1836
William Snodgrass NW¼-S23; 11-19-1836
Noah Bousman E½-SE¼-S23; 5-13-1837
William Patterson W½-SE¼-S23; 7-17-1837
Daniel B. Miller NW¼-NE¼-S24; 11-16-1836
Joseph Lollar NE¼-NE¼-S24; 11-19-1836
G. Gest SE¼-NE¼-S24; 1-14-1836
Samuel Poage SW¼-NE¼-S24; 8-25-1838
Samuel Helm NW¼-SE¼-S24; 6-17-1836
Daniel Jordan SW¼-SE¼-S24; 7-17-1837
Christian Nickey E½-SE¼-S24; 6-23-1837
Samuel Helm W½-SW¼-S24; 3-28-1836
Jonathan White NW¼-SW¼-S24; 5-20-1837
John F. Prugh E½-NE¼-S25; 5-16-1837
William Ellsworth W½-NE¼-S25; 5-16-1837
Edward W. Evans NW¼-NW¼-S25; 12-5-1832
William Patterson SW¼-NW¼; E½-NW¼-S25; 5-22-1837
John F. Prugh SE¼-S25; 5-16-1837
Thomas Wallace E½-SW¼-S25; 5-15-1837
William Patterson W½-SW¼-S25; 7-17-1837
William Warren E½-NE¼-S26; 1-21-1836
John Riley Warren W½-NE¼-S26; 1-10-1837
Joseph Lollar SE¼-S26; 11-18-1836
William D. Lane E½-SW¼-S26; 1-30-1837
William Warren W½-SW¼-S26; 8-18-1838

Page 257. T 21 N, R 14 E of 2nd P.M.

David A. Cox SW¼-SE¼-S27; 1-30-1837
Dolphin Warren SE¼-SE¼-S27; 12-21-1837
William Warren NE¼-SE¼-S27; 8-18-1838

John Thomas NW¼-SE¼-S27; 11-28-1838
John Thomas SW¼-S27; 1-30-1837
James Hale SW¼-NW¼-S28; 5-4-1835
Samuel Cain NW¼-NW¼-S28; 3-11-1836
John Kennier E½-SW¼-S28; 2-6-1837
Isaac Byers SW¼-NE¼-S29; 3-9-1835
Samuel Cain NE¼-NE¼-S29; 3-11-1336
James G. Birney SE¼-NE¼-S29; 11-26-1836
Joel Lewis NW¼-NE¼-S29; 3-1-1837
James G. Birney E½-SE¼-S29; 11-26-1836
Samuel Cornwell NW¼-SE¼-S29; 3-24-1837
Samuel Cornwell SW¼-SE¼-S29; 4-5-1837
Joel Lewis SN¼-S29; 11-27-1833
Elias Kizer SW¼-SW¼-S29; 10-7-1835
John Woodburn NE¼-SW¼-S29; 9-22-1834
Joel Lewis SE¼-SW¼-S29; 4-19-1837
John Baker E½-NE¼-S30; 9-3-1836
James Fagans W½-NE¼-S30; 6-1-1837
John Culp E½-NW¼-S30; 10-5-1837
John Fry W½-NW¼-S30; 3-1-1837
Thomas Baker, Sr. SW¼-SE¼-S30; 10-2-1835
Robert Armstrong NW¼-SE¼-S30; 2-9-1838
Jacob Kesler E½-SW¼-S30; 10-10-1837
William H. Laycock W½-SW¼-S30; 10-2-1837
William H. Laycock W½-NW¼-S31; SE¼-NW¼-S31; 10-2-1837
Benjamin Drake NE¼-NW¼-S31; 2-6-1838

Page 258. T 21 N, R 14 E of 2nd P.M.

James Montgomery & Isaac Cotton SE¼-S31; 1-28-1837
William A. Laycock SW¼-S31; 10-2-1837
James G. Birney E½-NE¼-S32; 11-26-1837
Samuel Cornwell W½-NE¼-S32; 4-5-1837
Abraham Balser NE¼-NW¼-S32; 11-13-1837
Robert Armstrong SE¼-NW¼-S32; 2-9-1838
Robert Ross W½-NW¼-S32; 9-29-1837
James G. Birney E½-SE¼-S32; 11-26-1836
George W. Manuel W½-SE¼-S32; 8-23-1838
John F. Kayler E½-SW¼-S32; 11-20-1837
Philip Lennard W½-SW¼-S32; 8-13-1838
Moses Rupert & John Berry NE¼-S33; 10-25-1836
Silvester Miller E½-NW¼-S33; 8-18-1838
James G. Birney W½-NW¼-S33; 8-30-1836
Joseph Beery E½-SE¼-S33; 3-1-1837
William K. Smith W½-SE¼-S33; 3-1-1837
William Warren E½-SW¼-S33; 8-18-1838
James G. Birney W½-SW¼-S33; 8-30-1836
John Mock NE¼-NE¼-S34; 10-17-1836
David A. Cox SE¼-NE¼; W½-NE¼-S34; 11-18-1836
Philip Shierling SE¼-NW¼-S34; 8-18-1838
Robert Balentine NE¼-NW¼-S34; 10-2-1838
Michael Lutz W½-NW¼-S34; 10-25-1836
Philip Shierlig E½-SE¼-S34; 5-22-1837
Joseph Young W½-SE¼-S34; 11-19-1836
William Weeks SW¼-S34; 4-1-1837
James T. Evans NE¼-NE¼-S35; 6-17-1836

Daniel Jordan SE¼-NE¼; W½-NE¼-S35; 7-17-1837
John Hock NW¼-NW¼-S35; 10-17-1836
Joseph Hickman SW¼-NW¼-S35; 12-1-1838
Robert Balentine E½-NW¼-S35; 10-2-1838
Joseph Lucas SE¼-S35; 12-15-1836
Philip Shierlig NW¼-SW¼-S35; 6-29-1837
Simeon H. Lucas E½-SW¼-S35; 10-5-1837
Simeon H. Lucas SW¼-SW¼-S35; 5-21-1838
William Patterson NE¼-S36; 5-26-1837

Page 259. T 21 N, R 14 E of 2nd P.M.

Wesley Ileff E½-NW¼-S36; 9-21-1837
James T. Evans NW¼-NW¼-S36; 8-18-1838
Michael Aker SW¼-NW¼-S36; 9-10-1838
William Patterson SE¼-S36; 5-26-1837·
George Ullrich & Andrew Weimer E½-SW¼-S36; 7-13-1837
Grover Gilliam W½-SW¼-S36; 11-9-1836

Page 259. T 22 N, R 14 E of 2nd P.M.

Abraham Statler Fr.S13; Lot 1-NE¼-NE¼-Fr.S24; Lot 2-SE¼-Fr.S24;
    W½-NE¼-Fr.S24; 8-20-1838
William Win Stanley NW¼-Fr.S24; 7-10-1839
Martin Eley E½-SE¼-S24; 9-21-1837
Benjamin Xenia Hutchins W½-SE¼-S24; 5-21-1838
William D. Jones. SW½-S24; 5-21-1838
Henry Inlow Lot 2-W½ pt.-Fr.S23; 3-27-1838
William House Lot 1-E½ pt.-Fr.S23; 8-20-1839
Jesse Hutchens NW¼-Fr.S26; 5-21-1838
Isaac Hutchins NE¼-Fr.S26; 5-21-1838
William Jenkins SE¼-S26; 5-21-1838
Alexis Edwards E½-SW¼-S26; 10-2-1838
William Youart W½-SW¼-S26; 8-29-1838
James Dye E½-NE¼-S25; 8-20-1838
Jacob Furrow W½-NE¼; E½-NW¼-S25; 11-27-1837
Jackson Parks W½-NW¼-S25; 6-20-1837
John Lefaver SE¼-S25; 8-20-1838
Jacob Smaell S½-SW¼-S25; 7-21-1837
John Wiggins N½-SW¼-S25; 5-21-1838
Amos W. Collins NE¼-Fr.S27; 1-14-1840
Edmund Rathbun SE¼-SE¼-Fr.S27; 6-8-1837
William Youart NE¼-SE¼-Fr.S27; 8-29-1838
Alexis Edwards Lots 1-2--W½-Fr.S27; 10-2-1838
John Walters Lots 3-4--W½-Fr.S27; 9-1-1838
George Swallow Fr.S28; 4-20-1838.

Page 260. T 22 N, R 14 E of 2nd P.M.

Isaac Wiley Fr.S32; 9-3-1838
Thomas Thomas SE¼-Fr.S33; 10-10-1836
Adam Pigman SW¼-NW¼; W½-NE¼-Fr.S33; 10-10-1836
Hiram Rathbun E½-NE¼-Fr.S33; 6-8-1837
Edmund Rathbun NE¼-S34; 3-8-1837
Hiram Rathbun NW¼-S34; 6-8-1837
Jacob Danner SE¼-S34; 6-9-1838
Thomas Thomas SW¼-SW¼-S34; 10-10-1836
John Henry Abicht E½-SE¼; NW¼-SE¼-S34; 8-9-1838
Jacob Karmann NE¼-S35; 8-9-1838

Charles Christian Lesch E½-NW¼-S35; 8-11-1838
Edmund Rathbun W½-NW¼-S35; 6-8-1837
Thomas Wilkison SW¼-S35; 6-1-1837
Jesse Marsh E½-NE¼-S36; 8-1-1837
Jonathan Maxson, of Clk. Co., O. W½-NE¼-S36; 8-2-1837
Dorsey Ryan E½-SE¼-S36; 9-10-1836
Joseph McFarland W½-SE¼-S36; 6-5-1837

Page 260. T 18 N, R 15 E of 2nd P.M.

Peter Deverage Fr.S5; 3-7-1835
Hiram Hill SE¼-NE¼-S6; 2-7-1834
Peter Deverage NE¼-NE¼-S6; 3-7-1835
Benjamin Pearce NW¼-NE¼-S6; 5-20-1836
Jesse Gray SW¼-NE¼-S6; 3-14-1834
Jonathan M. Ellis NW¼-S6; 5-19-1836
Malachi Nickolls E½-SE¼-S6; 2-20-1836
Waymouth Davis SW¼-SE¼-S6; 2-5-1834
Isaac Overman NW¼-SE¼-S6; 2-20-1836
Miles Davis SE¼-SW¼-S6; 12-19-1834
Jonathan M. Ellis NE¼-SW¼-S6; 2-22-1837
Jonathan M. Ellis W½-SW¼-S6; 5-19-1836

Page 261. T 18 N, R 15 E of 2nd P.M.

Aaron Hill SW¼-NW¼-S7; 3-14-1834
Aaron Hill NW¼-NW¼-S7; 1-23-1837
Aaron Hill E½-SW¼-S7; 10-6-1832

Page 261. T 19 N, R 15 E of 2nd P.M.

Richard C. Warwick S½-Fr.S4; 6-23-1832
John Murray Armacost N½-Fr.S4; 10-28-1835
Henry Davis E½-NE¼-S5; 9-19-1835
Andrew Frazier W½-NE¼-S5; 1-15-1838
Nicholas Higgins E½-NW¼; SW¼-NW¼-S5; 6-13-1836
John Harvey Farrens NW¼-NW¼-S5; 8-27-1836
Elizabeth Conkle E½-SE¼-S5; 7-6-1833
Charles Seevers W½-SE¼-S5; 6-13-1836
Nicholas Higgins SW¼-S5; 6-13-1836
Thomas Buckingham SE¼-NW¼-S6; 6-13-1836
Richard Conarroe W½-NW¼; NE¼-NW¼-S6; 1-21-1837
Nathan Freeman NE¼-SE¼-S6; 8-22-1836
William McKim SE¼-SE¼-S6; 1-5-1837
Jesse Markland NE¼-SW¼-S6; 10-19-1837
William Robinson NW¼-SW¼-S6; 4-10-1837
Caleb Manning SE¼-SW¼-S6; 3-1-1837
Joshua Robinson SW¼-SW¼-S6; 6-13-1836
Abraham Manning E½-NE¼-S7; 11-12-1836
Reuben Manning W½-NE¼-S7; 11-12-1836
Reuben Manning E½-NW¼-S7; 11-12-1836
Jesse Johnson W½-NW¼-S7; 4-4-1836
Abraham Manning E½-SE¼-S7; 12-12-1836
Reuben Manning W½-SE¼-S7; 11-12-1836

Page 262. T 19 N, R 15 E of 2nd P.M.

George W. Farrens NE¼-SW¼-S7; 10-17-1836
Caleb Manning SE¼-SW¼; W½-SW¼-S7; 11-12-1836
Stanton Bailey, Jr. NE¼-NE¼-S8; 9-16-1833
Ahaz Cartwright SE¼-NE¼-S8; 8-9-1836

Charles Seevers W½-NE¼-S8; 6-13-1836
Benjamin Bright SW¼-NW¼-S8; 6-2-1834
Andrew Frazier SE¼-NW¼-S8; 6-13-1834
Benjamin Bright NW¼-NW¼-S8; 1-5-1837
Thomas J. Markland NE¼-NW¼-S8; 10-17-1837
Richard C. Warwick SE¼-SE¼-S8; 7-24-1833
Ahaz Cartwright NE¼-SE¼-S8; 8-9-1836
Washington Markland W½-SE¼-S8; 10-17-1837
James Frazier NW¼-SW¼-S8; 10-10-1833
James Frazier NE¼-SW¼-S8; 6-20-1836
Richard Manning S½-SW¼-S8; 12-5-1836
John Gross Lot 1-N½-SE¼-S17; 10-10-1836
Hezekiah Lock Lot 2-S½-SE¼-S17; 7-26-1836
John Gross E½-NE¼-S17; 2-21-1839
Henry D. Farrens NW¼-NE¼-S17; 4-13-1837
John Wilson SW¼-NE¼-S17; 9-4-1837
Abner Anderson SE¼-NW¼-S17; 6-10-1835
Henry D. Farrens NE¼-NW¼-S17; 4-13-1837
Nathan Parker W½-NW¼-S17; 10-10-1836
Elias Ogan W½-SW¼-S17; 9-13-1836
Richard Williams E½-SW¼-S17; 9-22-1836
Nathan Parker E½-NE¼-S18; 10-10-1836
John B. Chenoweth W½-NE¼-S18; 10-14-1837
Loyd Brown NW¼-S18; 10-11-1836
Elihu H. Gist SE¼-S18; 9-26-1836
Eli Stockdale E½-SW¼-S18; 2-13-1837
John B. Chenoweth W½-SW¼-S18; 10-14-1837
John Armagost SE¼-NE¼-S19; 12-13-1837
Joseph Perkins NE¼-NE¼-S19; 9-22-1836
Joseph Perkins W½-NE¼-S19; 2-19-1836
Joseph Perkins E½-NW¼-S19; 2-22-1837
Jacob Armagost W½-NW¼-S19; 2-13-1837

Page 263. T 19 N, R 15 E of 2nd P.M.

William Murray SE¼-S19; SW¼-S19; 9-20-1838
William Chenoweth S½-Fr.S20; 11-7-1834
Jeremiah Loyd & Thomas Loyd NE¼-Fr.S20; 9-12-1836
Richard Williams NW¼-Fr.S20; 9-22-1836
Christophel Murray Armacost N½-Fr.S29; 10-28-1835
Luther Martin S½-Fr.S29; 10-28-1835
Jabez Murray Fr.S32; 11-7-1834
John B. Chenoweth NE¼-S30; 10-14-1837
Samuel Ogan E½-SE¼-S30; 4-23-1837
John B. Chenoweth W½-SE¼-S30; 10-14-1837
John B. Chenoweth E½-SW¼-S30; 10-14-1837
John Armagost W½-SW¼-S30; 12-13-1837
Jabez Murray NE¼-S31; 11-7-1834
Curtis Clenny E½-NW¼-S31; 1-23-1835
Benjamin Pearce W½-NW¼-S31; 5-19-1836
Jabez Murray SE¼-S31; 11-7-1834
Jabez Murray E½-SW¼-S31; 11-7-1834
Thomas Jeffrey W½-SW¼-S31; 4-8-1835

Page 263. T 20 N, R 15 E of 2nd P.M.

Francis Parrott & Thomas Parrott N½-Fr.S3; 9-19-1836
Perry Pease E pt.-S½; W pt.-S½-Fr.S3; 3-1-1837

Perry Pease   NE¼-S4; NW¼-S4; 3-1-1837
John Hole   E½-SE¼-S4; 9-5-1836
William Hole   W½-SE¼-S4; 9-5-1836
John Hole   E½-SW¼-S4; 2-27-1837
Samuel Cole   W½-SW¼-S4; 5-10-1837
John Wheatley   NE¼-S5; 11-7-1837
Benjamin Drake   E½-NW¼-S5; 6-15-1837
John Allbaugh   W½-NW¼-S5; 5-12-1837
John Ewing   SE¼-S5; 11-24-1837

           Page 264.   T 20 N, R 15 E of 2nd P.M.

William Bradford   E½-SW¼-S5; 11-24-1837
Nicholas Stutsman   W½-SW¼-S5; 11-26-1836
Andrew Emert   NE¼-S6; NW¼-S6; 10-8-1836
Elizabeth Stutsman   E½-SE¼-S6; 11-26-1836
Elizabeth Stutsman   W½-SE¼-S6; 12-5-1836
Andrew Emert   SW¼-S6; 10-8-1836
Isaac Hosier   NE¼-S7; 11-26-1836
William McGrew   NW¼-S7; 12-31-1836
David Stutsman   SE¼-S7; 11-26-1836
Jacob Belville   SW¼-S7; 3-27-1837
John Ewing   NE¼-S8; 10-25-1836
Peter Prough   NW¼-S8; 11-26-1836
Jacob Whitesel   SE¼-S8; 10-25-1836
Richard Goodwin   E½-SW¼; SW¼-SW¼-S8; 11-4-1836
David Stutsman   NW¼-SW¼-S8; 11-26-1836
Samuel Conklyn   NE¼-NW¼; E½-NW¼-S9; 2-13-1837
Thomas Welch   W½-NW¼-S9; 11-25-1836
Elizabeth Potter   E½-SE¼-S9; 8-15-1836
Samuel Conklyn   SW¼-SE¼-S9; 9-5-1836
Robert Finney   NW¼-SE¼-S9; 9-15-1836
Samuel Conklyn   SW¼-S9; 9-5-1836
Samuel Martin   Fr.S10; 11-4-1836
Perry Pease   Fr.S15; 3-1-1837
Joseph Combs   E½-NE¼-S17; 1-7-1837
Perry Pease   W½-NE¼; E½-NW¼-S17; 3-1-1837
Thomas E. F. Barnes   W½-NW¼-S17; 12-5-1836
Micajah Combs   E½-SE¼-S17; 1-7-1837
Perry Pease   W½-SE¼-S17; 3-1-1837
Joseph Wheatley   E½-SW¼-S17; 11-24-1837
John Wheatley   W½-SW¼-S17; 11-24-1837
John Cory   E½-NE¼-S18; 5-12-1838
Perry Pease   W½-NE¼-S18; 3-1-1837
James G. Birney   SW¼-S18; 1-23-1837

           Page 265.   T 20 N, R 15 E of 2nd P.M.

John Zercher   E½-NE¼-S20; 6-3-1837
Joshua Baily   W½-NE¼-S20; 8-21-1837
William Warwick, Jr.   E½-NW¼-S20; 7-27-1837
Mary Bailey   W½-NW¼-S20; 4-26-1838
Daniel Charles   E½-SE¼-S20; 3-1-1837
James C. Williams   E½-SW¼-S20; 3-1-1837
Joshua Freeman   W½-SW¼-S20; 3-1-1837
Philip Powell   SE¼-Fr.S21; 3-22-1837
Washington Rightnour   SW¼-Fr.S21; 8-27-1836
Stephen Allbaugh   W½-NW¼-Fr.S21; 8-27-1836

John Powell NE¼-Fr.S21; E½-NW¼-Fr.S21; 1-14-1837
Benjamin Pickett E½-NW¼-Fr.S28; 7-9-1836
Micajah Morgan W½-NW¼-Fr.S28; 2-6-1837
Nathan Thomas SW¼-Fr.S28; 3-1-1837
Philip Powell E½-Fr.S28; 11-30-1836
Benjamin Thomas NW¼-S29; 3-1-1837
Levi Hollingsworth E½-SE¼-S29; 8-21-1838
Eli Thomas W½-SE¼-S29; 5-23-1837
George Thomas E½-SW¼-S29; 3-1-1837
Henry Hill W½-SW¼-S29; 4-25-1837
Josiah Hutchens NE¼-NW¼-S30; 8-22-1836
James P. Crane SE¼-NW¼-S30; 10-24-1838
John Pike SW¼-SW¼-S30; 1-11-1833
James P. Crane NW¼-SW¼-S30; 10-24-1838
Micajah Morgan E½-SW¼-S30; 2-6-1837
          Page 266. T 20 N, R 15 E of 2nd P.M.
David Little SE¼-NW¼-S31; 3-17-1836
David Little SW¼-NW¼-S31; 8-22-1836
William McKim N½-NW¼-S31; 5-21-1838
Matthew Hill NW¼-SW¼-S31; 8-22-1836
Matthew Hill NE¼-SW¼-S31; 1-4-1837
William McKim SE¼-SW¼-S31; 10-18-1837
James Fleming SW¼-SW¼-S31; 5-21-1838
James Armstrong NE¼-S32; 5-21-1838
Amos Peacock NW¼-NW¼-S32; 7-2-1835
William Peacock SW¼-NW¼-S32; 1-30-1838
Amos Peacock E½-NW¼-S32; 3-1-1837
Thomas Price Murray SE¼-S32; 10-12-1835
William Powell, Jr. SW¼-S32; 1-20-1837
Clark Spencer W½-NW¼-Fr.S33; 6-3-1837
Smith G. Masterson Lots 1-2--E side-N½-Fr.S33; 1-4-1837
Thomas Price Murray S½-Fr.S33; 10-12-1835
          Page 266. T 21 N, R 15 E of 2nd P.M.
William L. Campbell NE¼-Fr.S2; 9-21-1837
Demas Lindley SE¼-Fr.S2; 6-19-1837
Reuben P. Graham NW¼-Fr.S2; 12-1-1836
Demas Lindley SW¼-Fr.S2; 11-11-1836
Demas Lindley NE¼-S3; 10-11-1836
Demas Lindley E½-NW¼-S3; 11-11-1836
Henry Handschy W½-NW¼-S3; 9-14-1836
Demas Lindley SE¼-S3; 10-11-1836
Jesse Beach SW¼-SW¼-S3; 1-1-1834
John Thompson NW¼-SW¼-S3; 3-17-1834
Jesse Beach E½-SW¼-S3; 9-22-1834
Jesse Beach NE¼-NE¼-S4; 1-1-1834
Henry Chandler S½-NE¼-S4; 10-17-1834
Arthur Hedgepeth(?) NW¼-NE¼-S4; 10-13-1836
Henry Chandler NE¼-NW¼-S4; 10-17-1836
John Ewing SE¼-NW¼; W½-NW¼-S4; 10-25-1836
          Page 267. T 21 N, R 15 E of 2nd P.M.
Thomas Devor SE¼-SE¼-S4; 1-1-1834
John Thompson NE¼-SE¼-S4; 2-14-1834
Milton Beach W½-SE¼-S4; 10-16-1835
Matthias C. Williams SW¼-S4; 7-2-1836

James Iliff & William T. Iliff NE¼-S5; 9-21-1837
Elias Willyard NW¼-S5; 4-14-1837
Cornelius Porter S½-SE¼-S5; 6-17-1836
William L. Campbell N½-SE¼-S5; 9-13-1837
Matthias C. Williams SW¼-S5; 7-2-1836
Jacob Puterbaugh NE¼-S6; 9-2-1836
Robert F. Kemp SE¼-NW¼-S6; 6-26-1837
William McFarlan NE¼-NW¼-S6; 7-8-1836
William McFarlan W½-NW¼-S6; 3-11-1836
Matthias C. Williams SE¼-S6; 7-2-1836
James Porter SW¼-SW¼-S6; 10-29-1833
Jesse James SE¼-SW¼-S6; 5-11-1837
Henry Surface NE¼-SW¼-S6; 5-12-1837
Robert F. Kemp NW¼-SW¼-S6; 6-26-1837
Matthias C. Williams NE¼-S7; 7-2-1836
Martin Fields SW¼-NW¼-S7; 1-10-1834
Martin Fields SE¼-NW¼-S7; 6-17-1836
Alsey Manes(?) NW¼-NW¼-S7; 11-3-1836
William Simmons NE¼-NW¼-S7; 4-5-1837
Joseph Wheatley SE¼-S7; 5-20-1837
Matthias C. Williams NW¼-S8; 7-2-1836
James G. Birney SW¼-S8; 9-5-1836
Jesse Gray SE¼-NE¼-S9; 9-5-1833
Thomas Devor NE¼-NE¼-S9; 10-7-1835
Joseph Anderson NW¼-NE¼-S9; 7-7-1836
Charles Henry Schwier SW¼-NE¼-S9; 8-22-1836
Matthias C. Williams NW¼-S9; 7-2-1836
Charles Henry Schwier E½-SE¼-S9; 8-20-1836
Henry Handschy W½-SE¼; SW¼-S9; 8-26-1836
Demas Lindley NE¼-S10; 11-11-1836
                Page 268. T 21 N, R 15 E of 2nd P.M.
William Anderson E½-NW¼-S10; 10-8-1836
Henry Handschy SE¼-SW¼; E½-SW¼-S10; 8-26-1836
Charles Henry Schwier W½-SW¼-S10; 8-20-1836
John A. Wiseman N½-Fr.S11; 7-8-1837
Daniel Lindley S½-Fr.S11; 7-6-1837
James G. Birney N end-N½; S end-N½; S½-Fr.S14; 9-18-1837
Spencer Brummitt SW¼-NE¼-S15; 1-27-1836
James G. Birney NW¼-NE¼-S15; 11-26-1836
James G. Birney E½-NE¼-S15; 1-23-1837
James Lambert SE¼-NW¼-S15; 1-27-1836
James Lambert SW¼-NW¼-S15; 10-29-1836
Spencer Brummitt NW¼-NW¼-S15; 11-12-1836
James G. Birney NE¼-NW¼-S15; 11-26-1836
Peter Brummitt E½-SE¼-S15; 2-16-1837
Absalom Noffsinger W½-SE¼-S15; 4-18-1835
Cortland Lambert E½-SW¼-S15; 10-29-1836
Demas Lindley W½-SW¼-S15; 11-11-1836
James G. Birney E½-NW¼-S17; 11-28-1836
William Birun W½-NW¼-S17; 2-2-1838
Richard Wheatley W½-SE¼; E½-SW¼-S17; 9-27-1836
Samuel Weaver NE¼-S18; 5-24-1837
William Weaver NW¼-S18; 5-24-1837
Elisha Bouer(?) E½-SE¼-S18; 2-8-1838

Edward Simmons W½-SE¼-S18; 5-11-1837
Edward Simmons E½-SW¼-S18; 4-5-1837
Samuel Poage W½-SW¼-S18; 6-20-1836
Henry Harshman E½-NE¼-S19; 8-11-1837
Samuel Chambers W½-NE¼-S19; 5-12-1837
Thomas Alexander NW¼-S19; 2-25-1834
Adam Shafer S½-NW¼-S19; 6-23-1837

Page 269. T 21 N, R 15 E of 2nd P.M.

Abraham Harshman NE¼-SE¼-S19; 12-15-1836
William Simmons NW¼-SE¼-S19; 2-2-1839
Henry Weyrick S½-SE¼-S19; 11-4-1837
Michael Brooks E½-SW¼-S19; 11-4-1837
Ezekel Cooper W½-SW¼-S19; 9-5-1837
Elijah Gorsuch E½-NE¼-S20; 9-13-1836
Andrew Emert NW¼-S20; 10-8-1836
Elijah Gorsuch E½-SE¼-S20; 9-13-1836
Jacob Harshman NW¼-SE¼-S20; 9-23-1836
Joseph H. Sutton SW¼-SE¼-S20; 8-5-1837
Jacob Harshman NE¼-SW¼-S20; 5-27-1836
Abraham Harshman SE¼-SW¼-S20; 12-15-1836
James G. Birney NE¼-S21; 1-23-1837
Henry Bailey E½-NW¼-S21; 9-13-1836
Cornelius Sutton SE¼-S21; 2-1-1837
Henry Bailey SW¼-S21; 9-13-1836
James Reeves SW¼-NE¼-S22; 11-3-1834
David Nickum NW¼-NE¼-S22; 1-27-1836
Valentine * E½-NE¼-S22; 12-12-1836. * Harlan
James Reeves SE¼-NW¼-S22; 8-30-1836
Elihu Harlan NE¼-NW¼-S22; 10-31-1836
James G. Birney W½-NW¼-S22; 11-26-1836
John Skinner SW¼-SE¼-S22; 3-13-1834
John Skinner NW¼-SE¼-S22; 8-30-1836
John Wallen NE¼-SE¼-S22; 10-11-1836
Andrew Stone SE¼-SE¼-S22; 11-10-1836
Andrew Stone E½-SW¼-S22; 12-10-1836
Amos Sutton W½-SW¼-S22; 8-5-1837
James Hinesley N½-Fr.S23; 12-5-1837
Robert Phillips S½-Fr.S23; 12-14-1837
John Mulford Fr.S26; N½-NE¼ & S½-NE¼-S27; 8-20-1836
Amos Smith N½-SE¼-Fr.S27; 5-1-1834
George Debolt S½-SE¼-Fr.S27; 10-24-1836

Page 270. T 21 N, R 15 E pf 2nd P.M.

Joseph Hinkle E½-NW¼-Fr.S27; 8-29-1836
George Debolt W½-NW¼-Fr.S27; 10-24-1836
Benjamin Debolt SW¼-Fr.S27; 1-13-1835
Joseph Wheatley E½-NE¼-S28; 9-27-1837
Thomas Sutton NW¼-NE¼-S28; 2-1-1837
Andrew Debolt SW¼-NE¼-S28; 1-13-1836
William Warren NW¼-NW¼-S28; 2-3-1834
George Kerschner SW¼-NW¼-S28; 9-23-1836
John Johnson E½-NW¼-S28; 3-17-1835
George Losear NW¼-SE¼-S28; 8-22-1836
Edward Johnson SW¼-SE¼-S28; 8-22-1836
Richard Wheatley E½-SE¼-S28; 9-19-1836

James Wilson SE¼-SW¼-S28; 8-15-1836
Joseph Wheatley NE¼-SW¼-S28; 9-19-1836
George Kerschner W½-SW¼-S28; 9-23-1836
John Riley Warren NE¼-NE¼-S29; 1-10-1837
John Gerhard, Jr. SE¼-NE¼-S29; 9-17-1838
Andrew Frazier W½-NE¼-S29; 1-15-1838
Joseph Harshman N½-NW¼-S29; 2-23-1835
Adam Bousman S½-NW¼-S29; 5-13-1837
David C. Goodman E½-SE¼-S29; 10-29-1836
William Goodman NW¼-SE¼-S29; 10-29-1836
William Cromas SW¼-SE¼-S29; 10-4-1838
Timothy F. Smith SW¼-S29; 10-20-1836
Joseph Harshman, Sr. SE¼-NE¼-S30; 4-16-1836
Henry Harshman SW¼-NE¼-S30; 8-11-1837
Henry Weyrick N½-NE¼-S30; 11-4-1837
Christopher Maness NE¼-NW¼-S30; 12-15-1836
Benjamin Glesner SE¼-NW¼-S30; 12-13-1838
William Ellsworth W½-NW¼-S30; 5-16-1837
William Warren NW¼-SE¼-S30; 9-18-1834
Moses Glessner SW¼-SE¼-S30; 12-13-1838
Reuben P. Graham E½-SE¼-S30; 12-1-1836
William Ellsworth SW¼-S30; 5-16-1837
Henry Hinkle NE¼-S31; 9-9-1836
Henry Gebhart NW¼-S31; 10-4-1836
Hiram Gilliam SE¼-S31; 11-9-1836
Samuel Sarber SW¼-S31; 10-3-1836

Page 271. T 21 N, R 15 E of 2nd P.M.

John Coffman E½-NE¼-S32; 10-21-1836
Jacob Grove W½-NE¼-S32; 4-28-1837
James Warren NW¼-NW¼-S32; 10-20-1836
Joseph McHannon, James B. Cecil, and John, Jacob, Sarah, & Elizabeth Cecil, surviving chn. of Magdalena Cecil, dau. of Jacob Coller, decd. SW¼-NW¼-S32; 4-10-1837
William Klais E½-NW¼-S32; 11-15-1837. See 2nd entry below
Daniel Faik E½-SE¼-S32; 9-17-1838
William Kedis NW¼-SE¼-S32; 11-10-1837. See 2nd entry above
John Wheatley SW¼-SE¼-S32; 11-24-1837
Samuel Cole SW¼-S32; 6-14-1837
Jacob Johnson SE¼-NE¼-S33; 4-10-1837
Jacob Johnson NE¼-NE¼-S33; 9-23-1836
Jacob Johnson W½-NE¼-S33; 3-2-1833
William Roth NW¼-S33; 4-28-1837
Joseph McHannon, James B. Cecil, and John, Jacob, Sarah, & Elizabeth Cecil, surviving chn. of Magdalena Cecil, dau. of Jacob Coller, decd. E½-SW¼-S33; 4-10-1837
Seth Macy W½-SW¼-S33; 5-1-1837
Aaron Simmons NE¼-Fr.S34; 9-29-1836
Adam Simmons SE¼-Fr.S34; 9-14-1836
Aaron Simmons E½-NW¼-S34; 9-29-1836
Jacob Fager W½-NW¼-S34; 2-6-1837
Adam Simmons E½-SW¼-S34; 9-14-1836
William White W½-SW¼-S34; 5-20-1837

Page 271. T 22 N, R 15 E of 2nd P.M.

Robert Armstrong Fr.S1; 6-6-1839

Peyton S. Symmes W½-NE¼-S2; 12-1-1836
Isaac Butler E½-NE¼-S2; 5-21-1838
Jason Humiston E½-SE¼-S2; 11-6-1838
Bell Woten W½-SE¼-S2; 1-16-1834
Bell Woten E½-SW¼-S2; 1-16-1834
Robert P. Thompson W½-SW¼-S2; 8-13-1838
Ellis Kincaid Fr.NW¼-S2; 11-6-1838
Page 272. T 22 N, R 15 E of 2nd P.M.
Robert P. Thompson Lots 1-2--E½-Fr.S3; 8-13-1838
Ebenezer Evans W½-E½-Fr.S4; 11-5-1838
Tobias Jatter Fr.S8; 2-22-1837
Thomas White NE¼-Fr.S9; 2-22-1837
George B. Vance SE¼-SE¼-Fr.S9; 5-21-1838
Edwin P. Hogarth NE¼-SE¼-Fr.S9; 8-10-1838
Jeremiah Snelbaker W½-SE¼-Fr.S9; 8-10-1838
John E. Bross E pt.-W½-Fr.S9; 5-21-1838
David H. Gregg W pt.-W½-Fr.S9; 5-21-1838
Abraham Lotz E½-NE¼-S10; 5-21-1838
John White W½-NE¼-S10; 11-5-1838
William Heckman E½-NW¼-S10; 4-1-1837
Benjamin Drake W½-NW¼-S10; 12-1-1837
Ernestus Putman E½-SE¼-S10; 3-27-1837
George A. Fairchild SW¼-SE¼-S10; 11-18-1837
John White NW¼-SE¼-S10; 11-5-1838
John Mitchell E½-SW¼-S10; 4-1-1837
Benjamin Drake W½-SW¼-S10; 11-4-1837
Jesse Hutchins E½-NE¼-S11; 2-13-1838
James Martendale W½-NE¼-S11; 6-12-1834
Conaway Stone NE¼-NW¼-S11; 2-22-1833
Abraham Lotz SE¼-NW¼-S11; 11-1-1837
William McFarling W½-NW¼-S11; 11-5-1838
John Eblen SE¼-SE¼-S11; 4-21-1837
Abraham Lotz NE¼-SE¼-S11; 5-21-1838
Abraham Lotz W½-SE¼-S11; 6-16-1836
William Cummings SE¼-SW¼-S11; 1-16-1834
William Cummings NE¼-SW¼-S11; 9-21-1835
Ebenezer Evans W½-SW¼-S11; 11-5-1838
James Cumins S12; 12-17-1836
William Felton Denny S13; 7-14-1837
William Felton Denney SW¼-NE¼-S14; 10-5-1833
John Eblen NW¼-NE¼-S14; 6-24-1834
William Felton Denney E½-NE¼-S14; 10-15-1836
John Eblen E½-NW¼-S14; 12-19-1836
John Beardshear W½-NW¼-S14; 5-21-1838
William F. Denney NE¼-SE¼-S14; 2-1-1837
Jacob H. Buffington NW¼-SE¼-S14; 12-15-1836
Alexander Classford SW¼-SE¼-S14; 12-26-1836
Page 273. T 22 N, R 15 E of 2nd P.M.
Jason Humiston SE¼-SE¼-S14; 11-5-1838
Samuel Woten SE¼-SW¼-S14; 10-15-1836
Benjamin Drake NE¼-SW¼-S14; 4-10-1837
John Beardshear W½-SW¼-S14; 5-21-1838
Isaac Beardshear NE¼-S15; 5-18-1838
Daniel Bocher NW¼-S15; 5-18-1838

Isaac Beardshear SE¼-S15; 5-18-1838
Daniel Booher SW¼-S15; 5-18-1838
James G. Birney NE¼-Fr.S17; 1-23-1837
James G. Birney SE¼-Fr.S17; 4-8-1837
James G. Birney SW¼-Fr.S17; 4-21-1837
James G. Birney S½-NW¼-Fr.S17; 4-22-1837
James G. Birney N½-NW¼-Fr.S17; 9-16-1837
John Watters Lots 1 & 3-E½-E½-Fr.S18; 9-1-1838
Elam P. Langdon Lots 2,4,5,6-W½-E½; Fr.SW¼-Fr.S18; 7-27-1839
Jesse Hutchens E½-NE¼-S19; 5-21-1838
Jacob Eley W½-NE¼-S19; 10-2-1838
John Hutchins E½-SE¼-S19; 5-21-1838
Andrew Gregg W½-SE¼-S19; 5-21-1838
Jacob Chrisman E½-SW¼-S19; 9-15-1838
Thomas Parks, Jr. W½-SW¼-S19; 6-19-1837
Samuel C. Carter NE¼-S20; 4-5-1837
Samuel C. Carter E½-NW¼-S20; 4-8-1837
William Hutchins W½-NW¼-S20; 5-21-1838
William V. Heard SE¼-S20; 5-21-1838
Christopher Furnas SW¼-S20; 5-21-1838
Christopher Gish E½-NE¼-S21; 11-20-1837
Turner Brown W½-NE¼-S21; 2-9-1838
David H. Gregg NW¼-S21; 5-21-1838
John B. Julien E½-SE¼-S21; 11-20-1837
Smith Gregg W½-SE¼-S21; 5-21-1838
William Gregg SW¼-S21; 5-21-1838
John Beardshear NE¼-S22; 5-21-1838
Jacob Snyder NW¼-S22; 5-18-1838
William Money E½-SE¼-S22; 2-28-1837
Thomas Peeden W½-SE¼-S22; 4-14-1837
Thomas Peeden E½-SW¼-S22; 8-12-1837
Matthew McKelvey W½-SW¼-S22; 5-10-1838

Page 274. T 22 N, R 15 E of 2nd P.M.

Jonathan Woten SW¼-NE¼-S23; 4-21-1837
John Eblen NW¼-NE¼-S23; 10-28-1837
Thomas P. Smith E½-NE¼-S23; 11-5-1838
William Money SW¼-NW¼-S23; 5-28-1836
Daniel B. Bingham NW¼-NW¼-S23; 5-21-1838
Samuel Woten E½-NW¼-S23; 10-5-1836
Jacob Snyder SE¼-S23; 5-18-1838
William Money NW¼-SW¼-S23; 6-24-1834
Jacob Snyder E½-SW¼-S23; 5-18-1838
Abraham Lotz SW¼-SW¼-S23; 5-21-1838
Samuel Stoner, Jr. S½-Fr.S25; Fr.S36; 10-31-1837
Samuel McKelvey NE¼-S26; 5-10-1836
Thomas P. Smith E½-NW¼-S26; 5-10-1838
John Millhouse W½-NW¼-S26; 11-1-1837
James Koon E½-SE¼-S26; 10-31-1837
Gideon Harrison W½-SE¼-S26; 12-12-1836
George Thompson SW¼-S26; 12-12-1836
Benjamin Drake E½-NE¼-S27; 4-10-1837
Thomas Peeden W½-NE¼-S27; 4-14-1837
Thomas Peeden SE¼-NW¼-S27; 5-7-1838
Nathan Beach SW¼-NW¼-S27; 5-21-1838

Jacob Stover N½-NW¼-S27; 5-21-1838
John Statter E½-SE¼-S27; 7-13-1837
Thomas Peeden W½-SE¼-S27; 4-14-1837
Absalom Hendricks NE¼-SW¼-S27; 9-23-1837
Thomas Peeden SE¼-SW¼-S27; 5-7-1838
Nathan Beach W½-SW¼-S27; 10-16-1837
Ezekiel C. Clough S28; 4-24-1837
Joseph Danner E½-NE¼-S29; 7-13-1837
George Free NW¼-NE¼-S29; 10-11-1837
Christian Lower SW¼-NE¼-S29; 4-13-1838
George Free E½-NW¼-S29; 10-11-1837
Henry Wats W½-NW¼-S29; 10-11-1837

Page 275.   T 22 N, R 15 E of 2nd P.M.

Stephen Jones SE¼-S29; 7-13-1837
Christian Lower, of Miami Co. (prob. Ohio) E½-SW¼-S29; 10-18-1837
Stephen Smith W½-SW¼-S29; 7-13-1837
Jesse Hutchens NE¼-S30; 5-21-1838
John Smaill NW¼-NW¼-S30; 7-21-1837
James Dye E½-NW¼; SW¼-NW¼-S30; 8-20-1838
Shadrick Chandler E½-SW¼; SW¼-SW¼-S30; 6-26-1837
James Dye NW¼-SW¼-S30; 8-20-1838

Thomas Singrey NE¼-S31; 5-29-1837
John Macemore E½-NW¼-S31; 5-29-1837
William Furrow W½-NW¼-S31; 6-1-1837
Elias Willyard SE¼-S31; 4-14-1837
Abraham Ackerman E½-SW¼-S31; 5-29-1837
Dorsey Ryan W½-SW¼-S31; 9-10-1836
Timothy Clough NE¼-S32; NW¼-S32; 10-31-1836
Moses Clough SE¼-S32; SW¼-S32; 10-31-1836
Jacob Harlan E½-NE¼-S33; 12-12-1836
Timothy Gates W½-NE¼-S33; 10-17-1836
Peter Fox, Sr. NW¼-S33; 3-24-1837
Martin Friend SW¼-SE¼-S33; 8-30-1836
George B. Vance NW¼-SE¼-S33; 8-30-1836
Henry Chandler E½-SE¼-S33; 10-17-1836
Rhoda Ingle E½-SW¼-S33; 10-31-1836
Thomas Singrey W½-SW¼-S33; 5-29-1837
James Dye NE¼-S34; 7-13-1837
John P. Campbell E½-NW¼-S34; 5-19-1837

Philip Free E½-SE¼-S34; 7-13-1837
Elihu Harlan W½-SE¼; E½-SW¼-S34; 10-31-1836
Isaac Berkheimer NW¼-SW¼; W½-SE¼-Fr.S35; 11-7-1836
George Laurence E½-SE¼-Fr.S35; 8-20-1838
Samuel Stoner, Jr. E½-NE¼-Fr.S35; 10-31-1837
Emanuel Flory W½-NE¼-Fr.S35; 10-26-1837

William L. Campbell & John P. Campbell W½-NW¼-S34; 9-13-1837
Ebenezer G. Campbell & James G. Campbell W½-SW¼-S34; 5-19-1837

Page 276.   T 23 N, R 15 E of 2nd P.M.

James Stone Fr.S36; 10-5-1833

- -

Land Office at Chillicothe
July 26, 1843

I hereby certify that the foregoing copies of entries of lands sol
and of lands remaining unsold, situate in the State of Indiana, so
or lately subject to sale at Cincinnati, have been carefully com-
pared with the original entries thereof in the Tract Book transmit
ted from the late Register's office at Cincinnati aforesaid and th
the same are correct copies of said original entries.

THOMAS SCOTT
Register

ARNOLD,Benjamin-38;Elijah-173-
174;George-70;Jeremiah-39;John-
49-81;Richard-24;William-35-38-
50-89
ASCEW,see Askue
ASH,George-88
ASHBROOK,Aaron-109
ASHBY,Bayless-14;Bladen-33
ASHFORD,William-140
ASHLY,David-176;William-55
ASHTON,William-124(2)
ASKUE,Amos-83-86
ASMANN,Henry-162(2);Herman-158
ASTON,John-72;Samuel-72
ATHEARN,see Athorn
ATHERTON,Amos-20;Elijah-19
ATKINS,William-126(4)-127
ATKINSON,Abraham-134;John-59;
Robert-108;Samuel-134(2);
William-42-132(2)
ATHORN,Prince-44
AUSTIN,Samuel-136;William-148-149
AVERILL,Philo-68
AYRES,Alfred-130;John-59;Samuel-
23;William-46

BABBITT,Edwin-166
BABBS,Noah-8;William-48
BABCOCK,James-77
BABINGER,Abraham-57
BABST,Anthony-159
BACCHUS,see Backhouse
BACKHOUSE,Allen-58-142;Isaac-70;
James-13-16(2);John-159;Marvin-
40(2)-68
BADGLEY,Joseph-187;Robert-87
BAGGS,Thomas-75
BAILEY,Andrew-17-34-72(2)-80-85-
92-97-124-143-162;David-31-114;
George-174-176;Henry-38(2)-39-
110(2)-111-198(2);Hiram-116;
James-82;John-102(3)-106-110-
134;Joshua-195;Leonard-132;Mary-
195;Richard-7;Staunton-38(2)-
121-193
BAIRD,James-68-94
BAKE,Jacob-22;John-23;Robert-
68(3);William-23
BAKER,see Balser,Bolser;Christo-
pher-121;Enoch-185-190;John-83-
87-190-191;Jonathan-80;Joseph-
136;Joshua-142;Mark-76;Martin-
142;Moses-82a;Richard-40-41;
Shelby-153(2);Thomas-191;Wil-
liam-87-153
BALDRIDGE,Samuel-104-106

BALDWIN,Amos-62;Charles-37;
Daniel-113-115;Elias-60;Isaac-
103;Jesse-106;John-103-113(2);
116;Jonas-71;Thomas-61-113
BALES,Dilwin-102(2);Nelson-175
BAIKLEY,Auson-155
BALL,Abner-85;Chester-183;Jacob-
23;William-154(2)
BALLENGER,Benjamin-103;David-157;
James-103-175(2);Jesse-108;
John-108;Joshua-102;William-102
BAISER,Abraham-191;Samuel-137
BALTIMORE,Philip-68
BANKS,Adam-87;Thomas-167
BANTA,Albert-108-117(4)-119(2);
Jane-52;John-43;Peter-52-57(2)-
97-137
BARBER,Isaac-108;John-13-123
BARCKMAN,Jacob-61-93
BARDLEMAN,Henry-157;John-157;
Joseph-157
BARKALOO,see Barricklow
BARKER,Hiram-132-147;Isaac-33(2)-
108;Joseph-43
BARKHURST,Isaac-123
BARLEY,Andrew-92
BARNARD,Frederick-119;George-40
BARNES,Alexander-172;Blackslee-
60;Isaac-105;John-116(2);Ste-
phen-127;Thomas-195;William-
105-183
BARNETT,Jacob-83;Philip-15
BARR,William-10(2)-12-41-52-53-
57-61-69-72-73(3)-77-112(2)-122
BARRACKMAN,Jacob-93
BARRETT,Caleb-88
BARRICKLOW,Farrington-7(2)-8(2);
John-5(2)-7-8(3)-11-13(2)-49
BARROWS,see Burrows;Stephen-43(2)
BARTEL,John-151-154
BARTON,Valentine-7;William-53-138
BARWICK,Chandler-167
BARYE,Lesmund-60
BASCOM,Erastus-133;Isaac-147;
Silas-71
BASSETT,Jonathan-64
BASYE,Lesmund-60(3)
BATES,Clark-63(2);Harvey-58;
Isaac-41;James-42;John-38;Seth-
62;Willis-6
BATKIN,William-65
BATTON,James-109
BAUER,see Bowers,Booher;Alvis-
143;John-153
BAUGH,John-189
BAUM,Martin-4-6-66

BAXTER,James-23-125(2);John-
118(2)
BAYLES,Daniel-96
BAYMILLER,Jacob-74
BAYNE,John-2;William-16
BAYS,Thomas-132
BEACH,Benjamin-77(2);Dwight-
177(2);Jesse-196(3);Job-57;Mil-
ton-196;Nathan-201-202;Solomon-
26-66;Timothy-175(2)
BEALOR,Frederick-153;Samuel-85-
88-97-101(2)
BEALL,Archibald-103-111-113(2)-
180;Curtis-117;James-167;John-
182;Josiah-20;Pleasant-182(2);
William-111
BEAMER,Henry-55
BEAN,William-52
BEAR,Ezra-147;Peter-72
BEARD,Enoch-114;Jesse-88;John-
28-99;Paul-114(2)-115-180;Thom-
as-86(2)-98(3);William-26-27(2)-
180(2)
BEARDSGEAR,Isaac-200-201;John-
200(2)-201
BEASLEY,Isaac-124;John-124;Thom-
as-127(2)
BEATTY,Charles-42-131-132;Hugh-
5;John-90-171;William-162
BEAUCHAMP,Noah-85
BECHEL,Sebastian-163(2)
BECK,Henry-64-67;John-101-173;
Samuel-97;Solomon-67;Wright-32
BECKETT,see Pickett;Benjamin-
43(2);William-93
BECKFORD,Moses-49
BECKMAN,Henry-142
BECKWORTH,Samuel-43
BEDFORD,Elias-50
BEDWELL,James-28
BEEKS,William-169
BEERY,see Berry
BEESON,Benjamin-86;Isaac-32-114;
Richard-120;William-97
BEIK,Joel-64
BELL,David-60(2)-126;Hugh-97;
Jacob-23(2);John-86(3)-88-111;
Joseph-45;Josiah-126;Samuel-26-
96(3);William-45-73-84
BELVILLE,Jacob-195
BENBOW,Edward-113
BENBRIDGE,Thomas-74
BENDEL,Philip-181(2)
BENEFIELD,John-98;Robert-98(2)
BENGE,Alfred-181
BENNETT,James-11;John-52-53;

Jonathan-53;Joseph-17-124;Rob-
ert-28(2);Samuel-170;Thomas-
142;William-73-84
BENNINGER,Martin-55
BENNY,Joshua-103
BENOIT,Anthony-136
BENSON,Henry-118;Michael-183-184;
Thomas-151;William-118-183-184
BENTLEY,Joseph-42(2)
BENTON,Joshua-32;Oliver-17;
Thomas-31
BERKHEIMER,Isaac-202
BERNARD,see Barnard;John-162(2)
BERRY,James-23;John-88-102-191;
Joseph-191
BERTE,see Burt
BEVENS,David-48;Owen-175
BEVERLIN,John-113
BIDDLE,Benjamin-73
BIGGS,John-29-161(6)-169(4)-
181(3)-183;Thomas-105-161
BILLS,Abraham-146;William-8
BINGHAM,Daniel-201
BINNEY,Joshua-103
BIRDZELL,William-134(2)
BIRGE,Alfred-182
BIRNEY,James-185(7)-186(3)-191(6)-
197(6)-198(2)-201(5)-195
BIRUN,William-197
BISBEE,Isaiah-80-78
BISHOP,Amos-187;Joel-49;John-
37(2)-157;Lewis-61-83;Thomas-45
BITTLE,Richard-181(2)-182-183;
William-181
BIXBY,Perry-152(2)
BLACK,Alexander-109-110;David-
22-61;Elwell-175(4);James-111(3);
John-92;Robert-102;Samuel-97;
William-97
BLACKBURN,Bryson-19;Edward-60
BLACKER,Robert-40
BLACKLIDGE,Harvey-172(2);Jacob-
83-90-91-171(2);James-91-172(2)
BLAIR,Robert-21-101
BLAKE,Thomas-49
BLANE,David-49
BLANEY,John-40-68
BLASDEL,Jacob-12(3)
BLATTNER,John-140
BLAZER,David-166
BLEDSOE,Abraham-4-16
BLODGET,Daniel-70-145;Joseph-145;
Nathan-55;Ora-145;Samuel-71
BLOOMFIELD,Lot-180
BLOUNT,Eli-120;William-105-106(2)
BLOYD,Jacob-63-86

BLUE,Benjamin-20;David-48(2)-49;
William-47-48
BLUNT ,see Blount
BOALING,Enoch-29
BOARDMAN,Amos-136;David-50-77-136
BOAS,Peter-4
BOCKUS,see Backhouse
BOCOCK,see Pocock;Lewis-41(2)-131
BODEKER,John-159(2)-161
BODINE,William-123
BODLE,Hugh-44
BOGERT,Ruliff-10(2)-52(2)-57
BOGGS,Thomas-75
BOHLE,see Bolay;Adam-138;Andrew-
139;Peter-163
BOHRER,Christian-153;George-153;
Sebastian-55
BOICE,John-52
BOISSEAU,Jacob-131;John-40(2)-42
BOLAY,see Bohle;David-139
BOLENDER,John-187
BOLINGER,Jacob-186;Stephen-163
BOLTON,James-92-109;William-92
BOLTZ,John-78
BOND,Benjamin-184;Edward-113(2);
Jesse-34-104;John-94;Joseph-
113(2);Lewis-19-20;Samuel-9(4)-
113-122;Thomas-19-98;William-33
BONHAM,Aaron-10-15;Benjamin-55;
Israel-15;James-123(2);Zede-
kiah-15
BONINE,David-31
BONNER,David-26;Samuel-26
BONTA,see Banta
BONWILL,Henry-91
BOOE,Benjamin-84
BOOHER,see Bower;Daniel-200-201
BOOING,Herman-159
BOOKER,Susannah-102
BOONE,see Booe;Benjamin-66;John-
115-184;Joseph-102
BOOTS,Martin-120
BORCHELT,John-155
BORDERS,William-126
BOREING,Ephraim-92
BOREM,Daniel-69
BOSON,John-42
BOSTICK,Enoch-149
BOSWELL,Isaac-32;Isom-188;Jacob-
32;Jason-129;Mariam-33
BOTKIN,Hugh-105(2)-107;James-176;
Peter-177;William-65
BOULSBY,Enos-66
BOURBON,Edward-115
BOURNE,Ezra-18;Samuel-18
BOUSMAN,Adam-185-199;Noah-190;

Washington-185
BOUTCHER,Samuel-124
BOVARD,Robert-41(3)-44
BOYEE,see Boice
BOWEN,see Brown;Ephraim-38-
39(2);James-126;Jeremiah-173;
John-136;Joseph-169
BOWERS,see Booher,Bauer;David-47;
Elisha-197;James-189
BOWLES,David-10-112;George-38-184
BOWISLEY,Enos-66
BOWMAN,James-70-145;Jacob-110;
Thomas-55-124
BOYD,Alexander-124;Elijah-41;
Henry-131;Jacob-147;James-42(2)-
100(2);John-131;Levi-151;Sam-
uel-100-101
BOYER,Benjamin-154
BOYLAND,Nicholas-40
BOYLE,James-44-48;John-156
BRACKEN,Levi-10;Thomas-10
BRACKENRIDGE,Thomas-14-123
BRADBURN,John-58-59-84
BRADBURY,Daniel-102-103;David-
103;Ezekiel-104;Gibens-54;Jo-
siah-103;Thomas-125
BRADFIELD,Cary-183;Elias-103
BRADFORD,David-62;Jesse-130;
Joel-3;William-195
BRADLEY,John-88;Turpin-151;
William-88
BRADSHAW,Robert-14
BRADWAY,see Brodway
BRAGG,Ephraim-189
BRAMBLE,Ayers-149;Laban-74-149
BRANDENBURG,Henry-26
BRANDON,John-146;Moses-146
BRANDT,Felix-44-69-72-74(3)
BRANNON,Lawrence-109;Thomas-12(2)
BRASHER,Charles-72;Jacob-9-72
BRAY,Henry-92;John-79-92;Thom-
as-92
BREES,Henry-158(2)
BREN,Jacob-156
BRENNAMAN,John-188
BREWATER,Henry-155;John-155
BREWER,Charles-70;Jesse-117-119;
Stephen-105-173
BREWINGTON,Benjamin-137;Charles-
75;John-75
BRIDGED,George-24
BRIDGES,John-63-82a;William-85
BRIERTON,Henry-133
BRIGGS,Abel-177(2);Abram-14
BRIGHT,Benjamin-194(2);Jesse-
129(2);William-146

BRINDLE,William-44-45(3)
BRINEY,Christopher-46-134
BRINKMAN,John-150-162
BRISBIN,Robert-23
BRISON,Hugh-13-81(2)-83;James-
188;John-22(2)
BRISTOW.Nero-127
BRITTAIN,Benjamin-116;George-
174;Henry-47(3);James-116(2)-117
BROADBURY,Simeon-171
BROCAW,Henry-73
BROCK,Elijah-115;Richard-180
BROCKAMP,Henry-159
BRODRICK,Anthony-14-53
BRODWAY,Josiah-29
BROMLEE,Samuel-73
BROOKS,Daniel-89;Eli-59-61-
160(2);Joab-25;Michael-198;
Moses-43-44-45-70-73(3)-79(2)-
91-117(3)-118(2)-119(8)-120
BROOKBANK,Thomas-155-156
BROSS,John-200
BROWN,see Bowen;Aaron-69;Amos-
3-4(3);Auson-3;Benjamin-32-54;
Clayton-179;David-28-76-78(2)-
103-148(2); E.-168;Eli-99;Eph-
raim-24-38-39-98;Ethan-2-44-
70(2)-73-87-101-119(3);George-
18(2)-101-128(2);Harvey-88;
Henderson-156-179(2);Henry-88-
100;James-70-100;John-9(2)-13-
14-15-26-62-65-66-77-88-89-131;
Joseph-37(2)-69-110;Loyd-194;
Matthew-63-66;Michael-91-96;
Paul-51-57(2);Philip-182-183(2)-
184;Robert-95(2)-96(2);Samuel-
89-98;Simon-158;Stephen-53;Thom-
as-25-26-65-95-125-127;Timothy-
160;Turner-201;William-26-28(2)-
34-39-87-145-147-173(2)-185
BROWNLEE,James-82a-85
BROWNSON,John-47(2);Reuben-86
BRUCE,Amer-9-49-51-75(2)-136(3);
Henry-50-51-91;James-51(2);John-
50-136(2);Stephen-50-136
BRUENGART,Sebastian-178
BRUMBLAY,John-75
BRUMFIELD,Jesse-184;Thomas-101
BRUMMITT,Peter-197;Spencer-197(2)
BRUNNER,John-139
BRUSH,Edward-81(3)-166;Jared-151
BRYAN,Benjamin-76;Henry-83-97-
102(3)-111;Joseph-70-145(2)
BRYANT,Thomas-145
BUCHANAN,James-8-82a;John-2
BUCK,Conrad-6(2);Sherman-17;

Warren-90;William-4
BUCKEL,David-137;Matthias-138
BUCKINGHAM,Enoch-19-20-60-61(2)-
143;Joshua-121(2);Thomas-193
BUCKLER,Joel-167
BUCKLES,Abraham-66
BUCKLEY,Isaac-64
BUCKMAN,John-155-159
BUELL,George-139(3)-143;Samuel-
40-151;Walter-100
BUFFIN,William-61
BUFFINGTON,Jacob-200;Jahiel-9-
46-47;John-9-46(2);Jonathan-46
BUEKLEY,Isaac-64
BULLA,Thomas-30(2)-31;William-
104(2)
BULLOCK,Stephen-82
BUNCH,Richard-37
BUNDY,Josiah-100-101-127(2);Sam-
uel-173;William-112
BURBRIDGE,Elijah-65;Robert-65
BURCH,Arnold-76;Charles-18;
Henry-70
BURCHAM,Daniel-71-146
BUREN,Daniel-69
BURGESS,John-30;Nelson-51(2);
Walter-27
BURGETT,Henry-19;Jacob-57
BURGOINE,Horatio-82a(2);William-
123(2)
BURKE,Elisha-15-16-79;Hardin-158;
Hausberry-158;James-7-40-75-130;
John-10;Stephen-16;Thomas-3(2)-
23-27(3);Ulick-15(2)-123;War-
ren-90;William-16
BURKDOL,Abraham-42
BURKELL,Solomon-86
BURKETT,John-150(2)
BURKHALTER,Abraham-65
BURKSHIRE,Deckey-48
BURNETT,see Barnett;Jacob-57-68-
69-70(3)-80-81-111(2)-162;
Robert-28
BURNS,Bernard-164;James-105;John-
66;Joseph-164;Robert-174;Thom-
as-7
BURROWS,see Barrows;Aaron-12(2);
Elhanan-151;Ephraim-74-149;
James-148(2);Stephen-43-72-73(2)-
76;William-103-106
BURT,John-159;Zepheniah-25
BURTON,Allen-71
BUSH,John-140-155(2)
BUSTER,William-16
BUTCHER,George-70
BUTLER,Amos-61(5)-62(3)-89-112(2);

Beal-28-67-109-112;Eli-111;
Enos-112(2);Hiram-109-112(2);
Isaac-200;James-7-175;Joseph-55;
Joshua-64;Nathan-183(2);Noble-
10;Stephen-51-58-75-76-89;Susan-
na-33-67;William-61-109
BUTT,Henry-155(3);John-154-155
BUTTER,James-175
BUTTERFIELD,Warren-130
BUZZARD,Samuel-126
BYERS,Isaac-191;James-136
BYRKILL,see Burkell
BYRKIT,Solomon-86

CABE,Elias-57
CADBURY,Henry-122
CADWALLADER,Abner-115;Amos-35;
Thomas-184
CADY,David-44
CAHILL,William-166(2)
CAIN,Abijah-34;David-79-144;
Hardy-34;Humphrey-149;Jacob-78;
John-103-108;Joseph-34;Joshua-
79;Samuel-24-120-191(2)
CAIRNS,William-57
CALDWELL,Bartholomew-50(2);James-
16-52-57(3)-84(2);John-16(2)-
50-87;Joseph-84-87;Manlove-87;
Samuel-55;Thomas-87;Wesley-135;
William-9
CALFEE,Henry-89;James-169
CALLOM,see Cullom
CAMBRIDGE,Levin-92
CAMMACK,James-39
CAMP,David-80-81
CAMPBELL,Ebenezer-202;Howell-88;
James-202;John-65(2)-80-93-
202(2);Joseph-179(2);Philip-176;
William-2-3-4(2)-6(2)-7-41(2)-
42-102-185-196-197-202
CAMPION,Hysen-24;Kepen-24
CANADAY,see Kennedy;David-67;
Joel-120;John-107;Robert-106(2)
CANAWAY,see Conaway
CANBY,Joseph-114
CANFIELD,Edwin-138;Noyes-49(2)-53
CANNON,see Kennon;Joseph-139
CAPPER,Thomas-23
CARBAUGH,Abraham-47
CARD,John-22
CARLEY,Justice-134
CARLOUGH,Abraham-10
CARLTON,Isaac-48;Jonathan-89
CARMAN,Jacob-192;John-127
CARMICHAEL,John-172
CARNEY,Edward-59-94

CARPENTER,George-147;Joseph-137
CARR,John-24
CARSON,see Cason;Adam-19;Aquilla-
43;David-67;Elijah-65;James-61;
John-20-78;Joseph-21;Robert-138;
Thomas-113(2)
CARTER,John-40;Mordecai-33;Sam-
uel-201(2);Thomas-87-122-181;
William-63
CARTWRIGHT,Ahaz-125-126-193-194;
John-29;William-25
CARVER,Christian-4;William-4
CARY,George-163
CASE,Aaron-154(2)-155-159;Henry-
58;Isaiah-116(2);Jacob-66-65-
95;James-51-137;Nancy-59;Nath-
aniel-114;Peter-155(2);Samuel-
58
CASON,see Carson;Elijah-65;Thom-
as-113;William-64(2)
CASSADY,John-14;Levi-35;Robert-
123;Wear-84;William-123
CATEY,Henry-112-172;William-174
CATHCART,James-86
CATHER,Robert-90(2)
CATTERELL,Bradbury-59
CATTERLINE,John-67
CATLIN,Horace-45;James-167
CECIL,Elizabeth-199(2);Jacob-
199(2);James-199(2);John-199(2);
Magdalena-199(2);Sarah-199(2)
CHADWICK,Samuel-184
CHAMBERLIN,Aaron-41;Horton-69(2);
William-3-4-41-51-54-122
CHAMBERS,Benjamin-5-9-47;James-
94-97;Manuel-17;Minor-70-144;
Samuel-198
CHAMNESS,Anthony-112
CHAMPION,Thomas-131
CHANCE,James-81-166;John-75-
166(3)
CHANDLER,Henry-196(2)-202;Robert-
131(2);Shadrick-202
CHAPMAN,John-59;Jonathan-91;
William-91-172
CHAPPELAW,William-123
CHARLES,Daniel-185-195;Samuel-
33-116-118
CHASE,Leonard-9;Salman-153
CHEEK,Francis-9;Page-9
CHEESEMAN,Richard-113
CHENAULT,Abner-87(2)
CHENOWETH,Abraham-39(2)-128;Jacob-
128(3);John-182(2)-194(5);Wil-
liam-39(2)-126-194
CHERRY,Isaac-188

CHIDESTER,Daniel-137
CHILDERS,Benjamin-78
CHITTENDEN,John-148
CHIVINGTON,John-23
CHOATE,Cautious-3;Seth-4
CHRISMAN,Jacob-201
CHRISTY,John-137
CHUNN,Thomas-110
CHURCH,John-155-160
CHURCHILL,Asahel-81-166;Joseph-75
CILLEY,Joseph-20(2)
CLANCY,Daniel-140
CLANTON,Edward-27
CLAPP,John-189
CLARK,Amaranda-93;Austin-73;Bar-
  zilla-43;Benjamin-18-110;Carle-
  ton-13;Daniel-31-103;Dennis-14;
  Ephraim-104;George-50-53-69-
  135(2)-138-144;James-117-121;
  Jedde-136(2);Jesse-34(3);Joel-
  45;John-54-72-88-107-148;Lewis-
  148-169(4);Nelson-177(4);Olive-
  83;Pharaoh-115;Rowana-93;Sam-
  uel-160;Thomas-17-58-92-98-161-
  169;William-20-26
CLARY,William-93
CLASSFORD,Alexander-200
CLAWSON,Abner-34-125(2);Edward-
  27;Josiah-34;Mahlon-129;William-
  34-173
CLEARWATER,David-62;Jacob-61;
  Reuben-60
CLEMENTS,Adam-139;Caleb-171;
  Isaac-112;Jacob-139(5);Jesse-
  77;John-48-169;Richard-90
CLENDENING,Evert-50;John-21
CLENNY,Curtis-115-194
CLEVELAND,Luther-152(3)
CLEVENGER,Daniel-110;Thomas-114-
  184
CLIFTON,Benjamin-13;John-13(3)-
  123
CLOSE,David-5(2)-6-8(2)
CLOUD,Baylis-15;Henry-47(2);
  James-14(2)-15(2)-17;John-17-
  178;Jonathan-99;Ramey-15;Wil-
  liam-14-21-57-84
CLOUGH,Ezekiel-202;Moses-202;
  Timothy-202
COATS,Isaac-119;James-185;John-
  119-186;Thomas-54-119-186-187;
  William-165-187
COBURN,Joseph-48
COCHRAN,Aaron-130;Enoch-133;John-
  71;William-48-135
COCKEY,Richard-20-61

CODDINGTON,William-169
COE,William-22
COEN,Edward-71;Josiah-170(2);
  Thomas-170
COFFEY,Spencer-160
COFFIN,Andrew-41;Duncan-189;
  Hervey-106;Hezekiah-54;Levi-
  184-186;Stephen-187
COFFMAN,John-199
COGGESHALL,Tristram-112(2)
COLE,Adam-71;Eleazer-72;Hart-
  shorn-163;Harvey-150;Hugh-147;
  James-15-81;John-73-74;Joseph-
  71-144-145;Martin-145;Samuel-
  74-130-195-199;Silas-145;Sol-
  omon-81;Thomas-46
COLEDIN,Caleb-136(2)
COLEMAN,Elias-38;Jonathan-99;
  Rolland-26
COLES,Thomas-48
COLLER,Jacob-199(2);Magdalena-
  199(2)
COLLETT,Charles-91(2)-95;Isaac-
  118
COLLIER,Thomas-90
COLLINS,Amos-192;Henry-8(2);
  Hugh-132;John-31-62(2)
COLLIVER,Richard-19-96
COLLUM,see Cullom
COLTHOFF,Frederick-159
COLUMBIA,John-51
COLWELL,see Caldwell
COMBS,Edward-154;John-70-82a;
  Joseph-195:Micajah-195;William-
  143
COMER,Robert-35;Stephen-113
COMMONS,see Cummings
COMPTON,Henry-21;Jacob-10;James-
  35
CONARROE,Richard-184-193
CONDON,Curtis-167
CONE,Charles-19;Gustavus-15;
  John-166
CONGER,David-77;Enoch-76(2)-
  77(2)-152;Josiah-182;Moses-58;
  Zachariah-76
CONKLE,Elizabeth-193
CONKLYN,Samuel-195(3)
CONLAN,Hugh-56
CONLEY,Isaac-27;James-43;John-
  97-173;Lemuel-153
CONN,James-122;William-89
CONNER,Abner-18;Daniel-7(2)-96-
  122(2)-134(2);David-96-120;Ed-
  ward-51;Isaac-7;James-12;John-
  7-58-59-81-82a-85(2)-88-141;

Reuben-82a;Richard-17;Timothy-134;William-82-82a-83-118
CONOVER,James-85;John-101-85
CONRAD,Christian-139
CONSLEY,Thomas-31
CONSTABLE,Mary-188(2);Thomas-188
CONWAY,Charles-118(2)-119;Daniel-47(2)-132;James-48-96(2);John-135;Robert-48(2)-132;Simon-48-68-132(2)
CONWELL,Elias-50;Francis-165(4)-168(3);James-80(2)-81-82a(2)-83(2)-158(2)-165(9)-166(8)-167(2)-168(8);Jeremiah-168
COOK,Andrew-50;Charity-34;Cornelius-106(2);George-122;Isaac-3-33-65-114;Jacob-3-117-140;James-106;John-2-167;Joshua-43;Mary-34;Nathan-100-174(2);Samuel-138;Seth-115;Thomas-65(2)-136(2);Ulysses-78;William-34-106;Wright-65
COOKSEY,Jonathan-162;Thomas-155-162;Zachariah-93-141
COOLEY,Isaac-169;Thadeus-12
COON,Isaac-22;James-201
COOPER,Christian-4-147(2);Eli-148;Ezekiel-198;Isaac-127(2);John-127-187(2);Moses-86;Thomas-41(2)-95-166
COPELAND,John-110;Jonathan-23;Samuel-187
CORBET,Jeremiah-127;Richard-126
CORBIN,Elijah-93
CORNELIUS,Absalom-15;George-137;Greenbury-101;William-8
CORNELISON,Andrew-125
CORNELL,Thomas-109
CORNWELL,Samuel-191(3)
CORT,George-125
CORY,see Curry;John-195
COSAIRT,Albert-4;Peter-104
COSSINS,Joseph-149
COTTON,see Lotton;Isaac-191;John-144(2);Nathan-68;Nathaniel-68;Ralph-46-68-70;Robert-71;William-68-69-70(3)-71(2);Zachariah-69
COULTER,John-21
COURCIER,John-124
COURTNEY,John-46
COVERDALE,Jacob-13;Perry-139-142
COWGILL,Caleb-107-117
COWLES,Rice-150
COX,Amy-121;Benjamin-33-105-118(2)-119-173-186-187(2);David-190-191;James-33;Jeremiah-30-33-

35-104-120-121(2);Jesse-105(2);John-67(2)-105-118(2)-167-187;Jonathan-105(2);Joseph-66(2)-100-121;Joshua-121-186(3);Levi-102;Martin-128(4);Simon-118;Solomon-121;Stephen-103;Thomas-105-165(3);William-67-80-105-106-174
COZINE,Martin-10-51
CRABB,James-112
CRAFT,Caleb-44-46(2)
CRAGUN,Caleb-89-164;Elisha-89
CRAIG,George-68(3);69(5);Jacob-61;James-172;Robert-5;Stephen-18-30
CRANDELL,Elihu-92;Elisha-92
CRANE,James-13-49-196(2);Jonas-15;Jonathan-25;Ruth-25
CRANER,Joshua-112;Thomas-112-173(2);Washington-175
CRAPPER,Bela-176;Joseph-176;Silas-175
CRAVENS,Joseph-120;Thomas-18
CRAW,Jonathan-54
CRAWFORD,Alexander-141;David-179(2);Samuel-102;Thomas-105-106;William-22
CRAWL,Joseph-42
CRAWLEY,James-165(2);Joseph-168;Milton-164-165
CREEK,John-26(6);65-96
CREEKMORE,William-165
CREW,Joseph-108;Josiah-184;
CREWELL,see Crowell
CRIPE,Abraham-87(2)
CRISLER,Allen-83(2);John-83;Thomas-83.
CRIST,G.-9(2)-25-65-82;John-81-83-167
CROATT,Joseph-42
CROCKER,Benjamin-18;John-53(2)
CROGGESHALL, see Coggeshall
CROMAS,William-199
CROMWELL,John-67;Vincent-24
CROOKS,James-23;William-61
CROOKSHANKS,Nathan-92;Nathaniel-15
CROSS,Aquilla-15(3);Cyrus-77
CROUCH,Andrew-97;Benjamin-52
CROWELL,John-21-171;Martin-42
CRUM,Abraham-88;Daniel-43-47(3);48-135
CRUMP,Rhoda-90
CRUMRINE,John-130(4);Peter-38
CRUTZ,Charles-40
CULBERTSON,Francis-111;Robert-

111-114
CULL,Hugh-32
CULLOM,William-45-73
CULLY,Thomas-64-65(2)-82
CULP,Cornelius-44;John-179-191;
Joseph-45-147
CULVER,Aaron-69;Michael-29-67
CUMMINGS,Alexander-61;Cornelius-
92;David-3(2)-10-45-46(2)-52-
53-54-71;Ezekiel-101;Isaac-32;
James-200;Nathan-101;William-
59-97-100-113-176(2)-200(2)
CUNDALE,John-49
CUNNINGHAM,Francis-127;James-42;
John-2(2)-3-53-144-149;Robert-
41;Samuel-53-66;William-66
CUPP,Philip-156
CURRY,see Cory;;Daniel-19-124;
Henry-164;James-6-22-90-132;
John-81-166(2);Thomas-166
CURTIS,Spencer-52
CUSMIERCIK,Albert-148
CUTTER,Cyrus-44-45-57

DACE,Robert-8
DAGGETT,Henry-15
DAILEY,Edmund-128(3);George-
183(2);James-24;Jesse-131
DAINES,Hiram-188-189
DALE,Alexander-84(2);Joseph-84
DAIMAZZO,James-71-144
DANBY,Thomas-57-97
DANIEL,Moses-44
DANNER,Jacob-192;Joseph-202
DARBY,Henry-135
DARE,see Dace;Abiel-23
DARLING,Jacob-53;John-53(2)-138;
Thomas-12-138
DARNEY,Hugh-148
DARST,see Durst;Jacob-21
DART,Amos-59;Diodat-132;George-
48;Joseph-60;Moses-59;William-
48-74
DASHIELL,Charles-75-121;John-
49(2)-75
DAUBENHEYER,Peter-147
DAUGHERTY,see Doughty;Ann-90;
Henry-59;James-75-84-100;John-
75;Sarah-76
DAUS,Anthony-162
DAVEE,see Davis
DAVENPORT,Jesse-30;Martin-28
DAVICE,see Davis
DAVIDSON,Alexander-156-160;Elias-
174;John-11-30-31-51-57;Moses-
174;Robert-13-55-123;Samuel-160;

Silvanus-174(2);William-174
DAVIES,see Davis
DAVIS,Allen-125;Benjamin-68-127;
Charles-87;David-111-140;Drew-
ry-38;Dunham-46;Elisha-154(2)-
159;Enoch-119-186;Giles-155;
Henry-80-126-193;Israel-17-18(2);
James-6-22(2)-29-155;John-12-
46-48-51-59-107;Jonathan-100;
Joseph-187(2);Leroy-182;Lewis-
5;Mathias-156;Miles-193;Moses-
116;Nancy-75;Nicholas-68(2)-
71(3);Paul-84;Peter-22(2);Reas-
on-87;Spencer-75(2);Stephen-21-
38(2);Thomas-69-71-148-149-186;
Timothy-9;Vincent-64;Ward-
141(2);Waymouth-193;William-60-
111-123-138(2)-140-180;Zachar-
iah-24-96
DAVISON,see Davidson
DAWSON,Charles-9-11-12-52-53,
James-173;Jesse-95;John-10-11(3);
12-53;Matthias-94-99;Thomas-95;
William-53
DAY,David-97;Stephen-152(3)
DEAKINS,James-62;Robert-181
DEAN,George-75;Thompson-137
DEARDORF,Peter-101
DEARKHUSING,John-141-153
DEARMAND,Alexander-14;Milton-
141(2)
DEATH,George-95;James-95;John-95
DEBAUN,John-165
DEBOLT,Andrew-198;Benjamin-198;
George-198(2)
DECKER,Christopher-159
DEFORD,Thomas-166
DEHAVAN,Samuel-168
DE FOREST,Delawzun-5
DELANY,John-90
DE LEBAR,Aaron-95
DELL,see Odell,Dill;James-104(4)-
112
DEMARD,see Demaree
DEMAREE,Henry-147-149;Jacob-14;
Peter-32-45(3)-68
DEMARIS,see Demaree
DEMENT,Richard-11
DEMOSS,John-9
DENMAN,James-85;John-22;William-
84-85
DENMOYER,Nancy-188
DENNIS,Elisha-86-97;Jacob-44
DENNISTON,John-95;William-22(2)-
95
DENNY,Adam-153(2);Mary-19;

Richard-66;William-200(4)
DENTON,John-107;Lewis-176;William-107
DERRICKSON,Joseph-117-183(2)
DESERKIE,Francis-69
DETRAZ,John-69
DEVERAGE,Peter-38-193(2)
DEVINGER,Barnet-157
DEVORE,Thomas-196-197
DEWEESE,Lewis-14-58
DEWITT,John-5-45
DEXTER,Isaac-8(3)
DICKENS,Joel-15-57-84
DICKER,Joel-84
DICKERSON,Daniel-41;Griffin-68;
John-40(2)-41-49-63-64-69(2)-
72(2)-73(2)-144;Robert-79-87;
Townsend-49;William-40-144;Zebulon-49
DICKEY,William-84
DICKMAN,Henry-155;Herman-155(2)
DICKS,Zachariah-109(3)
DIEL,see Dill
DIFFENDERFFER,Henry-2(2)-15
DIGGS,Armsby-118;Benjamin-178;
Henry-177;William-108(2)
DIKE,George-25
DILL,see Dell;Henry-50;John-187;
Nicholas-170-187;Valentine-142-170
DILLON,Jesse-102;Luke-102
DIIMAN,Andrew-42
DIMMITT,Miles-104;Thomas-103;
William-103(2)
DINKINS,Alexander-156
DISERINS,Francis-69
DIVERS,Patrick-52
DIXON,Arthur-82-85;John-5-6-52-
127(2);Mathew-82;Plat-84-85;
Silas-127
DOBBELING,Herman-142
DOBSON,Benjamin-35
DODDRIDGE,John-97-98-99(2);Philip-98
DODSON,Daniel-161;Edward-160;
John-98-118;Major-27-28;William-68(2)-161
DOLA,William-160
DOLEY,John-175
DOLPH,Benjamin-147
DOISON,see VanDolson;James-151
DONAHOE,Patrick-2-4-122
DONNER,Amos-43
DONNEY,see Downey
DORRELL,William-133
DOUGHTY,Ann-90;Edward-132;John-

77;William-104-173
DOUGLASS,Andrew-43-132;Jackson-
2;Robert-59;William-54
DOW,Joseph-71
DOWDEN,Samuel-11-138
DOWNEY,Alexander-132;Amos-43;
James-43-45-133;John-43;Richard-
43(2)-132(3)-133
DOWNING,see Dunning;Francis-18;
Samuel-127-128
DRAKE,Benjamin-4-130-154(3)-155+
177(2)-179(2)-180(3)-185-186(2)-
187-188(2)-190(2)-191-195-200(3)-
201;Dillard-6;Jesse-132;John-34;
Robert-5-40
DRAPER,Joseph-35
DRENAN,David-29
DREW,William-62(2)
DREWER,William-15
DRIGGS,Asel-177
DROGE,Charles-150(4)
DRULEY,Nicholas-27-28(3)-32; Samuel-28
DRURY,Edward-101(2);Samuel-88
DUBOIS,Abraham-8(2);Alexander-
63-182;Benjamin-8-44-46;Isaac-
63-182;Jacob-63(2)-108-109;William-24-60-63
DUFOUR,John-40(2)-130
DUGAN,John-31;Samuel-21;Thomas-2
DUGGINS,Henry-177
DUHME,Herman-154;John-157
DUKES,Stephen-129
DULL,see Dill
DUMONT,Abraham-70(2);Peter-112
DUNBAR,Seth-53-83;William-29
DUNCAN,Peter-90;Richard-80-170;
William-62-110
DUNGAN,Benjamin-95;James-95;
Joseph-96
DUNHAM,David-29-67;John-121
DUNLAP,James-131
DUNLAVY,Francis-57
DUNN,Gersham-77;James-23;John-
78-128(2)-132;Micajah-11;Silas-
97;Thomas-128;William-123(2)
DUNNING,Michael-134(3)-148
DURHAM,David-136;George-76
DURST,see Darst;Abraham-22
DUSKY,Dennis-21;Lemon-43
DUTIEL,Eugene-69
DUTTARROW,Henry-37;Peter-37
DUTTON,David-9
DWELLE,Elisha-156
DWIGGINS,James-36(2)
DWYGER,Edward-52

DYE,James-192-202(3)
DYER,George-115;William-98
DYKZ,Hyronimous-182

EADS,Jonathan-62;William-58(2)-
 60-63
EAGER,see Egar,Eggers,Eaker
EAGIN,see Agin
EAKER,William-25
EARHART,see Arehart
EASTON,Samuel-86
EASTOP,see Estep
EATON,Thomas-24;William-24
EAVES,Henry-72
EBLEN,John-200(3)-201
EDMOND,Christian-105-174
EDWARDS,Alexis-192(2);Benjamin-
 176(2);Eli-117;Jonathan-119-187;
 Joseph-133;Nathan-187;Robert-
 177;William-31-187
EGAN,see Agin,Egar;William-79-157
EGAR,John-82a
EGBERT,William-170
EGGERS,Daniel-29;James-24
EGGLESTON,Miles-60(2)
EHLER,Michael-76
ELDER,Dele-9;John-147;William-29
EIDON,Thomas-58
ELIASON,see Ellison,Allison;
 Joshua-111
ELLERMAN,Gerhard-153;Herod-146-
 151;John-142;William-30
ELLIOTT,Abraham-104(2)-107;Asa-
 28-29;Benjamin-36-92;Daniel-25;
 Exum-110;Israel-67-111;Isaac-38;
 Jeremiah-104;Job-37(2);Marshall-
 147;Nathan-36-126(2);Riley-53-
 54-137;Robert-8-35-43-132;Sam-
 uel-12(2);Seth-179;Spencer-107;
 Stephen-37;Washington-32(2);
 William-103(2)
ELLIS,Bevan-183;Enos-41-134;
 Isaiah-183;John-67-110-136;Jon-
 athan-193(3);Lewis-183(2);Otis-
 48;Shubal-118
ELLISON,see Allison,Eliason;
 Elisha-157(2);Obediah-54
ELLISTON,Amos-174
ELLSWORTH,William-190-199(2)
ELMORE,Achillis-88;Archelaus-107
ELTZROTH,John-117-118-119(2)
ELWELL,Abraham-63;Amasich-63
ELY,Adam-66;Jacob-201;Martin-192
EMANUEL,Joseph-148
EMBREE,David-100;Jesse-40(2)-
 44(2)-72(5)-73(2)-74-77(3)

EMERT,Andrew-195(2)-198
EMMARD,Peter-143
EMMICK,see Emrick;Jacob-129
ELMITT,John-66
EMRICK,see Emmick;David-70;John-
 130(3)
ENDERHEADON,John-162
ENDSLEY,Andrew-67;Hugh-67;John-67
ENDLEY,Thomas-98
ENGEL,John-57-78
ENGLISH,Charles-8;John-8;Wil-
 liam-6
ENT,Samuel-46
EPPIG,George-153
ERB,David-64
ERNNOUT,John-72
ESLEY,John-96-109
ESPEY,Hugh-5(5)-49;John-49;Rob-
 ert-5-6
ESTE,David-17-68-73(2)-178(2)-
 188(2);Obadiah-64-93
ESTEB,Isaac-27-28
EVANS,Benjamin-113-114;Ebenezer-
 200(2);Edward-190;James-191-
 192;Jared-53;Joseph-87-100-
 113(3);Samuel-12-104-124-151-
 190;William-81-182
EVELETH,Amariah-3
EVERETT,Isaac-119
EVERTON,Mary-30
EWART,Thomas-78;William-192(2)
EWBANK,John-11(6)
EWING,David-65(2)-89;John-63-
 195(2)-196;Robert-104-130(2);
 William-66
FABER,George-153(2)
FACTOR,John-153
FAGANS,James-191
FAGELY,Sophia-77
FAGER,Jacob-199
FAIK,Daniel-199
FAIRBANKS,Hiram-138
FAIRCHILD,George-200
FAIRFIELD,David-108
FALKINGTON,Stephen-13
FALL,George-125;Tetrich-47-48-135
 William-67
FALLEN,see Fullin;David-93
FALLIS,George-147(2);John-147;
 Martin-147(2);Richard-147;Sam-
 uel-147
FARLOW,George-98(2);John-28;
 Uriah-94;William-28
FARMER,George-10
FARQUHAR,Andrew-176;Mahlon-177
FARRELL,James-71-102

FARRANS,George-193;Henry-194(2);
    John-193;Matthew-90;Michael-14;
    Robert-73-74;Samuel-129(2)
FARRER,Thomas-93
FAULKNER,Jacob-151;Mary-76;Rob-
    ert-76
FAUROT,Jacob-81;John-81-158(2);
    William-157
FAUSSETT,Jacob-19-20(2)-124;Rob-
    ert-21;Samuel-124
FAY,Hiram-141
FEELAND,see Freland;John-53
FEELY,John-146
FEES,see Hees
FEGER,Joseph-57
FEHRMANN,Bernard-159
FEIST,John-137
FELIX,John-140
FELLOW,John-38
FELTER,see Fetter
FENDER,Gabriel-109;Henry-110
FENIMORE,Samuel-173-174
FENTON,John-43;Samuel-41-42
FERGUSON,Alexander-24;Arthur-66;
    George-63;Joseph-67;Nimrod-86(3)
    Sarah-112;William-18;Zachariah-
    109
FERREE,David-92
FERRIS,Isaac-138(8);Isaiah-54;
    John-9-49-81(2)-82-161(3)-162;
    Joseph-77;Josiah-54;William-34
FERRY,Gabriel-159
FETTER,Jacob-16
FETTIG,George-154
FIELDS,Jackson-190;Lansford-189;
    Martin-197(2);William-189(2)
FIFE,William-105
FIFIELD,Benniah-50
FINCH,Isaac-62;John-77;Jonathan-
    77;Moses-62;Nathaniel-59
FINCHER,Jane-99;John-99(2);Wil-
    liam-99
FINDLAY,James-6-8-9-17
FINNEY,John-130;Robert-195
FISHER,Daniel-67;David-27-67;Ed-
    ward-36;Jacob-178(2);John-26(2)-
    63-90-91-93(2)-116;Martin-97;
    Nathan-37;Thomas-37;Wilhelm-142
FISK,William-44
FITHIAN,Mason-104
FITZPATRICK,Bartholomew-80-162-
    164
FIX,John-98
FLACK,see Flake;Adam-51-75;Rob-
    ert-22
FLAKE,Armour-137;Michael-7-51(2)-

75-76-137;Nathan-72;William-7-51
FLANEGAN,Matthew-30
FLASH,Christina-128(2)
FLATER,John-126(2)
FLEMING,Alexander-47;Daniel-
    170(2);Jacob-188;James-196;John-
    74(3);Mitchell-19;Peter-30-67;
    Samuel-73(2)-74;William-46
FLETCHER,David-96;Jesse-96
FLEWELING,William-171
FLINT,John-23(5)-64;Joseph-86-98
FLOOD,William-82
FLOOR,Christian-141
FLORY,Emanuel-150(2)-202;John-129
FLOTRON,Francis-79
FLOWERS,Michael-18
FLOYD,Joseph-177
FOLAND,John-104
FOLSOM,Jeremiah-49;Richard-72
FONTS,see Fouts
FOOSNER,see Fusner
FOOT,Dan-40
FORBES,William-50
FORD,John-38;Nathaniel-125;Obed-
    iah-13;Samuel-148
FORDIN,James-90
FORDYCE,James-22-90
FORESTER,James-141(3)
FORRIS,see Voris
FORTNER,Levi-59
FORWOOD,Samuel-145
FOSDICK,Samuel-128(2)-155-163(2)-
    174-178-188(2)-189;Thomas-13
FOSSET-see Fausset
FOSTER,Isaac-54;James-55;John-
    12-39;Lowry-78;Thomas-139
FOTTRELL,Andrew-185(2)
FOUCH,John-80
FOULK,Aaron-137
FOUTS,Andrew-28;Jacob-29-30(3);
    Michael-103;William-27-30(2)-
    31-34
FOUTSCH,John-124
FOWLER,Benjamin-150(2);John-114;
    Philander-173;William-102-106
FOX,Elijah-100;James-100-135-148;
    John-98-100;Peter-202;Philip-98;
    William-29-104
FRAKES,Aaron-64;Joseph-48;Nath-
    an-72
FRANKFATHER,David-129(2)
FRASE,Adam-128
FRAZEE,Joseph-147
FRAZER,Andrew-193-194-199;David-
    117(3)-118-183;Eli-104(2);Fran-
    cis-184;George-96-114;Gideon-114;

James-114-184(2)-194(2);John-
12(2)-116-183(2);Joseph-183-184;
Mary-145;Samuel-47-74-145;Stan-
ley-175-177;Thomas-114-183(2);
William-47-74-99-134
FREAD,William-142
FRECH,Conrad-138
FREDENBURGH,Isaac-144
FREE,George-202(2);Philip-203;
Spencer-111-112
FREEL,James-19-96
FREEMAN,Isaac-137;Joshua-195;Na-
than-121-193;Richard-64;Solomon-
145(2);Thornton-116;William-
181-182
FREELAND,see Feeland;John-77;Rich-
ard-53
FRENCH,Henry-102;Jacob-102-112;
John-15(2);Joseph-152
FREY,Durs-55
FRIEND,Martin-202
FRIILING,John-164
FROLIGER,Arbagoost-139
FROMAN,Jacob-12-73-151;Paul-42-
72;Thomas-75
FROST,Barnet-114
FRY,see Frey;John-191;Theodore-
190;Thompson-190
FUDGE,David-183
FUGIT,John-58
FULGHUM,Frederick-38(2);Joseph-
36(2);Michael-38(2)
FULLEN,Samuel-92
FULLER,Isaac-13-78;James-11-80;
John-11;Samuel-82a(2);Sarah-11;
Thomas-11;Valentine-142-170
FULLIN,see Fallen;John-85
FULTON,David-42
FUNKHOUSER,Abraham-54
FURNAS,Christopher-201;John-26
FURROW,Jacob-192;William-202
FUSNER,Adam-142;John-143(2)

GAAR,see Garr
GABLE,see Goble
GAITHER,Basil-55-139
GALE,George-45
GAILAHER,Charles-173
GAILION,see Galyean
GALLOWAY,Joseph-127
GALYEAN,Jacob-103;Nathan-169;
Thomas-103
GANC,Aaron-89;Daniel-89
GANT,see Grant;Britton-16-58-141;
Calvin-169(2);George-124;Giles-
58-141;Stephen-162(2)

GAPEN,Eli-107
GARD,Aaron-29;Benjamin-24;Daniel-
156-179-190;David-12(2);Ephraim-
8;Josephus-29;Lot-29;Moses-178;
William-41
GARDNER,Eliab-85;Elial-26;Isaac-
25-26(2)-27-115-117;James-48;
John-103-144;Stephen-19-64-Wil-
liam-147
GARNER,Henry-18;John-13
GARR,Abraham-31-32
GARRETT,see Jarrett;Henry-37-
104(2);John-100(2)-111;Nathan-
23-100-111;William-98
GARRISON,Abraham-11;Elijah-10-15;
James-13(2);John-10-186;Lorenzo-
154;Samuel-80(2);Silas-11
GARSETT,Eli-110
GARVIN,John-93;Thomas-93
GARY,James-154
GASS,Joseph-117
GASTON,Robert-3
GATES,Noah-41;Timothy-202
GAVIN,James-61
GAYLEY,Sayrs-41
GAYMAN,David-58
GEBHART,Henry-199
GEIGER,Jacob-26
GEISSER,John-57
GEORGE,Andrew-79;Benjamin-17;
Henry-156;Hiram-163-164;John-
167;Samuel-86;William-79(2)-
89-159
GERARD,Peter-60;Stephen-146;Thom-
as-117-119-187;William-82a
GERHARD,John-199
GEST, G.-190;John-46
GIBBINS,John-6-44(2)-64
GIBBS,Charlotte-64;John-132(2)-
133-148;Robert-128
GIBSON,Christopher-13;James-8-
133;John-10-15-16;Levi-132;
William-48-133
GIFFIN,Samuel-135(2)
GIFFORD,John-72
GILBERT,Amos-45-68;John-131;
Jonathan-98
GILBRAITH,David-30-111;John-112;
Robert-100-110-111
GILDEWELL,see Glidwell
GILLESPIE,Joseph-97;Martin-71;
Robert-44(3)
GILLIGAN,Charmick-24;Cormack-24
GILLILAND,John-4-68-71-110;
Thomas-71
GILMAN,Jonathan-78-83. ;Thomas-86

-215-

GILLUM,Grover-192;Hiram-199;Jon-
  athan-83;Thomas-82a-175(5)
GILMORE,George-79;Jonathan-78
GILPATRICK,Rufus-190
GILPIN,Henry-176;Joseph-177;
  Thomas-177
GILTNER,Asahel-91-172;George-82-
  91-172
GINN,Gabriel-82a
GIRARD,see Gerard
GIRTON,Christian-23;Felix-32
GISH,Christopher-201
GISSER,Frederick-161
GIST,Elihu,194;Silas-35
GISTON,Christopher-23
GITTINGER,John-130
GIVAN,George-77;Gilbert-75-136;
  Joshua-77
GLAIZE,George-83-88(2)
GLASDON,James-12
GLASS,John-48;Robert-75-151
GLENN,Hugh-89-73;James-89;Jos-
  eph-89-147
GLENNY,Curtis-115
GLESNER,Benjamin-199;Moses-199
GLIDWELL,Martin-91;Robert-60-64-
  83
GLOSHON,John-164(2);Nicholas-163
GLOVER,Zachariah-84
GLOYD,Asa-76
GOBLE,Abner-22;Boni-22;Isaac-160;
  Robert-26;Stephen-59
GODDARD,Richard-4
GOFF,William-24
GOLAY,Elijah-41;Elisha-41;Lewis-
  78
GOLD,James-18(2)
GOLDING,George-137(2);James-153
GOLDMEIER,Henry-155
GOLDTRAP,John-20
GOLL,Joseph-152
GONDIER,James-62
GONELL,Cornelius-69
GOODERT,John-150(2)
GOODING,David-29
GOODMAN,David-199;William-199
GOODNER,Daniel-148(2);Jacob-6-
  45(2)-148;John-44
GOODRICH,Abijah-8;Rebecca-186
GOODWIN,Benjamin-167(3);Daniel-
  82;Enoch-155;James-11;Jehu-11;
  John-11(2);Joseph-176-182;Rich-
  ard-195;Samuel-91;William-120;
  Seth-58;   /44
GOOS,John-154
GOOTEE,James-13

GORDON,Charles-28-66-100;George-
  47;James-64;Orville-83-171(4);
  Rufus-5;Thomas-182;William-81(2)-
  166(2)-172(4)
GORSUCH,Elijah-198(2)
GOTT,William-127
GOTTSTEIN,Joseph-55(2)-57
GOUDIE,James-20-62;Samuel-20-61
GOYER,John-151
GRAFFIN,Jacob-111
GRAHAM,Abner-10;David-61;James-
  145;John-145;Reuben-196-199;Sam-
  uel-146(3);Stillwell-145;Tim-
  othy-146;William-145
GRAMANN,John-156
GRANDEN,Philip-11-108
GRANDY,Thomas-129
GRANT,Britton-58
GRASS,Joseph-117;see Gross
GRAVA,Francis-157
GRAVE,see Grove;Enos-32-37;
  George-47;Jacob-120;Jonathan-37
GRAY,Absalom-186;Alexander-172;
  David-24;Isaac-145;James-62-126-
  146;Jesse-193-197;John-62-73-
  82a;Joseph-127;Nathaniel-176(2);
  Robert-20;William-132-133
GREEN,Daniel-82a-168;Eli-7-9;
  Frederick-71-145;Henry-184(4);
  James-25-39(3);Jesse-108;John-
  2-116;Martin-5;Peter-188(8)-
  189(5)-190;Robert-64;Thomas-
  179(2);William-10-52-57-65
GREENER,John-140
GREENSTREET,Jesse-106;Thomas-109
GREENWALT,Atolf-159
GREENWOOD,Niles-53
GREER,Daniel-82a;James-25-85;
  William-65
GREGG,Andrew-201;David-200-201;
  Silas-95;Smith-201;Stephen-20;
  Thomas-20;William-201
GREGORY,William-136
GREINER,John-40
GRUWELL,Asa-99;John-94(2);Sam-
  uel-99
GRIFFIN,see Graffin,Giffin,Grif-
  fith;Jacob-111;John-161
GRIFFITH,Jackson-71(3);Mary-146;
  Stephen-86-98
GRIMES,James-32;William-32
GRIST,Simeon-93
GRISWOLD,William-153
GRO--NDYKE,Nicholas-15
GROGAN,John-57
GROSS,see Grass;John-125-126-129-

147-163(2);172-178(2)-179-182(4)-
190-194(2);Joseph-3
GROVE,George-7-47-150(4);Henry-7;
Jacob-120-199;James-150;see
Grave
GROVER,Ira-60
GUILE,Joshua-16(2)
GUILFORD,Nathan-46-47
GUION,Thomas-135(2)
GULICK,Joseph-44
GULLETT,Ezekiel-127;George-128;
Isaac-127-128;Robert-47
GULLEYS,Simon-124
GULLION,John-43;Robert-73-132
GULLIVER,Stephen-104
GUSTIN,Benajah-91;Samuel-91
GUTHRIE,Archibald-80
GWIN,John-106
GWINNUP,James-158(3)

HABADANK,William-155
HACKLEMAN,Abraham-62;Isaac-84;
Jacob-85-141;John-141
HACKMAN,Jacob-14;John-14
HADLOCK,James-43
HAFF,Frederick-73
HAFFNER,Joseph-80
HAFFORD,John-58
HAGEMAN,Simon-42
HAHN,Joseph-138(2)
HAINER,James-47
HAINES,Asa-176;Ezekiel-78;George-
76;John-35-71-115;Joseph-76;
Joshua-44-46;Matthias-44-46;
Stephen-176(2);Wright-175(2)-176
HAISLEY,Jesse-112(2);Joseph-112
HAIZIER,William-111
HALBERSTADT,Anthony-58-61;John-
60;William-143
HALE,James-191;John-120(4)
HALL,Amy-105;Charles-63;Daniel-
152;David-138;Gabriel-144;John-
55(2)-58-140;Joseph-11;Richard-
6;Samuel-42;Thomas-52;William-85
HALLEN,Joseph-113 ──→ 120(2)
HAILINAN,James-144(2)-149
HAISEY,James-160(2)
HAISTEAD,Robert-89-169(2);
Thomas-169
HAM,John-115
HAMBLIN,Levi-4-54
HAMILL,Samuel-49;Thomas-144-
145(3)
HAMILTON,Adam-84;Asa-8;James-2-
6-48-72-82a-143;John-7-44;Rob-
ert-2-54;Samuel-20;William-77(2);
Yale-82a
HAMMER,David-114;William-184
HAMMERIE,Balthasar-140
HAMMOND,Abraham-22;Amos-148;
Lewis-6;Michael-143-186
HAMPTON,Abraham-112;Andrew-33;
Jacob-33(4)-113
HAMSON,Thomas-155;see Hanson
HANCOCK,Elisha-75;Henry-136;Jos-
eph-88;Peter-76;William-75
HANDLEY,James-83
HANDORF,see VanHandorf
HANDSCHY,Henry-196-197(2)
HANN,Peter-17;see Hahn
HANNA,Abram-97;Henry-71-79;John-
65-66(2)-108;Joseph-63;Robert-
143;Samuel-48
HANNIGAN,Peter-50
HANSEL,Christopher-23(2)-24;Dav-
id-23;George-23;Thomas-52-53
HANSON,Benjamin-92;Bordan-102
HARBERT,Ebenezer-48(2);Samuel-
47-135;William-52
HARBOUR,Madison-187
HARBUCK,John-178
HARDIN,Charles-36;Henry-12;John-
31-99-142;Thomas-86
HARDING,Aaron-125;Eliakim-99;
H.-9;Henry-9
HARDWICK,John-174;Martin-105
HARDY,Charles-82a;Daniel-60
HAREGEDER,Benjamin-24
HARKNESS,Anthony-14(2)
HARKRIADER,Joseph-127(2)
HARLAN,Elihu-36-39-88-129-198-
202;George-65-109;Jacob-35-202;
James-129;John-96;Jonathan-181;
Joshua-36-65-109-129;Nathan-35-
130;Samuel-92(3)-93-96;Valen-
tine-36-96(2)-129-198
HARLEY,John-82
HARMAN,see Herman
HARNS,see Harris;Coonrod-187(2)
HARP,Nehemiah-81
HARPER,Ezekiel-53-135;John-10-
125;Joseph-10;Thomas-21-22;
William-91
HARPHAM,Henry-14-165-171
HARRELL,Chester-21;Gabriel-37;
Jesse-45;John-93;Moses-83(3)-
168;Stephen-82a;William-82a
HARRIS,see Harns;Benjamin-33-
175(2);Buckley-165;Caleb-4;Cor-
nelius-6;David-115;Elijah-127-
179;Harvey-39;Jacob-2-3-148(3);
James-103-112;John-118-176(3);

-217-

Josephus-186;Joshua-25;Obediah-113-114-115-183;Robert-2;Simeon-187(2);Willis-186

HARRISON,Charles-59;Gideon-35-201;Harvey-127;Job-59;William-97

HARSHMAN,Abraham-198(2);Henry-198-199;Jacob-198(2);Joseph-199(2)

HART,Abraham-150-151;Acklin-4;David-32;Isaac-142;Jeduthan-149(2);Stephen-167;William-124

HARTER,Joseph-21

HARTLEY,Norton-183

HARTMAN,Henry-97

HARTPENCE,James-14

HARTUP,James-31

HARVEY, B.-67-114(2);Caleb-67;Charles-90;Francis-29-67;Henry-101;Isaac-103;James-28-90;John-30-35-99(3)-100(2)-101(3)-102-104-111-173(2);Michael-114;Pryor-177;Robert-29-111;Thomas-64;William-90-101-114-143

HARWOOD,Philip-17

HASBROOK,Daniel-58

HASKIN,Jonathan-117

HASS,see Hess;Samuel-130

HASTIE,William-131

HASTINGS,Matthew-111;William-111

HATCH,Ralph-49

HATFIELD,John-22-23;Jonas-104;Thomas-104

HATHAWAY,Abiathar-85;Daniel-77(2);Manning-57

HATTON,Robert-131

HAUPTMAN,Frederick-55

HAVEKOTTE,Henry-159-160(2)

HAWKINS,Amos-35;Henry-113(2);John-35-79-80-88-157;Nathan-79-113-157(2);Reuben-161

HAWORTH,George-108;John-88-107;Joel-25-26-28(2)-29;William-108-118

HAYDEN,Stephen-24

HAYMOND,Cyrus-83;David-61

HAYS,Abijah-11-17;Caleb-42;David-61;Jacob-59;James-12-76(2)-151;John-18-59;Joseph-9-11-12;Samuel-88;Walter-11(2);William-63-148

HAZEN,Isaac-139(2);John-139;Nathaniel-152(2)

HEADLEY,John-149;William-149(2)

HEADY,Benjamin-68;George-144(2)-145;Stillwell-68

HEAP,William-124(2)

HEARD,William-201

HEASTON,David-117-181-187

HEATH,Daniel-134;James-21;Samuel-68-86-156

HEATON,Abraham-95;Daniel-95(2);Ebenezer-95(2);Jonas-107;Samuel-107;Seth-151;Thomas-91

HEAVENRIDGE,John-25

HEAVREN,James-82

HECK,Philip-60-142

HECKILBURN,Thomas-136

HECKMAN,William-200

HEDGEPETH,Arthur-196

HEDGER,Catherine-44

HEDGES,Charles-131(2);Nathaniel-131;William-41

HEDLY,see Headley;John-62

HEDRICK,Abraham-19;Jacob-62;Thomas-80-164(2)-165;William-19(2)

HEES,Francis-2

HEHEMAN,John-162

HEIMS,James-177;Samuel-120-190(2);William-58-82a(3)

HEIMICK,Jacob-99

HELTON,Alexander-182

HENDERSON,Elias-17-65(2);Hiram-123;Hubbard-35;Isaac-10;John-84-85-123(2);Nathaniel-65;Samuel-31-32;Shadrick-67(2);Silas-123;Thomas-58-62(2)-93-94-129-172;William-58-60(2)-84(2)-160

HENDRAY,Richard-98

HENDRICKS,Absalom-202;Henry-97;William-50

HENEKE,Joseph-164

HENLY,Jesse-28;Micajah-115

HENRY,Arthur-21-61;John-137;Joseph-164;Stewart-45;William-64

HENWOOD,John-97

HEPBURN,Edward-2(2)-12-40(2)-44(2)-69(2)-72(6)-73(5)-74-77(3)

HERBERT,see Harbert

HERMAN,Andrew-31;David-30-31;John-137

HERNDON,Elliot-58-85;Gideon-140(5);Nathaniel-58-59;Thomas-140(3)

HERRON,David-152(2);John-152.

HERSHEY,Christian-50(3)

HESS,see Hass;Bernard-155(2);Elisha-130

HESSLER,Jacob-71

HESTER,Thomas-114

HETTZEL,Samuel-127-128

HEUSTIS,Oliver-50-54

HEWITT,Robert-6;William-135-
136(2)
HIATT,Amos-185(2);Christopher-
118;Ebenezer-36;Eleazer-36;
George-135;Isaac-32;Jehu-179(2);
John-179;Jonathan-118-187;Moses-
119(2);Wells-139;William-32-33;
Zachariah-32-37-101-113-119(2)
HICKLE,Debolt-86
HICKMAN,Francis-186(2);Ithamer-
161;Jacob-186;James-179(2);John-
120-188;Joseph-118-180-186-192;
William-186
HICKS,Isaac-101;James-79(2)-
158(2);Samuel-188
HIDAY,Jacob-21
HIERS,John-82-167(2);William-95
HIGBIE,Abraham-149;Nancy-136-
137(2);William-8
HIGDON,Benjamin-154;Peter-11
HIGGINS,Amos-30;Jonathan-99(2);
Nicholas-193(2)
HIGHLAND,Richard-140
HILDEBRAND,Benjamin-147;Michael-
70(2)
HILDRETH,James-158;Jeffrey-167
HILER,Abraham-59;Peter-142
HILL,Aaron-30-193(3);Andrew-184;
Benjamin-34(2)-35-181(2)-182;
Benoni-121(2);Eli-78;Henry-121-
196;Hiram-193;James-44-103;
Jesse-87;Joel-110;John-176;Jon-
athan-98-135;Matthew-196(2);Na-
than-99-100-101-104;Philip-183;
Phineas-51-77;Robert-30-35-100;
Samuel-96;Thomas-30-77;William-
121
HILLMAN,Benjamin-96
HILLELICK,Andrew-22-23(2)
HIMES,George-79-117
HINDMAN,Thomas-79
HINDS,Benjamin-21-75;Henry-91;
James-8-122;Michael-90;Peter-
90;Reizen-151
HINESLEY,James-198
HINGEL-see Ruigel
HINKLE,Henry-199;Joseph-198
HINKLEY,Judah-19
HINKIN,Gerhard-161
HINKSON,John-14;Thomas-85
HINNENKAMP,Bernard-158
HINSHAW,Abel-183(3);Absalom-183;
Joseph-120;Phebe-180(2);Solomon-
184;Thomas-119-187-188
HIRT,Jacob-159;John-163;Joseph-
163

HISER,Daniel-6;Jefferson-5
HOBBS,Elisha-164(2)-169;Elizabeth-
159;Emery-14(2)-64-83;James-89;
Robert-164
HOBSON,George-105(2);Joseph-101
HOCK,John-192
HOCKETT,Hezekiah-114;Isaac-114-
180;Joseph-114;Moses-112(2);
Stephen-114(2);William-114-119
HODGES,Andrew-134(2);Benjamin-31-
125;George-139;John-105;Samuel-
188;Thomas-55-139
HODGSON,Daniel-118;Hur-114-115;
Isaac-180;James-136;Solomon-102
HODSON,Amos-114-119;Annual-180;
Enos-114;Robert-180;Zachariah-
106(2)
HOFARD,Martin-140
HOFFER,Frederic-138
HOFFMAN,see Huffman.
HOFFNER,Benjamin-83
HOGAN,David-9-50
HOGARTH,Edwin-200
HOGSHIRE,James-75
HOGSTON,Milass-183
HOILMAN,David-175
HOKE,John-129-130
HOLCHER,George-141
HOLCOMB,Rufus-76
HOLDEN,Martin-4
HOLDERMAN,Joseph-32;William-186
HOLDRON,David-15;Dennis-15
HOLE,John-195(2);William-195
HOLLAND,Francis-90;Henry-95;
James-129;Peter-129;Robert-
94(2);William-160(2)
HOLLCROFT,George-69-144
HOLLETT,George-31;Mark-31;
Thomas-31
HOLLIDAY,James-173;John-21
HOLLINGSHEAD,James-26
HOLLINGSWORTH,Abraham-26;Benja-
min-181;David-25-65-109;Eli-182;
Ezekiel-25;George-63(2)-84;Hen-
ry-25-106;Isaac-65;Jacob-65;
James-26-65-107;Joel-65;John-65;
Jonathan-65(3);Joseph-66-105(3)-
107;Levi-65-196;Pierce-180-181;
Richard-65;William-95
HOLLOWELL,see Howell;Jonathan-
123(2);Luke-178;Samuel-123;
William-54-123-178
HOLLRAH,Gerhard-172
HOLMAN,George-31-32(2);Jesse-7;
Joseph-27-110-111;William-27-32
HOLMES,James-35-36;Samuel-30

HOLT,Joseph-98
HOLTSCLAW,James-86;William-86
HOMAN, see Howman
HONOUR,Matthias-186
HOOKE,Michael-102
HOOL,John-152(2)
HOOPS,Jacob-18
HOOVER,Andrew-33-34(4)-103;David-
104;Henry-28-99-100-173;Jacob-
67-104;John-168;Peter-99(2)-
128(2)
HOPKINS,Augustus-175-177-178-
189(2);Benjamin-136;Thomas-122-
130;William-93
HORN,Jacob-39(2);Jose-38
HORNADY,John-64
HORNBACK,James-170
HORNBAKER,Benjamin-182
HORNBERGER,George-152(4)
HORNER,Jacob-64(2)-65(2);Job-117;
Levi-39-117;Michael-47;Samuel-
117(2)
HORNEY,Solomon-87-108;William-14
HOSKINS,Jonathan-117
HOTCHKISS,Luther-147(2)
HOUGH,Ira-113;John-92(2)-93;Jon-
athan-112;Joseph-22-26-110(2);
William-36-71
HOUGHAM,Aaron-95(2);Garvis-95;
Graves-95;Jonathan-96
HOUSCHANTT,Henry-140
HOUSE,Jacob-28-29;Joel-29;Lyman-
79;William-192
HOWARD,Ebenezer-62;Isaac-91;John-
9-30;Samuel-5-113-122
HOWE,Ebenezer-25-29;James-59;
Silas-6(2);Thomas-142(2)
HOWELL,see Hollowell;Chatfield-
23-24(2);Jacob-19;Jason-106;
Joab-19;John-24;Samuel-14-22;
William-14
HOWERY,John-77
HOWLETT,William-5
HOWMAN,Ebenezer-95
HOZIER,Isaac-195;Lewis-101;Wil-
liam-100(5)-111
HUBBARD,Auston-72;James-46;John-
46-134(3)-171;Joseph-186;Samuel-
171;Silas-36
HUBBLE,Richard-17(2)
HUBER,Henry-154;Michael-164(3)
HUDDLESTON,Job-97-105;Jonathan-
26- Thomas-10-122
HUDLOW,David-183
HUDSON,Corbly-59-60(2)-91;Mary-
91;William-17

HUEGEL,Joseph-163;Lewis-164
HUESTON,David-63;James-25;John-
133;Matthew-40(2)-83;Paul-77;
Priscilla-51;Robert-74;Samuel-
24(3)-66-125;Tenant-74
HUFFMAN,see Hoffman;Andrew-99;
Benjamin-50;Conrad-10;Daniel-46-
160-161;George-179(2);Henry-177;
Isaac-35;Jacob-177(2);Jesse-177;
John-64-154(2)-179-185;Jonas-98;
Robert-99;William-179(2)
HUFFORD,David-48-135
HUGHELL,Jacob-103;Joseph-172;
Thomas-171
HUGHES,John-53-85-96-135;Matthew-
63;Thomas-66
HULETT,Amos-174
HULICK,Barrent-9;Joseph-44
HULL,Jehial-187;John-123;William-
77-78-152(2)
HUMISTON,Jason-200(2)
HUMMEL,Michael-154
HUMPHREY,Arthur-3-4-6;Ebenezer-3
HUNNEMANN,Stephen-164
HUNT,Abraham-118(2)-184;Bazil-
107-176(4)-177(3);Bezaleel-176;
Charles-66(3);Edward-98-118;
George-66;Ira-112;James-176;
Jeremiah-51(2);Jesse-7-9-125;
John-7-24-27-32;Jonas-24;Jona-
than-17;Lebini-33;Lewis-134;
Miles-173(2)-174-176(3)-177(2);
Robert-10-52-54;Samuel-20-62(2)-
73-78-89(3);Smith-66;Thomas-12;
Timothy-66;William-28-37(2)-107-
176(3)
HUNTER,Henry-25(2);James-148-149;
John-45;Joseph-53
HUNTINGTON,Jonathan-8-71;William-
179-186
HUNTMANN,Henry-164
HURST,Perry-173
HUSER,Merritt-69
HUTCHINS,Benjamin-102(2)-107-116-
192;David-174;Denson-106;Isaac-
115-116-192;Jesse-192-201-202(2);
John-201;Jonathan-106-174;Jos-
iah-196;Thomas-116;William-201
HUTCHINSON,Milton-170(2);Sally-
42;Samuel-10;Solomon-10
HYTER,Abraham-13

ICE,Frederick-143
IFF,John-143-153
ILER,Jacob-40
ILIFF,James-197;Wesley-192;

-220-

William-197
IMEL,Robert-145;Thomas-145
IMRIC,see Emrick
INCE,James-50-52
INGLE,Rhoda-202
INLOW,Henry-192
INMAN,John-75;Stephen-50
IRBY,John-134
IRELAND,John-35
IRVIN,George-87-181;John-100-
181(3)-183(3)-184;Robert-181(2);
Stephen-128;William-101-111-
128(2)
ISH,see Ash;George-101(2)
ISSENMAN,Joseph-139
IVES,Hoel-39(2)

JACK,Adam-87;Robert-190(2);
Samuel-2-3(2)
JACKEWAYSE,Clark-73
JACKMAN,Atwell-166;William-58-
143;see Jackson
JACKSON,Andrew-87-89;Asa-136;At-
well-61;Enoch-10-11;Ezekiel-
11(5)-15;James-86-125;John-
107(2)-152;Joseph-106-125;Mor-
decai-131;Robert-52;William-120-
125(2)-128(2);see Jackman
JACOBS,Highland-141(2);James-30-
120(2);Jasper-121;John-120;
William-168
JACOBUS,John-12-122
JAMES,David59-93;Enoch-9(3);
Jesse-197;John-5(2)-47-48-69(2)-
116;Julius-44(2);Levi-4(2)-6(2)-
41-122;Pinkney-2;Thomas-59
JAQUITH,Asa-53
JARMAN,Azariah-74
JARRELL,see Jarrett;Elisha-
181(2);Manliff-183
JARRETT,see Garrett,Jarrell;Bent-
ley-109(2);Eli-110;George-109;
Levi-109;William-98-109
JASEN,John-59
JATTER,Tobias-200
JAY,Evan-174;James-116;John-113;
Samuel-107
JEFFREY,Job-117;Joel-117;John-
116;117;Thomas-184-194
JELLISON,Henry-126;Samuel-39(2)
JELLY,Andrew-42;Samuel-8(2)-10
JENKINS,Crocker-16-124;David-98-
173;Oren-124;Prince-16;William-
192
JENNINGS,Timothy-141(2)
JENNY,Abel-104

JESSUP,Abraham-34;Asa-143;David-
133;Eli-133;Ezra-133;Hezekiah-
37;Isaac-33-34-45-113(2)-133;
Jacob-34-113-117;Jonathan-100;
Nathan-112;Timothy-114;Walter-
133-148(2);William-39
JETER,Fielding-169(5)-170
JEWELL,John-190
JEWETT,Moses-135-136(2)-139;
Parker-176(2)
JINKS,Gideon-81(2)-166
JINN,see Zinn
JOB,James-84;Samuel-27(2)-28
JOHN,Enoch-19-20;Robert-20(2)
JOHNSON,Abel-74-150;Alexander-
186;Abraham-43;Archibald-84;Ben-
jamin-25-75(2);Caleb-57;Casper-
15;Cave-14;Charles-79;David-49;
Edward-55-83-139-164-165(2)-
198;Gabriel-70;George-49-63-
136-151;Hadley-170;Henry-151-
175;Isaac-76-93;Jacob-149(2)-
199(3);James-30-37(2)-146-150;
Jesse-113-114(2)-115-180-182-
193;John-41-50-63-114-142-184-
198;Jonathan-51-178(2)-183;
Joshua-106;Josiah-106(2);Lewis-
84(2)-85;Moses-132(2);Nathan-
51;Nelson-181;Phineas-59;Silas-
115;Stephen-112;Thomas-107-186;
William-4-79-117-150;Young-
150(2)
JOHNSTON,see Johnson
JOLLY,Lewis-14
JONES,Abijah-112;Abner-36;Abra-
ham-24;Amos-152-153;Andrew-28(2);
Benjamin-109;Christopher-2;Dan-
iel-105-107-174;David-125;Ed-
mund-110;Edward-110;Eliakim-76;
Elisha-170;Elizabeth-169;Garret-
91;George-31-32-79;Hillary-109;
Hubbard-43-48(2);Isaac-150;
James-13(3)-15-18(2);46-60-74;
John-51(2)-97-105-109-121;Josh-
ua-157;Lewis-3-4;Michael-48-
181(2);Nathan-36;Philip-19-91-
172;Robertson-18-59(2);Samuel-
103;Sarah-90;Simpson-89;Stan-
ford-172;Stephen-202;Thomas-147;
William-27-31(2)-32-90-109-156-
192
JORDAN,Daniel-190-192;John-28-
32(2)-105(2)
JUDD,Orrin-13;Phineas-13
JULIAN,see Julias;Isaac-101(2)-67
119;Jacob-104;John-82a-201;Rene-
119

KNOX,John-82a
KOBB,Richard-20-168
KOCH,John-155-160
KOONS,Jasper-30
KORCHER,Francis-137
KORDENBROCK,John-162
KRAMER,Gerhard-164;Henry-159
KRUTZ,see Crutz
KUHN,Philip-138-152
KUMKLE,John-130(2)-144
KUNT,William-67

LACY,John-101(2)-116;William-116
LADD,Christopher-82a(2)-83;James-
  107;Joseph-116;Moses-93;Noble-
  93;William-106(2)
LAFUZE,Samuel-24
LAIRD,James-90;Jesse-9
LAKE,Elijah-14;William-55
LAMB,Barnabas-174;David-98(2)-
  175-176(2);Esau-116;John-137;
  Josiah-113;Nathan-176;Thomas-
  34-102-110;William-176
LAMBDIN,John-14;Matthew-15;Sam-
  uel-15;William-70
LAMBERT,Cortland-197;James-
  197(2);Josiah-94-98-103;Nathan-
  iel-78
LAMBERTSON,Samuel-68;James-151;
  Thomas-75(2)-76-151
LAMBKIM,Ezra-44;Judson-44
LAMPTON,John-131
LANCASTER,Mallory-69;Wright-31-
  97-98
LANDERS,Kimbrow-72;Silas-138
LANDIS,David-24
LANE,Smith-85-98;William-190
LANGDON,Elam-201
LANGSTON,Bennet-66;Hiram-166
LANHAM,Henry-79
LARIDE,James-171
LARRISON,George-13-18;John-17
LAREW,Benjamin-45;Garret-45;
  William-2-100
LASLEY,David0181(2);Eli-174;
  Moses-174(2);Samuel-174
LASSELL,Joseph-40-148;William-
  148
LATHAM,David-69
LATHROP,David-15
LAUGHLIN,William-89
LAVERTY,John-121
LAWELLIN,Benjamin-120;Mashach-
  33-108-119;Michael-33
LAWMAN,Daniel-27;John-27
LAWRENCE,Abraham-139;Daniel-54(2)

55-139(2)-181;George-55-170-202;
  Isaac-54(4)-55(5)-152(2);James-
  54;Johannes-55;John-78-152;Mich-
  ael-145;Philip-54;Valentine-
  54(4)-55(4);William-131(2)
LAWSON,Wiley-189(2)
LAYCOCK,William-191(3)
LAYSON,John-99
LAYTON,David-51
LAZENBY,Joshua-38
LAZIEUR,Laurence-54
LEANLY,Bryan-27
LEAP,Samuel-68
LEARNED,James-44
LEASURE,Henry-134(2);William-148
LEATHERBURY,Charles-70-145
LEE,Abraham-19-24;Chester-178(2);
  David-69-144;Eli-93;Jacob-67;
  John-143;Joseph-23-76;Sarah-93;
  Stephen-80-94;William-144
LEEK,Hiram-45
LEEPER,John-11;William-22-55
LEESON,James-50(2);Richard-100
LEFAVER,John-192
LEFORGE,Jacob-140(2);John-58-59(2)
LEFTER,Uriah-167
LEGG,William-4
LEIGHTY,Jacob-139;John-55-139;
  Simon-178-179
LEITHNER,Gregory-57
LEMASTER,Isaac-9
LEMON,Adam-55;Lemuel-19-24(3);
  Martha-74(2);William-16
LENNEN,Peter-25-26(2);Samuel-26
LENOVER,James-T)0;Joseph-74
LENTZ,Nicholas-70(3)-71-145
LEONARD,Abner-21;Philip-188-191;
  Nathaniel-104;Samuel-99(2)-100
LESCHE,Bernard-157;Charles-193;
  John-157
LESTER,David-70(2)
LEVI,Isaac-18-42
LEVISTON,James-109
LEWIS,Abraham-27(2)-28(2);Benja-
  min-18;Caleb-109;David-80;Eben-
  ezer-16;Ephraim-55;Ezekiel-125;
  George-55-140;James-39-148(2)-
  185-190;Joel-191(3);John-46(2)-
  49-112(2)-145-180;Jonah-152(2);
  Jonathan-15-57(2);Joseph-102-113-
  181;Josiah-49;Matthew-161;Morgan-
  161;Nathan-80;Reuben-16;Richard-
  53-112-113;Samuel-41-172;Thomas-
  66(2)-143;William-50-54-55-66-
  68-95-109-115-124;Zimri-115
LIBBERT,John-146

-223-

LIDDIE,see Little
LIGGETT,John-75-151
LIGHT,Enoch-175(2)-178;Jacob-
45(2)
LIGHTNER,John-154
LIKELY,Henry-52
LILLARD,John-7
LILLY,Frederick-155(2);Thomas-102
LIMEBACK,Adam-3-5-122;William-131
LIMPUS,Elijah-80-83;Enoch-83(2);
Isaac-82a
LINDLEY,Abraham-41-71;Daniel-130-
197;Demas-130-196(5)-197(2);
Francis-149;James-112
LINDSEY,Elijah-8;George-46;James-
46-51(2)-137;Jeremiah-120;John-
4-70-75;Thomas-102;Vincent-46
LINN,Daniel-47;James-172;John-
124-William-91-172
LINTON,Demsey-180
LINVILLE,James-168;John-157-158
LIPSCOMB,John-161
LITTLE,David-196(2);Elias-46-
134;Jacob-27-97;John-143;Lewis-
27(2);Peter-97;William-12
LITTLETON,Thomas-53
LITTRELL,Samuel-96-109
LIVINGSTON,Adam-76;John-47-151
LLOYD,Humphrey-125;Jeremiah-194;
John-129;Joseph-15;Thomas-194;
William-123
LOCK,Benjamin-73;Hezekiah-194;
Isaac-176;John-146;Peter-40-68-
70-73(2);Richard-73;William-106-
174
LOCKHART,Moses-85
LOCKWOOD,Harvey-81(2)-166;Jared-
166;John-166
LODER,Daniel-74;James-74(2);
John-87
LOGAN,Daniel-93;James-61;John-60;
Samuel-82-93;Thomas-93;William-
64-65
LOGEE,Andreas-153
LOGG,William-4
LOLLAR,Ephraim-153;Joseph-190(2)
LOMAX,Abel-116;Joseph-174(2)
LONDON,see Loudon
LONG,Henry-110(2)
LONGFELLOW,Badger-182;James-35-
183;John-35(2)
LONGREAR,John-184
LONGWORTH,Nicholas-15-43-44-45-
46-48-59-68-69-71-73(5)-79(8)-
91-117(7)-118(4)-119(12)-120(5)
LONNEY,Thomas-5-122(2)

LOOKER,Samuel-13
LORD,Jesse-75
LORING,Israel-8;Thomas-129
LOSEAR,George-198
LOSEY,Solomon-146
LOSSET,Robert-21
LOSTUTTER,Peter-6(3)-8
LOTTON,Ralph-46;Thomas-132
LOTZ,Abraham-200(4)-201
LOUDERBACK,Abraham-94
LOUDON,Daniel-144-145
LOUGH,John-111
LOUGHMAN,Henry-42
LOUNSBURY,Daniel-171(2)
LOVE,Hanson-61;Israel-154;James-
154;Robert-126
LOVELACE,Seneca-40-41
LOVELL,Robert-100
LOW,Alexander-136
LOWDER,John-84-128
LOWER,Christian-202(2)
LOWES,James-17;Josiah-17;
William-17
LOWRY,William-86
LUCAS,Joseph-192;Simeon-192(2)
LUCK,Hezekiah-129
LUCKEY,Abia-131
LUDLOW,Stephen-12(2)
LUSE,Robert-20
LUTCHEN,William-76
LUTZ,Michael-191
LYBROOK,Henry-29;Philip-29(3)
LYKINS,Andrew-107(2)-117;James-
117;John-175;Jonas-175;Philip-
109
LYNAS,Joseph-13;William-58
LYONS,Mr.-39;Aaron-170(2);Ethel-
4;James-58-146-151;Joseph-72-
146;Joshua-141;Oliver-149;
Robert-5-43;William-141

McALLISTER,Alexander-111
McANALLY,William-141(2)
McBETH,Francis-134
McBOOM,William-27
McCABE,Archibald-74;John-83(2)-
149-168
McCAFFERTY,James-59
McCALLUM,Duncan-69(2)-132;James-
144;Neil-69
McCAIMAN,James-61
McCANN,Alexander-92;James-19
McCANNON,John-123
McCARTY,Abner-61(2);Benjamin-17-
18-61(3)-78-82(2)-82a(2)-86-108-
110;Enoch-62-141;James-72;Job-97;

-225-

McWHIRNEY,James-140(3);Samuel-140(2)
McWHORTER,James-91;John-91;Tyler-89

MABBETT,Anthony-28
MACEMORE,John-202
MACKLIN,John-25
MACY,Albert-174(2);James-22;Jonathan-102-106;Joseph-105-173-174;Robert-37;Seth-199;William-25
MADDEN,Solomon-112;Thomas-25-95
MAHONY,John-140
MAJOR,Daniel-13-123(2)-124-140-142-153;William-14(3)
MAKIN,Matthew-190
MALCOM,James-105-144
MALIN,Jacob-152;Joseph-146
MALLACK,David-93;George-93;James-93
MAISON,Aaron-162
MAISTON,Thomas-80
MANAN,Aaron-101;Jacob-82;Michael-82(2)
MANESS,Alsey-197;Christopher-199
MANLEY,John-92;William-92
MANLOVE,George-87
MANN,Allen-38-121;John-61-126(2);Samuel-39;Tobias-138
MANNING,Abraham-193(2);Amos-182;Ann-182;Caleb-193(2);Hezekiah-102;Reuben-193(3);Richard-194
MANSFIELD,Jared-40-130
MANTLE,George-50-52
MANUEL,George-191
MANWARING,Richard-14-60-91;Solomon-13-91;Thomas-18
MAPES,James-70
MAPLE,John-93;Stephen-165;William-80
MARBIE,Calvin-6
MARFORT,John-147
MARGERUM,Hermon-72
MARINE,Charles-116;Jonathan-113(2);Tibi-115;Ziba-115
MARKLAND,James-123;Jesse-193;Thomas-194;Washington-194
MARKLEY,John-177;Moses-177(2)
MARLIN,Charles-156-162;Cicero-163;Samuel-162;Wesley-156-157;William-80-156-162(4)-164(2)
MARLING,John-69
MARMON,Joseph-17
MARNAN,William-82
MARSH,Charles-133;David-132;

Jesse-193;Webster-71;William-42-66
MARSHALL,Aaron-106;David-15;Miles-106;Robert-82;Ruley-120;Samuel-76;Thomas-106;William-12
MARTIN,Aaron-32;Abner-67;Daniel-87;Eli-155;Elisha-186;Henry-66(2)-135;Isaac-33-96-100-101;James-26-55;John-128;Luther-194;Moses-83;Samuel-195;Stephen-89;Theophilus-74-150;Thomas-67;William-78-80-156
MARTINDALE,James-104(2)-200;Jesse-104;John-104;Martin-113;Moses-26-103-105(3)-112;William-104
MARTS,Peter-86
MASCHGER,Frederick-141;Henry-141(3)
MASON,Charles-126;Daniel-55-139;George-55(3);Horatio-81-83;Jacob-54;James-60;Joseph-139;Philip-55;Thomas-36-37
MASSEY,James-120(2);Peter-172;Isaac-33-120;William-116
MASTERS,Isaac-12
MASTERSON,James-128;Smith-128-196
MATER,Hannah-87
MATHEREL,Jane-45
MATLOCK,John-93
MATSTON,Thomas-162(2)
MATTHEWS,Aaron-166;George-59;Isabella-156;James-57;Michael-186
MATTOCKS,see Mallack;George-93;Giles-91;Jacob-92;John-93
MATTS,Isaac-42-43(2)
MAUDLIN,Benjamin-35-111
MAULSBY,David-174
MAXSON,Jonathan-193
MAXWELL,Hugh-26(2);Jacob-25;John-111;Moses-23;Richard-35(2);Thomas-167;William-82
MAY,Thomas-10
MAZE,Adam-108;David-92;Eli-108;Samuel-92-108
MEAD;Eli-52;Hugh-80-165;Luther-43
MEANS,John-76;William-41-144
MEDCALF,Isaac-28(2)
MEDORN,Christopher-123
MEISKER,David-75-76;George-42
MEEK,Bazil-32;Isaac-30;Jeptha-109;Jeremiah-30(2)-31-117-119;John-30(2)-34-35-106;Joseph-109;

Joshua-31;William-33
MEFFORD,Elliott-167
MEIROSE,Henry-160
MEISTER,Frederick-139;Joseph-153;
MELENDER,Peter-27
MELL,John-103
MELONE,Charles-83(3)-157(2)-
168(3);John-91
MELTON,David-84;John-114;Stephen-
117
MENDEL,Jacob-76
MENDENHALL,Elijah-173;Griffith-
34;Hiram-175(6);Isaac-99;James-
35;Mordecai-115;Nathan-175;
Richard-118-119;Stephen-37
MENNET,Samuel-69
MERCER,John-59
MEREDITH,David-125;Solomon-36
MERINE,see Marine
MERITT,Archibald-7(2)
MERRICK,John-153
MESSERSMITH,Sebastian-139
METTLER,William-127
MEWHINNEY,see McWhinney
MEYNCKE,Charles-124(2)
MICHAEL,Casper-52;Daniel-137;Ja-
cob-77;Jared-77;John-190;Philip-
52(2)-140
MICHOUD,Lewis-71
MIDDLETON,Samuel-38-39-126(2)
MILBURN,David-135;Joseph-46;
Robert-49-50-51
MILES,Benjamin-7(2)-49;George-90
MILEY,Henry-126
MILHOLLAND,George-162(2);James-
16(2);John-52-58;Mary-62;Thom-
as-16-58-162
MILLER,Abraham-23-97;Adam-57(2);
Alexander-67-69;Benjamin-182-
183;Daniel-23-29-38-53(2)-120-
190;David-132;Edward-133;Elijah-
149(2);Elizabeth-32;George-45-
98-171;Henry-7-15-67-142;Isaac-
98;Jacob-48-119-166(2);James-53;
Job-12;John-21(2)-22(4)-25-42-
43-78-80(2)-88-98-110-131-150-
153;Joseph-8;Levi-12;Michael-77;
Peter-97;Robert-25;Sebastian-
154(2);Sylvester-189-190-191;
Thomas-11-12-24-25-181-182-184;
Tobias-21;William-21-22-25-134-
159-164-180;Willis-75-99
MILLHOUSE,John-201
MILLIKAN,Allen-53;Eli-104;Mat-
thew-53;Samuel-110(2)
MILLIS,George-90

MILLMAN,Robert-174
MILLS,Aaron-115;Benjamin-49;
Cyrus-77;David-17;Henry-106-
173(3);Isaac-10-106(2);Jacob-
181(4)-184;James-49(2);John-69-
106-177;Jonathan-33;Joseph-173-
177(2);Moses-106;Peter-115;Rich-
ard-106;Seth-106;Thomas-116-
184(2);William-115
MILLSPAUGH,James-21;Nathaniel-16;
Peter-16
MILNER,John-19-92(2);William-31-
115
MILTON,see Melton
MINER,Benson-110;Joseph-85;Mary-
29;Richard-24;William-23
MING,Peter-40
MINNEMAN,Frederick-153
MINTS,William-60(2)
MISER,George-98-102
MISNER,Christopher-157;Elisha-
157-159;Henry-79;Jacob-40;
John-20-73
MITCHELL,George-135;Henry-144-
145;John-200;Samuel-37-133;
William-70-73-142(2)
MIXER,Ebenezer-40(2)
MOAD,Luther-43
MOCK,Jeremiah-188;John-191
MOFFITT,Charles-116;Jeremiah-
118(2)-119-121;John-107;Joseph-
118-186;Seth-118-185-186(2)-187;
Stephen-187;Thomas-110;Zimri-
185-187
MONEY,William-201(3)
MONFORT,Henry-117
MONIKER,John-167
MONKS,John-187
MONNET,Samuel-69
MONROE,George-93;Henry-3
MONTAGUE,Zacheriah-41;see below
MONTANYE,Lemuel-41-131(2);
Zachariah-131;see above
MONTGOMERY,James-51-94-95(2)-191;
John-51;Platt-98;Robert-99(2);
William-98
MOON,Malachi-35
MOORE,Adam-152;Alexander-33-34;
Arthur-57(2);Cyrus-40;David-105-
174;Erastus-2;Hugh-5-8-13-14-16-
42(2)-63-68(2)-93-99;Isaac-107;
Jacob-46;James-3-62-102-168;
Joel-28;John-103-118-126-127;
Jonathan-59;Patrick-110-180;
Roderick-2-53;Samuel-16-106(2);
William-63-131

MOORMAN,Archelaus-36;James-108-
116(2)-125(2)-126;Jesse-108-118-
178-179;John-116;Susanna-115;
Tarleton-108(2);Thomas-115(2);
Uriah-107
MORAN,Michael-14
MORCILION,John-69
MOREHOUSE,Nehemiah-74
MOREROD,Jean-41
MORFORD,John-152;William-159
MORGAN,Benjamin-14(2);35(2)-101-
123;Enoch-15-123;James-50(2);
Lorenzo-141;Micajah-36-196(2);
Michael-50;Mordecai-94;Thomas-
20-72-153
MORRIS,Achillis-101-105(2);Amos-
77-152;Benjamin-29;Caleb-104;
George-66;Isaac-101;James-87;
Jehosaphat-87-101;John-23-109;
Nathan-67-104;Robert-90;Walter-
42;William-60
MORRISON,James-33-116;Joseph-59;
Robert-32;Samuel-128-187-189
MORROW,Archibald-64-93;Charles-
168;James-93;John-33-93;William-
134
MORSE,Benjamin-52;Vallorus-133-
148
MORTON,Loring-58
MOSLEY,James-42
MOSS,Demas-51-70;Harvey-152;John-
23;Lemuel-75-77;Samuel-77;Wil-
liam-29(2);Zeally-3(3)-4
MOSSEY,Tence-33
MOULTON,Benjamin-133(2);William-
133(2)
MOUNTS,Caleb-2;David-82(3)-89-91-
160(3)-161(2);Hezekiah-85-91(2);
John-5-102;Peter-160;Providence-
122;Thomas-6-122
MOW,Adam-19
MUCHERLIERD,Barnet-157
MUIR,Mary-12(2)
MULFORD,Caleb-47;Ezra-147;Jere-
miah-43-44;John-198;Richard-52
MULLIN,Lannen-181
MULLONICK,Henry-174
MUMBOWER,Jane-176-177
MUNDEN,Jesse-86
MURDOCK,James-3(2)-65;Jesse-118
MURNAN,William-82
MURPHY,Amos-185;Benjamin-128;Eli-
131;Henry-14;Jerry-10;John-84;
Joshua-113;Mills-104;Robert-
128(2);Samuel-23;William-147
MURRAY,Andrew-166;Arnold-81-

166(2);Coburn-167;Elam-64;Jabez-
126(2)-194(4);James-44-138;Thom-
as-196(2);William-102-169-194
MUSGROVE,Eli-49;John-50;Moses-
50-75
MUTE,John-157
MYERS,Abraham-26;Bernard-164;
Christian-155;Frederick-76;
Henry-142;Jacob-45;Joel-134;
John-26(2)-27-45-67-109-110-
133(2);Jonathan-45(2);Marie-
153;Peter-179;Robert-15;Samuel-
158(2);Simon-45;William-45

NAGEL,Frederick-153
NAVE,Abraham-66(2)
NEAL,Enos-88-104(2);John-88;
Thomas-87-174
NEELY,Isaac-66;Thomas-67
NEFF,John-187;Orange-157;William-
157-158(10)-164-165(5)-166(4)-
167(2)-171(6)
NEISON,Adam-24-58;Charles-42;
David-80;John-71-122;Joseph-4-
22-29-122;Nathan-42;Sacker-15;
Thomas-152;William-19-86
NENTHORP,William-159
NESBITT,Andrew-187;Robert-134
NESTER,Philip-186
NEWCOMB,William-63
NEWCOMER,Peter-76
NEWHOUSE,James-82a;Samuel-82
NEWKIRK,Jacob-63
NEWLAND,Harrod-92(4);James-92
NEWMAN,John-171-172
NEWNUM,William-63
NEWTON,George-44;Henry-37;James-
37
NICEWONGER,Solomon-45-72
NICHOLAS,James-65;William-66
NICHOLS,Enoch-115;George-47(3);
Henry-91;James-65-66-84;John-
185;Lawrence-70(2)-145;Lewis-
134-137;Malachi-38-126(2)-193;
Matthew-95;Thomas-65;William-
66-97-157
NICHOLSON,David-45;James-173;
John-37
NICKERSON,Clark-176;David-45
NICKEY,Christian-190
NICKUM,David-198
NIEMAN,Herman-74-150;John-156
NIENABER,Gerhard-157;John-155-157
NIXON,Andrew-26;John-47-88(2)-135;
Marian-113;Miriam-113;Samuel-35-
184;Thomas-103-110-114;William-
35(2)

NOBBS,John-156
NOBLE,David-92;James-62(2)-109-
149;John-73;Joseph-68-71-72;
Lewis-96;William-73
NOFFSINGER,Absalom-197;Eli-39-128
NOLAND,Daniel-87(2)-97
NORCROSS,Reuben-105
NORDYKE,Benjamin-120
NORRIS,David-92;George-66;John-
61-92-94-109;Richard-7-10(2);
William-65-66
NORTH,David-180(2);Lot-6;Thomas-
6-181
NORTHUP,Perin-53
NORTON,David-67;Elias-115-116;
Jacob-52(2);James-115;John-
163(2)
NORVILL,Thomas-172
NORWELL,Benjamin-90
NOSTODT,George-187
NOYES,Israel-52(2)-53(2)
NUGENT,Benjamin-64;John-64;Rob-
ert-92;William-92
NULL,Henry-33;Michael-168-172
NURRE,John-159
NUTTER,Benjamin-29

OATHOUDT,Isaac-75
ODELL,see Dell,Dill;Daniel-51;
Gabriel-39;Hiram-127;Isaac-96;
James-180;John-49;William-35-
39-127-189-190;Wittoes-183
ODUM,David-87
OFFIELD,Lewis-14
OGAN,Elias-194;Samuel-194
OGDEN,Hezekiah-63;Isaac-23
OGLE,Eli-68;Hiram-68-70(3);Wil-
liam-21(2)-27
OGLEVEE,Joseph-48
OHLMAN,see Uhlhom;John-123-138-
156-160
OLCOTT,Thomas-51;William-51
OLDAKERS,Jacob-101
OLDHAM,Azariah-53;James-67;John-
96;Stephen-96
OLER,Henry-103;Simon-55
OLIVER,David-61;Jeremiah-110;
Nixon-21;Richard-135
OLMSTED,Ebenezer-75;John-75
O'NEAL,David-40;John-40;Michael-
57
ORCUTT,Joseph-188
OREN,Absalom-176;Ephraim-176;
Jacob-177(2);Levi-70
ORMSBY,Oliver-7-122
ORR,Andrew-23;David-22;John-22-

84-144;Joseph-68(2);Timothy-84
ORTMAN,Herman-164
OSBORN,Ambrose-39(2);Caleb-10;
Daniel-32-64-114(2);David-50-75-
106;Isaiah-106;James-63(2);John-
114;Jonathan-89;Thomas-19-63(2)-
94(2)
OSGOOD,Charles-12
OTTO,Henry-155;Jacob-124
OURSLER,Alexander-182(2)
OVERLY,Martin-120;Zachariah-130
OVERMAN,Cornelius-38;Eli-39-111-
114;Ephraim-30-38(2)-39;Isaac-
193;Jason-39;Jesse-35(2);Nathan-
30-39-111;Reuben-114
OWEN,Calvin-142(2);George-90;
Samuel-171
OWINGS,John-149
OWSLEY,Thomas-91(2)
OYSTER,Jesse-188

PAGE,John-59
PALMER,Daniel-25-51;John-54;
Joshua-65(2);Mason-158
PALMERTON,Ichabod-49
PARDUN,Walter-138
PARIS,George-109;James-13;Josh-
ua-15
PARK,Jackson-192;Jacob-11;Jona-
than-8-51;Joseph-11;Micajah-12-
62;Thomas-201;William-71-146
PARKER,Abraham-45;Anselm-58;Ben-
jamin-37;Henry-74-150;Housel-
16-58;James-99;Jeremiah-31;
Jesse-38(2);Joel-38;Joseph-11;
Moses-115;Nathan-194(2);Richard-
101;Thomas-38-39;Timothy-16-58
PARLEE,Benjamin-73
PARMER,Daniel-25
PARROTT,Francis-129-194;Robert-
11;Thomas-129-194
PARSON,Matthias-99;William-4
PARSONETT,James-100
PARVIS,Joshua-142
PASQUIER,Claude-131
PASUIS,see Paris
PATE,Adam-9;Charles-135(2)-146(2);
Daniel-49-50;David-146;George-
74-146(3);Henry-146;Jeremiah-72;
Lewis-146;Randol-146;William-
151(2)
PATMORE,William-146
PATRICK,John-151(2)
PATTERSON,Abraham-129(2);Hezekiah-
112;James-171;John-13-172;

William-111-150-151(2)-190(3)-
192(2)
PATTON,John-3(2)-4;Thomas-96;
William-92
PAVY,Samuel-146
PAWNER,William-21
PAYLEN,Henry-37
PAYNE,Aaron-52;John-5;Stephen-49-
75-77-80;William-162
PEABODY,Hiram-145;Stephen-70(3)
PEACOCK,Abraham-121;Amos-121-
196(2);David-104(2);William-105-
196
PEAL,Enos-104;John-116-125;
Mark-179(2)
PEARSON,Benjamin-34;Ebenezer-76;
Elliott-37;Henry-29;Isaac-118;
John-35-113-116;Matthias-103;
Moses-144(2);Nathan-31;Peter-
115;Thomas-114;William-114
PEASE,Harvey-144(2);Horace-154-
157(2);Perry-194-195(5)
PECK,Henry-64;William-148
PEDEN,John-127;Thomas-130(2)-
201(4)-202(2)
PEDRICK,Phillip-37
PEGG,see Pigg;John-100
PELAFISH,Christian-33
PEISOR,see Pilson;Peter-148
PEMBERTON,Joseph-33
PENTICOST,John-24(2)
PENWELL,David-2-17-62;Eli-2-4-17;
John-62-84
PERKINS,John-84;Joseph-194(3);
Robert-127(2)
PERRIN,Daniel-12;David-52;John-
85(2)
PERRY,Allen-151;Samuel-9
PETAFISH,see Pelafish
PETERS,Henry-46-69;Joseph-17;
Mary-40;Michael-69;Peter-69;
Stephen-46
PETERSON,Henry-150(2);John-13-60-
143;William-111
PETTIGREW,Daniel-78(2);David-78;
Ezekiel-153;Nathan-49-53-135;
Robert-24
PETTY,Daniel-118;Jesse-158;Josh-
ua-3
PHARIS,see Ferris
PHELPS,John-43-72;William-44-72
PHILLIPS,Augustin-152;Charles-
42(2);Gabriel-69;John-52(2)-87-
112;Robert-198;Sarah-76;Thomas-
105-178;William-2-42-131
PIATT,Benjamin-108;J.H.-11-51(2)-

108;Robert-12;William-78
PICKETT,see Beckett,Piggott,Puck-
ett;Benjamin-43-196;John-188;
Rebecca-119-120;William-40
PIERCE,Benjamin-193-194;Burket-
120-188-189(3);Isaac-173;Jacob-
164;Merely-184;Solomon-172;
Thomas-120-186(2)
PIERSON,see Parson,Pearson
PIGG,see Pegg;John-115(3);Valen-
tine-115(2)
PICCOTT,see Beckett,Pickett,Puck-
ett;John-119;Joshua-34
PIGMAN,Adam-92-192;Jesse-92
PIKE,James-183;John-196;William-
99;Zebulon-9(2)
PILES,Elijah-49
PILLRNESSEL,Herman-162(2)
PILSHER,Enoch-117
PILSON,see Pelsor;William-160-
161-163-170-172(2)
PINCH,Moses-62
PINGER,Christian-142
PINGRY,John-177
PIPER,James-63(2)
PIPPEN,Richard-158
PITMAN,Jo.-24
PITTS,Elijah-49;Randall-167
PLASPOHL,John-154(3)-155-157(2)-
164(3)
PLATT,Abraham-115-116-183;Elijah-
180;Gilbert-52-53;Nathan-40-68;
Samuel-184
PLEASANTS,George-71-146
PLEW,Jeremiah-126
PLUMMER,Baruch-93;John-29(2)-93-
159(3);Joseph-54;Levin-93(2);
Luther-138;Sewell-54;William-167
POAGE,Robert-189-190;Samuel-190-
198
POCOCK,see Bocook;Edward-41;
James-41-42
POCQUENEUR,John-139
POE,Willson-153
POIROT,Toussaint-139
POLEET,Squire-7(2)
POLLARD,Allison-175-176(2);John-
93
POILOCK,James-133;Samuel-35
POLLY,David-127;William-127
POND,Henry-160-169;Hiram-91-160;
Warren-169
POOL,John-35(2)-87-115;Thomas-35
POORE,Edwin-128
POPENOE,William-65
POPPE,Ahrend-155;Henry-142

PORT,Aaron-52;James-19;see Post
PORTER,Cornelius-197;James-102-
103-144(2)-188(2)-197;Joshua-82;
Moses-144;Nathan-124;Thomas-50
POST,Aaron-52;James-85;John-98(2);
see Port
POTEET,see Poteet
POTTER,David-129;Elizabeth-195;
John-109-116-117;Martin-144-149;
Thomas-112
POTTS,James-165(2);William-81
POUNT,John-162
POWELL,Benjamin-51;Isaac-156(2);
Jacob-6;James-169;John-196;Oner-
155(2)-156;Philip-127-195-196;
Simon-88;Wilie-63;William-2-196
POWERS,Alexander-79(2)-157;Benja-
min-107;Daniel-64-143;David-63;
Ezekiel-60;James-143(2);John-24;
Jonathan-22;Joseph-27-155;Thom-
as-64;William-60-158
PRATT,Daniel-71
PRAY,Enos-178
PREFOGLE,Peter-59-141
PRESTLEY,David-26
PRICE,Catherine-31;Edward-116;
James-17-59;John-90(2);Joseph-
143;Rice-121;Samuel-59-60;Thom-
as-11-117;William-34-115-174
PRICKET,John-70
PRINCE,David-52
PRIOR,Allen-109;Joseph-109
PRITCHARD,Ezekiel-47-127;James-
47;John-136(2);Samuel-37
PROBST,Frederick-146(2);Henry-
146-150(4)
PROTSMAN,John-71-144
PROVO,Asa-100-180
PRUDDEN,David-52-181(2);Isaac-
123;Sylvester-181
PRUGH,John-190(2);Peter-195
PRUITT,Adamston-160;Matthew-161;
William-145-158
PRUS,John-159(2)
PUCKETT,see Beckett,Piggott,Pick-
ett;Benjamin-178;Daniel-36-108-
182(3)-184(2);Isom-108(2)-178;
John-108;Joseph-108;Thomas-108;
Zachariah-107
PUDERBAUGH,David-190;Jacob-197
PUGH,Alfred-134;Caleb-9;Enoch-9-
12;James-176(3);Jesse-106;Jos-
eph-40-45;Robert-156
PUMPHREY,Blair-161;Nicholas-60-92
PURCELL,Benjamin-74-75-189(3);
John-13-189;Lawrence-75;Samuel-

72;Thomas-48-135;William-14-15
PURSLEY,Hudson-178;James-178(2)
PUTMAN,Ernestus-189(2)-200
PYLE,John-153

QUACKENBUSH,Peter-104
QUAIS,John-163;Nicholas-163(2)
QUICK,Cyrus-140;John-58(3)
QUIGLEY,James-2;John-2-3
QUIN,John-156-161(3)-162(3)

RABB,George-20
RADER,Jane-158;John-164(2)
RAIL,see Rayl
RAILSBACK,David-66-67(2)-109
RAINIER,Joseph-175;Stacy-182
RAINS,Joab-86-88
RAISTON,James-104
RAMBLEY,James-7-95;Thomas-95
RAMBO,Absalom-32;Isaac-110;
Jackson-32
RAMER,David-6;John-45;Peter-74
RAMSBURGH,Joseph-10
RAMSEY,Allen-59;David-185;James-
46-47-74-76-185(2);John-136;
Thomas-43;William-27-59-136
RAMSIERE,Jacob-68
RANCK,John-95
RAND,Thomas-72
RANDALL,John-126(3)-184;Jonas-30-
34(2);William-74-81
RANDOLPH.Jonah-177(3)
RAPP,Maria-138
RARDEN,Moses-19(2)
RASNICK,Lazarus-171
RASOR,George-80-163(2)
RATCLIFF,Cornelius-104(2);Job-
173;Thomas-106
RATHBUN,Edmund-192(2)-193;Hiram-
192(2)
RATTER,see Rutter,Ritter
RAVERS,Edward-149;John-157
RAWSON,Horace-118;Levi-187
RAY,Christian-101;Edward-79;John-
22-135;Lewis-80;Robert-74
RAYL,Elijah-5-122;James-131(2);
John-131;Thomas-41-131;William-
21-42
REAGAN,Nicholas-82a
RECKE,John-164
RECORDS,Thomas-43-137(2);Samuel-
43;William-51
REDDING,Matthias-72
REED,Adam-19;Andrew-61;Archibald-
95(2);Armstead-140;Daniel-19(2);
Hugh-25-65-83(2);Isaac-133(2);

ROOD,William-67-77
ROOKER,William-101
ROOT,Abraham-130;John-130;see Rute
ROPER,Hardy-46;John-31
ROSCHESHOSKI,Peter-148
ROSE,Abraham-62-64;Ezekiel-63
ROSEBROUGH,Robert-68-71
ROSENBAUM,Jacob-141
ROSS,John-23;Joseph-44;Robert-24-
  191;William-6(2)-87;Zedekiah-188
ROTH,John-137;William-199
ROTTINGHAUS,Henry-153
ROUGH,Peter-137
ROWND,Edward-77;John-77-152
ROUS,James-68
ROUSH,Jacob-29
ROWE,Conrad-51;Robert-52-57(3)
ROWLAND,Philip-74-149(2)-151;
  William-14
RCYER,Abraham-129(2);John-130(2)
ROYSDAM,Nathan-99
ROYSTER,Charles-83;Stanhope-20
RUBLE,George-177;Walter-108
RUDICEL,George-17-18-124(2);Jacob
  123(2);Michael-17-18-124;Philip-
  124
RUB,Henry-31;Richard-31-32
RUFFIN,William-20-24-61
RUFFUM,John-15
RUMBLEY,see Rambley
RUMSEY,see Ramsey
RUNYAN,Bonham-103;Peter-88-104
RUPERT,Moses-191
RUSING,William-63-64
RUSSELL,Enoch-81;James-81;John-
  85-165;Jonathan-165;Robert-81-
  83-165
RUSSEY,William-32
RUTE,Joel-181;see Root
RUTHERFORD,Robert-79
RUTHOP,John-150(2)
RUTTER,Allanson-40-41;Samuel-25
RYAN,Dorsey-127-193-202
RYCKMAN,Charles-167
RYLE,Larkin-72

SACK,Henry-163
SACKETT,Thomas-62
SAIGHMAN,William-14
SAILOR,see Taylor;Benjamin-82-
  82a(2)-84-85(4)-89;John-17-55-94
SALYERS,Charles-93;James-93
SAM,Adam-153
SAMPLE,John-63-178(3)
SAMPSON,Seth-2
SAND,Frederick-77

SANDERS,Jacob-108;Samuel-37-87-
  108;William-101-108
SANKEY,Thomas-21
SARBER,Samuel-199
SATER,Henry-17;John-17
SATTERTHWAITE,Benjamin-113
SAWDEN,William-137
SAXON,Alexander-85-168
SAYRES,Aaron-103;Leonard-17
SCANTLIN,Robert-20
SCEARSE,William-30
SCHAMBER,Conrad-141
SCHARBACK,Joseph-57
SCHENCK,Philip-69(2)
SCHIEDS,William-182
SCHLICHT,Adam-152
SCHLOSSER,Michael-159
SCHNETZ,Martin-55
SCHOCK,Gallus-159
SCHOOLEY,John-38;Stephen-156-160-
  161(3)-171
SCHOONOVER,Asa-172;Jeremiah-172;
  Joseph-172(2)
SCHREIBER,Anthony-159;Henry-159;
  Joseph-158
SCHWEGMAN,Henry-164(2);John-159;
  Joseph-159
SCHWIER,Charles-197(3)
SCHUTTA,John-155
SCOGGIN,Aaron-16-123(2);Eli-123
SCOLES,William-156(2)
SCOTT,Alexander-2;Archibald-122;
  Charles-58-83;Edward-157;Henry-
  138-139-142;James-2;Jesse-81;
  Job-157;Joel-94;John-104(2)-113-
  142(2)-157;Powell-108;Samuel-5-
  58;Thomas-69;William-40-41
SCOTTEN,Eli-168;Emery-90
SCRANTON,Joshua-43;Martin-44;
  William-49
SCROGGY,John-113
SCUDDER,Abner-42;Abraham-42;
  Henry-41-145(2);William-156(5)-
  160
SCURLOCK,Reuben-25-63
SEAL,James-21;William-21
SEANEY,Bryan-27
SEANGER,George-40
SEARCH,Phillip-108;William-108
SEARCY,Lemuel-3
SEARIGER,see Seanger
SEBASTIAN,Alexander-5(2)-122(2)
SEDAM,Cornelius-40(2)
SEDGWICK,Richard-28(2)
SEE,Jacob-67
SEELY,John-17;Morris-17;Robert-18

-233-

Thomas-14-60;William-90
SLAUGHTER,Thomas-91(2)
SLAWSON,Ezra-75;Simeon-70
SLEETH,John-99
SLOAN,Azor-147;George-133;Norman-
133-147
SLOO,Thomas-99-111
SLOOP,Thomas-31
SMALL,Abraham-87;Benjamin-30;Jac-
ob-192;John-34-39-103-202;Jonah-
87;Joshua-38(2);Josiah-87;Nathan
30;Obediah-38
SMATHERS,Benjamin-156(2)
SMILEY,James-22;Thomas-22
SMITH,Abraham-129(2);Adam-110;
Alfred-125;Amos-198;Andrew-185-
186;Anthony-139;Benjamin-33-89-
131(2)-186;Caleb-82;Charles-
165(2)-174;Christopher-22-23;
Cyrus-2-6;David-60-61;Durant-
186;Ebenezer-94(2);Eleazer-
115(3)-148;Elias-51;Enoch-13;
Ferman-61;Francis-123;George-
129-132;Henry-12(2)-74-129(2)-
165-163;Jacob-7-166;James-11-1:
134-149;Jeremiah-174;Job-182;
John-13-19-27-30(3)-34(3)-35(2)-
43(2)-64(2)-111-119-137-182;Jon-
athan-170(2);Joseph-59-89-107;
Margaret-185;Matthew-18-165;
Michael-133(2);Noah-2;Peter-4(2)-
27-66;Ralph-47;Richard-48-135;
Robert-23-74(2);Samuel-103-114;
Silas-71(2);Stephen-202;Summers-
166;Temple-173;Thomas-40-52-60-
69(2)-85-91-160-182-201(2);Tim-
othy-199;William-13(3)-40-47-77-
80-90-99-100-102-105(2)-112-114-
122-124-175-191;Zadock-95(2)
SNELBAKER,Jeremiah-200
SNELL,George-138;John-137
SNODGRASS,James-25;Samuel-35-82-
127;William-21-85-190
SNOOK,John-70
SNOW,Godfrey-77;Lemuel-18(4)
SNOWDEN,James-65-66;P.-90
SNYDER,Jacob-201(3);John-76-
123(2)-136;Michael-29(2)-66-67;
Samuel-76
SONGER,Peter-72
SOPER,Isaac-124
SOUDER,Benjamin-90
SOUTHARD,Benjamin-51
SPAHR,John-97(2)-98(2)
SPAKE,John-97-98
SPANGENBURG,Herman-123

SPANGLER,Jacob-74;Peter-150(2)
SPARKS,Amos-13;Jesse-123;John-18;
Joshua-18-60;Joseph-60;Matthew-
18(2);William-26-66-84-85
SPECKMAN,Henry-142(2)
SPEER,Alexander-79;Andrew-80;
James-59;John-22-48-131-145(2);
Martha-135
SPENCER,Mr.-111-112;Allen-17;
Clark-196;Elijah-87;John-172;
Joseph-29-86;William-47
SPOQUE,Hezekiah-131
SPORE,Daniel-6
SPRADLING,James-138;John-143;
William-60-142
SPRAY,James-104-108
SPRENGEIMEIER,Theodore-164
SPRINGER,Dennis-36;John-166;
Nathan-165
STAFFORD,Annanias-125;John-58-59-
89;Thomas-33-88;Tyra-170;
William-36
STAGE,Samuel-49-75
STAIR,Jacob-60
STALKER,David-177;Nathan-106
STALIMAN,Henry-153-164
STANDIFORD,James-47
STANLEY,Archelaus-174;James-174;
John-28;William-68-192;Zacher-
iah-28
STANSBAUGH,David-188;John-188
STANSBURY,John-17(2)
STANTON,Aaron-25-26(2);James-
25;Latham-25-93
STARBUCK,Edward-36(3)-37(3)-125;
John-93-175(2);Paul-33-36;Tris-
tram-116;Uriah-26-33-37;Walter-
175   /STARR,
STARK,Archibald-12/Barnett-87;
Charles-106(2)-107;John-28(2)-
109-125
STARRITT,William-17
STATLER,Abraham-192;John-202;
Joseph-77
STAYBACK,John-6
STEDDAM,Henry-102-115(2);John-
180;Samuel-115
STEDMAN,John-113
STEELE,Greenberry-168;Samuel-8-
89;William-79-104
STEETH,John-99
STEGALL,Jeremiah-116;Jonathan-
116;Lewis-116
STEHLIN,Martin-160
STEHR.Bernard-154
STEIMEMANN,John-159

STEPHENS,Benjamin-40-41;Charles
83;Elijah-82a(2);James-24-60-
64;John-11(2)-49;Joseph-64;Ran-
na-75;Reuben-6;Richard-79-158;
Solomon-75;Spencer-97-110;Wil-
liam-22-23
STEPHENSON,Andrew-136(2);Armoure
136;David-98;George-49-77;John-
49-77;Silvanus-132;Vincent-31;
William-59;Zadock-95
STEPLETON,Andrew-71
STERRETT,see Stervolt,Starrett;
Samuel-98
STERROLT,see Stervolt
STERVOLT,William-141
STETLER,Jacob-77;Jesse-37
STETTER,see Stetler
STEWART,Archibald-139-152;James-
8-16-22;John-8-185(2);Martin-5;
Samuel-20-31;Stephen-5-44-45;
Thomas-2-6-8;William-6-79
STICK,Samuel-189
STIERLEN,Gregory-57-140(2)
STILES,Byrd-64
STILWELL,David-165
STINES,Francis-163-164
STIP,Isaac-79
STOCKDALE,Eli-194;John-61;Thomas-
93(2)
STOCKINGER,John-141-142
STODDARD,see Stodder;Crim-96;
Orrin-96
STODDER,see Stoddard;Seth-40-
68(2)-71(2)
STOMS,Alfred-123;Jacob-14;Wil-
liam-15
STONE,Andrew-198(2);Asa-84;Con-
away-200;Daniel-101;Ethan-104-
111;James-73(3)-202;Jesse-77;
Peter-138;Samuel-73(3);William-
18.
STONER,Samuel-201-202
STOOP,see Sloop;David-91
STORMS,see Stoms
STORY,Edwin-145
STOTTLE,Anthony-159;John-159
STOUT,David-118;Elisha-93;Job-61;
John-130;Jonathan-19;Levi-117-
184
STOVER,Jacob-202;Samuel-110
STOW,Solomon-132
STRAIN,James-120
STRATTON,William-185
STRAWN,Jacob-28
STRINGER,Eli-62-82-89(2)-93;
William-169

STRONG,William-51
STROUBE,Christopher-20;John-20;
Nicholas-167
STROUD,Joseph-10;Joshua-12;
Reese-123
STUBBS,Samuel-158;Zepaniah-80
STUDY,Henry-103(5);Jacob-107
STUMP,Leonard-88
STURGES,James-88
STUTSMAN,David-195(2);Elizabeth-
195(2);Nicholas-195
SUGENT,George-112
SULER,James-29
SUISER,James-29
SUMEY,John-109
SUMMERS,David-57-188;Jefferson-
188(2);John-87-98;Joseph-17;
Simeon-98
SUMPTION,John-190
SUMWALT,Godfrey-108;John-107
SUNDERLAND,John-23;Peter-23
SURBER,Henry-134(2)
SURFACE,Henry-197
SUSSER,William-126
SUTHERLAND,John-34-46-47-74-76-
111(3)
SUTTON,Amos-96-198;Cornelius-198;
George-17-59;Hannibal-159;James-
95(2);John-105-148;Joseph-198;
Joshua-147;Reuben-10;Samuel-185;
Thomas-198
SUYDAM,Jacob-45
SWAFORD,Isaac-24;William-24
SWAIN,Charles-38;David-25;Elihu-
106(2);Frederick-77;Ira-174;
Silvanus-26
SWALLOW,Garret-46-47;George-192
SWAN,Levi-13-122;Mathew-11;
Robert-65(2)
SWANSON,Edward-67
SWEARINGEN,Isaac-17(2)
SWERER,Peter-173(2)
SWESEY,John-153(2)
SWETT,William-19
SWIFT,Christian-90;Christopher-
90;James-169-171;John-148;Mal-
achi-90;Minerva-53;Richard-172
SWIGGETT,Thomas-172
SWOPE,Michael-100
SYLVESTER,Job-53-54;Joseph-53
SYMMES,see Simes,Sims;Peyton-5-8-
9-14-20-43-62-111-129(3)-156-182-
200
SYMONS,see Simons

TABB,Warren-14
TALBERT,Job-26
TALBOTT,Archibald-21-62;Theodore-41
TALER,Asa-25(2)
TALKINGTON,see Falkington
TANN,Benjamin-125
TANNER,James-64;Thomas-50
TAPP,Newton-42(2)
TAPPEN,Samuel-25
TAPLEY,Aaron-2;Philip-44
TARTAR,Jacob-91-96
TASSET,Peter-150
TATEM,Matthew-24
TAWELL,John-112;see Tawitt
TAWITT,Parker-132;see Tawell
TAYLOR,Agnes-60;Benjamin-85(2)-
  89;Daniel-54-143(2);Griffin-
  79(5)-118;Isaac-15;Israel-189(2);
  Jacob-16;James-4-43-60-63;John-
  16-94-138;Robert-7-17-70-71-88-
  93-120(2);Thomas-31;William-106
TEAGARDEN,Daniel-171;Elizabeth-
  89;George-23;Henry-81-90-91;
  Susannah-94
TEAGLE,Joseph-113;Thomas-113
TEAGUE,Andrew-44;George-4(4);
  John-70(2)-68
TEAS,Gibson-183;Joseph-37-182(2)-
  183
TELFORD,Alexander-19(4)
TELLER,Henry-17
TEMPLETON,Daniel-61;John-63;
  Robert-60(4)-64-66
TENEY,Henry-46-76(2);Michael-46
TERREL,see Frel;James-19
TERRY,Ansel-169-170;George-
  124(2);Robert-55
TERWILLIGER,Cornelius-146
TETER,Fielding-81
TWARP,Abraham-57;Andrew-85-94;
  Boaze-88-168;John-35-60(3)-99;
  Thomas-113-115;William-52
THATCHER,Elijah-44-47-48-49-74;
  Harvey-148(2)
THAYER,Chester-132
THIEBAUD,Frederick-69
THOBLE,Henry-164
THOLKING,John-159
THOM,Stephen-55
THOMAS,Absalom-39;Antipas-29-118;
  Benjamin-35-125-180-196;Daniel-
  127;David-94;Eli-196;Enos-183;
  Ephraim-94;Francis-35(2)-113;
  George-196;Isaac-36-83;Isaiah-
  130;James-81;Jeremiah-41;Jesse-

62-111;John-32-39-82-138(2)-180-
  191(2);Lewis-97-112;Nathan-196;
  Richard-92-171(2);Solomon-36;
  Stephen-37-117;Thomas-63-86-
  192(2);William-180
THOMPSON,Cross-22;Enoch-61;
  George-39-138-201;James-111;
  John-27-28-36-45-82-181(2)-182-
  196(2);Joseph-80-164;Moses-128;
  Robert-38-200(2);Samuel-36;
  Smith-137;Theodore-51-76;Thom-
  as-78
THORN,Stephen-13;Taylor-126;Wil-
  liam-87-88(2)-100(3)-101(3)-113
THORNBURGH,Edward-114(3);Jona-
  than-105;Joseph-104-105-118;
  Morgan-105;Nathan-118-183(2);
  Walter-106;William-34-113
THORNTON,Edward-97;George-149;
  William-149
THRALL,Friend-146
THROCKMORTON,Charles-154-157-159;
  Joseph-80-154-159-162(2)-163;
  Theodore-80
THURBER,Edward-120-189(2)
THURSTON,Mordecai-76
TIBBETS,Abner-54-135;Benjamin-
  49;David-49;John-49(3)-135;
  William-53
TIBBS,Willoughby-15
TIDINGS,Edward-6
TILMAN,John-127-130
TIMBERMAN,Abraham-20
TIMMERMAN,John-157
TINDAL,Isaac-136;Robert-181(2)
TINKER,Ira-135;Samuel-132;
  Stephen-133
TIPSORD,Griffin-72
TITUS,Thomas-183
TOBBS,see Tabb
TODD,George-19;Henry-64;Nathan-
  50;Samuel-46-47-50-82-89(2)
TOLAND,see Foland
TOLES,James-126(2)
TOMLINSON,Jemah-189;Jesse-185(2)-
  186
TONEE,Edward-80;see Toney
TONER,Edward-80;Thomas-93
TONEY,see Tonee;James-28
TORLINE,John-154
TORRENCE,George-7-14-78-94(3)-
  122;John-69;William-11
TOWEL,John-112
TOWNSEND,James-111;Joel-73;John-
  30-32-57;Thomas-9;William-171
TRAVER,Levi-148

WALLACE,George-21;James-61-157;
  John-86(3)-97;Thomas-190
WALLEN,John-198
WALLERS,Samuel-93
WALLICK,Henry-6
WALLISER,Francis-57
WALLS,see Watts;Drury-113;Thom-
  as-15
WALSH,Esther-53;John-7;Patrick-53
WALTERS,see Waters;John-192;Val-
  entine-143;William-98
WALTON,James-43(2);Joseph-132
WALTZ,George-68;Job-168
WAMSLEY,Christopher-95;Isaac-124;
  Thomas-20
WARD,Caleb-151(2);James-96(2);
  Jesse-172(2);Joab-178(2);John-
  58-87-108;Obed-106(3);Samuel-
  142;Timothy-147(3);Uzal-25.
WARENSKI,Thomas-148
WARHAM,Jeremiah-167
WARNER,Anderson-165-171;Martin-
  166
WARNOCK,James-7;Joseph-8
WARRELL,Athwille-87;Joseph-99
WARREN,Benjamin-41;Dolphin-190;
  James-107(2)-199;John-189-190-
  199;William-190(3)-191-198-199
WARRICK,Richard-128-193-194
WARWICK,William-195
WASSON,Archibald-34;David-19-39-
  123;John-34;Joseph-34-67
WATERS,see Walters;Isaac-97;
  James-63-94;John-94-201;Samuel-
  93;William-120
WATKINS,Jeremiah-55;John-123;Jon-
  athan-18;Watkin-49;William-18
WATSON,James-5(3)-122(2);John-
  188;Joseph-133
WATTS,Henry-202;John-31(2)-64-
  72(3)-74(2);Joseph-99;Samuel-35;
  Thomas-15-74
WAY,Amos-9;Henry-108(3)-112(2)-
  116(2)-180;Huldah-115;John-118;
  Moorman-108;Paul-108(2)-116;
  Seth-102-112(2);Thomas-102;
  William-108(3)
WEATHERS,Jesse-48;John-48;Wil-
  liam-48
WEAVER,George-9;Jacob-120;John-
  120;Peter-31;Richard-10(2)-42;
  Samuel-197;William-197
WEBB,Edward-82a-83-94-95;Ezra-44;
  Forrest-84(2);James-90(2)-168;
  Jesse-84;Jonathan-82;Thomas-171;
  William-15-84

WEBER,Nicholas-61;Samuel-18
WEEKS,James-174;John-33;William-
  191
WEESNER,Micajah-112(2)-121
WEIGLER,Arnold-143(2);Charles-
  143(2);Henry-143(2);Julius-143(2)
WEILER,Conrad-152
WEIMER,Andrew-192
WEIR,William-85
WEIS,Valentine-170
WEIST,Christian-149;Henry-4(2)-
  4(2)
WELCH,Christopher-140;Henry-120;
  John-16;Thomas-195;William-19
WELCHONS,Daniel-102
WELL,see Will
WELLER,Lodowick-44(3)
WELLIVER,Isaac-94;Josiah-110
WELLMANN,Stephen-170
WELLNER,Charles-189(2)
WELLS,Horace-182;John-60-89
WENTHORP,see Nenthorp
WEST,Samuel-3
WESTCOTT,Ebenezer-77
WESTON,Benjamin-80(2)-165;
  David-167(2)
WETTER,Christopher-25-26(2);
  John-26
WEYMIRE,Jacob-98
WEYRICK,Henry-198-199
WHARTON,Richard-101
WHEATLEY,John-195(2)-199;Joseph-
  195-197-198-199;Richard-197-198
WHEELER,Charles-181-187;John-34-
  46(3);Madison-187;Piercy-137-
  151;Samuel-46;William-151;Wil-
  son-137(2)
WHERRETT,William-83(2)
WHETSEL,Henry-185;Hiram-176(2);*
WHETSTONE,Matthias-47. *Jacob-195
WHIPPLE,Jesse-122
WHITAKER,James-68-69-78-134(2);
  John-73(2);William-13
WHITE,Abel-61;Alexander-14-15-90;
  Benjamin-27-92(2);Caleb-3(2)-10-
  44-52-33-54-71-89;Daniel-74;Ed-
  ward-20-46;Hamilton-128(2);Hart-
  shorn-112;Iry-134;Israel-72;Ith-
  amer-20;Jacob-40-117;James-10-
  11-36;Joel-96;John-10-32-37-
  84(2)-92-200(2);Jonathan-190;
  Joseph-10-95;Peter-5;Robert-64;
  Tabitha-33(2)-36(2);Thomas-
  157(2)-200;William-13-42-199
WHITEHEAD,Jesse-139;John-32(2)-
  139;Lazarus-32-67(2);Michael-
  139(2)

WHITELOCK,Abraham-171;Charles-
171;Joseph-90-94(2);Thomas-171;
William-171
WHITEMAN,Lewis-8
WHITEMORE,William-70-145
WHITNEY,Joseph-59-142;Moses-17
WHITSON,Amos-177;Mary-179;Willis-
112-113-120
WHITTENGER,Henry-110;John-110
WHITWORTH,John-63
WICKERSHAM,Caleb-119;James-37-
129;William-178
WICKHAM,Nathan-13
WICTOR,Christiana-137;Francis-137
WIEMAN,George-160
WIGGINS,John-192;William-171
WIGGS,Susannah-38;William-38;
Windsor-38
WILCOX,Daniel-146;Isaac-8;James-
104
WILDRIDGE,Ralph-18(2)
WILES,Luke-42;Richardson-4.
WILEY,Allen-70-149;Anthony-94;
Cornelius-124;Delaney-149;Isaac-
66-192;James-17-81-82a-166-
167(2);John-25;Lemuel-144;Mel-
ville-145;Moses-13-16;Rensselaer
135;Spencer-81-140(2);Thomas-36-
129(3);William-4-5-122
WILFORD,Hugh-71
WILHEIM,Jacob-137
WILKINS,Charles-9;Francis-183;
Joseph-184;Philip-20
WILKINSON,Gideon-19(4)-124;John-
76;Joseph-7-122;Thomas-193
WILL,Henry-162;William-16
WILLCUTS,Clark-38-39-115-121
WILLEN,John-156
WILLETS,Elisha-97;Henry-103;Is-
aac-85-101(4);Jesse-97(2);Levi-
88-97(3);William-88-97
WILLIAMS,see Williamson;Abraham-
52;Absalom-99;Adam-172;Ann-181;
Anthony-24;Azariah-107;Caleb-51;
Charles-102;Cornelius-92;David-
16-123;Eleazer-128;Elmore-17;
Ephraim-105;George-25;Hezekiah-
107;Hiram-91-172;Isaac-109;.
James-85-121-195;Jesse-51-75-76-
127-167;Joel-63;John-27-90-93-
102-171-184(2);Jonas-85(2);Jon-
athan-102;Joseph-17-66;Joshua-
22;Martin-171;Matthias-196-
197(5);Nathan-102;Owen-112;Per-
ry-178;Ralph-64-81-90-166-171(2)
Richard-36-86-90-91-106-168-
194(2)
Robert-96;Samuel-36-185-187;
Stephen-116;Thomas-61-62-80(2);
Weden-165;William-2-31-33-91-102
WILLIAMSON,see Williams;David-74;
Eleazer-127;Joachim-149;John-
150;William-74
WILLIS,Jesse-106;Jonathan-184(2);
John-68(2);Jonathan-118;Robert-
173-177;William-24
WILLYARD,Elias-197-202
WILMER,Henry-72(2)-142
WILLMORE,Willis-115(2)
WILSON,Ammi-152;Bazel-161;Benja-
min-47(4)-63-135;Charles-169(2);
Daniel-63-74;David-6-167;George-
81-116;Hugh-71;Ira-152(3);Isaac-
63-86-87(3)-89-168-172;James-
120-135-147-155-159-199;Joel-
145-146;John-172-194;Jonathan-
109;Robert-4-164;Samuel-95-96-
97-157-164;Thomas-155(2)-161(2);
William-16-58-82a-86-87(2)-88-
89(2)-91-97
WILTSE,Henry-109
WINCHELL,Robert-82a;Ruggles-62
WINDER,James-90
WINDSOR,John-149
WINGFIELD,Bazel-100(2);Henry-31
WINKLEY,James-7
WINN,Thomas-133
WINSTANLEY,see Stanley
WINSTON,James-35;Pleasant-102-126
WISE,Parker-142;Samuel-142;
Solomon-92
WISEMAN,John-130(2)-155-190-197
WISHARD,James-132
WITHAM,Morris-22
WITHROW,John-35-36
WITTER,see Wetter
WOHLKING,Frederick-123
WOLBER,Frederick-142(2)-146(2)-
150; Henry-142-150-151
WOLF,John-143;Michael-35-103;
William-187(2)
WOLLISING,John-137
WONDERLICK,John-19
WOOD,Alexander-110;Andrew-100-
101;Benjamin-21;Cyrus-40;Dan-
iel-10;Eli-176;Isaac-20;James-
19-44;Jeremiah-91-143;John-17-
92;Joseph-48-112;Levi-165;Phil-
ip-28;Samuel-34-50-75-100(2);
Stephen-15-53(4)-75(2)-77-138;
Thomas-153;Winslow-50-75-110(2)-
152
WOODBERRY,Nathan-185(2)-186

WOODBURN,John-191
WOODCUCK,Joseph-30
WOODMANSEE,Asa-126(2)
WOODRUFF,Archibald-161;Josiah-131
WOODSON,Edward-94
WOODWARD,Bartlett-88;Cader-35-
187;Davis-53;John-101
WOODWORTH,Artema-81(2)-166;
Ryleigh-58;Samuel-178
WOOLCOTT,Daniel-147
WOOLLEY,George-41;John-16;Jos-
eph-15;Silas-16;William-72(2)
WOODMAN,Uriah-179(2)
WOOTERS,Nathan-179
WOOTON,Lewis-178(2)
WORMAN,Joseph-155(2);Thomas-64-
100
WORRELL,see Warrell
WORSTER,James-92
WORTH,Thomas-105
WORTHINGTON,William-90-109-110(3)
WOTEN,Bell-200(2);Jonathan-201;
Samuel-200-201
WRIGHT,Charles-3;David-118;Eli-
jah-116;Francis-185;Isaac-118-
119-178;Israel-178(2);Jacob-44;
James-33-105-108-118-178;Joel-
86;John-25-70-108(2)-110-118(2)-
144-180-185;Jonathan-34;Joseph-
108;Joshua-105;Lorenzo-137;Lyd-
ia-44;Nathaniel-74;Ralph-34-99;
Rees-177;Runnels-102;Samuel-54;

Solomon-118;Thomas-26-68-131(2);
Whiteley-67(2)-109;William-124-
171-177
WURTS,John-57
WYATT,David-28(2);Thomas-27;
William-28
WYMOND,James-147
WYSONG,Cyrenius-185(2);David-
181-187;Henry-117;Valentine-
119(2)-120

YANDERS,Simon-90
YATES,Edward-158;Noah-41;Wil-
liam-38
YEAGER,Harnit-177;Joseph-54-55-
139;Nicholas-139
YINN,see Zinn
YORK,Amos-133;Jesse-161;Joseph-
156(4);Joshua-162
YOST,Philip-17
YOUART,see Ewart
YOUELL,Cornelius-69
YOUNG,Elijah-110;Enoch-172;
Ephraim-81;Jonathan-57;Joseph-
191;Nathan-90;William-103-182
YOUNT,Daniel-86-88

ZEEK,Adam-31
ZETER,Lemuel-154
ZIMMERMAN,John-37
ZINN,George-73-151
ZOERCHER,John-195

www.ingramcontent.com/pod-product-compliance
Lightning Source LLC
Chambersburg PA
CBHW020456030426
42337CB00011B/131